AF820518

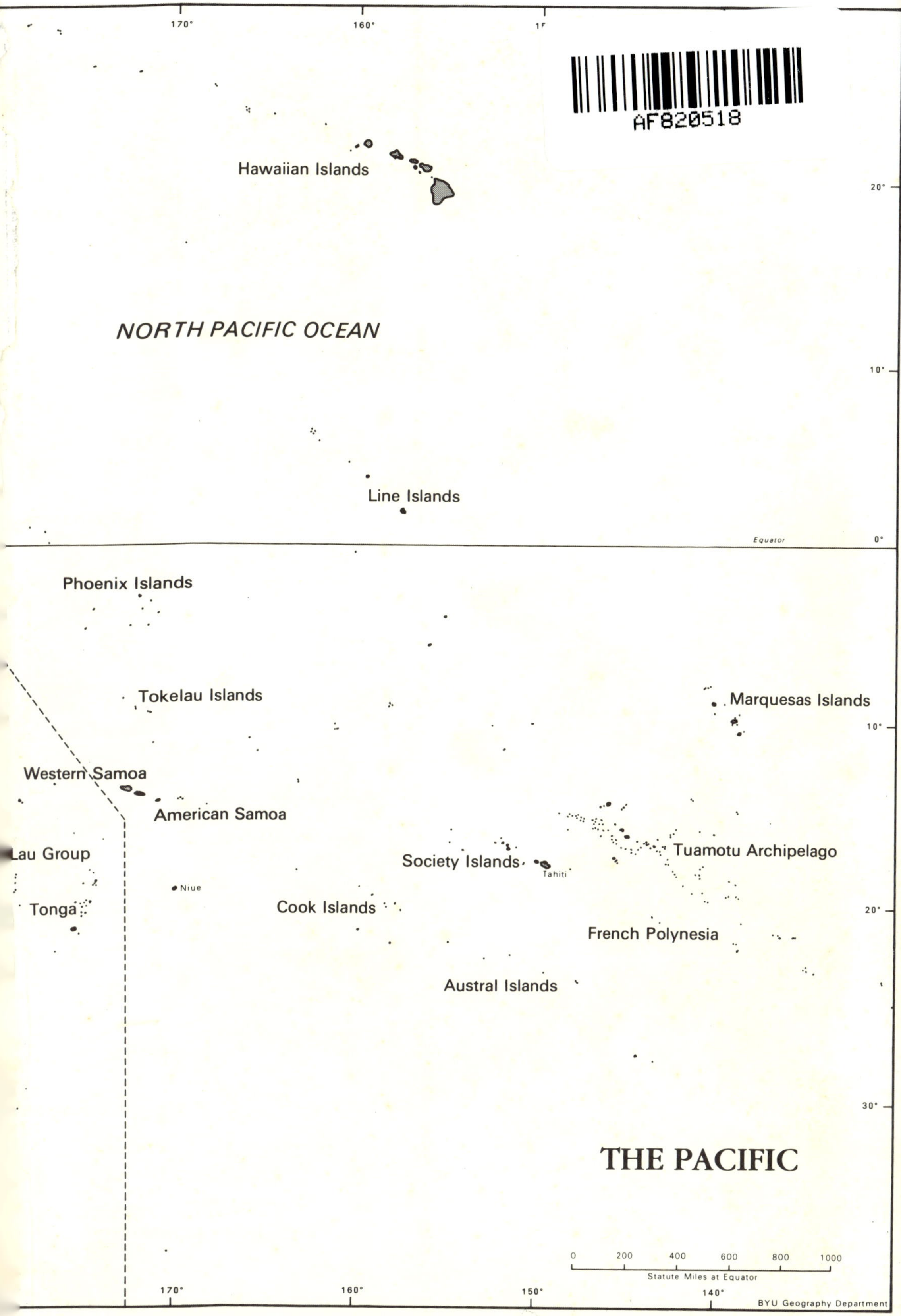
170°
160°
Hawaiian Islands
20°
NORTH PACIFIC OCEAN
10°
Line Islands
Equator
0°
Phoenix Islands
Tokelau Islands
Marquesas Islands
10°
Western Samoa
American Samoa
Lau Group
Society Islands
Tahiti
Tuamotu Archipelago
Niue
Tonga
Cook Islands
20°
French Polynesia
Austral Islands
30°
THE PACIFIC
0
200
400
600
800
1000
Statute Miles at Equator
170°
160°
150°
140°
BYU Geography Department

May 11, 1989

To LeRoy and Nedra,

You are fine people. We're happy you are here with us. I'm grateful for each of your contributions to BYU-Hawaii.

Sincerely,

Lanny

UNTO THE ISLANDS OF THE SEA

UNTO THE ISLANDS OF THE SEA

A History of the Latter-day Saints in the Pacific

R. Lanier Britsch

Deseret Book
Salt Lake City, Utah

©1986 Deseret Book Company
All rights reserved
Printed in the United States of America

No part of this book may be reproduced in any form or by any means without permission in writing from the publisher, Deseret Book Company, P.O. Box 30178, Salt Lake City, Utah 84130

First printing January 1986

Library of Congress Cataloging-in-Publication Data

Britsch, R. Lanier.
Unto the islands of the sea.

Bibliography: p.
Includes index.
1. Church of Jesus Christ of Latter-day Saints—Missions—Oceania—History. 2. Mormon Church—Missions—Oceania—History. 3. Oceania—Church history. I. Title.
BV3670.B74 1986 289.3'9 85-27463
ISBN 0-87747-754-X

To the
mission presidents
and missionaries
of the Pacific

CONTENTS

PART 4
NEW ZEALAND

PART 5
SAMOA

PART 6
TONGA

PART 7
FIJI AND OTHER ISLANDS

PREFACE

Anyone who has flown over or sailed the vast expanses of the Pacific Ocean must marvel that primitive man ever found and peopled the Pacific islands. How the early Pacific voyagers found Hawaii, Tahiti, Tonga, Samoa, New Zealand, and the thousands of other islands has only recently been understood. But who the ancient seafarers were, what their names were, and how they survived to establish homes and the peculiar cultures of the islands will never be more than partially understood.

Western man discovered the Polynesian Islands in the seventeenth and eighteenth centuries. Not long after Europeans found Polynesia, sailors, settlers, and missionaries arrived. Western man had a powerful impact on the peoples of Polynesia. He introduced not only the Christian religion, education and literacy, modern agriculture and industry, and western government, but also disease, debauchery, more advanced weapons, and confusing cultural patterns. The Polynesians had to make thousands of changes before they could adjust to the requirements of the new world that were thrust upon them.

While this period of adjustment was most vigorously underway, missionaries of The Church of Jesus Christ of Latter-day Saints arrived in the Pacific. Although this book is not a general history of the interactions of western civilization with Polynesian cultures, I've attempted to include as many facts about the interactions of western, Polynesian, and Mormon cultures as possible. Until 1950 (and to some extent, since then), much of the history of the Latter-day Saints in Polynesia is cultural history as well as religious history. Readers will note far more references to cultural matters than they would expect in a history of the Church in Canada, Britain, or Germany.

When I was first planning this book, I considered a format that briefly narrated the story of the Church in the Pacific and then turned to a series of topical chapters on such subjects as building missionaries, missionary methods, temple building, inspiring tales, ocean adventures, education, and so on. Although such an approach has merit, I concluded that most readers would prefer an integrated approach. Also, I suspect that many readers will want to read a thorough history of only one island group, such as Hawaii or Tonga. Therefore, I have written essentially separate histories of each of the main areas. The final chapter recounts the latest developments in Fiji, Guam-Micronesia, and other non-Polynesian areas.

I developed an interest in Polynesia while serving in Hawaii as a missionary for the LDS Church. After joining the history faculty at Brigham Young University, I was invited by Leonard J. Arrington, then LDS Church Historian, and the Assistant Church Historians, James B. Allen and Davis Bitton, to prepare a single volume titled *A History of the Latter-day Saints in Asia and the Pacific* for a multi-volume series that was to commemorate the sesquicentennial of the Church in 1980. The series was later canceled, but Deseret Book expressed interest in and support for my efforts. As I continued to research and write, the original volume proved to be too long for a manageable single volume; hence this book and later another on the Church in Asia.

I'm deeply grateful to Dr. Arrington and his associates for their encouragement and help. The staff members at the LDS Church Archives have become my close friends. They have not only helped me use materials I've requested, but they have also frequently brought to my attention items of great value that were unknown to me. Friends who have been especially helpful at the Church Archives are Ronald G. Watt, James Kimball, Fred Rowe, Glen M. Leonard, Linda Haslam, Gladys Noyce, and Bill Slaughter. Maurene U. Beecher provided direction and help through her editing. Gordon Irving has been of great assistance as director of the Church's James H. Moyle Oral History Program.

Dr. Arrington partially supported my field research with a Church Historian's Grant in 1974. Through his assistance I was able to visit the various island groups in quest of source materials. Leo Vernon provided BYU Research support, as did Martin B. Hickman, dean of the College of Family, Home, and Social Sciences at BYU. Ted J. Warner, former chairman of the BYU History Department, also provided considerable support for this project.

Several people have read parts of the manuscript. Special thanks goes to Marge Newton and Yves R. Perrin.

I've interviewed many people, some as oral histories. The names of these people are found in the footnotes. I'm thankful to all who have provided information in this way.

A number of Church leaders and their wives provided me and my wife with housing, transportation, and other help while we traveled in the South Pacific. We thank George Puckett, Ralph Rodgers, Baden Pere, Larry Oler, Charles Woodworth, Joseph Childers, Raymond Baudin, Ebbie Davis, and their wives. Bruce Lake, Stanley Peterson, Alton Wade, and Ward Magleby of the LDS Church Educational System have provided much useful information.

President Gordon B. Hinckley and Elders Loren C. Dunn, John H. Groberg, and Rex D. Pinegar have given considerable help and information.

The manuscript for this book has been through a number of drafts. Each draft has been revised on either a typewriter or a word processor. The young women (and, occasionally, young men) of the Faculty Support Center of the College of Family, Home, and Social Sciences have carefully and patiently typed the manuscript through all stages. Managers Diane Morita and Marilyn Webb deserve special thanks.

My father, Ralph A. Britsch, professor emeritus of humanities at BYU, has corrected the grammar and has made stylistic suggestions for the entire manuscript. I greatly appreciate his help, his expertise, his patience, and his love. I'm grateful for the careful editing of the manuscript by Jack Lyon of Deseret Book. Cartography is by Kelly Nielsen, Warren Muench, and Cindy Paine of the BYU Geography Department. My wife, JoAnn, has listened to every word of the initial drafts and has provided countless useful suggestions and refinements. Her good humor and encouragement through the years since I started this project in 1972 have been a tremendous support.

Many people have been involved in one way or another. I thank all of the research assistants who have helped along the way. Each has made his or her contribution to the completion of this study. Ultimately, the book has been my joy, my burden, and my grand hope to make a contribution to LDS Church history. It's been my labor of love. I'm sorry it's finished. The responsibility for its contents is totally mine.

INTRODUCTION

In the spring of 1843, only thirteen years after The Church of Jesus Christ of Latter-day Saints was organized, the Prophet Joseph Smith, Jr., called four men as missionaries to the islands of the Pacific. Those representatives started what has now extended to 140 years of LDS Church history in the Pacific, primarily in Polynesia. The history of the Latter-day Saints in this vast region is as varied as the islands and the people who live there. Since the 1840s, time has brought great changes in culture, government, technology, religion, education, communications, and transportation. Such changes have affected the history of the Mormons in this area. Missionaries and local members have found it necessary to adjust to the circumstances of the times.

Today the LDS Church in many parts of the Pacific islands is similar in level of activity, physical facilities, and competence of Church leaders to the well-organized stakes in Utah. The current advanced state of the Church in the Pacific is the result of years of cooperative effort on the part of missionaries, local Saints, and general officers of the Church who have supervised the area.

To a considerable degree the history of the Church in the Pacific is missionary and institutional history. Records of the lives and works of local Saints are not readily available to the researcher (although more could be done with local Church history by scholars who live in the various parts of the Pacific).

The Mormon missionary system differs in many ways from the missionary systems of other Christian denominations. LDS missionaries have always been self-supporting or supported by family or friends, unschooled in the ministry as the world knows it, untrained in languages. Mormon missions are short-term experiences, usually lasting two years but seldom more than three or four. Most LDS missionaries in the Pacific have lived with the people, eaten their food, slept on their floors, and bathed in their streams and pools. They have almost always avoided political involvements, except when friction between governments and the Church has drawn the missionaries into relations with political leaders. Except for the actions of Walter Murray Gibson, there have been no instances of usurpation, misuse of ecclesiastical or political power, or land grabbing in the annals of LDS Pacific history.

It is true that white missionaries have dominated the history of the Pacific missions, but thousands of local men and women have also served the Church as missionaries and local leaders. These people have contributed most, and have been the ballast for the Church. These usually unnamed Saints have built the Church, remained in their callings when circumstances became difficult, and made the Church succeed in their societies.

It is not clear from the records of the Church exactly when the leaders in Salt Lake City began thinking of the Polynesian people as descendants of Lehi, the Book of Mormon prophet. As will be seen later, Elder George Q. Cannon and his companions in Hawaii in 1851 were the first to tell the Polynesians of their birthright as children of Abraham and Lehi. Since that time almost all of the presidents of the Church have affirmed the position that the Polynesian people are of Israel. Because the Church believes that the descendants of Lehi are children of special promise, the leaders of the Church have expended vast amounts of manpower on missionary efforts among these people. As is now evident from the high percentage of Latter-day Saints in Tonga and Samoa and the respectable numbers of Mormons in other Polynesian areas, the years of missionary work have borne fruit.

The work of establishing the Church in the Pacific has been abetted by some significant advantages and hindered by some serious obstacles. Among the advantages are the Christian foundation laid by missionaries of other denominations who converted the people from non-Christian religions, translated the Bible, educated many of the people, established religious freedom, and introduced some of the amenities of modern life. Many of the obstacles to missionary success remain to this day: tropical storms, isolation, harsh geographical conditions, poor transportation and communications, and general poverty. But advantages and obstacles, successes and failures, wealth and poverty notwithstanding, the history of the Church in the islands goes on, founded on more than fourteen decades of interesting and inspirational experiences.

The sections of this volume are arranged in chronological order of the founding of the missions in each nation or area.

PART 1

FRENCH POLYNESIA

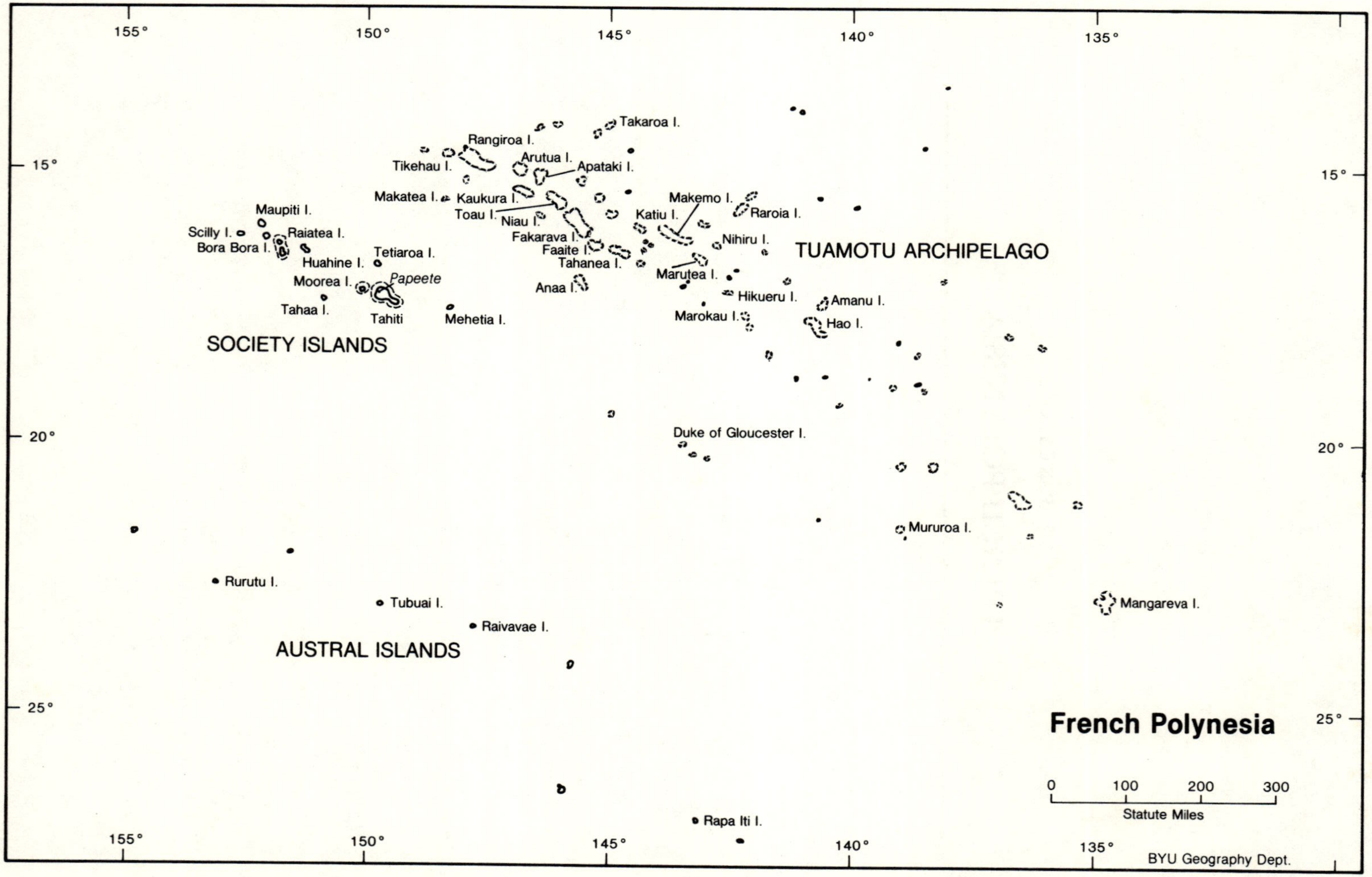

155°
150°
145°
140°
135°
15°
20°
25°
Takaroa I.
Rangiroa I.
Arutua I.
Apataki I.
Tikehau I.
Makatea I.
Kaukura I.
Toau I.
Niau I.
Fakarava I.
Faaite I.
Tahanea I.
Anaa I.
Makemo I.
Katiu I.
Raroia I.
Nihiru I.
Marutea I.
Hikueru I.
Marokau I.
Amanu I.
Hao I.
TUAMOTU ARCHIPELAGO
Maupiti I.
Scilly I.
Raiatea I.
Bora Bora I.
Huahine I.
Tetiaroa I.
Moorea I.
Papeete
Tahaa I.
Tahiti
Mehetia I.
SOCIETY ISLANDS
Duke of Gloucester I.
Mururoa I.
Rurutu I.
Tubuai I.
Raivavae I.
AUSTRAL ISLANDS
Mangareva I.
Rapa Iti I.
French Polynesia
0
100
200
300
Statute Miles
BYU Geography Dept.

CHAPTER 1

ESTABLISHING THE FIRST PACIFIC MISSION OF THE CHURCH

French Polynesia, 1844–1852

On May 11, 1843, Joseph Smith called Addison Pratt on a mission to the Pacific Islands, the first mission of the Church to that area. Elder Pratt was a reasonable choice, for when he was a young man he had sailed the Pacific Ocean and had at one time spent several months in the Sandwich Islands (Hawaii).

The call to serve had come from the Prophet,[1] and Brigham Young had ordained Addison a seventy and given him power over the elements. When Brother Young set him apart, he told Elder Pratt to avoid haste and passion, to see goodness in all. These were good words for one who would spend most of the next nine years serving the Lord among people who were greatly different from any with whom Latter-day Saint missionaries had worked.[2]

Of the four elders in Brother Pratt's missionary group, he was the best informed concerning the Pacific, but he was not the most experienced in Church matters. Noah Rogers was therefore chosen to head the new mission. The other two missionaries assigned were Benjamin F. Grouard and Knowlton F. Hanks. Elder Hanks did not live to serve in Polynesia; Elder Grouard would remain long enough to do the work of several good men.

When they departed from Nauvoo on May 23, 1843, the Church was only thirteen years old. Until that time no elders had been sent to foreign-language areas. It is not clear from the missionary records whether these elders were called to Hawaii or simply to any appropriate place in the Pacific. When they reached New Bedford, Massachusetts, Brother Pratt tried to find a ship going to Hawaii. Failing this, he booked passage on the *Timoleon,* a whaling ship bound for the Society Islands. It sailed on October 10, 1843.

Addison Pratt and Ben Grouard were accustomed to sea travel, but for Elders Rogers and Hanks, rough weather spelled misery and seasickness. However, more than the sea plagued Elder Hanks. Before he left Nauvoo he had suffered for some time from consumption, known today as tuberculosis. Day by day his condition worsened, and, finally, on November 3, he died. When his body slid into the water, the silent crew paid tribute to the first Mormon missionary to die and to be buried at sea.

More than six months passed before the *Timoleon* hove to in sight of the missionaries' first stopping place, Tubuai, in the southeast Pacific. It had sailed the Atlantic and around the Cape of Good Hope, on through the Indian Ocean, by the islands of Southeast Asia, and into the South Pacific. Elder Pratt and his two companions were eager to know what kind of people inhabited Tubuai Island. In the early morning hours of April 30, 1844, a canoe carrying two natives came aside the whaler. Elder Pratt shouted "Aloha." The natives shouted "Aroha" in return.

Tubuai lies 350 miles due south of Tahiti. It is a fertile island that produces a fine variety of fruits and vegetables. When the *Timoleon* dropped anchor, the first priority of all on board was to stock up on food and fresh water. President Rogers went ashore with the first boats, and a day later Pratt and Grouard followed. The Church had arrived on Polynesian soil. The three missionaries were well received by the people of Tubuai, who urged them to stay and teach the gospel. Pratt, whom they came to call "Paraita," was their evident favorite because he could communicate with them a little by using the Hawaiian language.

Elder Pratt's decision to stay, however, was not easy. His first intention had been to teach the gospel in Hawaii and then in well-known Tahiti. He was not sure he would be usefully serving by remaining on an almost unknown island, a mere three-by-six-mile oval with a small population. He sought the Lord in prayer, and when the answer came he not only felt that he should stay but he was convinced that if he left he would be running away from duty.

The *Timoleon* and Elder Pratt's companions remained at Tubuai for several more days and then sailed north to Tahiti, leaving him behind. Addison set to work with a will. He surveyed the little island and found that its natural resources provided well for its few inhabitants. An abundance of plants grew almost without care, and pigs, chickens, wild ducks, and hens abounded. Goats provided milk, and the sea gave up an amazing variety of fish and shellfish.

Addison Pratt (left) and Benjamin F. Grouard were the founders of Latter-day Saint missionary work in the Pacific islands. (Courtesy S. George Ellsworth.)

The people of Tubuai appeared to be without guile. Before long, however, Elder Pratt learned that these docile people could be whipped into a fury if their territory was infringed upon. When Captain James Cook discovered the island in 1777, the people had greeted him warmly. But twelve years later, when the mutineers of the *Bounty* attempted to create a colony there, a war ensued between the natives and the sailors. The mutineers were forced to leave and later settled Pitcairn Island.[3]

Although Protestant missionaries on the ship *Duff* had seen the island in February 1797, it was not until 1817 that William Ellis of the London Missionary Society landed there with serious intent to teach Christianity. He had little success. But beginning about 1822, native Tahitian missionaries began preaching Christian doctrine to the people of Tubuai. These Tahitians brought literacy and Christian civilization. At the time of the arrival of Addison Pratt and his companions, many of the older people of Tubuai could clearly remember heathen practices such as cannibalism that had been abolished some years before. But by 1844 the people of Tubuai all considered themselves Christians. London Missionary Society (LMS) missionaries had recorded the spoken language in writing and by 1840, only four years before the

LDS missionaries arrived, had printed a complete translation of the Bible.

Elder Pratt and his companions eventually clashed with the LMS missionaries because the Mormons were succeeding in what the Protestants considered their own territory. (The various Protestant groups had by this time parceled out the South Pacific among their different mission groups so that they could avoid competition and confrontations.) These confrontations notwithstanding, the LDS missionaries gained many benefits from the work of other church missions.

Elder Pratt, as we have said, had the advantage of some Hawaiian words that were cognate with the Tahitian language. But even he had a long way to go before he was blessed with fluency. He made slow progress with the language until King Tomatoa of Tubuai presented him with an English-Tahitian grammar. From that date, July 11, 1844, his linguistic ability improved rapidly.[4]

There lived at Mataura a small group of Europeans who had settled on the island and had taken, in most cases, native wives. These old "salts" were a pretty rough bunch, but they treated the Mormon missionary with respect. Gospel discussions with these people began as a friendly diversion to break the monotony of island life, but they steadily led into deeper and more serious teaching sessions on matters that were considered important for eternal salvation. Six weeks after Addison arrived on Tubuai, he recorded in his diary that the white people were much excited about the things he was teaching them.

On June 15, 1844, Ambrose Alexander, a white shipbuilder, applied for baptism and became the first person to join the Church in the Pacific islands. Five weeks later, on July 21, Elder Pratt recorded:

> Sabbath. After the morning service I gave an invitation to all those who felt it their duty to be baptized, to present themselves at a place appointed on the beach, and I would wait on them. The multitude assembled on the beach, there came forward and I baptized Charles Hill, John Layton, Wm. F. Bowen, Wm. Carrington, James Clark (foreigners), Nabota and his wife, Telii, Pauma, and Hamoe, the wife of Haamatua (natives), and confirmed them in the afternoon.[5]

The following Sunday Elder Pratt organized the Tubuai Branch of the Church, with eleven members. He ordained Charles Hill an elder and the other brethren priests, teachers, and deacons. Addison wrote:

> I cannot express the heartfelt gratitude that came over me when I saw the tears of penitence trickle down their sea-worn faces, nor the warm emotions that vibrated my heart while, on their knees, I heard

> them thank their Father in Heaven that I had been casually thrown upon this island and had become the humble instrument in his hand in bringing them to see their lost condition.[6]

But Elder Pratt could see that his principal responsibility was to the local people. So he moved to Mahu and worked on the language. By the end of July 1844 the work was well established on Tubuai, and in September Pratt began preaching in Tahitian. During his first year there he baptized a third of the island's population, sixty people, including all but one of the Caucasians on the island.[7]

THE OPENING OF THE LDS MISSION IN TAHITI

When Elders Noah Rogers and Benjamin F. Grouard left Elder Pratt on Tubuai, they sailed directly to Tahiti, arriving there on May 14, 1844. The island's beauty, climate, and friendly people had made it a favorite stopping place for whalers and other traders. Tahiti had first been discovered by Captain Samuel Wallis in 1767. He claimed the island as a British possession, but only a year later the French navigator de Bougainville made a similar claim for his country. Neither nation, however, convincingly established its claim to the island. In fact, it remained under control of the native Pomare dynasty until 1847. The most significant outside political influence came through the LMS missionaries.

When the LDS elders landed at Papeete, the capital of Tahiti, they found the political and social situation unsettled. Conflicts that had begun between the British and the French in 1835 had only recently come to a head. The French, who were looking forward to the day when a canal would be completed in Panama, desired a good port in the southeastern Pacific; Tahiti met all of their requirements. To move in directly and take the territory by force would have been too brazen; therefore, three French Roman Catholic missionaries were sent into Tahiti in 1835 and 1836 to establish a foothold. All three men were expelled from the island at the insistence of the LMS missionary, the politically active George Pritchard, who also acted as British consul. Pritchard detested the French, and Roman Catholicism. By 1836 the LMS had dominated Tahiti for almost four decades, and the British suggested that the Catholics should recognize the convention under which missionaries were to keep out of territory already occupied by a rival group. The arrangement was not acceptable to the French, who argued that they had a right both as Frenchmen and as Catholics to establish their church wherever they pleased.[8]

The conflict became serious when French Captain Abel Dupetit-Thouars demanded two successive indemnities in compensation for the mistreatment of the missionaries ousted in 1836. The local government could not raise the money. In default of payment the French made Tahiti a protectorate. In France the government accepted Dupetit-Thouars's arrangement in April 1843. The British government accepted the *fait accompli.*[9]

When Elder Rogers and Elder Grouard arrived and learned about the local situation, they were convinced the Lord had prepared the way for them, "for had the native government been in full force when we arrived, most likely the missionaries (who hitherto have been mighty men in this kingdom) would have so influenced the natives against us, as to prevent us from landing."[10] The French protectorate had declared complete religious freedom. But although the religious climate had improved, the domestic situation was still unsettled.

The elders considered their own safety a mixed blessing. It was true that they were secure in Tahiti, but the local people would not or could not listen to them. On the other hand, the way was not clear for them to sail to other islands. They began teaching the few Europeans and Americans on the island. The first baptisms on Tahiti were those of Mr. and Mrs. Seth George Lincoln, friends made during the long voyage of the *Timoleon.* One week later, on August 18, the missionaries baptized two American men. This success caused a stir among both foreigners and Tahitians. The LMS missionaries immediately began harassing the elders by repeating many of the false stories about Joseph Smith and the Mormons that were commonly circulated at the time. In September the anti-Mormon attacks were carried even to Tubuai. The Reverend Mr. William Howe sailed to that island "to set affairs in order," and while there he repeated many hateful things about Joseph Smith and the Church. Pratt had a direct confrontation with him, and, according to his own report, he came off the better in the encounter.[11]

Elders Rogers and Grouard busied themselves by preaching to the crews of whaling ships. The Lincolns, with whom they lived, made their home available for meetings and teaching sessions. But though a few Englishmen and Americans were baptized during October and November, both elders felt confined. Rogers, who presided over the mission, strongly believed they should take the gospel to as many islands as possible. Having heard from sailors that the island of Huahine, ninety miles to the northwest, might provide a fruitful field, Elder Rogers sailed there on October 17. On his arrival, he was disappointed to find that nearly all of the Caucasians ran grog shops and gambling houses. In addition, the Reverend Charles Barff, who was much loved and respected by the people, was not willing to yield any ground to a Mormon missionary. Elder Rogers's stay on Huahine, which lasted until late January 1845, proved a complete disappointment to him.[12]

In Elder Rogers's absence, Ben Grouard began to yearn for the strength and companionship of Elder Pratt, and in December he sailed to Tubuai. The two servants of God were thrilled to be together again after seven months' separation. Their friendship was particularly important because they had not received a single letter from home by the early part of 1845.[13] This situation seemed more serious because of reports they had received (which they counted as mere rumors) that Joseph and Hyrum Smith had been assassinated. It was not until July 1, 1845, that they received authentic information that confirmed the truth of these reports. Such tragic news, in addition to time and distance, made them feel estranged from their loved ones and the body of the Church. Nevertheless, they strengthened each other and continued the work.

Elder Pratt in particular had learned much about leading a body of Saints in so strange a place. On September 29, 1844, he wrote, "A little experience tells me that to baptize and build up a branch is a small matter compared to keeping it in order after it is built up, especially when it is constructed of such material as sailors and heathens. But the Lord helps me."[14]

Lacking a solid foundation in intellectual and spiritual matters, the people sometimes found themselves tempted to break the covenants made at baptism. Seeing this, Elder Pratt decided in September to divide his time between the two parts of his Tubuai Branch. From that time on he spent one week in Mahu and the next in Mataura.

Elder Pratt not only learned how much attention and effort were required to administer a branch successfully, but he also had a taste of political involvement. He reported that the queen and a number of her high-ranking associates were numbered among his flock. Curiously, Pratt's close association with these people placed him in a very awkward position, for he wrote, "If you will allow me to speak jestingly, I am prime minister of the island. My counsel is sought for in most law cases, though it is my endeavour to keep clear of them as much as possible."[15] In this way Elder Pratt discovered how easily his Protestant predecessors had become involved in politics simply because they desired to establish justice and harmony.

EXPANSION OF THE MISSION TO THE TUAMOTUS

By February 7, 1845, Elder Rogers and Elder Grouard were both back in Tahiti. But because they could see no signs of an imminent settlement between the French and the natives, they determined to sail to other areas in the vicinity, preferably to islands under local control.

Following this plan, Elder Rogers sailed northwest toward the Leeward Islands of the Society Group on April 22. The next day Elder Grouard sailed east toward the Tuamotus.

Noah Rogers's ship, the *Artroveda,* touched briefly on Moorea, only a short voyage from Papeete, and then went on to Huahine. There it was necessary to make repairs. It was not until May 29 that Rogers reached Mangaia of the Cook Islands. For a short time he thought he had found a suitable place to teach. But to his disappointment he learned that the four thousand people of the island were already under the influence of the LMS. He had a similar experience on Rurutu and, discouraged, returned to Tahiti on June 13. Depressed with the failure of his mission and fearful for the welfare of his family of nine children at Nauvoo, he took the ship *The Three Brothers* to the States. He arrived home December 29, 1845, and was united with his family only to die in the spring exodus from Nauvoo.[16]

Elder Grouard's experience on the low-lying coral atolls of the Tuamotus was almost the exact opposite of Rogers's. These islands offered a bleak existence. Little vegetation beyond the coconut thrived in the shallow soil of the archipelago. The diet there consisted principally of coconut and fish. The livelihood was meager and transportation was dangerous. Worst of all, the people had a reputation for ferocity and cannibalism. Most were hardly a generation removed from such practices.

When Elder Grouard landed on Anaa on May 1, 1845, he had a frightening experience:

> As we drew near the land I noticed that the beach was already lined with natives awaiting our arrival, and as we came nearer, I could distinctly hear them shout and jabber like a flock of ten thousand wild geese. . . . Leaping ashore, I found myself the next minute surrounded by some two or three hundred natives of both sexes and all ages: naked, half-naked, and dressed; hooting, hallooing, laughing, and jabbering like a legion of evil spirits. In my eyes they looked wild and savage-like; and I listened to their frightful noises, and not being able to understand what they said, I knew not but what I had become a victim for sacrifice in very deed.[17]

When the confusion subsided a bit, one of the chiefs, speaking in Tahitian (which some of the people could use if necessary), began a serious interview of the newcomer. He wanted to know Grouard's background and intentions. Elder Grouard told him he was an American who desired to stay among them and teach the gospel of Jesus Christ. This pleased the chief greatly. "Missionary," the chief said, "your talk is good, and the governor and chiefs are well pleased with it. You are the first missionary from the land of the white people that ever came to our poor land to live among us."[18] Before that time only Tahitian missionaries had been willing to make the sacrifice to live on Anaa.

Over the months ahead the Tuamotuans proved eager to hear Grouard's message, and he had much success. The second day he was on Anaa, Grouard met with the chiefs of the five villages of the island. He learned that there were only about one hundred nominal Christians among the two to three thousand inhabitants.

Only twenty-five days after he arrived, Elder Grouard baptized 6 converts. By mid-June, 24 had entered the Church. Soon after this, Grouard made a fifteen-day tour of the other villages on the island. He preached thirty-one times publicly, held many gospel discussions and conversations, and baptized 29 more people. From then on the Church grew rapidly. Another tour, which lasted into early August, brought 195 baptisms in the outer villages and another 65 at the home base. He now had 355 local converts. On September 21, Grouard organized five branches with seventeen officers and 620 members in good standing. All this had been accomplished within four months of the first baptisms.

This success and the bright prospects for many more converts led Elder Grouard to seek assistance from Brother Pratt. He worried, however, about the time that would be involved in sending for him. If Grouard sent a letter it might take eight months for Pratt to come to Anaa. After prayerful consideration he decided to go after his distant companion himself in a *pahi Paumotu,* a large native-built double canoe. Although this craft appeared fragile and dangerous, such ancient catamarans had conveyed the Pacific peoples from island to island for hundreds of years. Neither quadrant nor compass was available, but the natives could read the waves, the winds, the clouds, and the stars.

On October 14, Elder Grouard sailed for Tahiti with a crew of eighteen, sufficient food for the voyage, and a fair wind. Several days out, about evening, the little crew sighted the tiny island of Mehitia, where they wanted to put in for the night. In an effort to make better time they began running toward the island at full sail. A stiff gust of wind came up and carried the foremast away. Minutes later the mainmast blew down. The next few minutes nearly completed the disaster. The double canoe crashed into the reef and was broken up. Fortunately the people of the island saw the problem and rowed out to give assistance. No lives were lost, but the canoe was irreparably damaged. Although Elder Grouard's crew were experts in building *pahi Paumotu,* time was passing. During the next two weeks, while a new vessel was being constructed, Grouard used the delay to advantage, preaching the gospel to the natives of the island and baptizing two of them, but at the same time praying that a ship would appear to take him to Tahiti. His prayer was answered, and by rowing five miles out to sea he was able to hitch a ride to his destination. About twenty-four hours later the ship docked at Papeete. Elder Grouard had nothing but the clothes on his back, but the Saints at Papeete kindly ministered to his needs. Almost immediately he sent a message to Pratt on a vessel, the *Artarevedre,* which was making a round trip to Tubuai.

Captain Lajot's schooner, the *Artarevedre,* reached Tubuai on December 4, 1845. When Lajot delivered Pratt his mail, there were four letters: the first two were the only letters he had received from his wife in two and a half years; the others were notes from Grouard. From his wife he learned that she and the four girls were well but not too happy. She also described the death of the Prophet and circumstances in Nauvoo. From Grouard, Elder Pratt learned of his great success on Anaa and how desperately he needed help. Grouard wrote, "If you don't accept, I will come to Tubuai for you in this native vessel, for I am determined to have your assistance on Anaa come life or death; and if I should be drowned in consequence of starting in such a frail bark, my death will be upon your hands as you would not come with Captain Lajot."[19]

Elder Pratt dearly loved his friends on Tubuai, but he had accomplished all he felt he could there. He placed the Tubuai Branch in the hands of Elder Charles Hill, whom Pratt had considered his missionary companion since Hill's early conversion to the Church; and he promised the people he would return or send elders. He later did both. After enjoying several sumptuous yet tearful feasts and receiving gifts of the island's produce, Pratt, along with his friends Nabota and his wife Telii (who considered themselves his *hoas* or permanent companions), seventeen hogs, sixty hens, and one goat (all of which were Pratt's), boarded the *Artarevedre* for its return voyage to Tahiti. He sold his livestock in Papeete.

Once united on Tahiti, the elders worked a district called Tiarei for a month and then sailed for Anaa, arriving there on February 3, 1846. They set to work teaching school, preaching the gospel, and administering to the sick. In order to keep all the branches happy, Grouard and Pratt divided the island and then rotated their visits from place to place. Converts continued to enter the waters of baptism.

Elder Grouard, who seemed to prefer pioneering new areas to tending established branches, decided that he could serve better by visiting other islands in the chain. From June 5 until September 18 Elder Grouard traveled constantly and preached on at least nine other islands. From Faaite, Fakarava, Toau, Kaukura, Makatea, Tikahau, Rairoi [Rangiroa or Rahiroa], Arutua, and Apataki, he gleaned 116 souls.

On September 24, 1846, members of the Church from ten branches (the Tahiti branch was not represented)[20] assembled at Putuhara, Anaa, for the first Mormon conference in the Pacific. The total membership in the islands at this time was 866. Without doubt Pratt's decision to return to the body of the Saints in America was the most important matter discussed.

The next two months were little different for Pratt and Grouard from those that had preceded the conference. They continued their teaching, preaching, blessing, and baptizing. Then on November 14 the captain of the *Robroy* took Pratt to Tahiti. Addison Pratt knew that an important period of his life was coming to a close. He wrote while on his way to Tahiti:

> I shall never forget the parting with Brother Grouard. He and I have been yoked together in this mission for three and a half years. We have withstood the frowns of poverty, the opposition of men and devils, the abusive negligence of our friends in America (as we have received but three letters from there since we left), the frowns of hunger, traveling over the sharp coral rocks and slippery mountains with our toes out of our shoes, and our knees and elbows out of our clothes, living a part of our time on cocoanuts and raw fish, and sleeping on the ground for the sake of obeying the Savior's commands and preaching the Gospel to the natives of these South Sea Islands.[21]

By this time, in spite of such hardships, he and Elder Grouard had baptized more than a thousand souls into the kingdom.

When Elder Pratt landed at Papeete he found the harbor busy with ships of trade and war. The hostilities between the French and the Tahitians were unabated. But a few weeks later, at the end of December, the war finally ended. On January 1, 1847, a large number of natives assembled to hear the French governor address them. He told them, among other things, that "they could embrace any kind of religion they thought proper, and in so doing he would protect them from persecution."[22]

From New Year's Day until March, Elder Pratt spent most of his time in a district called Tiarei, about fifteen miles east of Papeete. One of his converts from Tubuai, Haametua, had come from there and had laid the groundwork for the establishment of the Church in Tiarei. Although Pratt felt that he was only marking his time until a ship sailed for California, he developed a branch of twenty-seven members at Huau. This early branch later proved to be important to the establishment of the Church on Tahiti.

On March 28, 1847, Addison Pratt sailed for Honolulu with Captain Lajot on the schooner *Providence.* They arrived at the Sandwich Islands (Hawaii) on April 28. Elder Pratt observed that the city was much more modern and European than it had been two and a half decades before. After a short visit there he continued on to San Francisco on the same ship. Arriving there on June 11, 1847, he made contact with a group of Church members who had come to California with Samuel Brannan aboard the ship *Brooklyn* a year before.

He was eager to know the location of the Church, his wife, and his daughters. No one had any answers. They did know that the Saints had been driven from Nauvoo and reported that Sam Brannan had gone by horseback to find the body of the Church and bring its members to his chosen Zion on the Pacific coast. The best Pratt could do was wait for better word.

When Brannan came back in the fall, he brought the surprising news that Brigham Young had chosen to remain in the Valley of the Great Salt Lake. Brannan also brought to Elder Pratt a letter from his wife. It was written at Winter Quarters, where she and the girls had suffered for two years with sickness, too little food, and many other hardships. Her letter told of her plans to move west as soon as she was able.

In May 1848, Addison, with a remnant of the Mormon Battalion, moved eastward into the Sierra Nevada mountains. They arrived in Salt Lake City on September 28. To Pratt's joy he found that his wife had arrived eight days before him.[23] They had been apart for five and a half years!

In October conference, Elder Pratt reported his and Elder Grouard's work and their plans, hopes, and desires for the Polynesian Saints. More missionaries were needed, and the sooner the better. The conference voted unanimously to send Elder Pratt and others to do the work.

Through the winter of 1848-49, Pratt conducted classes in Tahitian three nights a week; perhaps this was the first missionary training center of the Church.

Although a group of Tahiti-bound missionaries was ready to leave by midsummer of 1849, various delays held up their departure. Then, it was Pratt and James S. Brown who left first for the islands. Sailing from San Francisco, they landed at Papeete on May 24, 1850.

The same spring twenty-one more missionaries, seven of whom would preach, were called at April conference to serve in French Polynesia, as it later came to be called. Included were Louisa Barnes Pratt and daughters Ellen, Francis, Lois, and Ann Louise; Jonathan Crosby, his wife, Caroline (who was a sister of Mrs. Pratt), and their son Alma; Joseph Busby; Thomas Tompkins, his wife, and their two children (he was asked to take special care of the Pratts); a Brother McMerty and his wife and child; Sidney Alvarus Hanks (brother of Knowlton F. Hanks, who had died at sea during the earlier voyage); Simeon A. Dunn; Julian Moses; and Hiram E.W. Clark, age fourteen, who was under Sister Pratt's care. This company, prepared to teach the arts of civilization as well as the gospel, departed from Salt Lake City on May 7, 1850. They sailed from San Francisco on September 15, and, following a two-month voyage, they arrived at Tubuai on October 21, 1850.

ELDER GROUARD'S WORK BETWEEN 1847 AND 1850

Shortly before Addison Pratt left the islands, Elder Grouard decided to marry. He had written to his wife at Nauvoo many times but had not heard a word from her or about her. He became convinced that she had left him and the Church and returned to her former life in the Eastern states. Elder Grouard, now twenty-seven years old, rationalized that it was not good for man to be alone. Being wedded to his field of labor, as Pratt put it, he decided to take a wife and remain in the islands. Pratt performed the ceremony, uniting Grouard to Tearo, a native girl, in April 1846. Tearo was a member of the Church, "the prettiest and best girl on the island." A year or two later this marriage ended tragically when she, being seriously ill, died at sea, leaving Grouard with an infant daughter, Sophronia. Needing a mother to care for his child, Grouard married again; this time he chose Nahina, the daughter of a chief on Anaa. She gave birth to three sons.[24] He was never again to hear anything concerning his American wife.

While Pratt was away, Grouard remained busy. He selected John Hawkins, who was converted in the islands, to work with him. Hawkins was an avid teacher, and he expanded the work much farther into the Tuamotus. Grouard spent most of his time during Pratt's absence in Tahiti and Tubuai building and selling boats. When the company of missionaries arrived on Tubuai they found him hard at work on his third ship, a relatively large schooner with eighty tons burthen with a spacious cabin.

THE SECOND PERIOD AND CLOSING OF THE MISSION

Sister Pratt and all the members of the group were happy to see Elder Grouard after so many years, but they were dismayed to learn that since their arrival five months earlier, neither Addison Pratt nor James S. Brown had been allowed to come from Tahiti to Tubuai. The French governor had detained them in Tahiti, pending their fulfilling several requirements, one of which was a signed statement of the reasons for the Mormon mission in the French protectorate, something that would explain the doctrine, faith, and practices of the Latter-day Saints. A number of months passed before Pratt and Brown satisfied the governor, but in November 1850 they were finally given permits to stay in the French area. Their permits stated that they, like all other foreigners in the islands, could not live off the local people. Traveling without "purse or scrip" was no longer allowed. This restriction caused many difficulties during the remaining months of the mission.[25]

Elder Pratt, now free to pursue the work, took the first ship to Tubuai, arriving on January 28, 1851. President Pratt (he had been so appointed by Brigham Young) assigned Elder Brown to labor on Tahiti. On Tubuai, with the rest of the missionaries, Pratt helped construct the mission ship. The months from January to May were happy, family-filled days for Addison and his loved ones.

Louisa Barnes Pratt and Caroline Barnes Crosby contributed much to the mission. Their husbands were away on other islands most of the time. Occasionally they endured moments of fear for their own safety —for example, when natives unloaded a number of cases of liquor on the island and drank it up during the next day or so. They were busy conducting school for their own and the local children, holding women's meetings, and teaching American homemaking skills, such as quilting.[26]

In April, the mission ship, the *Ravaai* (the Fisherman), was ready to serve the mission by transporting missionaries from island to island and also to engage in interisland commerce to help provide financial support for the mission.

Missionary life was evidently too hard for two of the new missionaries and their families. In March 1851, only four months after their arrival at Tubuai, Joseph Busby sailed for home with his family. In May, Elder McMerty followed with his wife and child. President Pratt was disturbed by the "foolishness" of their coming so far only to "turn round and go back" just because of a little hardship. He asserted that these islands needed healthy, ambitious men, "young men who are neither sugar nor salt, as they are sometimes exposed to the wet."[27]

At the same time Thomas Tompkins was sent home with his family to search for a gathering place in California for the island Saints and to find financial assistance for the mission. Apparently nothing came of either purpose.

From the time of the *Ravaai*'s maiden voyage to Tahiti in May 1851, the mission encountered greater and greater opposition from both the French government (and the Roman Catholic Church, which

Louisa Barnes Pratt, wife of Addison Pratt, served as a missionary on the island of Tubuai. One of the first lady missionaries of the Church, she and her sister Caroline B. Crosby operated the first LDS school in the Pacific. (Courtesy LDS Church Archives.)

was supported by it) and representatives of the London Missionary Society.

The involvement of the French government in mission affairs had been of no real consequence until 1848. In that year, however, the government had begun restricting travel from island to island. Not only the LDS but also the LMS missionaries believed this was part of a plot to curtail their work. The restrictions effectively hindered the missionary efforts.

By the time Elders Pratt and Brown had arrived back in the islands in 1850, the French were firmly in control. For a time the law of religious toleration worked for the benefit of all non-Catholic missionaries. But the government, under Governor Bonard, had become uneasy about the presence of so many Americans within its domain. Furthermore, Roman Catholic missionaries, although not officially sponsored by the protectorate, seem to have received special favors and support. In historian Aarne A. Koskinan's words, "the French navy had unscrupulously interfered in the internal affairs" of the islands.[28] Indeed, the Roman Catholics, too, evidently served the government in some instances. The government's uneasiness about foreigners and its preferential treatment of Catholicism combined to create a near-impossible situation for the Mormons.

In addition, the government announced a law in March 1852 that placed all religious affairs at Papeete under state control and created a new office of district minister to direct and correlate the religious activities in Polynesia. At the same time, missionaries were ordered to keep to one district. They were also supposed to preach only when they had been asked to do so by written invitation of their congregations.[29] Neither Mormons nor Protestants adhered to these laws when they could avoid them.

A French historian, Charles-Andre Julien, has described the period from 1797 to 1870 in the Pacific as *la guerre des missions*, the war of the missions. Roman Catholic tradition demanded that "the maintenance of its traditional leading position was to be striven for by every possible means."[30] Unfortunately, in this war the Mormons did not have the strength numerically nor financially to fight a winning battle. As will be seen, before the conflict was over Grouard had been summoned to Papeete to answer trumped-up criminal charges, James S. Brown had been deported, and some local Saints had lost their lives on Anaa because they insisted upon practicing their religion.

At about the time Elder Pratt came back from Utah, bringing Elder Brown with him, Elder Grouard and one of the local converts, Brother

Whitaker, were charged with using seditious language at a conference held on Tubuai. Grouard noted, "Consequently a man-of-war was dispatched to bring us prisoners to Tahiti. . . . We had no public trial, but simply underwent an examination before the governor; and though some twenty affidavits had been elicited against us, they were so flimsy and contradictory, that simple affirmation of truth and innocence compelled an honourable acquittal."[31]

James S. Brown, a young, energetic veteran of the Mormon Battalion march to California, attracted too much attention to himself. While laboring on Anaa, he displayed an American flag, sketched a map of the Battalion route, made another map showing the location of the gold fields in California (he had been at Sutter's Mill when the first gold was discovered), and sympathized openly with the Polynesians when they complained of the French yoke. All this was carefully noted by four Catholic priests who had recently established themselves on the island. Brown was incredulous when a French man-of-war brought *gendarmes* to arrest him, place him in chains, and transport him to Papeete. On November 10, 1851, he was tried before the governor and some associates. Four days later Elder Brown was told that he must leave the protectorate on the next boat. Elder Grouard made sure the next boat was the *Ravaai*, the mission ship. They set out on the seventeenth and traveled south to Raivavae, which was outside the protectorate at that time.[32] Elder Pratt, who had been teaching there with little success, was replaced by Brown. Grouard and Pratt sailed on to Anaa and other islands in the Tuamotus and finally back to Tubuai, where they arrived on January 9, 1852.

Elder Brown remained on Raivavae and some other islands in the vicinity for almost a year. When he left Tahiti for home on November 26, 1852, he was deeply disturbed about the general condition of the Church in the islands. He observed, as did his companions who had left the same port in May, that among the population there was a general decline in morals. The prohibition on liquor had been repealed, more licentious dances were growing in popularity, and venereal diseases were at near-epidemic proportions.

But the event that almost broke Elder Brown's heart was the so-called Mormon revolt on Anaa. When he arrived on Tahiti he was carefully watched by the police. He did not at first understand why, but through notes passed to him by young men from Anaa, he learned that a number of Church leaders from that island were now on Tahiti, held prisoners for having been involved in the murder of a policeman and a Roman Catholic priest.

This event occurred after President Pratt, Elder Grouard, and their families had left the islands in May 1852, leaving only Brown and Hanks to carry on missionary activities. About this time four Catholic priests had begun to proselyte intensely among the people of Anaa. They gathered a congregation of around thirty members, most of whom were reported to be employed by the government. These priests also gained the offices of "district ministers" and forbade Mormon meetings. The Mormons were not supposed to read, sing, or pray. One evening while a prayer meeting was underway, a partially drunken *gendarme*, accompanied by two priests, entered the Mormon chapel at Putuahara and told the Saints to stop their meeting. One woman remained on her knees. The *gendarme* drew his sword and swung it over his head to bring it down on her. The tip of the sword caught on a cross beam, and one of the brethren grabbed a fishing spear and ran it through the *gendarme*, killing him. In the scuffle that followed, one of the priests was killed with the *gendarme*'s sword, evidently by one of the Mormons. The other priest escaped with serious cuts on his face. He managed to get word of these events to government headquarters in Papeete, and shortly a contingent of troops was on the little island. Before the troops left, five priesthood bearers, Tefatina, Reifara, Maru, Mafeuta, and Temutu, had been hanged from a beam tied between two coconut trees. A number of others, including several women, were chained and taken to Tahiti, where Brown later found them working in the mountains, building a road under very harsh conditions. It is no wonder that Elder Brown was deeply grieved to depart from the islands under these bitter circumstances.[33]

When Elder Brown left, only Sidney Alvarus Hanks remained of all the foreign missionaries who had come to the islands. He was in the east Tuamotus and out of touch with the rest of the mission. He evidently stayed in the islands until about 1857. In addition to him, there were a number of local elders and other priesthood bearers who carried on the work of the Church. John Hawkins, who had worked closely with the Utah missionaries before their departure, assumed the leadership of the Church in Tahiti for a time.

When Elder Grouard reported the status of the mission in Salt Lake City, he said there were between fifteen hundred and two thousand members of the Church on at least twenty islands spread over hundreds of miles of water. He said, "As a general thing they are faithful and zealous Saints."

CHAPTER 2

FORTY YEARS ALONE AND THE REESTABLISHING OF THE MISSION

French Polynesia, 1852–1899

After the expulsion of the missionaries in 1852, the Tahitian, Tuamotuan, and Tubuaian Saints kept the Church alive in the islands for forty years. Church President Brigham Young suggested to Walter Murray Gibson, a missionary who was sent to the Pacific in 1861, that he might call on the Saints in the Society Islands if it was convenient, but Gibson became involved in the Church in Hawaii and never visited French Polynesia.[1] No other LDS missionaries were sent to French Polynesia until 1892.

The story of the Saints from 1852 to 1892 is sketchy at best. Persecutions continued for many years. Government and Catholic harassment of the Saints on Anaa and other Tuamotu islands was so intense that it became dangerous for one to espouse Mormonism openly. This fact, in combination with an absence of an appointed authority who could resolve differences regarding doctrine and procedure, allowed dissensions to arise that ultimately broke the Church into factions—Mormons, Israelites, the Sheep, Abraham's Church, Darkites, and the Whistlers. Not until 1867, when the government extended general religious toleration throughout the protectorate, were any of the factions allowed to worship openly. By that time the LDS Church in French Polynesia was in a thoroughly disorganized state.[2]

James S. Brown returned as a missionary to Tahiti in 1892, after an absence of forty years. He observed that many unusual or erroneous doctrines had been adopted, such as holding daily meetings (which was not the accepted LDS pattern) and allowing only one man (or woman) to conduct services, lead the hymns, pray, and preach.

Several islands Saints stand out as stalwarts. Elders Tihoni and

Maihea are known to have withstood imprisonment and many other ordeals rather than deny what they knew to be true. Each of them tried to keep the Saints in his area active and faithful to the gospel.

John Hawkins, the inter-island sailor and trader who was converted to the Church by Addison Pratt, and who worked as a missionary while the Utah elders were in the islands, also tried to keep the Church going. He later joined with the Reorganized LDS Church, but for many years he served well in the original faith. According to F. Edward Butterworth, an RLDS missionary, Hawkins continued to work as an inter-island trader after the missionaries left. He kept his relationship to the Church a secret from the government, but he appointed five local brethren to work with him in the ministry. Each of the others established a store where Hawkins could supply goods and provide leadership support without being suspected by the police. He remained active as a missionary until at least 1864.[3] Two island Zions, "gathering places," were established. The Saints on Tubuai called Mahu "Tiona," or Zion. The Saints in and around Papeete gathered in a little mountain sanctuary near Faaa, also Tiona, three and a half miles west of the city. Exactly how many members of the Church lived there is not known. But they did conduct schools as well as regular church meetings. In the early 1870s this little community was under the care of local Tahitian elders and an East Indian (or part East Indian) member named David Brown.[4]

It was into this branch that two missionaries from the Reorganized Church came. Charles Wandell, an apostate Mormon who had joined the RLDS Church, and Gloud Rodger arrived at Tahiti on December 13, 1873. They visited the Tiona settlement and, unfortunately (from the LDS perspective) they convinced most of the Saints that they represented the church that had inherited the authority of the Prophet Joseph Smith after his martyrdom in 1844. They claimed that Brigham Young and the Utah Mormons were apostates and that the authority to lead the Church had been given to Joseph Smith III, who was the leader of the Reorganization. Before they went on to Australia to fill their missions, they baptized fifty-one people into their church.

The next RLDS missionary to claim authority over the Saints in the islands was William Nelson, who arrived in 1879. He was followed by Thomas W. Smith, an apostle in the Reorganized Church, who arrived as an assigned missionary in 1884. Before Mormon elders returned in 1892, Nelson and Smith had led a fairly large number of members into their church.

THE MISSION IS REESTABLISHED, 1892

After the closing of the LDS mission in French Polynesia in 1852, the mission in Hawaii (founded in 1850) was the only Pacific one to remain open for the next several decades. In 1888, however, missionaries were sent from Hawaii to Samoa to establish the LDS Church there. By the summer of 1891 the mission in Samoa with headquarters near Apia was well under way. Though the mission was only three years old, President William O. Lee decided it was time to open new fields of labor. In June he sent missionaries to Tonga. Then, with the blessings of the Church's First Presidency, he began making plans to send elders to Tahiti. Soon after Elder William A. Seegmiller of Richfield, Utah, arrived in Samoa on October 4, 1891, President Lee asked him whether he would be willing to help with the reopening of Church work in Tahiti.[5] He accepted the call and, eleven days later, when Tahitian Bibles and a dictionary arrived, he set to work learning the language.

Elder Joseph W. Damron, Jr., who arrived in Samoa on November 28, was selected to go to Tahiti with Elder Seegmiller. When the steamer *Richmond* left Apia harbor, both men were apprehensive about what lay ahead for them in Tahiti, but they wrote of their conviction that they could succeed in this new assignment.[6]

Their apprehension stayed with them through the entire voyage, in no way lessened by the natural beauty of Tahiti, which they could see as their ship glided to its mooring. How would they be accepted by the people, the government? Could they find any Mormons from the early era? "[In] all that crowd," wrote Elder Seegmiller, "not one did we know; it seemed strange, and we were indeed strangers." It was January 27, 1892. The Tahitian Mission of The Church of Jesus Christ of Latter-day Saints was open again after a hiatus of forty years.

The elders found a small room without much furniture, supplied with cobwebs and mosquitoes but priced low enough for self-supporting Mormon elders—six dollars a month. A week or two later they found something more to their liking, a three-dollar-a-month room.

As soon as they were settled, Elders Damron and Seegmiller began carefully studying the local situation. Through visits to Mr. Turnball, manager of a local firm, and Mr. William F. Doty, U.S. consul, they learned a little about the government situation. First, the territory was officially called *Establissements Français de l'Océanie.* The protectorate, as it had been known to earlier LDS missionaries, was now a colony. Between the 1840s and 1880s, the French had laboriously assembled the five archipelagos of the area (the Society Islands, the Marquesas, the Tuamotus, the Gambiers, the Australes, and the isolated island of Clipperton) into one governmental entity headed by a governor and council. Although the French had hoped the islands would bring them an economic advantage, by this time these hopes had not materialized.[7] Mr. Doty assured the elders that there were no restrictions concerning preaching the gospel or "carrying out our duty."[8]

Their initial fears concerning the local people were quickly alleviated. Even while the elders were at their first home, they were almost literally adopted by a Tahitian neighbor and his family who brought them fish, fruit, cabbage, breadfruit, and other food every day and helped in many other ways. The elders observed that there was a sizable Chinese population on the island. They later learned that in 1865 a planter had imported a fairly large number of Chinese to work on his cotton plantation. The plantation did not survive, but the Chinese did, and by 1892 they owned hotels and stores and were an important part of the populace. Europeans, mostly French by birth, numbered fewer than a thousand. Most of them were traders, merchants, or government employees.

One day, shortly after they arrived, Elders Damron and Seegmiller learned about a group of Mormons who lived outside of Papeete at Faaa. On February 8, Amaro, the Tahitian neighbor who had adopted them, took them there. They discovered that the supposed Mormons were actually RLDS. A Tahitian RLDS elder, Tupuni, explained that there were over two thousand members of the Reorganized church in the various islands.[9] This meeting was the first of hundreds of encounters between elders of the two churches. During the 1890s the problems between the two churches were of major importance; more on this will be discussed later.

In mid-February the elders made shoulder bags for their belongings and started on an extended walk around the island of Tahiti. Their trek helped them to learn the language faster and to get better acquainted with the culture.

Because they could speak neither Tahitian nor French, their missionary work moved slowly in the early months. Both elders were troubled by this and so informed the First Presidency. In order to improve communications between Salt Lake City and Tahiti (all communications had previously been sent through the mission president in Samoa), the First Presidency appointed Elder Damron temporary president of the newly organized Tahitian Mission and instructed him that he and Seegmiller were to report directly to Salt Lake City each month. Damron learned of his appointment on April 29, 1892.[10]

The First Presidency listened to the elders' pleas for help and called Elder James S. Brown, now sixty-five years old and missing one leg, to go to Tahiti as president of the mission. He was the only living member of the earlier mission group. Brown's son, Elando, and Elder Thomas Jones, Jr., were called to accompany the veteran elder.[11]

By June 1, when the three reinforcement elders arrived, Damron and Seegmiller had not accomplished much that was visible. But they were beginning to use the Tahitian language fairly well, and they did know the lay of the land. What they wanted now was to get some converts and especially to find members of the Church who had remained faithful since the early mission closed.

A friend of Brown's, Mr. Dorence Atwater, who had been U.S. consul for twenty-five years, allowed them all to stay in a very comfortable home in Papeete; a number of RLDS members who knew Brown visited him and renewed old acquaintances.

Not long after his arrival, President Brown was invited to use Mr. Atwater's hall for religious services. Atwater, however, suggested that the elders should obtain the governor's permission before going ahead. Mr. Atwater introduced Brown to the director and secretary of the interior, "who immediately asked me if I was not the same Brown who had difficulty with the government many years ago." Brother Brown said that he was. Three days later the elders were informed that they would not be "permitted to labor as ministers" among the people of the colony. After consulting the American consul, writing letters, and seeking French legal counsel, they learned that they could legally preach if they notified the appropriate authorities, the mayor or local magistrate, in writing before holding each service. Brown said that because of this restriction they were "practically shut out from holding meetings."[12]

Then, on August 22, President Brown received a letter from an old Church member named Tehahe, or Opu, who lived on Tubuai. It proved to be the opening the elders had been hoping for. Tehahe warmly invited the elders to come to Tubuai, as he said that "they had been left in the dark many years without one ray of light."[13] That day they were also visited by an employee of a wealthy part-Tahitian named Mapuhi, who lived in the Tuamotu Islands. Mapuhi claimed to be a member of the Church and wanted to see the missionaries. He

Tamaiti or Tatio or Faretaha i rani (known by all three names), was baptized by Addison Pratt at Tubuai. He remained faithful to the Church until his death in the 1920s. Photo taken in 1921. (Courtesy L. H. Kennard.)

later proved to be a true Latter-day Saint. He shared with the elders and Saints his three schooners and his home, which the missionaries described as a seven-room mansion, larger than the fine homes of Papeete. Mapuhi had joined the Church as a small boy when Sidney Alvarus Hanks ministered in the Tuamotus. As a young man he had learned the trade of shipbuilding, and by trading pearls and pearl shell with the island people, he had become known as the "pearl king."

As soon as transportation could be arranged, President Brown, in company with Elder Seegmiller, sailed to Tubuai. When they landed at Mataura on September 20, the elders learned that representatives of the RLDS church had preceded them. The people were noticeably cool toward them; in fact, President Brown reported that very few people were hospitable. About a week after their arrival, they moved five miles around the island to Mahu. There "the clouds over the mission began to break." Many of the Polynesians began to talk openly with President Brown and to bring food. The next Sunday Brown and Seegmiller met with a number of people in an open-air meeting. In that gathering Elder Brown "explained how the authority had continued in the church from the Prophet Joseph to the present organization." Following the meeting several people asked for baptism and, two days later, on October 4, Elder Seegmiller baptized twenty-four persons. Brown's journal entries noted numerous baptisms over the next few weeks: October 10, "nine baptized"; October 14 and following, "baptized several"; November 8, "baptized eight"; November 14, "eight members were added to the Church"; November 16, "added five more souls to the Church by baptism." On November 23, Elder Seegmiller baptized the school teacher at Mataura and two of the governor's daughters.[14] Before the end of November, sixty-five Tubuaians claimed membership in the Church.

On November 24, President Brown sailed from Tubuai. He placed Elder Seegmiller in charge of the branches. Serious problems remained to be settled regarding property ownership, and some of these matters were not resolved for many years. Seegmiller and the reestablished Church also had frequent conflicts with the Catholics, Protestants, and the Reorganized church. These problems notwithstanding, when President Brown left the island, he was convinced that the Lord had blessed them for their perseverance, prayers, and hard work.

Elder Brown had scarcely landed in Papeete on December 1 when he learned from his son, Elando, that Elders Damron and Jones, who had left Papeete shortly after J. S. Brown departed for Tubuai, were having success in the Tuamotu Islands. A conference of all the Saints in that area was planned for early January 1893, and Brown's help was needed.

Brown learned that after he and Seegmiller had sailed for Tubuai, Brother Mapuhi had come to Tahiti. The elders were eager to sail with him to Takaroa, his home island, and see the Saints of that part of the colony. They sailed from Papeete on October 26, in Mapuhi's 105-ton schooner, *Teavaroa*. After stopping briefly at a couple of islands where the RLDS were in the majority, the *Teavaroa* docked at Takaroa on November 1.[15]

On this island Elders Damron and Jones found a branch of one hundred Church members who had resisted the RLDS missionaries. After the elders met with these Saints, these faithful island people concluded that authorized messengers had indeed finally come from the Church in Salt Lake City. On November 6, they officially accepted Damron and Jones as their missionaries. By early December, thirty-three people had been added to the Church.[16] The Takaroa Branch was organized, holding regular meetings, and even building a stone meetinghouse. Brother Mapuhi was the motivating force behind this effort.

Gradually a more complete picture of the Church in the Tuamotus began to emerge. One day Elders Damron and Jones heard about

Saints on Anaa, and another day they learned of Saints in Katiu. In December they discovered that all the Tuamotu Saints were led by an old man, now blind, named Maihea. He said he had received his authority while Pratt and Grouard were in the islands. This venerable leader from Anaa had called a conference of all Tuamotu Saints to be held on the island of Faaite beginning January 6. When Damron and Jones learned about this, they wrote to Tahiti and asked their mission president to make every effort to join them at the scheduled conference. By leaving Papeete on December 15, Elders James S. and Elando Brown arrived at Takaroa on the twenty-sixth. Several days later, they, in company with Damron and Jones and six boatloads of local Saints, sailed for Faaite.

The fleet of Takaroa Latter-day Saints arrived at Faaite on December 31. It was evident from the large number of canoes and boats in the lagoon that others had already arrived. Elaborate preparations had occupied the local members for weeks before the gathering. Available food of all kinds—pigs, coconuts, fruits, fish, canned goods, and so forth—was amassed for the expected throng. But more exciting than the anticipated feasts, the renewal of friendships, and the exchange of information and gossip, was the joy of having men among them who were missionaries of the Mormon Church.

According to Elder Damron, not many minutes after they came ashore, Elder Brown and his companions were visited by a delegation of older men who were led by Maihea. Maihea came almost immediately to the point by asking a series of questions: "Are you the real Iatobo (James) that brought us the Gospel forty years ago? Second, Are you now representing the same Gospel as before?" He also asked the location of different villages on Anaa, the island where Elder Brown had labored while on his former mission. Being convinced, he said with joy: "We receive you as our father and leader, but had you not come back personally we would have refused to receive any foreign missionaries, as so many false teachers have been in our midst and decoyed many from the Gospel of Christ."[17] Maihea then related how he and his people had prayed constantly that God would again send them missionaries with the light of truth and the Holy Spirit to bless them. Their prayers had been answered after forty years of waiting.

During the conference meetings the elders learned that there were now ten branches with 425 members, most of them comparatively recent: only seventeen veterans of the early mission were known to be still alive or faithful to the Church. The missionaries ordained Tehina of Anaa and Karere of Katiu as elders. A number of other Polynesian elders were sustained in their positions as branch presidents.

Following the January conference the Browns, father and son, sailed for Anaa, where they taught the gospel until April. Elders Damron and Jones remained in the vicinity of Takaroa, and Elder Seegmiller remained on Tubuai.

During the absence of the missionaries from Tahiti, a new group of elders arrived on March 21, 1893, from Salt Lake City. The new recruits included Frank Cutler, Thomas L. Woodbury, Eugene M. Cannon, Carl J. Larsen, I. Frank Goff, Fred C. Rossiter, Jesse M. Fox, and Edward Sudbury. The new missionaries rented a home and set to work studying the Tahitian language. In early May, President Brown returned to Tahiti and gave the missionaries their teaching assignments.

Basically the missionary method consisted of from one to four elders traveling alone or together from island to island, meeting with the people, living with them in their huts or homes, eating their food, blessing the sick, organizing branches, baptizing an occasional convert, debating with leaders of other denominations (particularly the RLDS), trying to escape the inconsistent but heavy hand of the government, and in general attempting to uplift the Saints morally and spiritually. Local Polynesian elders generally presided over the branches.

In July 1893, about thirteen months after he had arrived in the islands, James S. Brown turned the leadership of the now firmly established mission over to Joseph W. Damron. On July 8, Brown, accompanied by his son Elando and Elder Edward Sudbury, whose health was poor, sailed from Tahiti.[18]

When Brother Brown arrived home in Salt Lake City, he reported to the First Presidency and made several suggestions, specifically that ten more missionaries be sent to Tahiti by the next spring, that these missionaries be prepared financially to support themselves and avoid living off the members, that the mission have a ship, and that a headquarters building be obtained in Papeete. Concerning the ship, he explained that inter-island travel was so unpredictable and dangerous that a vessel of one hundred tons should be procured to serve the mission's needs. Many decades passed, however, before such a boat was purchased by the mission. Brown's request for a mission headquarters, fortunately, was met much sooner.[19]

After Brown left the islands, the work proceeded without any serious problem until late March 1895, when a relatively new political administrator of the Tuamotu islands, E. A. Martin, decided to create difficulties for the Mormons and, later, for all of the non-French religious groups, specifically the RLDS and the Seventh-Day Adventists. Martin accused the Mormon elders of being "beggars, spongers off the natives, idlers who had nothing to do in our own country." These accusations were leveled at Elders Eugene M. Cannon and Carl J. Larsen on March 30, while they were en route to Takaroa for a semiannual conference. On that same day, Administrator Martin dispatched a command that the regular conference not be held. According to Elder Cannon, Martin declared that he had not sanctioned the conference and that those who had called it would be "taken to judgment" if his order was not followed. Martin also ordered the missionaries in the Tuamotus to cease teaching the gospel. His orders were followed.

During the next six months President Frank Cutler spent countless hours writing legal petitions; meeting with Mr. J. Lamb Doty, U.S. consul (who was a great friend to the Mormons); and arguing the Church's case directly before Governor Martin of the Tuamotus and Governor Papinaud of the French colony. Cutler assured Governor Papinaud that Latter-day Saints "obey, honor, and sustain the law" and support the local government. His main request was for a license to preach. Such a license was never granted, but because of pressure applied through Consul Doty, Governor Papinaud ordered his subordinate, E. A. Martin, to desist from his unfriendly acts and to allow the Mormon elders to continue their work. The missionaries were, of course, very happy to have the obstacles removed from their way, but six months had been lost.[20]

The colonial administration of the *Establissements Français de l'Océanie* was incredibly topheavy. There were during this time over five hundred paid officials to administer a colony of fewer than fifteen thousand people. Indeed, during the 1890s and until World War II, there was a persistent "tendency of the French to use Tahiti as a 'dumping ground' for bad officials."[21] Governors were frequently changed. The police were seemingly ever present.

One positive result of the Martin affair was that President Cutler found it necessary to reevaluate the status of the Church in the islands in order to write convincing letters to the government. President Cutler learned that Mormons made up one-fifth of the total population of the Tuamotu Islands. There were at that time 255 Mormon families. He also found that the RLDS and Roman Catholics each had approximately 1,000 followers in the Tuamotus and that the Protestants and Mormons each had about 700. At the end of 1895 there were sixteen LDS branches in the Tuamotus and two branches on Tubuai, but there were only five members on the island of Tahiti where over ten thousand people lived. There were in the whole mission a total of 1,043 Church members, including children. It now seems ironical that the LDS mission was called the Tahiti or Society Islands Mission during this era; it might better have been called the Tuamotu Mission.[22]

EXPANSION INTO NEW ENDEAVORS AND FIELDS

President Cutler, like his predecessors, was too involved with the problems of initial establishment to be concerned with moving into new areas. The task of expansion fell primarily to Daniel T. Miller, the next president of the mission. Though newly married, he arrived alone in Papeete on September 6, 1896. He was twenty-six years old when he received his call, but he was unusually well prepared to lead the missionary work in Tahiti. Miller was a linguist who could read and speak French (which would be useful in Tahiti), German, Greek, and Latin.[23]

Miller continued the translation program that was already underway. President Cutler had translated or supervised the translation of several items, including the Articles of Faith and the Lectures on Faith, numbers two and three.[24]

President Miller first broached the subject of translating the Book of Mormon and Doctrine and Covenants to the First Presidency in June 1897. Because his missionaries were having so many confrontations with the Reorganized Church, especially about matters discussed in B. H. Roberts's book *Succession in the Presidency of the Church*, Miller suggested that parts of this book should be the first item for translation, and next should follow the Doctrine and Covenants. Brother Miller also mentioned the importance of getting the Book of Mormon into Tahitian because the Catholics were "mistranslating" parts of it to mislead the people. The First Presidency gave its blessing, and before long these and other projects were underway.[25]

On June 18, 1898, Elders Chamberlain and Neff began translating the Doctrine and Covenants. They, along with President Miller and Elder Willey, started work on the Book of Mormon at about the same time. They finished the Tahitian Book of Mormon on July 7, 1899, but it was not published until 1904. For reasons not shown in the historical records, the Doctrine and Covenants translation from this early era was never published.[26]

The development that helped most in proselyting was the establishment of a language-learning program that President Miller put into effect in 1898. Through the coordinated study of grammars, vocabulary, scriptures, and conversation with the natives, Miller had many of his missionary students out among the people, carrying full loads within six months. Their accomplishment astonished many long-time foreign residents of Papeete.[27]

Along with the language program and translation work, the energetic President Miller saw the need for the mission to have a geographical center. Until his time there were no headquarters where new missionaries could be welcomed and where they could go when they were tired or sick or to pick up mail, tracts, supplies, and so forth. Nor was there a meeting house in Papeete. Unlike the Tuamotus and Tubuai, where the Church had fine stone chapels built or under construction in all seventeen branches, the Saints in Papeete had, with some difficulty, been renting halls for services. In the spring of 1897, Miller and his companions began looking for property to purchase. They hoped to build a small meeting hall with a mission office and sleeping room adjoining it.

During April conference at Hikueru in the Tuamotus, President Miller explained to the Saints the need for a building in Papeete. The Saints in the Tuamotus were relatively prosperous. Most of their income was derived from diving for pearl shell and from making copra (dried coconut meat). For the chapel they made donations of $602.80 and promises of another $400. With this money in hand, Miller continued to look for a good piece of property.

He did not find an ideal piece of land, but in August he obtained deed to a lot at Fautahera, on the outskirts of Papeete. It was twenty meters by thirty-five meters, donated by a friend of the Saints named Arai. The completed buildings were quite small, consisting of a meeting hall, an office for the mission president, and a study and sleeping room. Nearby, outside, they built a small cook house, which also doubled as a dormitory for missionaries.[28]

Soon after he arrived there, President Miller recognized the need to expand missionary efforts on Tahiti. He saw that it would take far fewer elders to proselyte the ten-thousand-plus people concentrated there than were required to handle the people on the scattered Tuamotu Islands. With this in mind he assigned several elders to begin proselyting the villages of Tahiti. Many of these places had been visited before, but almost always by elders who had only recently arrived in the mission and who could not speak Tahitian. By the summer of 1899, pairs of missionaries were living in three districts of Tahiti, and people gradually began joining the Church.[29]

In his effort to make Tahiti the actual administrative center of the Church, D. T. Miller decided to hold the April 1899 mission-wide conference at Papeete. The cost of coming to the conference was prohibitively high for most members in the Tuamotus, but fairly large groups did come from Takaroa, Hikueru, and two other islands. Local elders and sisters spoke, sang, and prayed. A warm, optimistic feeling pervaded the proceedings. In fact, President Miller reported that he had the same feeling he had enjoyed at general conference in Salt Lake City.

During this meeting President Miller called three Polynesian couples to fill short missions. All of them served honorably and did so at some sacrifice. Toae, who had previously served as a branch president, later became the first Tahitian Latter-day Saint to visit Salt Lake City and return to his home country. Timi and his wife were sent as the first LDS missionaries to Mangareva, in the Gambier group. Rua and his wife also served well. These local missionaries seem to have been the first "couple missionaries" in the Society Islands Mission, though other local elders had served as missionaries before them.

In August 1897, President Miller told the First Presidency about his decision to send elders to Moorea, only twelve miles west of Tahiti, and to the Leeward Group (*Iles Sous le Vent*) of the Society Islands with their approximately six thousand people. The major islands of the latter group are the twin islands of Raiatea and Tahaa and the islands of Huahine, Bora Bora, and Maupiti, all volcanic islands. Raiatea and Tahaa are particularly well-watered and fertile.

Raiatea, a well-populated island, was the political center of the Leeward Group in pre-missionary times. London Missionary Society preachers had converted most of the natives of this area to Protestant Christianity early in the 1800s. When the French subjugated Tahiti, Moorea, and the Tuamotu and Austral Islands, they had not been able to bring the Leeward Group under their control. In a treaty of 1847, France had agreed with Britain to respect the independence of the Leeward Islands. The treaty, however, had been revoked in 1888, and the area was officially annexed to the French colony in that year. Nevertheless, it was not until a war proved the greater military strength of France that the people of Raiatea submitted to colonial rule in 1897. This development made it possible for the Latter-day Saints to move into the area in the same year. The Roman Catholics, RLDS, and Seventh-day Adventists soon followed. By May 1898 twenty-two inhabitants of these islands had been baptized Latter-day Saints. From this time on, the Leeward Islands were, with the exception of only a few years, tracted regularly by the LDS missionaries.[30]

After founding the work on Moorea and the Leeward Islands, President Miller turned his attention to the 8,000 people in the Cook Islands and the 4,443 residents of the Marquesas Islands. He and his colleagues studied the religious and political situation in the Cook Islands as carefully as possible before moving into that area. Language materials in Rarotongan, the language of the main island of the group, were obtained, and by March 18, 1899, Elders Osborne J. P. Widtsoe and Mervin W. Davis were studying them. On May 19, these two elders sailed for Rarotonga. They arrived at Avarua, the capital, on May 23. The following day they found a quiet spot on the green volcanic hillside near Avarua and dedicated the island of Rarotonga to the preaching of the gospel of Christ. Although the Tahitian language is related to Rarotongan, or Cook Island Maori, as it is now called, the elders still had to study the language for several months before they were able to teach effectively.

By the fall of 1899 the elders were familiar with the local religious situation. They found the people friendly but very devoted to their LMS form of Protestantism. The queen and other political figures used not-so-subtle pressure to keep the people within the quasi-official church. John Williams had first introduced Christianity to these islands in 1823, and from that time until the 1890s, when Roman Catholics and Seventh-day Adventists entered the area, the LMS (now called Cook Island Christian) had operated without any religious rivalry.

Elders Widtsoe and Davis began holding meetings but ran into direct opposition from the queen. Elder Davis later wrote, "After our first meeting the edict of the powerful Queen backed by the Protestant prejudice went forth prohibiting the people from attending other meetings than those held in the Protestant Church."[31] This opposition, in combination with a lack of interest, "put an end to our meetings."

The contrast between the supervision of the Cook Islands by the British and of Tahiti by the French was striking. There were only two or three British officials in the entire group, in comparison with about five hundred officials in the French colony. In October 1900, New Zealand took possession of the Cook Islands—this, according to Elder

Davis, with "the full consent of the native people." English rule had not entirely suppressed the old native form of government, but affairs had been rapidly moving in that direction. The elders hoped more religious freedom would be a major result of these changes.

On July 18, 1900, Elders Widtsoe and Davis arrived on the island of Aitutaki. They published two tracts in Rarotongan and dedicated the island and its people to the reception of the gospel. They visited most of the people and found them friendly, but, as had happened on Rarotonga, the Protestant minister used his influence to interfere with the Church's progress. Even though no converts were made on Aitutaki, "conditions were more in our favor" there than on Rarotonga.[32]

On February 27, 1900, Elder Benjamin A. Johnson joined Widtsoe at Rarotonga, and on May 23, 1901, Elder Thomas Loveland arrived there. Johnson and Loveland later replaced the two senior elders when the latter departed for home in December 1900 and September 1901. Although all four missionaries worked earnestly to establish the restored gospel, they did not succeed. There were no baptisms.

The First Presidency of the Church was interested in the progress of the work in both the Cook Islands and the Marquesas Islands. When they recognized that hard work and patience were not accomplishing anything in these places, they directed President Edward S. Hall to close all those parts of the mission where the elders had been for a year or more without making any converts. As a result the LDS missionaries were withdrawn from the Cook Islands in November 1903. A number of years passed before Mormon elders reintroduced the gospel there.[33]

The story of the first attempt to plant the Church in the Marquesas Islands is no happier than that of the Cook Islands. President Miller had great hopes for this area and seriously began to plan the opening of this field in 1898.

When Elders Edgar L. Cropper and Eli Horton landed at Taiohas, Nukuhiva, on May 30, 1899, following a lengthy and frequently interrupted voyage of seven hundred and forty miles from Tahiti, they found that the people were already committed to either the Roman Catholic or Protestant religions. Moreover, the Bible had not been translated into Marquesan, and almost no language study helps were available. The first missionaries to bring Christianity there had been from the LMS, but for political reasons they later pulled out, leaving the area to the French Protestants. But because the Roman Catholic orders were more energetic, by the 1890s an estimated 2,800 Marquesans claimed to be of that faith.[34]

The Mormon missionaries did everything possible to try to learn the language. A Marquesan man helped them to get a Catholic prayer book, another book that contained the Gospels of Matthew and John, and a third publication that contained a short life of Christ. They did not have a grammar or a dictionary, but with these aids and the help of some local people they learned the Marquesan language.

More disappointing to the elders than the language problem was the spiritual indifference that prevailed. Even though Cropper, Horton, and those who followed them held sacrament meetings and even preached the gospel in Tahitian to appeal to the people from Tahiti and the Tuamotus who were living there, they did so with almost no success. Since the First Presidency had asked President Hall to close all areas that had not produced a convert in the last year, the Marquesas conference of the Society Islands Mission was closed by July 1904.[35]

When Miller left the islands in July 1899, the mission was well established. Sunday schools, which had been introduced by Cutler, were organized in many of the branches. Records were being kept—poorly in most branches, but they were providing a semblance of documentation for the leaders in Salt Lake City and for later histories. And by this time the mission did have a headquarters building. A sad note was that Elder Miller's wife, Hattie, whom he had married only one month before sailing for Tahiti, died of appendicitis in August 1898. After his return home he became a language professor at Brigham Young College in Logan, Utah. He never remarried.

CHAPTER 3

A TIME FOR CONSOLIDATION

French Polynesia, 1899–1919

William H. Chamberlain followed Daniel T. Miller as president of the mission. He and the mission presidents who succeeded him followed the general pattern that had already been established. They assigned several pairs of elders to Tahiti (if there were enough missionaries in the field to justify it), sent several pairs into the Tuamotus to travel from island to island, and appointed a pair or two to the Leeward Islands. Every so often in the halls of government a question regarding the Church would be raised that had to be answered. But for the most part, until World War I, the mission moved at a steady if rather slow pace.

LIFE AND SURVIVAL IN FRENCH POLYNESIA

Novelists and screenwriters have created a romantic image of life in the South Pacific. It is true that some larger volcanic islands such as Tahiti have provided a fairly easy livelihood and a casual social and moral climate. Nevertheless, life on most Pacific islands was and is tedious and often difficult. The Tuamotu Islands provide an excellent example of the struggle that island life can present. These low-lying coral atolls sustain little vegetation besides coconut palms, pandanus trees, and scrub bushes. Coconuts of various stages of maturity provide the basic staple of every person's diet. They provide liquid for drinking, a milk for thickening and making pudding, coconut meat for food and sacrament emblems, a kind of sisal for making twine, fronds for making baskets, hats, mats, and roof thatch, a substance for making liquor, and a trunk for constructing houses and boats. Before the coming of Europeans and canned foods, nearly all atoll dwellers survived on coconuts and sea products. Even today months can pass without any contact with the outside world.

Transportation was a serious problem for natives and missionaries alike during the period under consideration, and it has not improved very much since then. Hardly a month went by without the missionaries or members having narrowly escaped drowning (and not all did escape), having waited through a long doldrum, or having had some other miserable experience at sea. In addition, they frequently had to wait for months to find a ship that was going where they wanted to go. Most inter-island boats were small, filthy, and uncomfortable. The distances to be traveled were usually vast. For example, the distance is the same from Papeete to Hao as from Salt Lake City to Los Angeles. Covering such distances in open boats is a pleasure only for rugged sportsmen.

Island life offered little variety. There are no seasons, only variations in the weather. The food was monotonous. The people were generally so few in number that almost no new social contacts were available among them. Life in the Tuamotu Islands offered almost no privacy. The intimate aspects of husband-wife relationships were an accepted part of life for children as well as for adults. Moral standards such as those expected by the LDS Church then and now, and by other Christians, were almost totally alien to the local peoples, the long years of missionary effort notwithstanding. Youthful sexual experimentation was common in 1900 and remained common in the 1950s.[1]

How to handle offenses against the Christian moral requirement was a difficult question for various presidents of the island missions. In 1897 President Miller asked the First Presidency how he should deal with such matters. He received much the same counsel as that given to President Thomas S. Court in Samoa eight years later: "A policy will have to be followed best suited to the conditions there existing,"[2] and "where the people are in part the victims of their environments, mercy should be allowed to have full claim."[3]

In addition to lax morals, limited diet, and general boredom, in 1903, 1905, and 1906 the people of the islands were terrorized by extremely destructive cyclones. The worst of the three storms began on January 14, 1903, and lasted for almost two days. During the storm 517 people in the Tuamotus lost their lives; among these were 100 Latter-day Saints.[4]

Two LDS missionaries survived the main blast on the island of Hikueru. Their story, as told by Heber J. Sheffield, is one of the most exciting and harrowing of all South Sea adventures; space will allow only a brief synopsis of the events. Over seventeen hundred people had gathered on Hikueru to dive for pearl shell. The winds rose to ninety miles an hour and created waves so large that they rushed over the highest point of the island, which was thirty feet high. The temporary shacks of the visitors as well as the more permanent houses were destroyed. The people who lived through it—and 375 on Hikueru did not—were saved by tying themselves near the tops of coconut palms and holding on all night as the wind, water, and debris swept past. When the tumult ended, the tops of all the palms were gone, as were all houses, government buildings, and almost all food. The only building left standing was the coral-stone LDS chapel. The meeting house on Takaroa also survived. After the cyclone the people suffered greatly for want of food and water. Elders Sheffield and Joseph E. Allen and an RLDS minister, J. W. Gilbert, worked together to build a water distillery that produced 250 gallons a day. It saved many lives. These men and the island governor organized the people to bury the dead, distribute the meager amount of food, and help in many ways. Most of the people had lost all of their possessions. The elders came through the disaster with only the trousers they were wearing.[5]

Anthropologist Bengt Danielsson has pointed out that the cyclones of 1903, 1905, and 1906 caused an almost complete break with the past on the island of Raroia. The same thing happened elsewhere in the Tuamotus. In effect, the tidal waves washed away the old-style houses, implements, and other objects. Old family books containing many genealogies were also washed away; relics of the past were all gone, and more modern substitutes had replaced them. Waves destroyed what natural beauty had existed on the islands: ten years later missionaries were still commenting on the bleakness of the atolls since the great cyclones.[6]

An important part of Tuamotu life was pearl-shell diving. The missionaries frequently recorded their impressions concerning its good and bad effects upon the people. In the romantic and sentimental lore of the Pacific, the Tuamotus are frequently called the "Pearl Islands." Even in the best days of pearl and mother-of-pearl diving this was a misnomer: only a few of the seventy-eight Tuamotu Islands have provided the right environment for mussels to survive and thrive.

Because of this sensitive ecological system, the French government began restricting the yearly diving area before the turn of the century. These restrictions caused the people to gather to a different island each year, usually from August or September through November or December. Shell diving is risky work. In most years of the early part of the century, five to ten divers drowned.

The stakes were high but so were the returns. In 1898 and 1900, elders reported that good divers could earn as much as one hundred dollars a day. Others averaged from sixteen to thirty dollars. But most of the people did not know how to use their profits wisely. Church and government leaders lamented the fact that most money gravitated quickly to the hands of traders. Thousands of dollars in francs were consumed in liquor and gambling, with prostitutes, or on useless trinkets. Traders competed with one another for the bounty. They sold foreign goods to the divers at outlandish prices and brought most of the local people into serious debt. This was an ongoing problem for many of the Tuamotu Saints.

On the brighter side, at least four fine coral rock chapels, some with organs, were constructed on Takaroa, Hikueru, Morokau, and Anaa with funds raised almost entirely from diving. (On one occasion the Takaroa Saints earned five thousand dollars in three days of diving.) Because of their work as divers the Tuamotuans were usually wealthier than the people of Tahiti and the Leeward Islands.[7]

The gathering for the diving season also created an unusual opportunity for the Mormon missionaries as well as other ministers. The large number of Church members so assembled required attention and care, but the large number of non-Mormons likewise offered a good audience for the gospel message. Several converts were baptized during almost every diving season.

A NEW MISSION HEADQUARTERS IN PAPEETE

After the turn of the century, there was a gradual trend toward centralization of the Church in Papeete. Most of the members were still in the Tuamotu Islands, but the growth on Tahiti and the Leeward Group helped to make Papeete more important to the Church. By 1904 the mission president saw the need for a much larger facility. Early in 1905 President Edward S. Hall purchased for 9,000 francs a lot on the corner of Brea and Dumont d'Urville streets. By October 1906, the missionaries had completed a new mission home and meeting hall.[8] Having new, respectable headquarters did much to elevate the Church in the eyes of missionaries, members, and nonmembers alike.

Related to the building of a respectable headquarters was the idea of creating a gathering place for the Tahitian Saints. The first mention of this appears in the mission historical record on March 13, 1906, when President Hall and three elders were reported to have left Papeete to inspect some land at Tarauau "with the hope of buying it to colonize the saints on." A gathering and colonizing movement was underway in Samoa at this time, which may have stimulated President Hall to consider a similar move.[9] He also might have seen the advantages of having the Saints gathered in the two earlier Tionas.

After Hall's time the idea of a gathering place evidently received little or no attention until 1913 or 1914, when the First Presidency either asked or permitted President Fullmer to seek a suitable site to colonize. Mission clerk Ira Hyer wrote that "colonization has long been talked of in this mission and it now looks as though we will soon have a gathering place." The mission leaders made a decision during April conference in 1914 to try to buy a tract of land in the district of Haapepe.[10]

In a meeting of the First Presidency and Council of the Twelve on June 18, a purchase price for land was discussed, and it was decided that the amount asked was double its true value. The brethren decided to offer $10,000 if necessary, in order to obtain the land. Unfortunately, the conclusion to this matter does not appear in the mission records, nor is there further mention of gathering. We can only guess that the offer for the land was not accepted by the sellers and that the movement for a colony subsequently lost momentum. It is also possible that the outbreak of World War I soon after affected the plans.[11]

Between 1905 and 1915 the Church in the Pacific moved along at a steady but less than exciting pace. The number of members edged up slowly, the number of branches leveled off at twelve, and the number of Melchizedek Priesthood holders grew slightly—from seventy to seventy-two. The table on the next page illustrates the statistics during the years 1910 to 1919. (Statistics are lacking from 1898 to 1910, when the Church began requiring annual statistical reports.)

There is no clear historical evidence why these years were without greater numerical growth. The mission presidents, Frank Cutler, William A. Seegmiller, Franklin J. Fullmer, and Ira Hyer (acting), were all veterans and were well qualified to lead the mission. Perhaps the mission had reached a leveling-off time, a time for consolidation. In fact, there is evidence that this was happening by 1914.[12]

French Polynesia Mission, 1910-1919[13]

Year	Total Members*	Convert Baptisms	Melchizedek Priesthood	Total Branches	Total Missionaries
1910	1,115	11	70	14	10
1912	1,301	61	68	12	11
1914	1,345	5	71	12	8
1915	1,373	0	72	12	13
1916	1,398	18	74	12	15
1917	1,493	58	77	12	15
1918	1,539	26	79	12	16
1919	1,563	16	79	12	11

THE IMPACT OF WORLD WAR I

The years of World War I were different from the preceding decade and a half in a number of ways. First, the war changed many aspects of life inside and outside the Church; and second, the mission president during these years, Ernest C. Rossiter, was a uniquely creative and spiritual man who fostered growth in several unusual ways.

News of the outbreak of war reached Papeete in early August 1914, and because France was involved, the news was momentous, for it meant the colony was also at war. On about August 10, the old French gunboat *Zelle* was dispatched to subdue an unarmed German freighter in nearby waters. The freighter's crew and passengers were taken prisoner, as were all German citizens in the colony. Tahiti and French Polynesia played a minor but active part in the war. Over a thousand Polynesians, several of whom were LDS, served in the French forces in Europe. Papeete was shelled by two German war vessels on September 22, 1914. The heart of the Papeete business district was burned to the ground, and even the LDS mission headquarters took an indirect hit. Prices in the colony went topsy-turvy, but generally they inflated rapidly. Most foreign goods were difficult to obtain until the war ended in 1918. Police surveillance became heavy, and considerable control was exercised over news media. Non-French citizens were not allowed to teach school, a policy that closed three LDS mission schools that were operating on Tubuai, Takaroa, and Hikueru.

The mission had two uncomfortable encounters with the

government during the war years. First, the missionaries sent through the mail the mission newspaper, the *Heheuraa Api* or *The New Revelation*, which contained news of German successes during the early months of the war. The police did not want such news distributed within the colony and seized the entire edition of the paper. For a time it appeared that the paper, which had been published since 1907, would be banned until after the war, but through fasting, prayer, and persuasive arguments President Rossiter was able to convince the governor to allow the paper to be issued. The other incident occurred in 1918, when Brother Toae in a speech in his branch compared the organization of the priesthood with the German army. When word of this indiscretion reached antagonistic ears, it was reported to the governor. He checked the circumstances involved and, fortunately, dropped the issue.[14]

A surprising result of the war was that the number of missionaries increased rather than declined. The main reasons for this increase were that the United States was not involved in the war until 1917 and that missionaries were not allowed in the British Isles or on the Continent after the beginning of the war. The elders who otherwise would have been sent to Europe went to French Polynesia instead.

President Ernest C. Rossiter and his wife, Venus, had arrived in the mission on March 7, 1915. They were both remarkable people.

President Ernest C. Rossiter (seated center); his wife, Venus; and a group of French Polynesia missionaries. (Courtesy LDS Church Archives.)

Brother Rossiter had filled a mission in France, and his knowledge of the language gave him a distinct advantage over other mission presidents since the time of Daniel T. Miller, who also spoke French. Rossiter was able to smooth over several rough spots with the government simply because he understood what was being said and because he could explain the Church's position clearly. He did have to learn the Tahitian language, but he mastered it quickly.

Venus Rossiter was a talented pianist and organist. She was also a brave and hardworking young woman. She frequently traveled with her husband into the Tuamotus, something no previous mission president's wife had done. Her descriptions of life and circumstances in the islands, sent in letters to her mother that were published in the *Deseret News,* were fair, objective, and sympathetic.[15] During her years in the mission she composed a number of songs, taught organ lessons, and helped prepare a new edition to the *Gospel Hymn Book.*

The best example of President Rossiter's effectiveness as a leader occurred during 1916. It illustrates well both the difficult circumstances of life in the islands and the willingness of the people to respond to an inspired leader.

Mission conference was held at Takaroa in early April that year. While President Rossiter and his wife and the missionaries were there, they became aware of considerable tension that existed among the people. Church members and nonmembers were involved in a complicated land dispute. Neither the local governor nor the governor of the colony had been able to settle the matter. On a Sunday shortly before Rossiter planned to sail to another island, Toae a Mahia, who served as branch president, asked President Rossiter to remain and adjust matters among the people. Rossiter knew little about the traditions and laws regarding such matters and did not want to become involved. But while he was discussing the problem with them, he felt impressed to tell the people that if they would truly repent there might be a way to solve the land problem. After saying this he was troubled because he did not understand what he had told the people. In the afternoon he again told them to repent, but he also explained that he would fast and pray until Monday afternoon and then he would explain all that would be required of them. The next day he outlined a plan: the members were to obey the Word of Wisdom, unmarried couples were to be married (ten couples soon obeyed this injunction in a festive ceremony at which most of the island's people were present), the members were to obey the law of tithing, and they were to do their best to get out of debt. Rossiter reported that none of the

Temporary village constructed during pearl-shell diving season at Hikueru Island, Tuamotu Archipelago. Around 1919. (Courtesy L. H. Kennard.)

members were free from debt; in fact, some owed as much as fifty thousand francs ($10,000).

The missionaries were delighted when almost all of the Saints began keeping this counsel. Their greatest problem was getting out of debt—that would take time. Even Rossiter did not immediately know what to do about their financial difficulties. It was not until the beginning of the pearl diving season in August that Rossiter and the missionaries with him devised a plan. They proposed that all the members from Takaroa who were pearl-shell divers be completely under the direction of the missionaries, who would allocate food, clothing, and money during the divers' annual trip to Hikueru. The balance would be used for paying off debts. The Takaroa Saints all accepted the proposal. But Rossiter now went to Papeete and chartered a ship to transport the people, and, so that the LDS divers would not have to pay inflated prices for food, old Brother Mapuhi, who was still an active trader, purchased four thousand dollars worth of supplies to provide for the divers and their families. In past years various merchants had transported the divers free if they promised to sell all of their shell to them. Then, once the Polynesians were obligated to them, the merchants would pay below-the-market prices for the shell.

The missionaries and members constructed a warehouse in which

This impressive chapel was built by the Saints in Takaroa, Tuamotus. The principal financial force behind it was Brother Mapuhi. Photo taken October 1921. (Courtesy L. H. Kennard.)

to store the shell, and they divided it into sections for each diver. The elders allocated fifteen shells daily to each diver for food and personal expenses and stored the rest. The missionaries also emphasized the need for cleanliness in the villages. After the island governor visited the Latter-day Saints, he complimented the Church and told Rossiter that as long as he continued to do such work he could be assured of the governor's support.

When President Rossiter sold the shell, it brought nearly one hundred thousand francs ($20,000). This money was used to pay old debts. It also helped the people resolve the land problem. The following year the Saints followed the same procedure. They earned less money (65,000 francs) but continued to pay their debts. After they had followed the same plan in 1918, the mission secretary wrote about the success of the cooperative venture in the mission historical record. "For the past three seasons," he wrote, "President Rossiter has taken charge of the affairs of a good many of our saints to assist them in paying their many and longstanding debts and to free them from bondage. No one could begin to imagine the enormous task that it was. . . . But . . . he was able with the help of the Lord to assist them in paying off $75,000 of their old debts—all this over and above their living expenses, taxes, a full tithing, transportation to and from the diving islands, and all other incidental expenses. All of which we know could never have been accomplished except for the divine assistance of our Heavenly Father."[16]

But President Rossiter is best remembered by the people of the islands for his spiritual insight and gift of healing. To this day many stories circulate through the mission concerning miracles, even the raising of the dead, which were performed under his administration.[17]

President Rossiter led out in the strengthening of the Church organization. He translated or encouraged others to translate a number of useful Church publications, and he strengthened the auxiliaries. (The Relief Society had been started by 1894, the Sunday School in 1896, and the Mutual Improvement Association by 1914, but no mention is made in the records concerning the Primary.)

The Rossiters received their release on June 17, 1919. Venus Rossiter sailed a month later; her husband remained in the mission until November 22, so that he could complete some translations and tour the mission one last time.[18] Although he then thought his work was done in Tahiti, he served another mission there during World War II.

CHAPTER 4

FROM WORLD WAR I TO 1950: MAINTAINING THE STATUS QUO

French Polynesia, 1920–1950

"I don't know whether I have told you about Tahiti or not," wrote Leonidas H. Kennard, Jr., in 1920 to his wife and children, "but this is not a savage island, for here vessels call from all over the world and regularly from San Francisco and New Zealand. There are a lot of good-sized business firms here and nearly anything can be had, but things are quite high-priced. . . . There are quite a lot of ships here; nearly all have gas engines in them. There are a lot of automobiles and trucks and an ice plant. We have had ice cream a few times using condensed milk. There is a telephone and electric lights."[1] President Kennard, who had arrived in Tahiti on February 3, 1920, had served his first mission to French Polynesia more than two decades earlier. His letters home reveal mixed reactions to the islands and the people there. On the one hand he detested the loose moral practices, which involved some of the Church members as well as others. On the other hand he loved the local Saints and admired their courage, warmth, uncomplaining acceptance of life, and interest in religion in a land where faith, he said, usually had little place.

On August 16, 1920, President Kennard wrote home from the shell-diving island of Hikueru. He observed many changes in Hikueru since his first mission, as well as in Tahiti:

> When I was in these islands first, the people did their climbing trees with a short pair of hobbles made of bark or coconut leaves; now they use climbing spurs. They used to eat fish and coconuts mainly; now they live on imported food largely. They used to make their canoes out of logs; now they buy lumber to make them. In diving they used to have nothing to protect their eyes from the salt water; now they use watertight glasses. The only lights were lamps;

> now there are electric lights and 2 picture shows even in the Tuamotus. There used to be no way to travel but sail boats; now nearly all boats and ships have gas engines and travel whether the wind blows or not. . . . In Papeete there is a wireless station so if I had to and was at Headquarters I could telegraph home or could receive a telegram from here, so you see this part of the world is progressing.[2]

Life was becoming easier in the French colony at that time, but most citizens of the area were not well-off economically by European or American standards. Costs for food and most goods were high, and the romantic image of the perfect, "natural" life existed more in the minds of writers than in the lives of the people. The islands, which had lost population until 1910, were undergoing a natural increase by 1920. By 1926 the total population of the colony was 35,862; in 1931 it was 39,226. About 7,000 people lived in Papeete in 1930—a little less than half the population of Tahiti.[3]

Even though life was more convenient for those who could afford it, and even though the population was on the rise, most Polynesians of the area continued to make their livings by subsistence farming in the Society Islands and by making copra and diving for pearl shell in

The Hikueru chapel in the Tuamotus. Dedicated in 1927. (Courtesy LDS Church Archives.)

the Tuamotus. The level of education continued to be lower than the French or the various mission societies would have liked.

The Tahitian Mission of the LDS Church did not make a great deal of progress between 1920 and the end of World War II. Although the missionaries to the area were as faithful in their efforts as their predecessors had been, few converts were made during this period, nor was there much change in expansion, organizational development, physical facilities, education, and welfare. There were some bright spots: chapels and recreation halls were constructed, a number of translated works were published, and three general authorities of the Church visited the mission. But the period can best be described as a maintaining of the status quo.

The reasons for so little growth were many and varied. Among the most serious of the deterrents were difficulties with the French government, the small population base, the depression of the 1930s, and World War II.

The accompanying table gives a statistical picture of the Church in French Polynesia from 1920 to 1950. The gross increase in members was thirteen, but the most accurate growth figure is from 1926 to 1939, during which time the Church grew by 503 members. The fact that there were many deaths and births during this long period is not reflected in these statistics, but the membership must have changed considerably. Notice the large drop in total membership between 1924 and 1926. At that time the mission staff conducted a careful census and discovered that the records had often taken no account of deaths; when they were now properly recorded, there was a large drop in total recorded members. Even in 1921, President Kennard wrote that he believed there were only 1,200 members, although the records listed 1,625.

In considering the period from 1920 to 1950 in French Polynesia, it is difficult to separate the proselyting activities of the missionaries from their efforts to strengthen the existing members. After 1950, the Church introduced lesson plans as aids for teaching the gospel to nonmembers, but during this time the programs used to attract nonmembers into the Church were simultaneously employed to strengthen the local Saints. Several examples illustrate this point:

In 1920, Elder LeRoy Mallory, a talented musician, started a band on the island of Takaroa. Within a year and a half he had trained the musicians so well that they became the most popular musical group in the islands. They stayed together for several years, frequently travel-

French Polynesia Mission, 1920-1950[4]

Year	Total Members*	Convert Baptisms	Melchizedek Priesthood	Total Branches	Total Missionaries
1920	1,591	15	88	14	14
1921	1,625	29		14	18
1922	1,665	33	93	16	16
1923	1,689	29	100	16	5
1924	1,721	17	98	16	11
1925	1,493	14	102	16	6
1926	1,065	10	93	16	11
1927	1,079	26	96	16	13
1928	1,109	58	95	16	14
1929	1,149	48	98	15	15
1930	1,181	26	98	16	12
1931	1,222	47	98		11
1932	1,297	28	104		9 average
1933	1,311	30	107		7 average
1934	1,346	21	111		7 average
1935	1,387	30	114	16	11
1936	1,385	33	114	17	16
1937	1,492	27	120	20	22
1938	1,493	33	123	21	18
1939	1,568	49	132	22	25
1940	1,511	20	130	22	0**
1941-45		No statistics available			2
1946		28	76	15	6
1947		No statistics available			
1948	1,160	31	85		12
1949		No report submitted			
1950	1,604	67	104	20	11

* Includes unbaptized children of members

**16 average

Brass bands were popular among Church members in French Polynesia, Samoa, Tonga, and New Zealand from the early years of the Twentieth Century. This band was from the island of Takaroa, Tuamotus. Mission President LeRoy Mallory is seated in the middle (without a bow tie). He loved music and encouraged the formation of bands and orchestras. Photo taken around 1935. (Courtesy LDS Church Archives.)

ing from island to island in the Tuamotus and occasionally going to Tahiti to perform. When Mallory returned to Tahiti as mission president during the 1930s, he started the band again. Once again the band served the Church and the colony by providing music for many special occasions.[5]

Another example of the dual purposes of the mission-Church enterprise was the tradition of making semiannual conferences missionary efforts as well as regular meetings of the Church.[6] For instance, the *haapiiraa*, variously translated as gospel class, lesson, doctrine, or teaching, was used as a teaching activity. It sometimes took the form of a memorized dialogue between teacher and student and sometimes that of a question and answer session on a particular subject. The haapiiraas usually focused on a specific subject, such as "The Plan of Salvation," "The Life of Christ," "Zion Established on the Tops of the Mountains," "Baptism for the Dead," or "Conversion."

Church leaders frequently used haapiiraas as a Mutual Improvement Association, or *Feia Api* activity. (*Feia Api* means "new group" or youth group.) Missionaries sometimes trained a group of young people in a particular subject, and when they had mastered the material, the whole group, missionaries and all, would travel to an area where the Church was not established and perform the haapiiraas for an assembled crowd of nonmembers. This was one of the most frequently used methods of teaching the gospel.

Another missionary undertaking that was both a mission and Church effort was the mission newspaper (sometimes called a magazine), *Te Heheuraa* or the New Revelation. Beginning in 1907 and continuing with only occasional interruptions, this paper served the needs of Church members and nonmembers alike. Every issue contained information about the Church in Tahiti, Utah, and the world in general, as well as news of world events. Gospel lessons and inspirational articles were also included. The missionaries sold subscriptions to this periodical by traveling from house to house throughout the islands. Although the number of subscribers fluctuated, by 1929 over thirteen hundred people received the paper.[7]

Every mission president during this period believed publishing was an important part of the mission's responsibility. The mission bought a printing press early in the century. Missionaries, with the help of local members, set the type and did the printing, cutting, collating, and binding on a number of book-length works as well as many tracts, leaflets, and flyers. All mission roll and record books as well as several editions of the hymn book were published on the mission press. Even the lesson manuals for the priesthood, as well as those for the Sunday School, Relief Society, and other auxiliaries, were either locally created or translated from English materials and published at mission headquarters.

Among the important, larger early projects was *E Buka Haapiiraa no te Autaluea-raa*, translated from Orson F. Whitney's *Gospel Themes*. Two years later, in 1925, President Ole B. Peterson's translation of George Q. Cannon's *History of Joseph Smith* was published in a three-hundred-copy edition.[8] Later publishing efforts included a three-hundred-copy edition of Nephi Anderson's novel *Added Upon* (1939) and a five-hundred-copy translation of Kelsch's *Ready Reference to the Bible and Scriptures* (1940).[9]

Another major project that took much of the time of Elder Doyle L. Green and President Kenneth R. Stevens from 1938 to 1940 was a second translation of the Doctrine and Covenants. This version, like the first, which was made around the turn of the century, was never published.

Bands, conferences, haapiiraas, plays, publications, radio broadcasts, and other methods were used to strengthen the Saints and proselytize among non-Mormons.[10] But over the years growth in the Church was minimal.

In addition to problems with the French government, the limited population, the depression, and World War II, there were other difficulties that made progress slow. The branches were sprawled over a vast amount of ocean. Because transportation was so irregular, some of the smaller branches went for one, two, or even three years without having a visit from a missionary. Because so much time passed between supervisory visits to these islands, branches frequently fell into disorder. In 1927, President Alma G. Burton wrote that keeping the outlying branches in order was "an almost endless task [that] leaves us but little time for work with investigators."[11] His comment was typical of many made by mission presidents over the years.

The missionaries evidently seldom did house-to-house tracting with the intention of getting into a prolonged series of gospel discussions that would lead to the conversion and baptism of an investigator. Instead they sold mission newspapers, planned and attended conferences, directed plays, built chapels, and talked with the Saints. Somehow, during this period, the Leeward Group, where a fairly good start had been made earlier in the century, was almost left out. Elders occasionally "tracted round" these islands and sold newspaper subscriptions, but they rarely attempted to do any long-range work.

The missionaries devoted much of their time to the supervision of the districts and branches. The local members ordinarily acted as branch presidents, counselors, auxiliary leaders, teachers, and so on, but all of these people were supervised by the missionaries.

Another problem the mission faced was the fluctuating and generally small number of missionaries. The average force, from 1920 to 1950, including the mission president and his wife, was ten foreign missionaries. This group was usually assigned as follows: an office staff, consisting of the president, his wife, the mission secretary, and one or two elders who operated the printing office and edited the newspaper; and from three to five pairs of elders to care for all other areas of the mission.[12]

CHAPEL BUILDING TO 1948

The Tahitian Mission had many legal problems in acquiring land. Because the French government considered the Church to be an American organization, it was difficult for the mission presidents to buy or lease land. Government policy required the Church to obtain

LDS missionaries throughout the South Pacific traveled hundreds of miles in open boats such as the Manahiki, shown here. President L. H. Kennard, Jr., wrote, "I made a trip of more than 200 miles on this boat." Elders on board are (left to right) Grant Lee Benson, LeRoy Mallory, and Jesse Heslop. Around 1920. (Courtesy L. H. Kennard.)

permits to buy any land. In 1925, President Ole B. Peterson created the "Foreign Lands Corporation," designed to legally own all Church properties. During the next year President Burton had all titles and deeds to Church-owned properties put in the name of the corporation.[13] This organization continued to hold all Church properties until the 1950s, when other arrangements had to be made.

Between 1920 and 1948, the Church built at least twelve chapels, five recreation halls—called *Fare Putuputuraa*, or gathering places—and a number of small homes for the elders. Most of the buildings in the Tuamotus were constructed of coral stone, but there were some *niao* or coconut-leaf structures. Surprisingly, the construction of chapels did not slow down during the depression years of the 1930s.

THE VISITS OF DAVID O. MCKAY (1921) AND RUFUS K. HARDY (1939)

The first visit of a general authority of the Church to the islands was on April 11, 1921, when Elder David O. McKay of the Council of the Twelve Apostles and Elder Hugh J. Cannon arrived in Papeete. Elder McKay was on an early leg of an around-the-world tour of LDS missions.

Because President Kennard had no advance knowledge of when Elder McKay would arrive, he was away on Tubuai for a conference. Elders McKay and Cannon did not stay but decided to go on to New Zealand on their steamer, the *Marama*. "These brethren," wrote the mission secretary, "came with the intention of visiting the Tuamotus in speedy steamers." Such ships were not available. Short of chartering a vessel, which they were unable to do, it would have taken two or three months to visit the Tuamotus.

While Elder McKay was in Tahiti he became convinced that the mission needed a vessel to transport the mission president, missionaries, and members from island to island. After arriving in New Zealand, he was joined by President Kennard, who spent two weeks there to discuss the condition of the mission in detail. In addition to their conversations about the mission, they also decided the mission should buy an eighty-ton schooner. Although bids were received from two companies in New Zealand and one in Papeete, a ship was not purchased for the mission at that time. Estimates for a desirable ship came to about $40,000. This large capital outlay was more than the Church leaders in Salt Lake City were willing to spend at that time.[14]

Elder Rufus K. Hardy, member of the First Council of the Seventy and veteran of many years of missionary work in New Zealand, arrived in Papeete on May 2, 1939, eighteen years after Elder McKay's stopover. Elder Hardy was the second general authority of the Church to visit French Polynesia. While he was in the islands he "had an outstanding influence," according to President Stevens.[15] He chartered a schooner and toured the islands of Niau, Fakarava, Takaroa, Nihiru, Hikueru and Hao in the Tuamotus, Tubuai in the Austral Group, and Tahiti.

The white-goateed general authority had strong opinions about the operation of the mission. Before he departed on June 22, 1939, he gave President Kenneth R. Stevens and the missionaries a number of suggestions. He recommended that the local Saints be placed in as many leadership positions as was possible. This, he reasoned, would leave the missionaries free to do more proselyting.[16] Elder Hardy also encouraged the elders to stop living in the homes of members, to get out among the people and to islands where the Church was not permanently established. He did not like the haapiiraa method of presenting the teachings of the Church and encouraged more direct gospel teaching from missionary to investigator.[17]

CHURCH RELATIONS WITH THE GOVERNMENT

On August 31, 1928, the following entry was made in the French Polynesia Mission Historical Record: "Mr. Lulu Spitz, a Papeete business man and also a campaign leader of one of the parties seeking to be elected as Tahiti's Representative to France, called at the Mission House, with the report that the Elders had influenced the natives in their voting, at some of the Tuamotu islands."[18] In response President Burton explained to Mr. Spitz that the Church had always stayed out of politics and that all of the LDS missionaries were strongly advised to keep their political opinions to themselves. In short, he said the report of the Church meddling in the election was false.

Mr. Spitz explained that there was an official government report that had been sent to the Minister of Colonies and that asserted that the Mormon Church was a detriment to the French government of the islands. Although this report concerned Brother Burton, it did not trouble him deeply because it was not unusual. The mission had frequently encountered opposition from the government before and, as will be seen, continued to have difficulties thereafter.

For example, in 1931 the Church was denied a building permit for construction of a small bamboo house for the elders at Mataua. Only after the Tahitian who leased the land to the Church applied for the permit in his own name was the permission to build granted.[19] In December 1931 a problem arose over return fare deposits for steamship transportation. Whereas the government had been willing to accept the Union Steamship Company's bond for the LDS missionaries before this time, it required return tickets or a bank deposit for all aliens who entered the colony. Now, when funds were so scarce during the depression, the government demanded that the money for the return ticket be held on deposit in Papeete.[20] Another example was the suppression of the mission newspaper for several months during 1933 because it was published in a foreign language—Tahitian—instead of French.

Church-government relations were probably at their worst during 1932 and 1933. On October 24, 1932, President George W. Burbidge and the Church attorney, Mr. Leonce Brault (who served the Church without remuneration until 1948), visited the secretary to the governor about entry visas for two elders. The mission force was down to five, and help was badly needed. The secretary told President Burbidge that the request for visas was refused, and when Burbidge questioned the secretary he was told that the government had proof that President Burbidge and his wife had been holding secret political meetings with Dr. Cassiau and a Mr. Ahnne. Further, Burbidge had supposedly sent word to Takaroa, by way of Tuamata a Mapuhi and Toae a Marie, for all the natives to vote for a certain candidate who was in the opposition party. The anti-government candidate, incidentally, had received most of the votes. In addition, the Church was accused of taking too much contribution money out of the islands.

All of the accusations were false, but it was difficult to convince the governor. Burbidge explained that he had visited Dr. Cassiau for a complete physical examination but that he did not know Mr. Ahnne. Concerning the Takaroa problem, he explained that Taumata a Mapuhi and Toae a Marie had come to Papeete to be set apart for Church positions. Regarding the money matter, President Burbidge calculated that the Church brought fourteen times as much money into the islands as it took out. But these explanations were not sufficient to satisfy the governor. He asked for a detailed explanation as to why the mission and missionaries were in the country in the first place. President Burbidge submitted the names of all the missionaries and explanations as to the number of members who needed leadership, what the Church hoped to accomplish, and so forth. Still the governor delayed giving permission. Meanwhile, the two new missionaries arrived on November 5. They were given local passports only after several days' delay. But even then they were not authorized to preach and take an active role in the mission.

The problem of visas and of how many missionaries could enter French Polynesia was finally resolved—more by a change of governors than by a satisfactory decision. In February 1933, the governor told Burbidge he could send his missionaries wherever he desired, and he would even allow new missionaries into the country; but he also explained that the French government did not favor the expansion of foreign missions. President Burbidge had the satisfaction of remaining in the mission until the next July, when a new governor arrived in Papeete. On July 6, Burbidge had an interview with him and found him to be a most hospitable and broad-minded person. To Burbidge's joy the governor said, "There never has been a governor who has had the power to stop missionaries from coming into the Islands as long as they conducted themselves properly, had sufficient income to live on and obeyed the rules and regulations of the Islands." It was to the Church's advantage that the new governor had visited Salt Lake City, met President Heber J. Grant, and heard the Tabernacle organ while en route to Tahiti.

From 1933 to 1939, the number of missionaries increased rapidly, for two reasons. First, the governor of French Polynesia was friendly and willing to allow the increase. Second, as has been mentioned earlier, the First Presidency reduced the length of time missionaries were asked to devote to this service.[21]

Mission leaders frequently wondered why the French officials evidently did not like the Church. Two observations may be made. First, the government did not dislike the Church so much as it believed that the Church was an American organization that dispersed pro-American propaganda. The French did not like the American influence in the islands; this remains true today.

Second, though the governors of the islands during the 1930s and 1940s were usually broad-minded men (the earlier example being an obvious exception) who were willing to work with the Church leaders on important matters, most difficulties were caused by bureaucrats who were motivated by self-interest or political objectives, or who were influenced by other religious groups. Because the governors were strongly swayed by the bureaucrats, the Church frequently found itself in trouble.

THE IMPACT AND INFLUENCE OF WORLD WAR II

When war broke out in Europe on September 1, 1939, French Polynesia was immediately involved. All mail was subject to inspection, and printed materials such as the Church newspaper were censored. Boat schedules were no longer posted, for fear of sabotage. Before many months food prices climbed, and, later, food became scarce. In March 1940, imports from the United States ceased, and many canned goods and other merchandise became unavailable. By the summer of 1940, steamers were calling infrequently, and returning elders, along with others who wanted to go to New Zealand or America, found themselves wondering whether they would ever be able to leave the islands.[22]

On July 1, 1940, word arrived of France's capitulation to the German forces. Rumors concerning French Polynesia's fate traveled swiftly, and no one felt secure. George Cobb, the American consul, advised President Stevens to call all of the Mormon missionaries from the Tuamotus into Tahiti.[23] As the elders returned to Papeete, they brought reports of difficult conditions in the outlying islands. By July 27, all of the Mormon missionaries were safely on Tahiti.

By that time, President and Sister Stevens, their children, and six elders had been released. They sailed for home on August 6. Newly appointed President Eugene M. Cannon and his wife had arrived on August 3.

President Cannon modified the MIA program and made it fit the pattern of the Church in America, introduced couple dancing (which was considered evil by most churches in the islands), sent the twelve remaining elders to work around Tahiti and in the Leeward Islands, and did everything he could to build up the Church.

The people of Tahiti and French Polynesia were in a state of political turmoil during the latter part of the summer of 1940. The main concern of most Tahitians was that British supply ships coming to Papeete were discontinued until the people there decided whether they would support the Allies or the German forces. In an effort to arrive at a consensus concerning this matter, a plebiscite was held in early September, wherein the people were to vote either for DeGaulle and the Free French or for Petain and the Vichy Government, which had collaborated with Germany. The Free French received 5,564 votes and the Vichy government 18. The governor of French Polynesia and thirty-four other Vichy supporters resigned and handed the reins of government to provisional leaders E. Ahnne, G. Lagarde, E. Martin, and G. Bambridge. This new governing body assured all church leaders that they would not interfere with religious affairs.[24]

Two months later, on October 14, President Cannon received a telegram from President Heber J. Grant directing him to send the missionaries home as soon as possible. Identical telegrams were sent to New Zealand, Australia, Tonga, and Samoa. Brother Cannon's reaction was typical of those of the presidents throughout the Pacific. He wrote, "Oh, how we hate to close up this mission, although we have felt it coming for a year. There has been little headway for some 40 years. The Lord's will be done."

The missionaries were already gathered near headquarters and under normal circumstances should have been able to depart from the islands within a few days or weeks. But because ships came to Papeete so infrequently, President Cannon decided to try to make connections with a Matson ship at Pago Pago, Samoa. These plans were scuttled when one of the elders underwent surgery for appendicitis. His recovery took longer than expected, and by the time he was able to leave, the Samoa connection had been missed. President Grant strongly encouraged President Cannon to use regularly scheduled transportation, but since no ships were expected at Papeete for at least six months, President Cannon chartered a large diesel-powered sailing ship, the *Benicia*, under Captain Charley Brown, to transport the fourteen missionaries to Hawaii. As the schooner left Papeete on November 19, 1940, a thousand Saints and nonmembers bade a tearful good-bye to their beloved friends and leaders.[25]

Seven months passed before Ernest C. Rossiter and his wife, Venus, arrived in Tahiti for their second mission there. They found Ani a Mariteragi, president of the Papeete Branch, and his wife living in the mission home and taking charge of the affairs of the mission. They had handled finances and other matters well, but the members seemed to be confused and disorganized, feeling that they were "sheep without a shepherd." President Rossiter said that once his arrival was announced over the radio, the members rallied around and soon brought order to the Church.[26]

Rossiter's second mission was made difficult by war conditions, rationing, martial law, friction between the Free French and the Vichy faction, and the fact that his wife was seriously ill with asthma during most of their stay. The First Presidency encouraged her to return home early in 1943; in fact, they suggested that President Rossiter come home too. But she remained in Tahiti until November 1943, and President Rossiter stayed until late in 1944.

In the absence of elders from Zion, President Rossiter called a number of local missionaries to act in the supervisory positions the foreign elders had held. He also called several pairs of sister missionaries to teach the gospel. Those listed were Tuehe a Timo, Teipo a Maire, Julliet a Haapairai, Keha a Malumui, Garoro a Turoa, Haea a Mapuhi, and Tefanaki a Tukarua.[27]

Semiannual conferences were held as usual, but the war made attendance difficult for many of the Saints because of financial limitations and because permits to travel from island to island were required by the government.

During the war the Church made some headway with the government. President Rossiter, who spoke French well and was able to converse freely with the French officials, developed a more personal working relationship with the governor than had existed before. He was even invited to attend a reception at the governor's mansion, an honor that had not been given to any previous mission president.

In August 1942 the first of two shipments of food, twenty-two cases, arrived in Papeete from the Church welfare program. In March

1943, thirty-four more cases of food arrived. Both the government and the Church members appreciated this help during the difficult war years.

In the fall of 1944 President Rossiter became quite ill, and in December he was flown to Hawaii and hospitalized. Although he recovered his health, he did not return to French Polynesia as mission president. His replacement, Edgar Bentley Mitchell, Jr., arrived in Papeete on February 17, 1945.

THE BEGINNING OF THE POSTWAR BUILDUP OF THE FRENCH POLYNESIA MISSION

Until June 3, 1946, when the first four foreign elders arrived in Papeete after the war, all missionary work remained in the hands of the local members. But even after the new missionaries arrived, it took them a number of months to be of any real value because they could not speak French or Tahitian. The government was not eager to have the mission force built up again, but after President Mitchell explained the precedents that had been established prior to the war and claimed the right to bring in replacements to take the places of the missionaries who had left in 1940 to fight for their country and for France, the governor finally granted written permission for twelve missionaries to enter the country to replace the elders who had sailed on November 19, 1940.[28] By August 14, 1947, the mission was up to full strength.

President Mitchell's most important undertaking was the construction of a new mission complex. A number of pieces of property had to be purchased in order for the large structures to be built. President Mitchell began negotiations for, and bought for $16,698, the largest piece of land, that held by Mr. Jean Malarde, August 1946. He wrote, "This marks the beginning of a new era in the Tahitian Mission. It also marks the beginning of a new era in Governmental relations with the Church. A year ago a purchase of this magnitude would never have been permitted. The present administration has given their recognition of the Tahitian Mission by mentioning in the permit for purchase of this property that the Foreign Lands Corporation was given permit to purchase said property for the Tahitian Mission of the Church of Jesus Christ of Latter-day Saints."[29]

Actually this purchase did not mark the end of difficulties with the government, nor did it end all problems in acquiring land. But Mitchell correctly discerned that this was the beginning of a new era for the Tahitian Mission. From that time on, difficulties notwithstanding, progress was rapid in terms of physical, spiritual, and numerical growth.

By October 31, 1947, Leland Carver, a former missionary to Tahiti, who had been appointed by the Church to come to Tahiti and assist with the building project, began directing the crushing of rock for use in building. On December 28, 1947, Frank Fullmer, who supervised the building project, arrived on a ship that was loaded with four hundred tons of building material and equipment, including a dump truck, a station wagon, two cement mixers, block machines, a roof-tile machine, a variety of tools, cement, and so on. The groundbreaking was held January 1, 1948. Harold W. Burton was architect for the new building.

On August 14, Elder Matthew Cowley, president of the Pacific Missions of the Church and member of the Council of the Twelve, laid the cornerstone. While Elder Cowley was in Papeete he encouraged all members and missionaries to work closely together, not only to build the new headquarters, but also to show the nonmembers an example of love and cooperation.

While Elder Cowley was there he also directed several changes in the mission. He organized the first mission presidency; that is, he called two missionaries, Elders Wilcox and Magnusson, to serve as counselors to President Mitchell. Elder Cowley also suggested that the young members of the Church should learn to perform the more appropriate dances of their people, the dances that tell a story. He encouraged the members of the Church to gather the legends of their people and to hold them sacred.

In another area, Elder Cowley admonished against the tradition of having missionary elders decide who could partake of the sacrament and who could not. The people were to be taught correct principles and then be left to decide for themselves whether or not they were worthy to partake of the Lord's Supper.

While Elder Cowley was in the Tahitian Mission on this first of several visits, he toured the Leeward Islands and Tubuai. His trip to the Tahitian Mission ended on August 23, 1948. After Brother Cowley had departed, President Mitchell concluded that he had done much to "liberalize the thought of both the natives and the missionaries of this mission."

The building project consumed much of the missionaries' time, but Mitchell was eager to open new areas. Even though missionaries had lived on Tahiti for a number of decades, the Papeete Branch was the only visible result of their labors. With the intention of improving

The Faariipiti Chapel, Papeete, was the first major construction project in the Islands after World War II. It served as the first stake center but was razed in 1978 to make way for a larger, more modern replacement. (Photo by R. Lanier Britsch.)

on this situation, during 1948 President Mitchell assigned elders to work in several areas of Tahiti permanently. By the end of the year, beginnings had been made at Papara, Paea, and Punaauia, and a branch had been organized at Pueu. In October 1947, two missionaries were sent to Huahine in the Leeward Group, and by February 25, 1948, they had completed a small bamboo meetinghouse. In September 1949, following Mitchell's release, the elders on Tubuai reported that they were reopening the Huahine branch there; the branch had been closed for twenty years. In October 1949, elders were sent to organize a branch at Makatea.[30]

When Bentley Mitchell left the islands on June 30, 1949, he felt deeply satisfied with the work that had been accomplished under his direction. He was replaced by Franklin J. Fullmer, who held the callings of mission president and building supervisor until January 3, 1950, when LeRoy R. Mallory and his wife Muriel arrived to begin their second calling as mission leaders.

The dedication of the new chapel and mission home was an extremely important occasion for the Tahitian Saints. They were so excited that they began coming into Tahiti from the outlying islands in September 1949, four months ahead of the announced date. Elder Cowley arrived for the dedication on January 18, 1950, and found the Saints buzzing with anticipation. When the morning of January 22 arrived, the members and friends of the Church began to assemble early in the morning. By two o'clock every available seat both inside and outside the chapel was taken, and the streets were crowded with people. It was estimated that over three thousand people were in attendance. As the governor of the islands arrived, *La Marseillaise* was sung. He turned the key in the front door and officially signified the beginning of use for the chapel. Later in the program Elder Matthew Cowley dedicated the new buildings to the Lord and invoked His blessings on all that would take place there over the coming years.

With the dedication of the new facilities, the Tahitian Mission was prepared to move ahead and achieve unprecedented growth and development during the coming decades.

CHAPTER 5

YEARS OF GROWTH AND CHANGE

French Polynesia, 1950–1984

Since World War II, the Church in French Polynesia has grown so rapidly and changed so significantly that missionaries from earlier eras would hardly recognize any carryovers from prewar days. The past thirty years have been very different from the plodding decades from 1900 to 1940. New methods of doing missionary work, changes in teaching, leadership, and administrative procedures, and improved lesson materials for use in priesthood and auxiliary classes have improved the quality of teaching in the Church. The French Polynesian members are stronger in the faith and more diligent in keeping the Lord's commandments than at any other time in history.

There are two overarching reasons for the rapid growth of the Church in French Polynesia during the past thirty years. First, the missionaries, who have greatly increased in numbers, have used new and more effective proselyting methods. Second, there has been a shift in population from the Tuamotus to the Society Islands, that is, Tahiti, Moorea, and the Leeward Group. The mission presidents since World War II have generally placed more emphasis on proselyting among the people of these islands than elsewhere in the mission. The chart on the next page illustrates the extent of the population shift toward the western islands since 1946.

Although a number of mission presidents before the war recognized the advantages of tracting and teaching where the bulk of the people were, it was not until 1948, during the time of President Bentley Mitchell, that serious proselyting with the intention of establishing permanent branches took place on Tahiti. But even though a beginning was made in the outer areas of Tahiti at that time, it was not

French Polynesia Census Figures[1]

Island or Group	1946 census	1967 census
Tahiti	24,820	61,519
Moorea	2,838	4,370
Leeward	12,645	15,337
Subtotal	40,303	81,226
Tuamotu & Gambier	6,696	6,664
Austral	3,921	5,053
Makatea	1,826	55*
Marquesas	2,988	5,174
Total	55,734	98,378

*Phosphate works closed 1966

until 1953 that missionaries began to make inroads among the people beyond Papeete.

The table on the next page presents the basic statistics for the French Polynesia mission from 1951 to 1971.

The gross increase over the two decades was 3,050 members. The number of Melchizedek Priesthood holders increased almost 200 percent, and the number of branches by 50 percent. In 1967, Latter-day Saints made up 4.5 percent of the total population of French Polynesia.

THE MALLORYS, THE BAND, AND THE "PARAITA"

President LeRoy Mallory and his wife, Muriel, arrived in Tahiti in early January 1950. During two previous missions President Mallory had organized brass bands on the island of Takaroa. After the excitement of the Papeete chapel dedication on January 22, 1950, had subsided, Mallory began making arrangements to organize his third mission band. By the end of the year, thirty-seven musicians were making music in an organization that became an effective missionary tool. President Mallory also organized a small string orchestra.[3]

French Polynesia Mission Statistics, 1951-1971[2]

Year	Total Members	Convert Baptisms	Melchizedek Priesthood	Total Branches	Number of Missionaries	
					foreign	local
1950	1,604	67	104	20	11	—
1951	1,700	74	116	27	7	20
1952	1,753	27	126	27	13	—
1953	1,824	32	130	27	11	—
1954	2,028	153	136	28	8	—
1955	2,149	63	140	30	10	—
1956	2,163	32	145	17?	12	—
1957	2,313	64	147	21?	12	—
1958	2,451	87	150	23	15	1
1959	2,920	146	163	27	14	1
1960	2,953	89	187	27	17	4
1961	3,352	296	201	28	20	6
1962	3,583	—	216	33	18	—
1963	3,870	48	239	35	17	3
1964	4,063	65	252	27	17	3
1965	4,234	91	276	27	26	10
1966	4,376	71	287	28	21	4
1967	4,479	65	305	29	40	10
1968	4,555	118	293	31	47	10
1969	4,864	92	323	31	48	—
1970	4,834	111	335	31	54	6
1971	4,750	158	314	30	—	—

During Mallory's presidency the mission realized a long-hoped-for dream. In 1950 the Church bought the *Fandango,* an eighty-two-foot two-masted schooner in San Pedro, and had it sailed to Tahiti for the use of the mission. The *Fandango* arrived at Papeete on April 8, 1950, after a three-week voyage from California. Captain E. K. Kenny, a non-Mormon, was the only professional sailor aboard. The crew was made up of new and returned missionaries to French Polynesia, among them being former President E. Bentley Mitchell.[4]

The *Paraita,* the Pratt, was the French Polynesia Mission ship from 1950 until 1961. It improved communications but cost more than the Church could justify. (Courtesy Yves Perrin.)

After four months of negotiations with the government, the *Fandango* was placed under French registration on July 29, 1950. It was officially owned by the Tahitian Navigation Society, which was created by the Church to operate the ship. With the raising of the French flag, the ship was rechristened the *Paraita,* the Pratt, after the Tahitian name of Addison Pratt, one of the first LDS missionaries to French Polynesia. The first voyage for serious purposes began on August 9, when President Mallory and others sailed to Tubuai for a conference. After that time the beautiful craft was used regularly for taking the mission president and other officers to conferences and for transporting missionaries and members from island to island. Occasionally, the government requested that the ship sail to one island or another to take officials, police, or medical personnel there.

An example of the boat's usefulness occurred in September 1951. President Mallory spearheaded an all-mission youth conference to be held at Takaroa. The young people of many branches made extensive preparations for the three-day meeting. In this instance the *Paraita* conveyed the Mallorys, an elder, and fifty youths, including the band, a basketball team, the string orchestra, and several MIA officers.

The youth conference was the first of its kind to be held in French Polynesia. The conference was similar to such meetings elsewhere in the world. Workshop sessions, dance lessons, basketball and other sports, and a testimony meeting (in which every youth spoke) made up the program. Since that time several similar youth programs have been held in the mission and stake.

The *Paraita* tremendously improved communications in the mission. Missionary transfers were no longer a major hurdle, nor was it difficult for the mission president to attend conferences in the districts. But the ship was expensive to operate. Although specific financial records are not available, the cost of sailing the ship was so high that President John Orton made arrangements in 1954 to have the boat used part-time as a freight vessel. This caused more problems than it solved, and in 1956 the boat was reconverted to a strictly passenger craft. The *Paraita* served the mission well until July 1961, when it was sold. It continued in service for several more years as an inter-island transport ship but was then found unsafe and was put out of commission.[5]

In 1959, as a consequence of many years of faithful membership in the Church, thirty Tahitian Saints made great sacrifices to set aside the money for a trip to Hawaii to receive temple blessings. The French government granted permission for the group to sail to Hawaii only after hearing persuasive arguments from the non-Mormon harbormaster. The Saints wrote to President David O. McKay and the First Presidency and obtained their permission to sail to Hawaii in the church-owned *Paraita.* Finally the ship was put in drydock for painting, inspection, and engine repairs.

On July 23, 1959, only two or three days before the group was set to sail, Ernest C. Rossiter, twice a mission president to Tahiti, arrived in Papeete by air. Elder Rossiter announced that President McKay had sent word to cancel the trip.

The surprised Saints could not understand the reasons for President McKay's decision. The captain of the *Paraita,* Raituia T. Tapu, who was to become the first president of the Papeete Tahiti Stake, later recalled that Rossiter quoted President McKay as saying, "They won't make it, and if we allow them to come we'll be in trouble with the French government. So you go stop them." Brother Rossiter asked the members how they felt about President McKay's warning.

Brother Tapu then said, "Well, he's the prophet. If he says so, we say amen." Following a unanimous vote to cancel the trip, the meeting ended.

When Brother Tapu went to the boat the next day, the engine mechanic told him that an important gear was badly worn and would last only one hundred to one hundred and fifty hours. Then the ship would be entirely dependent on the wind. The following day, which would have been the day for sailing to Hawaii, the ship was taken out of dry dock and anchored in the harbor. Two days later Brother Tapu received a telephone call from the harbormaster, who said the the boat was sinking.

It was soon discovered that the exhaust pipe from the kitchen was rotten. The repairmen had painted over some rotten wood and a rusty pipe, which had broken, and the water had rushed in. The fire department soon arrived and pumped the water out.

Brother Tapu's comment captures the meaning of the whole experience. He said, "So what would you say if we were two or three hundred miles away on a lifeboat? That's why I always had a testimony for President McKay. A true prophet of the Lord."[6]

THE INTRODUCTION OF IMPROVED TEACHING PLANS

During the time of Presidents Mallory and Othello P. Pearce (the latter served on an interim basis from June 1952 to March 1953), progress was made on some fronts—for example, the Pearl of Great Price was translated by two foreign elders, Richard B. Pearce and Jay Larson, and a Polynesian elder, Taumata a Tukeravehe—but few converts were joining the Church.

On March 4, 1953, John K. Orton became president of the Tahitian mission. Shortly after he arrived, he visited the Saints, members, and missionaries in the Tuamotus and on Tubuai. He was moved to take an unusual course of action, which he described in this way:

> At this time all the missionaries were called into headquarters, and a new plan was discussed and decided upon. The new plan, simply stated, was to remove the missionaries from the outlying islands and to concentrate their work in Papeete, where there is the largest portion of the population.
>
> We had had no baptisms up until August. From August till the first of the year we had 32 converts. We have returned the outlying islands to the native Priesthood holders to administer and the biggest portion of the missionaries' time in proselyting.[7]

Although more was required to make the outlying branches self-sufficient than simply handing the administrative responsibilities over to the local priesthood holders, Orton's basic plan was largely responsible for the rapid growth of the Church in the islands over the next ten years.

For the first time in the history of the mission, the missionaries were given a set of lessons for investigators that proceeded from point to point in an orderly explanation of the restored gospel. Because of health problems, President Orton served for only one year. But he had created such momentum that in 1954, by following his plan, the missionaries gleaned 153 converts from the Tahitian field, the largest number to that time.

The shift of Church members and the growth of branches in Tahiti-Moorea and Leeward districts was dramatic. In early 1947 there was only one branch on Tahiti and there were none in the Leeward Islands. By 1967 there were ten branches in Tahiti and Moorea, and eight in the Leeward Group. On the other hand, the number of branches in the Tuamotus dropped from eighteen to twelve during the same era.

During 1954, serious missionary work (that is, work that was intended to bring about lasting branches of the Church rather than simply good public relations) was started on Raiatea and Tahaa, and in 1955, in Huahine of the Leeward Group. In January 1955, President Larson Caldwell and Elder Joseph Childers organized a Sunday School at Utoroa, Raiatea, one week before the first two converts were baptized and confirmed members of the Church. Thirty-six investigators attended that first meeting.[8]

The year 1955 was unusually fruitful. It began with a two-day visit from the Prophet, President David O. McKay, and his wife, Emma Ray. Then, during the year, the first French language church meetings were held, a new chapel was dedicated for the new Cumora Branch at Tahaa, a new and popular youth chorus called the Pupu Himene was organized, and new lesson manuals were developed and translated.

THE VISIT OF PRESIDENT DAVID O. MCKAY

January 18, 1955, was "one of the most important days in the life of this mission and in the lives of all here," wrote President Ellis V. Christensen of President McKay's visit. President McKay was on an extended tour of the South Pacific, a tour that would culminate with the selection of the temple site in New Zealand.

When President McKay was in Papeete, he held several meetings with the Church members, met with the press, and also visited the governor of the islands. He created a new and stronger urge among both the members and the missionaries to do missionary work. "Everyone's faith was strengthened by his visit."[9]

President McKay asked the mission president to assign some missionaries to learn the French language and to begin proselyting among the French-speaking people of the islands. Elders Thomas Stone and Everett Williams, who arrived in the mission on March 17, were assigned to learn the French language and begin teaching. By May 8, they were out tracting among the people. In June, a French-language Sunday School was organized in connection with the Papeete Branch. Thirty-six members and investigators, most of them youths, attended. At almost the same time an MIA class was started for the same people. Since that time mission presidents have placed ever-increasing emphasis on the use of the French language. A French-speaking branch was organized on October 13, 1957, with one hundred and twenty members, and in recent years Church meetings have been held bilingually.[10]

Since 1955 the Church in French Polynesia has made a number of large strides toward following more fully the pattern prescribed by Church headquarters. The large strides include the organization of the first elders quorum; the instigation of the labor or building missionary program, and the construction of three chapels under that program, as well as the building of a number of other Church structures; the first and later temple excursions to New Zealand; the founding of an elementary school in Papeete; and the organization of the first stake in French Polynesia in May 1972.

Smaller steps include the organization of the LDS Scouts of Tahiti; the sending of a crippled Chinese boy to the Primary Children's Hospital in Salt Lake City for treatment; the sending of students to Liahona High School in Tonga; the use of free radio time for the presentation of gospel teachings and music in both Tahitian and French over Radio Tahiti; and the continued publication of a newspaper called the *Ve'a* ("Messenger"), which reached both members and nonmembers. The Church also made use of dramatic productions and "Soirées," singing and musical productions, to entertain audiences and to raise money to meet branch expenses; and a number of Tahitian Saints were called to fill local and foreign missions.

When the membership of the Papeete Branch grew to around four hundred and the combined number of elders on Tahiti and Tubuai rose to 125, President Christensen decided that an elders quorum organization would be justified. On September 9, 1956, Taumata Mapuhi was sustained as the first elders quorum president in French Polynesia. He chose Tinomana Hauata and Joseph Benacek to serve as his counselors. The new quorum included all the elders on Tahiti and Tubuai, four hundred miles away. One of the first projects of the quorum was to develop plans for a temple excursion for worthy elders and their families.[11]

THE BUILDING MISSIONARY PROGRAM IN FRENCH POLYNESIA

For six years after the large and beautiful Papeete chapel was dedicated, it remained the only modern meeting house in the mission. There were a number of old-style, coral-rock chapels in the Tuamotus and on Tubuai, but on Tahiti and the Leeward Islands the Saints continued to meet in frame or *niau* (thatched) buildings.

During March 1956, Elder Wendell B. Mendenhall, chairman of the Church Building Committee, visited Tahiti, After seeing the niau chapels at Paea and Pueu, he was shocked by the conditions under which the Saints carried on the activities of the Church.[12]

The Paea chapel on Tahiti was built by labor missionaries. It is typical of buildings constructed under that program between 1957 and 1965. (Photo by R. Lanier Britsch.)

Not long after this, the First Presidency and the expenditures committee of the Church approved the building of five chapels in the French Polynesia Mission. The first project was to be a new chapel at Paea, a few miles around the island from Papeete.

The story of the Paea Branch is typical of the development of the new branches of the Church since World War II. The Church first gained a foothold there through the efforts of one family. In early 1949, President E. Bentley Mitchell helped Brother Maoriora Anihia to organize a small home Primary composed of his own and some neighbor children. Later the group began meeting in a borrowed home. In 1950 the Saints there built a niau chapel, which was dedicated on April 29. The next day the first convert to the Church from Paea was baptized. Two local missionaries, Tu and Teaki Menemene, were assigned to the area, and they accomplished much during the seven months they worked there. Gradually, year by year, the branch increased in size until by the mid-1950s there was an obvious need for a better facility.

After Brother Mendenhall's visit in March 1956, President Christensen began looking for an appropriate piece of land for a chapel large enough to seat one hundred people, with an adjoining cultural hall and from four to six classrooms. On March 6, 1957, negotiations for land were concluded. This was the first purchase of land in the name of the newly formed "Council of Administration of the Tahitian Mission of the Church of Jesus Christ of Latter-day Saints." This Council of Administration, more commonly called the Board of Directors, was essential to the mission at that time, French law requiring each religious organization to have an official Board of Directors that was recognized by the governor. The move to form the Council of Administration was also motivated by the French government's refusal to recognize the old Foreign Lands Corporation as anything but a foreign business company. The recognition by the French government of the Council of Administration is the closest the Church has come to legal recognition by the government in Tahiti.[13]

As in Tonga and Samoa, local young men were called to labor as building missionaries. When the fifteen workers were assembled at Paea, people came from near and far to visit with and see the builders who were "working without pay." Although most of the labor missionaries were unskilled when they began work on the Paea chapel, before long they had learned how to lay brick, do carpentry, drive trucks, install plumbing, and put in electrical wiring. Their families at home supported them, and the local branch provided their

A few chapels similar to this one were used in Tahiti until the 1970s. (Courtesy LDS Church Archives.)

food. (The full story of the building missionary program is recounted in the Tonga and Samoa chapters.)

Work began in early April 1957, and the completed building was dedicated on April 5, 1958.[14] After the Paea chapel was finished, the building missionaries moved to Uturoa and then to Avera, Raiatea, in the Leeward Group.

After the abolishment of the building missionary program, a number of new modern chapels were constructed throughout the islands. Even before the Paea chapel was erected, the Church had installed a number of concrete slabs for basketball and other sports. These recreation areas were also used for dancing and other entertainments. In 1954 a covered basketball pavilion was built near the Papeete chapel. Called the *Fare Basket,* it became an important gathering place for youth and also served as a missionary tool.

Mission President Karl M. Richards, who served from 1966 to 1969, purchased a considerable number of building lots. Government officials informed him that after certain plans to open the Leeward Islands up to tourists were completed, the value of land would inflate rapidly. President Richards heeded this warning and bought needed and suitable property wherever he could find it. Just as the government officials predicted, the value of land in this area skyrocketed after Richards bought the lots for the Church.

By the early 1970s, the Church owned nineteen permanent and fourteen temporary chapels, twelve recreation halls, eleven basketball courts, and seventeen missionary quarters.[15] Since that time the number of buildings has continued to expand almost yearly.

THE FIRST TEMPLE EXCURSION TO NEW ZEALAND

Temple work is of great importance to believing Latter-day Saints. Many members of the Church in French Polynesia desired to travel to Hawaii or New Zealand long before they were able to save enough money to make either expensive trip. Saints from New Zealand, Tonga, and Samoa began visiting the Hawaii Temple shortly after it was opened in 1919. But because of the high travel costs of and the tight government restrictions on travel, only a few Tahitians were able to receive temple blessings before December 1963.

When the first elders quorum was established in 1956, the presidency immediately began planning ways to get members to the temple. The abortive *Paraita* trip to Hawaii has already been reviewed. After that time President Mapuhi and his counselors devoted much time and energy encouraging members to prepare themselves financially and spiritually to travel to the new temple in New Zealand, four hundred miles closer than Hawaii. By 1963 sixty-nine people had made preparations to enter the House of the Lord.

The temple-goers left Tahiti in two groups. The first consisted of President and Mrs. Thomas R. Stone, Taumata and Vahinerii Mapuhi, and several others who left Papeete on December 16. When they arrived in Auckland they were greeted by Ruth Mitchell, wife of the late E. Bentley Mitchell, who had done most of the translating of the temple ceremony into the Tahitian language. She had traveled from the United States to be with the French Polynesian Saints on this special occasion. The second group arrived on December 24 and went immediately to Temple View, the location of the temple. On Christmas Day, 1963, the Tahitian Saints received their own endowments. Between that day and January 3, they spent almost every waking moment in the temple.

It is not possible to measure the results of such an experience in the lives of a group of people. But the "temple members," as they were called in the islands, believed that they were better and stronger members of the Church because of this experience. One man, eighty-four-year-old Tahauri Hutihuti, had saved for thirty years to obtain enough money to make the trip. When he returned, he said he hoped to go again. The mission record included this appropriate observation on the excursion: "The members who returned from New Zealand today are literally radiant and beaming and filled with the spirit of the gospel. We know that they will be a real strength to our mission."[16]

Subsequent excursions went to New Zealand in 1965, 1967, and 1968, and two went in 1969. From that time until the Papeete Tahiti Temple was constructed, the excursions were regular annual affairs.

THE MAUPITI ISLAND TRAGEDY

The sea is powerful and insensitive to the people who must live near it and use it as a source of food and a means of transportation. Time and again it has claimed the lives of the people of Polynesia. The worst sea tragedy for Latter-day Saints in the Pacific—worse than the shipwreck of the *Julia Ann* in the 1850s, which took four lives—was the shipwreck of the *Manuia* on May 23, 1963. A sad irony is that "Manuia" means good luck or good fortune.

Latter-day Saint missionary work in the Windward Islands was, as we've noted earlier, successful only after World War II. But as branches grew, so did the need for new chapels. On May 22, 1963, a new building was dedicated for Haapu Branch on the island of Huahine. Members and friends of the Church gathered there from many islands. The occasion was made special not only by the presence of government officials, but also by Elder Gordon B. Hinckley of the Council of the Twelve, who spoke and pronounced the dedicatory prayer. After the formal services "everyone was happy and we held a big, big, big party," recalled Claire Manea years later.

It was late evening before the fifty members and friends from the little island of Maupiti pulled themselves away from the celebration and climbed aboard the old but seaworthy *Manuia* and started their voyage into the night. The rolling sea was normal until the little ship passed between the islands of Raiatea and Tahaa. From there on, bubbles like suds passed, and every experienced seagoer knew that rough seas were ahead. By the time they reached Maupiti the ocean was very rough. Dawn had not yet come, although it was not far away.

Seamen's guides warn sailors, especially those who have never docked at Maupiti before, to use a pilot. The channel through the coral reef into the calm waters of the lagoon is known as the most dangerous pass in all of French Polynesia. On that morning the waves were so

The first group of Tahitian Saints to go to the temple in New Zealand, 1963. (Courtesy LDS Church Archives.)

high the passage could hardly be seen. The old men on board said, "Captain, don't go in, don't go in!" But before he could rethink his course, the *Manuia* rose high on a great swell, the rudder and propeller hung for a moment out of water, and the captain lost control of the ship. It hit the reef with a terrible crash and then rolled over in the massive waves. Three times it rolled over. In those first horrifying moments the superstructure of the craft was torn off and set adrift. This finally proved fortuitous, for twenty people were able to cling to it and preserve their lives.

Because of the pounding waves and turbulent churning and turning of the black waters, the rescue was slow. Men needed not only bravery but also great skill to maneuver their canoes and little boats. Few boatmen dared to brave the passage. Most surfed their boats across the reef.

When the losses were assessed, fifteen lives had been lost—all died who did not know how to swim. Ten women, five of whom were mothers, three small babies, a four- or five-year-old girl, and one man perished in the sea. The loss was tragic for everyone on the island. The crying, moaning, and, for some, hysteria were terrible. All but two of the Relief Society sisters of the little Maupiti Branch drowned.

When President Kendall Young received word of the tragedy, he immediately informed Elder Hinckley. They had flown back to Tahiti after the dedication ceremonies. Elder Hinckley was scheduled to fly back to Salt Lake City that night. He canceled his flight home and asked President Young to arrange transportation to Maupiti. The best they could find was an old P.T. boat of World War II vintage. They bought wood for coffins, gathered mattresses and blankets to sleep on deck, asked eight or ten priesthood and Relief Society people to come along to help, and sailed toward Maupiti, 160 miles away. The old boat arrived at Maupiti the next afternoon, a day after the accident.

Only nine of the fifteen bodies had been recovered. Because of the humid heat and their poor condition, they had already been laid to rest in the tropical soil. The village of Vaitea, with its seven hundred stricken residents, deeply appreciated the comfort and concern shown by Elder Hinckley's visit. He wept as he saw and held the little children who were left motherless. After visiting the new graves and consoling the survivors, the brethren held a funeral service in the little chapel.

The wood they had brought for caskets was given to a man who had used his supply for that purpose. The missionaries bought cloth for new clothes—many belongings had been lost with the ship—and the Church sent needed supplies with the next boat.

Some of the survivors were helped onto the old P.T. boat and taken back to Tahiti for better medical attention. Among those was Claire Teriitehau. She had been interested in the Church for many months, interested enough to go to the dedication at Huahine, but had not been baptized. Her life had been saved by her fiancé, a man named André Manea. While she was on board the ship, Sister Young, the mission president's wife, asked Claire if she would like a blessing under the hands of Elder Hinckley. Claire asked for a blessing. Elder Hinckley "said many things, but one thing I especially remember that Apostle Hinckley told me was that I would join the Church and that I would be needed by the Lord. I didn't understand what he meant when he said it, but now I do because I have many callings in the Church. . . . I was baptized because I had that experience. The things that happened are a great testimony to me." Such were the words of one who survived the tragedy. Claire was baptized on July 1, 1963.

Elder Hinckley was deeply affected by these events. In words of great meaning he wrote, "This has been a terrible day, I'm glad I came. . . . I shall never forget Maupiti."[17]

"ECOLE PRIMAIRE ELEMENTAIRE-S.D.J."— THE LDS ELEMENTARY SCHOOL

The first LDS schools in French Polynesia were established in 1914, but because of World War I they were closed. From that time

LDS Elementary School in Papeete, 1964. The new Tahiti Temple now shares this site. (Courtesy Yves Perrin.)

until the 1960s, several mission presidents discussed with the governors of the islands the possibility of establishing LDS schools. In each instance the suggestion was rebuffed because of French laws demanding that all schools had to be operated and taught by French-speaking citizens.

In 1961, President Kendall W. Young, who had served his first mission to France, rekindled the idea of a school. After two years of serious negotiations with the government and after convincing Church authorities in Salt Lake City that the idea was desirable and feasible, President Young moved ahead with plans for construction of an elementary school. After President McKay agreed to that proposal, he turned the project over to the Church's Pacific Board of Education for implementation.

The groundbreaking in Papeete took place on May 25, 1963, only two days after the Maupiti tragedy, with Elder Gordon B. Hinckley representing the First Presidency. A search was made in France for the right person to direct the new school. The man selected was Louis Bertone, who was a convert of three years, a recognized administrator, and a veteran of many years' service in the French military. Brother Bertone, with his family, moved to Papeete in October 1962.

Bertone had to watch many details and make many decisions. After he submitted careful plans to the government about the size of the proposed building, the hiring of teachers, teacher housing, courses to be taught, transportation, and hundreds of other details, his request for authorization to open the school was granted on February 6, 1963. Sixteen months after the groundbreaking in May 1963, the physical plant was completed by twenty-five building missionaries. The dedication took place on September 18, 1964.

The school opened its doors to four hundred students on Monday, September 20, 1964. All classes were taught in French. Because French law required that half of the teachers be from France, the first staff was composed of six teachers from various parts of France and six from Tahiti. After its beginning the school was enlarged from twelve to seventeen classrooms, and teacher housing was constructed. In 1978 there were 530 students in the school.

In 1969, Brother Bertone resigned to retire in Utah. His successor was Raymond R. Baudin, a professional engineer and teacher. Baudin had served on the faculty since the school opened. During his tenure as principal he improved the curriculum, implemented in-service

A group of Saints laying the floor of the new LDS Elementary School, Papeete, 1963. (Courtesy LDS Church Archives.)

training for the faculty, and continued to strengthen the quality of religious education.

After the primary school opened, several other important developments came in the area of Church education. During the 1960s, 1970s, and early 1980s, many LDS and non-LDS students were sent, through Church arrangements, to the Church College of New Zealand, to Liahona High School in Tonga, and to the Brigham Young University – Hawaii Campus. More recently the Church Educational System has instituted the home-study seminary program in French Polynesia. In 1978, 213 students participated in this program.[18]

When the primary school in Tahiti was founded, it served a number of worthy purposes. However, time brought changes in the situation in French Polynesia, and the school outlived its usefulness. The Church did not operate a high school into which its elementary school graduates could enter. This became a problem when the government high schools required either graduation from government elementary schools or the successful passing of an examination to prove that the prospective student's education was equal. Not all of the LDS children passed the examination, and some of their parents began taking them out of the LDS school and registering them in public schools. Two other factors worked against the continued success of the LDS school. The government had opened many new schools since the early 1960s, making the LDS school less important. Another factor was that many children lived considerable distances around the island from the school and transportation was a problem. Enrollment dropped severely during the late 1970s and early 1980s. Administrators, that is, Principal Yves Perrin, Area CES Administrator Bruce M. Lake, and the Council of the Twelve finally decided it would be best to close the school. The elementary school in Tahiti was closed in June 1982.[19] It was fortunate that the school property served well as a site for the new Papeete Tahiti Temple.

THE CREATION OF TAHITI STAKE

Although French Polynesia was the first Pacific area to receive the restored gospel, it was the last among the old missions (Hawaii, New Zealand, Samoa, and Tonga) to be organized as a stake. Historic development and geography account for the delay. Until the 1950s the Church was strongest in the outer islands. Now it seems unlikely the Church may ever have enough members in the Tuamotus to support a stake. Considering that the Church has been firmly established in

Tahiti itself only since the mid-1950s, progress toward the first stake was actually quite rapid.

Three mission presidents, Thomas Stone, Karl M. Richards, and Ralph Richards, gave the major energy and impulse toward stakehood. They organized the Tahiti-Moorea district along the lines of a stake. They went further in finding a man to be stake president than is usual in such a situation. Raituia T. Tapu, mentioned earlier as captain of the *Paraita,* was induced to return to Tahiti from Laie, Hawaii, where he had served as a high councilor. He had had more Church administration experience than any other Tahitian at that time.

In the spring of 1972 the First Presidency and the Council of the Twelve approved the creation of Tahiti Stake. Elders Marvin J. Ashton of the Council of the Twelve and Franklin D. Richards, assistant to the Twelve, organized the stake on May 14, 1972. It was, incidentally, the first stake created in a French-speaking country. The new stake consisted of all the former branches on Tahiti and Moorea.

EXPANSION INTO OTHER FIELDS

In 1961, President Kendall Young visited Noumea, New Caledonia, and organized a small branch of Tahitian Latter-day Saints. (A more complete recounting of this story is found in chapter 28.) More recently, President Karl M. Richards and Raymond R. Baudin, the latter the first native French mission president, established, then reestablished missionary work in the Marquesas Islands, northeast of the Tuamotu group. The population base is small and the Roman Catholic Church is strong in the Marquesas, but it is anticipated that the LDS Church will be able to establish permanent branches there in the near future.

THE FIRST AREA CONFERENCE IN TAHITI

On March 1 and 2, 1976, President Spencer W. Kimball and President N. Eldon Tanner, along with nine other general authorities, met in Papeete, the final stopping place on their strenuous circuit of nations in the South Pacific. Twenty-three hundred Saints and friends of the Church gathered for the two days of meetings. President Kimball expressed his strong love for the Polynesian members and encouraged them to share the love of the gospel with their neighbors and friends. He also spoke to the Tahitian Saints, as he or one of the general authorities had done at almost all other Pacific conferences,

The first Tahiti Stake presidency, 1972. From left to right: Raymond Baudin, Raituia T. Tapu, and Fernand Caumet. (Courtesy Yves Perrin.)

about creating local Zions. "The gathering of the Saints," he said, "is for you and me." And, interpreting the concept, stressed, "To the Tahitians these beautiful islands are Zion."[20]

In Tahiti, where relations between the Church and the French government have been strained from time to time, President Kimball's meeting (along with President Baudin of the mission and President Victor D. Cave of the stake) with Charles Schmitt, governor of French Polynesia, was important to the continuation of good feelings. Governor Schmitt showed his respect for the Church by attending the last session of the conference.

The area conference had the effect the Church leaders desired. Missionary work improved, largely because more local elders began accepting calls, and numbers grew. But growth is one thing and development is another. By mid-1981, the Tahiti Papeete Stake was prepared for a division. An apostle was assigned to go to Tahiti to divide the stake, but he was reassigned elsewhere at the last minute, and the division was delayed for a year. But on June 20, 1982, Elder James E. Faust called thirty-one-year-old Lysis G. Terooatea, a former bishop and high councilor, as the first president of the Pirae Tahiti Stake. On the same day, Jean-Michel Vehiatua Carlson, also age thirty-one, a former bishop, high councilor, and counselor in the stake presidency, was called to lead the Papeete Stake. At about the same time Victor D. Cave was called as regional representative over the Tahiti

Papeete Stake Center. (Courtesy Yves Perrin.)

Region. When one adds together some changes in the temporal affairs department, the closing of the elementary school, the creation of the second stake, and the calling of Tahiti's own first regional representative, June 1982 was a historic period that marked the maturity of the Church in that area.

In tiny Tubuai and the atolls of the Tuamotu Archipelago (population 7,660 in 1971), however, the small numbers of Saints will have to do with branches for now, as they have done for well over a hundred years.

THE PAPEETE TAHITI TEMPLE

"While he [Joseph Smith] was yet alive and while the saints were yet in Nauvoo he was inspired to call the first missionaries to these beautiful Society Islands of the Pacific. From their dedicated labors in those early years there came a great harvest." So prayed President Gordon B. Hinckley in the dedicatory prayer of the Papeete Tahiti Temple. He continued, "Since that time there have been seasons of prosperity and seasons when problems were many and the harvest was lean. But through all of these years thy work has grown as with faith thy servants have labored among the Tahitian people and found

Pirae Stake Center, Tahiti. (Courtesy Yves Perrin.)

those who have come into the fold of the Church. There is now strength and maturity among many thousands of the Saints in French Polynesia, for which we express gratitude unto thee. As a capstone to all of this effort we now have this beautiful and sacred house to present unto thee."

Although the Saints of French Polynesia are now moving ahead with greater vigor than ever before, the dedication of their small 8,500-square-foot temple was the culmination, the capstone, of many years of labor and dedication to the restored gospel. Hundreds of Tahitian Saints had sacrificed to travel to the temples at New Zealand, Hawaii, or other locations to receive their temple ordinances. The financial cost was almost always extremely high when compared with other parts of the world. Numerous stories tell of Tahitian members who lived on very humble food for long periods of time or who made other sacrifices in order to save enough money to travel to the temple.

Also, the Tahitian Latter-day Saints had shown their zeal for genealogy work when they participated in and encouraged the collection of oral genealogies and histories during the early 1970s. Yves Perrin was hired by the Genealogical Department of the Church to collect Tahitian family histories and genealogies on tape and to transcribe that information for research purposes. The Buka Tupuna—

Oral Genealogy Program—continued until 1975, under the direction of Stewart Shaver.

If mere numbers were the sole determiners of where and when temples should be built, Tahiti, with its 6,400 members, would have to rank fairly low on any list. But because the Lord and his servants measure their purposes by a different standard—the standard of covenants and needs—the Saints in Tahiti now have a temple in their midst. Perhaps more than any other temple, the Papeete Tahiti Temple exemplifies the concept of taking temples to the people rather than having the people travel to the temple.

The First Presidency of the Church announced during general conference in April 1980 that a temple would be built in Tahiti. At that time, they also announced that temples would be constructed in Samoa, Tonga, and Sydney, Australia. Along with the temples in Hawaii and New Zealand, which had been built many years before, the new temples would bring to five the number of temples in Polynesia.

About 3,000 people attended the groundbreaking in Tahiti when President Spencer W. Kimball turned the first soil on February 13, 1981. As already noted, the former site of the LDS Elementary School in Papeete was selected for the new temple. Fortunately, the school was constructed in such a way that the temple could be placed in an area that remained open.

Although ground had been broken and the land had been dedicated, construction did not begin for more than a year. Once underway, however, the white edifice rose from the ground in beautiful majesty. The combination of white masonry walls and glazed blue-tile roof is striking. As on all new temples, a statue of the Angel Moroni graces the top of the spire. By October 1983, construction was complete and ready for visitors and final dedication.

Elder Jack H. Goaslind, Jr., of the First Quorum of the Seventy, who was area executive administrator of Church operations in French Polynesia, and regional representative Victor D. Cave, hosted a number of dignitaries on a special V.I.P. visitors day on October 10, three days before the new building was opened to the public. Temple President Joseph E. Childers and his staff did everything possible to make Alain Ohrel, high commissioner of the republic and highest-ranking official of the French government in French Polynesia, as well as other distinguished guests, feel comfortable in the new structure. These special guests added dignity to the occasion. When the regular open house began on October 13, more than 1,800 guests filed through the first day. By the time the ten-day open house ended, over

Groundbreaking for the Papeete, Tahiti Temple in February 1981. In the foreground are Elder Jack H. Goaslind, Jr., then Area Executive Administrator, and President Spencer W. Kimball. (Courtesy Yves Perrin.)

16,500 (approximately 16 percent of Tahiti's populace) people had toured the temple. The building did much to allay fears and strange ideas regarding Latter-day Saints and the concept of temple work.

President Gordon B. Hinckley and a company of general authorities including Elders L. Tom Perry and David B. Haight of the Council of the Twelve, Rex C. Reeve, Sr., of the First Quorum of the Seventy, and Presiding Bishop Victor L. Brown joined Elder Goaslind on October 27 for the first of six dedicatory sessions. The sessions were attended by 2,500 worthy Latter-day Saints.

In his dedicatory address President Hinckley spoke at length regarding the tragedy that had occurred at Maupiti twenty years before. Referring to the women among the fifteen who died, he said,

Papeete Tahiti Temple. (Copyright © The Church of Jesus Christ of Latter-day Saints. Used by permission.)

"I hope with all my heart the husbands [of those sisters who died] are worthy to come to this house and have their beautiful wives sealed to them." Between the dedication sessions he met Claire T. Manea again. Both shed tears. She and her husband, André Manea, have dedicated their lives to the Church. At the time of the temple dedication André was first counselor to President C. Jay Larson of the Tahiti Papeete Mission. In a very real way they represent the firm dedication of thousands of Saints in French Polynesia—both living and dead—who have dedicated all they have to build up the kingdom of God in the islands of the sea.[21]

The history of the Church in French Polynesia has been largely a series of struggles to overcome impediments caused by nature, economics, governments, society, churches, and international events. The first one hundred years, from 1844 until 1945, were unimpressive from a numerical standpoint, but they were, nevertheless, full of examples of personal sacrifice, fortitude, and character on the part of local Saints and missionaries alike. The years since World War II have seen rapid growth and significant changes. New methods of proselyting and contemporary administrative and teaching techniques, coupled with excellent new physical facilities, have replaced the outmoded ways of earlier times. The Saints of French Polynesia are now stronger in faith and more diligent in keeping the Lord's commandments than at any other time in history.

PART 2

HAWAII

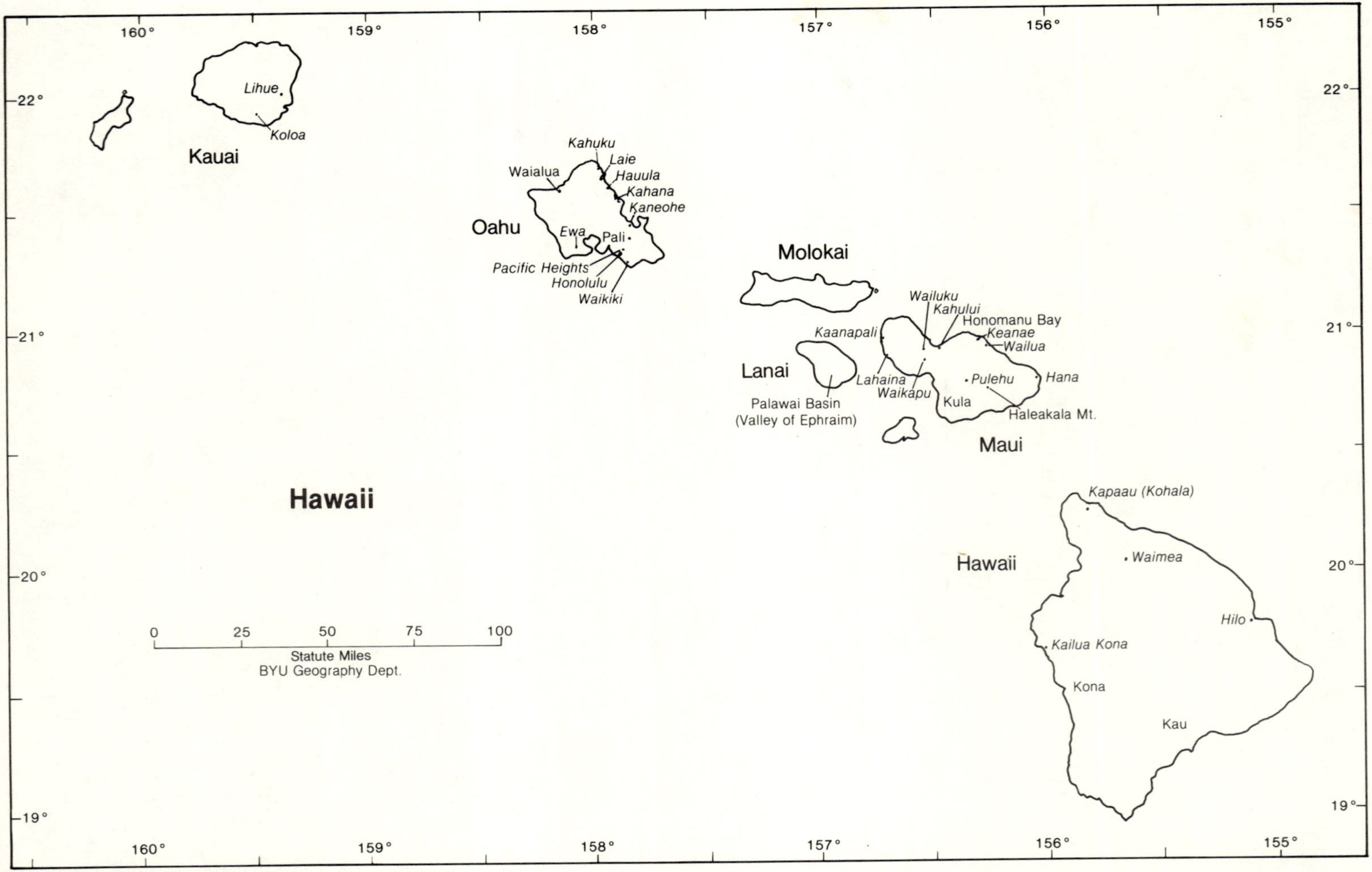
160°
159°
158°
157°
156°
155°
22°
21°
20°
19°
Kauai
Lihue
Koloa
Oahu
Kahuku
Laie
Hauula
Kahana
Kaneohe
Waialua
Ewa
Pali
Pacific Heights
Honolulu
Waikiki
Molokai
Lanai
Palawai Basin
(Valley of Ephraim)
Kaanapali
Wailuku
Kahului
Honomanu Bay
Keanae
Wailua
Lahaina
Waikapu
Pulehu
Hana
Kula
Haleakala Mt.
Maui
Hawaii
Kapaau (Kohala)
Waimea
Hilo
Kailua Kona
Kona
Kau
Hawaii
0
25
50
75
100
Statute Miles
BYU Geography Dept.

CHAPTER 6

THE FOUNDING OF THE CHURCH IN HAWAII

Hawaii, 1850–1854

The year was 1850. Only three years had passed since Brigham Young led his modern Israel from Illinois to the Valley of the Great Salt Lake. And only two years earlier gold had been discovered at Sutter's Mill in northern California. The cry of gold had raced across the frontier of the yet uncompleted nation, across the territories of the United States, and into every city, town, and hamlet in the country. The desire for easy wealth brought hopeful miners west in such numbers that by 1850 twenty-five thousand people called California home, even though it was a temporary home for many.

President Brigham Young was not enticed by the prospects of greater wealth obtained by mining. In fact, he once told his people, "If you Elders of Israel want to go to the gold mines, go and be damned!"[1] But the financial obligations of some of the pioneers, particularly of the elderly, were brought to his attention, and the prospect of clearing these debts by mining convinced him that a few carefully chosen men should go to California in search of gold.

Even though the homes, gardens, farms, and shops of Great Salt Lake City were still new and much remained to be done, President Young sent a group of able-bodied men to California as gold-digging missionaries. The wealth they garnered would not all be their own: their purpose was to obtain money to strengthen Zion. It was among these men that the story of the Latter-day Saints in the Sandwich Islands—Hawaii—had its beginning.

The chill of fall had come upon the hills of northern California when Elder Charles C. Rich, an apostle, rode into a little mining camp called Slap Jack Bar on September 24, 1850. It was here on the middle fork of the American River that a group of the gold-mining elders had

Honolulu Harbor around 1850. The scenes the first LDS missionaries to the Sandwich Islands saw must have been similar to this. (Courtesy LDS Church Archives.)

staked their claims and were digging. Elder Rich, Brigham Young's personal representative to all the Latter-day Saints in the Pacific Coast area, did not take long to get to the reason for his visit: he wanted some of the men to fill missions to the Sandwich Islands.

The next morning he selected and set apart eight men to fill missions and preach the restored gospel in Hawaii. Among those called were Henry William Bigler, who was at Sutter's Mill when gold was discovered there in January 1848; George Q. Cannon, who later served in the First Presidency of the LDS Church; John Dixon; William Farrer; James Hawkins; James Keeler; Thomas Morris; and Thomas Whittle.[2] In addition, Hiram Clark, who had filled two previous missions to Great Britain, and Hiram Blackwell were called from other mining camps. The fifty-five-year-old Clark was appointed president of the mission. They sailed from San Francisco on November 15, 1850, and, after a rough voyage, arrived in Honolulu on December 12.

The dirt, grime, and foul smells of the *Imau of Muscat* were probably difficult to escape even after the landing in Honolulu. Before sleep fell upon the missionaries that night, they were laying plans to hold a special service to dedicate themselves to the Lord and to seek his blessings in converting many.

In the early morning of December 13, the elders walked up Nuuanu Valley to the beautiful King's Falls. There they bathed, their first good bath in a month, and then hiked another mile up the verdant valley. Finding a secluded place about a thousand feet above sea level, in an area now called Pacific Heights, they built an altar of stone, about three feet high and three feet around. Together they sang some hymns and prayed for the Lord's Spirit. After expressing to one another their feelings concerning their mission, they knelt together as President Clark offered a prayer that dedicated Hawaii to the preaching of the gospel. Clark asked the Lord to "open the way that we might be enabled to preach the Gospel on these islands . . . have his Spirit . . . to guide us . . . preserve us from the adversary and from every evil, and that the honest in heart might embrace the truth."[3]

After pleading with the Lord to prosper their efforts, the missionaries next tried to learn as much as they could about the people they wanted to teach. They assumed that they had been sent to the islands to preach the gospel to white persons, the *haoles*; therefore, later in the day, they surveyed the situation to see how many whites were available for proselyting. Actually, there were very few. Since there was obviously not enough work to be done among the haoles in and around Honolulu, the missionaries decided that they would divide into pairs and go to other islands to preach. It was decided that Elders Blackwell and Hawkins should go to the big island, Hawaii; that Cannon, Keeler, and Bigler should work on Maui; that Dixon and Farrer should go north to Kauai; and that Clark, Morris, and Whittle should remain in Honolulu. On December 14, President Clark, concerned about the safety of the elders, visited the British Consul and was told that the laws of the kingdom would provide protection for the new missionary force. With this assurance, they began to sail for other parts of the islands. Thus began the dissemination of the message of Mormonism among the people of the Sandwich Islands.

Not all the elders began preaching and performing missionary labor immediately. For some reason President Clark advised Elder Morris to go to work at a profession. Almost at once upon his arrival he took employment with the British Consul, William Miller.[4] Clark and Whittle, who did want to teach, arranged to preach in a free room in the market area of town. They placed a notice of their meeting in the *Polynesian,* a weekly newspaper, but attracted little attention. In short, the work got off to a slow start on Oahu.

On Kauai the work hardly fared better. After an uncomfortable voyage, William Farrer and John Dixon arrived there on December 21, 1850. Two days later, after holding some unsuccessful meetings, they sailed on to Koloa. They worked at setting up meetings with the small white population at the plantation, but after three weeks they had had no success in gaining interest. Because they had received some rather discouraging letters from President Clark and others, Farrer and Dixon decided Farrer should return to Honolulu and find out what the other elders were planning to do. At this point, because the haole population was paying so little attention to his message, Farrer was starting to work on the Hawaiian tongue but "could not make much progress in learning the native language for want of some person to teach us."[5]

Elder Farrer arrived in Honolulu on January 28. When he reported that he had not achieved anything among the whites, he found that Clark and Whittle were similarly discouraged.[6]

Seven days later Elder Cannon arrived in Honolulu from Maui; President Clark had asked him to come. Dixon also came to Honolulu from Kauai. Cannon had been very much surprised to receive President Clark's letter, which said that Whittle was returning to North America and that he, Clark, wanted Cannon to be his companion and clerk. This was not to Cannon's liking because matters had been moving in a positive direction in Maui.

Elder Cannon recounted to the president that the Sunday after

Lahaina as it appeared at the time when George Q. Cannon and his companions were there in the 1850s. (Courtesy LDS Church Archives.)

they arrived they asked the Rev. Mr. Taylor, who ministered at the Bethel Chapel, for permission to use his facilities. Taylor granted their request, but after their afternoon service was over, it was evident that if any good were to be done they would have to appeal to a larger population that the available whites. "Preaching to them with the hope of convincing them of the truth seemed a hopeless labor," wrote Elder Cannon some years later.

It was at this point that several of the elders decided to work with the Hawaiian people. Elder Cannon later recounted the event this way:

> The question arose directly, "Shall we confine our labors to the white people?" . . .
>
> For my part I felt it to be my duty to warn all men, white and red; and no sooner did I learn the condition of the population than I made up my mind to acquire the language, preach the gospel to the natives and to the whites whenever I could obtain an opportunity, and thus fill my mission. I felt resolved to stay there, master the language and warn the people of those islands, if I had to do it alone; for I felt that I could not do otherwise and be free from condemnation; the spirit of it was upon me. Elders Bigler and Keeler felt the same.[7]

Cannon, Bigler, and Keeler had begun studying the language within two days of their arrival. It was only three weeks before that Cannon was blessed with the gift of understanding the language. His ability to speak came a litle more slowly but still very quickly.

At the end of three weeks the Maui missionaries were almost destitute of funds and found it necessary to leave their rented home. Just when they were parting, a kind old Hawaiian lady named Nalimanui, who had been their neighbor and laundress, came to them and offered a room of her own to them. They were very touched and blessed her for her kindness.

Elder Cannon had some powerful spiritual experiences during the short time he stayed with Nalimanui. He made further progress in the Hawaiian language, but more importantly he also received direct instructions from the Lord about the future of the Hawaiian people and the Church. In 1900 Elder Cannon said he heard the Lord's voice "more than once as one man speaks with another, encouraging me and showing me the work which should be done among this people if I would follow the dictates of His Spirit."

The doctrine that the Hawaiian people and all other Polynesians are heirs to the blessings promised to the posterity of Abraham had its origin through George Q. Cannon. While he was at Lahaina, he received a knowledge directly from the Lord that the Hawaiians were

George Q. Cannon served his mission to Hawaii between 1850 and 1854. He later served as counselor to four presidents of the Church. (Courtesy LDS Church Archives.)

Nalimanui provided shelter and food for Elder George Q. Cannon and his companions at Lahaina, 1851. (Courtesy LDS Church Archives.)

of the house of Israel. From this time on Elder Cannon and his associates began to teach that the Hawaiian people were an offshoot branch of Israel through the posterity of Lehi, the Book of Mormon prophet.

It was at this time that Elder Cannon received his instructions from President Clark to come to Honolulu. After he had explained to President Clark what had transpired in Maui, it was apparent that it would be better for him to return there.[8] The following day, about January 29, 1851, Elder Dixon decided to return home with Elder Whittle.

Young Elder Cannon was disgusted with the talk of going home, and he told the elders so. "The Lord," said Cannon, "would hold me accountable for not doing my duty to that people." Feeling Cannon's enthusiasm and dedication, Elder Farrer decided to go to Maui to be Elder Bigler's companion.[9]

Cannon and Farrer arrived back on Maui on January 30, only four days before Elder Blackwell visited them on his way to Honolulu from Hawaii. There were so few haoles to teach on the big island that Blackwell had decided that he had done his duty, and on February 1, had sailed from Hilo and stopped off at Lahaina, Maui, a day later. His companions there were surprised that he had left his assigned area. Blackwell told them that he had worked at the Hawaiian language a little but thought it would take him at least a year to learn it, and even then he doubted that the Hawaiians would accept the gospel.[10] He was even considering going home. He had wanted his colleague Brother Hawkins to come along with him, but Hawkins said he had been sent to the big island and would stay until he received other directions.[11] Blackwell sailed on to Honolulu the same day and from there returned home with Dixon and Whittle at the end of February.[12] Elder Hawkins stayed on in Hawaii for a number of months and worked at acquiring the language.

On February 10, 1851, President Clark baptized a sixteen-year-old boy, the first Hawaiian to be baptized in the Islands. At about the same time Clark baptized a man named Blake, who was a printer. Blake had resided for a time in the Marquesas Islands, northeast of the Society Island group. In mid-February Clark also became acquainted with a Brother Clifford, who had been baptized in the Society Islands by Elder Addison Pratt. Together they discussed the possibility of missionary work in the Marquesas Islands. They finally decided that Blake would accompany Clark there.

Greatly excited by this plan, President Clark proceeded to Maui. His intention was to persuade the elders there to go with him, but he failed. Nevertheless, President Clark left his field of duty on February 27, 1851. He sailed that day for Tahiti with the intention of going from there to the Marquesas group, but because of transportation problems he never made it to those islands. Failing this, he eventually returned to California.[13]

As we have said, Dixon, Blackwell, and Whittle left Hawaii at about the same time. Elder Morris sailed during April. Hence by that time, hardly more than four months after the mission opened, half of the original ten missionaries had left the field.

THE WORK ON MAUI

The efforts of George Q. Cannon were the first to bear significant fruit in the Hawaiian Islands. He left his companions at Lahaina on March 4, 1851, and, despite bad weather, made his way during the next three days over a rough road but through beautiful scenery to Wailuku. He recorded in his diary that he had the feeling, as he traveled, that he was to meet someone who would be interested in his message and who would be willing to care for his needs. A series of unusual incidents brought him into contact with a Hawaiian judge named Jonatana H. Napela, a man of considerable influence in the area. Cannon stayed with Napela for several days and spoke to him and several of his friends about the restored gospel. These men were

Jonatana H. Napela assisted the first LDS missionaries in Maui. A stalwart in the community and in the Church, he worked side by side with George Q. Cannon in translating the Book of Mormon into the Hawaiian language. (Courtesy LDS Church Archives.)

much interested in the differences between Protestantism and Mormonism.

Cannon returned to Lahaina after a few days but was eager to get back to his new friends in Wailuku. When he returned there he found that the Reverend Mr. Conde, whom he had encountered during his first visit, was more upset with the Mormon incursion than before. Cannon reported that Conde "used all his influence against me among his congregation, and one Sunday he came out in public and delivered a most abusive discourse against the Prophet Joseph Smith and our principles, in which he gave an entirely false statement of the cause of his death, and also warned the people against me."[14]

Elder Cannon was present on this occasion and understood what Conde had said in Hawaiian. Conde had not expected this and was embarrassed when Cannon asked him to retract the lies he had spoken. Conde refused to do so. The two men discussed matters for more than half an hour, with many Hawaiians listening, among them Mr. Napela and his friends. The result was that more interest was aroused locally than before.

Napela continued to study Mormonism after this confrontation. Conde threatened to have his judgeship taken away from him if he persisted in his interest in Mormonism. Napela was not concerned, but Cannon, who had been staying with Napela while in Wailuku, decided that it would be wiser to go to another area for a while and let matters settle at Wailuku. Much time passed before the elders resumed the work there.

He chose to go to an area called Kula, which means "the country near the base of a mountain." The mountain, in this case, is Haleakala, a 10,025-foot extinct volcano of renowned beauty. Kula was especially important to Hawaii's economy at this time because Irish potatoes were grown there to be exported to California for sale to gold miners. This trade was dropping even while Cannon was there.

During the following week, Elder Keeler joined Cannon at Kula. They had not seen each other for two months. Both men were elated with their prospects for conversions, and on the next Sunday four people were baptized. A week later six more were baptized, and within a few days the membership in Kula was at nineteen. Among the new converts were a man named Kaleohano, who was Cannon's host, and also Pake, who had been a friend from his first arrival.

Elder Keeler, who gained courage faster than he developed linguistic facility, went on around the island attempting to teach the gospel. Three weeks into July he came back to Kula and asked Elder Cannon to come with him to a place called Keanae. They were accompanied by newly converted Saints who were enthusiastic about the gospel. Cannon wrote:

> Our arrival at Keanae created great excitement. The people had been watching for us, and seeing us approach from a long distance, had gathered to meet us. . . . We obtained the Calvinistic meeting-house the afternoon of our arrival, and there was a large attendance to hear the preaching.
>
> This was on Wednesday, and from that time until Monday we were constantly speaking, baptizing, confirming and counseling the people. During that time there were upwards of one hundred and thirty baptized. The Spirit of the Lord was powerfully poured out, and all rejoiced; I never enjoyed myself so well before in my life.[15]

About the last day of July, Elder Cannon returned to Kula, where on August 6 he organized the first branch of the Church in Hawaii, the Kula Branch. The site was the village of Kealakou. Two teachers and three deacons were ordained, and one of the teachers, Kaleohano, was appointed clerk of the branch.[16]

Within two weeks Elder Cannon returned to Keanae and organized four branches in that area, at Keanae, Wailua, Waianu, and Honomanu. This extraordinary event took place August 19 at a meeting of all the Saints from the area. The day before, Sunday,

Hawaiian Saints gathered at old Pulehu chapel, Maui. Late 1800s. (Courtesy LDS Church Archives.)

Cannon and Keeler had administered and passed the sacrament to one hundred and ninety members of the Church and then baptized fifteen more people after the meeting.[17]

THE WORK ON OAHU

Success did not come so quickly to the elders on Oahu. Bigler and Farrer had more difficulty learning the language than did Cannon. Farrer, the more advanced of the two, started trying to teach the gospel to the Hawaiians in late April. His first missionary campaign took him among the Hawaiians in Koolau, Kahana, Hauula, Laie, Kahuku, Waialua, and into the Ewa district. He retraced his steps and returned to Honolulu in early June.

Bigler and Farrer remained in Honolulu until June 16; then they decided they would probably improve in the language if they left the city atmosphere. In Kaneohe, on the windward side, they worked hard at the language and at trying to interest people in their work but had little success at either. In early July, Farrer once again worked in the direction of Laie. At Hauula he met a friend from Honolulu, Mr.

J.W.H. Kauwahi, who invited him to his home at Laie. For several weeks Farrer stayed there, studied the language, and talked with the people. He performed his first baptism on August 17. His convert was his host, Mr. Kauwahi. Farrer also baptized a man from Hauula named Kealoha.[18]

NEW MISSIONARIES ARRIVE

On August 18, 1851, Elder Farrer received a letter from Elder Bigler in Honolulu, asking him to come there as soon as he could because new missionaries had arrived and wanted to meet together. When Farrer arrived there the next day, he met Elders Philip B. Lewis and Francis A. Hammond. Together they boarded a schooner that took them to Lahaina, Maui. The new missionaries explained that they had arrived at Lahaina with their wives and Elder John S. Woodbury (whose wife had remained in California temporarily because of illness) on August 10. Lewis, forty-seven, and Hammond, twenty-nine, were seasoned veterans in Church service. Lewis had been called by Apostle Parley P. Pratt,[19] president of all Pacific area missions, to preside over the Sandwich Islands mission.

Cannon and Keeler, it will be remembered, were at this time having their greatest success. After holding their conference and organizing the four branches at Keanae, they traveled the sixty or seventy miles to Lahaina. All of the missionaries except James Hawkins, who was on Hawaii, arrived and met together on August 20, 1851.[20]

At their first meeting, held that day, Lewis was sustained as mission president, and the following day it was decided that he should remain at Lahaina. Elder Hammond, who had lived at Lahaina during his years as a sailor, decided to stay there too and set up a shoe repair shop to support himself, his wife, and his child.[21] Woodbury was assigned to go to Hawaii and work with Hawkins. The other missionaries would continue working as they had done before. Lewis, whose wife had come with him, was financially burdened, so he decided to teach English for a while until he could acquire the native language.

It was obvious to the new elders that the course taken by Cannon and his companions was the best way to succeed. The new elders were surprised that so much had been accomplished.

Cannon and Farrer, as well as Bigler and Keeler, felt a certain relief that they did not have families to "fetter" them.[22] Within a few days the old elders returned to their areas of labor, and in early September, Elder Woodbury joined Elder Hawkins on Hawaii.[23] President Lewis decided that Honolulu was the logical place to establish the mission headquarters.

DIFFICULTIES ENCOUNTERED IN THE WORK

A constant battle continued between the LDS missionaries and the ministers of the other religions. This struggle has never entirely ended. Ministers occasionally used threats and other means of persuading new converts to Mormonism to return to their former churches. The first serious confrontation of this kind occurred in the Kula and Keanae districts of Maui. When Cannon returned there in September 1851, he found that the local minister of the Koolau area had stopped all of the LDS meetings and even threatened the Hawaiians that if they continued in their new-found beliefs they would be bound and sent out of their area. The local representative of the king backed these threats. Enemies of the Church claimed that other government officials supported them, and because of the seriousness of the matter, it was decided that Elder Cannon should visit Honolulu and attempt to clear up the difficulties.

Early in October Elder Cannon arrived in Honolulu. In company with President Lewis, he visited the appropriate government ministers, both U.S. and Hawaiian, and tried to get written assurance that the Latter-day Saints had permission to preach and establish their Church. He did not obtain it, but the elders were able to use a portion of a letter from the Rev. Mr. Richard Armstrong, minister of public instruction, to document the legality of the Mormon cause. Cannon later talked to Princes Alexander and Lot and received assurance from them that the LDS people would be protected.[24]

Elder Farrer on Oahu experienced harassment that was similar to what had occurred on Maui. He used Cannon's experience to fight for his position, and he put down the opposition without too much trouble.

By the end of the first year, missionary work was moving along at a rapid pace. Cannon and Keeler had established the Church well in Kula and Keanae and had recently moved back to Wailuku, where they had continued success. Farrer and Bigler were doing well on the windward side of Oahu. By the first anniversary of the establishment of the mission, Elder Hawkins had spent most of a year on Hawaii and had been joined briefly by Elder Woodbury, who decided to go to the dryer side of the island. On November 10, Hawkins joined the Maui elders and labored with them for many months there. Woodbury, who was joined by Elder and Sister Perkins, worked on Hawaii for a time. They were later sent to work on Molokai.

Elvira Woodbury (who had been forced to remain in California because of ill health) and William J. and Patsy Perkins had arrived on November 30, 1851. After their arrival no other missionaries came until February 17, 1853.

THE WORK DURING THE SECOND YEAR

The second year of the mission brought uneven progress. The missionaries settled into a pattern of traveling from place to place; living on poi (either taro poi or potato poi), fruits, fish, chicken, and pork (the latter two on special occasions); and sleeping in the homes of friends or under trees if no friends were found. They did most of their own sewing and often repaired their own shoes.

They struggled to keep their new converts interested and active, but they were frequently frustrated because they could not get the Hawaiian people to understand their logic. During November and December of 1851 a number of Farrer's converts fell away. He found their excuses for doing so to be capricious and without a basis in "reason." On December 13, he wrote, "It appears to me—that it will be a hard job to do much with this people and get them to understand principle of which they are very ignorant, but perhaps when we get a thorough knowledge of the language we may be enabled to get them to understand principle better."

From the beginning the elders taught the gospel in its fulness. They stressed first principles and basic ideas but did not hesitate to teach other aspects of the restoration. They treated the Hawaiian members as complete equals.

TRANSLATING THE BOOK OF MORMON

From the beginning the elders had recognized the necessity of having written materials in Hawaiian available for their converts. At first nobody had the ability to produce such translations, but in late January 1852, Elder Cannon began translating the Book of Mormon.[25] A few months later, in June, Elder Farrer started work on Orson Pratt's pamphlet on the coming forth of the Book of Mormon. By August this small work was completed and ready for publication.[26] Cannon's work on the Book of Mormon, being much larger and much more demanding of accuracy and correct interpretation, took longer. On the last day of January 1854, just two years since the project was commenced, the book was complete and ready for publication.[27]

Much took place at the October conference in 1853. The Saints had grown in number to over three thousand, notwithstanding the unfortunate deaths of almost one hundred and eighty who had succumbed to smallpox. Fifty-three organized branches were represented at the meetings. The first matter of business discussed was the necessity of printing the Book of Mormon.[28] The missionaries wanted to print it and a number of other items, such as a synopsis of the scriptures, some portions of the Doctrine and Covenants relating to Church government, a selection of hymns, and various tracts and pamphlets. Having their own press seemed the least expensive course as well as the most convenient means of achieving their ends. A Hawaiian high chief named Levi Haalelea had become interested in the gospel and was attending meetings regularly. A man of considerable influence and wealth, he was also a member of the king's privy council. Less than a month after the conference, he indicated his willingness to help finance the press, and in January 1854 he loaned the mission $500 for one year with interest.[29] On December 2, 1853, Elder Dennis, a convert to the Church in Hawaii and a man of considerable means and great generosity, promised to lend the mission $1000, to be paid back when possible.

One of the elders, William McBride, was not well and was released to return home with a commission to buy a printing press in California. McBride sailed from Hawaii on January 21. When he arrived in California, he discovered that no presses were available, and so a press was ordered from Boston. It was finally sent from New York, arriving in Honolulu on October 6, 1854.

Elder Cannon, who was a printer by trade, had been released, and no one in the mission knew how to operate the new press. It was stored for six months. In the interim a letter arrived from Elder Parley P. Pratt, who was still presiding in California, asking that the press be sent to California, where paper and experienced printers were more readily available.

Only five months after he had arrived home in Utah, Elder Cannon was called back to California. There he set up the press and supervised the printing of the Book of Mormon in Hawaiian, completing the task late in 1855.[30]

Evidently Cannon had problems, perhaps financial, for he did not quickly finish the binding and shipping of the volume. Henry Bigler recorded receiving twelve cases of unbound copies on November 24, 1857. He was angry with the customs officer who said "they could hardly be considered religious books" and would not allow them to be entered duty free. Then about six months after the books arrived, the missionaries were called home on account of the Utah War, and the books were stored to await the eventual return of the elders.[31]

CHAPEL BUILDING AND LOCAL LEADERSHIP

The missionaries were not content, even during the early years, to allow their converts to remain without basic facilities. Meetinghouses were constructed in many parts of the islands, the earliest in August 1852. During that month two chapels were dedicated on Maui. The next month another chapel was completed at Keanae, Maui. Elder Farrer described it as being "a frame building 56 feet long by 21 wide, built after the native fashion and covered with lauhala." The roof was of thatched pili grass. This description seems to fit most of the early meetinghouses. In some instances frame houses were rented and fitted out with rude benches. Finding property on which to build was not always easy, but some help did come from kind Polynesians who had influence, such as Mr. Haalelea.

Not many months passed after the first branches were organized before Hawaiian men were ordained elders in the Melchizedek Priesthood and sent on six-month missions to their own people. Hawaiian missionaries were called in fairly large numbers, beginning with the October 1852 conference. A year later twenty-two local elders and priests were called, and the following April ten more joined the ranks as missionaries. Their efforts yielded much fruit during the first year or two until about 1854, when the work slowed down on all fronts. Hawaiian Church members were not left as passive onlookers. From the beginning they were involved in responsible ways.

On December 31, 1854, there were thirty-one foreign missionaries in Hawaii, and fifty-three branches.

Several Hawaiian Saints stand out as examples of devotion to the work. Elders Jonatana Napela and J.W.H. Kauwahi were strong members, and there were many others who almost matched their stature. Brother Napela was a member of the Maui conference presidency. He also founded the first language-training school for missionaries in the Pacific area. On April 9, 1853, he suggested that the newly arrived missionaries should come to his house to live for a time so that he could teach them the language.[32] On Saturday, April 16, he began his school by having them read aloud from the Hawaiian Bible. In the evening Napela made them recite again. Two days later Elder Ephraim Green wrote, "I have all ways bin a hard working man all the days of my life but this is the hardist work I ever dun to set and study all day. Our teacher is very atentive. Sum of the Brethring have got so thay can read quite well but cant tell the mening of what thay read."[33]

EARLY EDUCATIONAL EFFORTS

The economic and sanitary conditions of the Hawaiian Saints troubled the missionaries, and they sincerely wanted to help them rise above their situation.[34]

In August 1853, the elders concluded that there were sufficient numbers in the Church to deserve LDS schools separate from the government institutions. They based this claim, which was made to Richard Armstrong, minister of public instruction, on the idea that there was already a double system of Protestant and Catholic schools supported by the state. In effect this was almost true because the local people of each area in the nation had the right to elect the boards of directors for their schools, and it was only natural that they would choose people of their own denominations.[35]

It is not known how many schools were finally founded by the LDS missionaries during these early years, but schools were operated on Oahu, Kauai, Maui, Molokai, and Lanai. Some local opposition arose on Molokai when Elder Woodbury and the Saints organized their school there. The problems were quickly resolved when the local Protestant missionary told the Hawaiians they could attend any school they wanted to.[36]

TENSIONS RELATING TO THE DOCTRINE OF POLYGAMY

Word of plural marriage had preceded the first Mormon missionaries to the islands, but it was not a serious issue during the first two and a half years of the mission. From August 1853 on, however, the tensions between the Church and the government of Hawaii increased. Until that time very little had been said about the doctrine of plural marriage. The missionaries did not include it in their discussions at all until April of that year, and then did so only because they thought it would be wiser to teach the doctrine themselves than to allow their converts to learn about it from their enemies.

There is no evidence that the Hawaiian Saints were ever counseled to enter the practice of plural marriage or that any did. But the fact that the concept of polygamy had been introduced to the Hawaiian Saints came to the attention, naturally enough, of government officials and contributed to further friction between them and the Saints.

The same false stories about the Saints in Utah, especially the stories about Brigham Young, were circulated in Hawaii as were spread all over America and the Western world. Many newly converted members fell away because they could not stand the harassment from their former associates and friends.

The most direct result of the discussions of plural marriage was refusal by the government to grant to LDS Church officials the right to perform marriages. This was a serious problem that continued until 1877. There were no cases that proved Mormons to be violating the law; nevertheless the ruling stood. The Saints deeply disliked having to go to Protestent ministers for their marriages, but this humiliation had to be endured.[37]

A number of other confrontations arose that brought the mission president into contact with government officials. One Hawaiian brother, Elder Kauwahi, a native lawyer at the time seeking election as marshal of Kauai and favored to win, was arrested for breaking the marriage laws of the kingdom. In truth he had been divorced for several years before he remarried and entered the Church. Nevertheless, he was arrested, placed in prison for a time, tried, fined, imprisoned again, and finally allowed to appeal to the supreme court. The missionaries were convinced that this was all done to discredit one of the most intelligent and influential Hawaiians in the islands because he had become a Mormon.[38]

THE GREAT SMALLPOX EPIDEMIC

Some of the saddest incidents in the mission's history took place during a terrible smallpox epidemic in late 1853. The elders, who were evidently immune to the disease, spent their time administering to the sick. But many good members of the Church died on Oahu. Fewer suffered from the disease on the outer islands, but the effects were sorely felt there as well. Several of the elders were perplexed by their observations that the Lord had taken the best and strongest members from their midst.[39] In an effort to try to find meaning in these difficult losses, B. F. Johnson wrote about his feelings at the time:

> So went most of our dearest and most zealous brethren and friends—our most active help in the ministry—and my heart wept, and my whole soul cried out to the Lord for that poor people. I was in great affliction, and marveled that the Lord would permit all his most faithful servants to die, so dear to us, and whose help we so much needed. I pondered the subject prayerfully until the light of the Lord shone upon my understanding, and I saw multitudes of their race in the spirit world who had lived before them, and there was not one there with the priesthood to teach them the gospel. The voice of the Spirit said to me, "Sorrow not, for they are now doing that greater work for which they were ordained, and it is all of the Lord."[40]

In this way did one elder receive solace for his grief. He was convinced that the gospel was now being preached to the Hawaiian people who had died prior to the introduction of the gospel in that land.

By 1854 the Church was well established in Hawaii. Over fifty branches were organized on all the major islands. Chapels had been built, schools had been opened, local Saints had been given responsible positions in the Church, and literature had been published in the Hawaiian language. There were over four thousand Hawaiian members of the Church, and the future looked promising for further expansion of the faith in the islands.

CHAPTER 7

LANAI: AN ISLAND ZION

Hawaii, 1854–1864

The Latter-day Saint missionaries to Hawaii came armed with the same religious beliefs that had motivated and guided their colleagues in other parts of the world. Since the 1830s, Church doctrine had required the Saints everywhere to "flee from Babylon," the sinful world, and come to "Zion," where the pure in heart could dwell in peace. The missionaries who left the Utah gathering place to teach the gospel in Hawaii carried with them these concepts and the idea of a separate gathering place.[1]

The principle of gathering was developed among the Mormons in New York, Ohio, Missouri, and Illinois, where Church members expected to dwell together in righteousness and prepare for the Millennium. The result of this doctrine was the establishment of a number of gathering places.

THE DECISION TO GATHER ON LANAI

When the Hawaiian membership grew to 3,008, and the antagonism of the government, Protestant and Catholic missionaries, and others became strong against the Church in Hawaii, the missionaries decided to find a temporary gathering place there. This action had been suggested by President Brigham Young before it was officially acted upon at October conference in 1853. A committee of elders was appointed to search for a suitable location or locations. They were hoping to find a place that was somewhat removed from the larger centers, a place where strong Saints could develop without outside harassment.[2]

About two weeks after the conference, on October 19, at the suggestion of Elder Hammond, who had previously been there, the committee visited the little island of Lanai. They hoped it would be a suitable gathering place for the Hawaiian Saints. B. F. Johnson described the excursion:

> The following morning . . . we started to explore this island, which is nearly circular in shape, and about 20 miles in diameter, and had been upheaved, a melted, dripping mass of rock. . . . In ascending this island mountain about one mile was rugged and rocky, but another mile of smooth and beautiful grasslands brought us to a summit or rim of a basin or valley, which as a concave occupied its whole top; and as we gazed down upon it we were charmed with its beauty. Never had we seen a valley of such symmetry and beauty, and as we proceeded, we found the soil very rich, the only question of importance being the needed supply of water to sustain the population through the dry season. . . .
>
> We were told of springs over a high ridge. . . . At the bottom we found a number of small basins dry in the clay banks, filled by the seeping waters. . . .
>
> Exploring the interior portion of the valley we found beautiful fields of sweet potatoes, with melon vines and beans that had grown year after year. . . .
>
> We could not see how to procure water for a settlement, as to construct tanks would be expensive and take time.[3]

When the committee members returned to Lahaina, Maui, they held a meeting to consider their findings and their impressions about Lanai. Most of the group liked the site.[4]

In February 1854, Elder Francis A. Hammond met with Chief Levi Haalelea, the owner of some Lanai land, and the chief made the following offer: "He said he would give us the privilege of going onto his land there for the space of four years and try what we could do, without any charge, and after that if we wanted it longer we should then pay something for it."[5] Other sites were considered after this time, but the thinking of the elders moved more and more in the direction of Lanai.

In early June, President Lewis received a letter from President Young in which he discussed the concept of "temporary or subsidiary gathering places" and asked the Saints in Hawaii to find a suitable location and to proceed to settle it.[6] With this prodding from Brigham Young, the committee decided to use the Palawai Basin, Lanai, as their local Zion.

THE BEGINNING OF THE LANAI SETTLEMENT

When Elders Green, Hammond, and Johnson arrived on Lanai on August 28, 1854, they were greeted by twenty-one Hawaiian "pioneers" who had moved there to participate in the gathering, and by fifty Saints who were already permanent residents of the island. Where and when the latter group were converted is not clear. Both the missionaries and the local Saints regularly referred to the new settlers as pioneers. Other parts of Lanai were already inhabited, but the land where the new settlement was placed was essentially barren. Elder Johnson proposed that Palawai Valley should be called the Valley of Ephraim and that the city be called Joseph. All agreed.[7] They knelt together, and Johnson, who was first counselor in the mission presidency, prayed and dedicated the land and people to the Lord.

Elder Green divided the pioneers into groups of ten, with captains at the head of each group. Because nine or ten of the Lanai residents wanted to be considered pioneers, they were also grouped together, making a total of three captains and groups. When this was done they began clearing land to plant their crops.

Conditions on Lanai were difficult because there was so little food available, and water had to be obtained from a spring located more than a mile from the new settlement. Family and friends had to provide food for the pioneers by transporting it by canoe or boat from Maui. It was an almost all-male community for the first eight months or so. Families were to come later, after a good crop had been raised to support them.

Settling this community was not very different from settling in Utah or Idaho. In Utah each village and town was started from barren wilderness. Almost every comfort of life had to be created. Land had to be cleared, water had to be obtained, homes had to be built, and streets had to be laid out. The same kinds of work had to be done on Lanai. First, a decision had to be made concerning how large the city should be and where the roads should run. Since Elder Green was in charge, he made this decision. On Tuesday, October 3, 1854, he wrote: "This morning Br. Hammon left for Maui. I tuck my cumpas and commenst to lay out a town at the fut of the mountain and laid out one stret runing south to the sea three mildes to a fine litle harbour whare we land our boats hear we intendt to build a store hou[se] to leave our produse. I then laid out three more streats thruing [turning] the town in to blocks fore acres each with the streats fore rods wide. This is a butiful location for a town."

The next task was to assign lots to the pioneers and properly locate their houses upon them. Timber had to be acquired either in the mountains above the town or from other islands. Since water was in short supply, cisterns were dug, faced with rock, and cemented. The oxen, mules, and donkeys had to be controlled, and so a corral was built. The pigs were provided with a pen, but the chickens and turkeys were allowed to forage for themselves.

Homes for the pioneers, like the meetinghouse, were in Hawaiian style. Elder George Q. Cannon described these homes, called *hales,* in this manner:

> These native houses are built by putting posts in the ground on which a board is laid as a plate for the rafters to rest upon. When the frame of posts and rafters is built, poles . . . are lashed horizontally, about six inches apart, on to the posts and rafters. The house is then thatched by fastening a durable grass, which they have in that country, on to the poles. When finished, a house looks, in shape and size, like a well built hay stack. . . .
>
> Inside the house they have no board floors. The ground is covered with grass, on which mats are laid. The making of these mats constitutes one of the chief employments of the women, and a good housewife in that country is known by the quality and fineness of the mats in her home. Such a woman is very particular to have no dirt brought into her house; for the mats answer the purpose of beds, tables and chairs.[8]

Pioneering was difficult. Burning, clearing, plowing, hoeing, and digging hardly ever stopped. Over the next year the pioneers planted an amazing variety of seeds, slips, and starts. The list included wheat, oats, barley, grapes, sweet potatoes and Irish potatoes, beans of several kinds, peas, squash, pumpkins, bananas, corn, melons, peaches, plums, quinces, pears, tomatoes, cabbage, and "many kinds of garden seed."[9] There was some success, and the experiment was deemed worth the effort. The wheat produced well, as did the corn. Over fifty acres were planted during the first year.

In addition to the hard work the project had its lighter moments. The pioneers enjoyed hunting wild goats in the mountains, and on a number of occasions during the first year they came back with goats for meat. Fishing was also important—a routine but enjoyable part of every Hawaiian's life. The pioneers held several feasts that delighted the hearts and stomachs of all who participated.

On several occasions Elder Green wrote about the beauty of his island home. "This morning the sun has risen clear and spreads its golden rays over the Sandwich Isles and all nature seems to rejoice at its appearance." Then in June 1855, when corn had been harvested and dried, he continued, jocularly imitating the style of the Book of Mormon: "And it came to pass that I Ephraim being born of Yanky parence and som what lurnd in all the arts of that people proceded to make a cake which was choice above all uther cakes that I had ever seen even in my own land and thus ended the thurtieth day of June 1855."

CHANGES IN THE LANAI SETTLEMENT AND IN THE MISSION

The July conference of 1855 was a very important meeting. As was standard practice, all of the haole elders came together. They met on Lanai and made a number of decisions, among them to release President Lewis and Elders Green, Hammond, A. Allred, Woodbury, and Linn. Silas Smith was chosen as the new president of the mission. They also decided to start a school on Lanai, where Elder Ward E. Pack would teach the Hawaiians English. In addition, the mission decided to assume the debts of the Lanai experiment.

The following year, from July 1855 to July 1856, was not as successful as the elders had hoped. The crops on Lanai were poor, and the Saints throughout the other islands generally refused to move from their homes to the new colony. Strong sermons on the necessity of gathering out of Babylon or out of Egypt were given regularly in all parts of the mission, but with little effect. Only the very strongest converts were willing to move. Concerning this trend, Elder Joseph F. Smith said, "The gathering at the island of Lanai has gleaned out most of the faithful and diligent brethren, and that, perhaps, is one cause why the Saints feel so discouraged on the other islands."[10]

At the July 1855 conference it was evident that growth had slowed to a near standstill. There were 4,650 members in the islands at that time.[11] By April conference, 1856, when the elders took a careful census of the Saints, there was actually a drop in the total. Strong men were laboring in Hawaii at this time, but the opposition to their work grew. President Silas Smith tried to be positive but noted: "We are forced to acknowledge that despite all our exertions to strengthen, build up and increase the Church on these Islands, there is a very manifest falling away, both in numbers, and in the faith and good works of those who pretend to hold on to the work."[12]

During the next year matters became worse. A number of previously active and successful branches suffered from widespread apostasy. Apparently the only area that remained strong was Lanai, and even there, problems arose.

From July 1856 on, President Silas Smith's letters were often negative. He told President Young that the newness of the Church had worn off and that people were no longer attracted to its new ideas and doctrines. Within the Church many "weak" Saints, those who didn't attend meetings regularly, give freely of their means, or support the leaders, were critical of the Church because debts, such as the costs of seeds and tools for Lanai, had not been paid off. Others complained about the failure of the crops on Lanai, this notwithstanding the fact that people were starving in all parts of the islands because of an extended drought that had begun in 1856 and lasted into late 1857.

In May 1857, President Smith reported that "the past six months has been for us a season of unprecedented opposition from Apostates, Editors, and hireling Priests who have spared no pain to belie and misrepresent the Church, and do all in their power to impede its progress."[13]

During the summer of 1857 more elders were called to labor in Hawaii. At the head was Henry W. Bigler, one of the first group of missionaries sent to Hawaii. Two other veterans of the Hawaiian mission were also called—John S. Woodbury and James Keeler. Bigler could hardly believe how much things had changed since his release in 1854. When he attended church in Honolulu, he felt as if "everything [were] dead or dying."[14]

On October 4, 1857, a conference was held at which twelve missionaries were released to return home to Utah or California. Silas Smith was released, and William Bigler was sustained as president of the mission. A number of business matters were discussed at the conference, and it was resolved that Lanai was not adequate for the Church's needs and that a new gathering place should be sought.[15]

THE UTAH ELDERS ARE CALLED HOME

For the next month the work moved along at a slow pace, with little promise of improvement. Then on November 20, 1857, the mail arrived. One letter was from President Brigham Young, dated September 4. In part it read: "The reports from the Sandwich Islands have for a number of years agreed in one thing, that is, for the majority of the Saints on these Islands have either been dead or dying Spiritually. . . . I think it best for all of the Elders (with one or two exceptions) to come home . . . as soon as possible."[16]

In a letter to his nephew, Elder John R. Young, President Young went into detail concerning the difficulties the Saints were having with the United States government and the possibility of war (the Utah War). This did not surprise the elders, because newspapers had kept them abreast of the issues.

This call to return home was not peculiar to Hawaii. Most missionaries throughout the world were called home. President Young was concerned for the welfare of Utah, but he also wanted the men of the Church home to take care of their wives and children. The majority of the missionaries were married and were anxious to return home as quickly as possible.

When President Bigler announced to the Saints the following Sunday the impending closing of the mission, it was a cause of much grief among the faithful few.

On December 9, 1857, the remaining elders who had been released in October sailed from the islands. Following their release, they had worked at various occupations to earn the money necessary to pay for their passages. After they were gone, only eleven Zion missionaries were left, and they were doing their best to earn enough funds to pay their way home.

President Young was concerned about leaving the Hawaiian Saints without proper leadership, but he said that he "presumed that the Books of Mormon [in Hawaiian], the native Elders and one or two now from here will answer on that mission for the present."[17] He has been criticized for pulling all of the missionaries out of Hawaii. An important fact to remember, though, is that he was acting on the counsel of President Bigler and Elder Woodbury, who had told him, on December 3, 1857, that they did not think it was necessary for anyone to stay.[18]

Not long after the Utah elders departed, Chief Haalelea offered the Lanai Saints all of his holdings, around 10,000 acres, for the small sum of $300. But because of financial problems the Saints did not purchase the land. In any event they were not driven from Lanai by Haalelea. It may be surmised that he either received rent or simply remained patient with the Lanai Saints.[19]

Unfortunately almost no records exist that tell the story of the Hawaiian Saints from May 1, 1858, until July 1861, when Walter Murray Gibson arrived in the islands. There is no question that the total number of members declined during those years and during the years that followed. Fifteen Hawaiian elders were appointed to positions of authority, such as conference presidencies. At the last mission conference with the Utah elders present on April 25, 1858, there were still 3,067 members of record. At the next conference in

Walter Murray Gibson. (Courtesy LDS Church Archives.)

October only 632 members were reported. Though this probably reflects poor record keeping more than it does the actual decrease in the number of Saints, it must be said that 1858 and the next several years to follow were dark indeed.[20]

THE ERA OF WALTER MURRAY GIBSON

Three years passed after the Utah elders left Hawaii before an authorized representative from the center of the Church visited there. And then, unfortunately, it was the adventurer Walter Murray Gibson who stepped into this divided and disoriented setting to take charge of the Church in the islands.[21]

The story of Gibson's life reads more like a novel than like history. He was born at sea, reared in North Carolina, went to sea at an early age, and married while he was still under twenty. His life was filled with adventures, the most important being his fitting out an expedition to visit the East Indies. This voyage ended in disaster because

Gibson was considered by the Dutch in Indonesia to be hostile to their governing of that territory. He spent some time in prison, escaped, and returned to the United States, where he sought redress of his grievance against the Dutch government.

He was not successful in this effort. It appears from his own writings that he was interested in establishing some kind of personal kingdom in the Southeast Asian area. This desire eventually consumed his every thought and action for many years. It was this grandiose scheme that brought him into contact with the Latter-day Saints.

In 1856, before he joined the Church, Gibson conceived the idea of relocating the Mormons from Utah to the island of New Guinea. He thought the U.S. government would like this plan because the Latter-day Saints were a thorn in its side, as is attested by the later Utah War. Gibson discussed his proposal with Utah's representative to Congress, John M. Bernhisel, and the plan was also presented to President James Buchanan. Buchanan considered the project impractical and too expensive, and the government was not further involved.

In 1859 Gibson traveled to Salt Lake City, where he was hospitably received. He was frank about his intentions. The *Deseret News* reported that he had come to "influence" President Young to move the Saints to New Guinea. During the days following his arrival in Salt Lake City, he lectured on the East Indies. This was his principle means of financial support in Utah and elsewhere.

But Brigham Young was not convinced that the Saints should move. In fact, he told Gibson that if he really wanted to help the people of the East Indies, he should investigate the gospel and be baptized; then he, Brigham Young, would ordain Gibson an elder and send him there on a mission. Gibson appeared to take President Young's advice seriously. He remained in Salt Lake City during the winter and was baptized a member of the Church during January 1860.

GIBSON BECOMES A MISSIONARY

Later that year Gibson was sent on a mission to the Eastern States, but he returned to Salt Lake City only six months later, on November 4. He had not been able to get the East Indies out of his mind. Only three weeks passed before he persuaded President Young to send him on a mission to Japan and Malaysia. The authority he received was very broad: Brigham Young said that "Gibson was going forth fully authorized to negotiate with all the nations of this world who would obey the gospel of Christ."[22]

Gibson's route to his mission field took him to San Francisco and on to Hawaii. While in San Francisco, Gibson wrote several letters to President Young, reporting on the good works he had performed. But other observers of his actions did not report any open representation on his part that he was a Latter-day Saint.

When Gibson arrived in Honolulu, he identified himself as a world traveler and an expert on Malaysia and the East Indies. Two months passed before he publicly affiliated himself with the Hawaiian Saints. In fact, in October 1861 some reporters from the *Pacific Commercial Advertiser,* a Honolulu newspaper, asked Gibson whether he was a member of the Church. He told them that "he himself believed in no creed or sect whatever."[23] He later wrote the same thing in his diary.

Because there was not a president of the Hawaiian Mission when he arrived, Gibson assumed this title for himself. He was not satisfied, however, with the limited nature of the office, and so he enlarged the scope of the title and became the "Chief President of the Islands of the Sea and of the Hawaiian Islands, for the Church of the Latter Day Saints." Gibson was not appointed to this position by Church leaders in Salt Lake City, but he did write to President Young and reported his activities, at least some of them. In effect, Brigham Young gave Gibson tacit authority to lead the Church in Hawaii, but President Young did not have the full picture of what Gibson was doing.

Captain Gibson assumed control of the Church in Hawaii during September 1861. When the regular October conference of the Hawaiian Saints was held, Gibson was there and in charge. One of his first official acts was to sell certificates of membership and of office to all members who desired to remain active in the Church. Gibson continued this practice throughout the three years of his "presidency."

But selling offices in the Church was just the beginning of the changes he made in its organization. He also ordained seventies (an office of priesthood reserved for stakes), bishops, an archbishop (the Church had none elsewhere), a quorum of twelve apostles, and a first presidency. Each of these officers paid well for his position. None of these offices was normal in a mission, and apostles and a first presidency were reserved for the top leadership of the Church.

GIBSON ACQUIRES CONTROL OF LANAI

Gibson had learned about the Mormon settlement on Lanai shortly after arriving in Honolulu in July 1861. Haalelea, who owned the land, was still willing to sell his portion of the island, that is, the Valley of

Palawai. The price he asked at this time was $500 for 3,000 acres. Gibson decided that the Church should have this property.

By the end of September Gibson had men searching for water, planting new crops, repairing the huts, and rebuilding the "City of Joseph." Gibson insisted on work from his Hawaiian charges, and he received it. Everything he did, however, was for his own benefit and aggrandizement. Lanai was merely a means to a selfish end. Consider the following quotations from his diary: "I could make a glorious little kingdom out of this, or any such chance, with such people; so loving and obedient. . . . I would fill this lovely crater with corn and wine and oil and babies and love and health and brotherly rejoicing and sisters kisses and the memory of me for evermore."[24]

Late in January he wrote, "I view him [the Hawaiian] and treat him as an interesting yet feeble younger brother, a subject of an oceanic empire. . . . Who or what shall I fear where I am King— and I shall keep within my Kingdom. . . . I am King; not of oceanica, not of Malaysia, not of Hawaii nei, not of Lanai, but of Palawai on this day of grace. But this is but the baby of my Kingdom. Oh smiling Palawai, thou infant hope of my glorious kingdom."[25]

Under Gibson's direction chapels were sold, Church lands on other islands were sold, homes of members were sold, lands owned by members were sold, and other private property was sold, sometimes at ridiculously low prices, in order to raise enough money to buy the lands desired by Gibson.

Throughout his campaign to raise money, he told his Hawaiian brothers and sisters that they were giving their means so that a gathering place could be acquired for all of them. He then had the titles of the property placed in his own name. In April 1864, Gibson proved his bad faith by refusing to sign the Lanai property over to a delegation of Church leaders when he was asked to do so. For this reason he has been accused of stealing the Island of Lanai from the Church. He did not actually steal the property, but he defrauded the members of the Church by telling them that he would serve their interests and then doing otherwise.

GIBSON'S EXCOMMUNICATION FROM THE CHURCH

Gibson almost completely controlled the Church in Hawaii for three years. Then a number of Hawaiian elders who could remember how the earlier missionaries had behaved toward them became discontented. These people left Lanai and jointly wrote to some of their former missionary friends, to Alma L. Smith in particular. Their letters contained questions about Gibson's actions and his strange use of authority. These questions were brought to the attention of the First Presidency, who immediately dispatched a select committee made up of apostles Ezra T. Benson and Lorenzo Snow and former missionaries Joseph F. Smith, Alma L. Smith, and William W. Cluff to go to Hawaii to investigate Gibson's activities.

When these brethren visited with Gibson on Lanai, they found that his practices were out of harmony with the accepted patterns of Church government. On April 12, 1864, four days after Gibson was excommunicated, Elder Benson wrote:

> We reached his house on Sunday morning and found him and his daughter in possession of good health, but apparently more surprised than rejoiced at seeing us. We found that in the district of Palawai 6,000 acres of land had been bought by the Church, and that besides this Captain Gibson had got possession of all the government land on the island of Lanai. The Saints had been constrained to turn over all their substance, horses, sheep, goats, poultry, houses and lands to the Church to gather up to Lanai giving their time for the cultivation of the soil and this many had done receiving their food once a day from the hands of the head bishop.[26]

Several weeks later, on May 4, 1864, Joseph F. Smith wrote a letter to George Q. Cannon adding the following details:

> On arriving at Palawai, we found Captain Gibson snugly settled in a small village of some fifty grass houses. . . .
>
> We found that he had ordained twelve apostles. High priests, seventys, elders, bishops, and "priestesses of temples," all of whom had to pay a certain sum corresponding to the various degrees of honor bestowed upon them. What the "priestesses of the temple" signified we were at a loss to know, but we soon found it was only to gull the poor natives and obtain their money. Gibson had bought the district of Palawai (6,000 acres) by the donation of the Saints, assuring them he was doing it all for them for the Church. He persuaded them to give all they had to the Church and made it a test of fellowship. Many could not bear it and were excommunicated, while the faithful remained and became wholly dependent on him for both food and clothing.
>
> Brothers Benson and Snow required him to sign the land over to the Church as it was deeded to him and his heirs. This he flatly refused to do informing them he should take his own course, that he was not sent here by the Church, had received no counsel from Brigham Young, had acted upon his own responsibility in what he had done, and he was not beholding to the Church.

> He also told them he should ask no counsel of them, but would pursue his own course for the future. . . . He declared he should use his influence to keep the natives in his power, and persuade more to come there if he could, that they should receive no benefit from the land they had bought only as they would become subject to him. It is useless to say more. He was cut off from the Church.[27]

After Gibson's excommunication, Elders Benson and Snow departed almost immediately for home. Elder Joseph F. Smith was left to preside over the Hawaiian Saints, along with Elders Alma L. Smith and William W. Cluff.

Gibson, meanwhile, was left on Lanai with those Saints who would remain with him. His influence had been strong among them, but when it was learned that he had been officially cut off from the Church, the people of Lanai left him very quickly. In October 1864, only six months later, it was reported that there were only fourteen members of the Church still living under Gibson's direction on Lanai. These people requested to be cut off from the Church in October 1864, and their request was granted.

One might wonder whether the Church attempted to recover the lands it had purchased on Lanai. Although the native Saints did make a half-hearted attempt to do so, the missionaries made no legal effort to win back the land. The reason for this was twofold. First, Joseph F. Smith, who was in Hawaii earlier when the decision had been made to look for a new gathering place, would have had to institute such a litigation, but he did not believe that Lanai was worth fighting for. His feelings about the matter had apparently not changed since 1857. Second, Elder Smith was convinced that the costs of a court battle would be greater than the value of the land. Thus Gibson was left alone to do as he desired with the Palawai plantation. He had difficulty accomplishing much there after the Saints left because his subservient laborers could not be replaced from another source.[28]

The decade from 1854 until 1864 began on a positive note. There were over four thousand members of the Church in the islands in August 1854. A year later that number had grown slightly, but from that time on the number of members began to drop. Two years later, in October 1857, there were only 3,122 members of record. It was unfortunate that the Lanai colony drew away the main strength in the branches at the very time when the newness and message of Mormonism were losing appeal.

But still more tragic was the effect Walter Murray Gibson had on the Church. The Hawaiian Saints had already suffered from the absence of experienced leaders, and Gibson's self-serving takeover of the Church did much to corrupt the remaining members and the order of the Church. Considerable effort was required by later missionaries to rebuild the Church and to regain the losses of the years from 1858 to 1864.

CHAPTER 8

LAIE: THE PERMANENT GATHERING PLACE IN HAWAII

Hawaii, 1864–1892

When Elders Ezra T. Benson and Lorenzo Snow left the islands, the Church was in almost total disarray. Many chapels had been sold. Lands had been turned over to Walter Murray Gibson, as had crops and livestock. Bitterness filled the minds and hearts of many Hawaiian Saints. The task before the remaining elders was to rebuild, as far as possible, the Church structure that had existed before the Utah elders departed in 1858.

The first work before the elders was to organize branches and regulate the affairs of the Church. Twenty-four-year-old Joseph F. Smith, who was president of the mission, developed the idea of establishing a new gathering place somewhere in the islands where the Saints could be taught how to work and to live the gospel principles. This suggestion was passed on to President Brigham Young.[1]

President Young's attitude toward the Hawaiian Saints is important. He was reluctant to believe that much should be done in Hawaii. His letters to Joseph F. Smith reveal that he was disturbed by the unfaithfulness of the Hawaiians and wanted to see some indication of repentance before he committed more Church resources.[2]

A mission conference was held during the first three days of October 1864. Only two hundred Saints were present, but they manifested a spirit of determination to live the gospel. President Smith told the Saints that they were gathered together "to inaugurate a reformation." He then read the names of fifty men and women whom he deemed worthy to be rebaptized if they were willing to make their commitments again. This practice of rebaptizing members was a symbolic renewal of the first baptismal covenant. The first rebaptisms were performed in Utah in 1856 as part of a so-called reformation but were discontinued before the end of the century.[3] These fifty were baptized that night after the meeting. The following day sixty-three more names were read, and these Saints were rebaptized.

At the close of the conference Joseph F. Smith announced that he, William W. Cluff, and John R. Young had been released to return home, and that Alma L. Smith and Benjamin Cluff would temporarily preside over the mission.

THE FOUNDING OF LAIE

The suggestion to find a new gathering place came from Joseph F. Smith, but the follow-through for the project came from Brigham Young. In October 1864 he called Francis A. Hammond, the former Hawaii missionary, and George Nebeker, who had never been there, as co-presidents of the mission. Brigham Young told presidents Hammond and Nebeker that they were to teach the Saints how to labor and how to live the principles of the gospel. The clearest statement of the purpose of the new settlement was made in a letter from him to King Kamehameha V, which was sent with Hammond when he made his second trip to Hawaii in March 1865. President Young wrote that the missionaries were going to Hawaii as "religious teachers, but . . . they will not confine their labors to spiritual matters only. According to the precepts of our religion, the spiritual and temporal are so intimately blended that we view no salvation or system of salvation as being complete, which does not provide means for the welfare and preservation of the body as well as the salvation of the Spirit. . . . Mr. Hammond, and my other friends . . . will therefore endeavor to teach your Majesty's subjects . . . practical salvation."[4]

The disappointments suffered by the Hawaiian Saints during the Gibson experience led President Young to establish the new gathering place on a different basis than Lanai. The new home of the Saints would not be purchased with their own contributions, but obtained and owned by the Church's leaders in the islands and held for the benefit of the local Saints.

President Young told Hammond and Nebeker that the Church would support them and loan them money to buy land, but that it would be in their names. The financial arrangements were supposed to be reasonable enough that the new gathering place could pay for itself and return the original loan payments to the Church.

When Brothers Hammond and Nebeker arrived in the islands, they found the economic situation there to be in a serious state of fluc-

George Nebeker directed the affairs of the Hawaiian Mission and Laie Plantation during its early years. (Courtesy LDS Church Archives.)

tuation. The American Civil War had rung the death knell for the whaling industry, but it had helped to create the Hawaiian sugar industry. The war years had given rise to much land speculation throughout the islands and had also raised the value of sugar. The end of the war brought a depression in the sugar market; it was not ruined, but it was unstable. Many speculators lost all they had, and others were eager to sell their properties even at a loss.[5] The time was right for the purchase of good property.

Elders Hammond and Nebeker arrived in Honolulu on December 23, 1864, and began a careful search for land. Their quest led them to Kauai during early January and then back to Honolulu.

By January 16, they knew the situation well and were satisfied that they could "buy all the land" they wanted; it was only a question of time. That day they decided that Nebeker should sail for home immediately and bring their families back. Hammond was to buy property as soon as it was feasible and get crops started.

On January 20, 1865, Hammond talked to Thomas T. Dougherty, who owned 6,000 acres of land on the north side of Oahu. His plantation was called "Laie." After visiting Laie, Hammond met with Mr. Dougherty on January 26, 1865, and made an agreement to purchase the plantation. Elder Hammond recorded the final transaction in this way:

> Called on Mr. T. T. Dougherty and offered him 12,000 dollars for "Laie" with all the stock, horses and improvements thereon—he would not take less than 14,000 dollars. I finally after a little consideration consented to give it. I agreed to send him a draft for 3000 dollars in ten weeks from date and pay 5000 dollars more by the 1st of July/65—6000 dollars in two years from date bearing at 12 per cent per annum—giving a mortgage on the place for security. I take possession immediately.[6]

Hammond believed he had made a good bargain, and he had. This property became the center of Zion in the Pacific.

Dollar costs are, of course, relative to time and subject to the constant effects of inflation and deflation. Yet from any point of view the cost of the Laie plantation was nominal. Perhaps $2.33 an acre seemed high to Brigham Young, who objected to the cost, for he was accustomed to settling land that was virtually free. But for fertile and productive land that had been bought and sold over generations, the price was low. The tract was wedge-shaped, had three miles of coast, and ran to the top of the Koolau Range behind. There was sufficient water available to handle current needs. In addition to these benefits, there were many head of livestock, 600 cattle, 500 sheep, 250 goats, and 20 horses, which added to the value of the purchase. A large frame home and five Hawaiian houses, all furnished, stood on the land. There were five acres of cotton that promised to bear a crop.[7]

Two other advantages made Laie attractive. It was close to the capital city—only thirty-seven miles from Honolulu—but not too close. Second, it was already the location of an active branch of seventy Latter-day Saints.

After setting affairs in order in Honolulu, President Hammond followed his companion and sailed for home on January 30, 1865. He left Elders Alma L. Smith and Benjamin Cluff in charge and assigned them to move to Laie and begin planting cotton. Hammond hoped that by March they would have one hundred acres planted. He was eager to report his progress to President Young.

When Hammond arrived back in Salt Lake City, he and Elder Nebeker were charged with the responsibility of selecting a group of mechanics, farmers, and others with skills that could be taught to the Hawaiians. In nearly all instances the missionaries were called with their wives. Those called included four former missionaries and their wives: Ephraim and Mary Green, James and Harriet Lawson, Eli and

Louisa Jane Bell, and William and Emma Wright. All four men had served in Hawaii during the 1850s. Other missionaries who had not been to Hawaii before were Charles and Mary Boyden, Alfred and Mildred Randall, Caleb and Anna World (and their six children), Philip Pugsley, Maria Louisa Nebeker, Mary Ellen Cluff, and Talitha Smith. The latter three were wives of missionaries already in the field or assigned to it. A number of children were taken along when the company went to the islands. The entire group, when settled in Hawaii, numbered forty. The families were part of the plan. President Young wanted the Hawaiians to see how proper Saints conducted their lives.

As another part of the plan, President Young hoped both cotton and sugar could be produced in Hawaii and shipped to Utah to take care of the Saints' needs.[8]

GETTING SETTLED AT LAIE

When Elder Hammond returned to Hawaii after his trip, he found that his colleagues had worked hard, but they had already encountered problems with insects and unfavorable weather that were to plague them in the years to come. "The late planting of corn and cotton looks well," he wrote, "but all of the first planting has been destroyed by the wind and worms."[9]

Hammond was a dedicated man who worked long hours. His diary reflects only one goal in his mind—that of serving the Lord. His task was not easy, for he had to make decisions concerning land-use policy, where to build roads, where to plant, and where to build fences. He had to decide whether livestock should better be sold or cared for, and whether to plant corn, rice, Irish potatoes, or sugar cane. On Sunday, May 7, 1865, he preached to the people "on the necessity of connecting temporal matters with spiritual matters, taught them the doctrine of obedience being the foundation of all happiness —and told them the object of our coming unto them again, that it was to improve their temporal condition."[10]

Between the time of Hammond's return to the islands and May 18, when he again took ship and returned to San Francisco to help bring the company of missionaries across, a serious matter was under consideration in the king's court. Brigham Young had sent a rather lengthy letter to King Kamehameha V (quoted in part above), in which he detailed the Latter-day Saint attitude toward the Hawaiian people, that is, the belief that they are descendants of Lehi, the Book of

Mormon prophet. The letter elaborated on both the temporal intentions and proselyting purposes of the mission.

Even though the laws of the kingdom allowed religious toleration, the king and his advisers did not feel that these laws applied to the Latter-day Saints because many of their teachings were foreign to the recognized doctrines of Christianity. "As long as your friends limit themselves to carrying on their agricultural and mechanical operations," wrote John O. Dominis, the king's private secretary and husband of later Queen Liliuokalani, "they will be protected in their industry, but they can never be recognized here on a footing with Christian missionaries as teachers, as those words are ordinarily understood."[11] This problem, fortunately, was resolved without serious difficulty. Within a year or so the king had died, and the matter was not raised after that. But as a result of this governmental action the Church was still denied the right to perform marriages for a number of years.

When President Hammond arrived in San Francisco, he found that the main body of Hawaii-bound missionaries had departed from Salt Lake City the same day he sailed from Honolulu. The company arrived in San Francisco a few days later and sailed for Honolulu on June 22, making Laie by July 7.

PROGRESS TO 1868

The settlers divided the land and built homes. Some Hawaiians were able to construct frame homes, but most lived in traditional grass houses. President Nebeker lived in the "mansion," a large home that was on the property when it was purchased. Each native family was loaned enough land for a home and garden. The land was owned by the Church and rented on a share basis. In an effort to make the landholding system clear to the local Saints, President Nebeker announced in the following April conference, 1866, that the Laie plantation "was purchased by the servants of God and it [is] entirely under their control and direction. It is expected of the native brethren that come here to go to work [to] prove their condition by laboring under the direction of the servants of God and receive a just remuneration for all their labors."[12]

Almost as soon as the homes were brought under construction, a chapel was begun. It was not a large building, only 24 by 36 feet, but it was of frame construction and was a great improvement over the bowery or the crowded situation in the mansion.

Following the pattern of the Church elsewhere, the Saints in Laie, both foreign and local, felt the need to educate their young. On October 20, 1865, Mildred E. Randall opened two schools, one for the haole children and the other for the Hawaiians. English was the language of instruction in both courses, but some Hawaiian was used with the native children when necessary. The difference in their abilities in English was the reason given by the mission president for the separate schools. Sister Randall continued the schools until November 1866, when she returned home to Utah.[13]

In August 1867 the missionaries decided to share the responsibility of teaching the children. By that time the veteran elders who could speak Hawaiian were traveling regularly to the other islands and preaching to the Saints, but it was decided that whoever was left at home in Laie would man the school.

About mid-April 1867, local elders were called to serve as missionaries, adding real strength to the work. This pattern became the regular procedure over the coming years.

In May 1867, Elder Lawson and his family were released from their missions. When Lawson reported to President Young, he painted a dark picture of affairs in Laie. He was particularly concerned about the subsistence of the missionaries and their families. As a result Brigham Young suggested to President Nebeker that if anyone should come along who would buy the plantation and cover expenses, he should sell it.[14] This suggestion was gently worded, but it still placed the existence of the Laie project on unsure footing. Nebeker believed that he could not sell the land without taking a serious loss. He and the other missionaries were also afraid that if they put the land up for sale, it would discourage the Hawaiian Saints living on the land and others as well, whether a sale was made or not. The risk was too high. Brigham Young agreed, and it was decided to move ahead with the sugarcane planting and milling.[15] Cotton planting had proved unsuccessful. After the spring of 1868 the continued existence of Laie as a gathering place for the Hawaiian Saints was never in serious question.

THE PLANTATION YEARS TO 1892

The year 1868 was an especially good one for the Hawaiian Mission. Most of the missionaries and Saints were in harmony with the objectives of the mission, and the work moved forward. Under the leadership of Jonatana H. Napela, the Hawaiian men of Laie were organized into work teams. Nebeker found a nearly new mill and bought it for around two thousand dollars, and the Church went into the sugar-milling business. A stone building was constructed to house the mill, and on November 12, 1868, after seven months of preparation, it was put into operation.

The first cane crop was exceptionally heavy. The total product of the first harvest was around a hundred tons of sugar. But the following year, 1869, was a dry one. The crop was smaller and of inferior quality. In fact, the production of sugar over the following years was disappointing almost as often as it was satisfactory.[16]

Several problems plagued the plantation. Most serious was the insufficient water supply. This problem was overcome in the early 1880s when a flume more than two miles long was constructed to bring water from the mountains, and an artesian well was drilled. A consistent sales outlet for the sugar had to be arranged. Nebeker, acting on the suggestions of Brigham Young, tried to establish marketing relationships with Salt Lake City merchants, but without success. Over the years most of the sugar produced on the Laie plantation was sold to Waterhouse and Company in Honolulu, who in turn shipped it to San Francisco. Mr. Waterhouse became the principal financial backer of the Laie operation. At one time he held a substantial mortgage on the plantation. In fact, the Laie plantation was almost always deeply in debt to this company until the 1890s. Relations between Waterhouse and the Church, however, were generally satisfactory to both parties.

When Harvey H. Cluff took over as mission president and plantation manager in 1879, he soon recognized that the once-new mill was now dilapidated and that it would be necessary either to ship the cane to another mill or to build a new one. He decided that the latter course would be better because it would keep the local Saints employed. An entirely new building with larger, more modern equipment was constructed a few hundred feet toward the mountain from the old mill. This facility served the plantation for a number of years.

But other problems besides those connected with the sugar business also developed at Laie. During his presidency, from June 1873 until September 1874, Fred A. Mitchell became seriously concerned about the sale of *awa*. Awa (pronounced ah-va) is a mild narcotic made from the root of a kind of pepper plant. Its sister drink, called *kava,* is used in ceremonies in island countries throughout the Pacific area.

On New Year's Day 1874, a great feast was held at the Laie chapel. At its conclusion President Mitchell, who was somewhat dictatorial,

The second or new sugar mill at Laie. (Courtesy LDS Church Archives.)

stood at the door in the traditional fashion of the old lords of the land (*konohikis*) and declared that there would be no more drinking of awa or selling it to persons outside of the plantation. This ultimatum was a real shock to the assembled group, because they had used part of the plantation land to cultivate the awa plant, with the intention of selling most of the crop for profit. But Mitchell said it had to be destroyed. This pronouncement almost caused a riot in the chapel.

President Mitchell's decision was motivated by the fact that the Word of Wisdom was receiving much emphasis in Utah. In 1867 President Brigham Young had strongly suggested that men who were participants in the newly created School of the Prophets should stop using habit-forming substances and donate the money saved to bring "the poor" home to Zion. Women of the Relief Society also joined in the movement to abstain from tea and coffee and donate the savings to the railroad fund of the Perpetual Emigration Fund.

But there was not uniformity of thought among the elders in Hawaii on this matter. Coffee trees were cultivated on the Laie plantation, and some of the elders felt there was little difference between the two crops. Why Mitchell was so adamant about awa but not coffee is not clear. Nevertheless, he refused to allow the Laie Saints to sell even their existing crop of awa.

The issue would probably have died a natural death were it not that a Chinese landholder had offered to sell his land to the Laie Saints. This property, called Kahana, 3,600 acres of good land eight miles from Laie, seemed to the upset Hawaiians the answer to their problems; by purchasing it apart from the Church they could remove themselves from the iron hand of Mitchell. The cost was to be $6,000.

Mitchell wanted to take Church court action against the dissidents as early as April 1874 but did not. When the Hawaiian Saints went through with their plan to buy Kahana, however, he called a meeting of the priesthood in late June to consider the matter. Elder Harvey H. Cluff recorded the event in this way:

> The meeting was filled to overflowing . . . President Mitchell . . . asked those who had combined together if they still were determined to go ahead with the organization and draw off from Laie, to which they answered in the affirmative. Whereupon President Mitchell "moved that they be disfellowshipped from the Church of Jesus Christ of Latter-day Saints" and when put to vote there were only about thirty voted for the motion including the foreigners. At this Brother Mitchell asked to sing, at which the congregation went into demonic yells, and the greater part of the audience rushed out before the benediction was offered.[17]

The next day Mitchell sent a letter to all the Saints in the mission telling them not to support the Kahana project in spirit or with contributions.

Not many days after the Church court, a number of angry Hawaiian Saints wrote to President Brigham Young and expressed their feelings. The chief complaint centered on President Mitchell's "giving away to passion so easily, with his indisposition to listen to more than one side." The feeling among the Hawaiians was that the plantation belonged to Mitchell and that they had "no lot in Laie." The Saints also said they did not realize that buying new land for themselves was an offense that could bring disfellowshipment to twelve of their number.[18]

The immediate result of these events and this letter was Mitchell's release as mission president and the calling of Alma L. Smith to replace him. But the long-term result was the founding of Kahana village, a settlement eight miles closer to Honolulu than is Laie. Within a year after its purchase, Kahana had become an established village, with a chapel, branch presidency, and full status in the eyes of the mission presidency. By the early 1880s Kahana was the second-largest Mormon settlement in the islands. Almost half of the Laie Saints moved to this new "native" gathering place after the problems at Laie. This loss of membership at Laie made plantation operations there difficult for a while. Another result was the continued cultivation of the awa plant; in the early 1880s part of the Laie plantation land was still being used for the cultivation of awa.[19]

Laie did not grow rapidly over the years, for most local Saints preferred to live in or near their ancestral villages, but the missionaries never stopped preaching about the importance of gathering. The actual size of Laie village through the years is very difficult to establish; almost no official records exist that disclose such information. During the 1870s population estimates fell between 377 (1874) and 275 (1877).[20] Descriptions of Laie settlement in the 1890s lead one to conclude that there were not many more residents then than in the late 1870s.

Church growth throughout the mission was more impressive. According to Andrew Jenson there were one thousand members in 1866. The April 1872 total was 2,627, but by 1879 the number had grown to 4,408. This figure seems more impressive when it is set against the total Hawaiian population at that time—44,088. One-tenth of the Hawaiians belonged to the Church. But after 1878 growth was slow. In 1894 there were eighty-one branches in the mission, but the total membership was only 4,899.[21]

The erratic growth of the Church over the years was a source of constant anxiety to the foreign missionaries. It was not unusual to have from two hundred to four hundred convert baptisms in a six-month period, but often the converts seemed to be like shallow soil on which the seed was cast. One missionary commented that the Polynesian missionaries "seem to make converts by persuasion and by getting the best of their opponents in argument rather than by convincing the sinner of the error of his ways and teaching him the true plan of salvation."[22]

In April 1874 the mission president discovered that the Hawaiian elders were teaching a number of incorrect doctrines and procedures. Alma L. Smith wrote, "During the last six months the foreign Elders have had a big job on their hands in discovering, ferreting out, correcting and undoing many false and erroneous doctrines and principles introduced by the native elders who have been sent out as missionaries during the last number of years." Among the changes the elders discovered were several modes of baptism, a number of styles of administering to the sick, and the empowering of a number of native officers with the authority to forgive sins. This last divergence included a widespread practice of having the guilty person appear before one of the appointed officers, confess sins of any kind, and receive a certificate stating his "sins were all forgiven" and he "was clean and spotless from the crown of his head to the soles of his feet." Besides these changes, Smith wrote that there were many "other false, heathenish, idolatrous, and superstitious ideas and notions" that had crept in.

No Hawaiian elders were called to serve missions for the next year. The use of the local brethren as missionaries was gradually resumed, but never on the same large scale as from 1872 to 1875.[23] Generally the Hawaiians traveled with foreign companions after this time. The immediately obvious result was a significant drop in the number of baptisms over the next two decades. Later, in 1890, twenty local elders were called into the mission field. Total membership grew from 4,119 in 1890 to 4,899 in 1894.

The Hawaiian Islands made great material progress between 1865 and 1895. Much happened within the Church in Hawaii, but many developments in Hawaii in general also helped to change the complexion of the Church and the mission.

Not only the convenience of life but also the population of the islands changed significantly during these years. As the sugar industry developed, it was early recognized that three things were necessary for success: a market, capital, and labor. The United States became the principal sugar market. Capital seemed to be no problem. But labor was a serious matter. Because the Hawaiian population was falling steadily, owners and government officials found it necessary to go outside the kingdom for laborers. In 1864 the Hawaiian government

An early "grass shack" style chapel. (Courtesy LDS Church Archives.)

organized the Bureau of Immigration. Foreign labor was recruited, and immigration in general was encouraged. By the end of 1865, 1,306 Chinese workers had come to Hawaii under contract. Three years later, about 150 Japanese laborers were brought in.

The influx of foreign labor was steady for the next two decades. By 1890, when the total population was 90,000, over 55,000 laborers had been imported into Hawaii. Although some contract laborers returned home to China or Japan, the 1890 total included 15,000 Chinese, 12,000 Japanese, and 9,000 Portuguese; by that time the polyglot, polyracial nature of Hawaii had been established. The Caucasian population also grew rapidly during these years. The Hawaiian segment seems to have started a population climb in the middle or late 1870s. Unfortunately, however, the Hawaiians had descended by then to the lowest rung of the nation's economic and social ladder.

THE CHURCH AND THE HAWAIIAN GOVERNMENT

David Kalakaua was elected king by the Hawaiian legislature on February 12, 1874, and he reigned until 1891. During his time relationships between the government and the Church were friendly. Many of his goals and desires, such as the growth of the Hawaiian population and the concept of Hawaii for the Hawaiians, were also espoused by the Latter-day Saints.

On April 30, 1874, ten weeks after his election, missionaries received notice that Kalakaua would be in Laie the following day; he was touring the island of Oahu with a large retinue. The Laie Saints made elaborate if frantic preparations, but they were ready when the king arrived. He seemed to like what he saw, for he complimented the citizens of Laie for their industry and for the beauty of the community. The number of children there impressed him most. He told the assembled crowd that there were more children there than at any other village of similar size he had visited.[24]

Kalakaua and his wife, Kapiolani, visited Laie on many occasions. They made most of their visits as private citizens. Kapiolani attended Relief Society once in a while and was evidently pleased with what she saw and heard. In fact, the king and queen founded a national "Female Relief Society," patterned after what they had seen in the LDS Church, to help the poor of the kingdom.

Kalakaua was succeeded by Queen Liliuokalani. Her reign was brief, hardly more than two years, because of a revolution (a small one at that) that brought an end to the Hawaiian kingdom during its ninety-ninth year. The United States government took control of Hawaii in 1893 and finally annexed the area in 1898. Hawaii officially became a territory of the United States on June 14, 1900.

Liliuokalani was a fine, well-educated lady. She was a devoted Christian and a strong leader. She was, like her predecessor, a friend to the Latter-day Saints. On many occasions she visited Relief Society in Honolulu and at Laie. According to Jenson's "History of the Hawaiian Mission," Queen Liliuokalani requested that LDS services be held at the palace on March 13, 1892. After this, LDS services were regularly held there until she was deposed. Liliuokalani was a close friend of Libbie Noall, the mission president's wife, and sought her advice on a number of occasions.[25] The queen was baptized into the Church by Abraham Fernandez in 1906, but she also joined other churches during her later years—making her commitment to the LDS Church questionable.

ORGANIZATIONAL DEVELOPMENTS AND CHAPEL BUILDING

During the years from 1865 to 1895, the pattern of the Church in Hawaii came to resemble much more closely that found in Salt Lake

Auwaiolimu chapel in Honolulu, late 1880s. (Courtesy LDS Church Archives.)

The Laie chapel was dedicated in 1882. It stood on the same promontory where the Hawaii Temple now stands. (Courtesy LDS Church Archives.)

City. All the auxiliaries of the Church were organized: Sunday School (1871),[26] Relief Society (1875),[27] Mutual Improvement Association (1876),[28] and Primary (1883).[29] Choirs and other musical organizations were founded. Chapels and a school were created, and printed material was prepared in the Hawaiian language.

From the early days the Saints of Hawaii engaged in the work and sacrifice necessary to build chapels. Apparently the post-1865 chapels were not generally much better than those of the 1850s. The Laie chapel was the first substantial building. Constructed of rock, it served for almost twenty years, but in 1881 it became obvious that with the growth of the Church in the islands and the increasing size of the semiannual conferences, it would be necessary to build a new meeting hall.

Much planning and fundraising was done before construction commenced. When the cornerstone was laid, King Kalakaua attended and donated $100 to the project. Six months later, on October 6, 1882, the meeting hall was ready for dedication and the king was once again in attendance. He, like the rest of the assembled throng, was impressed by the large structure.

The chapel stood on the choicest spot in all of Laie, the same site where the temple now stands.[30] President Edward Partridge, Jr., dedicated the building, after which the king was invited to speak. He did not talk long but told the Saints that they were his best subjects in "fulfilling the laws and keeping the peace of the kingdom."

In 1885 there were twenty-five chapels in the mission, but of that number, only the Laie chapel could be considered a permanent structure. Others were flimsy frame buildings or makeshift grass pavilions.

The second permanent building constructed was the Honolulu chapel, completed in 1889 with Elder Matthew Noall as the head builder. It was not as large as the Laie building, but it was a credit to the Church. The Honolulu Branch, with its 891 members, was probably the largest branch of the Church outside Utah at that time.

THE LAIE SCHOOL

The efforts of Mildred E. Randall as an educator during the first several years of the Laie colony were admirable. After her departure, the elders struggled to keep the school open by trading the responsibility among those who were not assigned to the outside areas. This method proved unsatisfactory.

Word of the educational needs of the mission was sent to Salt Lake City, and in the spring of 1873 Sister Randall was called to fill a second mission, a teaching mission, in Laie. She arrived in Hawaii on June 3, 1873, and by the sixteenth of the month had started a school in the Laie chapel, the small rock building. Only four students were enrolled, all Hawaiians. By January 1874 the numbers increased to around twenty pupils and leveled off there. She was a demanding teacher and taught the courses in English. Subjects studied were spelling, reading, writing, mental and written arithmetic, and geography, as well as recitations, dialogues, and singing.

Financially the school was not a success. Sister Randall was expected to support herself from the tuition paid by her pupils. She wrote, "I charge them 20¢ per week per scholar, which is 5¢ cheaper than other schools of the same grade that have assistance from the government. But I am here on a mission to benefit the people all I can and not to oppress them by charging exorbitant prices for what I can do for them. I only want a living, and that in the most economical style."[31]

If all her pupils had paid their tuition, her pay would have been $16.00 a month. Her release from this second mission came June 20, 1876.

The next teacher of the Laie English School was Jane E. Molen.

Laie Elementary School after the Hawaii Temple was completed. (Courtesy LDS Church Archives.)

After her release the school closed for a time. Then in April 1883 Marvin E. Pack was appointed teacher of the school "about to be established at Laie."[32]

After that, the school grew rapidly and required the full attention of one missionary, usually an elder. By 1885 there were fifty students enrolled, aged six to eighteen. In 1887 Elder Fred Beesley petitioned the government school board in Honolulu for financial aid. To the joy of the missionaries, the board agreed to pay a teacher fifty dollars a month and supply maps, charts, and other materials if the Church would provide a building.[33] After that time the school continued to grow and make steady progress.

JOSEPH F. SMITH'S TWO-YEAR EXILE IN HAWAII

For two years, from February 9, 1885, until June 25, 1887, Joseph F. Smith, who since October 1880 had been second counselor in the First Presidency of the Church, lived in the Hawaiian Mission. President Smith had previously filled two missions to Hawaii. Shortly after his second mission in 1864, he had been called and ordained an apostle (in 1866).

President Smith went to Hawaii to escape the persecutions growing out of the polygamy problem. The U.S. marshals were particularly interested in finding him because as an officiator and recorder in the Endowment House he had detailed information and records about plural marriage.

When the pressure became too great, President John Taylor told President Smith to leave four of his five wives and go to Hawaii. He took Julina, his "legal" wife, with him and departed. Although the two years he spent in Hawaii were a great blessing to the missionaries and Saints of the islands, they were years of suffering and trouble for the Smiths.

The major benefit to the Hawaiian Saints of President Smith's residence was his great spiritual leadership and administrative experience. He regularly taught the missionaries and their president concerning the order of the Church. He encouraged better record keeping and stricter attention to statistical matters. He frequently spoke in Sunday meetings and also in every conference session while he was in the islands.

In Hawaii, President Smith made an inspiring prophecy that has become an important tradition among the Hawaiian Saints. Though it was recorded many years after the event, the best evidence indicates that the ideas expressed were, indeed, those of Joseph F. Smith.[34] This prophecy grew out of the problems of the times. The Saints of Laie were discouraged about the plantation in 1885 or 1886 and brought their complaints to President Smith. After listening to the people for a while, he arose and said:

> My brothers and sisters, do not leave this land, for this place has been chosen by the Lord as a gathering place for the Saints of the Church of Jesus Christ of Latter-day Saints in Hawaii nei. Do not complain because of the many trials which come to you, because of the barrenness of the land, the lack of water, the scarcity of foods to which you are accustomed, and the poverty as well. Be patient, for the day is coming when this land will become a most beautiful land. Water shall spring forth in abundance, and upon the barren land you now see, the Saints will build homes, taro will be planted, and there will be plenty to eat and drink. Many trees will be planted and this place will become verdant, the fragrance of flowers will fill the air, and trees which are now seen growing on the mountains will be moved by the Saints and will grow in this place near the sea, and because of the great beauty of the land, inland birds will come here and sing their songs.
>
> And upon this place the glory of the Lord will rest, to bless the Saints who believe in Him and His commandments. And there are some in this house who will live to see all these things fulfilled, which I have spoken from the Lord.
>
> Therefore, do not waver, work with patience, continue on, stand firm, keep the commandments and also the laws of the gathering, and you will receive greater blessings, both spiritual and temporal, than you now enjoy or have enjoyed in the past. May the Lord be with us all.

In later years the Laie plantation developed in almost precisely the manner in which President Smith had predicted. His words gave the discouraged Saints the reassurance they needed to carry on.

In March 1887 Julina Smith sailed from Hawaii. She took with her a one-year-old child, E. Wesley, who had been born at Laie. He later served twice as president of the Hawaiian Mission. In late June, President Smith departed for home. He had been called back because of the ill health of President Taylor, who died on July 25, 1887.[35]

AN ASSESSMENT OF LAIE'S EARLY YEARS

The first twenty-five years of Laie as a Mormon colony brought growth and change to the mission and to the members of the Church. The plantation was not an economic success, and the missionaries were generally discouraged with the slow progress of their Polynesian brothers and sisters. They often wondered and asked whether the entire operation was not a failure from the beginning.

The economic outlook was seldom bright at Laie. Church leaders in Salt Lake City frequently sent loans to help redeem the credit rating of the plantation. In fact, one of the mission presidents reported that the entire Laie sugar crop would hardly keep some of the large mills operating more than a day or two. But the plantation had not been purchased to make men rich. The goal was to help the local Saints develop character while they developed skills, or at least while they earned honest livings.

Beyond the economic issue lies the question of social progress. Did Laie do what it was supposed to do for the Saints? There is strong evidence that those who gathered to Laie did improve. They lived cleaner lives, in a physical as well as a moral sense, than they had done when the community was first founded. They were not perfect, but they were evidently coming closer to the mark than most of the people who lived outside the little community.

Spiritual progress is difficult to evaluate. In the Latter-day Saint way of thinking, it is closely related to temporal welfare. This concept was recognized in Hawaii both when Brigham Young decided to found a gathering place and throughout the early years of the community. There were also other outward evidences of spirituality. The Relief Society sisters frequently reported that many kind and Christian acts were taking place. The sisters struggled to improve themselves. By the late 1890s Alice R. Woolley, wife of President Samuel E. Woolley, said she believed that the Hawaiian Relief Societies could hold their own with most of those at home and that there were many good and faithful Saints in the Islands.[36] It must also be added that over the years the Hawaiian elders and other priesthood bearers had devoted many years to the service of the Lord as missionaries and in other priesthood capacities. Virtually all of the branches were presided over by Hawaiian Saints.

CHAPTER 9

GROWTH OF LAIE PLANTATION AND THE BUILDING OF A TEMPLE

Hawaii, 1892–1919

Matthew Noall and his wife, Libbie, had not been back in Utah from their first mission for very long when they were asked to return to Hawaii to take charge of the mission. The Noalls arrived in Hawaii on December 18, 1891, and took control early in January 1892. Dissensions had earlier arisen between the local Saints and the missionaries, and among the missionaries themselves. President Ward E. Pack had been unable to solve these problems, and the responsibility of bringing peace to the mission now rested upon twenty-eight-year-old President Noall. Through meetings, discussions, and constant supervision of the principal troublemaker, Noall resolved the matter within a month or two after his arrival.

Among the first problems confronting President Noall was the threatened failure of the mission-owned "company" store that was operated in the old mansion house. Chinese merchants had moved into the area and were drawing off business. In order to compete, Noall built a new store, which was completed February 29, 1892.

Next President Noall wrote to the First Presidency for permission to build a new mission home. The old place was deteriorating, and he hoped that a new home would bring credit to the Church. While he waited for an answer, President Noall set about handling some other problems. For one, local residents leased some of the Laie land for *kalo* (taro) patches, and those who were less than honest were failing to make full payment on their land. Also, there were arguments concerning boundary lines between home lots. Noall surveyed the land carefully and established uniform rents that were due at a set time. Some of the Saints did not like these new procedures, but they worked.

President Matthew and Libbie Noall. (Photo from the *Improvement Era.*)

Soon after he arrived, President Noall also began working on the financial accounts of the plantation. He found that few records existed earlier than 1890 and that even those for 1890 and 1891 were far from accurate. By 1895 he had corrected the records and had established that the plantation and all of the Laie property were worth $116,220. The gross value increased about $26,000 during Noall's administration. The plantation produced profits sufficient to allow Noall to send $30,000, over three years, to President Woodruff to help with financial problems at the Church headquarters in Salt Lake City.

Three developments contributed to the plantation's success. First and most important was a new processing agreement made between Laie plantation and the newly formed Kahuku Plantation Company, which had built a large, modern sugar mill very close to Laie. The Kahuku company agreed to cut, haul, and process Laie's cane crop for half the end product. This arrangement was modified almost yearly, but the general terms of the agreement did not change much.

A second change that increased profits was the cultivation of more acres of cane. This was made possible by a third factor, an improved water supply. More water was obtained by building a reservoir and adding more ditches and flumes. Later President Woolley continued the expansion of land and the search for water. Steam-powered pumps were added in the late 1890s, which made it possible to open some higher land than had previously been inaccessible.

By April 1892 Noall had received permission from the First Presidency to build a new mission home. He drew the plans, and soon the new home was under construction. On October 6, 1894, Lanihuli House, as it was named, was dedicated. It was the physical center of the Church in Hawaii until the temple was completed and took its place in 1919. The Lanihuli House was described at the time as a "building modern in all its designs." It was an interesting combination of current mainland styling and some Hawaiian modifications. It can best be classified as Hawaiian Victorian.[1]

THE WOOLLEYS BEGIN THEIR MISSION

Samuel E. Woolley was working for the Iosepa Agriculture and Stock Company, the Church Hawaiian colony in Skull Valley, Utah,[2] when he received a letter from the First Presidency asking him to take his wife and four children and go to Hawaii as mission president.

The Woolleys arrived in Honolulu on August 31, 1895. Brother Abraham Fernandez, one of the local Saints, met the Woolleys, loaded

Lanihuli House was Hawaiian Mission headquarters from 1894, when Matthew Noall completed it, until 1919, when the mission office was moved to Honolulu. (Courtesy LDS Church Archives.)

them and their luggage into his cart, and drove toward Laie. When they arrived at the foot of the Pali, the famous cliff overlook on Oahu, they were met by missionaries from Laie, who had a team and wagon from the plantation. After the transfer they made their way into the night and watched as the moon rose over the sea. President Woolley later wrote that it was a beautiful night, very bright. They arrived at Lanihuli at midnight and found their way to bed. In this way they began a mission that lasted almost twenty-five years, a mission that would include many changes in the Church and the plantation and that would last long enough for Brother and Sister Woolley to see their children grow to maturity. Woolley himself started his mission at age thirty-six and ended it in his early sixties. He spent his most productive years in the service of the Lord in Hawaii.[3]

President Woolley was an energetic leader. His daily journal entries almost always begin with "up at daybreak" or "at work early." To him, "early" meant anytime after 2:00 A.M. but before 6:00 A.M. He believed in the original idea and philosophy of the Laie community: the purpose of the settlement was to help the Hawaiians both temporally and spiritually. For many years the population of Laie had remained static, because the land would not provide a living for many more than the ninety to one hundred employees and their families. Woolley could see that if Laie were to grow as a gathering place, the plantation would have to be enlarged. Accordingly he brought existing properties under cultivation and bought new land, continuing this process until he was released.

One of the most important capital improvements Woolley made at Laie was the installation in June 1898 of a steam-powered water pump. By 1930 this pump and four others that had been acquired had a capacity of around eight million gallons daily.[4]

The expansion of land made it possible for the population of Laie to grow gradually. By the early 1920s Laie had nearly one thousand people. By 1930 there were 432 people employed in various parts of the operation. From 1900 until the early 1920s the plantation paid its own way every year and supported the financial needs of the mission as well.[5]

Woolley made one of his land acquisitions in a rather unusual way. Around 1905 and 1906, a wealthy and influential sugar magnate, J. B. Castle, who controlled the Kahuku Plantation Company, developed an enterprise that encompassed a major part of the windward side of Oahu. Already the owner of lands on the Kahuku side of Laie, he then acquired those that adjoined the Laie Plantation on the Honolulu side and formed a new company called the Koolau Agricultural Co., Ltd. Not happy about having his lands divided by the Laie plantation, he decided he wanted the upper part of the Church's property.

President Woolley resisted Castle's offers to buy because he believed Laie was a sacred trust from the Lord. Castle continued to bring pressure on him to sell the *mauka* (upper) lands, but Woolley did his best to delay a decision.

In 1906, Castle used the milling contract between the Kahuku company and the Laie plantation as a bludgeon to achieve his purposes. In effect, he told the Church that if it would not sell the lands, water, and rights he desired, the 1906 cane crop would be the last the Kahuku mill would process. This action would have put Laie Plantation out of business.

All Woolley could do was pray and wait. Curiously, nothing happened. Somehow, year after year, Woolley continued to make arrangements with Kahuku Plantation Company to mill the Laie cane, and the Kahuku company continued to mill it. Years passed and J. B. Castle died. The Koolau Agriculture Company properties were put up for sale, and in 1918 Woolley, acting as agent for the Laie Plantation, bought this property. This new land, eight hundred acres, purportedly valued at a half million dollars, almost doubled the sugar-cane acreage of Laie Plantation.[6]

Under President Woolley's watchful eye and skillful leadership, the erstwhile small-time farming enterprise of the nineteenth century grew into a major twentieth-century operation. The sugar crop of 1894-95 was 339 tons. Woolley's best crop of 3,103 tons of sugar, an almost tenfold increase, was produced in 1917-18, while World War I was underway.[7] Woolley was encouraged to produce all the sugar possible to help with the war need; he met the challenge.

THE JUBILEE—THE FIFTIETH ANNIVERSARY OF THE HAWAIIAN MISSION

December 12, 1900, was the fiftieth anniversary of the arrival of the first ten Latter-day Saint missionaries in the Hawaiian Islands. On this date began a celebration lasting several days to commemorate the founding of the mission. The Jubilee committee invited President George Q. Cannon, first counselor in the First Presidency, who had been the acting leader of the first missionaries, to attend. President Cannon, his family, and William W. Cluff and others arrived on the evening of December 10, 1900.

The next four days were a whirlwind of meetings and receptions. Six meetings were held at the Orpheum Theatre on Fort Street on December 12 and 13. President Cannon spoke at each session. To his own satisfaction he was able to speak a few words in the Hawaiian language, though it had been many years since he had used it. Before he departed the islands on January 5, 1901, he was speaking the language almost fluently.

The speeches, music, feasts, and receptions were important, but perhaps more so were the words of encouragement, wisdom, and exhortation that President Cannon gave at various meetings held after the official celebration was over. He also gave blessings to many Saints who sought him out. Even ex-Queen Liliuokalani asked him to come to her home, where she knelt before him and asked for a special blessing. President Cannon wrote in his journal, "I felt very free in blessing her, and the Spirit rested upon us both."[8]

Three significant revelatory experiences occurred while Brother Cannon was in the islands. On Sunday, December 23, he spoke to the Saints at Laie Branch concerning the blessings the Lord still held in store for them. President Woolley wrote, "He said if they would be faithful enough that the time would come when some would be given the power to seal husband and wife for time and eternity so that their children would be born under the New and Everlasting Covenant."[9]

President Cannon was moved to discuss the same subject a week later in Honolulu. Taken together, these expressions of President Cannon later gave rise to the tradition that he had prophesied that a temple would be built in Hawaii.

The second revelatory clarification occurred at Lahaina, Maui. On the morning of December 27, President Cannon, in company with President Woolley, Elder Cluff, and others, started out to find the place where Nalimanui had lived when she offered him food and shelter. President Cannon wrote, "I wanted to find the site of this house and the garden where I sought the Lord in secret prayer and where He condescended to commune with me, for I heard His voice more than once as one man speaks with another, encouraging me and showing me the work which should be done among this people if I would follow the dictates of His Spirit. Glory to God in the highest that He has permitted me to live to behold the fulfillment of His words."[10]

The third experience took place at Waikapu, Maui. It concerned the Latter-day Saint teaching that the island peoples are descendants of Abraham through Lehi and are heirs to all the blessings of Abraham and his posterity. This idea had been accepted by Latter-day Saints ever since the time of Elder Cannon's first mission, but the fact that it had its inception through him was not well known until President Cannon explained it to the Saints at Waikapu on December 28, 1900. President Woolley wrote that Cannon "told them they were of the seed of Abraham, he knew it because the Lord told him so at Lahaina."

The first fifty years had brought success. Two hundred and ninety-nine mission calls had been accepted by foreign elders and their wives during those years. Some missionaries had served two or even three missions. It is not possible to number the Hawaiian elders who served during these years, except to say that their numbers may have been larger than those of the foreign missionaries. And beyond the missionaries were the many thousands of faithful Saints who had served in the numerous presidencies, choirs, teaching and clerking positions, and other responsibilities that the Church requires of its members.

PROGRESS OF THE HAWAIIAN MISSION TO 1920

The progress of the mission during the first two decades of the twentieth century was remarkable in many ways. Not only did the Saints move forward temporally, but they also entered a new era of spiritual strength.

Although Laie had been the pride of the Church in the islands before 1900, it was after this date that the little community on Oahu became a showplace. Trees that were hardy enough to withstand the brisk winds of the windward side of the island were found and planted, along with many varieties of shrubs and flowers. The roads were paved and kept clean. By 1913 there were eighty LDS families living there, and many nonmember Chinese, Japanese, Korean, and Portuguese farmers and gardeners as well.

Life in Laie was modest. Yearly rent was twenty-five cents per family. This charge was levied only to remind the residents that the land was owned by the Church. But there was another "cost" that contributed much to the environment of Laie. In a 1911 address, President Woolley said, "History says this land was a place of refuge in ancient times, and I want it to continue so to be. . . . The price of a house and lot at Laie is *proper living*."[11]

The Laie School brought credit to the Church and the community. Though not large, it served a growing number of children, both Church members and nonmembers. After the turn of the century, the mission staff put more effort into the school to maintain well-trained teachers who could stay in Hawaii for several years. The school buildings were steadily improved, and by 1920, even though the campus had been moved several times to make way for other developments, the physical plant consisted of six separate cottages for the six grades. A Honolulu newspaper wrote concerning the Laie school in 1920, "This high-class establishment is for the use of 150 children of the settlement and represents, as in other sections of the islands, about every race on the face of the earth."[12]

Between April 1913 and April 1914, six meetinghouses, two amusement halls, and one additional building at the Laie School were added to the inventory of Church buildings. This was done at a cost of $16,600. A year later President Woolley reported that there were fifty-two meetinghouses in the mission, valued at $66,000. These were in addition to the Laie plantation and property and some missionary homes.

Growth in financial and physical status was satisfactory, but growth in the number of lives touched by the gospel was more important. The following table illustrates the pattern in numbers of members by year from 1910 to 1920:[13]

Hawaiian Mission Statistics, 1910-1920

Year	Total Membership	Convert Baptisms	Melchizedek Priesthood	Branches	Districts	Missionaries
1910	8,170	275	332	76	9	37
1915	9,443	118	353	62	11	46
1920	11,078	291	384	64	12	51

Membership growth was never spectacular, but it remained steady over the years. It was more rapid when larger numbers of missionaries were called into the field after 1919. In 1913 the missionaries calculated the proportion of Latter-day Saints in the islands and concluded that 22 percent of the Hawaiian population was LDS.

The temple was the most important factor in motivating the Saints to keep the commandments of the Lord. It is impossible to show a direct relationship between the behavior of the Saints and the promise of the temple, but it is interesting to observe that only one person was excommunicated from the Church in 1918, whereas earlier in the century as many as fifty had been cut off in one year. The cause for excommunication had usually been immoral conduct. By the time the temple was dedicated, the Hawaiians evidently had developed much moral strength.

FROM PLANTATION TO TEMPLE

By today's standards, there were hardly enough members of the Church in Hawaii in 1915 to populate two stakes, to say nothing of justifying the operation of a temple. But population was not the only issue involved in the decision to build a temple in Hawaii. As early as 1900 President Cannon had seen the need for the Hawaiians to have the blessings of being sealed as families for time and eternity. After that time temple work was discussed frequently in mission and other conferences. President Woolley regularly encouraged his people to live lives of purity so they could enter the temple someday. In April 1915, President Woolley told the Saints in conference, "Have we searched out our genealogies? Are we prepared for a temple to be built? . . . Who knows but what the Lord wants to build a temple in this land? I tell you that there are people here today who if they continue in the work of the Lord, shall enter into the temple or other temples; and the time will come, in my judgement, that a temple will be built here."[14]

Two months later, President Joseph F. Smith selected a temple site at Laie and dedicated it to the Lord. Elder Reed Smoot, who was with the prophet, recounted President Smith's words: " 'I feel impressed to dedicate this ground for the erection of a Temple to God, for a place where the peoples of the Pacific Isles can come and do their temple work. I have not presented this to the Council of the Twelve or to my counselors; but if you think there would be no objection to it, I think now is the time to dedicate the ground. . . .' Never in all my life did I hear such a prayer. The very ground seemed to be sacred, and he seemed as if he were talking face to face with the Father. I cannot and never will forget it if I live a thousand years."[15]

At general conference in Salt Lake City the next October, President Smith presented the Laie Temple proposition to the Church. In explaining the designs of the brethren in building such a structure, he said it was being built "so that the good people of these islands may reach the blessings of the House of God within their own borders."[16]

When the plans for the temple were announced, Polynesian members of the Church all over the Pacific began making preparations to attend the temple. In New Zealand, Tonga, Samoa, and French

Bishop Charles W. Nibley and President Joseph F. Smith are seated left and right in the center of the front row. Elder Reed Smoot stands between them on the back row. Samuel E. Woolley is on the far right. This photo was taken in 1915 when Joseph F. Smith dedicated the ground for the Hawaii Temple. (Courtesy LDS Church Archives.)

Polynesia, mission presidents encouraged the members to work, earn, and save, and to look forward to the time when they could partake of the blessings of the temple.

The firm that was chosen to design the Hawaiian Temple was Hyrum E. Pope and Harold W. Burton, the same architects who had designed the Alberta Temple in Canada, which was already under construction.

Brothers Pope and Burton evaluated the situation in Hawaii to determine the types of building materials that were available there. They discovered that few local materials could be used; however, there was an abundant supply of lava, which could be ground into aggregate for use in concrete. It was therefore decided to construct the entire building of concrete and steel. The Hawaiian Temple they designed would be a monolith, adorned with beautiful friezes and lovely fountains and gardens.

President Woolley wanted the temple completed within a year from groundbreaking. But because of construction problems, it was not finished until July 15, 1919, over three years from the official groundbreaking in early February 1916.

The principal people involved in the building process were Pope and Burton, architects; Ralph E. Woolley, construction supervisor (he was the son of President Woolley); Leo and Avard Fairbanks, sculptors; and LeConte Stewart, the artist who painted the scenes in the various rooms. Stewart's work was not actually completed until July 1919. The end product was immediately recognized as one of the most beautiful structures in the islands. It was early proclaimed by newspapermen and other public relations people to be the Taj Mahal of Hawaii.

Perhaps the delays were good for the Saints in Hawaii. The added time made it possible for them to raise their share of the $250,000 the building finally cost.

The last year and a half before the temple was dedicated brought several changes in Church leadership. On November 19, 1918, President Joseph F. Smith died. The Saints in Hawaii were deeply saddened by his death. He, more than any living man, was their advocate within the councils of the Church. Every active member of the Church in Hawaii had looked forward to the day when he would come among them again and dedicate the temple. He was succeeded by President Heber J. Grant, who dedicated the temple.

Two other changes occurred in Church leadership positions in Hawaii. First, in July 1918, President William M. Waddoups, then forty years old, arrived in Hawaii as the first president of the new temple. He had maintained a close relationship with the Hawaiian Saints in Utah after completing his first mission from 1900 to 1903. He had served as an ordinance worker in the Salt Lake Temple in 1917 and was in this way prepared to direct the operation of the temple in Hawaii. He began teaching the members how to prepare their genealogies and to understand the purposes of the temple. He toured the islands, holding training sessions and speaking in the branches of the mission.

The other change was the appointment of a new mission president. This came as a shock to some of the Saints. President Woolley had been in office for so long that some members had been born, reared, educated, and married during his time. He too felt regret in having to relinquish his calling. Although he was released as mission president, he continued to manage the plantation until 1921, when Antoine R. Ivins was hired by the Church to handle that responsibility.

Woolley's replacement was E. Wesley Smith, a son of President Joseph F. Smith and his wife Julina. Born at Laie on April 2, 1886, he had filled a mission to Hawaii from 1907 to 1910. When he arrived in Honolulu on June 25, 1919, he established the mission headquarters in that city. Honolulu, now grown to a population of between 45,000 and 55,000, was rapidly becoming the location of the greatest concentration of Mormons in the islands. It was also the most convenient place for transportation and other aspects of mission administration. From 1919 on, Honolulu and Laie became respectively the administrative and spiritual centers of the Church in Hawaii.

The temple was dedicated on November 27, 1919, Thanksgiving Day. President Grant, who presided at the services, was accompanied by his counselors, Anthon H. Lund and Rudger Clawson. Other general authorities who were there included Stephen L Richards of the Council of the Twelve and Presiding Bishop Charles W. Nibley. Great preparations, both physical and spiritual, had been made for this most important of events in Hawaiian Mission history. When President Grant spoke, he expressed his deep personal regrets that President Smith could not be there to conduct the services. His dedicatory prayer was one of thanksgiving to the Lord for His mighty hand in caring for His Saints and restoring the gospel. He expressed gratitude to the Lord for George Q. Cannon, Joseph F. Smith, and J. H. Napela. He gave thanks "that thousands and tens of thousands of the descendants of Lehi, in this favored land, have come to a knowledge of the gospel." He prayed that the way would be opened for the Polynesians in Hawaii as well as in New Zealand and the other island groups of the Pacific to come to "this holy house and become saviors unto their ancestors."

On December 2, the temple was opened for baptismal work for the dead. Within the week, the full services of its facilities were offered to the worthy Saints.

The completion of the temple symbolized in many ways the end of an era of Church history in Hawaii. President Joseph F. Smith, who represented the first generation of missionaries, was now gone. President Woolley, who had worked so diligently to create a beautiful and productive Laie, had been released. The mission headquarters were now moved from Laie to Honolulu, and a different kind of administration was about to begin.

Perhaps more than any other event, the death of Ma Naoheakamalu represented the passing of the old era. She was a very old lady by 1919. She had taken care of President Smith when he was deathly ill while serving his first mission in the 1850s. When he returned to the islands, he had shown his warm love for her, treating her as though she were his mother.

Ma Naoheakamalu, blind and unable to walk, was present at one of

Hawaii Temple as it appeared immediately before dedication in 1919. (Photo by architects Pope and Burton in *Improvement Era.)*

Ma Naoheakamalu, Joseph F. Smith's Hawaiian mother. Some sources refer to her as Ma Manuhii. (Courtesy LDS Church Archives.)

the five dedication services at the temple. The week following the dedication, she received her own endowment in the temple. Elder Wilford W. King, mission clerk, reported the touching event in this way:

> She had to be carried and helped all the way. While in the temple she testified she heard President Joseph F. Smith say "aloha" ("love to you") to her and it caused her to weep for joy.
>
> The next week she returned to her home in Honolulu and shortly after took sick. She called for Pres. E. Wesley Smith to come and see her. On his entering the room she sat up in bed and said, "Auhea ke keiki" (meaning "where is the boy?" the son of President Joseph F. Smith). President Smith took hold of her hand. She clasped it to her breast, kissed it and wept. Then she said in her own tongue, "It is enough, I am satisfied and ready to go now." She had been to the temple, a thing for which she had lived and she had now felt the hand of the son of the man she loved so much and she was ready to return to her Maker. She passed away the next morning.[17]

Her death came on December 11, 1919. And with her passed an era of the history of the Church in Hawaii.[18]

CHAPTER 10

FROM "HAWAIIAN" CHURCH TO INTERNATIONAL CHURCH

Hawaii, 1919–1950

By 1900 the Hawaiian part of the population of the Islands had fallen to one-fourth of the total (numerous Chinese, Japanese, Portuguese, Filipinos, and Koreans had immigrated), yet as late as the 1930s missionaries to Hawaii worked primarily with this small segment of the population. The Church was known as a Hawaiian church, yet Hawaii no longer belonged to the Hawaiians. But by 1950 the racial mixture of the Church had changed greatly. This happened for two primary reasons: First, the second generation, and in some cases, the third generations of Chinese and Japanese in Hawaii were becoming culturally American. Those of the first generation still acted and thought much as though they were in their native lands, but the children born in Hawaii (by 1930, 75 percent of the 139,631 Japanese in Hawaii had been born there) were Americans. This fact made it possible for LDS missionaries to teach the gospel to these people in English. The second reason for significant racial change in the Church was the influx, beginning in the 1920s, of a fairly large number of Samoans. These people came to Hawaii to work in the temple, but for various reasons many chose to stay permanently.

CHURCH GROWTH AND INSTITUTIONAL DEVELOPMENT TO 1940

The Hawaiian Mission received an ample share of elders and sisters during most of the 1920s, having yearly averages of between fifty-one and sixty-three missionaries for the decade. Church membership in the Islands passed the 14,000 mark in 1926, but the number of members did not grow appreciably until after World War II. The Depression and World War II made progress more difficult. In the 1930s the number of missionaries dropped to an average of thirty-three per year; the Second World War brought about even more serious reductions. By late 1944 no young men were serving missions in the Pacific area. Older couples and local missionaries staffed the missions.[1]

TEACHING THE GOSPEL IN HAWAII

Tracting was a regular method of finding prospective investigators. Often the missionaries to Hawaii found it too easy to spend time in the homes of the members. This was a problem in two ways. The Hawaiian members loved the elders. In many cases they felt deeply hurt if the missionaries insisted that they could not continue calling on them. On the other hand, some elders found it easy to fritter away their time learning to play the ukulele or listening to stories about the old days in the islands.

After the temple was completed at Laie, many tourists visited there. A bureau of information was established there so that missionaries could distribute tracts and other information to visitors. Different mission presidents held varying views toward the information bureau. Most felt that a great missionary work was being performed there; in fact, it was sometimes considered the highest honor among the missionaries to be assigned to the temple. The temple brought much acclaim to the Church in Hawaii, and it was a great aid to the missionary cause.

The methods used by the missionaries to spread the gospel changed to meet the circumstances of the times and included radio broadcasts, missionary basketball teams, and youth programs.

There were sixty-two branches and eight districts (previously called conferences) in the mission in 1929. Some of these branches were still headed by missionaries instead of local members. The Saints were organized into districts in much the same pattern as was followed in the stakes of Zion. In 1927 President Waddoups, who was temple president and mission president at the same time, organized mission boards for all of the auxiliaries—the Sunday School, Relief Society, Primary, and Mutual Improvement Association. These boards traveled with their presidencies to the semiannual district conferences and directed, encouraged, and guided the efforts of the mission. Still later, at the all-mission conference of April 1931, President Castle H. Murphy, excited about the prospect of having a stake in Hawaii, organized the Oahu District Council. It was patterned after the high councils of the stakes of Zion. In 1928 the Laie District had been combined with the Honolulu District; thus the new council was selected from members on the entire island of Oahu.

Within a few months after the Oahu District Council was organized, President Murphy established similar councils in each of the eight other districts of the mission. Four years later, in June 1935, a stake was organized on Oahu. Because of the experience gained in the stake-like organization, the change from district to stake was fairly easy.

The years from 1920 to 1940 were transition years. The older Hawaiians frequently preferred to speak and read in the Hawaiian language, whereas the young people, who had been schooled in English since childhood, preferred English. This led to a problem in providing appropriate lesson materials for each group. Most of the classes and organizations were carried on entirely in English with materials provided from Salt Lake City. But it was still necessary as late as 1930 to provide translated lessons for the older Hawaiians.

When the Church Welfare Program was instituted in 1936, the Hawaiian Saints planted papaya groves and taro farms and stored goods and necessities for a time when they would be needed. They were needed and used during the early days of World War II, when grocery stores were closed by military order.

Some welfare efforts were undertaken during the war years, but in 1947 one of the most creative welfare projects anywhere in the world was begun. A monthly *Hukilau* was held to attract visitors to Laie but more particularly to raise money for welfare purposes. The word *Hukilau* derives from the Hawaiian form of fishing in which people on the beach pull *huki,* a fish net, with leaves, *lau,* attached to it. Following this activity, in which the tourists participated, a Hawaiian dinner and a program were presented to the tourists. The *Hukilau* brought a steady and considerable amount of money into the welfare savings of Laie. This project was continued well into the 1960s when the Polynesian Cultural Center eclipsed it and brought it to a conclusion.

General authority and general board member visits became quite frequent from 1920 to 1940, and each visit was a special spiritual occasion. The peoples of Hawaii, in true Aloha spirit, withheld no effort to make these visits memorable for both themselves and their guests. In 1935 President J. Reuben Clark, Jr., of the First Presidency, wrote these thought-provoking words concerning his visit, along with President Grant, to the islands:

> As one witnessed day after day and night after night among the Saints congregating together to meet him . . . their every word and look evidenced that to them President Grant was indeed the Prophet of the Lord, the Seer and the Revelator, one was shocked and saddened in the contemplation of how poor and destitute we Anglo-Saxons are in real depth of feeling, and how inhibited and niggardly we are in showing the feeling we have, in contrast with the overwhelming richness of the sentiment and emotion which the Hawaiians possess and with the understanding prodigality with which they shower these blessings upon others. Truly we feel little and show less; they feel much and show all.[2]

One of the high points among visits of the general authorities was that of Elder David O. McKay and his traveling companion Hugh J. Cannon, the son of President George Q. Cannon. While in the islands Elder McKay was informed of the need many Church leaders felt for a Church college, the first time that the idea of a Church college for Hawaii was considered.

The spiritual highlight of the visit was one in which only a few people participated. While on the island of Maui, Elder McKay and the party visited Pulehu in the Kula district, where George Q. Cannon had baptized his first converts in 1851 and organized the first branch of the Church in Hawaii the same year. This was sacred ground to Elder McKay and the others present—Hugh J. Cannon, Mission President E. Wesley Smith, Elder Samuel H. Hurst, and a Hawaiian elder, David Kailimai. President Smith recounted the event in these words: "While there Elder McKay felt impressed with a desire to offer a prayer to the Lord in the spirit of thanksgiving for the privilege they had of being there, and for the many . . . who had embraced the Gospel. We bowed in prayer, Elder McKay being mouth. It was a moment never to be forgotten, for indeed the spot is sacred. Elder McKay said, 'I feel certain that President Cannon and President [Joseph F.] Smith are near for the veil was very thin.' Elder [Hugh J.] Cannon was deeply impressed, and with tears filling his eyes and in a choked voice said, 'There was no veil.' "[3]

This incident was told to a group of assembled Saints at the Wailuku chapel that night, February 8, 1921. J. Pia Cockett, who later became one of the grand old men of the Church, wrote of the event in his notebook, adding more details: "While he [Elder McKay] was praying, the Hawaiian Elder [David Kailimai] was privileged to see in a vision two hands clasped in the form of greeting. He thought Cannon and Hurst were shaking hands. He opened his eyes and saw they were apart. He closed his eyes again and after the prayer he told what he had seen. [At that point Elder McKay made the statement quoted above.]"

For many years Elder Cockett was under the impression that the clasped hands that had been seen were those of George Q. Cannon and his son, Hugh J. But in 1936 this story was retold to President McKay when he visited Hawaii again. He corrected Brother Cockett by saying, "Those hands were the hands of the two fathers, George Q. Cannon and Joseph F. Smith, in the presence of the two sons, Hugh J. Cannon and E. Wesley Smith."[4]

The site of the little chapel in Pulehu is still considered sacred ground. Late in the 1920s a monument was planned and then erected to mark the spot where these early events had taken place. On October 26, 1930, the Kula Monument was dedicated by President William M. Waddoups, under the direction of the mission president, Castle H. Murphy. It is a granite shaft with a bronze marker telling its purpose.

The creation of the Oahu Stake in 1935 brought about regular and more frequent visits by general authorities. After June 1935 quarterly stake conferences necessitated four visits by general authorities each year.

Providing appropriate chapels and meeting facilities was a constant challenge for the mission presidents and the members. Chapels on the outside islands were seldom more than one-room, single-wall frame structures. If they had classrooms they were usually small extensions on the side of or under the main hall. In most instances the chapel served for both worship and recreation. On MIA nights, the benches were pulled back to the walls, and activities took place there. As leaders became more conscious of the Church's image and became cognizant of the impossibility of providing the full program of the Church in makeshift chapels, a considerable amount of money and effort was put into chapel construction. During the 1920s the record was especially impressive. Three new chapels were completed in 1921, four in 1923, four in 1926, and seven small chapels in 1928.

The most impressive building before 1940 was the Kalihi chapel in Honolulu. It was a large and commodious structure that was capable of accommodating several hundred people for meetings or conferences. President Anthony W. Ivins of the First Presidency dedicated this edifice on August 3, 1924.

Construction slowed during the depression years, but in 1935 President Castle H. Murphy purchased property at 1560 South

The tabernacle on Beretania Street was dedicated by President David O. McKay, then second counselor in the First Presidency, in 1941. It was designed by architects Pope and Burton. (Courtesy LDS Church Archives.)

Beretania Street in Honolulu. Six years later a new tabernacle was completed there. Designed by Pope and Burton, the same men who designed the temple in Laie, it was impressive then and remains a beautiful architectural attraction. The tabernacle on Beretania Street, often called a temple by visitors to the islands, did much to enhance the image of the Church both among members and outsiders. This tabernacle was the headquarters for the Oahu Stake. Stake President Ralph E. Woolley, who had supervised construction of the temple over twenty years before, was the contractor. The cost of the building was approximately $275,000, more than $70,000 of which was raised by Hawaiian Saints. President David O. McKay dedicated it on August 16, 1941.[5]

Four months after the tabernacle was dedicated, the Japanese bombed Pearl Harbor, and the war halted any further construction until 1945.

When E. Wesley Smith was called as mission president in 1919, the mission and the plantation were made separate responsibilities. President Samuel E. Woolley remained plantation manager until May 1921, when Antoine R. Ivins was sent to Laie to preside. His responsibility was a secular one. The role the plantation had played earlier diminished to one of little significance. It was simply a business propo-

President and Sister David O. McKay arrive in Honolulu to dedicate the Oahu Stake tabernacle, 1941. (Courtesy LDS Church Archives.)

sition that employed many Latter-day Saints along with some non-members.

The plantation, however, could not hold its own in the world sugar market. By 1927 it was falling into debt, and in an effort to recover its losses, Brother Ivins decided to sell some beach-front property belonging to the plantation. The $275,000 brought in by this sale failed to meet fully the debts of the plantation, and it also angered some of the old-timers of Laie, who did not believe the Zion's Securities Corporation, which had been set up by President Grant in 1922 to manage all nonreligious properties of the Church, had the right to sell the land. Apparently some of Laie's residents, under the impression that the land belonged to the people who lived on it, did not believe that any property could be sold without their approval. This was proved to be incorrect in a court case brought before the Land Court of the Territory of Hawaii, which was decided in favor of Zion's Securities Corporation on February 28, 1928.[6]

Economic problems continued on the plantation until 1931, when Brother Ivins entered into a lease arrangement with the Kahuku Plantation Company to have it take over all of the sugar lands. This arrangement was renewed from time to time down to the late 1960s. In summary it may be said that in 1931 the Church got out of the management end of the sugar business. Since Elder Ivins's release to become a general authority in 1931, several other men have managed the residential portions of Laie. At this writing the Church still maintains control of a major portion of Laie, but it has not assumed an economic responsibility for the Saints of Laie since 1931.

One other institution passed from Church control during this time. The elementary school in Laie had been the pride of the mission for many years. Many missionaries taught school there, most of them women after 1900. In 1927, however, the government of the Territory was given control of this institution. Church leaders determined that missionaries could better spend their time in full-time proselyting. Furthermore, the Territory had sufficient money available to pay the cost of educating Laie's children.

Another change that occurred in Laie was the growth of a small settlement of Samoans there. The precise date of the first pilgrimage of a Samoan Saint to the Hawaiian Temple is not known. As early as 1922, however, President E. Wesley Smith noted in his yearly report the presence of one Samoan family that was living in Laie. A year later President Eugene J. Neff, the new mission president, noted that "a number of Samoan Saints have immigrated to Hawaii." He found it necessary to create a Samoan Society "in order to keep them together and active in Church work."[7]

It is difficult to trace the development of the Samoan community after 1923. However, by 1929 there were 125 Samoans living in Laie. How many lived elsewhere on Oahu, if any, is not known. Although 125 people seems a relatively small number, it was 24 percent of Laie's 1930 census figure, which was 521 total population.

Apparently the Samoan population in Hawaii did not grow during the depression years nor during World War II. After 1951, because of an unusual arrangement with the U.S. government that made it possible for people in American Samoa to travel to Hawaii free of charge on one voyage of the U.S.S. *President Jackson,* the population grew quickly again. This rapid influx brought the permanent Samoan population of Laie to around 300 in 1955.[8]

As implied above, the main attraction of Samoans to Laie was the temple. Hawaii also offered a more pleasant and more luxurious way of life than Western or American Samoa. When migrants came, they cooperated to help bring other members of their families to the Hawaiian mecca.

Once there they found work on the Laie Plantation or did labor as it could be found. The Samoan tradition of family ownership and cooperation has been both a help and a hindrance to these people in the American setting. Communal ownership has sometimes caused problems for Samoans. The cultural adjustments notwithstanding, the Samoan Saints have added greatly to the Church in Hawaii.

THE CREATION OF THE OAHU STAKE

Halfway through the thirty-year period under consideration, President Heber J. Grant organized the Oahu Stake. Today this seems a small matter, considering the present rapid growth of the Church and the constant divisions and creations of stakes, but in the 1930s it was a matter of some weight and concern to the highest councils of the Church.

Perhaps the most serious question to be considered was whether both the Hawaiian Mission and the proposed stake would each have sufficient workers to succeed after a division took place. Surveying the Church to find a precedent for a stake and mission operating in the same area, the general authorities found that the California Mission and the stakes created there were similar and worked effectively. On November 20, 1934, the First Presidency wrote to President Murphy to learn his feelings about the idea. They told him that the matter had been discussed for over a year among the First Presidency and Council of the Twelve and that they agreed that a stake should be organized in the islands.[9]

President Murphy was elated with the suggestion. He had worked steadily in that direction ever since 1931. By 1934 he had placed the mission firmly on a stake-like basis. On June 20, 1935, President Grant; J. Reuben Clark, Jr., first counselor in the First Presidency; and a number of other dignitaries were welcomed to Hawaii with one of the most lavish greetings the Hawaiian Saints had yet mustered. Music, leis, feasts, tears, and laughter blended into a spiritual occasion that is still remembered by many kamaainas (old-timers) today.

After the First Presidency and their party had visited the outer islands, the special conference was held on June 30, 1935. The Oahu Stake, as the new unit was named, was the first stake to be organized outside continental North America. The first stake president called was

A group of Church dignitaries at the creation of Oahu Stake, 1935. Seated left to right: Sister Grant; President Heber J. Grant; Sister Clark; President J. Reuben Clark, Jr.; general board visitors Edith G. Young, Anna G. Midgley, Sister Richards, Preston D. Richards. Standing left to right are Joseph Anderson, Sister Musser, J. B. Musser, Olivia Waddoups, temple president William Waddoups, Verna Murphy, mission president Castle H. Murphy, Romania Woolley, Oahu Stake president Ralph E. Woolley, and counselors Edward L. Clissold and Arthur K. Parker. (Courtesy LDS Church Archives.)

Ralph E. Woolley, son of President Samuel E. Woolley. He selected as his counselors Edward L. Clissold and Arthur K. Parker.

The progress of the Church in Hawaii pleased President Grant greatly. He and President Clark believed that after eighty-five years of experience in the Church, "the Hawaiians had earned the right to the gift of a greater power and fuller local responsibility in the administration of Church activities upon the islands."[10] It was a source of deep satisfaction to them that the distribution of Church offices in the new stake, both at the stake level and in the wards and branches, between the Hawaiians and the other racial groups in the Church "was essentially proportionate to their relative numbers." In addition, President Grant believed that the organization of the Stake would lead to an "almost coercive effect upon the launching of the Gospel in the Eastern hemisphere."[11]

THE JAPANESE/CENTRAL PACIFIC MISSION

When President Grant arrived in Hawaii to organize the Oahu Stake, he was introduced to nine Japanese of Hawaii, generally called Americans of Japanese Ancestry (AJA), who had been baptized members of the Church the day before.[12]

President Grant's entire Hawaiian experience pointed him to the

President and Sister Hilton A. Robertson, center second row, sit among Japanese-American members and missionaries of the Japanese Mission in Hawaii, 1937 or 1938. (Courtesy LDS Church Archives.)

conclusion that work had to be seriously undertaken among the Japanese, Chinese, and other Asians in Hawaii. From President Murphy, who had felt compelled to start missionary work among the Chinese and Japanese in 1932, he learned of the various ethnic Sunday Schools in Honolulu, but the Japanese organization, which held all of its meetings in the Japanese language, seemed to impress him most. For a year or two before this, Elwood L. Christensen, a former missionary to Japan, had conducted services with the small but growing Japanese congregation.[13] Both President Grant and President Clark related prophetic visions of the role Hawaii was to play in the expansion of the Church into Asia. President Clark wrote, "It would seem not improbable that Hawaii is the most favorable place for the Church to make its next effort to preach the Gospel to the Japanese people; and it would further appear that a strong colony of Japanese Saints in Hawaii could operate from there into their homeland in a way that might bring many Japanese to a knowledge not only of Christianity, but of the restored Gospel. There are evidences that the fields are ripening; if so, they will be ready sooner or later for the harvest to begin."[14]

The same reasoning was applied to the Chinese, Filipinos, and Indians of Hawaii. This vision of things to come has been fulfilled to a remarkable degree.

The mission of the Church in Japan had been closed after operating from 1901 to 1924. While President Grant was in the islands, he talked with President Murphy and others about reopening the Japanese Mission, but in Hawaii rather than Japan. Over a year passed, and then, in November 1936, Hilton A. Robertson and his wife, Hazel, both of whom had served missions in Japan (in fact, Elder Robertson had been mission president at the time of the closing of the mission), were called to open the Japanese Mission in Hawaii. They arrived in Honolulu on February 24, 1937.

On the following Sunday the Robertsons met with the little band of thirty-five Japanese Saints and investigators. Among them was Sister Isune Nachie, who was now very old. She had joined the Church in Japan before the mission's closure and came to Laie in 1923 to do temple work. President Clissold described her as a true Saint. Others who were there were Dr. Tomizo Katsunuma, who had been converted to the Church while attending Utah State University at Logan, Utah, and Kay Ikegami, who also proved to be a faithful leader.

The first three missionaries to the Japanese Mission in Hawaii arrived in October 1937. They were Melvyn A. Weenig, Preston D. Evans, and Roy W. Spear. Weenig was later called as president of this mission in 1946. By the end of the first year the total membership of the mission was seventeen: nine males and eight females; but four converts had been baptized and a good beginning had been made.

J. Christopher Conkling has prepared the following table about the growth of the Japanese/Central Pacific Mission.[15]

Growth Patterns, Japanese/Central Pacific Mission

	1937	1938	1939	1940	1941	1942	1943	1944	1945	1946	1947	1948	1949
Missionaries	5	19	32	54	55	18	13	7	4	34	66	89	77
Baptisms	4	13	26	37	48	156	72	48	34	30	15	52	67
Total Membership	17	30	60	101	150	302	375	437	484	522	532	604	671

As can be seen, the number of missionaries increased fairly rapidly after 1937, and the number of members began to rise steadily as well. During 1938 the work was expanded to the island of Hawaii, and in January and February 1939, missionaries of this mission were sent to Maui and Kauai, respectively. From the beginning, the greatest success came among the young AJA. Sunday Schools, Primaries, and MIAs were organized wherever the missionaries worked.

During the entire lifetime of the mission, the elders and sisters were encouraged to learn the Japanese language. In retrospect this seems almost unnecessary, but it was considered wise at the time even though nearly all of the converts were among the English-speaking young people. The major concern was that when the youths had been influenced by the missionaries, they would want to introduce the missionaries to their parents. It was hoped that an ability to speak the Japanese language would help to influence the older people, if only to convince them that their children should become Latter-day Saints.

Another reason for learning the Japanese language was the hope that the Japanese Mission in Hawaii would someday be the base of operations for the reopening of Japan. Although affairs did not work out in precisely this way, the missionaries of Hawaii did teach the Japanese language to the first missionaries called to reopen Japan. In 1948, while waiting for permission to enter Japan, the first five elders studied the language on Oahu under the tutelage of Paul V. Hyer and his companion, both of whom had learned to speak Japanese while serving as missionaries in Hawaii.

The Robertsons were released in September 1940, and President Jay C. Jensen and his wife were called to direct the work. President Jensen had been a missionary in Japan during the early mission. He continued the patterns of proselyting established by President Robertson.

The churches of Hawaii, LDS and non-LDS, grew in number during World War II. Many of the new members were AJA. They, like many others, found themselves turning to religion more than before. It is fortunate that the Church had developed an organization ready to benefit from this new interest in American or Christian religions. A glance at table 3 reveals that the Japanese Mission membership more than doubled during 1942, the first year of the war.

Concurrent with the greater interest in religion among the AJA was another development that may have contributed to the rapid growth during 1942. The missionaries were going home, and no new elders were on their way to replace them. It is probable that the missionaries put more pressure on their prospective converts to make decisions to be baptized than they might have done otherwise. Whatever the reasons, the number of converts expanded rapidly during 1942 and continued to grow throughout the war even though the missionary force was greatly diminished.

President Edward L. Clissold, who was first counselor in the Oahu Stake presidency, was called to replace President Jensen in December

1942. He served as acting president until 1944, when his assignment as a Reserve Naval officer took him away from Hawaii. He was also temple president during these years.

One of the first changes Clissold made was the name of the mission. Because the term *Japanese* was held in derision, President Clissold felt that a more innocuous name would be better for the image of the mission; hence, he chose the "Central Pacific Mission (CPM)" as the new name. This remained the name of the mission from 1943 until it was combined with the Hawaiian Mission in 1950.

As the number of full-time missionaries dropped, President Clissold had to encourage the Japanese members to join with the long-established branches. In 1944 President Castle Murphy was again called to Hawaii, this time to act simultaneously as president of the Hawaiian Mission, the Central Pacific Mission, and the Hawaiian Temple. He was also servicemen's coordinator.

The conclusion of the war brought marked changes to the mission. In 1946 Melvyn A. Weenig and his wife were called to preside over the CPM, and before the year was over there were forty-five missionaries serving in it, a number that Weenig did not believe adequate to handle the work. Over the next two years the mission force increased, but the number of baptisms did not grow accordingly. The immediacy of the war was past, and the AJA turned back toward their Japanese heritage.

But even though numbers of converts did not grow rapidly after the war, the AJA converts of earlier times remained loyal. According to Conkling, they "were the most faithful [Saints] in the world."[16] Among those who were converted to the Church by the Japanese/CPM were Adney Y. Komatsu, later to be the first AJA to be a mission president and then a general authority of the Church; Tomosue Abo; Kenji Akagi; Russel N. Horiuchi; Kotaro Koizumi; William Nako; Arthur K. Nishimoto; Edward Okazaki; Satoru Sato; Ralph Shino; Sam Shimabukuro; Walter Teruya; and still more to come at this writing, all of whom have been called to serve as mission presidents to Japan, as regional representatives, or temple presidents in Tokyo. Hundreds of other Japanese from Hawaii have served in Japan as missionaries.

One of the aspirations of President Weenig and his missionaries was to extend their mission to Japan. This did not prove to be the destiny of the CPM. It did, however, produce many missionaries who were called to Japan. It was to Edward L. Clissold, not to President Weenig, that the responsibility of reopening the Japanese Mission was given.

Elder Adney Y. Komatsu, the first person of Japanese ancestry to become a General Authority of the Church, was Area Administrator of the South Pacific for a period of time. (Courtesy Adney Y. Komatsu.)

President Clissold had been assigned to Japan as a member of the occupation forces at the end of the war. While there, he participated with the LDS servicemen and reported their missionary activities to President McKay after he returned home. In 1948, the First Presidency decided that Clissold and Weenig should go to Japan together, but because of restrictions of the occupation forces, only one man could be sent. Because Brother Clissold was already familiar with conditions in Japan and knew many important people there, he was sent to reopen the mission in Japan. He arrived there in the spring of 1948.

After the war, the efforts of the CPM were centered almost entirely upon young people who did not speak Japanese and were part of a new Hawaii. For this reason Church leaders in Hawaii and Salt Lake City began to question the need for a separate mission for Japanese Americans. Finally, in 1950, the First Presidency decided to combine the CPM and Hawaiian Missions.

WORLD WAR II AND ITS EFFECTS UPON THE CHURCH IN HAWAII

The leaders of the Church in Salt Lake City were much concerned about the war and watched its development carefully. In October 1940 the First Presidency ordered all LDS missionaries home from New Zealand, French Polynesia, Tonga, Samoa, and Australia. Some of these missionaries were transferred to the Hawaiian Mission.

Except for the loss of the full-time foreign missionaries after 1941 and the more restricted way of life caused by the war, the Church was not significantly hindered in its progress in Hawaii. Because of military restrictions, during January and part of February 1942 no Church meetings were held. After that there were blackouts for a time that made night meetings impossible, but for the greater part of the war the Church was able to carry on as usual. A curfew hampered evening activities for a while, but even this precaution was short-lived.

The Church contributed to the war effort by leasing to war agencies the two large amusement halls in Honolulu. President Waldron wrote, "Our church gained great respect from the military and the government officials in Hawaii at the time of Pearl Harbor for we were prepared to render much needed aid. In the organization of Civil Defense, our priesthood quorums and missionaries gave needed assistance. Our Boy Scouts worked in the vital communication system, and the Relief Society helped the Red Cross care for the wounded and sewed and rolled bandages for the hospitals."[17]

The missionaries made a significant contribution to the defense effort. A special historical issue of *Ka Elele O Hawaii* titled "Hawaiian Mission Review" and published in late 1942 summarized the activities of the missionaries. The editors wrote:

> Our elders were pressed into service as policemen, armed guards on vital bridges and highways, communications operators to send and receive important military messages, air-raid wardens, first-aid instructors, observation-post watchmen, ship-charters, and grave diggers. Many missionaries were donating as much as eighteen hours a day to emergency duty! Even today, after a year of warfare, many missionaries are still taking their regular turns at the switchboards of "Communication Headquarters." Others are permanent "Block Wardens," assigned to check on blackout restrictions, to keep track of all people living within certain districts, and to go into active duty in case of air-raid alarm.[18]

The Church also stressed the welfare program and "victory gardens" as a means of better caring for the needs of the people.

The war brought hundreds of LDS servicemen and women to the islands. These people not only participated in the activities of the Church but also contributed to its operation in many ways. One special facility was prepared for the service personnel: A large home located on a lot adjoining the new tabernacle became a recreation and rest center for LDS service people and their friends. The place was

President George Albert Smith with members of the Church in Hawaii. They represent five races. Left to right, Samoan, Filipino, Japanese, Chinese, and Hawaiian. 1950. (Photo from the *Improvement Era.*)

named *Malamakoa,* which means in Hawaiian "take care of the soldier."

Although World War II was a trying experience for the Saints of Hawaii, it was not an unhappy time from a Church point of view. Many people grew because they were given new or greater responsibilities.

In May 1947 Castle H. and Verna Murphy were released from their fourth and last mission to Hawaii. They had begun their service in Hawaii in 1909 and had served over fifteen years as missionaries, mission president and mission mother, and temple president and matron, and as friends of the people of Hawaii.

The man who replaced President Murphy was E. Wesley Smith, the same man who had begun this era of missionary and Church history. Once again while he presided, the number of missionaries grew rapidly, proselyting was emphasized, and the number of convert baptisms increased. By 1950 Hawaii was well into a new phase of its history.

Church leaders had decided that the Hawaiian Mission and the Central Pacific Mission should be combined into a new entity called the Hawaii Mission, so called in order to denote its geographical location but not a particular race of people. This merger took place on April 1, 1950. It retained this name until 1974, when, in keeping with a general naming policy churchwide, it was renamed the Hawaii Honolulu Mission.

December 1950 marked the centennial of the Hawaiian Mission. The ceremonies and festivities celebrating this event, however, had been held the previous August when President George Albert Smith visited Hawaii. A pageant was then presented, feasts were held, and there was much rejoicing in song and dance. Newspapers and special programs recounted the accomplishments of the Church in the islands. Marvelous progress had been made during the Church's first hundred years.

CHAPTER 11

LAIE: A MISSIONARY TOOL

Hawaii, 1950 to 1984

In 1951 President Ralph E. Woolley was released as stake president after having served for sixteen years. Edward L. Clissold was called as his replacement. Few stake presidents in the Church have assumed the office with as many years of administrative experience as President Clissold brought to the post.

When President Clissold was called to preside, he, his counselors, and the stake high council concluded that the Saints within the stake had made sufficient progress in administrative matters to be given the financial responsibilities as well as all other parts of their stewardships. By placing the tithing and budget records in the hands of the bishops, the stake leaders helped to teach many people the order of the Church.

Not long after he became president, Brother Clissold observed another problem in his stake: a concentration of leadership in Waikiki Ward at the expense of other wards and branches. Before the war there were probably not more than 150 or 200 haole members of the Church in the islands. This number increased rapidly during and after the war, and many of the haoles gravitated to the Waikiki Ward even though they lived elsewhere on Oahu. President Clissold and his associates were not pleased to have so many leaders and potential leaders of the stake concentrated in one ward, so they asked all members to attend the wards in which they lived. This suggestion was not well received by some haole members of the stake. Nevertheless, the problem was alleviated when Elder Marion G. Romney visited the stake for quarterly conference and asked the Saints to follow the order of the Church, but a few have persisted in attending Waikiki Ward ever since even though they live outside the boundaries of the ward

During the 1950s a number of Americans of Japanese and Chinese ancestry emerged as important leaders of the Church in Hawaii. Many of these men and women had been too young to assume major leadership responsibilities before this time, but after 1950 they became more conspicuous in bishoprics and high councils.[1]

When President Clissold was sustained in his calling, there were sixteen wards and branches and nearly eleven thousand members in Oahu Stake. In four more years the stake was again divided. On August 28, 1955, the Honolulu Stake was organized with Bishop Jay A. Qualey, Jr., as the first president. Continued progress and expansion made it possible to reorganize once again on February 4, 1962, when the Pearl Harbor (presently the Honolulu, Hawaii West) Stake was begun with George Q. Cannon, Jr., formerly a member of the Hawaii Mission presidency, as stake president.

The development of stakes in Hawaii since 1962 has been steady. Eight stakes have been organized since that time, and all of the islands are now covered by them.[2] The organization of the Hilo, Kona, Maui, and Kauai stakes indicates that the Saints there were prepared by the three-quarter point in the century to handle their own administrative responsibilities. Aside from the blessing of having high priests and bishops in their midst, there are actually few differences between a stake and a well-organized district. Nevertheless, in the hearts and minds of the members, stakehood is a parallel honor to full citizenship.

Statehood and the privileges of U.S. citizenship were also important to LDS Hawaiians. The Congress of the United States passed a bill admitting the Territory of Hawaii as the fiftieth state of the Union on March 12, 1959. The words of a multi-racial native son who said, "Now we are all haoles," captured the feeling of acceptance of most Hawaiian residents as they became in a full sense part of the United States of America. Statehood spurred the development of the already important tourist industry. As a Honolulu banker remarked, "Statehood had the effect of a multi-million dollar advertising campaign—for free. Everyone suddenly discovered Hawaii."[3]

Concurrent with the growth in tourist trade, and partly because of it, many mainland-based corporations began establishing offices in Honolulu and other parts of the Islands. Many faithful Latter-day Saints were among the men and women sent to Hawaii by corporations and small businesses. Several of these haole business people have been called as stake presidents.

The most important developments in the Church in Hawaii during the last twenty-five years have been in education. Latter-day Saint education in Hawaii developed through several stages. The first schools in Hawaii were established by the early missionaries, and Hawaiian children were included in these schools from the beginning. But in 1927, the Laie elementary school was turned over to the territory, and until 1955, when the Church College of Hawaii began, the Church did not operate any schools in Hawaii.

In 1929 the Territorial Legislature of Hawaii passed a law that allowed students one hour per week of free school time to attend religious education classes taught by the denomination of their choice. In 1938, the first Religious Education (R.E.) classes of the Church were started at Kohala. Once underway, the program expanded rapidly. The Hawaiian and Japanese missions as well as the Oahu Stake participated in and supported the teaching efforts. By 1941 there were eighty-five classes in seventy-one different schools, with an average weekly attendance of 1,468. Approximately half of these students were not members of the Church.[4]

In November 1941, Alfred C. Nielsen, who had been principal of Cyprus High School Seminary in Magna, Utah, was sent to Hawaii to act as supervisor of R.E. classes in elementary and high schools. He was also made director of an Institute of Religion to be organized at the University of Hawaii. Unfortunately, two weeks after his arrival the Japanese attacked Pearl Harbor and schools were closed until February 1942, but the program was never suspended. It was finally necessary to call for volunteers to teach the classes, but Brother Nielsen and his replacement, Frank W. McGhie, who arrived in the summer of 1945, succeeded in filling most of the posts on Oahu. In this manner the program was carried on until the war ended.

In April 1948 the Supreme Court of the United States handed down a decision that released-time religious education classes that met in public schools were not constitutional. Immediately the commissioner of schools in Hawaii decided that the R.E. classes had to cease. However, it was finally decided by the school commissioner that schoolrooms could be used for R.E. purposes thirty minutes after classes ended for the day. This delay allowed students to leave for home instead of staying for R.E. class, thus making it almost impossible to continue the program.[5] The major effectiveness of the R.E. program ended in 1948, but classes were continued in some parts of the islands into the early 1960s.

The early morning seminary program was introduced in Hawaii in 1953. It began in Honolulu and was supervised by Frank W. McGhie.[6] By the 1963-64 school year, 927 students were registered in seminary classes in Hawaii,[7] and by 1975 1,133 students were enrolled.

The Institute of Religion program at the University of Hawaii did not succeed until 1959, when Trevor Christensen took over the program. Since then the number of students at the Institute has expanded enough (152 institute students in 1975) to justify the construction of a new institute building near the campus.

The most significant LDS educational program, the Church College of Hawaii, was President David O. McKay's school: It was his idea; it was born of his vision and persistence. During President McKay's tour of Hawaii in 1921, he visited the temple, the plantation, and the elementary school at Laie, where he attended a flag-raising ceremony at the school. Elder McKay was deeply moved by the event and later wrote:

> As I looked at that motley group of youngsters, and realized how far apart their parents are in hopes, aspirations, and ideals, and then thought of these boys and girls, the first generation of their children, all thrown into what Israel Zangwell has aptly called the "Melting Pot" and coming out Americans, my bosom swelled with emotion and tears came to my eyes, and I felt like bowing in prayer and thanksgiving for the glorious country which is doing so much for all these nationalities. But more than that, when I realize that these same boys and girls have the opportunity of participating in all the blessings of the Gospel which will transform the American into a real citizen of the Kingdom of God, I feel to praise His name for the glorious privileges vouchsafed to this generation.[8]

With these thoughts in his mind, Elder McKay; his host, President Smith; and his companion, Brother Cannon, traveled by boat to Maui, arriving there the next morning. It was on this day that the sacred vision of the clasped hands occurred. It was also on this day, after many hours of meetings and discussions among the visitors and the Maui-based missionaries, that Elder McKay made a decision to recommend the founding of a new college to be built at Laie for the young Saints of Hawaii.

On a number of occasions during the next thirty years, President McKay spoke to the leaders of the Church in Hawaii concerning his school in Laie.[9] When he became president of the Church in 1951, President McKay took action immediately. Until then he had suggested, proposed, recommended, and encouraged the stake leaders in

Hawaii and the First Presidency on this matter. Now he directed that steps be taken to establish the school.[10]

Finally, on July 21, 1954, the establishment of a college in Hawaii was officially announced by the First Presidency. Dean Reuben D. Law of the College of Education at Brigham Young University was appointed the first president of the school.

A group of advisers was appointed to oversee the creation of the school. This body, known as the Continuing Committee, was composed of Edward L. Clissold, chairman, president of Oahu Stake; Ralph E. Woolley, past president of the stake and a successful businessman, contractor, and civic leader; D. Arthur Haycock, president of the Hawaii Mission; George Q. Cannon, counselor of the mission presidency and later president of the Pearl Harbor Stake; and Lawrence Haneberg, later a counselor in the Honolulu stake presidency. This group later became the board of trustees of the institution.

The Continuing Committee and President Law worked as quickly as possible to get ready for the opening of the college. The First Presidency proposed that the school be called "The Church College of Hawaii." In some ways the name became a problem. Outsiders frequently asked, "Which Church?" or "Who runs the college?" Nevertheless, CCH came to stand for a special educational institution with unusual purposes. These purposes and goals were made clear by President McKay when he dedicated the land on which the college is built.

Only a year after plans for the college were announced, President McKay journeyed to Laie to preside at the groundbreaking ceremonies of CCH. During the services he recalled his vision, thirty-four years before, of a school at Laie. Concerning the people who would teach in the college President McKay said, "No man or woman should teach in this college who doesn't have in his or her heart an assurance, not a mere belief, an assurance, that God has had a hand over this entire valley, that that dedication offered years ago was inspired, that this land is a choice land. It's part of America, part of Zion."

Then, in a spirit of prophecy, President McKay spoke of the destiny of the Church College of Hawaii: "You mark that word, and from this school . . . will go men and women whose influence will be felt for good towards the establishment of peace internationally.[11]

A major purpose of the college was missionary work. In his prayer dedicating the land for the college, President McKay said, "We dedicate our actions in this service unto thee and unto thy glory and to the salvation of the children of men, that this college, and the temple, and the town of Laie may become a missionary factor, influencing not thousands, not tens of thousands, but millions of people who will come seeking to know what this town and its significance are."[12]

At the time of the groundbreaking, President McKay met with the Continuing Committee and asked when the college would open. He was told that the target date was September 1956. To this President McKay replied, "I would like it to begin in the fall of 1955." In Brother Clissold's words, "There was a feverish several months of labor, but the school opened its doors on September 26, 1955, according to [President McKay's] wish."[13] Temporary war surplus buildings provided the first classrooms and offices.

There were 153 students and twenty faculty and administrators on hand when the first day of classes began. Since that time CCH has grown to 1,800 students with almost one hundred faculty members. The administrative organization and curriculum were quite broad for a new two-year school. There were nine divisions: Agriculture and Industrial Arts; Art and Music; Business Administration and Secretarial Training; Education; Home Living; Language Arts; Religion; and Social Sciences. Within these divisions were twenty-three departments.[14]

The permanent physical plant of the Church College of Hawaii was erected by building missionaries who were called by the Church to contribute two or more years to the construction project. The land for the college was dedicated in February 1955, but construction did not begin until December. The entire undertaking was directed by Joseph E. Wilson. At the height of the work, over fifty mainland missionaries or supervisors and their wives were working on the job. An additional seventy-five to eighty local building missionaries from all parts of the islands also participated. Local Saints from Laie also helped in different phases of the work. The wives of the builders cleaned all of the windows and laid around 174,000 square feet of floor tile. The completed buildings, designed for a student body of 1,000 to 1,200 people, cost around four million dollars. Since 1958—besides a number of dormitories—a library, a student center, a large activities center, and a new administration building have been constructed.

Dedication services for the initial and largest section of the college were held on December 17, 1958. President David O. McKay presided at this well-attended meeting. In his dedicatory prayer he stressed the missionary nature and purposes of the college. He paraphrased and quoted from the Doctrine and Covenants, section 88, verses 77-81, wherein the Lord outlines the kinds of knowledge men should seek and then explains why they should have this knowledge. President McKay prayed:

Aerial view of the Brigham Young University—Hawaii Campus. (Courtesy J. Elliot Cameron.)

> Thou hast emphasized the responsibility which rests upon thy people to carry the message of the restoration of the gospel to all nations. Thus doth thou emphasize the fact that it is not sufficient merely to testify to the world of the restoration, but to present the principles of the gospel in an intelligent manner that the honest in heart may be convinced of the truth, and may be led from paths of error into the way of righteousness.
>
> To this general and glorious purpose, therefore, our Father, we unitedly assemble and authoritatively dedicate The Church College of Hawaii.

In a later paragraph he once again mentioned the missionary responsibility and purpose of the school. He said, "May there radiate from these buildings an aura of light as tangible as personality radiates from each individual, influencing all to live clean and upright lives, to seek truth diligently, to be inspired so to live that others seeing their good deeds may live to glorify thee, our creator, our Father, our God."[15]

The Church College of Hawaii began as a two-year institution that granted associate degrees. In October 1959, after visits from evaluation teams, CCH was fully accredited as a two-year college. In that same year the Church's Pacific Board of Education authorized the expansion of the college to become a four-year teacher-training institution. Emphasis in the four-year course of study centered on the liberal arts curriculum.

The Church College was administered by four presidents during its nineteen years of existence separate from Brigham Young University. President Reuben D. Law served during the most difficult years. He had the problem of designing a new institution and working with an advisory board that was at times difficult to please, but he also had the satisfaction of seeing his ideas and theories about education brought into reality.

Dr. Richard T. Wootton, formerly a member of the faculty and director of the counseling center at the college, became the second president in June 1959. During his tenure in office the college achieved accreditation and four-year college status, new dormitories were added, the student body more than quadrupled, the faculty tripled, two student wards of the Church were organized, and the Polynesian Cultural Center was opened. The Polynesian Cultural Center was not Dr. Wootton's direct responsibility, but he was much involved in its planning and construction. More will be said of this later.

The third president of the college, Dr. Owen J. Cook, assumed office in August 1964. During his years as president the school was placed on a firm financial foundation. He was instrumental in obtaining approval for the Aloha (Student) Center and also for the construction of a number of married-student dormitories. Under his direction the first summer school was held in 1966. Dr. Cook left CCH during the spring of 1971 to accept a position as superintendent of schools in Colton, California.

In January 1969, the First Presidency announced the establishment of a Language Training Mission at CCH. The purpose of the mission was to teach Asian and Polynesian languages to missionaries going to East Asia and the South Pacific. The LTM remained at the college until 1975, when it was consolidated with all other language training programs at BYU in Provo, Utah.

The next president of the college was Dr. Stephen L. Brower, who came to CCH in July 1971, having recently been released as mission president for the Church in Colombia and Venezuela. During his tenure the college came to a crossroads where it was necessary to determine the direction, goals, priorities, and programs of the school. President Brower envisioned a college in which the sacred and secular parts of life were closely integrated. He was also concerned about the kinds of training programs and majors that were available for the students from Polynesia. He believed that too much emphasis had been given to the liberal arts and that the students needed training in specific technical skills. In his effort to make the curriculum more practical, he apparently infringed upon the established domains of some of the faculty, for some of them seriously opposed his efforts. Several faculty members left the college because they were not able or willing to adjust to the new regime.

Curriculum was not the only problem he was forced to confront. Influences of student radicalism, the drug culture, and other elements of the "counter culture" had crept onto the campus, and it was President Brower's problem to rid the school of such dissidence.

After unsuccessfully attempting to enlist the cooperation of the student-body officers in an effort to create a higher standard of behavior on campus, President Brower disbanded student government and asked the local stake officers to call student-body leaders through the priesthood to plan and direct student programs and activities. President Brower was once again sharply criticized for his action.

President Brower clarified the formal relationship of CCH with the Polynesian Cultural Center. Again his concern was with the missionary role of the college as it related to the Cultural Center.

In summary it can be said that even though Dr. Brower's presidency was a period of turmoil and change, it was also an era of significant progress for the school. He served as a catalyst that brought the purposes and objectives of the school into focus. He helped the faculty and student body understand their responsibilities as members of a Latter-day Saint institution.

On July 1, 1974, the Church College of Hawaii became a satellite branch of Brigham Young University,[16] and its name was changed to the Brigham Young University–Hawaii Campus. The Hawaii Campus is not a branch college; it is an administrative branch of the Utah school. Faculty members and administrators at the Hawaii Campus continued to determine the school's curriculum and to administer a separate budget. The school was to be administered by a dean (since changed to president) who was responsible to the president of BYU. The first dean of the Laie school was Dan W. Andersen, a specialist with many years of experience in the field of international education. Under President Andersen the student body grew to nearly two thousand, the current enrollment ceiling. Dr. J. Elliot Cameron, a vice-president at BYU–Provo, succeeded Dr. Andersen on August 1, 1980. During the Andersen-Cameron years, not only the student body but also the number of buildings grew. Included were a new library, a large activities center (the second largest indoor seating facility in Hawaii), and a new administration building, which served the needs of both the university and the Polynesian Cultural Center.

THE POLYNESIAN CULTURAL CENTER

In 1951 Elder Matthew Cowley and Edward L. Clissold entered into a discussion about the needs of the Maori Saints who regularly came to Laie to do temple work. Living costs for them were high. To counter this problem Elder Cowley suggested that the Maoris should build a large Maori house, a communal dwelling, where they could live inexpensively while at Laie. Also, he thought these people might do some entertaining, attract some tourists and thus make a little money to sustain themselves. But nothing immediately came of their discussion.[17]

When the college was constructed and students began to come to it from the South Pacific, President Clissold wanted to help them find ways to support themselves. He talked to a number of businessmen and encouraged them to establish businesses and industries in the Laie area. Some businesses were brought to Laie as a result of Brother Clissold's work, but not enough jobs were provided to take care of the students' needs.

As President Clissold and leaders at the college thought about the needs of the students and their abilities as dancers, singers, and living representatives of Polynesian cultures, they conceived a plan to create a living center of Polynesian culture and entertainment. The students, according to the plan, would provide a large part of the employees for the center, and thus their financial needs could be met.

President Clissold was in a strong position to accomplish the task of building the center. At that time he was stake president, manager of Zion's Securities Corporation in Laie, and a member of the Pacific Board of Education, which directed CCH. He was able to cut much red tape and move the work along quickly. Formal direction of the endeavor was given by the First Presidency to the Pacific Board of Education with Wendell B. Mendenhall as chairman.

The original center was constructed almost entirely by building missionaries. Covering sixteen acres, it was a cluster of huts with a lagoon winding among them. Included were six different villages: Hawaiian, Samoan, Tongan, Fijian, Maori, and Tahitian. Native craftsmen constructed the buildings to accurately represent the homes and other structures of the various Polynesian areas. The landscaping, too, was as authentic as possible.

Construction of the center began in early 1962 and went on for almost two years. On November 12, 1963, over one thousand people gathered at the center to hear President Hugh B. Brown dedicate the newly completed facilities. Although the directors of the undertaking, Brother Clissold and Brother Mendenhall in particular, were sure the new operation would be successful, many skeptics in Honolulu, some of whom held high positions in the tourist industry, prophesied doom for the center. An eighty-mile round-trip journey from Honolulu to Laie and back is too far, they argued. Tourists don't really want an authentic cultural experience, particularly if the dancers are dressed modestly, said other critics. But the Church leaders were right and the skeptics were wrong. Within four years after its official opening, the center was hailed as a grand success by Honolulu newspapers and leaders of the tourist industry. During 1975 more than 850,000 people visited the Laie, Hawaii, complex. By that time the show had been sold out each night for seven years. Only two free attractions in Hawaii drew more visitors—the Honolulu Zoo and Volcano National Park on the big island. In 1975 about half of the tourists who visited Hawaii

A hospitable host at the Polynesian Cultural Center. (Courtesy Polynesian Cultural Center.)

went through the PCC. By 1984, the PCC was the top-paid attraction in the islands, drawing over one million visitors a year.

The cultural center is a nonprofit organization of the Church. Its principal purpose was to provide employment for students at BYU–Hawaii (over 700 students worked there in 1984) and to generate money to help support that institution. The center has been successful in doing both of these things. In addition to the money earned for these purposes, the PCC has also produced sufficient surpluses to make a sizable contribution to the large expansion project that was completed during the summer of 1976 and dedicated on July 4 of that year.

The expanded facilities cover forty-two acres and include a 2,500-seat theater, a dining pavilion the size of a football field, a large departure building called *Hale O Navaa* (house of the canoes), a number of new cultural attractions, and service and administrative buildings. Since then, PCC administrative offices have been moved to the Snow Administration Building on the BYU–Hawaii Campus.

During the early years, the cultural center's main purpose was to provide student employment and financial support for the school. In 1973, however, when the new expansion was approved, the First Presidency modified the role of the PCC. The highest priority of the center was then seen as giving large numbers of people favorable contact with the Church. This priority recalls to mind the words of President McKay (quoted earlier) as he dedicated the ground for CCH, now called the BYU–Hawaii Campus: "We dedicate our actions to this service unto Thee and unto Thy glory and to the salvation of the children of men, that this college, and the temple, and the town of Laie may become *a missionary factor, influencing* not thousands, not tens of thousands, but *millions of people* who will come seeking to know what this town and its significance are." (Italics added.)

Another missionary tool, conceived and developed by Norman Nielsen and Steven Bennett of the PCC staff, was a free guided tour of Laie, the BYU–Hawaii Campus, and the temple grounds. To make the experience interesting, two replicas of 1910 Honolulu trams were purchased, and a monologue was prepared that told of the history of the Laie plantation, the purposes of the college, and a few ideas concerning the temple and why Latter-day Saints construct such edifices. The final stop on the tour was at the Temple Bureau of Information. By 1975 thousands of PCC visitors were participating in these free tours. According to Robert E. Crandall, then president of the Hawaii Mission, about 10,000 copies of the Book of Mormon were being distributed at the Temple Information Bureau each year, most of which were sold to people on the PCC tours. With the expansion of the center, the time soon came when "millions of people," as President McKay prayed, were being influenced each year by the BYU–Hawaii Campus, the temple, and Laie.

The building missionary program in Hawaii extended beyond the college and the Polynesian Cultural Center. The builders completely remodeled and enlarged the visitors' center (information bureau) at the temple, constructed homes for missionaries and workers who served at the temple and for the temple president, built homes for the faculty at CCH, and constructed a number of maintenance buildings and other auxiliary buildings for the college. Between 1960 and 1963, the big years of the building program, the building missionaries constructed seven chapel complexes on Oahu and another seven similar but smaller chapels and cultural halls on the outside islands. Other chapels were built during the remaining two years of the building missionary program.

LAIE, THE PLANTATION, AND ZION'S SECURITIES CORPORATION

Laie plantation was managed by Antoine R. Ivins from 1921 until he was called into the First Council of Seventy on October 8, 1931. One of his last official actions was to lease the cane lands to Kahuku Plantation Company until 1953. After Elder Ivins left, the plantation and community lands held by Zion's Securities Corporation (ZSC) were managed by William Waddoups; Frank and Ralph E. Woolley; and then, after 1951, by Edward L. Clissold. Brother Clissold served as manager and then chairman of the local ZSC board until 1970. The manager of the Laie lease lands of ZSC from the late 1950s and during the 1960s was Howard B. Stone, who had served as mission president in Samoa. His experience in Samoa helped in his dealings with the Samoan Saints of Laie.

The community of Laie was a company town. Until recently, virtually all of the property, with the exception of BYU–Hawaii Campus, the PCC, and lands used for Church purposes, such as chapels, belonged to ZSC. In recent years the economic and social functions of Laie have changed. Laie was originally purchased by the Church as a place where the Hawaiian Saints could be taught the arts of civilization, moral behavior, and good work habits. It later became a gathering place in the same sense as was Utah. In other words, Laie was to be simply a place where the Saints could gather out of the world. From the time of President Noall and President Samuel E. Woolley, the main purpose of the endeavor seems to have been to provide employment for the families living in the little village. During all this time the leaders of the mission continued to encourage the Hawaiian Saints to gather to Laie.

After the temple was constructed, the leaders of the Church in Hawaii stopped trying to persuade the Saints from the outer islands to move to Laie. There was not work for them there. The main immigrants to Laie after the temple was completed were Samoans and a smattering of Maoris, Tahitians, and later a fairly large group of Tongans.

By the early 1950s the Laie community had run the full gamut from a paternalistic sociological experiment to a modern, up-to-date, full-fledged business proposition. Rents for house lots in Laie had been as small as twenty-five cents a year in early days. Later they were only one dollar a month. When President Clissold took over ZSC in 1951, he found that many thousands of dollars in back-due rents, taxes, and other debts to the corporation were on the books. After evaluating the situation, he and his associates decided that the best course of action would be to have all of the Laie properties appraised and then to assign rental prices according to the real value of the land. They followed this procedure. They established three rent rates in accordance with the services provided to the various lots. The less valuable property continued to be leased at approximately the same low rate as before, but better lands were rented at higher charges. At that time ZSC also instituted a policy of rewriting all leases every five years. In this way rent rates could be adjusted to reflect changing economic conditions. The new system, unfortunately, worked a hardship on some Laie residents.

CONTINUED EXPANSION, THE REDEDICATION OF THE TEMPLE, AND THE HAWAII AREA CONFERENCE

In 1976 the Hawaii Temple was closed for remodeling. By June 1978, however, it was completely refurbished and ready for rededication. Having the First Presidency in Hawaii for these services would have made the rededication a major historical event, but the leaders of the Church made the occasion even more significant by holding the first area conference in the United States during the same week. President Spencer W. Kimball presided at the nine sessions of the rededication on June 13 through 15. He then presided at a priesthood solemn assembly in Laie on June 17, before meeting with the Saints in the area conference the following day. His talks to the 8,500 members and friends of the Church who gathered at the Neal Blaisdell Arena in Honolulu were similar to his speeches to the Saints at general conference: "Enough has been said. It is now time to 'do it.' " As he had admonished the Church since he assumed his prophetic role in 1973, he reiterated to the Saints of Hawaii his major theme: "We urge you to quicken your pace, lengthen your stride, move forward in your local ecclesiastical work." Many members who participated in the temple rededication, the solemn assembly, and the area conference described the eight days of meetings as the most spiritually stimulating period of their lives.[18]

With the creation of Kauai Hawaii Stake in July 1977, all the islands were encompassed in stakes. (By 1983 there were thirteen stakes in Hawaii.) The responsibilities of the mission president were reduced somewhat, but at approximately the same time the mission was expanding its efforts into a new part of the world, Micronesia. Although Guam had been under jurisdiction of the Hawaii Mission since 1970, it was not until 1975 that serious proselyting work was started there.

In the spring of 1980, the Micronesian part of the Hawaii Honolulu Mission was made an independent mission. Farron C. Lossee, who was a counselor in the Hawaii-based mission presidency, was appointed mission president (see chapter 28). As a result of this administrative change, the Hawaii Honolulu Mission was once again geographically limited to the area the mission encompassed when it was opened almost 130 years before. The geographical limitation notwithstanding, the 32,500 Saints in Hawaii remained a foundation stone of the Church in the Pacific. The thirteen stakes and forty-one wards, the temple, the BYU–Hawaii Campus, and the Polynesian Cultural Center were symbols of growth and expansion in Hawaii and the Pacific world.

PART 3

AUSTRALIA

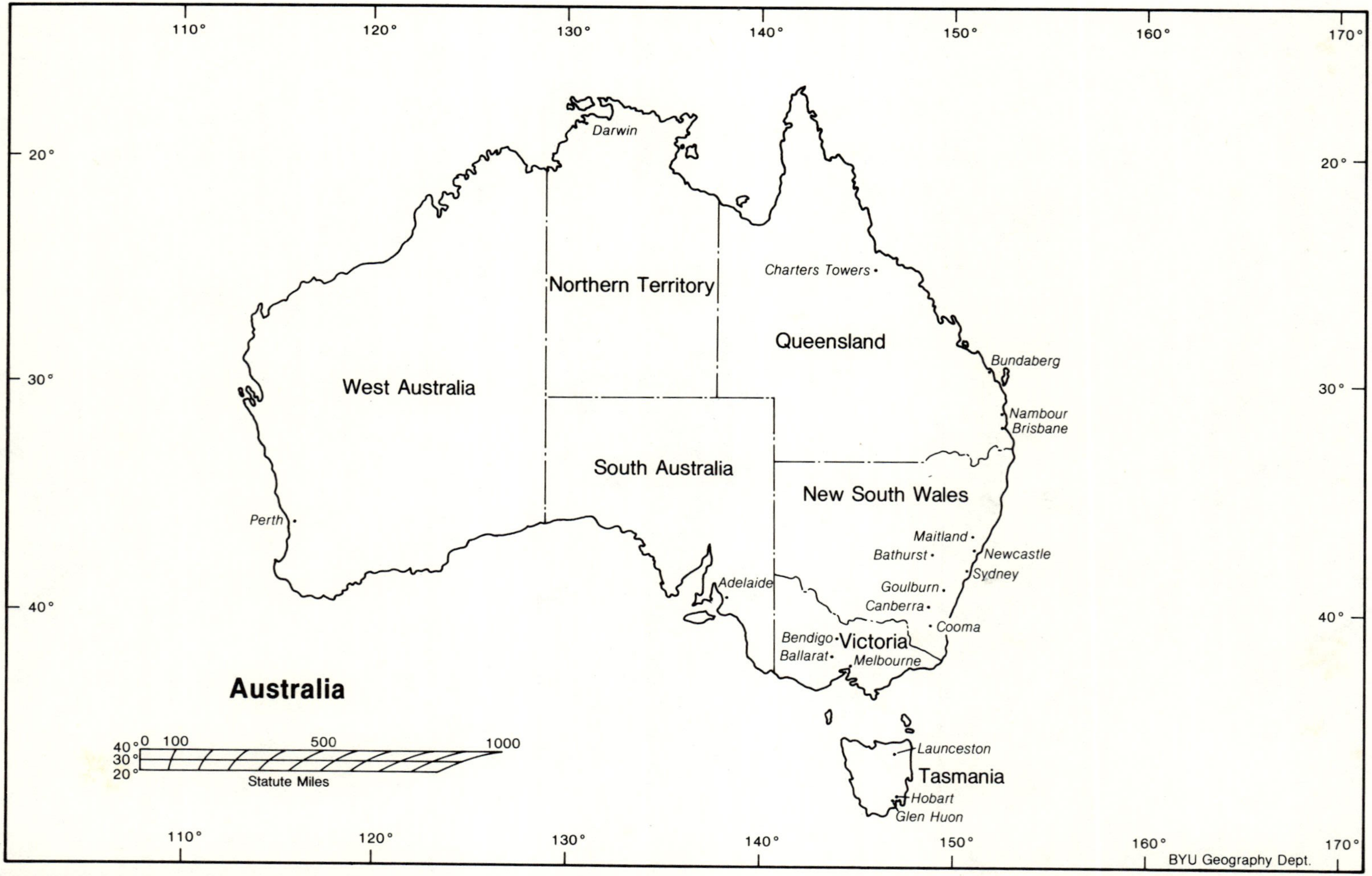

110°
120°
130°
140°
150°
160°
170°
20°
30°
40°
Darwin
Northern Territory
Queensland
Charters Towers
West Australia
South Australia
Bundaberg
Nambour
Brisbane
New South Wales
Perth
Maitland
Bathurst
Newcastle
Sydney
Adelaide
Goulburn
Canberra
Cooma
Bendigo
Victoria
Ballarat
Melbourne
Australia
0
100
500
1000
Statute Miles
Launceston
Tasmania
Hobart
Glen Huon
BYU Geography Dept.

CHAPTER 12

LAYING THE FOUNDATIONS IN THE LAND "DOWN UNDER"

Australia, 1851–1897

In comparison with the seven-month voyage of the first missionaries to French Polynesia or the eighty-six day trip of the second contingent of elders going to serve in India in 1852-53, the forty-nine days John Murdock and Charles W. Wandell spent at sea before arriving at Sydney, Australia, on October 30, 1851, seem relatively few. Sydney, Australia's oldest city, a western-style metropolis that boasted most of the modern features found in England or the United States, was different from other major centers in the Pacific and Asian area. In fact, Sydney and the other major cities of southeastern Australia were founded primarily by Britishers from England, Scotland, and Ireland.

The first colony in Australia was founded near Sydney in 1788. Within seventy-five years, settlements were established on several widely separated harbors, hardy colonists had created five states, and the vast, almost uninhabited interior had been explored. The most densely populated areas were (and are) New South Wales, Victoria, and South Australia, followed by Queensland and Western Australia. The island of Tasmania was settled by the 1850s, but the Northern Territory remained almost untouched.

In contrast with the United States, religious freedom was not an important factor for migration to Australia. In fact, Australia presented some conditions that hindered the spread of Christianity. Initially, Australia was a penal colony, and Port Jackson, later renamed Sydney, was created essentially as a place of exile for convicts. To be sure, many were not hardened criminals but simply underprivileged people or political agitators who had run afoul of the existing social order. The total number of convicts, both men and women, transported to Australia between 1788 and 1867 was around 160,000, and the land was "far from favorable soil for Christianity."[1] (By the turn of the twentieth century, only a few of the people could trace their ancestry to convicts because so many free settlers had migrated to Australia.)

However, Australia also presented some advantages for church people. Most of the settlers were from the British Isles, and they brought with them varieties of Christianity that were virtually the same as those of Great Britain. The newcomers transferred their British ways with relatively few changes; only the geography was different. But as time passed, their Christianity as well as other aspects of their culture changed.

One major change was the step-by-step reduction of the Church of England's status as an official state-supported religion to one of financial equality with the other major denominations. This was finally followed by the removal of all state support for public worship. This final step occurred in South Australia in 1851, in New South Wales in 1862, in Victoria in 1871, and in Western Australia in 1895. The gradual elimination of state involvement in religion made LDS missionary work easier than it might otherwise have been.

THE AUSTRALIA MISSION

Although John Murdock and Charles W. Wandell were called by Brigham Young and Parley P. Pratt to open missionary work in Australia, they were not the first LDS missionaries to preach the restored gospel "down under." The first was William Barrett, who was ordained an elder in July 1840 by George A. Smith and commissioned to teach the gospel "whenever and wherever he might have opportunity to do so." Young Barrett, a youth of seventeen, was ordained because he was leaving England for Australia, but whether he preached there with any success or baptized anyone remains in question. Two years later, Andrew Anderson, an early English convert, went to Sydney with his family. In 1845 he reported establishing a branch of eleven members.[2] By the time Murdock and Wandell arrived, however, Anderson had apparently moved to another place.

Elders Murdock and Wandell sailed from San Francisco on September 11 and arrived in Sydney, New South Wales, on October 30, 1851.[3] Within two days of their arrival, they engaged a printer to produce two thousand copies of a pamphlet, Parley P. Pratt's *Proclamation to the People of the Coasts and Islands of the Pacific.* To their satisfaction they found that this item sold quite well.[4]

Between November 1851 and July 1852, Elders Murdock and

Wandell expended considerable energy, time, and money on the publication of printed material. In addition to the *Proclamation*, they published Orson Pratt's long-used pamphlet *An Interesting Account of Several Remarkable Visions* (2000 copies); a selection of fifty-one *Latter-day Saints' Hymns* (500 copies); a clip-and-paste booklet by Charles W. Wandell titled *History of the Persecutions!! Endured by the Church of Jesus Christ of Latter-day Saints, in America* (64 pages; 2000 copies); a tract by Wandell replying to some local anti-Mormon literature, titled *Reply to Shall We Believe in Mormon?* Murdock and Wandell and the elders who followed them pursued the publishing course so sedulously that by April 1855, the editor of *Zion's Watchman* (an Australian publication) calculated that they had distributed 24,000 tracts and several hundred pounds sterling worth of books.[5]

Peter Crawley, a scholar of early LDS imprints, wrote, "The importance of these tracts goes far beyond the Australian mission, however. They are the earliest publications associated with that enormous effort in the early 1850s that spread the Mormon missions beyond North America and Western Europe, harbingers of publications that within the half-decade would come from San Francisco, Cape Town, Madras, and Calcutta."[6]

Zion's Watchman was begun after Elders Murdock and Wandell departed for home. The first issue was a four-page production used by the elders to fight anti-Mormon literature that was being circulated. *Zion's Watchman* was published from August 13, 1853, until April 1856, when time and manpower shortages stopped further publication.[7]

But Elders Murdock and Wandell also occupied themselves in public preaching. During their first two weekends they preached at the Sydney race course, the most public place they could find. But because fifty-nine-year-old Murdock's health prevented him from continued outdoor preaching, they rented a hall, "the Old Assembly Room," and began holding three meetings there each Sunday. A month after they opened the mission, they baptized their first converts. Joseph Popplewells was baptized on December 3, 1851—and his wife, Emily, and a friend, Bridget Gallimore, joined soon after. By the end of the year twelve names were on the records of the Church.[8]

The Sydney Branch was organized on January 4, 1852, with twelve members, including two priests, one teacher, and one deacon. By March 27, there were thirty-six members of the new branch, including two elders in the Melchizedek Priesthood.

The reports the elders sent home and to the *Millennial Star* in

England about the social and religious situation were somewhat contradictory. On the one hand, they said they could not get into private homes to preach because the gold rush, which was in progress at the time, was reported to have made people extremely suspicious of strangers. Wandell also said that Australians did not like Americans, and that the elders were not able to obtain free food and lodging.

On the other hand, they held three well-attended meetings every Sunday, preached five evenings a week, sold a large number of books (when they had them available), and baptized a fairly large number of people in a relatively short period of time. By June 2, 1852, when Elder Murdock sailed for home after turning over the presidency of the mission to Elder Wandell, there were forty-seven members of the Sydney Branch.

After Elder Murdock left, President Wandell expanded into new areas. Missionary work by several new converts made expansion possible. By July 1852, there were five local elders and two priests devoting full time to missionary service. Elder John Jones and John McCarthy opened the city of Maitland, about eighty miles northeast of Sydney, to the preaching of the gospel. They went there in response to a letter from an interested immigrant family from England and soon baptized three persons.[9] Other elders were sent to open other fields. For example, an Elder Batter was sent to Melbourne following the July 1852 conference of the mission.[10]

Between July 1852 and March 1853, the Church grew at a steady pace. A branch was created at Melbourne, Victoria, with twenty members; twenty people were converted in the Hunter and Manning Districts; and the Sydney Branch grew to sixty-three. By that time, March 1853, Elder Wandell was ready to return home. Because he did not have directions from Church headquarters in Utah, he set apart his counselor, John Jones, as mission president. This action was sustained by the Australian Saints in conference on March 23-27.[11]

If Elder Wandell had known that a group of ten new missionaries would be arriving within a week after his departure, he no doubt would have delayed appointing Brother Jones as mission president. The members of the Church received word that new missionaries had arrived on March 30, 1852. These brethren, lead by Augustus Farnham, who had been appointed to succeed President Wandell, were called at a special conference of the Church held in Salt Lake City on August 28 and 29, 1852. This conference is best remembered for the announcement that the doctrine of plural marriage would be made known to the world. Until that time the doctrine had not been openly preached outside of Utah.

Elder Farnham replaced Brother Jones, took over the reins of presidency, and assigned the missionaries to various areas. Elder John Jones accepted the calling of branch president over the Sydney Branch. William Hyde went to the Hunter's River district, then to Moreton Bay, later called Brisbane; Elders Frost and Smith went to Victoria; Elders Dowdle and Norton went to Adelaide and the Swan River settlement; Elders Graham and Eldredge opened the southwest part of New South Wales; and Elder Fleming remained in Sydney as President Farnham's counselor. Elder John Hyde, the remaining member of the group, was bedridden with throat cancer until his death in August 1853. He was the first LDS missionary to die in Australia.

Year by year the missionaries opened new cities, towns, and rural areas to the preaching of the gospel. Getting from one place to another was not easy, but it was no harder than in the United States.

Different missionaries had different impressions of Australia and its people. Elder Wandell concluded that he had never seen harder-working, more orderly people. William Hyde, on the other hand, advised member families in Wales not to travel to the United States by way of Australia (evidently the cost was less expensive this way even though the distance was much greater), for, said he, Australia was the "shortest cut to hell."[12]

Not long after the Farnham group arrived, the news of the polygamy issue reached Australia. It caused much unfavorable comment both outside and inside the Church. The issue was never put to rest until the Church changed its position in 1890, and there were reverberations from it well into the twentieth century.

GATHERING TO ZION

The principle of "gathering to Zion" was not taught in Australia until the Sydney branch had been organized for a few months. Then both Elder Murdock and Elder Wandell taught the members that they had an obligation to immigrate to Utah to be with the Saints. By October 1852, Wandell had a plan to establish an "emigrating fund" and to send a company of Saints by January 1, 1853.[13] His plans did not materialize quite as fast as he hoped, but on April 6, 1853, he led the first company of Australian emigrants from Sydney to California. Thirty Saints were in the group.

A view of beautiful Sydney Harbor. (Courtesy Ralph A. Britsch.)

It is not possible to reconstruct the entire story of Australian emigration. We do know, however, that at least ten companies left Australia between 1853 and 1859, and there were five hundred or more emigrants in these groups. Between 1860 and 1897, another ten to fifteen groups embarked for Zion, but these companies were generally smaller than the earlier ones. Perhaps as many as seven or eight hundred Saints left Australia to gather in Zion between 1853 and the turn of the century.[14]

The principle of gathering was important to the Latter-day Saints even before they moved to Utah. But after 1847 almost all missionaries were instructed to help converts come to the Utah Zion. Actually there were one or two exceptions to this rule. In his general epistle to the Church in December 1847, President Brigham Young told the Saints "on the Society and other Islands of the Pacific Ocean . . . to tarry where they are, for the time being, or until further notice." In contrast, he counseled members of the Church "in Australia, China, and the East Indies generally . . . to ship to the most convenient port in the United States, and from thence make to this point."[15]

Once the Church was established in Australia, the missionaries never slackened in their drive to send or to take their converts to Utah. President Farnham wrote, "So far as we can judge, we consider it best to push them [the Saints] to Zion as quick as circumstances will permit, for this is a very bad pasture in which to herd sheep."[16] "Epistles" were circulated among the Saints that informed new members that it was a commandment from the Lord to gather. Great "blessings, honor, glory, and exaltation" were promised to those members who would leave the "confines of Babylon" and go to Zion. It was only after the turn of the century that this policy changed.

But immigrating to Utah was a costly proposition. The price of a ticket usually ranged from sixty to one hundred and sixty dollars for an adult. Several of the missionaries observed that only the poor were willing to emigrate, which made it doubly hard to organize and prepare the Saints for emigration.

Not only was the trip to America costly, but there was also a certain amount of danger involved.[17] One group of Australian Saints met with disaster aboard the *Julia Ann,* a new seaworthy vessel, commanded by an able man, Captain Pond. When the *Julia Ann* sailed from Sydney on September 7, 1855, she carried fifty-six passengers, among whom were twenty-eight Latter-day Saints. On the night of October 3, the vessel struck a reef about twelve miles from Scilly Island, an atoll about two hundred miles west of Bora Bora in French Polynesia. Before many hours the ship was completely broken up. Five people, two women and three children, were washed into the sea and drowned. Brother John McCarthy later described the tragic moments in this way:

> I saw mothers nursing their babes in the midst of falling masts and broken spars, while the breakers were falling twenty feet high over the wreck. One lady, Sister Harris—preparatory to leaving the ship with her two children, the eldest of which was two years old—tied the youngest, a babe six weeks old, to her breast; the vessel immediately afterwards broke in two parts across the main hatch, and the water, rushing in, engulfed herself and the child amid the struggling waves and timbers of the wreck.
>
> There was another lady, Sister Humphrey, who had three children. When the vessel struck she told her friends to protect her children and convey them safely to Great Salt Lake City, for her earthly career was run. Shortly afterwards, she, with one of her children, was swept by the sea into the foaming surf, and they were seen no more.[18]

By constructing a raft and repairing one of the ship's quarter boats, the survivors were conveyed to Scilly Island, where they remained, living on sea turtle and wild fowl, for eight weeks. At the end of the seventh week repairs were completed on the quarter boat, and Captain Pond and nine men began rowing eastward. After four days of hard rowing they landed on Bora Bora, and within a few days the passengers of the *Julia Ann* were safely in Tahiti. They finally arrived in San Francisco in two groups in April and June 1856.[19] Tragedies such as this were uncommon; nevertheless, President Brigham Young cautioned all groups to be careful.

The high cost of transportation and relative danger notwithstanding, the Saints of Australia continued to gather to Utah until after the turn of the century, and even then, although the leaders of the Church discouraged further emigration, many Australian members continued to move to Zion. This strengthened the Church in Utah and the Mountain West, but emigration caused the Church to progress very slowly in Australia. A high percentage of strongly committed Saints were among those who left for Salt Lake City. In many cases entire branches departed for America.

In retrospect one cannot but feel that the membership of the Church in Australia would be larger if emigration had not been encouraged. On the other hand, it must be remembered that the Church was fighting for survival in Utah in these early years and needed the added strength and numbers that the new converts provided.

There is another justification for emigration. There are many examples that show that the Saints who remained in Australia did not necessarily build up the Church. Rather, they found themselves in a lifelong struggle to maintain their own faith. Too often they saw their children marry outside the Church, sometimes to people who were not only nonbelievers but who were antagonistic to Mormonism.[20]

After the Farnham group arrived, President Farnham rented an upstairs room at No. 12 Cooper's Terrace, Parramatta Street, in Sydney, to use as a mission office. He called Elder Josiah Fleming to act as his counselor and directed the missionaries, both foreign and local, to fan out all over southeast Australia. President Farnham wrote to the First Presidency several times during 1854 and 1855, asking for more missionaries. Several groups of elders arrived in Australia before problems in Utah caused a near shutdown of missionary work in 1858. (More on this later.)

The missionaries started work in New Zealand and Tasmania during 1854. In August 1854 President Farnham wrote to Brigham Young about reports that certain Maori chiefs were dissatisfied with the versions of Christianity they had been taught. President Farnham, like Elders Murdock and Wandell before him, believed that the time was right to open missionary work in New Zealand.[21] He did not let the matter die but pursued it at the next conference of the mission in October. There, the missionaries decided to send President Augustus Farnham and Elder William Cooke to New Zealand to investigate the possibility of sending permanent missionaries. On October 20, the two missionaries, accompanied by Thomas Holder, sailed for New Zealand on the steamer *William Denny*. When they arrived at Auckland seven days later, they found all the hotels filled with new immigrants. They finally found an unfurnished flat and stayed there a few days. They preached in and around Auckland but soon departed to Wellington, a city on the south end of the North Island. On December 11, 1854, President Farnham sailed from New Zealand for Australia. Elder Cooke labored and established a branch of the Church at Karori. When President Farnham reported to President Young about his trip, he painted a positive picture. He and Elder Cooke had found a number of people who were willing to listen to the gospel message; he also said that the Maoris were a "fine race" who would probably accept the gospel as soon as tracts and literature were translated into their language.[22] From this time until January 1, 1898, the mission was known as the Australasia Mission. (For more on New Zealand history, see chapter 16.)

Missionary work in Tasmania was begun by Robert Owen, a missionary to India, who left his post there before he was released, came to Australia, and then, without the full support of President Farnham, went to Tasmania. He sailed there on October 24, 1854. He had little success.

During 1855 the Farnham group was given permission to return home whenever they decided to leave. By the end of the year only six Utah elders remained in the country. Most of the elders returned home as leaders of emigrant companies. The last two missionaries to leave were President Farnham and Elder Fleming, who sailed on May 28, 1856, with one hundred and thirty Saints. President Farnham appointed Elder Absolom Dowdle president of the mission.

Between October 26 and December 12, 1856, sixteen new missionaries arrived, some of whom were sent to work in New Zealand; but from that time until 1859 affairs worsened. Seven of these new missionaries left the field before they were released because of internal dissension. However, some of the other elders had remarkable success. For example, Elder Amasa Potter and his companions in two years taught the gospel in twenty-three different cities and established branches in seven of them. This was in the face of ever-increasing persecution because of plural marriage.

In April 1858, the LDS missionaries received word concerning the possibility of war in Utah. They decided that their first loyalties were to their wives, children, and the Church at home. A fact that helped them decide to return home was a serious drought in Australia that had done terrible damage to livestock and farms.[23]

When the missionaries left, they turned the leadership of the mission over to the local Saints. Unlike Hawaii, where the departure of the missionaries caused serious difficulties within the Church, the local Australian members stepped in and ably handled the administration of the Church as long as there were enough Saints to carry on. The practice that caused the Church to fall into disorganization in Sydney and the other branches was emigration. Branch leaders kept leaving one by one. By 1863 the Church was in an almost totally disorganized state. Only about two hundred Saints remained in the country, and they were scattered all over southeastern Australia.

Local elders assumed callings as mission president and did their best to hold things together. Thomas Ford served well until his death in 1863, and then his counselor, William Broadbent, took over. In 1867, a new convert, Robert Beauchamp, began preaching in Melbourne and attracted good-sized audiences. He kept the Melbourne branch organized and thriving for a short time, but he immigrated with his family to Utah in 1868. A year later the First Presidency called him to return to Australia as mission president. He labored well for three or four years and sent at least four emigrant companies to Utah. But because he became involved in moral problems, he dropped out by 1874 and the Church was left in a state of confusion.

Elder William Geddes was appointed mission president in 1874, but he returned to Utah in 1875 after working in Victoria and Tasmania. In December 1879, Elder Elijah F. Pearce took charge of the Australasia Mission. He made his headquarters in Christchurch, New Zealand. The move reflected the shift of emphasis that had taken place in the mission. From that time until New Zealand became a separate mission in 1898, Australia was in a secondary position. Most of the missionaries were assigned to New Zealand, and by far the larger number of converts were baptized there. Three or four branches continued to operate in Australia during the years 1879 to 1898, but instability was the rule.

In August 1897, the First Presidency decided to separate the

Australia and New Zealand portions of the mission. This decision was motivated by the obvious need to place more emphasis on proselyting in Australia. The population there was over six million, more than three times that of New Zealand. On October 28, 1897, the Australasia Mission was divided, the action becoming effective on January 1, 1898. Andrew Smith, a missionary in Australia, was appointed the first president of the Australia Mission. The number of missionaries was immediately increased, and by 1900 there were twenty-one American elders serving in Australia.

CHAPTER 13

HOLDING OUR OWN AND A LITTLE MORE

Australia, 1898–1925

The division of the Australasian Mission into two parts, Australia and New Zealand, came on January 1, 1898. This division brought an end to the administrative ties that had existed between the two countries and brought a second "beginning" to the Australian Mission. From 1898 on, the missionaries and Saints of Australia had the benefit of direct guidance and supervision by a local mission president. Such local leadership helped the Church to move ahead more rapidly after 1898 than before.

Although the growth of the Church was relatively slow in Australia during the first twenty-five years of this century, it was not because of any significant opposition from the Australian people. True, there were occasional incidents in which antagonistic ministers from other faiths persecuted Mormon missionaries, but the predominant attitude of the Australian people was one of friendliness, tolerance, and willingness to allow the missionaries to carry out their work. The Australian people were, and are, deeply committed to religious freedom.

The accompanying table illustrates the growth pattern of the Church in Australia from 1910 to 1925:

Australian Mission Statistics, 1910-1925[1]

Year	Total Members	Convert Baptisms	Melchizedek Priesthood	Total Branches	Number of Missionaries
1910	660	59	3	8	46
1911	701	27		11	39

Year	Total Members	Convert Baptisms	Melchizedek Priesthood	Total Branches	Number of Missionaries
1912	724	43	11	10	44
1913	884				
1914	863	37	21	10	33
1915	913	39	25	10	28
1916	946	20	26	10	37
1917	974	37	27	10	36
1918	964	65	30	10	21
1919	976	31	30	10	20
1920	988	58	32		21
1921	1,025	30	34	8	26
1922	966	64	36		35
1923	1,053	90	36		27
1924	1,115	102	36	7	40
1925	1,169	65	40		40

Why did the Church grow so slowly during this period? Four principal reasons may be given: emigration, the small number of missionaries in the country, the vastness of Australia, and the lack of an effective proselyting plan. Around the turn of the century, the First Presidency changed its long-standing policy of encouraging members in foreign countries to migrate to Utah. The purposes of having a central Zion had been fulfilled, and it was now time to build up the Church throughout the world. This change of policy notwithstanding, it was difficult for both missionaries and members to reverse quickly a course that had continued for sixty or more years. Although immigration to Utah, or the "stakes of Zion," slowed down after 1900, an average of fifteen members still left Australia every year. Had they stayed, their added strength and zeal might have helped the Church to grow more rapidly.

The missionaries were as successful in Australia as in other parts of the world (they averaged 1.55 converts per year). The problem lay in the small number of missionaries in a very large country. Between 1910 and 1925 the average was thirty-one missionaries a year. This sounds large in comparison with the smaller groups of elders who served in Samoa, Tonga, and French Polynesia, but Australia is roughly the size of the United States, and by that time it was fairly well

Missionaries arriving in Sydney around 1900. (Courtesy LDS Church Archives.)

populated. By 1901, Sydney had 481,830 inhabitants; the state of New South Wales had 1,400,000 people; Melbourne boasted a population of 496,079; and the state of Victoria had 1,200,000 people. Australia's population in 1901 was 3,773,801, most of it located in the southeastern area from Brisbane to Adelaide, a distance similar to that from Washington, D.C., to New Orleans. By 1921 the national population had increased to 5,435,734.

From 1907 until well after this period, the Church in Australia was divided into six conferences (or districts). These conferences corresponded to the six states of the nation: Queensland (which is larger than Texas), New South Wales, Victoria, Tasmania, South Australia, and Western Australia (the last area to be opened to LDS proselyting, and nearly the size of Alaska). There were usually only from four to six missionaries in each state.

Missionary work was not started in Perth, Western Australia, until 1907, and it took some time before a branch was well established there. During one period, the Western Australia Conference went three years without a visit from the mission president. In 1902 it had taken President James Duckworth four months to visit the conferences in eastern Australia, Victoria, South Australia, and Tasmania. The mission headquarters for all of Australia were at Sydney, New South Wales, several thousand miles away from Perth. The transcontinental railroad connecting Perth and Adelaide was not built until 1917. Until that time it took the missionaries as many as twenty days to sail from Sydney to Perth.

The proselyting methods employed, like those used in most other parts of the Pacific, were not very effective. This was true until the 1950s. The main differences between early proselyting methods and those used since 1952 are the step-by-step teaching plans and the more forceful use of challenges.

During the early decades of this century, the missionaries usually lived in the large urban areas such as Sydney, Melbourne, Adelaide, or Hobart, or in the surrounding communities. The senior or presiding elder served as both the president of the conference and the leader of the missionaries. Sometimes other missionaries served as branch presidents, especially in new branches. Thus the missionaries devoted much time to branch and conference business.

A typical day consisted of several hours of tracting in the morning, then lunch and visits with members and investigators during the afternoon and evening. The missionaries used some evenings for attending meetings such as Mutual Improvement Association, and others for holding street meetings. In Sydney, they almost always devoted Friday evenings to street meetings because the stores remained open that night and brought large numbers of people into the streets. For many years the missionaries who lived within reasonable traveling distance from the mission headquarters gathered there early Friday evening for a report meeting and meal and then walked downtown together to hold a public meeting. Street meetings always began with a hymn followed by a prayer offered by one of the missionaries. After the prayer, an elder spoke on some gospel subject. There were almost always hecklers in the audience who made jokes, asked difficult questions, or created a disturbance in other ways. But some of the missionaries still believed that the street meetings were the most effective method of getting people interested in the gospel message.[2]

The missionaries handed out hundreds of thousands of tracts. In 1907 alone they distributed over 225,000 tracts throughout Australia. This was in addition to the circulation and selling of a large number of Church books. But the very fact that so many pieces of Church literature were distributed and so few converts were made that year (there were only ten convert baptisms in 1907) speaks poorly for tracting as a method of bringing people into the Church. The Book of Mormon seems to have been used very little as a proselyting tool.

The missionaries spent much time visiting investigators and members. These visits did not follow the same pattern as that used by later missionaries, when each meeting was held to accomplish a specific purpose or to teach a lesson. During the early days, missionary visits were primarily for friendshipping. President Marion G. Romney, who served his mission in Australia from 1920 to 1923, recalled later that there was a danger of the elders covering too much ground when they did get into a gospel conversation or lesson. "In that day we gave them everything from pre-existence to final exaltation in one lesson."[3]

As late as the 1930s, but more frequently during earlier decades, the missionaries went traveling and tracting in the countryside "without purse or scrip." These preaching trips seldom lasted more than two or three weeks, but they were tests of faith for the elders and tests of the kindness of the Australian people. The missionaries seldom went without meals, but they were frequently drenched in rainstorms and often walked twenty or thirty miles a day.

Only occasionally did such trips into the rural areas bring about results. Clarence H. Tingey, who served in Australia from 1917 to 1919, and again in the late 1920s and early 1930s as mission president, has estimated that fewer than 10 percent of the Church members lived

The Toowoomla branch, Australia, consisted of two missionaries, two boys, one man, and ten women in 1913. (Photo from the *Improvement Era*.)

outside the bounds of the major urban centers.[4] Although these Saints were not members of regular branches, they did create a foundation for later groups, branches, and finally wards that have developed throughout the continent. The courage of the Saints who lived their lives without the blessing of an organized branch deserves praise. The mission records mention families, single persons, and small groups of Saints who carried on the best they could. Elder Tingey remembered a group of seven women and one ten-year-old boy who somehow remained together and faithful to the Church at Charters Towers, a small mining town in northern Queensland. They had no priesthood to bless them, direct their meetings, or administer the sacrament, but they remained faithful to the principles of the gospel.

While Clarence Tingey was serving as conference president in Queensland, he was asked to visit a family who had written for information about the Church. Elder Tingey traveled by train to a barren part of the country, approximately 180 miles west of Brisbane. After a ride of a few miles by wagon, he arrived at the home of his investigators. He found them to be poverty stricken, and the father of the family, Lance Brown, was completely deaf. Brother Tingey proceeded to teach the entire family the gospel. To do this he had to learn a certain amount of sign language. After two days Tingey needed to return to Brisbane. Mrs. Brown, learning of his intention to leave the next morning, said, "Elder Tingey, we've discussed matters very frankly, and we want you to baptize us before you leave in the morning." Elder Tingey replied by telling the Browns to pray about their decision and to ask the Lord for direction. He promised them that he would do the same thing. Then he added, "Furthermore, Mrs. Brown, you will know that God lives."

At five o'clock the next morning Elder Tingey was awakened by the rumbling of wagon wheels outside of his bedroom window. When he looked out, he saw the family all dressed in white. They obviously had their answer. After driving to a dry river bed, they finally found a pool of clear water where Elder Tingey baptized Brother Brown, his wife, and their three oldest children. He confirmed them all immediately after.

Following the baptisms, Elder Tingey left. Eight years later, when he returned to Australia as mission president, Brother Tingey met Sister Brown at a Sunday service in Brisbane. She greeted him, saying, "Elder Tingey, I know that God lives." Brother Brown had died, but the family had remained faithful to the Church and had moved into Brisbane. Later some members of this family immigrated to the Blackfoot, Idaho, area. Like the Browns, a number of Australian converts lived the gospel without the help of organized units of the Church. Their willingness to build the Church alone contributed to the strength it developed in later years.[5]

The Brown family's request for baptism after only two days was unusual. More frequently the missionaries met with investigators for months or years.

ISSUES, PROBLEMS, AND DEVELOPMENTS

The Latter-day Saint missionaries in Australia were usually treated kindly; however, there were some notable exceptions to this general pattern. Ironically, the most difficult problems were caused by representatives of the "Josephites," members of the Reorganized Church of Jesus Christ of Latter Day Saints (RLDS). Their opposition to the Mormon mission was especially strong in the Brisbane area, where the RLDS were most numerous, but problems also arose in other areas. In 1902, 1903, 1913, and 1918 the RLDS anti-Mormon assaults were heavy. In 1902 the elders in Brisbane reported that some members of the branch had gone over to the RLDS and that the little branch hung by a thread because of the opposition. In early 1903 the missionaries wrote, "No one says more terrible things about our character than the Josephites." These attacks were evidently directed by the two RLDS apostles who were living in Australia at that time.[6]

An upsetting situation developed between the Latter-day Saints and the RLDS in Adelaide, South Australia, in 1913. RLDS members circulated through crowds at LDS street meetings, spreading false stories and heckling the elders. They then took the platform after the Mormon elders had finished and continued their abusive verbal assaults. The elders reported that the RLDS caused several mobbings and breakups of open-air meetings. As a result of these disturbances, the Adelaide police asked the Latter-day Saints not to hold further street meetings.[7]

The most serious confrontation between representatives of the two churches came in 1918. During that year the Mormon elders in Brisbane agreed to debate with some representatives of the RLDS on the question of the succession of the presidency of the Church. The debate was held in the RLDS hall, before a primarily RLDS congregation. The Mormon elders were not well enough prepared, nor were they skilled debaters. And because they did not know the issues well enough, they clearly lost the debate. As a result of this interchange and the issues it raised, twelve members of the Mormon Church fell away and were later excommunicated. After that encounter the LDS missionaries reported very few direct dealings with the RLDS. This was probably because the LDS elders could see that no good could be accomplished through argumentation and debate.[8]

World War I had an upsetting effect on Australia's economic and social life. Consumer goods were scarce, and food and petroleum products were rationed. Many young Australian men entered the armed forces and fought in Europe. But most Australians, like most Americans, did not feel the war's tragic impact until it was almost over.

The effects of the war on the Church were not serious, but it created some inconveniences. Manpower was the worst problem; men were needed to lead the branches, and men were needed from America to serve as missionaries. The number of missionaries dropped from around thirty before the war to only eighteen by late 1919.

The Church was ready to send more missionaries to Australia by late 1919. In fact, the Home and Territories Department of the Australian government had agreed in September 1918 to permit twelve new missionaries to enter.[9] After the war ended, however, the issue of Mormon missionaries received considerable attention in London. Because of the efforts and lobbying of certain anti-Mormon forces, the British government turned down all applications for entry made by Mormon missionaries. This was done by continuing the policy that had existed during the war of refusing entry to missionaries in general, but now limiting the policy to exclude only LDS missionaries while allowing others. This policy was then extended to Australia, New Zealand, Tonga, and other parts of the British Commonwealth and the British protectorates. Through the efforts of LDS Church leaders in Utah and Britain, and with the help of United States government officials, the ban was eventually lifted. By April 1920, the government of Australia decided to allow LDS missionaries into the country in the same numbers as before the war.[10]

From 1918 to 1923 the Church was confronted with still other problems. During 1918 a movie titled "The Mormon Maid," which the elders described as "an immoral, villainous, and slanderous picture, purporting to be an exposure of 'Mormonism and its hidden secrets,' " was shown in theatres throughout Australia. "We get some pretty warm times over it," wrote an elder in Tasmania.[11]

During 1922, President Don C. Rushton reported to the Presiding

President and Sister Don Carlos Rushton. (Photo from the *Improvement Era*.)

Bishopric that the Church had "been assailed by the papers that have copied stories from the English papers, but in most cases we have been allowed to reply." President Rushton was referring to a strong anti-Mormon attack that Winifred Graham had launched in England. She revived many old falsehoods about the Church and polygamy and led many to believe that hundreds of English girls were led away to lives of slavery in Utah. This material was reprinted in Australia and caused some problems for the Church.

As a result of this anti-Mormon attack, and perhaps as part of it, the Ministerial Society, as President Rushton called the group, "tried hard to have us turned out of Australia, and to prevent us from building churches."[12] Before the end of 1923, however, the Church had been declared "a religious denomination" by the executive council of the state of Victoria.[13] When President Rushton submitted his annual report for 1923, he said the Church was in better favor with the government than at any other time in the history of the mission. During 1924, President Charles Hyde applied for and obtained permission to raise the quota of missionaries to forty.

THE VISIT OF ELDER DAVID O. MCKAY TO AUSTRALIA

During August and September 1921, Elder David O. McKay and his traveling companion, Hugh J. Cannon, visited Australia as a part of their around-the-world missions tour. During his month in Australia, Elder McKay traveled over four thousand miles and visited all of the conferences but Perth, Western Australia.[14]

THE BUILDING OF CHAPELS

By 1925 the membership of the Church had grown to almost twelve hundred members, who composed eight branches and six conferences (or districts). These branches varied in size but averaged 150 members. Even Sydney, the largest conference, had only 300 members. It is more surprising that the branches were able to build chapels by the mid-1920s than that they had not done so before that time.

The first branches in Sydney, Brisbane, Melbourne, Adelaide, and Hobart were established during the 1890s. Brisbane was first, in 1893, and Enmore Branch in Sydney followed in 1895. Tiny branches were established in other cities before 1900. In Brisbane the complete organization of the Church was developed, with a Sunday School in 1894, MIA in 1895, and Primary and Relief Society in 1898. None of the other branches grew fast enough to organize these auxiliaries so early. As late as 1922 there were no other organized Relief Societies or Primaries.

Brisbane Branch developed first. The Brisbane members initially held their meetings in the home occupied by the missionaries. When the branch became too large for them to continue meeting there, they rented an old store and used it for a meeting hall; and when the branch outgrew the store, they moved to the Alliance Hall in Woolloongabba, a subcity within greater Brisbane. But by 1904, the branch was so large and the members' desire to have their own place of worship so great that they bought a lot on Gibbon Street, Woolloongabba, in August; by December 4, the members and missionaries had erected a chapel. The building served the needs of the Brisbane Conference for many years. It was also the only LDS-owned meetinghouse in Australia until the 1920s.

The Saints in other Australian branches also wanted to own their own chapels. Throughout the country, with the exception of Brisbane, they had rented rooms and halls from fraternal organizations or civic groups. The Saints in Adelaide purchased a building lot in 1914, but, lacking the necessary money and because of World War I, they were unable to move ahead with building until 1922. The members of Melbourne Branch organized a building-fund committee in 1919 and began holding choir concerts, bazaars, and other benefits to raise funds for a new chapel. After three years of efforts, President Don C. Rushton laid the foundation stone for the Melbourne chapel on November 4, 1922. Less than two months later, on December 31, 1922, the Saints dedicated their new hall.[15]

In January 1923, the new chapel in Adelaide was completed. On January 13, 1924, the chapel in Enmore, Sydney, was dedicated by President Rushton. In 1925 the Saints in Hobart, Tasmania, dedicated their new building. The members of the Church in Perth, Western Australia, built a new chapel by June 1925.

By the time the Perth chapel was completed, the Saints in every conference had their own meetinghouses. The buildings were modest rectangular brick structures with chapels upstairs, classrooms below, and small missionary quarters behind. President Rushton directed the construction of three buildings. President Charles Hyde directed the completion of two more chapels by mid-1925, and a third meetinghouse at Glen Huon, Tasmania, in 1927.

By 1925 the Church was firmly established in Australia. The governments of some states recognized the Church as a legitimate religious organization. The branches were generally well organized and were led for the most part by local members; at least the auxiliaries were usually directed by Australian Saints. The Australian government allowed forty missionaries into the country and put no restrictions on printed materials or proselyting methods. The circumstances seemed right for rapid growth and development of the Church. No one, however, could have foreseen the coming of the Depression and World War II and the delaying effects these events would have on the development of the Church.

CHAPTER 14

CONSTRUCTING A STRONG SPIRITUAL AND ORGANIZATIONAL FOUNDATION

Australia, 1926–1950

Between 1926 and 1951, Church membership in Australia grew from 1169 to 2187. The average number of converts was fifty-eight per year. During the same period almost 360 Saints immigrated to Canada and the United States. The most intensive period of movement was between 1945 and 1950, when 120 Latter-day Saints—5 percent of Australia's Church membership—left the country.[1]

Even though the Church did not grow rapidly in Australia during the quarter century from 1926 to 1950, the missionaries and members constructed a strong spiritual and organizational foundation for later leaders and members to build on.

THE DEPRESSION YEARS

President Charles H. Hyde served twice as mission president. His first term was from 1911 to 1913, and his second from 1924 to 1928. Brother Hyde was a warm, kind man, neither argumentative nor aggressive. But he was orderly, and during his second mission he devoted much of his energy to teaching the importance of accurate record keeping. He also placed the mission on a firm, businesslike basis.[2] He wanted to open new areas to the preaching of the gospel, and he did send elders into one or two new towns during 1928, but he was hampered by having only thirty-one or thirty-two missionaries during the last two years of his mission. In 1927 he wrote the First Presidency and said, "We are holding our own. . . . We cannot do the country work [rural tracting] we would like to because of the shortness of elders. Those we have devote most of their time in looking after the saints."[3]

President Tingey, who succeeded Brother Hyde in November 1928, felt the same need for more missionaries, but more missionaries were not forthcoming. Instead, conditions grew more difficult. The great economic depression that began in 1929 affected Australia as it did the rest of the industrialized world. Because of difficult financial conditions in America, many Latter-day Saint families were unable to support their sons on missions. As a result, the numbers of elders declined steadily until 1935.[4]

Even though conditions became difficult, President Tingey refused to slow down the work of the mission; he led his missionaries to greater success than had ever been achieved before.

In 1929 President Tingey recognized that the Church leaders in Salt Lake City would be unable to meet the missionary needs of the Australian Mission. Late in that year he wrote, "To partially overcome this condition we are organizing local Branch Presidencies wherever possible, relieving missionaries from some detail among the Saints, permitting expansion into new fields."[5] In later years this move to assign local Saints to leadership positions proved to be one of the most important changes in administration during the first half of the century. President Tingey did not succeed in turning all branch presidencies over to local men, but he called enough Australian priesthood holders into leadership positions that when World War II began, the local members were prepared to take care of their own Church needs.

President Tingey introduced several other changes. Finding the monthly reports inadequate, he asked each missionary to write him a personal letter with each report, explaining his feelings, asking questions about the gospel, telling about spiritual experiences, and so forth. In return, President Tingey wrote letters back to each elder as often as possible. Through this means the missionaries learned of the mission president's personal concern for them, and they found out how strongly he desired them to succeed.

In an effort to distribute more copies of the Book of Mormon, the missionaries held special fast days once a month. President Tingey reported that the number of Books of Mormon distributed increased considerably.

In 1930 the missionaries and President Tingey conceived and launched the *Austral Star,* the first mission publication since the days of *Zion's Watchman.* Although it was started primarily to serve the needs of the missionaries, local Saints contributed many articles and notices. Early issues also contained suggested lessons for monthly

President and Sister Charles H. Hyde, 1929. (Photo from the *Improvement Era*.)

missionary visits to the members. Also included in the *Star* were regular question-and-answer articles, originally written by President Tingey but later written by other presidents; brief notices of changes in each of the districts and branches; and other articles designed to educate and inspire readers. The *Austral Star* was published until the mission was divided in 1955. After that time other publications came into being.[6]

In 1929 a Primary was organized in Brisbane—the first in the mission for nearly three decades. In the following year a Primary was created in the Hobart Branch.

The first all-mission conference was held at Melbourne from April 1 to 7, 1930. This series of meetings, banquets, games, and dramatic productions commemorated the centennial of the founding of the Church. Many members participated in meetings with the largest group of Saints ever assembled in Australia.[7]

During 1930 the Saints of the Australian Mission sent their first full-time missionary into the field. Ezra Oswald Watson of Glen Huon, Tasmania, accepted a call to serve a mission in New Zealand. Not long after Elder Watson's call, two other Australians, Horace H. Woodford and J. Kenneth Rule, accepted missionary assignments for two years in their native land.[8]

In 1931 President Tingey created genealogical organizations in each of the districts. The leaders of these organizations were charged with the responsibility of teaching the importance of temple work, genealogical research, and the concept of the eternal family.[9]

Because of the innovations that President Tingey introduced to the mission, and because the missionaries were working longer hours than they had done before, the mission was more successful than it had ever been. The number of convert baptisms per missionary rose to 3.1 during 1931 and 1932 and averaged 2.6 during 1933 and 1934. It must be remembered that the number of full-time missionaries was steadily dropping during these years. By 1933 the mission staff was down to eighteen missionaries. "The greater proportion of their time," wrote Brother Tingey, "is required in protecting existing organizations." In an effort to further shore up the proselyting efforts, President Tingey called eleven Australian elders to serve for a full two years as part-time missionaries. He assigned them to proselyte and to maintain contact with the Saints through a system of "block-teaching." All eleven greatly aided the full-time elders in their work.[10] But even the use of local part-time missionaries did not completely solve the manpower problem.

The missionaries devised various methods for keeping in touch with and strengthening the members who lived in outlying areas. The most successful was weekly correspondence Sunday School lessons. Over two hundred Saints received these lessons during 1933.

Church relations with the government improved between 1926 and 1935. Probably the most important event was the achievement of official recognition for the Church. Prior to 1931, legal status had been granted to the Church in all states but New South Wales and South Australia. However, a large percentage of the Church members resided in New South Wales, and they did not like having to be married or buried by a Catholic father or a Protestant minister. President Tingey arranged to meet with Prime Minister Bevan of New South Wales, who introduced him to a cabinet member who, however, refused to consider granting legal status to the Church because of its past practice of polygamy. After corresponding for several weeks and receiving nothing but negative replies, President Tingey told the official that he was going to obtain a writ of mandamus. The cabinet officer agreed to reconsider. He asked President Tingey to cut section 132 of the Doctrine and Covenants from every book distributed in New South

Wales. The President refused to do so, but he offered to sign a sworn statement attesting that the Church had not practiced polygamy or taught the principle since 1890. This was agreed to, and since that time mission, district, and branch leaders have been recognized as church officials with the authority to marry and bury their members. South Australia granted the same rights soon after recognition was given to the Church by New South Wales in early 1931.[11]

Shortly afterward, President Tingey was released from his mission because of the ill health of both his and his wife's mothers. He assigned L. DeVon Mecham to act as mission president until a replacement could be called by the First Presidency. During Elder Mecham's term, the Australian government changed its immigration quotas, and it appeared for a time that missionaries along with all other aliens might be prohibited from entering the country. The reason for the tighter restrictions was the high cost to the government of supporting people who were out of work. Twenty-five percent of Australia's working force was unemployed during the height of the Depression. Most of these people were supported by the government dole. Because the greatly diminished national income resulted in decreased tax money, the government was hard pressed to meet the needs of its people, and it ultimately decided to keep most foreigners out of the country. Since the banning of Mormon missionaries would have seriously hampered the Church's effectiveness among its own people, acting President Mecham traveled to the national capital of Canberra to discuss the matter with the Secretary of Home Affairs. He was assured that if immigration were stopped, he would be notified immediately and be given whatever assistance was possible. Brother Mecham returned to Sydney with the strong impression that the national government generally held a favorable opinion of the Mormons.[12] From that time on, the position of the Church evidently gained favor in the eyes of the Australian people. Not long after Brother Mecham's visit to Canberra, the general authorities learned that President and Sister Tingey were free to resume missionary work, and in February 1932, after only ten months, they returned to Australia.

FIVE YEARS OF GROWTH—1935-1940

By December of 1935 the mission force had grown from fifteen to twenty-nine. And by the end of 1936 the total number of missionaries was forty-seven (the quota was then fifty). From 1937 through most of 1940 the number of missionaries remained at about that level.

The additional missionaries made it possible for the Church to expand in a number of areas. President Thomas D. Rees, who began serving as mission president in June 1935, sent missionaries to towns where work had been stopped earlier in the decade because of the Depression. He also opened several new fields. During 1935 a new branch was formed in Nambour, north of Brisbane, and branches were reorganized in Bendigo, Victoria, and Newcastle, New South Wales, both of which had been closed during the worst years of the Depression. In 1936 two other branches that had been closed during the Depression were reopened, at Goulburn, New South Wales, and Ballarat, near Melbourne. In addition, new branches were started at Bundaberg, north Queensland, and at Como and Bathurst in New South Wales. During 1936 the Saints at Nambour raised money and bought a chapel. President Rees dedicated the building on September 23, 1936. By the end of 1937, there were seven branches in New South Wales, the newest of which was Woollahra Branch in Sydney.[13]

By the end of 1937 President Rees wrote to the First Presidency: "This mission is growing. People everywhere are willing to listen to the elders. As a rule the elders are treated with courtesy and respect as they visit from door to door." He reported that he had created the new mission positions of mission Sunday School superintendent, genealogical supervisor, MIA superintendency, and a Primary presidency, and in most cases had called local Saints to fill the assignments.

Yet there were some areas of concern. First, the newly reorganized branches at Bendigo and Ballarat were again closed because there were not enough members to continue holding services. But beyond this, there was the more serious, ongoing problem of a high percentage of the young women marrying outside the Church. There was nothing that President Rees could do about this problem because women in the Church drastically outnumbered the men; from 1925 to 1950, there were 31 percent more women than men. Not until the late 1950s did the ratio of men to women become equal.[14]

On February 21, 1938, Elders George Albert Smith and Rufus K. Hardy arrived in Sydney. They visited all of the major branches in the southeastern part of the country, discussing the construction of chapels and counseling with missionaries concerning their work.

During 1938 the Australian Mission started using basketball teams and radio broadcasts as proselyting tools. President Tingey had been the first LDS missionary to give a religiously oriented, although not Mormon-oriented, talk on radio. This was in 1934, and he had been so successful that the station manager had invited him to speak again. Almost four years passed, however, before the missionaries were able to arrange to be on other stations. During 1938, several elders appeared on radio programs to talk about the United States. Usually they were able to get in a word or two concerning their reasons for being in Australia. In 1939 the mission succeeded in getting several stations to play religious music by the Mormon Tabernacle Choir on Sundays. In 1940, a number of stations in various parts of Australia began airing "Music and the Spoken Word," by Richard L. Evans and the Tabernacle Choir. "This broadcast," wrote President Judd, "is fast becoming one of the most popular programs on the air here in Australia."[15]

In a country where sports were well liked, the Church used basketball as its most important tool for making friends. Elders in the Melbourne area entered tournaments and were very successful. President Judd wrote:

> They emerged victorious in the basketball series and have received the name among most of the people of Melbourne of being typical examples of clean, fine, and upstanding manhood. One year ago the people had exactly the opposite opinion of the Elders. [This was an overstatement.] Mr. Burge, director of the Y.M.C.A. at Melbourne said, "I have never associated with a cleaner group of young men in all my life."
>
> Through basketball the Elders have been able to tell of Mormonism in interviews over the radio and have received more favorable publicity for the Church in the newspapers than it received in all the years of its organization in Australia. . . . The elders report that basketball has done more good than all other types of work combined. As a direct result we have already received a number of baptisms.[16]

During 1939 elders in South Australia and New South Wales also organized teams. Two of the three teams won championships in their districts. In 1940 the missionary teams in Victoria and South Australia both won their state championships. Other elders made many friends in Sydney by coaching over three hundred members of basketball teams there.[17] One of the teams was featured in a movie about the game that was seen by more than a million people. The elders continued to play basketball, and also softball, through most of 1940, but the momentum created was cut short by World War II.

WORLD WAR II AND THE EVACUATION OF THE MISSIONARIES

Germany invaded Poland on September 3, 1939. Prime Minister Menzies of Australia announced to his people that Australia was at war. In an effort to help the mother country, the Australian government took steps to enlarge the production of supplies, foodstuffs, and war equipment. Australians also raised, trained, and equipped an army to serve with the British overseas. By November 1939 the government had introduced compulsory military training for home service. At the end of the year the Australians sent a division to Palestine to be trained before joining British forces in France.[18] Before long another Australian division was sent abroad, and many "Aussies" saw action in the Middle East and in other parts of the European Theater of war.

The war did not have a marked effect on the Church in Australia during 1939. Toward the end of that year President Judd mentioned merely that "many members are enlisting in the Australian forces." But on December 24, 1940, he wrote to the First Presidency that conditions in general were adverse. First, in May 1940, the First Presidency had informed him that because of international tensions "there would be no more missionaries sent to Australia for the present." Second, because so many priesthood holders were joining the Australian army, the branches were in "a depleted condition," and in many branches there were not enough men to fill the positions. Third, the government had placed a ban on certain imports, and included on the list were many kinds of printed materials. "We found it impossible to import any tracts or Books of Mormon," wrote Brother Judd. But far more important than these three problems was a fourth: Because of the steadily deteriorating condition of world affairs, the First Presidency decided to call all Pacific area missionaries except the mission presidents home to United States territory.

On October 14 President Judd received a telegram from President Heber J. Grant that told him to return all elders as soon as possible, to use American ships if they were available, to install local officers in the branches, to give honorable releases to all elders who had served for more than two years, and to notify others that they would be reassigned to missions in the United States.[19] President Judd immediately notified all the missionaries, and within twenty-four hours most of the elders were on their way to Sydney. President Judd arranged for most of his missionaries to sail to Hawaii, via New Zealand and other stops, on the S.S. *Mariposa.* Twenty-seven elders sailed on October 19, only five days after the evacuation had been ordered. The five elders who were laboring in Perth, Western Australia, which is 2,800 miles from Sydney, were unable to arrive on time but sailed on the next American boat, which left on January 10, 1941.

When the missionaries left, they lost track of many investigators and friends. They left the Church records in an uncompleted state, and the local priesthood had to try to construct the information that was needed. President Judd said that this was especially difficult because the local brethren "had not had any previous experience in the handling of the Church records."[20] By the night of January 10, 1941, the Australian Mission was in the hands of James Judd, his wife, and the Saints of Australia. The Judds remained there until March 25, when they were replaced by Elvon W. and June Orme.

Elvon W. Orme had a lifetime interest in and familiarity with Australia. Elvon's father, Charles Alvin Orme, was serving as mission president there when the younger Orme was born. Brother Elvon Orme was only thirty-one years old when he went to Australia as mission president. President Orme had planned to marry June Cannon the following June, but they moved their wedding day to February 26. The following day he was set apart as mission president and she as mission Relief Society president and mission secretary. They left Salt Lake City on February 28, 1941. Theirs was an unusual honeymoon.

The Ormes soon learned that most of their energies would be required to keep the existing organizations intact. By the time of their arrival, Australia had been at war for a year and a half. Speaking of the number of men who had joined the Australian military forces, President Orme said that "the place was depleted."

Early in the war, Australian government officials passed a Manpower Act that stipulated the ages, occupations, types of training, and so on that would qualify Australian men for military service or for exemption from the service. President Orme's problem was keeping enough Australian elders exempt from the draft to man branch presidencies. Since Protestant and Catholic churches were able to operate with only one minister, the government found the Mormon need for three leaders a bit strange. Nevertheless, President Orme received permission for three men to stay home to operate each of the branches. President Orme made every effort to staff the branches and district positions with men who were too old to be drafted in any event.

Brother Orme also decided that he himself needed counselors. He called Archibald Campbell of Queensland as his first counselor and Arthur H. Butler from Melbourne as his second counselor. When

Brother Campbell died a year or two later, Brother Butler was moved to first counselor, and William Edward Waters was called as second counselor.

President and Sister Orme found it necessary to travel constantly. The government carefully restricted travel because of fuel shortages and rationing; everyone traveled according to a government-established priority number. But because President Orme had become acquainted with the personnel and workings of the United States consular office in Sydney during his first mission, which had ended only six years before he returned as mission president, he was able to obtain help in gaining a fairly high travel priority number. He never had trouble getting where he wanted to go.

The war was a time of frustration and fear, but progress was made during this period. LDS women volunteered many hours to the Red Cross, and Relief Society sisters helped improve the status and image of the Church in the eyes of civic leaders in many parts of the country. A number of LDS American servicemen acted as missionaries for the Church and for America. Several times President Orme and his counselors were asked by U.S. military officials to straighten out problems and tensions between the U.S. Army and Australian citizens and were able to act successfully as mediators.

But the most important achievement during the war was the development of confidence among Australian Church leaders. Although some of the mission presidents after the war were tied to their old habits and concepts of leadership and continued to place missionaries in some positions in which local leaders should have been asked to serve, the Church in Australia was ready to assume independent leadership.[21]

President Orme was not well when he was called as mission president. During his stay in Australia he underwent surgery for serious internal disorders. Finally, in 1945, his health became so poor that he was released. On June 30, 1945, a month after the war ended in Europe and a month and a half before it concluded in the Pacific, President Orme set apart his counselor, Arthur H. Butler, a lifelong member of the Church, as acting president of the mission. Brother Butler, counselor and president of the Melbourne District for many years, was the first Australian to serve as mission president of that country. Sister Edith Butler acted as mission Relief Society president.[22]

President Butler served as acting mission president for only a little more than two months and was then replaced by Thomas D. Rees, who had served as president during the late 1930s. President Rees and his wife did much to return the mission to its pre-war status. Four new American missionaries arrived before 1945 ended, and there were twenty-eight elders by the end of 1946. During the next two years the number of missionaries grew to seventy-seven, dropping to thirty-three by the end of 1950 because of the Korean conflict.

President Rees sent elders into all of the well-established areas as well as to a number of towns where smaller groups had stopped holding meetings during the war. New missionaries gave attention to Launceston, Ballarat, Bendigo, Goulbourn, Bathurst, and Bundaberg. President Rees had helped the missionaries to open several of these branches during his previous mission.

He and Sister Rees remained in Australia for only a year and a half, but while they were there they traveled constantly. They helped the Enmore Branch establish the first welfare committee ever organized in Australia. Following the organization of this committee, members of the Enmore Branch set up a storehouse of goods in the meeting-house.[23]

President and Sister Charles B. Richmond took over the mission on April 23, 1947. At the same time, Elder Matthew Cowley of the Council of the Twelve Apostles and president of the Pacific Missions arrived for his first tour of the Australian Mission. He was the fourth general authority of the Church to visit the land "down under." He returned once a year for the next two or three years.

Partly at the prompting of Elder Cowley, but also because it was the logical thing to do, President Richmond continued the effort that had been started almost two decades before of placing as many local members in leadership positions as possible. Still, some missionaries held positions as Sunday School, MIA, and Primary teachers. Also following the pre-war pattern, President Richmond encouraged the use of radio and basketball as means of gaining publicity for the Church. By 1950, thirteen radio stations were broadcasting "Music and the Spoken Word." Some elders also appeared on the "Amateur Hour," a popular nationwide radio show. In the postwar years, however, the missionary basketball teams were often banned from championship play because they were not made up of Australians. Nevertheless, basketball was a help to the missionary cause.

When George Aaron Christensen and his wife took the lead of the mission in April 1950, the missionary staff was large and growing. The government was willing to allow almost any number of elders and sister missionaries. The districts and branches were fully organized, and all appeared to be well. Then, on June 25, 1950, Communist North

Koreans invaded South Korea, and the following day President Harry S Truman ordered United States military forces to help the Korean government. On June 29, the Australian government announced that it had put a naval squadron at the disposal of the United States, and the next day a Royal Australian Air Force fighter squadron was also put at the disposal of the United States. The Korean conflict disrupted life in both countries, and it also temporarily slowed down the work of the Church in Australia. The Church appeared to be at a "take-off" point in 1938 and 1939, but the Second World War slowed progress. In 1950 there was every reason to believe that the "take-off" was imminent, but once again war slowed the work. This time, however, the Church was better prepared to meet the problems head on and to overcome them quickly. The 1950s were yet to be a decade of wonderful growth.

CHAPTER 15

SINCE 1950: YEARS OF RAPID GROWTH AND CHANGE

Australia, 1951–1984

The 1950s began on a negative note. In June, war broke out in Korea, and by the year's end the number of full-time missionaries dropped considerably. All the missions of the Church were similarly affected. Between 1951 and 1953, the total number of LDS missionaries fell from 4,847 to 2,189, and the situation would have been worse if the First Presidency had not called on the seventies quorums in 1951 to provide one thousand missionaries.[1] Some of those thousand men were assigned to Australia, where they performed excellent service. But the Australians, also seeing the need to support the missionary cause, provided thirty-seven part-time missionaries by the end of 1951 and eight full-time missionaries, 20 percent of the force, by the end of 1953.[2] In 1954 the Church and the Selective Service System implemented a quota that allowed one missionary to be called from each ward and branch in the United States. This procedure allowed the number of missionaries in Australia to rise to ninety. The next year the number of missionaries jumped to 151. But that number was only a small beginning for the great growth that was to come in the next few years.

The Korean conflict did not have the same delaying effect as World War II. Local leaders picked up the slack in many areas where the missionaries had led out. Three new branches were organized during the Korean conflict, and construction was commenced on several new chapels. A number of new committees were organized in many of the branches. The mission presidents placed greater demands on the missionaries, whose efforts paid off in 1952 with an average of 3.4 baptisms per missionary. This was the best record to date in the history of the mission. In 1953 the missionaries baptized 4.5 converts per missionary. This was an exciting era in Australia. In 1952 the Church Radio, Publicity, and Missionary Literature Committee developed a plan for Churchwide use titled *Systematic Program for Teaching the Gospel.*[3] From it the missionaries in Australia developed the "Australian Mission Proselyting Plan." This new program, introduced in 1954, used many new proselyting techniques, especially visual aids. The plan, like most others of the time, helped the missionaries to lead investigators through a series of logical steps, using the scriptures as a basis, to the conclusion that the teachings and claims of the Church are indeed true. The plan not only helped the investigators to understand the gospel, but it also gave the elders and sister missionaries more confidence as teachers.

Early in 1951 the headquarters of the Australian Mission under the direction of President George A. Christensen were moved from Enmore, Sydney, to Melbourne.

THE VISIT OF PRESIDENT DAVID O. MCKAY TO AUSTRALIA

David O. McKay became president of the Church on April 9, 1951. He had a broad vision of missionary work, and during his presidency the Church grew from 1.14 million to 2.8 million members. President McKay visited Australia from January 31 to February 8, 1955.

These Saints from Tasmania traveled over four hundred miles by land and sea to meet and hear President David O. McKay speak in Melbourne in 1955. (Photo from the *Improvement Era.*)

"The turning point for the Church in Australia was President David O. McKay's visit in 1955," said Philip Mitchell, a third-generation member of the Church from Hobart, Tasmania. "The media were baffled; they couldn't understand why people who had not seen the prophet before cried when he alighted from the plane. What they could not appreciate was that this was the Prophet, and the Spirit was bearing witness to the Saints."[4] The Australian Saints were thrilled to see and hear the Prophet and to shake his hand. During the eight days of his visit President McKay held conference-type meetings in Brisbane, Adelaide, Melbourne, and Sydney. He also held several missionary testimony and training meetings. In his addresses to the members, President McKay bore witness that salvation can come only through Jesus; he taught the importance of unity in the Church, and he urged the Australian Saints to remain in Australia. He implied that a temple would soon be constructed somewhere closer in the Pacific area. (On the next leg of this trip President McKay selected the temple site in New Zealand.) At the laying of the cornerstone for the new Ipswich chapel, twenty-eight miles inland from Brisbane, President McKay counseled the members that they were part of a partnership in the building of a chapel, noting that a church building, no matter how pretty it looks, "is nothing but a shell unless you build your own souls."[5] Saints and friends gathered from all parts of Queensland to be part of this great occasion.

President McKay was deeply touched when he learned that a handful of Saints had driven 1,700 miles from Perth, Western Australia, to attend the meeting in Adelaide. He also paid tribute to eighteen members who traveled by land and sea from Tasmania to be with the Prophet in Melbourne. Before he left Australia President McKay had met with and shaken the hands of most of two thousand Saints, two-thirds of the Australian members.

But President McKay did not limit himself to meetings with members and missionaries. He devoted considerable time to interviews with newspaper and radio people and to visits with the governors of Victoria, New South Wales, and Queensland. Sir Dallas Brooks, governor of the State of Victoria, was so impressed by President McKay that he extended his scheduled fifteen-minute appointment to nearly an hour. When their visit ended, Governor Brooks walked with President McKay down the steps of the Government House to the car, an act seldom performed by a person in his position.[6]

When President McKay, his wife, and Franklin J. Murdock, his

President David O. McKLay places the cornerstone on the Ipswich chapel, Australia, 1955. (Photo from the *Improvement Era*.)

traveling companion, departed from Sydney Airport, they left behind many statements, ideas, and visions of how things could be. President McKay also gave utterance to a number of prophecies that were fulfilled in later years. Here are three examples: In Queensland, on February 1, President McKay, President Charles V. Liljenquist of the Australian Mission, their wives, and a number of other Church leaders visited Chermside Valley, not many miles from Brisbane. As they stood on a high rise overlooking this beautiful landscape, President McKay turned to President Liljenquist and asked whether there had ever been missionaries of the Church there. President Liljenquist answered that he did not know of any. On hearing this, President McKay said, "Now is the time to send missionaries into this [Chermside] valley. It is ripe and ready for harvest."[7] Within two years there was a branch of over one hundred members in Chermside Valley. By 1958 these new Saints constructed a chapel.[8]

President McKay also predicted that as new chapels were completed, the membership of the Church would double in a short time, which it did.[9]

To show his faith in the value of new buildings, President McKay soon announced a large new construction program. And to manifest his belief that "a spiritual awakening [was] imminent," he, in counsel with other general authorities, decided to divide the Australian Mission and to form a new mission. This plan was officially announced in Salt Lake City on April 30, 1955. Elder Marion G. Romney supervised the actual mechanics of the reorganization during July. The new mission, known as the South Australia Mission, contained Victoria, South Australia, Western Australia, and Tasmania, with mission headquarters at Melbourne. The Australian Mission consisted of New South Wales and Queensland. Mission leaders had to work out many problems over the next several years, such as arranging a high missionary quota (it grew from 100, to 200, to 300, and finally to 700 missionaries in 1962), purchasing a new mission home in Sydney, gaining permission for construction supervisors to enter the country, expanding quotas for the free importation of Church literature, and so on.

CHAPEL BUILDING IN THE 1950s

Church construction following President McKay's visit was directed by Elder Wendell B. Mendenhall. Brother Mendenhall had already been involved in constructing a number of chapels in other parts of the Pacific. The operating guidelines for the construction program in the Pacific Islands were not entirely appropriate for Australia because the economic situation among members of the Church in Australia was far superior to that of the members in the islands. Also, there were more than adequate numbers of skilled craftsmen in Australia, which was not true in Samoa, Tonga, or French Polynesia. For these reasons the Saints in Australia contributed more money and provided fewer labor missionaries, usually two or three per building, than elsewhere in the Pacific. The Australian Saints contributed much time as volunteer workers, but they donated most of the local 30 percent of the building cost in cash. Fourteen men were called as construction missionaries from the United States during the first three years of the program. These brethren functioned as general contractors and building superintendents.

The first phase of the chapel-building program got underway on January 10, 1956, and was completed in late 1958. During this time nineteen chapels were constructed from Perth in the west; to Hobart, Tasmania, in the south; to Brisbane in the east. The new buildings were very different from other churches in Australia, whether Mormon or otherwise. Early LDS chapels, most of which had been constructed during the 1920s, consisted primarily of meeting halls and a few classrooms. The new buildings, some of which were quite large—

This chapel at Orange, New South Wales, is typical of many that were constructed by building missionaries. (Courtesy Donley Despain.)

much larger than the membership seemed to warrant—contained not only chapel meeting areas, but also cultural halls, kitchens, baptismal fonts, classrooms, and offices. Many nonmembers toured the new structures and expressed appreciation for their beauty and utility.

Many Australian Saints made great sacrifices for the building program. In one instance a widow gave her total inheritance to help a building get underway. In another, a sister donated the savings she had intended to use to go to the temple, to help pay her branch's assessment for the Sutherland chapel. (Fortunately she was somehow still able to get to the temple.) Three men in Parramatta branch repaired old cars and sold them to raise money for their building fund. Some branches regularly held special fast days and contributed the money saved to the building fund. Other branches held bazaars, gave choir concerts, served banquets, washed cars, put on dramatic productions, and so on, to raise the much-needed money for the new structures.[10]

As President McKay predicted, the size of many branches doubled before the new buildings were completed. The number of branches also increased rapidly between 1955 and 1959, growing from twenty-three to thirty-two. The growth was so rapid that the mission presidents soon realized that the nineteen chapels of the first phase would be but a beginning. By the end of 1958 they had purchased an additional fifteen building sites.

The building program, in short, had a marked effect on the growth of the Church in Australia, but buildings alone did not bring such growth. By the end of 1959 there were 233 full-time missionaries serving in Australia. These missionaries were using improved teaching methods, and they were using the most effective public relations program ever employed in Australia. The "Mormon Yankee" basketball team took several championships between 1955 and 1958. During 1956, the Mormon Yankees played several international Olympic teams while the Olympic games were being held in Melbourne. The Church also used radio and television more effectively during these years. It placed the Tabernacle Choir broadcasts on more stations, and several quartets of elders sang on radio talent shows and had an opportunity to talk about their purposes as missionaries in Australia. Between 1955 and 1959 membership in Australia grew from 3,506 to 7,071, an increase of more than 100 percent.

Between 1959 and 1976 the Church completed an additional fifty-six chapels, and many others have been built since then. The labor missionary program continued to operate into the 1980s. The number of participants was relatively small, but several young men were usually engaged on each chapel. Since the early 1960s, the building program had done well to keep up with the growth of new branches, wards, and stakes.

THE NEW ZEALAND TEMPLE

While the Australian Saints were busy raising money and building chapels from 1955 to 1958, the members of New Zealand were building a temple. On February 17, 1955, only a few days after he returned home from the Pacific Islands, New Zealand, and Australia, President McKay announced the plan to build the New Zealand Temple (see chapter 20). Prior to this time Australian Saints had traveled to Hawaii or the United States mainland to participate in temple ordinances.

During the temple construction period, Church leaders in New Zealand published a newsletter to report progress and to keep Church leaders in other parts of the Pacific posted on plans and developments. As the time for completion and dedication approached, leaders in Australia as well as in the Islands encouraged faithful members to prepare to go to New Zealand for the ceremonies. The cost was generally easier for Australians to handle than it was for Samoans,

Tongans, and Tahitians. But it was still expensive, and some Australian members made significant sacrifices to be able to attend the dedication.

On April 17, 1958, three days before the dedication, 126 Australian Saints, almost all leaders in their districts and branches, left by air to attend the special event. When they returned home, they created a strong corps of dedicated people who desired to see stakes organized in Australia, like the one formed in New Zealand following the dedication.

THE ORGANIZATION OF STAKES

By 1960 there were over seven thousand members of the Church in Australia, most of whom lived in the major southeastern cities. Because the leaders of the Church there understood the gospel and the order of the Church, the First Presidency and Quorum of the Twelve decided to organize a stake in Sydney. Elders Delbert L. Stapley and Marion G. Romney officially created Sydney Stake, later changed to Sydney Australia Greenwich Stake, on March 27, 1960, with Dell C. Hunt as president. This stake was the two hundred ninety-third in the world and the third outside North America, the first two being the Oahu, Hawaii Stake, and the Auckland, New Zealand Stake. Later that same year Elder Spencer W. Kimball, of the Twelve, organized stakes in Brisbane and Melbourne. Brisbane Stake was formed on October 23, 1960, with William E. Waters, a veteran Church leader, as president. The next week, on October 30, Elder Kimball called Boyd C. Bott as president of the new Melbourne Stake. Since that time thirteen other stakes have been created in Australia.[11]

The stakes have contributed to the rapid growth of the Church in Australia since 1960 because they have relieved the mission presidents of local responsibilities in many of the districts and branches. The stakes have organized their own local missions to augment the work of the full-time missionaries. Also, by placing the Church in the hands of the Australian members, they have been able to dispel much of the "American Church" image. Recently some of the Australian stakes have been able to call relatively large numbers (1 percent of stake membership) of local elders and sisters to fill full-time missions in Australia and abroad. In 1976 President Allen M. Swan of the Australia Adelaide Mission reported that 25 percent of his missionaries were from Australia. "This permits us to assign an Australian with an American companion where possible, which is having a decidedly favourable effect on our public image."[12]

FURTHER DIVISIONS OF MISSIONS

Since 1960 the history of the Church in Australia has been primarily one of steady growth and development. The growth of the Church has made possible and necessary the organization of not only sixteen stakes but also three additional missions since the first division in 1955. The third mission, the Australian West Mission (now called the Australia Adelaide Mission), was created from the South Australia Mission. President Milton J. Hess was asked to establish the new mission home in Adelaide, South Australia. The mission included South and Western Australia and the Northern Territory, which had been opened to proselyting in 1960. In 1973, President Harold B. Lee asked President J. Martell Bird of the Australian Mission in Sydney to remain in the country for an extra year to open a new mission in Brisbane. The creation of the Brisbane Mission came about at least in part because President Kimball, acting as chairman of the Missionary Committee, asked especially geographically large missions to have a maximum of two hundred missionaries. This decision was motivated by concern that the mission presidents should be able to interview and counsel with all missionaries regularly. As a result of this decision, the Australian Mission was reduced from three hundred to two hundred missionaries during an eight-month period from 1972 into 1973. When the mission force reached two hundred, President J. Martell Bird surveyed the mission and concluded that two hundred missionaries were not enough to handle all of New South Wales and Queensland. President Bird sent his conclusions to the First Presidency and the Missionary Committee, and they agreed that a new mission was needed.

The new Australia Northeast Mission, soon to be renamed the Australia Brisbane Mission, was officially formed on July 24, 1973. President Bird recorded an unusual spiritual experience in connection with the purchase of the new mission home. He and Sister Bird decided to try to find an appropriate home in the Hamilton, Albion, or Albion Heights areas, north of the Brisbane River. The principal advantage to having the mission home in this area was that it was a fine part of the city, close to the business district on one side and the international airport on the other. But after searching for many days on their own, they were unable to find the kind of house they desired.

President and Sister Bird concluded that they would have to look for a home in other areas of the city. But even though they eventually made substantial down payments on three different houses, each deal fell through for one reason or another. Finally they asked an "estate agent" to go through the prime area again, this time knocking on doors of all homes that looked appropriate, even though the homes were not listed for sale. In August 1973, the agent called President Bird to say that he had found the right place. Before long the Birds had closed the deal for a fine concrete and steel home, one that President Bird described as beautiful and practical. They even purchased the existing furniture, linens, towels, soap, and food with the home. It is perfectly situated between the business center and the airport and has an excellent view of the city. Before this, President Bird rented office space for the mission staff in a building that was only about five minutes' drive from the new home.

A few weeks later, President and Sister Bird visited Sister Waters, widow of the late first president of Brisbane Stake. In the course of their conversation Sister Waters asked where the new mission home was situated, and President Bird told her it was in Albion Heights. Sister Waters then said, "Of course, I should have remembered. It was the last time that President and Sister McKay flew from Sydney to Brisbane. President Waters and I were with them. As our plane approached the Brisbane Airport, President McKay, looking out the window, pointed down and said the mission home for Brisbane area would one day be established on the north side of the Brisbane River and pointed to the Albion/Albion Heights area. Yes, I should have known where you would locate the mission home!" President and Sister Bird did not even know that President McKay had indicated a mission home would be established in Brisbane. President Bird wrote, "We did, however, then realize why the three previously selected houses had not materialized and the deals had fallen through."[13]

The fifth mission, the Australia Perth Mission, was organized on July 1, 1975, with Bruce J. Opie as its first president.

USING THE PROGRAMS OF THE CHURCH

Prior to World War II only three general authorities of the Church visited Australia. Since then, primarily because of the organization of stakes, general authorities and general board members have made hundreds of visits to the stakes and missions. From 1960 until the mid-1970s, general authorities visited each stake twice a year. In addition, since 1967, when regional representatives of the Twelve were first called and regional meetings were begun, general board members have regularly visited the Saints in Australia in greater numbers and helped them develop the full program of the Church.

The Mackay Branch choir practices for the opening meeting of their newly completed chapel. (Courtesy Donley Despain.)

The Sydney Distribution Centre was established in the late 1960s and continues to serve the needs of the Church by distributing lesson materials, equipment, furnishings, and so forth.

During the 1970s the Saints there participated in general conferences through closed circuit broadcasts of the priesthood sessions and by radio broadcasts of selected sessions of other conference meetings. Australian Church public relations workers have been quite successful in getting the Church before the people. The Saints and nonmembers had the opportunity to become acquainted with President Spencer W. Kimball when, in June 1975, the Australian Broadcasting Commission interviewed him via transcontinental telephone lines. Also participating in the interview was President Ian G. Mackie of the Sydney Australia Greenwich Stake. The interview was part of a half-hour program dealing with the Church, aired over seventy radio stations across Australia.

General authority and general board member visits, better distribution of Church materials, and improved public communications helped increase the use of Church programs. But some of the most important work accomplished during the last decade or two has been done within the walls of homes and classrooms and in the cultural halls and open parks of Australia. Since the early decades of this century, Church leaders in Australia have lamented that a high

LDS chapel building missionaries made many friends in Nundel, New South Wales, when they worked unceasingly to save the city from a forest fire. (Courtesy Donley Despain.)

percentage of the young members have married outside the Church. The overbalance of women to men has been discussed before. The ratio of men to women in the Church is now about equal, but leaders remain concerned about the large number of young people who do not find marriage partners within the Church. Many stories could be told, however, of faithful fathers and mothers who are holding weekly family home evenings wherein they are teaching their children the principles of the gospel. Hundreds of Sunday School teachers and Young Women's advisers, as well as Aaronic Priesthood advisers, are regularly teaching thousands of young Australian Saints about their responsibilities to themselves and to the Church.

To supplement the efforts of parents and teachers, ward and stake leaders throughout Australia, in cooperation with mission presidents and district and branch leaders, have planned and held many special youth and Young Adult conferences.[14]

IMMIGRATION OF SPANISH-, GREEK-, AND ITALIAN-SPEAKING PEOPLES

Since World War II, 3.1 million immigrants have arrived at Australia's ports and airports, an average of 180,000 migrants a year for twenty-seven years. Thousands of these people have joined the

Church. Some of them are now sending their sons and daughters on missions to their former homelands—Finland, Italy, Latin America. Two immigrant converts to the Church have served as mission presidents in Italy. President Ivan Radman, born in Yugoslavia, was called from Adelaide. President John Grinceri immigrated to Australia with his family from Italy while he was a young man.

A large number of people have fairly recently emigrated from South America, and there are some Church members among these people. In fact, a number of LDS Latin American migrants to Australia have qualified for entry visas because they learned skills and crafts while working as labor missionaries in South America. In 1974 a Spanish-speaking branch was formed in the Sydney area, and by 1984 the Fairfield Second and South Harbour Wards, Sydney, were Spanish-speaking wards. Spanish-speaking missionaries have been serving in Sydney and Melbourne, and Italian-speaking missionaries have been proselyting in Sydney, Melbourne, and Adelaide.[15] Greek-speaking missionaries have also served in Sydney. (Harbour Second Ward, Sydney, is Tongan. There is also a Samoan branch in that area.)

MISSIONARY WORK

Since 1955, and even before, the missions of Australia have employed the most advanced techniques available in teaching the gospel. In the fall of 1972, however, the Missionary Department assigned the Sydney mission to experiment with a new series of discussions. Twelve missionaries learned the new discussions, which would later be published and distributed to all missions of the world as the *Uniform System for Teaching Families.* This pilot program was applied in only six areas throughout the world. When the new plan was accepted Churchwide, the Australian missionaries took pride in the part they had played and were grateful to have had the opportunity to make a contribution to the new program.[16]

The Saints in Australia have been led by two general authorities of the Church. From July 1961 until July 1964, Elder Bruce R. McConkie, then of the First Council of the Seventy, presided over the South Australia Mission. During the summer of 1976, Elder Loren C. Dunn of the First Quorum of the Seventy, who had formerly served as a missionary in Australia, was called to serve as president of the Australia Sydney Mission. More recently several other general authorities have supervised Australia as area executive administrators.

The first Australian to serve as president of an Australian mission was Bruce J. Opie, who led the Perth Mission from 1975 to 1978. President Opie joined the Church in 1960, and by 1964 he had been called as a bishop in Melbourne. During his first eighteen years in the Church, he has served as counselor in a bishopric, bishop, high councilor, first counselor in Melbourne Stake Presidency, president of Melbourne Australia Moorabbin Stake for four years, and mission president. Professionally, President Opie is a highly respected town planner. Most recently he has served the Church in Hong Kong as the director of temporal affairs. During 1967 and 1968 he was federal president of the Royal Australian Planning Institute.

THE FIRST AUSTRALIA AREA CONFERENCES

"Saints from Victoria, Tasmania, South Australia, and Western Australia converged here [Melbourne] by the thousands in February for their first area conference. As with other area conferences in the South Pacific, this was one great spiritual outpouring, culminating months of planning, rehearsing, and expectations." So wrote Malcolm R. Taylor, Melbourne area public relations director, in the May 1976 *Ensign.* He expressed the feelings of Saints not only in Melbourne but also in Sydney and Brisbane. Saints traveled over two thousand miles from Perth and the surrounding area to attend the meetings in Mel-

Sydney Opera House, where the first area conference in Australia was held in 1976. (Courtesy Ralph A. Britsch.)

bourne; one family came two thousand miles from Darwin, on the north coast, to the meeting in Brisbane; still another family came from Indonesia.

The conferences in Melbourne and Sydney followed the general pattern of area conferences elsewhere in the world. In both cities the Saints presented cultural programs depicting the history of the development of Australia. President Spencer W. Kimball presided at each major session and keynoted the conferences. He was aided by President N. Eldon Tanner and eight other general authorities. Over thirty-five hundred people attended the meeting held Sunday morning, February 29, in Sydney's beautiful opera house and in the overflow facilities. A choir composed of 350 voices sang "Come, Come Ye Saints." This choir was over half as large as the entire congregation had been when President McKay met with the Saints in Sydney in 1955.

The Sunday morning session in Sydney was carried live over ten television stations. It was estimated by network authorities that over three million people viewed the meeting. Response was so favorable that a major network rebroadcast the session in Western Australia, where the members had been unable to see the live telecast because of a technicians' strike.[17]

CHURCH GROWTH AND ADMINISTRATION SINCE 1976

The first area conference in Australia brought not only spiritual growth to the members, but also real growth in numerical terms. The conference made a big difference to the Australian Saints' perception of themselves. In the past they had seen themselves as members of small congregations. Now they saw themselves as part of a major church. During the years immediately following, convert baptisms increased, and the growth since that time has hardly faltered. Real growth in convert baptisms has averaged around 7 percent per year. The number of stakes doubled in five years, from eight in 1977 to sixteen in 1981. Within the five missions and the stakes there are ninety-eight branches and ninety-four wards. Although it is difficult to establish the exact membership in Australia in 1984, there are at least forty-three thousand active Latter-day Saints. This figure shows considerable growth from the approximately thirty-four thousand members in 1977.

But total numbers are only a partial indication of growth. Percentage of participation in Church meetings and activities has increased significantly. For example, sacrament meeting attendance has increased from 33 percent in 1977 to over 40 percent (very close to Churchwide average) in 1983. And the percentage of adults paying a full tithing has increased from 17 to 29 percent over the same period.

The second area conference in December 1979 helped to build and strengthen the Saints, but changes in Church administration also account for the impressive growth since the mid-1970s. In 1975, as part of a new program of area supervision and administration, Elder Robert L. Simpson, then an assistant to the Twelve, was assigned to direct the affairs of the Church in Australia, New Zealand, and the South Pacific Islands. He moved to Auckland, New Zealand, and directed the work from an office he established there. He frequently traveled to Australia (as well as to other parts of his vast area) to meet with local leaders of both ecclesiastical and temporal affairs. Because his area was so large, part of it was divided in 1976, and he was left with Australia and New Zealand. However, because of the great growth in both countries, the area was too large for one man to handle. A regional office for temporal affairs was established in Sydney, but administering even the temporal affairs for both countries from a main office in Auckland proved difficult. In 1981, the membership of the Church in Australia exceeded that of New Zealand for the first time since the 1850s. Australia, because of its five times greater population, held the greater prospect for growth. Also, because it made little sense to send materials to Auckland from Salt Lake City and then pay duties and other fees to move them again to Australia, it was considered best to establish the main temporal affairs office in Sydney.

Elder Loren C. Dunn of the First Quorum of the Seventy directed Church affairs in Australia and New Zealand from 1978 until the end of 1979, when Elders Rex D. Pinegar and Jack H. Goaslind, Jr., of the First Quorum of the Seventy were assigned as area executive administrators for Australia/Papua New Guinea and New Zealand, Fiji, and Tahiti, respectively. Thus, the area was divided once again.

The work of the Lord has moved forward rapidly under each executive administrator, but as the areas have been reduced in size, the administrators have been able to give more attention to the growing departments, regions, stakes, and missions under their care. In 1981, the First Presidency organized area councils throughout the world. The area council consisted of the executive administrator, the regional representatives within the area, the director of temporal affairs, and the comptroller for the area. (Even before this time councils of leaders had met together to develop plans and to oversee the affairs of the Church. Elder Loren C. Dunn recalled an unusually

A view of Sydney, Australia. (Courtesy Ralph A. Britsch.)

spiritual meeting in the late 1970s when he and Elder Simpson met with all of the regional representatives, stake presidents, and mission presidents from Australia. The Spirit manifested the purposes of the Kingdom to all who were there. This council meeting brought all the major leaders of the Church in Australia together for the first time and created a much greater harmony of purpose.) These men created the "Five Year Plan" and updated it annually, reviewed all land purchases and building projects, looked into development needs, and supervised all aspects of the Church in the area. Yet the executive administrator did not have control over the area budget, nor did he hire Church employees. Such matters were handled by the Presiding Bishopric International Office in Salt Lake City. There was clearly at least one more major step needed in the decentralization process that had been underway since 1975.

In June 1984, the First Presidency announced that area presidencies were being called to direct thirteen geographical areas throughout the world. President Gordon B. Hinckley, second counselor in the First Presidency, "emphasized that the Church's growth requires flexibility in administration as the institution pursues its unchanging divine mandate to preach the gospel of Jesus Christ to all the world."[18] The appointment of presidencies, with a president and two counselors, follows a general pattern of Church government. The

The first Pacific Area presidency: Robert L. Simpson (top), Devere Harris (left), and Philip T. Sonntag. (Copyright © The Church of Jesus Christ of Latter-day Saints. Used by permission.)

initial presidency appointed to guide the Pacific Area (Australia, New Zealand, Pacific Islands, Hawaii) included President Robert L. Simpson and his counselors Devere Harris and Philip T. Sonntag, all of the First Quorum of the Seventy. As with the area executive administrators between 1975 and 1979, this presidency was asked to live in their area. They took residence in Sydney, Australia.

The duties of the area presidency included responsibility for all departments and affairs of the Church within their area. This included but was not limited to Membership, the Church Educational System, Finances, Real Estate, Translation Services, Social Services, Genealogy, Welfare, and so on. Few administrative changes in recent decades have had greater ramifications regarding the decentralization process in a worldwide church. For the first time since the days of almost autonomous mission presidents (generally those who served prior to the 1950s), who handled most temporal and ecclesiastical matters within their own missions, the temporal and ecclesiastical parts of the international Church have been combined under the leadership of one body with authority to administer all affairs. Through this change, all departments of the Church were caused to directly serve the purposes and needs of the priesthood in fulfilling the mission of the Church.[19]

THE SYDNEY AUSTRALIA TEMPLE

The regional representatives and stake presidents from Australia learned that a temple was to be built in Sydney, at a meeting held in the board room of the Church Administration Building in Salt Lake City. The announcement was made public a day later, on April 2, 1980. No one who was well acquainted with the Church in Australia was surprised. The Church was mature in that land, and building a temple there was the logical next step. The three regional representatives, Ian G. Mackie, Donald W. Cummings, and P. Bruce Mitchell, were all native ''Aussies,'' as were the remainder of the leaders of the Church.

Under the direction of the regional representatives, a campaign was organized to raise funds for the new structure. By October 1980, only six months after the temple was announced, the Australian Saints had raised close to one million dollars, their full share of the project.[20]

Raising the funds for the temple was one thing, but getting the building under construction proved to be quite another. The first site selected for the structure did not satisfy Church leaders in Australia. Hence, after looking a good deal, the present location was selected. But because of various kinds of delays, most of them related to legal matters, the groundbreaking was not held until August 13, 1982.

Formerly a boys school, the temple site is a beautiful property in the Carlingsford section of Sydney, overlooking the western part of the city. Six old buildings yet remain on the 8.5 acres the Church bought. One of these structures has historical significance and has

Sydney Australia Temple. (Copyright © The Church of Jesus Christ of Latter-day Saints. Used by permission.)

been given by the Church to the Shire Council. The other buildings have been renovated and are now used for Church purposes. Their character fits in perfectly with the surrounding environment. In addition to the temple, the Church will also construct a meetinghouse on the property. The Church was able to acquire the property largely because it was able and willing to make optimum use of its potential.

The groundbreaking services were conducted by Elder Bruce R. McConkie of the Quorum of the Twelve. He formerly served as mission president in Australia. The actual groundbreaking was attended by a relatively small group because of limited space. But in the evening a fireside was held at which both Elder Pinegar and Elder McConkie spoke to a packed stake center audience of over fifteen hundred. "There could scarcely be a more memorable day in the entire history of this great nation," said Elder McConkie in his address. "We have done something which will do more for the salvation and exaltation of the people of this great land than practically any other single thing we could have done." Clarifying the role of temples, Elder McConkie noted that the gathering of Israel referred to in Isaiah, with mention of the mountain of the Lord's House "in the tops of the mountains," is figurative language for places where temples will be built. . . . The gathering of Israel is into the stakes of Zion in the nations of the earth. This temple is a fulfillment, as far as Australia is concerned, of that prophecy of Isaiah. It is just as literal a fulfillment as the building of the temple in Salt Lake.

"I cannot use language that is too emphatic. There is no way to overemphasize what we are presenting—the fact that a House of the Lord is about to rise in Australia will be the crowning event for the Church here at this time, when the blessings and ordinances are made available."[21] Elder McConkie assured the Australian Saints that as soon as the numbers of members warrant it other temples will be built there. "There is no reason why we can't have temples in Adelaide, Melbourne, Brisbane, Perth, or wherever the number of saints justifies it."[22]

The 12,500-square-foot structure was completed in August 1984. An open house was held from September 6 to September 18. Thousands of nonmembers toured the new structure and felt the peace and serenity within. After being closed for final cleaning and preparations, the temple was dedicated in multiple sessions that were held on September 20, 21, 22, and 23, 1984. President Gordon B. Hinckley, second counselor in the First Presidency, conducted the services and read the dedicatory prayer. Over six thousand members attended those services.

With the completion of the temple, the Australian Saints are moving on to still greater growth as the center of a new geographical administrative area of the Church. Their major task remaining is the perfection of themselves and greater numbers of their fellowmen both within and outside the Church.

PART 4

NEW ZEALAND

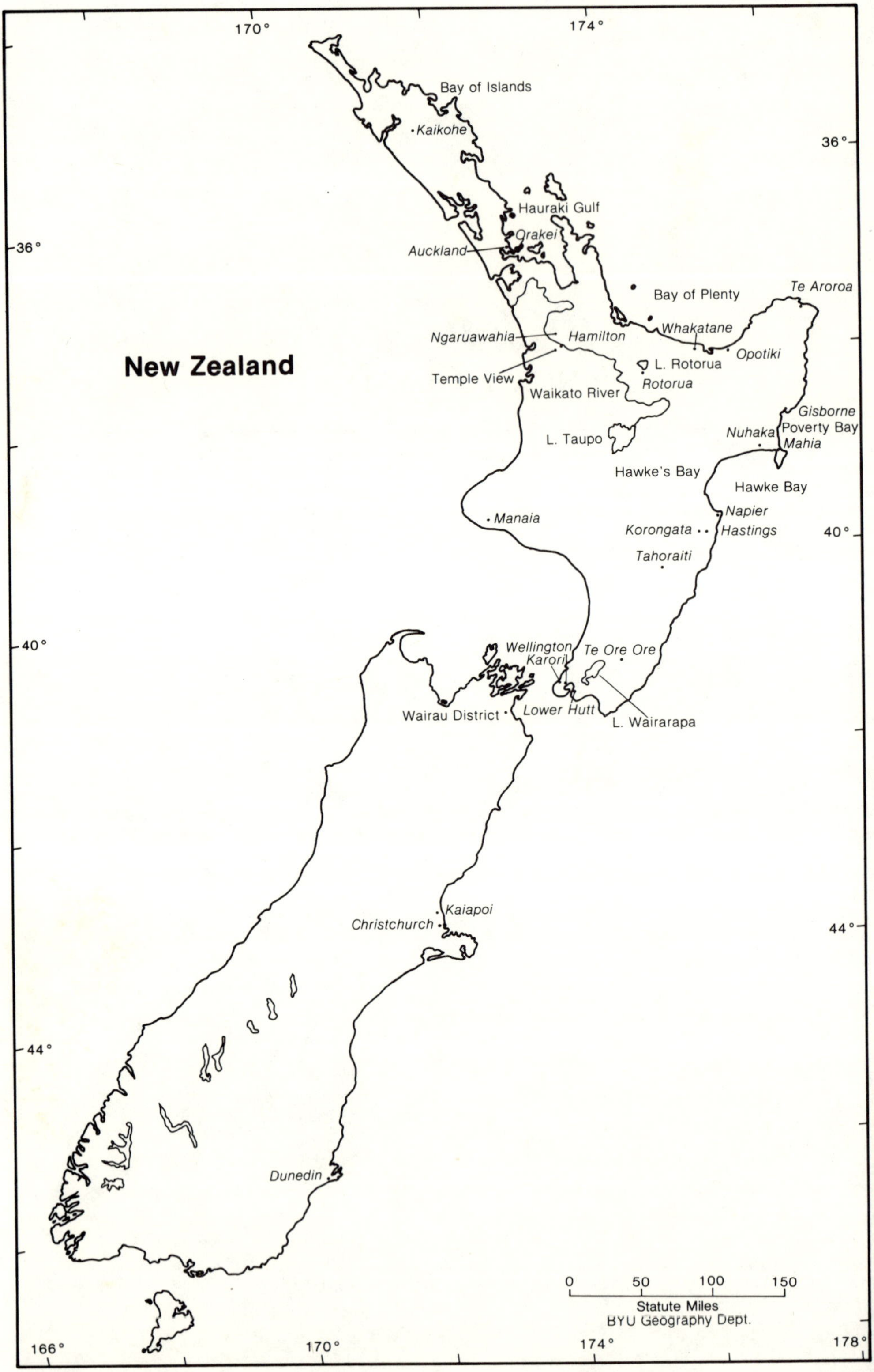
New Zealand
170°
174°
36°
40°
44°
166°
178°
Bay of Islands
Kaikohe
Hauraki Gulf
Orakei
Auckland
Bay of Plenty
Te Araroa
Whakatane
Opotiki
Ngaruawahia
Hamilton
Temple View
L. Rotorua
Rotorua
Waikato River
Gisborne
Poverty Bay
Nuhaka
Mahia
L. Taupo
Hawke's Bay
Hawke Bay
Manaia
Napier
Korongata
Hastings
Tahoraiti
Wellington
Karori
Te Ore Ore
Wairau District
Lower Hutt
L. Wairarapa
Kaiapoi
Christchurch
Dunedin
0
50
100
150
Statute Miles
BYU Geography Dept.

CHAPTER 16

PAKEHA THEN MAORI: ESTABLISHING MORMONISM IN NEW ZEALAND

New Zealand, 1854–1884

In New Zealand, as in Hawaii, the first Latter-day Saint missionaries perceived their call to be to the Caucasians of the country. Only after almost three decades of slow progress among the *pakeha* (whites) did the elders turn to the local Polynesian people, the Maoris, and have real success. It is tempting to recount only the years of success and to ignore the times of struggle prior to the 1880s. But those events also deserve a telling.[1]

We have already discussed the founding of the Australian Mission.[2] In those pages the story of the first missionaries to New Zealand is briefly told. Mission President Augustus Farnham, Australian convert Elder William Cooke, and Thomas Holder, a priest, sailed from Australia on October 20, 1854, and arrived in Auckland, New Zealand, on October 27. After preaching in Auckland, in Nelson, on the north tip of the South Island, and in Wellington at the south end of the North Island, President Farnham returned to Australia. He left Elder Cooke in charge of the New Zealand part of the mission. When New Zealand was opened to preaching the gospel, the First Presidency changed the name of the mission to Australasian, which name was used until the end of 1897.

William Cooke spent all of the next year and part of 1856 teaching the gospel in and around Wellington. He was only moderately successful. He baptized ten people during early 1855 and organized a branch at Karori, near Wellington, sometime before April 1.[3] Two more converts joined the Saints during the next year. The first two people baptized in New Zealand were Martha Holder and her daughter Louisa, who were probably the mother and sister of Thomas Holder.[4]

A view of the beautiful countryside near Raglan, New Zealand. (Courtesy Ralph A. Britsch.)

The records of the Church do not reveal what happened to the Saints and the branch at Karori until 1870. We will return to them later. Elder Cooke returned to Australia in 1856, and from then until the arrival of Carl C. Asmussen, an elder of Danish birth, in 1867, the record is silent. Asmussen was not new to New Zealand. He had immigrated there earlier and established a jewelry business in Christchurch. While he was there he found a pamphlet titled "How to Be Saved," by Lorenzo Snow. Later he returned to his native Denmark, met the LDS missionaries, and joined the Church. On his return trip to New Zealand, Asmussen stopped off at Liverpool, England, where he met with and was ordained an elder by Franklin D. Richards. Elder Richards charged him with the responsibility of teaching the gospel in New Zealand when he returned there.

Elder Asmussen began teaching while aboard ship. His first convert was a German, and shortly after he arrived at Christchurch he baptized two brothers, William and James T. Burnett. William had previously been baptized but had fallen away from the Church. From all indications his new commitment was firm. Elder Asmussen ordained William an elder and James a priest, and the three of them set to work preaching, teaching, and expounding on the restored gospel.[5]

In mid-April 1867, a little over a month after these three arrived at Christchurch, Elder Asmussen wrote to Brigham Young that they were regularly holding public meetings and that many people had expressed interest in their message. Asmussen mentioned, however, that he was skeptical about having many positive results; the people seemed more interested in the Church as a curiosity than as the true restored gospel.[6]

Elder Asmussen remained in New Zealand for only three months and then returned to Copenhagen. He appointed William Burnett to take charge of Church affairs and his brother James to assist him. The Burnetts enthusiastically pursued their callings and by September had baptized two more converts. They now had five members and held meetings every Sunday, but only a few attended.

The Burnetts evidently did most of their work at Kaiapoi, near Christchurch. By January 1868, William wrote of "the spirit of gathering" that the members at Kaiapoi shared. All, apparently, hoped to go to Utah as soon as they could raise the money. In March 1870, however, they were still at Kaiapoi. At this time they were waiting for Elder Robert Beauchamp, the only officially called and appointed missionary in the Australasian Mission, to come from Australia to preach the gospel. The Burnetts had sold books, distributed tracts, and loaned copies of the *Millennial Star*, the Church periodical published in England, but they prayed that "when brother Robert Beauchamp will come, the people will listen to him."[7]

President Beauchamp was also expected by a larger group at Karori, near Wellington. There Brother Holder and his family had remained faithful to the Church since Elder Cooke had left them in 1856. In fact, they had loaned books and information to friends and were now eager to have President Beauchamp visit them and baptize a number of converts. Foremost among the new converts was English-born Henry Allington, a school teacher at Karori. He was first introduced to the gospel through the Book of Mormon and the writings of Orson Pratt and had become so committed to the Church that for two years before this time he had acted as a missionary among the people of the area. Before President Beauchamp arrived, Brother Allington wrote that he believed there were twelve people who were ready for baptism.[8]

When President Beauchamp arrived at Karori, he was not disappointed. Within two weeks of his arrival on April 8, 1870, he had baptized six people and said he expected to baptize "quite a number" the next Sunday. Among the first to be baptized was Henry Allington.

During his first twelve days in New Zealand, President Beauchamp ordained Brother Allington an elder and called him as president of the Karori Branch (there were twenty members), which he also organized.[9] At this time the Wellington newspapers began to criticize the Church, and one writer even suggested mobbing the elders and Saints. But no violence against the Church resulted at this time.

From Karori, Elder Beauchamp went to Kaiapoi, near Christchurch. The Burnett brothers were especially happy to see him. His visit lasted only from May 13 to 24, but he fed them spiritually. He also baptized several other people and reorganized the Kaiapoi Branch. Because there were now two functioning branches, President Beauchamp decided that it would be proper to organize a conference (district) in New Zealand. All three members of the new presidency were already engaged in branch callings, which they retained. William Burnett was now called as conference president, James T. Burnett became first counselor, and Henry Allington became second counselor.[10] President Beauchamp's visit must be counted as one of the great short missions of the Church. When he arrived in New Zealand, there were only nine baptized members of the Church. But when he sailed for Melbourne, there were forty-one Saints in good standing, as well as two branches and a conference.[11]

The first conference meeting of the New Zealand Conference was held on January 8, 1871, at Wellington, with William Burnett presiding. About this time the members of the Karori Branch organized a Sunday School for the fifteen children of the branch.

Considering the small size of the branches in New Zealand, it is strange that following Beauchamp's first visit and several times during the next year, Wellington newspapers wrote long and abusively about him and the Mormon cause in general. When President Beauchamp returned to Wellington—Karori—in October 1871, to hold the second conference of the New Zealand Conference, the *Wellington Advertiser*, reflecting the same attitudes as the *Post* and the *Christian Messenger* of the same city, made a strong and irrational attack against Brother Beauchamp. The following is the concluding paragraph:

> We trust, however, that he [Elder Beauchamp] will be sent forth from their [the people's] doors, as a thing too filthy to be touched, and that the unwhipped vagabond may be forced to earn his living by honest labor. . . . We hear that the foul-mouthed wretch intends holding forth at Karori tomorrow, and we urge upon husbands and brothers not to allow the ears of their female relations to be polluted by the foul language poured forth by this disgrace to mankind. We should be sorry to promote a breach of the peace, but we trust the vagrant will be pelted with rotten eggs.[12]

The articles in the *Advertiser* and other newspapers had the effect their writers desired, and mobs gathered to harass and destroy the property of the Saints. On more than one occasion mobs followed the members to their homes and threw rotten eggs at them and their houses. One night the mob brought tar and feathers but failed to find Elder Beauchamp. That same night they broke several windows in one of the Saint's homes by throwing two- or three-pound stones. Fortunately, nobody was hurt.

All this abuse was eventually brought to the attention of the government. A member of parliament, Mr. Haughton, asked the premier whether he was aware of the Mormon disturbance and the possible political effects the Latter-day Saints could have. Mr. William Fox, the premier, answered that he was not aware of any wrongdoing by the Mormons and that neither he nor his government would become involved until it was proven that the LDS were creating problems.

This kind of abuse notwithstanding, the Saints held their conferences and continued to influence a few good people to join them in their cause.

Shortly after they joined the Church, Brothers Allington and Burnett mentioned their desire to gather to Zion. The persecution heaped on the Church must have strengthened their resolve to immigrate to Utah. On December 30, 1871, a company of eleven Saints (two families) sailed from Auckland for America. In April 1872, Henry Allington led his wife, his two children, and five other members of the Church aboard the *Nevada*. They arrived in Salt Lake City forty-four days later. There are occasional references to other emigrants from New Zealand to Zion, but it is not possible to calculate the total numbers who left. As was true in Australia, many of the emigrants had been the strongest members of their little branches, and these branches were definitely weakened. In fact, it was reported in 1876 that only one Saint was still living in Wellington-Karori; all the rest had moved to Utah.

Four years passed before another full-time missionary arrived in New Zealand. Whether he came as a result of James T. Burnett's March 13, 1875, letter to President Brigham Young, in which he said, "There is an opening for a missionary" in the area of Christchurch, or from some other cause, is not known. In any event, in November 1875, Thomas Steed was sent from Melbourne to work in the New Zealand Conference of the Australasian Mission. After visits in Wellington and Karori, Brother Steed traveled south to Kaiapoi, where he found James T. Burnett in charge of a dozen-member branch.

Elder Steed eagerly set to work tracting and conversing with people "from morning to night" on the principles of the gospel. As might have been expected, he soon aroused some sentiment against himself. One of the local newspapers advanced the idea that Steed "had come from Utah to carry off a cargo of New Zealand beauties and ship them to Brigham Young for wives."[13] This article excited some young men of the area so much that they threatened to throw Elder Steed in the Waimakariri River. Through gentle, friendly talk he convinced the ringleader that neither he nor the rest of the Mormons were bad people.

Less than a month after Steed's arrival, four elders came directly from Utah. Two of them, Frederick and Charles Hurst, had been baptized in Australia and had immigrated to Utah. Their mother lived in Wellington, New Zealand, and they had a happy reunion with her. The other two elders were John T. Rich and William McLachlin; the latter was appointed leader of the conference. All but one of the elders worked in the Christchurch area during 1876. On January 23, 1877, the New Zealand elders were surprised and sorry to receive word that they were all released to return home to Utah.

During most of 1877 and until August 1878, the Saints in New Zealand were once again on their own. When Thomas A. Shreeve arrived in Christchurch on August 23, 1878, the mission began an era of continuous missionary activity that has extended to the present.

THE SECULAR AND RELIGIOUS HISTORY OF NEW ZEALAND TO 1880

The islands now called New Zealand were first discovered by the Dutch explorer Abel Tasman in 1642. Captain James Cook was the first European to chart these islands, during his voyage of 1769. Few other white men visited the islands until the 1790s, when some sailors, traders, and vagabonds began establishing small settlements on the North Island on the Bay of Islands.

The delay in colonization until 1840 was caused primarily by two factors: First, the British government had doubts about the wisdom of such an enterprise; and second, the local inhabitants, the Maoris, were greatly feared because of their practice of cannibalism. In the 1830s, however, desire for land became greater than the fear of the Maoris, and settlers came to the country in greater numbers. By 1840 the New Zealand Land Company had been organized for the purpose of colonizing the islands. During that same year the British government decided that too many of the Queen's subjects had immigrated to the new country to leave them without an orderly form of government. Hence British sovereignty was extended to New Zealand, and a lieutenant governor was appointed to guide the political destiny of both pakehas and Maoris. The officers of the Colonial Office in England placed New Zealand under the control of the governor of Australia until the new government was securely established. In May 1841 New Zealand became a separate Crown Colony.

Many pakehas were not happy to have the new government established. At least the general reaction to William Hobson, the first British governor, was far short of enthusiastic. He was an able administrator and had an honest concern for all the people of New Zealand. The pakehas, however, concluded that Hobson was too concerned about the rights of the Maoris. This conclusion arose from Hobson's having signed the "Treaty of Waitangi" on February 6, 1840, a document that stated his hopes and intentions for the new political system. It also promised the Maori people that in exchange for their acknowledgment of the sovereignty of Queen Victoria, they would be given the rights of British subjects and full, exclusive, and undisturbed use of their lands. Hobson demanded that he and his successors be the only legal parties to whom the Maoris could sell their land. Obviously his intent was to protect land, the only real economic asset of the Maoris, from exploitation and to establish a biracial society in New Zealand, with equality of rights for both races. But although the racial situation in New Zealand today approaches complete equality, Hobson's ideal commonwealth was not immediately achieved.

During the 1840s, pakehas systematically colonized both islands. The steady foreign encroachment by the pakehas, in combination with some indications that the new government was not entirely fair and equal in its dealings with the Maoris, caused some tribes to rebel. Several serious battles were fought between 1843 and 1848, and then twelve years of peace preceded the next and more critical outbreak of war.

During the late 1840s the pakeha part of the population pressed the government, both in New Zealand and in England, for a constitution and for more local representation. In 1852 Sir George Grey, the governor, introduced a constitution that set up a pseudo-federal system in New Zealand. It called for a basically representative form of government. When the first House and Council met in 1854, the primarily British settlers demanded "responsible government"—government on the British parliamentary model, with the ministers chosen from the House and responsible to it. This request was granted in 1855, and in May 1856 New Zealand was launched as a self-governing colony.[14]

It is appropriate here to discuss the role of religion in New Zealand prior to this time. When pakehas first began settling in the Bay of Islands region during the 1790s, there were probably about 200,000 Maoris living on the North Island. During the next forty years this number declined by half. Wars among the tribes had always been endemic, but the introduction of the musket and other firearms, as well as diseases that were new to the Maoris, caused increased misery and loss of life.

The early Protestant missionaries attempted to counter the forces of war and disease and were somewhat successful. Samuel Marsden, senior Church of England chaplain in the penal colony at Sydney, Australia, was the first churchman to vigorously advocate missionary work among the Maoris. He became acquainted with some Maoris in Australia and was convinced that they were intelligent, upstanding people who were ready to hear and accept Christianity. Marsden organized a group of mission workers, among whom were several mechanics and farmers, and finally, after several years of delays, sailed for New Zealand. He led the small body of missionaries in the first Christian service known to be held in New Zealand, on Christmas day 1814. Grattan encapsulates the missionary efforts of the next several decades in these words: "The missionaries set about reducing the language to written form, teaching the people to read and write, printing portions of the Bible and tracts in Maori, teaching the practical arts, particularly agriculture, and encouraging the Maoris to divert their energies from war to peaceful pursuits."[15] Before the middle of the century, several other missionary groups—Presbyterians, Methodists, Baptists, and Roman Catholics—had entered the field. The emphasis of their work was on the good of the Maoris and not on the well-being of the white intruders.

The missionaries were very successful. They introduced the potato and the pig, both of which greatly benefited the Maori economy, as well as many other varieties of food. Farming machines too were brought to the Maoris, who quickly mastered the science of agriculture. But the greatest success was in converting the Maoris to Christianity. In 1854, shortly after George Grey completed his term as governor of New Zealand, he reported that "all but about 1 per cent of the Maoris had made a profession of Christianity."[16]

In 1854 the first Latter-day Saint missionaries landed in New

Zealand. On the surface it would appear that the time was right for immediate success in teaching the restored gospel to the Maoris as well as to the pakeha or Caucasians. Success with the Maori, however, was delayed until the 1880s. There were several reasons for this delay. The most serious was the series of Maori-pakeha wars that occurred between 1860 and 1872. Although there was never a full-scale uprising of all Maoris, and though the total number of people killed on both sides was less than three thousand, these wars, which were a result of the Maoris' certainty that they had been unjustly dealt with in land transactions, were very disruptive for all people on the North Island. It is doubtful that LDS missionary efforts could have succeeded under the circumstances, especially considering the anti-pakeha feelings among many of the Maoris during this time.

A second reason why the Maoris were not ready for Mormonism in the 1850s was that Christianity, as taught by the Protestants and Roman Catholics, was still new, and most Maoris were satisfied with their teachings. By the 1880s, however, all this had changed, and in addition to large-scale defections from the orthodox faiths because they embodied pakeha doctrines,[17] the Maoris themselves devised several important new religious-political movements, and a number of smaller religious cults of a millennial kind. Among the more important movements was the King Movement, which, although it was primarily political, embodied concepts from the Bible. The most violently anti-pakeha movement, but one that was more religious in composition than the King Movement, was Hauhau or Pai Marire. It too was partially based on elements from the Bible, but it revived ideas and practices associated with the Maori *tohungas* (priests) and ritual dances and incantations to ward off pakeha bullets. A third movement, the Ringatu Church, which still claims over 3 percent of the Maori population, was started by Te Kooti during the 1860s. Te Kooti is revered by his followers as a prophet and saint. Although Ringatu was founded as an outgrowth of the King Movement and Hauhau, it came to combine Christian and Maori traditions, and it emphasizes faith healing. One of the distinctive features of this religion, which gave it its name, is the upraised hand, "te ringa tu," which is equivalent to the "Amen" of Christians.[18] In the late 1870s another Maori prophet, Te Whiti, arose and preached peace. In addition to these well-known Maori prophets and religious leaders, there were many minor figures who had local importance and impact. More than one of these men had roles to play in the acceptance of Mormonism by the Maori people.

MORMON MISSIONARY SUCCESS AMONG THE MAORIS

By the 1880s, when the Church began a concerted effort to influence and convert the Maori people, New Zealand's pakeha population had grown considerably. In fact, the total pakeha growth between 1858 and 1871 was from 59,000 to 256,000 people. This growth continued to the end of the century, when the total population was 772,719 (in 1901). At that time there were only 43,143 Maoris. The Maori decline, which had started at the beginning of the century, continued until 1893. The LDS missionaries came among the Maoris at a time when they were depleted, beaten, and badly in need of spiritual regeneration. The elders were eager to take care of these Maori needs, but time and considerable effort were required before the Mormon-Maori connection was made.

In his fine study of Maori Mormonism, Ian Barker asserts that LDS missionary progress among New Zealand Europeans was "minimal," and for this reason the mission leaders made a decision, based on previous experience with other Polynesian people, to proselyte among the Maoris.[19] Barker is only partially correct. It is true that relatively few Europeans had joined the Church prior to the move to actively proselyte the Maoris. It is also true, however, that very few missionaries had been sent to New Zealand since 1854 and that each of the elders who were called had succeeded in converting a relatively large number of people. Most LDS missionary work was conducted on the South Island, in and around Christchurch, until 1880, when the headquarters was moved to Auckland. In each year from 1878 on, there were three to six elders preaching the gospel. This number usually included several local converts. By the end of 1880, the small number of elders had accomplished a great deal. There were seven branches organized; three of these had Sunday Schools and two had Relief Societies. There were 133 baptized members and sixty-five children of record. In addition, thirty-three members had emigrated to Zion since 1878. From about 1881 on, the emphasis of New Zealand missionary work was on the Maoris, but it is not correct to assert that the pakehas would not have come into the Church or that the missionary work among them had been a failure.

Until 1897, New Zealand was part of the Australasian Mission. In 1879, however, there were no missionaries in Australia, and the mission headquarters were moved to New Zealand. From then until the mission was divided, the mission president always lived in New Zealand.

The decision to take the gospel to the Maoris was not a sudden one. Since 1853 Church leaders had been aware of these people and their good qualities. In that year, Augustus Farnham wrote concerning the Maoris: "I am informed the chiefs of the tribes say the [Protestant and Roman Catholic] missionaries do not preach to them the right gospel; that they are keeping back the part they need. And they do not feel to receive their teaching. From what I can learn, the field is ready to harvest."[20]

Although President Farnham did go to New Zealand, he did not have time to work with the Maoris. Several other elders made contact with various tribes, particularly on South Island, where relatively few Maoris resided. James T. Burnett reported working with Maoris in the Canterbury region in 1872. Again, in 1876, Elder Burnett, in company with Utah Elders Thomas Steed and Fred Hurst, visited a *Pa* (stronghold or village) near Kaiapoi. There Elder Hurst, who had learned enough of the Maori language to use it, conversed with some of the chiefs and talked with them about the restored gospel.[21] But nothing came of this or several later encounters.

On January 14, 1881, three new Utah elders arrived in Auckland. They were William M. Bromley, who was called as mission president by the First Presidency; Nicholas H. Groesbeck; and John S. Ferris. They joined George Batt and John P. Sorensen, who were already serving. Batt, who had been serving as acting mission president, was situated in Auckland, and Sorensen, a Dane who was converted in Utah and who had formerly lived in New Zealand, was working in the Napier area along Hawkes Bay (or Hawke Bay). Several local converts were assisting in the work when the new elders arrived.

It is not clear from the historical record why Joseph F. Smith of the First Presidency told Elder Bromley that the time had come for the Maoris to receive the gospel.[22] There is some evidence that Church leaders in Salt Lake City had discussed the Maoris during the preceding several years. In an article that appeared in the *Juvenile Instructor* in 1876 (pp. 187-88), the writer counseled his young readers in this way: "Let us then not look down on the Maori, but let us strive to elevate him, and instruct him in all that is good and beneficial, and above all impart to him a knowledge of the true faith, and teach him the way to eternal life and salvation." This writer, known only by his pseudonym of Hugh Knough, then suggested that the Maoris "are undoubtedly of the seed of Jacob." He was not sure how this seed found its way to New Zealand, but he suggested that Israelites might have come "from time to time from Asia," or they "might be descendants" of the two loads of ships that Hagoth led to sea. Such articles as this one may have influenced President Smith. Or perhaps he was motivated to tell Elder Bromley it was time to teach the Maoris because he had recently received a letter from George Batt in which he said that the Maoris were ripe for conversion. Brother Batt wrote, "They [the Maoris] are looking for something important to take place. Who knows? It might be the Mormon Elders taking them the word of the Lord as revealed through the Prophet Joseph Smith, even the Book of Mormon."[23] Considering President Smith's relationship with the Hawaiian Polynesians and his belief that they were children of Israel, it is not surprising that he felt a concern for the Maoris and was inspired to tell Elder Bromley that the time had come to establish the work among them.

On March 6, 1881, Elder Bromley, along with several local pakeha elders, the most important of whom was William J. McDonnel, made his way to Orakei village, about four miles from Auckland. There they met with Chief Paora Tuhare of the Ngati-paoa tribe. The chief was not eager to talk with the elders, but he did agree to consider a document outlining the beliefs of the Latter-day Saints. He also agreed to send this document to the king in the Waikato area and to Te Whiti, the great Maori prophet who lived in the Taranaki on the west coast. President Bromley wrote the needed document, and Elder McDonnel had it translated into Maori and printed two thousand copies. But even though the missionaries returned to Orakei on March 20 with the statement of principles that Chief Paora asked for, they did not succeed in converting any members of that tribe at that time.[24]

Pursuing this plan further, Elder John P. Sorensen went to the Taranaki area and met with Te Whiti, but Te Whiti refused to accept the Maori tract. This meeting, held on June 17, distressed Sorensen so much that he shook the dust from his feet as a witness against Te Whiti. Obviously this attempt to convert the Maoris ended as a disappointment.

At approximately the same time, Elder John S. Ferris traveled to Opitiki, a few miles east of Whakatane, on the Bay of Plenty. By December he reported to President Bromley that he had distributed tracts among the Whakatohea and adjoining tribes, but he could not report any headway.

The first Maori to accept the gospel in New Zealand was one of the king's attendants named Ngataki from the Waikato area, just south of Auckland. He became acquainted with Elder McDonnel, who had charge of the "graving" or dry dock at the bottom of Hobson Street in

Auckland. After four days of steady gospel discussions, McDonnel considered Ngataki ready for baptism and performed the ordinance sometime in October 1881.

More than another year passed, however, before a significant breakthrough came. During that time several new groups of pakeha elders arrived from Zion, and a few returned home, some with groups of emigrants and some because of sickness. The missionaries who stayed continued to work with various Maori tribes as well as with the pakehas, particularly of South Island.

In December 1882 President Bromley traveled from Auckland to Cambridge, about one hundred miles south, to spend the Christmas holidays with Elder and Sister Thomas L. Cox. Elder Cox was a local convert who made his living as a shoemaker. Hannah Cox was, like her husband, a sincere friend of the Maori people. Together they visited among the Maoris, taking care of their needs and also teaching the gospel. Brother Bromley was quite surprised to see Elder William McDonnel when he arrived at the Cox place early on the morning of the twenty-fourth. Elder McDonnel explained to the others that he had had some dreams that made him believe the Maoris were ready to accept the gospel. Later that same day, Elders Bromley, Cox, and McDonnel went out into the country to visit a Maori village. After talking with several groups of Maoris, they decided to head back to Brother Cox's home. Along the way, Elder McDonnel noticed a Maori house on the brow of a little hill and a man standing near it. He climbed the hill and handed the man a tract in the Maori language and turned to walk away. The man grabbed him by the collar and told him to stay and give his message. By then, Elders Bromley and Cox had climbed to the house. The man turned out to be a Maori chief named Hare Teimana. The three elders spent several hours teaching Hare Teimana, his household, and some other Maoris about the restored gospel. Before they concluded, they bore witness that they held the same power to act in the name of God that Christ gave to the ancient apostles. On hearing this, Hare Teimana asked the elders to bless his daughter Mele (Mary), who was seriously ill. They did so, and she immediately showed signs of recovery.

The next day the three elders returned to the same place. Hare Teimana told them of a night vision he had beheld a month or two before. Several versions of this vision are extant, but they agree on one major point—that messengers from God were coming and that they were working with or under the direction of the ancient apostle Peter. One version says that Hare Teimana recognized Elder McDonnel and his companions when he saw them for the first time. In any event, because of this vision and the obvious healing power these men held, a number of Maoris were converted to the Church. That day, three people applied for baptism. "We went to the Waikato river," wrote President Bromley, "and there on Christmas night, at 10:30 P.M., with the bright rays of the moon for a light, and the Spirit of God to comfort us, we baptized and confirmed at the water's edge two men and a woman." The three new converts were Hare Teimana, Pare Teimana (his wife), and Hare Te Katere (Harry T. Carter). They were only a small promise of the rapid growth that was to come.

The next Monday, New Year's Day, Elder Cox baptized five men and one woman, making nine converts in all. Elder Bromley wrote that "these are people of influence and very intelligent."[25] He appointed Elder Cox to preside over the Waikato district and the mission among the Maoris of that part of the country.

Over the next weeks and months Elder Cox steadily added new members to the Church. Some of his converts were Maoris of talent and stature among their people. For instance, on January 9, Elder Cox baptized Pepene Eketone, a man who had intended to enter the ministry of the Church of England. Educated in English and Maori colleges, Eketone was a government interpreter. His linguistic abilities proved useful to the Church.

At about the same time, President Bromley appointed Elders Alma Greenwood and James C. Williams to travel throughout the Waikato area and teach the gospel to the Maori people. They spent a month traveling from village to village and ultimately baptized four Maoris who lived near Cambridge. But they were generally unsuccessful. Cox's little branch was the only early site of LDS success in the Waikato. Other Christian churches were having similar results there. This was the King Country, the location of the most disaffected Maoris in the nation. The people here did not like or trust pakeha government or pakeha religion. This attitude extended to the Mormons as well as others. Fortunately, not all Maoris felt the same way. Latter-day Saint success came in areas where the Maoris had remained friendly or neutral during the Maori-pakeha wars.

Before going on, it is important to note that during February 1882, Elder Cox, under the direction of President Bromley, ordained the first Maoris to the Aaronic Priesthood. He called a meeting at his home of a select group of men, including some young ones. After carefully explaining what the priesthood was and elaborating on each office, Cox asked Hare Teimana, Hare Te Katera, Hari Wirihana, Pepene

Eketone, Epiha Harepa, Te Opira, Maora, Peter Temuhitu, Eihona, Tapa Tewhapa, and Ohahatutute Omahana whether they would like to be ordained to various offices in the Aaronic Priesthood. They discussed this offer among themselves for a few minutes and then asked whether they could have a few days to consider the matter. On the next Sunday, February 25, they met again. Through Brother Eketone, who acted as interpreter, Elder Cox asked the men what their decision was. Hare Teimana spoke first; he said he "thought we ought to make the old people the Priests." He was obviously thinking of Maori practices wherein the seniors held the greatest authority. Brother Teimana suggested that Hare Te Katera, an older chief, should be given the priesthood and placed in charge of the Church members. When asked how he felt about this suggestion, Katera said he desired to have the priesthood. "He believed that the Holy Ghost would enlighten his mind and teach him what to do," wrote James C. Williams, the clerk of the meeting. None of the other brethren felt they were ready yet to hold the priesthood. Elders Cox and Williams then ordained Brother Katera to the office of priest. Immediately after, he was sustained as president of the new Waotu Branch of the Waikato Conference. The branch had twenty-seven adult members and one child.[26] By March 17, less than three weeks later, the branch had grown to sixty-one Maori members, forty-five of whom had been baptized by Brother Cox.

On March 21, 1883, President Bromley assigned Elder Alma Greenwood to leave the Auckland area and preside over the Wellington District. President Bromley counseled Elder Greenwood to expend most of his efforts in teaching the gospel to the Maoris. Only three days after he arrived at Wellington, Elder Greenwood, in company with Elders Farr and Hansen, traveled to Carterton, one of the principal cities of the Wairarapa district or valley. On April 3, the elders visited Waitapu, thirty miles down the valley from Carterton. Here they became acquainted with chief Manihera Rangitakaiwaho, who, with his family and a number of Maoris, listened intently to the message of the Restoration. Two days later, the elders baptized the first Maori convert from this area.

On April 22, Elder Ira N. Hinckley, Jr., joined Elder Greenwood as his companion. The experiences they had together over the coming months were remarkable. These two must be credited with the first significant and lasting success among the Maoris. Over the next several months Elders Greenwood and Hinckley centered most of their attention on Manihera, an influential chief of the Papawai tribe, "knowing that if he would embrace the truth, it would be of great utility in opening our way to the natives."[27] In July 1883, Chief Manihera introduced the elders to some close friends at Te Ore Ore, where a large number of Maoris lived. Within this household of friends was a man named Ihaia Hopu Whakamaeru, who was an invalid, "haggard and emaciated." Ihaia, who had been a minister in the Church of England for forty years, listened long and carefully to the Mormon message, and in the evening he asked to be baptized. He urged Manihera to join the Church too. Manihera, after making some excuses, decided to do so, and a day was appointed for the baptism.

Concerning the baptism, Elder Greenwood wrote:

> On the 21st of July, 1883, we were instrumental in leading thirteen Maoris into the waters of baptism, Ihaia and Manihera being among the number. Although the former had been an invalid for a number of years, and constantly confined to his bed four months previous to his baptism, he walked a quarter of a mile down to the river on a bitter, cold day and was immersed in ice-cold water. Next day his health was improved. . . .
>
> The Spirit of God, immediately subsequent to their baptism and confirmation, rested powerfully down upon them. . . . Everywhere and any time they met any of the Maoris, they were preaching the truth to them, as after events proved this was the effectual opening of the gospel to the natives of New Zealand.[28]

Soon after this baptismal service, Elders Greenwood and Hinckley ordained Manihera and Ihaia priests in the Aaronic Priesthood, and in December 1883, the two new members were called to preside in Papawai and Manaia, respectively. Ihaia, who had formerly served as a mediator between Maoris and pakehas during times of war, was now a public official and was well respected among all the surrounding tribes. On December 9, they were ordained elders, four other Maori brothers were made priests, and two were ordained teachers. That same day, all the Saints of lower Wairarapa were combined to make the Papawai Branch, the first all-Maori branch in the mission. Manihera was called as branch president.

One might wonder whether these Maori Saints, so new in the Church, were really capable of understanding the workings of the Church organization and the finer details of doctrine. The missionaries found the Maoris to be well-versed in the Bible, particularly as to the historical and biographical parts. But the elders did not simply baptize, ordain, and sustain the new leaders. "We spent much time in minutely educating the new converts in the principles of the truth," wrote Elder

Greenwood. "Our task . . . was very irksome, being compelled to employ two Bibles (an English and Maori); passages necessary to substantiate the gospel were searched out of the English book and afterwards pointed out to the Maoris in their own Bible. We drilled and educated them to that extent that they could vanquish any foe."[29]

Elder Greenwood was proud of the progress of his Maori converts; he wrote, "Not many months passed away before the [Maori] Saints could administer the sacrament, assist in confirmation, take general charge of meetings, and perform the duties of their callings with equal, and in some instances, better proficiency than that of the white Saints in the world with the same experience."[30]

Six days after the organization of the Papawai Branch, the missionaries, along with Elders Manihera and Ihaia, traveled again to Te Ore Ore. There they all preached the gospel to a considerable number of Maoris who had already decided to join the Church. Following the meeting, sixteen Maoris, eight men and eight women, were baptized. The next day, December 16, 1883, Elder Greenwood directed the organization of the Te Ore Ore Branch. Elder Ihaia Whakamaeru was called as branch president, which position he held until his death in April 1886, and other men were called as his counselors, secretary, and treasurer.

Leaving Te Ore Ore on December 19, the elders traveled seventy-five miles north to Tahoraiti by late afternoon on the twentieth. Nine buggies were required for the entire entourage. When they arrived, the missionaries were greeted in the most elaborate Maori fashion. There was a great show of emotion, with much loud noise and many warlike gestures on the part of the key greeter. During the next three or four days the missionaries taught the gospel to hundreds of Maoris and baptized four converts into the Church. In this way the gospel was introduced at Tahoraiti.

Although the details of Elder Greenwood's and Elder Hinckley's mission are fascinating, we must abridge most of their activities. Having been invited to the Hawkes Bay district by letters and even by a telegram from Chief Hohepa Otene Meihana and his friend Tomoana, a member of the national parliament, the elders left about one hundred Maori members of the Church in the Wairarapa valley and traveled north to the Hastings area to see the Maoris there, who were "anxiously" awaiting their arrival. Within a few days, Chief Hohepa Otene Meihana asked for baptism, and shortly after, on May 5, 1884, thirteen other Maoris joined the Church. Elder Greenwood wrote that "Brother Otene Meihana was very ambitious in the work, having an ardent desire to bring all his race into the truth, and through his labors the word of God was carried to many persons."[31]

During May and June 1884, the elders taught the Maoris of every settlement in the Hawkes Bay section and made many converts. On June 29, they organized two branches, one at Taonoke with Hohepa Otene Meihana as president, and the other at Korongata, where Oterene Rapi was called to preside. There were a total of seventy-one members in these two branches. For the next two months Elders Greenwood and Hinckley alternately visited the two branches every other Sunday. They taught the leaders and members carefully, and the Maoris "soon became sufficiently advanced to enable them to preside intelligently over those who were under their watchcare."

At that time the two elders were joined at Hawkes Bay by President William Thomas Stewart, who had replaced President Bromley almost a year before. Together the three men left the Hawkes Bay branches and headed north along the coast. It was their intention to go all the way back to Auckland, but they had so much success that they were delayed for several months. Andrew Jenson recounted the events of the next few weeks in this way:

> When they reached Wairoa, northeast of Napier, they held seven meetings in seven different places among the natives, but none applied for baptism, though most of them were favorably impressed. At Nuhaka they baptized 15 and blessed three children on the 4th of September. At Kopuawhara, Mahia, they baptized and blessed 42 on the sixth. On the 7th they arrived at Muriwai, Poverty Bay, and were well received and on the 9th, they baptized 25 natives, which was the greatest number baptized at any time since the opening of the mission.
>
> Tuesday, September 9. President Stewart telegraphed to John C. Stewart to go to Mahia immediately and take charge of those who had been baptized. . . . Elder Stewart reached Mahia on the 4th of October and continued the good work in that district. By the end of the year about 270 souls had been baptized in that country. [That is in the area of the Mahia Peninsula. By that time another one hundred had been baptized in the Poverty Bay area.][32]

The growth of the Church was so rapid that some non-Mormon Maoris called a meeting to see what could be done about it. The result was that more Maoris entered the waters of baptism. Between September 23 and November 30, 1884, four additional branches were organized—at Muriwai, Papawhariki, and Marahea (Poverty Bay), Tikokino (Hawkes Bay), and Kopuawhara and Tauapata (Mahia district). In December, three more branches were added to the growing list. In late November Elders Greenwood and Hinckley were released to return home, and the Maori mission was placed in other hands.

New missionaries were arriving in New Zealand regularly from mid-1884 on. President Stewart appointed them to work with the new members in the various branches and to continue teaching prospective converts. President Stewart was probably the most successful missionary at this time. During November he and his companions baptized sixty-two people, and in December they added sixty more names to the Church records.

When the accomplishments of the year were assessed, President Stewart reported 545 baptisms for 1884 and a total membership of 1,076; 265 were pakehas and 811 were Maoris. Elder Charles O. Anderson wrote home describing some of the new members:

> Here [Hawkes Bay] are some very rich natives belonging to the Church, and all come riding in the finest kind of buggies drawn by stylish and spirited horses. . . . The Maoris of this portion of the country are altogether different from those in my district, both morally and otherwise, and all those who have been baptized are such as previously belonged to the Church of England or other sects of Christendom. They have large farms which they cultivate in wheat, oats, potatoes and vegetables. . . . They are also possessors of a large number of horses, cattle and sheep.[33]

Almost all of the converts from the Hawkes Bay, Mahia, and Poverty Bay areas were born of the Ngatikahungunu and Aitangaa-mahaki tribes. Large numbers of the former tribe entered the Church, and they have provided many of its finest leaders. The Poverty Bay Saints have been almost as influential.

CHAPTER 17

MAORI TOHUNGA AND THE GROWTH OF THE CHURCH

New Zealand, 1885–1897

By the end of 1884 the missionaries had firmly established the restored gospel among the Maori people. In August 1885, there were sixteen Maori and four pakeha branches of the Church, and this number continued to grow steadily for the next fifteen years. At the close of 1887, there were 2,573 Latter-day Saints, and by the turn of the century there were nearly four thousand members of the Church in New Zealand. Most of the Maori tribes had been introduced to the gospel. In 1901 there were seventy-nine branches.

Even though Polynesians of all island groups have taken well to the restored gospel, the Maoris appear to have been prepared in special ways for the coming of the Mormon missionaries.

In pre-Christian missionary times, the Maoris had a well-developed form of religion. Tohungas or priests supervised worship. Sometimes these men would give oracles, cure diseases, and admonish their people.[1] After the establishment of Christianity, some old tohungas continued to carry on their former practices but now claimed to receive their revelations from a different source. In other instances family patriarchs, village elders, and chiefs acted as prophets and were "regarded with feelings of reverence and were credited with possessing supernatural powers."[2] No fewer than five such men made prophecies about the coming to New Zealand of the true church. As a result of such prophetic utterances, a number of Maoris ultimately joined the Church.

Two of these prophecies can serve as examples. In 1830 an aged patriarch named Arama Toiroa, who lived in the area of Mahia, gathered his children, grandchildren, and relatives together. (At that time most of his descendants had joined the Church of England.) To them he said, "My dear friends, you must leave that church, for it is not the true church of the God of heaven. The church you have joined is from the earth and not from heaven."

Upon hearing this his people asked, "Where then can we find a church where we can worship the true God?"

Arama Toiroa answered, "There will come to you a true form of worship; it will be brought from the east, even from beyond the heavens. It will be brought across the great ocean and you will hear of it coming to Poneke Wellington and afterwards its representatives will come to Te Mahia.

"They will then go northward to Waiapu but will return to Te Mahia.

"When this 'Karakia,' form of worship, is introduced amongst you, you will know it, for one shall stand and raise both hands to heaven.

"When you see this sign, enter into that church."

Fifty-four years passed before Arama's words were fulfilled. Brother Whaanga described the day when the gospel was first preached to Arama's people:

> In journeying northward they reached . . . Korongata, where many of us were assembled on the Sabbath day.
>
> Amongst the people who were there was a grandson of Arama Toiroa whose name was Te Teira Marutu.
>
> The meeting was conducted by Elder Stewart and his friends. The services were opened with singing and prayer, and a Gospel address was delivered, after which they sang again, and Brother Stewart arose to dismiss with prayer. In doing so he raised both hands and invoked God's blessing upon the people.
>
> As soon as the grandson of Arama Toiroa saw this he arose and declared that this was the church of which his forefather prophesied which would surely be firmly established amongst the Maori people.
>
> He and his wife applied for baptism, and they and their children were thus initiated into the Church by Elder Stewart.[3]

Subsequently the missionaries returned to Mahia and held meetings with other descendants of Arama Toiroa. After seeing the sign, these people said, "This is indeed the church for us, for did not our revered forefather, Arama Toiroa, prophesy about it?"

Largely as a result of this prophecy, every person in Korongata joined the Church, and a large number of Maoris in Mahia entered the waters of baptism.

In 1845 a second prophet, Toaroa Pakahia, spoke words similar to those of Arama.[4] And again in 1877, Apiata Kuikainga, an ancestor of Stuart Meha who was a faithful leader of the Church in New Zealand for many years, predicted that when the true church came, its ministers would teach salvation for the dead. In 1885, when this doctrine was preached to the Meha family by Elders George S. Taylor and Edward Newby, they all desired baptism.[5] In 1881 Elder John Ferris wrote that Maoris had told him that "more than a year ago the king [Tawhiao] said a white man would come across the sea and preach to them the true gospel, and they affirm that they believe he [Ferris] is the man."[6] Elder Ferris wrote to the *Deseret News* in Salt Lake City that three Maori chiefs considered him to be the man spoken of by the king two years before. He had come from "a far country and would give them the good church."[7] The complete text of King Tawhiao's prophecy was later quoted in the *Improvement Era* in 1932: "Our church is coming from the east—not a church paid with money. Its ministers go two by two; when they pray they raise their hands. They will not come to go among the Pakeha (Europeans) but will dine, live, talk, and sleep with you. The sign will be the writing of the names of males, females and children. . . . Those churches that have already come are nothing, but when these come that I speak about, do not disturb them—that will be your church!"[8]

The Latter-day Saints interpreted the "sign of writing names" to be a reference to genealogical work and work for the dead. During 1885 and 1886, seven branches, having 537 souls, were raised up in the Waikato.

The best known prophecy is that from Paora Potangaroa. In March 1881, Elder Matthew Cowley reported, a large convention was held among the Ngatikahungunu tribe. Many Maori chiefs assembled at Te Ore Ore, near Masterton, to discuss political, social, and religious problems. The established churches were well represented, but the chiefs shared a feeling of discontent about the lack of unity among them. Why, the natives asked, were there so many different churches within the bounds of Christianity? Which one should the Maoris join so that unity could again be restored among them?

After considerable debate and discussion the chiefs decided to place the question—specifically "Which of the churches is the church for the Maori race? Which of them should we join?"—before the most respected and wisest chief among them. This was Potangaroa, who, when asked the question, answered with one word, "Taihoa," which means "wait." He retired to his home and meditated, fasted, and prayed about the problem for three days. When he returned to the convention he addressed his people, saying, "My friends, the church for the Maori people has not yet come among us. You will recognize it when it comes. Its missionaries will travel in pairs. They will come from the rising sun. They will visit with us in our homes. They will learn our language and teach us the gospel in our own tongue. When they pray they will raise their right hands."[9]

Potangaroa then asked Ranginui Kingi to write his words as he continued to answer the question that had been put to him. He called the transcription of his words "A covenant for remembering the hidden words which were revealed by the Spirit of Jehovah to Paora Potangaroa." Quoting from Elder Cowley, who translated the document: "First, this is the day of the fulness (1881)." Brother Cowley pointed out that later that year the fulness of the gospel was taken to the Maoris. Actually, President Bromley and his colleagues first visited a Maori village, Orakei, on March 6, 1881, ten days before the "covenant" was given to the Maoris at Te Ore Ore. "Second, the year 1882, would be the year of the 'sealing' (or the year they would learn the sealing ordinances). Third, the year 1883 will be the year of 'the honoring'—of 'great faith'—as it is written: 'render therefore to all their dues: tribute to whom tribute is due; custom to whom custom; fear to whom fear; honor to whom honor.' (Romans 13:7)." In that year the Maoris began to honor the true God by rendering their dues to him and entering The Church of Jesus Christ of Latter-day Saints. Members of the Ngatikahungunu tribe, especially, began to enter the Church in large numbers. It will be recalled that the Te Ore Ore Branch was organized on December 16, 1883.

The document concludes in these words:

> This covenant is to be remembered by the generations which follow after us. And the fruits of that which is set forth above (in the covenants) are—we are the lost sheep of the House of Israel. (We will learn of) the scepter of Judah; of Shilo; of the king of peace; of the day of judgment; of the kingdom of heaven; of the sacred church with a large wall surrounding; of the increase of the race; of faith, love, peace, patience, judgment, unity. All this plan will be fulfilled by the people of Ngatikahungunu Tribe during the next forty years.
> March 16, 1881
> Ranginui Kingi[10]

Elder Cowley identified the "sacred church with a large wall surrounding" with the Salt Lake Temple. He also pointed out that the only Maoris to participate in all the ordinances of the gospel during the next forty years (until 1921), including the temple rites, were members of the Ngatikahungunu tribe. Later many members of other tribes participated in all blessings of the gospel.[11]

There is no question as to the authenticity of the prophecies of Potangaroa or of the document that Elder Cowley used. Potangaroa was well known in his time.[12]

Shortly after leaving New Zealand in 1884, Elder Alma Greenwood wrote about Potangaroa's influence. "Many of the natives were led to investigate the new and somewhat strange religion, which had come in their midst. This, too, was in accordance with some predictions previously made by a Maori prophet: that in 1883, a new religion would come [at this time "Mormonism" was unknown among the Maoris of the Wairarapa], and all other religions would be inferior to the new one. The prophecy and its literal fulfillment gave the gospel prestige and influence among that people."[13]

There were a number of other reasons for the Mormon-Maori connection. The Maori prophets had identified some of the characteristics of the Mormon missionaries: In addition to traveling in pairs, eating, sleeping, and visiting with the Maoris in their homes, the elders also learned the Maori language so that they could understand the Maoris and their thinking. The elders willingly endured various privations and discomforts in order to remain among the Maori people. As Ian Barker states it, "The habitual enthusiasm, friendliness, devotion and sincerity of most of the elders impressed the Maoris. Both Mormons and Maoris placed high premiums on hospitality and friendliness."[14]

But the foregoing were only surface reasons for the Mormon impact on the Maoris. Ian Barker captures the essence of the Mormon-Maori connection in these words: "Important features of Mormonism appeared to have deep roots in Maori tradition. Conversion to Mormonism did not involve a sharp break with the past that conversion to Christianity had. To the Maori, the adoption of Mormonism implied a restoration of traditional sacramentals in a modified form. Historical, social, mythological and religious similarities enabled the elders and the Maoris to establish bonds of sympathy and understanding, which in no small part contributed to Mormon successes."[15]

Of great importance to the Maoris, as they discovered Mormonism and used it to make the adjustment to the pakeha world, was that the elders did not reject *Maoritanga*, Maori cultural traditions, in their entirety.

Before 1865 the typical Maori probably would not have made any connection between the Maori God *Io* and the Mormon God Jehovah. Before that date Io was a secret deity who was known only to a few high-ranking tohunga. Io was the one god, the creator, omniscient, omnipotent, and uncreated. Io reigned supreme over many other gods who carried out various functions in heaven and on earth. In the hereafter, the dead were ushered through one of four doors, rather than through the Pearly Gates or into hell. The Maoris always believed that men would be sent to many mansions, some to glory but most to one or another degree of happiness in accordance with their works and disposition. The *atua* or lower gods were generally identified with elements of nature, but there was a latent anthropomorphism within the Maori religion. While sectarians struggled to remove all vestiges of such belief, the Latter-day Saints not only condoned but strongly affirmed that God the Father and Jesus Christ were immortal men, who looked like men, even though they were Gods. All this seemed to make more sense to many Maoris than did the doctrines of mainline Christianity.[16]

The Maoris had intense interest in and love for their families. The Mormon concept of eternal families immediately appealed to many Maoris. They had long revered their dead, and when Christianity was brought to them, the Maoris feared for the pagan spirits of their ancestors. But unlike the orthodox missionaries, who could suggest no alternative to eternal damnation, the elders taught a message of hope and salvation.

Not only did the Mormon missionaries teach about salvation for the dead, but they also taught the Maoris the doctrine of eternal increase. The resurrection was to be literal and physical.

The Maori tohungas had sought and received revelations from God. They considered it their responsibility to be seers and lived so that they could carry out this function. The tohungas also performed healings and exorcised evil spirits. These functions were also performed by village elders and patriarchs after the introduction of Christianity. Continuous revelation, healing, and exorcism were generally discounted by the Protestant and Catholic missionaries as being superstitions from a bygone era, or as parts of the gospel that were no longer in vogue. The Mormon elders, however, taught the necessity of contemporary revelation as well as of all other gifts of the Spirit as taught in the New Testament. A main tenet of the restored gospel was that the priesthood had again been given to man.

Some Latter-day Saints suggested even before LDS missionary work was started among the Maoris that the Maoris were of the house of Israel. This suggestion may be explained by the fact that following the introduction of Christianity, the Maoris soon identified themselves with Judah. Then, as the competition for land became more intense between them and the pakehas, and particularly as the Maoris began to realize that they were coming out on the short end in most transactions, the persecutions of Judah became all the more real to them. When the elders began teaching about the history of the Church, it became evident that the Mormons, too, were a persecuted people. This helped to establish a bond between Mormons and Maoris—they understood each other.

But there was much more to the idea that the Maoris were of Israel than merely shared persecutions. Far more important was the Mormon belief that the Maoris, like their Polynesian brothers and sisters elsewhere, were literally of Abraham through his posterity who migrated to the American continent, as is told in the Book of Mormon. Although the relationship between the Polynesian peoples and the adventurer Hagoth (Alma 63:5-8) is not clear—he being a Nephite and the Polynesians appearing to be Lamanites—Church leaders have time and time again referred to the Polynesians as children of Lehi. LDS missionaries believed and taught that the Maoris were chosen sons and daughters of Abraham.[17] The elders expected the Maoris to accept easily the restored gospel and to assume their rightful place as leaders in the Church. There was almost no racial prejudice on the part of the Mormons toward the Maoris.

Although the first Maoris who were offered the priesthood were hesitant to accept it, it was not long before they assumed nearly all of the positions of leadership in the branches. Many Maoris were ordained to positions in the priesthood. In this way, the Mormon Church became their own church. They led it, taught the members, blessed their own sick, and guided their own families through personal revelation.

THE TRANSLATION AND PUBLICATION OF THE BOOK OF MORMON INTO MAORI

Before the translation of the Book of Mormon was begun in earnest, various elders had undertaken smaller projects, such as translating tracts, the Word of Wisdom, the Articles of Faith, and the sacrament prayers. Late in 1885 or early in 1886, President William T. Stewart, with the help of Ezra F. Richards and a part-Maori named James Jury, began translating the Book of Mormon. But the project was discontinued on February 23, 1886, because the missionaries did not know enough Maori, and James Jury did not know enough English. "The native language itself is more or less deficient," wrote President Stewart, "and it will require a most thorough acquaintance with its idiomatic construction to enable a translator to convey the teachings of so important a work as the Book of Mormon in that forceful manner desired."[18]

During May 1886, President Stewart sailed for home, having been released from his assignment. William Paxman assumed the leadership of the mission in New Zealand. Maoris were still coming into the Church in large numbers during his first year as president. He traveled widely and held many district conferences. In March 1887, President Paxman led the third all-mission conference, near Gisborne. To his and his wife Katie's sorrow their little daughter Sarah died March 10, the day before the meetings began. Some meetings were canceled on the eleventh to make time for the funeral and burial. Sarah was the first LDS missionary's child to die in New Zealand.[19]

Two days later, following considerable discussion among the assembled missionaries, President Paxman asked the Maori priesthood holders whether they would support, both financially and spiritually, another attempt at translating the Book of Mormon. The response from the brethren was overwhelmingly positive. Every man who spoke was "very anxious to have the work published immediately."[20]

President Paxman appointed Elders Ezra F. Richards and Sondra Sanders as translators and Sister Katie Paxman to be their cook and assistant. Because of other responsibilities they did not begin the work of translating until April 26. But from that time until November 24, 1887, when they completed the first draft, they devoted most of their time to the project.

With the assistance of Henare Potae, Te Pirihi Tutekohi, and James Jury, the two elders revised the first draft between December 5, 1887, and March 24, 1888. Sister Georgiana Marriott, the wife of one of the missionaries, copied most of the new manuscript. At April conference in 1888, President Paxman displayed the accomplishment of the missionaries and local members. He asked Elder Sanders to read a sample to the people. The assembled members of the Church voted to have two thousand copies of the book published as soon as possible.

The Star Publishing Company of Auckland was contracted to print and bind the Maori Book of Mormon. The final cost of 371 pounds was borne entirely by members of the Church in New Zealand. President Paxman delivered the manuscript to the publishers in September, and they returned the printed and bound volumes to him for distribution by the next April conference. President and Sister Paxman were released to return home at that time. He left New Zealand a very happy man, for he had completed his favorite project.[21]

HUI TAUS, MAORI EMIGRATION, AND THE DIVISION OF THE MISSION

The first all-mission conference was held in March 1885. It included all of the Australasian Mission, of which New Zealand was the most prominent part, but Australia was hardly represented, if at all. Conferences in New Zealand followed the pattern used elsewhere in the Church. The Relief Society was not organized in 1885, but before many years had passed, special meetings were held for the women. Missionary sessions were usually held daily, but most important were the general sessions for all the members and other interested friends who chose to attend.

In each district, local and mission leaders held a hui pariha, quarterly conference. At some point before the turn of the century, the national meeting came to be called the *Hui Tau* (Annual Meeting). *Hui* means meeting, conference, or gathering. From 1887 on, the Hui Tau was always held at the time of April general conference in Salt Lake City, on or about April 6. From the beginning, feasts and socializing were part of the Hui Tau, but as years passed the event gradually became more elaborate, with games, sports, Maori dancing, oratory, dramas, and so forth. During the twentieth century the Hui Tau not only served the spiritual and social needs of the New Zealand Saints, but it also helped preserve Maori culture.

The spirit of gathering to Zion touched not only several hundred pakeha Saints in New Zealand before the turn of the century but also a few Maoris. Arama Toiroa, in his prophecy of the coming of the Church, had also said, "Many of you will join the church and afterwards one will go from amongst you the same way that the ministers came even unto the land afar off." In 1893, Hirini Whaanga, a descendant of Arama and a respected chief among the Ngatikahungunu tribe, developed a great desire to "gather" to Zion. His family protested, but he reminded them of Arama's prophecy and received their support.[22]

In June 1894, Hirini, his wife Mere, and six other members of their extended family sailed from New Zealand for Utah. They were in company with Elders Lars Christian Rasmussen and Douglas Gibson.

When they arrived in Utah, the Maori family lived briefly with the John C. Stewarts in Kanab and then settled permanently in Salt Lake City, where Hirini and his wife occupied themselves doing temple work for their ancestors. In 1898, when Hirini was seventy years old, the First Presidency called him back to New Zealand as a missionary. He willingly accepted the call and served for over a year. During that time he also gathered the names of many ancestors and did their temple work on his return to Salt Lake City. He died there in 1905.[23] Other Maori Saints also immigrated to Utah during the 1890s and the early twentieth century, but details about their activities are not available. The First Presidency generally discouraged immigration of island people to Utah.[24]

The 1890s were a busy time for the president of the Australasian Mission. During that decade missionaries of the Church were assigned to several important cities in Australia. By 1897 it was evident to the First Presidency and Council of the Twelve that Australia was not receiving the leadership and attention that the missionaries and members there needed. With this in mind the First Presidency directed George Reynolds, mission secretary, to instruct President Ezra F. Richards that Australia was to be made a separate mission. The official division took place on January 1, 1898.[25]

CHAPTER 18

THE MAORI AGRICULTURAL COLLEGE AND INSTITUTIONAL DEVELOPMENTS

New Zealand, 1898–1919

The period from 1898 until 1919 among the Maoris was not without growth, change, problems, successes, and excitement. But this era was very different from the one that preceded it. The first two decades of this century were most notable for the steady institutional development of the Church in New Zealand. Mission leaders and local Saints were faced with the problems of providing chapels and meeting halls, caring for the educational needs of the Maori children and youth, winning legal and popular recognition for the Church, and bringing the Church organizations closer to parity with the approved organization in Zion.

The growth of the Church in New Zealand in numbers of members from 1901 to 1919 was 1,316. This was fewer than half the number of converts who came into the Church between 1881 and 1901, but certainly it was a respectable rate of growth in comparison with other Pacific missions of the Church at that time. The accompanying table illustrates the statistical status of the Church in New Zealand from 1901 to 1919:

New Zealand Mission Statistics, 1901-1919[1]

Year	Total Members	Convert Baptisms	Melchizedek Priesthood	Total Branches	Total Districts	Total Missionaries
1901	4,457		175	79	15	49
1905	5,238	126	174	91	14	54
1910	5,521	250	205	105	17	56 + 14 local
1915	6,488	194	220	105	17	47
1919	5,773	188	191	41	10	53

Several figures need to be explained. The drop in membership between 1915 and 1919 relates to record keeping. A careful census of Church membership was taken in 1916, which resulted in a more accurate total. The drop in total branches between 1915 and 1919 resulted from the consolidation of a number of small groups (which had been called branches in prior reports) into larger branches. The convert baptism figures are not exactly correct. They probably reflect many baptisms of eight-year-old children of members. The small number of Melchizedek Priesthood holders reflects an attitude that was common in all the Pacific missions, that is, few Polynesians were entrusted with the Priesthood, even though in New Zealand almost every branch was presided over by a local man with local counselors. The total number of missionaries remained stable during this quarter century.

The importance of the missionaries in the Church during this era cannot be overemphasized. Although local Saints were deeply involved in the work of the Church, the missionaries supplied the necessary experience. It is difficult to say whether the elders and sisters were actually too involved in local Church affairs. The Maori and European Saints loved them, but their very activity may have slowed the numerical enlargement of the Church. In 1906, for example, there were sixty foreign LDS missionaries in New Zealand. Of this number, one was mission president, one was mission secretary, one was mission architect, three or four were assigned to "temporal work," that is, as chapel builders, four were schoolteachers, and fourteen were district presidents who occupied almost all of their time in ecclesiastical affairs. And the companions of the district presidents were limited in the tracting, preaching, traveling, and teaching they could do. Over half of the mission force was tied up in nonmissionary or semimissionary service. The situation did not improve quickly; in fact, it seemed to go the other way. In 1912, President Orson D. Romney reported that of forty-one missionaries, "only 13 of this number do missionary work. The balance are kept busy looking after the welfare of the Maori Saints." He said that he believed that because the Maori Saints did not have the privilege of emigrating, "they should have first consideration."[2] This is not to say that the work performed by the nonproselyting missionaries was not important but that the preaching of the gospel to nonmembers was not carried out with as large a force as might have been.

Maori elders were called as missionaries even before this era, but beginning about 1900, many Maoris were called to serve missions of from three to six months. The mission goal was to have one local elder serving from each district at all times.

The methods the missionaries used to teach the gospel to prospective converts were not much different from those in other parts of the Pacific. That is, they did much tracting, held "hall" meetings when assembly places could be arranged for, visited with people who were friendly to the Church, and occasionally locked horns with ministers of other faiths in open debate. In 1899 a new teaching medium was introduced by President Ezra F. Richards. He imported a "magic lantern" (a primitive slide projector) and a number of slides of Salt Lake City, Church headquarters, Church leaders, and natural wonders and industrial developments of Utah and the West. From then until 1905 (and occasionally after that), the mission secretaries made frequent references to the positive effects the "lantern lectures" had on the Maoris and pakehas of New Zealand.

From the time of the great acceptance of the gospel by the Maoris in the 1880s, little attention had been given to the much larger pakeha part of the population. In 1900, President John E. Magleby renewed and emphasized the work among these people. Until the early 1880s the elders had used street meetings as a method of gaining interest among the Europeans. Now, President Magleby encouraged those elders who were assigned to teach pakehas to begin holding street meetings again. This practice created some problems. In Auckland, an unruly crowd of approximately five hundred people rushed the elders and attempted to crush them. The police broke up this crowd, but unfortunately similar incidents happened a number of times during May and June 1901. The police finally refused to give the elders help. The question of whether the police had an obligation to protect the elders became a hotly debated subject in the Auckland newspapers. To the elders' surprise, public sentiment was generally on their side.[3]

In the south, at Christchurch and Dunedin, the elders had similar experiences. Peace was restored because the newspapers and the mayor of Christchurch insisted that the elders be given their right to speak.[4]

In December 1902, President Charles B. Bartlett called at the office of the Registrar General in Wellington and asked him to place the names of the elders on the list of legally recognized ministers so that they could perform marriages. After considering the request for a week, the Register General refused to grant President Bartlett's request,[5] forcing him to follow a legal procedure that did get the elders' names placed on the register but that took many months.

Not until the next December did LDS missionaries perform a legal marriage. When the matter was finally settled in February 1904, only two missionaries, the president and one other, were allowed to perform the rite.[6]

Over the years a number of small problems arose between the Church and the government. The most serious occurred in 1917, when certain officials decided to stop LDS missionaries from entering the country. We will discuss this matter more fully later.

However, the image and position of the Church were generally improving in New Zealand during this era. Not only was the Church gaining acceptance among outsiders, but it was developing well within. The Primary and MIA were slow in coming to New Zealand, but the Relief Society, the *Hui Atawhai*, was organized June 8, 1901, and began making a significant contribution to the lives of the Maori Saints. On that day Elder David M. Haun created the first Maori Relief Society at TeHoro Branch, Bay of Islands District. Sister Mangu Reweti was sustained as president, and Sisters Ere Hari and Kewa Waa were called as counselors. Two months later President Magleby organized three additional Relief Societies in the Mahia area. By 1904, fifteen branches had Relief Societies, and the number continued to grow over the years. In order to improve the Relief Societies and help the Maori sisters, President Magleby called Emma E. Wright, the wife of one of the missionaries, to serve as president of the Relief Society of the New Zealand Mission. Sister Takare Takana was chosen to be Sister Wright's counselor and companion. Together they traveled from branch to branch and area to area teaching the Maori sisters the principles of compassionate service and how to operate their organizations. In April 1908, Adelaide Hardy, wife of President Rufus K. Hardy, was sustained as Relief Society president. From that time until 1931, when the first local woman, Wiremu Ihepera Takare Duncan, was sustained in that calling, the wife of the mission president presided over the mission Relief Society.[7]

The first Mutual Improvement Association was started by the pakehas of the Auckland Branch in 1907. The first Maori MIAs were organized at Tahoraiti, Omahu (Mahia), and Gisborne in 1918. Korongata followed the next year. The Primary got off to a good start at Nuhaka on December 28, 1913. Sister Bessie Greening was sustained as the first president. Real growth of the Primary organization did not come, however, until the late 1920s.

Progress was also made on other fronts during the early years of the century. Many branches organized choirs. A number of chapels

Maori Sunday School at Korongata (near Hastings), New Zealand, 1909. (Photo from the *Improvement Era.*)

were constructed. The missionaries who were assigned as "temporal" workers supervised the construction of about one meeting hall each year for the first decade. The district and mission-wide huis (conferences) became more elaborate and useful. Since none of the chapels were large enough to seat all of the participants, mission leaders rented large tents to use as assembly rooms.

An interesting sidelight related to the huis was the trend toward holding these meetings in conjunction with some large non-LDS event or celebration. This plan worked for several years, but the hui committee of 1903 voted to stop holding the meetings in this way. From then on, the Hui Tau was always held separately from all other groups.

Even though 8 or 9 percent of the Maoris had joined the Church by the turn of the century, they had not become perfect, of course. Some Maoris continued or resumed the practice of tohungaism (something like witchcraft), continued to hold overly elaborate funeral *tangis* (in which too much drinking and emotional display were attendant), followed poor health practices, and were lax in observing the Word of Wisdom and law of chastity. The latter two problems seem to have continued until after World War II. The others declined with the gradual dissolution of *Maoritanga*, Maori traditions.

By the turn of the century, tohungaism, which had formerly been more respectable, had deteriorated into something akin to witchcraft. This practice found its way into the Church, where several branch presidents were guilty of engaging in it. From 1898 until 1903 there were frequent references in the mission records to talks by mission presidents and elders about the evils of tohungaism. The practice was widespread among the members for a while but seems to have died a natural death.[8]

As early as 1902, President Magleby suggested the creation of a Maori periodical to "carry the Gospel message to all parts of the land as well as build the Saints up in their most holy faith."[9] In 1906, President Hoagland made the idea a reality. He proposed to publish the paper every two weeks, part in Maori and part in English. On January 31, 1907, the first issue of the *Elders' Message* was published. The format was closer to that of a magazine than of a newspaper.

In February 1908, the new mission president, Rufus K. Hardy, decided to publish two papers, one in English and one in Maori, to be alternated every other week. The Maori paper would be called *Te Karere, The Messenger.* President Hardy planned to publish parts of a forthcoming translation of the Doctrine and Covenants in *Te Karere.* He reasoned that when all the parts or sections had been published, the mission printers could then bind additional copies and distribute the completed book. President Hardy assigned Elder William H. Dixon to translate the Doctrine and Covenants. By the time President and Sister Hardy left New Zealand on May 12, 1909, Elder Dixon had published a number of sections in *Te Karere.* This mission periodical was later recombined with the English *Elders' Messenger. Te Karere* served the needs of the missionaries and Saints until the 1950s.[10]

The New Zealand Mission occupied rented headquarters until 1909. Various mission presidents spoke or wrote about their desire for better facilities, but until President Hardy took charge of the matter, nothing significant was done. During the summer of 1908, President Hardy purchased a lot on upper Queen Street, in the heart of Auckland. By the time he closed the deal in August, plans were underway to build an assembly hall with a mission home and office adjoining it. A printing shop was to be placed in the basement under the assembly hall. On January 30, 1909, the two buildings were completed and ready for dedication. Charles Hardy, president of the Auckland Branch for many years, dedicated the mission home on that day. On January 31, Mission President Hardy dedicated the hall and all other parts of the facility. This assembly hall was the first chapel constructed for the use of the pakeha Saints in New Zealand.[11]

CHURCH SCHOOLS AND THE MAORI AGRICULTURAL COLLEGE

It was not until 1877 that the New Zealand government passed statutes that established free compulsory and secular education. Of importance was the fact that education was to take place in English, for Maoris as well as pakeha. The cities received the first and greatest attention; the Maori *pas* or villages, where most LDS Maoris resided, were given less consideration.

Because elementary or primary schools were not usually available for the children of the Maori Saints, the missionaries opened the first LDS primary school at Nuhaka on January 11, 1886. It must have been evident to the missionaries that an education, preferably in English, was mandatory for the young Latter-day Saints if they were going to compete with the dominant pakeha part of the population.

Elder Sondra Sanders was the first teacher; he was soon replaced by Sister Georgiana Marriott, another missionary. The school was a rude substitute for institutions that were better supplied; Sister Marriott used a homemade blackboard, and the children shared slates during the early months of the school's existence.[12] Before many months there were forty children in the school.[13]

By the end of 1888, the mission leaders had created additional schools in Waiapu, Mahia, Waikato, and Hauraki. The elders not only became teachers, but they also worked physically to keep some of the schools open. George B. Andrus, who served as a missionary-teacher during the first years of this century, raised vegetables such as sweet potatoes, squash, cabbage, corn, beans and turnips for his Maori students to eat, and if there was any produce left over, he sold it to pakehas to obtain money for school supplies.[14]

Most of the schools were conducted in Church meetinghouses. Evidently few or no schoolhouses were constructed for educational purposes alone.

The number of schools decreased during the 1890s, but interest picked up after the turn of the century. In the early 1900s the mission operated schools in ten different locations, but by 1911 this number dropped to seven. Some schools were still operating as late as 1917, but they were gradually phased out as government education was provided in the rural areas.

It must be said that the Church schools seem to have been below the standard of excellence that the government desired. None of them were recognized by the Department of Education. The reasons for their marginal success are fairly obvious: the missionary-teachers were

Elementary school group in front of a rural LDS chapel. Around 1910. (Courtesy LDS Church Archives.)

seldom professionally trained, and, perhaps more important, their length of service was usually short. Beyond this, the schools were poorly financed and supplied. Finally, missionaries were almost always educated in American schools, and their training was very different from that of the British system that was used in New Zealand.

In 1913, the New Zealand Mission opened the doors of its new and impressive educational institution, the Maori Agricultural College (MAC). The MAC's place in the history of the Church in New Zealand, important as it was, is difficult to assess. On the one hand the school seems to have been a failure if numbers of graduates are considered important. On the other hand, there is evidence that the graduates of the MAC have done much to build the Church in New Zealand and have contributed to the strength of their communities.

The idea of establishing a college[15] was generated a decade before the MAC finally came into existence. In April 1904, when President Charles B. Bartlett first spoke publicly about plans for the school, he said he desired one where Maori boys "can be taught the principles of the Gospel, as well as book learning, and in doing this it will give us a better hold on the rising generation and will make them stronger in the faith."[16] President Bartlett went on to say that too many LDS boys had

A farm scene at the 130-acre site that later became the Maori Agricultural College, 1909. (Photo from the *Improvement Era.*)

gone to schools run by other churches and that many had been lost to the Church in this way.

When Louis Hoagland became mission president in June 1905, he immediately began championing the cause of the proposed school. He began looking for an appropriate piece of land during 1906. By September he wrote (with the additional signatures of about ten other missionaries and one Maori leader) to President Joseph F. Smith asking for funds to buy land. Hoagland's first and most important justification for the school was that the LDS Church was losing its young people. He said the Church's opponents were content to let the LDS have the old people if they could get the young people in their schools. President Hoagland added that President Bartlett had promised the Maori Saints a school two years before, and he stressed that this promise had been renewed at every conference since then. He, Hoagland, did not wish to cause a breach of confidence.[17]

President Hoagland evidently made his case well, for the First Presidency promised financial support for the proposal. On March 28, 1907, Rufus K. Hardy, who was later called to the First Council of the Seventy, and his wife, Adelaide, arrived in New Zealand to replace President Hoagland. President Hardy was authorized to follow through on the project. The Hardys were accompanied by Benjamin and Emma Goddard. Goddard was a former New Zealand missionary. On April 1, 1908, Hardy's offer on 130 acres of land near Korongata, six miles from Hastings, was accepted by William and Thomas Thompson, and soon after, missionaries and members were assigned to begin working the land. They decided to plant sixty-five acres in grain and rent the remainder. J.B. Walker, a prominent Auckland architect, was engaged to design the school. President Orson D. Romney finally received approval from the First Presidency on August 18, 1911, to begin construction. W.H. Hay and Son, of Hastings, won the contract at a bid price of $48,000, and started building in November.

Preparations for the dedication of the MAC began more than a year before the actual event. President Romney invited any of the general authorities to attend, but none could arrange to come. When members and nonmembers began arriving at Korongata a week before the appointed time, mission leaders and the hosts at Korongata began making additional arrangements beyond the large initial projections. The crowd was large; invitations had been sent to every Maori family in the country encouraging them to be at the Hui Tau and dedication. Two thousand people camped on the college grounds, and when the school was dedicated on April 6, over three thousand people were

The college chapel at the Maori Agricultural College was the grandest structure on campus. (Photo from MAC Catalog.)

there. Possibly a third of the people were not members of the Church.

President John Johnson, who arrived in New Zealand in October 1912, described the efforts necessary to feed the throng: "One can scarcely conceive the amount of labor required to cook for and feed two thousand people three times a day. All the cooking was done by means of a large steam engine, and the preparation of the meats, vegetables, etc., was done by organized committees of potatoe peelers, butchers, dishwashers, waiters and carvers. There was seating capacity in the dining tent for nearly one thousand people, and first and second tables were set for each meal, after which the workers were waited upon."[18]

The MAC campus consisted of five buildings: the assembly hall, which doubled as a chapel and contained four classrooms; the dormitory, which had twenty-seven bedrooms with two or three beds per room, a large kitchen, a dining room, and six bathrooms; a manual training building where woodworking and other arts were taught; a duplex for the faculty families; and a laundry and ironing building.[19]

But more important than the buildings was the philosophy of education that directed the teachers and president of the school. The founders of the college did not lose sight of its original purposes. Religious education was the main reason for the school's existence. But in addition, the mission board of education decided that the college could best serve the needs of young Maoris if its program was a practical one. Consider the aims printed in the first Catalogue and Announcement of the MAC:

> The specific aims of the college are to teach Maoris the principles of agriculture that they may better utilize their valuable land holdings; to instruct them in the manual arts that they may build their own houses, barns, bridges, etc.; to train them in the secular branches of education that they may cope successfully with their associates in the commercial and social world, and to furnish them an opportunity to possess themselves of that education that will imbue them with a better understanding of the obligations of life and a higher appreciation of its opportunities.

In several ways, the purposes of the MAC embodied the general ideals and objectives of the "Young Maori Movement" and other non-LDS social-political organizations that were attempting to better the lot of the Maori people. Since the Treaty of Waitangi in the 1840s, the pakeha part of the population had operated on the assumption that the Maori race would eventually die out. The whites had "alienated" millions of acres of Maori land over the decades; by 1918 Maoris controlled only 5 million acres of the original 66 million acres of land guaranteed them at Waitangi. Conversely, the Maori population by 1901 had risen to 43,143.[20] This trend continued, and as Maori numbers rose, a small part of the white community began to feel some pangs of conscience for wresting so large a portion of the Maori lands from them.

The first stated objective of the MAC was to teach the Maoris the principles of agriculture so that they could better use their land holdings. Unfortunately, skills alone could not immediately open the door of opportunity for the Maoris. There was a strong prejudice against Maoris within most lending institutions. It was generally believed that Maoris were neither wise in the use of money nor industrious in its pursuit. Hence, even though a Maori boy might obtain the training necessary to succeed in the pakeha world on pakeha terms, he generally had to pay such impossibly high rates of interest on loans for needed supplies and equipment that he was shut out from his own lands. It is ironical that pakehas frequently criticized Maoris for not making better use of their property. Church leaders hoped that education would break down some of the barriers that the Maori Saints faced.

Maori Agricultural College Rugby team, 1918. (Photo from the *Improvement Era*.)

Students paid little to attend the MAC—nine pounds for those boys who did not live in the dormitory and eighteen pounds for those who were residents. The MAC offered a broad curriculum as well as many extracurricular activities such as sports, debate, and oratory. The school had a band and glee club. Livestock was raised nearby, and farming skills were emphasized. All teaching was done in English. In 1919, personnel at the college, in addition to the president, included "directors" of livestock and farming, manual training, athletics, and music. Two additional elders worked on the farm.

The MAC had its own branch of the Church, where the boys, who ranged from age twelve to age eighteen, participated in classes, singing, priesthood work, and sacrament meetings.

The MAC had a grand beginning and served well the needs of its students. But the very Saints whom the mission leaders expected to give the school the strongest support did not send as many of their sons there as they might have done. The student body was small, usually only from twenty-seven to thirty students. The largest class seems to have been the last class to enter in 1930, a group of around eighty boys.

Finances were a problem from the beginning. Different tactics were used to solve this problem. In 1914 the Church bought an additional 136 acres of land so that the school could come closer to self-sufficiency through profits from the land. This helped a little, but not enough. From time to time mission leaders asked for donations to help defray expenses, but a lack of funds continued to plague the school throughout its history.

Money was not the only problem. The New Zealand Department of Education was not impressed with the faculty or the curriculum of the school. Too many of the faculty members were untrained missionaries who were familiar with neither the parlance of education nor the educational system in New Zealand. The various presidents of the MAC constantly worked to overcome these dual problems but with only minor success.

The MAC occupied a tremendous amount of the mission president's time. Mission records are filled with accounts of meetings, travels to and from, and problems related to the college. There were also such emergencies as the faculty home burning down on two different occasions. The MAC did much for the few boys who took advantage of it, but the outlay of work, money, and worry required of the mission were heavy.

THE WAR YEARS

What is not said about World War I in the mission records is more significant than the few words that are written on the subject. The Great War began in 1914, and New Zealand was soon drawn into the conflict because of its dominion status as a part of the British Commonwealth of Nations. Yet even though New Zealand was at war from 1914 until November 1918, the effects of war were hardly evident. In fact, the economy improved, and an attitude of "business as usual" prevailed. True, before the end of the war, over 100,000 New Zealand men had served overseas and 16,000 had been killed or had died abroad, but all this was accomplished without noticeable changes in New Zealand's economy or style of living. Among the servicemen were a number of Latter-day Saints. Maoris fought side by side with the pakeha troops. During the war years, military training was introduced at the MAC, where a cadet corps was trained in marksmanship, marching, and related skills. However, both within and outside the

"Through the efforts put forth by this group of children . . . we have accomplished a great deal during 1917. In March . . . we staged a concert. Through the concert we bought and paid for a new church organ, costing $125, of which the mission contributed $25." Thames, New Zealand. (Photo from the *Improvement Era*.)

Church, life went on much as usual. The war brought more prosperity than hardship.

During the war years the mission and missionaries of the Church underwent considerable harassment, little of it related to the war itself. In August 1913, shortly before the war began, elders in Wellington reported that the government was planning to investigate the Church to see whether it deserved the privileges accorded all other churches. This investigation was the result of what the missionaries called "lurid tales from parts of England." A period of persecution of the Church was nearing an end at about this time in England, and it is not surprising that some of the false accusations against the Church and the missionaries made their way to New Zealand.[21]

Either the problems vanished for two or three years after 1913 or the missionaries stopped writing about them. In 1917, however, matters deteriorated again, and the Church faced trials at the hands of mobs and government officials. In Christchurch (where the elders had refrained from holding street meetings for many years), the missionaries attempted to hold open meetings again, only to be driven home by an angry mob. It is true that in Auckland, where the elders had likewise held no street meetings for years, they got along quite well when they started the practice again. But soon two elders were arrested there for distributing tracts and for dispersing literature that did not display the name of the printer and date of publication.

In May 1917, a number of anti-Mormon articles appeared in various newspapers within the Dominion that caused a new surge of prejudice against the elders and the Church and created serious problems that took many months to resolve. On June 25, President James N. Lambert went to the docks to meet eight new elders, but when the *Niagra* came in, there were no missionaries on board. The president learned that the eight elders had not been allowed to board the ship in Honolulu, but he could not find out why. Not until July 13, when he was at the Union Steamship Company asking when the next ship would be in, did he learn that the New Zealand government had sent out an order forbidding LDS missionaries to come. Lambert sought the help of a Maori member of Parliament, Dr. Maui Pomare, who assisted the Church on many occasions, and of Mr. Winslow, American consul in Auckland. Winslow learned from William Ferguson Massey, prime minister, that the elders had been stopped at Honolulu because Massey's government objected to the LDS "inculcating [its] doctrines into others" and because it had been reported to them that the Mormon elders were "guilty of inducing women to go to Utah."[22] No

Group picture of the Maori missionaries who were serving in 1917. (Photo from the *Improvement Era*.)

New Zealand Latter-day Saints had immigrated to Utah during the previous two years.

Consul Winslow encouraged President Lambert to prepare a letter for him to forward to Washington, a letter setting forth the Mormon position and purposes. From August 12, 1917, until late February 1918, President Lambert carried on a vigorous campaign to change the exclusion order. His efforts took him to Wellington many times; there he met with Mr. Massey and convinced him that the Church had been treated unfairly. President Lambert held many other meetings with various cabinet officials and undersecretaries. A number of non-Mormons helped the Church by writing letters about its standards and beneficent purposes. Finally, in February 1918, G.W. Russell, minister of internal affairs, directed his undersecretary to approve a quota system so that elders could be brought into the country on a replacement basis. Lambert suggested that sixty-five elders would be an appropriate number, and this maximum was used by the government until 1947.[23] After this problem was resolved, mission-government relations were generally amicable. At times the mission presidents even reported that government officials were pleasant to work with.

Between 1917 and 1919, President Lambert assigned two elders to work with several Maori brethren, particularly Wi Duncan and Stuart Meha, on language and translation projects. Francis Kirkham wrote a

Maori grammar that was published by the mission for the elders' use. It helped many missionaries improve their Maori over the next few years. Of greater importance were the translation projects President Lambert assigned to Elder Matthew Cowley. Elder Cowley had perfected his knowledge of Maori to an unusual degree. Those people who knew him while he served his first mission said he spoke like an educated native. Elder Cowley revised the Book of Mormon translation and prepared it for a second edition. When that task was completed, President Lambert asked him to translate the Doctrine and Covenents and the Pearl of Great Price. Elder Cowley later commented to his sister that he marveled that he "was the one that was supposed to have done the translating." The Spirit of the Lord was upon him while he performed this labor.[24]

Elders W. J. Maw, Harold Hinckley, Sidney J. Ottley, and M. Chard Moody (left to right) traveled from fifteen to sixty miles a day by bicycle among the villages of Hawkes Bay district to teach the gospel in 1916. (Photo from the *Improvement Era*.)

The final results of Elder Cowley's efforts were printed in 1918 (the Book of Mormon) and 1919 (the Doctrine and Covenants and the Pearl of Great Price), but already the Maori language was rapidly declining in use. Older members of the Church appreciated the Maori scriptures, but most young Maoris were becoming fluent in English by this time. In 1918, Elder A. Leonard Ellidge wrote home that it was difficult to find Maori speakers who could teach the missionaries how to use the language. He believed the Maori language would die out within forty years. Time proved his prediction to be almost true.

By the end of 1919 the Church in New Zealand had made considerable institutional progress. All of the auxiliaries had been organized, a college was operating, the branches generally had adequate housing, the mission had a respectable headquarters building, and, in general, the work of the Lord was moving well. It was a fact, however, that much remained to be done to bring the Church in New Zealand abreast of the Church in Zion. Only Nuhaka Branch was fully organized. The districts were presided over by pakeha elders rather than Maoris. There was not a recreation hall in any branch. Much had been accomplished by the Saints since 1898, but much still remained to be done.

CHAPTER 19

YEARS OF STRUGGLE, DEPRESSION, AND WAR

New Zealand, 1920–1948

Following the First World War, social and economic conditions were less than satisfactory for most New Zealanders. From October 1918 until January 1919, the country was hit by a severe epidemic of Spanish influenza that left 6,600 people dead. A high percentage of those who died were Maoris, and many Church members succumbed. Although there were a number of converts during 1918 and 1919, the membership dropped by over two hundred during this time.

Following the prosperous war years, the economy began a downward trend that did not fully reverse itself until the late 1930s.[1] At the conclusion of almost every year, the mission presidents recorded that tithes were lower than hoped for or expected. The number of tithepayers rose during the 1920s and 1930s, but the total dollar amounts contributed reflected hard times. The New Zealand of that time has been described as a large farm. Its major industry was

Waikato elders' quarters and branch chapel, 1918. (Photo from the *Improvement Era.*)

dairying and related activities. Unfortunately, the price of New Zealand's butter and cheese was dictated by the world market, and local efforts to make economic adjustments did not help.

Despite difficult economic conditions and considerable social unrest in the country, the Church continued to grow during the 1920s and 1930s. Total growth during these years was almost three times that of the first two decades of the century, even though the number of missionaries dropped during the Depression years. Surprisingly, the largest number of converts was made in 1932, when the mission force declined to eleven missionaries. The following table provides the statistics for the years 1920 to 1950:

New Zealand Mission Statistics, 1920-1950[2]

Year	Total Members	Convert Baptisms	Melchizedek Priesthood	Total Branches	Total Districts	Total Missionaries
1920	5,868	141	194	41	21	58
1925	6,306	228	207	50	13	51
1930	7,256	228	273	*65	15	29
1935	8,597	178	401	83	13	38
1939**	9,579	273	409	89	13	66
1945	10,229	174	440	89	14	0
1950	11,961	351	518		16	89

*Estimate
**No report in 1940

MAJOR CONCERNS

The records of the New Zealand Mission for 1921 reveal most of the ongoing programs and problems dealt with between 1920 and 1935. During 1921 the mission president was concerned with the problems of getting the approved quota of missionaries into the country, with diseases and sicknesses among the missionaries, and with the rise and popularity of Tahupotiki W. Ratana, a faith healer who was attracting much attention outside of, as well as inside, the Church. Reorganites and other anti-Mormons also caused problems. The mission president planned the annual Hui Tau and hosted Elders David O. McKay and Hugh J. Cannon at that event and elsewhere. He helped plan the second *ope,* excursion, to the Hawaii Temple. He also headed the board of education of the Maori Agricultural College. In addition to all of this, the mission president conducted district conferences (*hui pariha*) all over the country; traveled great distances to bless and comfort the sick, dying, and bereaved; supervised the acquisition and maintenance of Church property; and directed the keeping of the financial, statistical, historical, and membership records of the mission of 1921.

During 1919, President Lambert had trouble getting visas for new missionaries in spite of the agreement of 1917-18 that allowed the Church a quota of sixty-five missionaries. His successor, Elder Fred Schwendiman, discovered that although the mission had notified the New Zealand government when elders had left the country, the government failed to notify authorities in Washington that more missionaries were eligible to come. From that time on, mission leaders reminded the appropriate officers to keep their part of the agreement.

In the first decades of this century death struck a relatively high number of elders. One elder died in the influenza epidemic of 1918-19, and several more died during the first five years of the 1920s. Typhoid took three or four missionaries before an immunization was introduced in 1925. During the first four months of that year, New Zealand suffered a serious epidemic of poliomyelitis, then called infantile paralysis. Schools, theaters, dancehalls, and churches were all closed. The annual Hui Tau was cancelled, as were all district conferences. Missionary work, aside from blessings of the sick, came to a near standstill. Diphtheria caused much severe illness especially among young people, including the children of the MAC faculty and other missionary families. As the years passed, disease caused fewer problems, but it was a matter of concern through this entire period.

Before 1920, very few Maori Saints had attended the temple. Hirini Whaanga and his wife Mele immigrated to Salt Lake City in the 1890s, and after that time several other Maori Saints, notably Stuart Meha, visited the temple. When the First Presidency announced plans to build the Hawaiian Temple, they made it known that this temple was to serve the needs of all Pacific Island peoples. From 1915 until the new temple was completed, New Zealand mission leaders encouraged the local Saints to save their money and prepare spiritually and morally to attend the temple. In the later months of 1919, President James N. Lambert solidified plans for twenty-seven Maori Saints to go to the dedication. But evidently he was not in close touch with either Hawaii or Salt Lake City for he learned on December 31, 1919, that the dedication services had already been held November

27-30. Lambert was given instructions, however, to bring the temple Saints to Hawaii after Hui Tau the next April or May. The Hawaii-bound Saints sailed on May 5. President Lambert and the Maori Saints took almost $500 that had been collected by the Relief Society sisters to the temple as a donation toward its construction.

The final size of the temple group was smaller than was originally planned—six couples and two single men. Included among the travelers were Wiremu Karaka, Hohepa Heperi, Wiremu Takana, Wiremu Duncan, Eriata Nopera, Rahiri Harris and their wives, and Waitokorau Tamaihana, and Hui Hui Pera. Most of these people are well-known to the older Saints of New Zealand. Before they returned home, these Saints did a great deal of work in the Hawaiian Temple, and two couples even traveled on to Salt Lake City to visit the temple there. While he was in Salt Lake City, Wi Duncan met President Heber J. Grant, who ordained him a high priest. Duncan was the first Maori to receive this blessing.

From 1920 until the mid-1930s, it was traditional to send an *ope,* an excursion, to the Hawaiian Temple each year following Hui Tau. During some years the groups did not materialize, but in most, fifteen to thirty Saints made the long sea-journey to receive the blessings of the temple.

THE VISIT OF ELDER DAVID O. MCKAY

Elder McKay's coming to New Zealand was in answer to requests for a visit by a general authority that had been made as early as the turn of the century. President George S. Taylor, who replaced President Lambert in 1921, received word that Elder McKay and Hugh J. Cannon were scheduled to arrive at Wellington on April 20. President Taylor immediately contacted the members of the Hui Tau committee, who delayed the annual meeting until April 23-25. Every member of the Church who had the means to attend traveled to Huntly, in the Waikato area. When Elders McKay and Cannon arrived there, they found a typical, although large, Hui Tau setup. Two large tents, one for meetings and one for eating, were the main features of the landscape, and a playing field, a *marae,* had been prepared for athletic activities. The nearby chapel also served as a meeting hall for smaller sessions of the conference.

When Elder McKay stepped from the automobile, he was greeted with enthusiastic cries of "Haere Mai, Nau Mai," and a Maori Haka, a warlike greeting. Two hundred or more Saints then formed a line, and even though President Taylor told the Saints to shake hands in the pakeha way, Elder McKay insisted on shaking hands and hongi-ing, rubbing noses and foreheads, with every person in the line. As later groups arrived, this ritual was repeated a number of times.[3]

The Hui Tau began at 10:00 in the morning of April 23. Elder McKay spoke at least seven times during the three days of meetings. The third day of meetings was held on the Australian-New Zealand holiday called ANZAC day. This day was set aside to commemorate the valor and sacrifices of the Australian and New Zealand servicemen at Gallipoli, during World War I. Elder McKay talked especially to the bereaved ones who had lost sons, husbands, brothers, or relatives during the war.

Many wonderful things happened during the Hui Tau and also during the remainder of Elder McKay's visit in New Zealand, but the most remembered incident was his first talk at the conference. As he began speaking he said: "O, how I wish I could speak to you in your own language to tell you what is in my heart, but since I cannot, I am going to pray that while I speak in my own tongue you may have the gift of interpretation and discernment. While you may not understand my words, the Spirit of the Lord will bear witness to you of my words that I give to you under the inspiration of the Lord." Gordon C. Young, one of the missionaries who were there, later described what happened as Elder McKay continued to talk:

> He spoke several sentences and then Stuart [Meha] would interpret into Maori. Then he'd make another statement in English and Stuart would interpret. All at once everything was quiet, and all over the congregation the Maoris—not the Europeans but the Maoris—called out, "Stuart, sit down, don't interpret; we can understand what the Apostle is saying." They didn't [all] speak English, and they didn't understand anything President McKay was saying before, but now they were calling out to Stuart to sit down. He was rather disconcerted. . . . Stuart didn't know what to do so he started to interpret again. The calls came again, "Stuart, sit down. Don't interpret." So Stuart just sat down, and President McKay went on and gave one of the most beautiful talks I have ever heard in my life, and those people all understood what he was saying.[4]

Because Elders McKay and Cannon traveled to Samoa and Tonga from New Zealand and then returned, their New Zealand visit fell into two parts. But before they finally departed for Australia on August 2, 1921, they had toured most of the districts of the mission and met with hundreds of the Saints.[5]

THE RATANA MOVEMENT

The Ratana movement caused the Church some serious problems during the 1920s.[6] In 1927 President J. Howard Jenkins reported that Tahupotiki Wiremu Ratana, a faith healer, had drawn many Anglican Maoris and Mormon Maoris into his church. But Wi Duncan and other dedicated Saints succeeded in turning most of the Mormon-become-Ratana-followers back toward the LDS Church. President John E. Magleby, who replaced Jenkins in 1928, noted the return of around two thousand Maori Saints from the Ratana church. Since these people had not been excommunicated, it was not necessary to rebaptize them. After 1929 Ratana seems not to have been a problem for the Church.[7]

ORGANIZATIONAL CHANGES

Until 1928 the Primary Association was not well organized in New Zealand. Branch Primaries had been created early in the century, but they had been on-again, off-again (mostly the latter) auxiliaries. But the Primary received serious attention from President Jenkins in early 1928. He called Sister Arta Ballif, wife of MAC Principal Ariel S. Ballif, as president of the Primary. The first Primary to be established during the 1920s was the Nuhaka Primary, created on February 8, 1927. This was a few months before the Ballifs arrived in New Zealand on June 19, 1927. Before they left for home three and one-half years later, Sister Ballif had supervised the organization of fifty-two Primaries. During the 1930s the mission presidents made frequent references to the important role this auxiliary played in attracting new members to the Church and in holding the young people.[8]

By the late 1920s all the auxiliaries were well organized. The Mutual Improvement Association (MIA), like the Primary, had a strong influence for good among the youths inside and outside the Church. Athletics brought many young men into the Church.

Although mission presidents had been encouraged to turn leadership positions over to the local Saints, they had found it difficult to change the pattern of appointing missionaries as district presidents. But other district offices were held almost exclusively by New Zealanders. When President Magleby returned to New Zealand to serve his second term as mission president, he determined to place more authority in the hands of local priesthood bearers. On September 2, 1928, he called Eriata Nopera to be president of the

Hawkes Bay District. Having received permission to do so from President Heber J. Grant, President Magleby ordained Brother Nopera a high priest. He was only the second Maori to be ordained to this office in the priesthood. Brother Nopera chose Stuart Meha and Wilson Paewai to serve as his counselors. In a letter to the missionaries, written about this time, President Magleby "issued a declaration that local brethren and sisters should be used wherever possible so that they would become self-supporting and not dependent on the Elders to keep the branches moving."[9] Before the end of September, President Magleby reorganized the Mahia District and called Paora Hapi to be district president. He too was ordained a high priest. On October 14, Hohepa Heperi was sustained as president of the Bay of Islands District and ordained a high priest. Each of these men chose Maori counselors and clerks.[10] In July 1929, President Magleby called Turi Ruruku to serve as president of the Wairau District. He too was ordained a high priest. Over the next two or three years, two other districts were reorganized and placed under local elders. By the end of 1928, President Magleby reported that activity had picked up in the Maori-led districts. He believed this was a direct result of the change to local leaders.

This group of Maori Church members traveled to the Hawaii Temple in 1929. Mission President John E. Magleby (center, first row) faced a number of unreasonable obstacles from the New Zealand government before the group was allowed to leave. (Photo from the *Improvement Era.*)

THE CLOSING OF THE MAORI AGRICULTURAL COLLEGE

Although the Maori Agricultural College served well the needs of many Maori boys during its history, the principal problems of a lack of Maori members' support, poor financial backing, and failure to meet the standards of the New Zealand Department of Education continued to hinder the school's success till the very end. The MAC was not officially registered by the department of education until the last year of its operation. For this reason, the Maori boys who attended were not eligible for government-supported scholarships, which amounted to around US $175 a school year. Too many young Latter-day Saint boys chose (or their parents decided for them) to attend Te Aute, a fine school which was operated by the Church of England.

During the three and one-half years that Ariel S. Ballif was at the school, he brought about significant improvements that made the MAC a respectable institution in the eyes of government officials. Annoyed at the passive attitude of the Maori Saints, President Ballif expressed his feelings about the school in *Te Karere,* in January 1930:

> In the past three school years every effort has been put forth by the President of the mission and staff to place the M.A.C. on the standard that you have asked for. You have asked for teachers that the Government would accept; that has been arranged. You have asked us to prepare the boys for the Government examinations; that has also been arranged. You have complained at the amount of work that the boys have had to do at the college, stating they did not have enough time to study; this year they will be freed from the tying jobs and ample time [will be] given for study. Everything that has been asked for in reason and possibility has been granted. Yes, this year we will receive our first visit from the Secondary Department Inspector. From this we anticipate, with every reason to believe, that our college will be a registered Secondary School this year.

Elder Ballif's expectations were realized; the school was approved. The government authorities were impressed with what they observed when they visited the college during March and April 1930.[11]

However, on October 2, 1930, the First Presidency wrote to President Magleby and informed him of their decision to close the Maori Agricultural College. The reasons they gave Magleby included the general Church policy of retreat from the education field, the confidence they had in the New Zealand system of public education, and the high cost per capita to operate the school. The MAC was to close its doors after the 1930-31 school year.[12]

Before the final year was completed, the Hawkes Bay area was hit by a terribly destructive earthquake. On February 3, 1931, Hastings, Napier, and the surrounding territory were rocked by the most severe earthquake on record in New Zealand. Houses, stores, shops, and schools crumbled to the ground. Fires burned out of control because water lines had been broken.

The MAC was on vacation at this time. After it was all over, President John E. Magleby sent a message to the First Presidency: "Elders unhurt, Saints quite secure in earthquake area; college buildings standing; worthless; dangerous."[13] The MAC closed its doors forever.

Many of the most important Maori leaders of the Church in later years were MAC graduates. Some of the wealthiest Maori members, especially in the Hawkes Bay area, were MAC alumni. When the Zion elders were recalled from New Zealand in 1940 because of World War II (a topic we will discuss later), they were largely replaced by former MAC pupils. MAC "Old Boys," members of the alumni association, filled many positions of responsibility, such as district presidencies. When Matthew Cowley, then an apostle, returned to New Zealand, he said concerning the MAC graduates: "I went around among the native people, I discovered that the leaders of the natives . . . today are not those who went to the Church of England . . . or . . . Catholic schools —the leaders in the native race are the young men who learned at the feet of the Mormon elders at the Maori Agricultural College."[14] Perhaps no higher tribute could be given to the Maori Agricultural College and the elders who taught there.

THE DEPTHS OF THE DEPRESSION

LDS Church records in New Zealand say little about the Depression except that the number of missionaries dropped by 60 percent and tithes fell to a low level. From 1920 to 1928, an average of twenty new missionaries arrived in New Zealand every year. But from 1929 through 1934, the number of new missionaries who arrived dropped to only eight per year, and for one eighteen-month period, only one new worker came to that country. Between 1932 and 1935, no elders were assigned to work on the South Island, although acting President Harold T. Christensen visited district conferences there. The few missionaries who were in New Zealand during the early 1930s devoted almost all of their time to the members. Even after more elders started arriving, as late as 1936, they spent 75 percent of their time with members and only 25 percent proselyting.

Many members of the Church were on government relief. The mission did what it could to provide employment for them. For instance, some Maori members who were still on relief in 1936 were assigned to build several LDS chapels in the Hawkes Bay District.[15] The New Zealand government was helpful to the Church during the Depression years because the mission tried diligently to help the members help themselves. Most Mormon villages were examples of cleanliness and order.

More impressive than the problems of this era were the successes. The mission Hui Taus grew in size and evidently in quality. Many high-ranking Maoris—for example Mita Taupapaki, chief of the Te Arawa tribe—attended the yearly festivities and expressed support and interest in the Church's activities, particularly in the MIA and Primary. A mission genealogy committee was organized in 1932. President Christensen appointed Stuart Meha to head that work and to encourage district genealogy workers. Auxiliary conferences were held in a number of districts during these years. Obviously, neither the members nor the small band of missionaries decided to give up. Growth continued during the Depression.

On July 13, 1933, Rufus K. Hardy returned to Auckland after more than twenty years and began his second term as mission president. His second mission lasted only sixteen months because he was called to be a member of the First Council of the Seventy. Elder Hardy was the first New Zealand missionary to be called as a general authority of the Church.

President Hardy pursued a course that was similar to that of his earlier mission. He strongly encouraged the missionaries to learn the Maori language and devoted great energy to building relationships with the Maori community. That he was successful in this is attested to by the fact that when he visited Wahi to pay his respects to the dead Maori king, Rata Mahuta, he was allowed into the village in spite of an edict that no Europeans were to be allowed for the five days of the Tangi. At Hardy's approach, "the residents of the king's village came forward and instructed the policeman to let [Elder Hardy] pass, stating that [he] was not a European, but one of them."[16]

SIX YEARS OF GROWTH—1935-1940

There were a number of similarities between the developments of the Church in New Zealand and those in Australia during the years from 1935 to 1940. In both missions the local Saints recovered from the worst effects of the Depression. It was also during this time that

Elder Matthew Cowley, apostle to the Polynesians. (Courtesy LDS Church Archives.)

the New Zealand Mission, like Australia, began using radio, movies, and athletics, particularly basketball, to improve the image of the Church and to attract young people to the gospel. This short period saw the beginning of changes that were not to come to fruition until after World War II.

Some developments in New Zealand, however, were quite different from anything that took place in Australia. For example, President M. Charles Woods, who became president of the mission in 1935, saw a need to proselyte among the people of the European towns. Late in 1936 he wrote: "I believe that there are no Maoris in New Zealand who do not know of the Church . . . and who have not had more or less to do with some of the saints. Hitherto the European and Maori work has been done separately. . . . For the past nine months the elders have all been instructed to do as much work with the Europeans as possible and to contact all people in their districts.

. . . European towns are being systematically tracted."[17] Woods noted, moreover, that tracting was not a useful means of spreading the gospel among the Maoris.

The next year President Woods said that he was working to unify the mission, "not drawing so definite a line between Maori and European work as had hitherto been the case."[18] He opened the South Island and revived several old districts among the scattered pakeha Saints.

When Matthew Cowley took over as mission president in 1938, he emphasized work among the Maoris once again. In retrospect, this seems to have been an inspired move. During World War II, the local Saints were forced to rely on themselves. President Cowley's work among the Maoris before the war helped them to be ready for what came. Notwithstanding, President Woods had seen the signs of historical change and was a decade or so ahead of the times. Following the war there was a marked shift from work with the Maoris to energetic proselyting of the pakehas.

On June 16, 1937, Elder and Sister William E. Waddoups, who had served for many years as president and matron of the Hawaiian Temple and who were now touring the missions of the Pacific as genealogy specialists for the Church, arrived in Auckland.

President Waddoups outlined a number of guidelines that were to be followed in submitting genealogy records for temple work. As a result of their extended visit, which ended August 23, 1937, the mission created a genealogical office, which was initially situated in the home of Te Ao Wilson, counselor to Stuart Meha, president of the Mission Genealogical Society. Brother Wilson was assigned to check all records that were submitted. This was the first attempt to bring uniformity to genealogy work in New Zealand.[19]

A unique innovation of the New Zealand Mission was President Woods's decision to call a number of young Maori girls on missions to help the Primary Associations. This was in addition to the many local elders and priests who had been called to serve regular or short-term missions over the decades.

THE VISIT OF ELDERS GEORGE ALBERT SMITH AND RUFUS K. HARDY

The visit of Elders George Albert Smith and Rufus K. Hardy to New Zealand was a major historical event. These two general authorities of the Church, an Apostle and a member of the First Council of the Seventy, helped the Saints of New Zealand feel that they played "an important part in the affairs of the Church as a whole," Cowley wrote. They first arrived in New Zealand on February 18, 1938, accompanied by incoming President Matthew Cowley, his wife Elva, and daughter Jewell. That same evening the general authorities sailed on to Australia, but they returned to New Zealand for a month-long visit in time for Hui Tau (the first in three years because of polio epidemics) in April. Their visit was somewhat marred because Elder Hardy contracted a serious bladder ailment and missed all but one session of the conference.

The Hui Tau, which took place from April 13 to 17, was held at Ngaruawahia, the beautiful pa of Princess Te Puea Herangi. This stately leader of the Waikato Maori tribes had hosted her Mormon friends ten years before. Now, even though she was not a baptized member, she again opened her doors and provided the needed facilities for this important event. She even donated twenty-five pigs and two tons of potatoes for food. Princess Te Puea publicly commended the Church for its work among the Maori people. Approximately 2,500 Saints and friends attended.

It was at this Hui Tau that President Cowley established the course he would follow for the remainder of his mission, a mission that lasted for over seven years. He told the people assembled that "he deplored the increased use of the English language among the Maoris to the detriment of their own beautiful language." He encouraged the elders to learn the language of the people among whom they were serving—the Maoris. This counsel may seem to have slighted the existence of the whites of New Zealand, but since eight thousand of the nine thousand New Zealand Mormons were Maoris, it is understandable.

Elder George Albert Smith, who later became President of the Church, spoke a number of times and helped the Saints to understand the gospel. One of his sermons focused on authority, priesthood, and proper use of Church positions. Wisely he counseled that it is "what we do [that] determines our place in the Celestial Kingdom, and not what we have conferred upon us."

An interesting sidelight to the Sunday program was a meeting of forty-seven mothers, each of whom had at least ten children. Together they had given birth to 605 children. Amazingly, thirteen of these women had fifteen or more children each, for a total of 218. Truly, the decline of the Maori race was past.

Although Elder Hardy, who had served in New Zealand for so many years, was unable to guide Elder Smith through the country,

President Cowley and his assistants took him to most of the districts of the North Island and introduced him to the local situation.

After the Hui Tau and general authority visit were over, President Cowley called many local elders and sisters to fill missions, and he also asked district presidents to call "week-end" missionaries to visit little villages and hold Sunday services. President Cowley traveled constantly. In June 1938, he reported that during the previous fifty-one days he had journeyed five thousand miles, "visited almost every branch in the mission, and traveled with the elders through their respective districts."[20] His visits created a "spirit of unity throughout the entire mission."[21] During 1939, President Cowley traveled 35,000 miles by car, train, and boat.

WAR, WITHDRAWAL OF THE MISSIONARIES, AND THE LONG STRUGGLE

In New Zealand, as in Australia, there were many indications that the Church was about to "take off" during 1939. The mission force was up to sixty-six, the largest number since 1917, and the Church was gaining acceptance and public approval throughout the country. Many radio stations regularly broadcasted recordings from the Salt Lake Tabernacle Choir and Organ, the "Fullness of Times" series, and interviews with LDS missionaries and leaders. Elders were asked to speak to civic clubs. Missionary basketball and baseball teams brought attention and admiration to the Church. The Church had an attractive exhibit at the New Zealand Centennial Exhibition.

Once again the annual Hui Tau was held at Ngaruawahia. Although the event was celebrated four years late, the mission held its Golden Jubilee Hui Tau at this time. Tennis, basketball, rugby, oratory, choir, drama, *te rongo pai*—the chanting of memorized scriptures, a tradition that dated back to the 1800s—and many other activities occupied the time of the participants. The usual meetings were held, with the exception of separate meetings for the pakehas that were conducted in English.

At this time, when everything seemed to be going so well for the Church, war broke out in Europe, and because of her ties to Britain, New Zealand was embroiled in the conflict. Everywhere there was a call to arms.

When 1940 ended, President Cowley reported that some Church activities, such as the Hui Tau, district conferences, MIA Gold and Green Balls (dances), athletic events, radio broadcasts, and the like had

The old Queen Street chapel in Auckland. (Photo from *Improvement Era.*)

been carried on much as usual in spite of the war. But many things had changed. The proceeds from the dances—more than seven hundred pounds—had been contributed to the New Zealand Patriotic Fund. The Saints had held special fast days and contributed the monetary value of the uneaten meals to the same cause. Many of the younger members of the Church were now overseas, wearing the uniform of their country.

In May 1940, the First Presidency informed the Australian Mission that no new missionaries would be sent for the duration of the war, and on June 16, President Cowley received a similar message. Two days later he notified all missionaries in New Zealand concerning the First Presidency's decision and warned them of the possible consequences. "Every minute is precious and must be used to the best advantage. We must prepare for any emergency. A call may come at any time for all of us to return home."[22] Furthermore, President Cowley asked every missionary to obtain a notebook and to make a record of names and addresses of all friends and investigators. He reasoned that such a record would be helpful to the missionaries who came later. He also told the elders to help the Saints to perfect their local organizations. President Cowley calculated that with completion of normal mission terms, by June 1941 there would be only four missionaries from Zion in New Zealand, in addition to the president and his family. In effect, the withdrawal of the missionaries was underway.

The anticipated call to leave for home came on October 14, 1940. President Cowley received the same notification as did the other four Pacific mission presidents. It told the president to send the missionaries home on American ships as soon as possible, and to decide whether to send his wife and family home but in either case to stay there himself until further notice. On October 22, the Zion elders, thirty-four in number, boarded the *Mariposa* and sailed for Hawaii by way of Samoa. Proselyting came to an immediate standstill, "but the activities of the Church continue[d] as usual under the leadership of the local Priesthood."[23] Elva and Jewell Cowley remained in New Zealand with President Cowley. A year later, in 1941, the Cowleys adopted a Maori boy named Tony.

For the next five years President Cowley worked at holding the Church together. Because of gasoline shortages and other travel restrictions, he was unable to visit the ninety branches of the mission with any regularity. There were instances where branches faltered and where activity dwindled. But President Cowley did all he could to keep the work moving.

In late 1941 or early 1942, United States servicemen began coming to New Zealand. The mission home became a home away from home for many servicemen and women. Allied military hospitals were established in New Zealand, and President Cowley ministered to the needs of numbers of LDS who were recuperating there.[24] He called special fast days to raise money to help servicemen and the war effort. Gold and Green Balls were held from time to time to raise money for the Patriotic Fund. Aside from these events, no large gatherings, such as the Hui Tau, were allowed during the war.

For some reason no mission records were kept during the war years. President Cowley had only one assistant, Kelly Harris, who acted as editor of *Te Karere* and later as mission secretary. Office work did not receive top priority during a time when human problems seemed so much more important.

The Cowleys received word of their release in the fall of 1944. But because of transportation problems, Reed A. Halverson and his family, who replaced the Cowleys, did not arrive at Wellington until July 24, 1945. When President Cowley led his little family on board a U.S. naval ship to embark for home on July 30, they concluded a mission that had begun seven and one-half years before. About two weeks later, the Second World War ended.

President Cowley arrived home in Utah in September 1945. He did not have time to re-establish his law practice before he was called to fill the vacancy in the Council of the Twelve Apostles that had occurred when President Heber J. Grant had passed away in May 1945 and George Albert Smith had left the Council to become the new President of the Church. The Maori Saints were especially grateful to have a representative of their people among the general authorities. It was not long before Elder Cowley was known not only as the friend of the Maoris but also as the Apostle to the Polynesians.

THE POSTWAR YEARS

The first five Zion elders who were called to New Zealand after the war arrived in February 1946, and by April 1947 fifty missionaries were proselyting there. In 1947 the government removed the quota limitation of sixty-five missionaries and allowed the Church to bring in an unlimited number of foreign elders and sisters. For the first several years after the resumption of mission activities, the missionaries were assigned to work in much the same manner as before the war. They were urged by their mission presidents to learn Maori; they were assigned as district presidents; they were encouraged to work primarily with the Maori people. They were also assigned to clear up branch problems and to help with organizational changes. Records received much attention. The early postwar missionaries devoted much time to tracing down members who had moved from rural to urban areas, for during the war years, as President Halverson wrote, the membership had migrated considerably.[25] In April 1946, the first postwar Hui Tau was held. It seems to have been little different from those before the war.

By the end of 1947, President Halverson was keenly aware of the serious need for a new mission home and numerous chapels. In July 1948, President Halverson was replaced by Gordon C. Young. During Young's presidency, many of the changes were put in motion that set the contemporary period apart from pre-war time.

CHAPTER 20

THE FRUITION OF MORMONISM IN NEW ZEALAND

New Zealand, 1948–1984

In probably no other country in the Pacific area is the contrast between the prewar and postwar status of the Church more marked than in New Zealand. The general shift from Maori church to pakeha church is the most obvious change in the Church in New Zealand since the war.

Many other changes have occurred in the Church in New Zealand, and on the surface it appears that these new developments have taken place because a large number of pakehas joined the Church and brought businesslike, efficient, institutionalized methods with them. This is only partially true. Many of the developments reflect worldwide changes in Church procedure, changes that have applied everywhere. But several of the most important improvements in New Zealand directly reflect the Church's continued interest in and love for the Maoris and their contributions. The New Zealand Temple and the Church College of New Zealand would probably not have been built for the pakeha people of New Zealand alone; in fact, both projects were announced before significant numbers of pakehas came into the Church.

Yet the influx of pakehas made it possible for the Church in New Zealand to adapt and respond more easily to the rapidly changing programs of the late '50s to the '80s. Until 1948 the Church was in the hands of old-style leaders, many of whom had served in their callings for more than twenty years. The meetinghouses were all old, and many were dilapidated. The mission presidents were traditionally the ultimate leader of the Church, and in some ways they were honored and almost idolized to a greater degree than some of them desired. The missionary elders held too many district and branch positions. In a way it seemed like the elders' church. Immorality was a problem, and too many couples were living together without legal marriages. Since 1948, leaders have been working to develop within the New Zealand Saints the kinds of skills and abilities that are necessary to operate the contemporary Church.

A TURNING POINT—THE PRESIDENCY OF GORDON C. YOUNG

Gordon Claridge Young, his wife, Virginia, and their two youngest children arrived in New Zealand on July 23, 1948. President Young was sent to New Zealand at a difficult time. The mission had only recently been put back on its feet through the efforts of President Reed A. Halversen. He, of course, had faced problems, some of which dated back to the late 1920s. Because President Halverson was so busy reestablishing the mission, he was forced to let some other things go. When President Young arrived, a total reorganization of the districts was needed. He divided three of the largest districts, released the local district presidents (whose average terms in office were over twenty years), called missionaries to fill these positions along with local counselors, and set up the district organizations after the pattern of stakes. President Young saw this move as an opportunity for more people to serve. Some of the local leaders, however, felt they were being demoted and insulted. A few of the old district presidents would not speak to President Young after they were released. Time healed most of the wounds, but President Young did not have an easy tenure as mission president.

Later, in an effort to strengthen the Maori part of the Church and also to help four of the most respected older leaders know of his love for them, President Young set apart Hohepa Heperi, Stuart Meha, Rahiri Harris, and Syd Christy as special missionaries. These were *Rangatiras,* men of high rank who were respected both in and out of the Church. They traveled wherever they desired, and everywhere they went they were treated well. They did much good among their own people and evidently enjoyed their callings.

The release of the old district presidents was only the beginning of President Young's unpopularity. At the end of 1948 he wrote, "There are many throughout the mission who are living in adultery with its undermining and disintegrating effects." He planned to warn the people that he intended to take action against some of the blatant offenders. He intended to make every effort to redeem the guilty persons, but he did not want the Church weakened further by sexual immorality. "Immorality is an easy sin among the Maori people," he wrote, "and has never been stressed sufficiently as a sin to make them realize the necessity of refraining from this great breach of moral law."[1] President Young seems to have been justified in this assertion. Only seven people were excommunicated during the 1930s, and evidently none in the 1940s before his time. He started slowly and took action against only six people during the first one and one-half years he was president, but in 1950, he and his missionary colleagues removed sixty-seven people from the Church. (Not all were for immorality, but most of them were.) Over the next two years the leaders excommunicated another ninety people. Because of these actions, many Maoris did not like President Young, and he knew it. Nevertheless, he felt compelled to bring about a reformation among them.[2] By the time his mission was over, President Young counted at least 168 couples whom he had "straightened out"—almost one couple a week for his entire mission.

According to President Young, no one disliked "unpleasantness" more than he. But he felt compelled to make changes and to call the people to repentance. Shortly after he started his mission, he was called north to Awarua to preside at the funeral of his old friend Henare Peri. When he arrived at the old chapel, he found it in a sorry state. The windows were broken out, the door was gone, and blackberry bushes had crept in and taken over. But soon two women arrived and cleaned up the place and later members of Henare's family began to assemble. President Young learned that thirteen or more years ago there had been a family feud between Henare and his brother Atawhai that had broken up the branch and resulted in the inactivity of all its members. Now, because they hardly had a choice, members of both sides of the family filed into the little frame chapel. After a hymn and prayer, President Young stood up. He later described his experience in these words:

> When I started to speak I lapsed into the old Maori form they call *Mihi,* you talk right to the dead just like you are talking to the living. I said, "Henry, you've gone, you've gone to the other side of the veil and I can't do anything for you," but there on that spot, on that day, the Lord put his finger on me and I said, "but you who are left, so help me God, I'm going to try to help you." And from then on I just simply didn't stop. I straightened out that branch before I left. Everything was back in order and I didn't do it with kid gloves. I seemed to have a feeling of urgency to get things done.[3]

After this, President Young returned to Auckland and called the members of its two small branches together. One branch was composed almost entirely of Maoris, and the other had pakehas and island people. The Maoris did not care to become members of the same branch with the others. But to the combined Auckland members President Young said, "We're not Maoris and Samoans and Tongans and Cook Islanders and Europeans, we're Latter-day Saints and we're to be together, not pulling in different directions, having these little family feuds."[4] Although he did not combine the two branches until a new chapel was constructed during 1951 and 1952, he did reorganize the branches, and within a short time attendance at Sunday meetings increased by over 300 percent.

President Young felt inspired to shift the emphasis of missionary work from the Maoris to the pakeha segment of the country. "There was not a Maori in New Zealand who had not heard the gospel time and time and time again, and here were 1,750,000 Europeans who didn't even know anything about the Church," said President Young. At that time, in fact, the Maoris comprised only 6 percent of the national population. The elders, however, were not enthusiastic about this change because working with the Maoris had been a warm and generally pleasant experience. Now they were forced to knock on doors and meet frequent rebuffs. But the change was made. Some Maori members also thought that President Young had lost his love for them. This was not true; he simply saw a greater vision of what the Church could be in New Zealand.

While President Young was in New Zealand, he supervised the construction of a number of small chapels, helped the missionaries adapt the Anderson-Bankhead Plan for teaching the gospel to the needs of New Zealand, bought and refurbished a large new mission home (which the next president sold because he thought it was too big), obtained approval for the new Queen Street chapel which was constructed on the old mission office-chapel site, directed the annual Hui Taus, placed the Church on its feet in the Cook Islands, purchased the land for the new Church College of New Zealand (CCNZ), and obtained permission from the New Zealand government to build the school.

President Young's work on the Church College of New Zealand deserves further comment. Ever since the Maori Agricultural College was closed in 1931, the Old Boys and others had talked of building a new school. President Cowley, who had been a member of the MAC board, supported the idea, and when he was called as an apostle, he encouraged the other general authorities to approve the plan. Following his first visit to New Zealand as president of the Pacific Missions of the Church (a position he was given in December 1946), Elder Cowley reported to the Twelve that he had met with representatives of the MAC Old Boys Association and that they and he strongly favored building another Church school in New Zealand.[5] When Gordon Young was set apart as president of the mission, George Albert Smith, president of the Church, gave him a verbal assignment to find land for a new school.[6]

It was 1949, however, before President Young found time to start looking for land, and then he learned that all land prices had been frozen in 1942, and, further, that with the exception of veterans, no one could buy or sell houses or property. Even when real-estate deals were transacted for veterans, the price of property was established by a government land sales court. These facts notwithstanding, President Young started looking for land. He centered his efforts in the Hamilton area.

President Young became a familiar figure at all Hamilton real-estate agencies. "Any land?" "Nothing, Mr. Young, nothing." He did not give up. Finally, after a number of fruitless eighty-five-mile trips from Auckland to Hamilton, on May 23, 1949, his luck changed, and before the day was over the Church had the promise of 215 acres of choice land. An agent told President Young about a friend of his who wanted to trade for a smaller piece of land. (He was not a veteran and could not sell property, but he could trade.) When President Young saw the property, he visualized the college on it. "The Lord showed me the college on that hill—I knew I had found the college grounds."[7]

When President Young met Bert Meldrum, the owner, Meldrum refused to sell his land because he could not buy more. To his objections President Young replied that he would obtain a letter from the prime minister absolving Meldrum from section 51 of the returned servicemen's act so that he could buy another piece of property. Young later succeeded in doing this and the Church gained title to the Meldrum property on Tuhikaramea Road for 4,800 pounds.[8] It was the first parcel of land purchased by the Church to create the village of Temple View.

Buying the land was but the first step in a long process that almost became a saga for the mission leaders. Following World War II, New Zealand was short of almost all building materials. The government controlled all basic products such as cement and steel. Through negotiations with Prime Minister Fraser and then with his successor, Mr.

Holyoak (both of whom became solid friends of the Church), and their various cabinet ministers, President Young and his successors were able to arrange for the Church to import cement and other products, materials, and machines necessary for building. The government reduced or waived import duties on most items, even motor vehicles.

Because lumber was in short supply, the mission bought a stand of timber and a sawmill near Kaikohe. President Young also obtained permission from Salt Lake City to buy wood-finishing equipment and to establish a joinery in the old Auckland chapel so that church builders could make window sills, door frames, and woodwork for the new Queen Street chapel. The machinery was later moved to the college.

Although the college and temple were constructed in the years following Gordon Young's presidency, he, along with his associates in the mission, laid the foundation for almost everything of importance done by the Church during the next decade or two. He helped lay the groundwork for stakes and he built many buildings, but, most importantly, he prepared the Saints morally to be ready for the temple when it was ready for them.

THE CHURCH COLLEGE OF NEW ZEALAND, THE TEMPLE, AND THE LABOR MISSIONARIES

Probably no one foresaw what the later size and scope of the college would be when it was first approved by the leaders of the Church. Elder Cowley wanted a school that enrolled girls and Europeans as well as Maori boys. President Young envisioned a few classrooms and the stadium. But the completed campus exceeded everyone's original plans. Seven years after construction began, there were not only the originally planned five classroom wings and six dormitory buildings, but also the Matthew Cowley Administration Building with its offices, student store, and post office; the David O. McKay Building, which contained a cafeteria, a nine-hundred-seat auditorium, a double gymnasium, and a swimming pool; a shop building; and twenty homes and four duplexes for the faculty and staff. (The Cowley and McKay buildings were not approved until February 1955.) But the most significant addition, though technically not a part of the school, was the new temple.[9]

When the general authorities approved the founding of the Church College of New Zealand, they allocated three million dollars for buildings and for work on the grounds. When the college was ded-

Hui Tau activity in front of a carved Maori house, 1953. (Photo from the *Improvement Era*.)

icated, the cost for construction was nearly seven million dollars. The New Zealand Temple cost another one million dollars. The school, the temple, and the homes made a village that was named Temple View in 1958. The relatively low cost of construction was made possible through the labor or building missionary program. Hundreds of Saints, male and female, Maoris and others, contributed anything from a day's labor to as much as eight years' work to the New Zealand Construction Project. Most labor missions, however, were from one to two years in length.

School construction began in 1951, but because of labor shortages, little was accomplished until the volunteer labor program was adopted at the April 1952 Hui Tau. At that time the New Zealand Saints voted to support volunteer laborers with food and money until the school was completed. Within a few days of the Hui Tau, forty laborers reported to the building site. Through the combined efforts of the mission president, Sidney J. Ottley; the construction supervisor, George Biesinger (who had been sent from Salt Lake City); and Wendell B. Mendenhall (who initially had no official role in the project but who took an interest in construction of the school while he was visiting his missionary son in New Zealand), the project got under way. Brother Mendenhall ultimately became the chairman of the Church Building Committee. He worked with Brother Biesinger for about two months trying to get the buildings started and then returned to his home in California, where, with the support of President McKay, he arranged for seven skilled builders to go to New Zealand on building assignments. These men became supervisors of crews of laborers. They trained Maoris, Samoans, Tongans, and other volunteers to be carpenters, brick masons, cabinet makers, electricians, concrete workers, and so forth. By 1954, the school was well enough along to host the annual Hui Tau. Five thousand people crowded into the classrooms to sleep and eat. The assemblies were held in the joinery or shop building, the first building to be completed. By this time, May 1954, so much interest had been created outside the Church that missionaries were called to act as guides for visitors to the project. Thousands of visitors came to the campus and learned what the Church stood for and how its members worked together. When President McKay saw the success of these missionaries, he said, "The school is open; we are now teaching." He also may have been referring to the number of people who were learning trades.

About this time, in February, President McKay appointed a curriculum committee to plan the course work for CCNZ. Members of the committee were Ariel S. Ballif, who was soon to be called as mission president; George Biesinger, construction supervisor; A. Ray Olpin, president of the University of Utah; William C. Carr, member of the Brigham Young University faculty; and Wi Pere Amaru, of New Zealand. These men met frequently in Utah and formulated plans for curriculum and for the construction of the McKay and Cowley Buildings.[10] Later a local board was appointed, but its members were replaced in 1957 by the new Pacific Board of Education, with Wendell B. Mendenhall as chairman.

In January 1955, President McKay visited all of the Island missions, including Australia. His purpose for coming was twofold: to encourage the Saints and strengthen missionary work, and to select a site for a temple. When he visited the construction site, two important things happened. Although he had left home with the thought of curtailing the building program, he was impressed by the spirit of the workers and by what had been done. He decided to enlarge the school and build the Cowley and McKay Buildings. Further, while he was being shown the land near the school, Brother Mendenhall drove him to the site where the temple now stands. Brother Mendenhall wrote,

"We directed our course around the back of it [the hill] to the farm lands. After we stepped from the car, and we were looking around, President McKay called me to one side. By the way he was looking at the hill, I could tell immediately what was on his mind. . . . He asked: 'What do you think?' I knew what the question implied and I simply asked in return: 'What do you think, President McKay?' And then in an almost prophetic tone he pronounced: 'This is the place to build the temple.' "[11]

Of course, negotiations followed between representatives of the Church and the owners of the property, and before too long the Church had the land. The temple piece connected the CCNZ land and another 729-acre plot that President Ottley had acquired in late 1952.

President McKay did not announce plans for the New Zealand Temple until after he had returned home to discuss his findings with the Quorum of the Twelve.

It was at that time, February 1955, that the status of the laborers was changed from that of volunteers to missionaries. From then until the 1960s, many men in the Pacific and in the United States were called to serve labor missions.

Seeing the opportunity to make the college, the village, and the temple a harmonious whole, Church architect Edward O. Anderson suggested that the same materials be used on the temple as had been employed on the college. Over two years of devoted work were required of the labor missionaries to complete the sacred structure. Toward the end it appeared to the construction supervisors that the temple could not be completed in time for the scheduled dedication services in April 1958. The workers had already given their time, energy, and skill from daylight until dark for many months, but now they worked even longer and were joined by many short-time volunteers from throughout the mission. At the peak of the building program, over four hundred labor missionaries were engaged simultaneously at the college and temple. Through cooperation and sacrifice they completed the project on time. The entire program had actually been much more a spiritual than a temporal one.

President and Sister McKay were accompanied to New Zealand by Elders Delbert L. Stapley and Marion G. Romney of the Council of the Twelve; Elder Gordon B. Hinckley, assistant to the Twelve; their wives; and others. Wendell B. Mendenhall, then chairman of the Church Building Committee and chairman of the newly formed Pacific Board of Education; Edward L. Clissold, president of Oahu Stake and a member of the Pacific Board; George R. Biesinger, project supervisor;

and E. Albert Rosenvall, president of the temple, were present. Thousands of Saints from throughout the South Pacific assembled for the three days of services which began on April 20. Maoris, Samoans, and Tongans provided songs, dances, and ceremonials in the natural amphitheatre at the college, and President and Sister McKay were greeted with the ceremonial challenge by a Maori warrior.

At the actual dedication ceremonies, choirs from the various island groups performed, as did other choirs from New Zealand. Session by session, the various racial-linguistic groups gathered in the temple. In the dedicatory prayer, President McKay thanked the Lord for the services rendered by the builders and prayed for His acceptance and protection of the building and its occupants. He also "expressed gratitude that the descendants of Father Lehi were guided to these islands, to become associated with other leading and influential nations of the world."[12]

On April 26, President McKay dedicated the new college. Many national political and civic leaders, including the prime minister, Walter Nash, were in attendance. In February the first group of students, numbering 342, had entered CCNZ. Although the buildings were not quite completed, Dr. Clifton D. Boyack and his faculty of forty-one were eager to get the school going.

Young Maori members perform a traditional dance at the annual Hui Tau, 1953. (Photo from the *Improvement Era.*)

President McKay gave the students and faculty a profound challenge to pursue the highest values and truths. He said:

> Character is the aim of true education; and science, history, and literature are but means to accomplish this desired end. Character is not the result of chance, but of continuous right thinking and right acting. True education seeks to make men and women not only good mathematicians, proficient linguists, profound scientists, or brilliant literary lights, but also honest men, with virtue, temperance, and brotherly love. It seeks to make men and women who prize truth, justice, wisdom, benevolence, and self-control as the choicest acquisitions of a successful life.[13]

Using the words of Emerson, President McKay said, "Character is higher than intellect. A great soul will be fit to live as well as to think." He challenged the college community to produce men and women who had character and intellect.

Since 1958, the college has grown in size and in numbers of students. After 1965 the student body has generally been between 550 and 725 pupils. The curriculum is broad and useful for the needs of the primarily Maori student body. Although skills and trades are emphasized, the imposition of American administrative methods caused some problems during the first several years of its operation. The new school was very poorly received by the New Zealand government and by the New Zealand populace. It appeared to them to be an American school with American teachers teaching American propaganda to New Zealanders. A major task at CCNZ has been to change the American image of the school. By the late 1970s no Americans were employed at CCNZ. The school now meets the needs of New Zealand's educational traditions as well as providing some innovations, such as graduation after four years of class work, which the New Zealand system does not offer. The school is fully accredited to send its students on to university work and also to prepare them to sit for the School Certification Examination, which is equivalent to high-school graduation in the United States. CCNZ graduates have a good record in the certification exam. CCNZ is a respected educational institution in a country that demands excellence in the educational field.

Its position of respect notwithstanding, there has been considerable discussion of late regarding the school's future. Although CCNZ was founded at a time when its need was questionable in secular terms, there was a religious need for the school in the 1950s. Many LDS families were not providing the kind of home life then that would develop strong LDS adults. How well life in student dorms, even with the best dorm parents, could substitute for regular family life appears questionable, but the merits were thought to outweigh the drawbacks, and the school was founded.

One of the most difficult administrative decisions in recent years has been to keep the Church College of New Zealand open even though it clearly cannot be justified with older or present policy guidelines. Recently, Bruce M. Lake, who was then serving as CES zone administrator over the New Zealand Area, had his staff study the cost and implications of closing CCNZ. He presented four options to the Church Board of Education. Option one was to continue on the present basis. Option two was to close the school. There was considerable precedent for such an action in Tahiti, American Samoa, Mexico, South America, and elsewhere. The third option was to accept government education grants that are received by all other private schools in New Zealand. The fourth option was to accept the conditions of the Private Schools Conditional Integration Act of 1977, which provides for the government to take over such schools. After taking over the school, the government would have paid for the salaries of teachers and administrators, books, maintenance, and all other school costs. The school would have been operated by a local committee. And the school could have continued to hire only LDS teachers and to teach LDS religion classes. But because the CES board does not believe in such close arrangements with governments, the decision was made to refuse that arrangement and to continue to operate the school on the present basis.

But why wasn't CCNZ closed? All students in New Zealand have access to fine free public education. The school obviously meant more to Church leaders than education alone. To close the school would have dissolved a stake and would have affected the New Zealand Missionary Training Center (which was started there in 1977). Even though costs to operate the school will double in the next several years, the Church has evidently decided that the school stands for much more than education. It is the flagship of the Church in New Zealand. It, along with the temple and the village of Temple View, is the focal point of the Church in that land.[14]

THE CREATION OF STAKES AND DIVISIONS OF THE MISSION

The year 1958 was a time of significant change for the Church in New Zealand. The temple and college were put into operation. The Auckland Stake was created in May, followed by the division of the

Air view of Temple View including the Church College of New Zealand (near), the New Zealand Temple (center), and faculty/staff housing (right).

mission and the establishment of the New Zealand South Mission, with headquarters in Wellington. Within a short time the mission presidents were asked to stop holding the Hui Tau. Everything seemed to be changing.

From the time of Gordon C. Young on to President Ariel S. Ballif, each mission president made changes in the district organizations that would lead to stakehood. President Young patterned the district organizations after stakes but called missionaries again as district presidents. President Ottley continued many of the efforts of President Young, but it was President Ballif who expended almost limitless time and energy in holding leadership seminars, training classes, and personal teaching sessions with priesthood leaders all over the country. He removed almost all the missionaries from branch and district positions and placed the burden of authority on the local people. He organized elders quorums and district councils and did everything else he could to prepare for stakes. Shortly before he was released, President Ballif saw the fruits of his efforts when Elder Marion G. Romney, his brother-in-law, organized the Auckland Stake from the Auckland and Waikato districts on May 18, 1958. It was the first stake ever organized outside North America and Hawaii. George R. Biesinger was called as president, with William Roberts and Stanford

The New Zealand Temple. (Courtesy Ralph A. Britsch.)

W. Bird as counselors. Since that time fourteen additional stakes have been organized, and others are reported to be under consideration. The first stakes organized after the Auckland Stake were at Hamilton and Hawkes Bay (both 1960) and Wellington (1965).

Foreigners have sometimes observed that a seemingly large number of Americans and pakehas have been appointed to the top stake positions. Actually, since the first several stakes were organized, and experienced American leaders were used, the Maoris and other local Saints have assumed a large proportion of the stake presidency, high council, and bishopric assignments. Many Maoris have pakeha names, thus making it difficult to take an accurate census of racial distribution.

During May 1958, the New Zealand Mission was divided, and Alexander P. Anderson become the first president of the South Mission, later named the New Zealand Wellington Mission. At that time Robert L. Simpson replaced Ariel Ballif as president in the north. President Simpson was later called as a counselor in the Presiding Bishopric of the Church, and at the time of this writing (1984) serves as a member of the First Quorum of the Seventy. He was the first area executive administrator of the New Zealand–Australia–South Pacific area. He was the third New Zealand mission president to be called as a general authority.

The Wellington Mission allowed the president there to emphasize proselyting in areas that had previously been worked lightly or not at all. The dividing line between the two missions was drawn from a few miles north of New Plymouth, on the west coast, in a northeasterly direction to Hawkes Bay, near Te Avaroa. New emphasis was directed to the South Island, and a stake was organized in 1977 at previously anti-Mormon Christchurch.

The Church Missionary Committee sent larger groups of missionaries to New Zealand, following the mission division. By 1960, both presidents, Simpson and Anderson, had about 150 elders and sisters under them. This level was not always maintained, but the total number of missionaries was higher than before 1958. Between 1958 and 1966, Church membership grew from around seventeen thousand to nearly twenty-six thousand. By 1966, 1 percent of the population of New Zealand was LDS.

On July 1, 1976, the First Presidency and leaders of the Church organized the New Zealand Christchurch Mission from the Wellington Mission. In January 1982, the Wellington Mission was closed, leaving only the Auckland and Christchurch Missions.

The creation of stakes and division of the original mission changed many administrative functions within the Church. The stakes, as independent units completely separate from missions, have removed much of the administrative burden from the mission presidents, though not all. Stakes finance their own programs, build their own chapels, call their own local missionaries, and report to regional representatives. Sometimes there has been overlapping between the stake missions and the full-time missions, but to make better use of missionaries in both groups, stake and mission leaders have coordinated their efforts and cooperated with each other. Most recently the full-time mission presidents have encouraged their missionaries to bring families, rather than just single young people, into the Church.

The Church has had regular coverage on New Zealand radio and television. Several documentaries were produced by national stations to explain the rapid growth of the Church during the 1960s. Such interest has continued.

When the mission was divided in 1958 and the first stake created, the Hui Tau was discontinued in the Auckland Mission area. President Anderson, who had been present at the 1921 Hui Tau when Elder McKay said he hoped the Hui Tau would always be held, continued to hold South Mission Hui Taus. These gatherings were held at Lower Hutt, a suburb of Wellington. The meetings were successful, but the First Presidency suggested that President Anderson and his assistants stop holding Hui Taus and devote their time to quarterly district conferences. Thus the Hui Tau, once a unifying, binding force among the New Zealand Saints, came to an end. More frequent visits from Church leaders in Salt Lake City and more local responsibility took the place of the annual social and spiritual occasion.[15]

THE COOK ISLANDS

The Cook Islands, which until 1965 were a New Zealand dependency, are an internally self-governing nation linked to New Zealand and the British Commonwealth. New Zealand handles foreign relations, defense, and, to an extent, the finances of the Cook Islands. The native people of the thirteen inhabited islands are primarily Cook Island Maoris. English is used by many of the people, but the local Maori dialect is the predominant language.

Latter-day Saint missionaries first attempted to establish the restored gospel in Rarotonga, the principal island of the group, in 1899, but after three years they gave up the effort.[16] The dominant church, the London Missionary Society, which is now called Cook Island Christian, made work difficult then and still holds 75 percent of the people as adherents.

Following that disappointing failure, the Latter-day Saints allowed over four decades to pass before seriously attempting to establish the Church there. At a time when missionary work was generally curtailed because of World War II, President Matthew Cowley of the New Zealand Mission asked Fritz Bunge-Kruger, a baker who had established a business at Avarua, Rarotonga, to use his influence to establish the Church there. President Cowley ordained him an elder and set him apart as a missionary on May 12, 1942.

When Elder Bunge-Kruger and his family arrived at Avarua, they surveyed their friends and acquaintances carefully and selected a few who they believed would be interested in the LDS message. Within a month the Bunge-Krugers had taught the gospel to a close friend named Samuel Glassie and his family. These five people were the first converts in the Cook Islands.

Brother Glassie knew the Cook Island Maori Rarotongan language well, and soon he and Elder Bunge-Kruger were out teaching the local people. Brother Glassie also translated some tracts and other information that he and Brother Bunge-Kruger published on a duplicating machine that President Cowley supplied them. The dominant churches were upset by their success and circulated anti-Momon information, but the little group of Saints continued to grow. The new converts were Manu Cummings and his family. Brother and Sister Cummings became faithful leaders of the Church.

The little group of Saints held sacrament meetings, and then, stage by stage, they added Relief Society, Primary, and Sunday School. When Fritz Bunge-Kruger left the Cook Islands in June 1946, there were thirty-seven other members of the Church.[17]

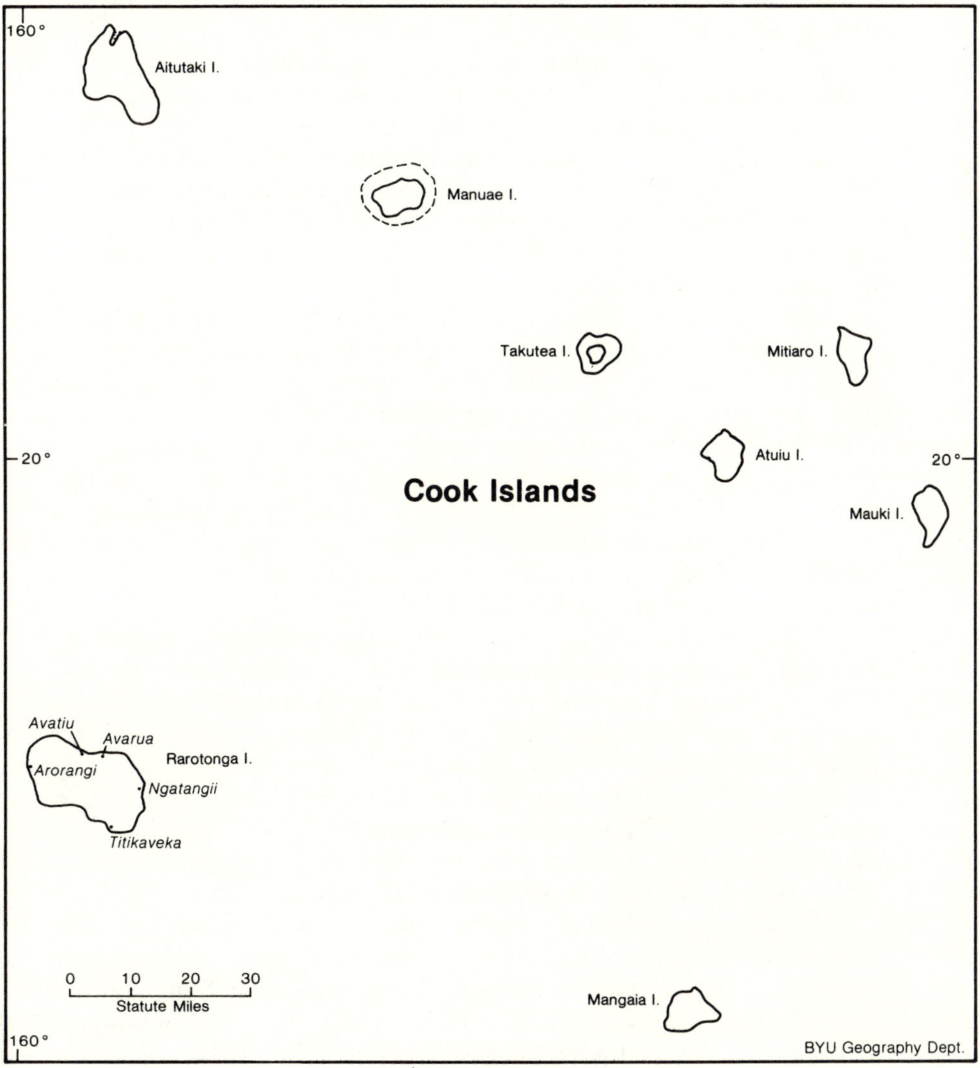

In 1947, President Reed A. Halverson sent first a married couple, Elder and Sister Trevor Hamon, and then Elders Donlon DeLaMar and John L. Sorenson to Avarua. They built a thatched-roof chapel and partially organized a branch, but by the end of 1947 the little group was dissolved because the members were scattered over too wide an area. The Saints did continue, however, to hold auxiliary meetings in their villages. In the meantime, Elder Matthew Cowley visited Rarotonga, and on July 1, 1947, he dedicated the Cook Islands to the preaching of the gospel.[18]

The missionaries made some progress during the next several years. Living conditions were extremely poor both for elders and for local residents, but 160 Cook Islanders had joined the Church by the end of 1949. In that year additional elders opened the work in Aitutaki Island, 140 miles north of Rarotonga, and found some interested hearers. The mission bought a new Fordson truck for the elders on Rarotonga, which they used to bus members and friends from all around the island to meetings.[19]

One reason the Church moved ahead fairly slowly was the difficulty mission leaders had in acquiring land for a permanent chapel. All the land in the group was and is owned communally by the Maoris and may only be leased. Churches can obtain leases for more than sixty years, but the government supervises leases carefully, especially if the church seeking the lease is not Cook Island Christian, Roman Catholic, or Seventh Day Adventist. With great effort (and some monetary enticement), President Gordon C. Young succeeded in signing a renewable thirty-year lease of two and one-half acres, a short distance out of town in an area called Avatiu.[20]

By the end of 1951, Church membership stood at nearly two hundred on Rarotonga and Aitutaki. During the next three years, membership edged up only slowly, partially because the area did not receive as much attention from New Zealand Mission leaders as was needed. The main problem was transportation, or rather the lack of it. Recognizing this problem, the First Presidency decided in May 1954 to transfer the Cook Islands to the Samoan Mission.[21] This was the first of six transfers, most of which were motivated by an effort to improve communications and transportation to and from the area.

When the Cook Islands became part of the Samoan Mission, there were six elders assigned to the area. This level of manpower was maintained over the next several years. President Howard B. Stone traveled there many times during his presidency and supervised a number of changes and improvements. He organized branches on Rarotonga and

Aitutaki, opened work on several new islands (among them were Mangaia and Mauke), helped the elders translate "Joseph Smith's Own Story" into Cook Island Maori, and directed the construction of the first concrete-block chapel and missionary home at Avarua, Rarotonga. These two structures were built by Elder Charles R. Dana, a building missionary supervisor, and a crew of ten builders from Samoa. Between September 7 and November 25, 1955, these builders constructed a small modern chapel and recreation hall (with classrooms) and a three-bedroom home. They rushed to complete the job so that they could get out of the country before the hurricane season, which extends from December to May in most years.[22] Two years later, building missionaries constructed a modern chapel at Aitutaki.

As far as the members of the Church in the Cook Islands were concerned, the highlight of the decade was the one-hour visit by President David O. McKay to the Saints and friends of the Church when his plane stopped for refueling on Aitutaki. Sixty-six members and eighty-five nonmembers visited with him and held a brief palm-shaded meeting in January 1955. He shook everyone's hand and departed for Tahiti.

By the end of 1956, President Stone had sixteen elders working on five of the Cook Islands. As the membership continued to grow, leaders in Samoa, the Cook Islands, and Salt Lake City became convinced that the interests of the local Saints could be met better if the area were made a separate mission. On November 20, 1960, Elder John Longden, assistant to the Quorum of the Twelve Apostles, visited the Cook Islands and made Joseph R. Reeder, who was just completing a term as president of the French Polynesia Mission, president of the new Rarotonga Mission. Headquarters were established at Avarua.[23]

The new mission consisted of only six branches and several hundred members. Local leaders directed the three branches on Rarotonga, while missionary elders headed the other three branches. During the six years that followed, two new branches were added; a thirty-eight acre farm was leased; cash crops were produced for the Saints; three new chapels were constructed at Arorangi, Titikaveka, and Ngatangii villages in Rarotonga; a monthly bulletin was published; and the Book of Mormon was translated into Cook Island Maori. The Book of Mormon was published in 1966, shortly after the island group was made part of the New Zealand Mission.[24]

Even though missionary work was being done on eight islands and some branches were growing, religious and family opposition caused most Cook Islanders to refuse to listen to the Mormon message. Because of the insular nature of the mission and the numerically small population of most of the islands (it varies from three hundred to twenty-nine hundred on all islands except Rarotonga, which has about twelve thousand people), people felt the pressure of their families and friends so strongly that they did not have the courage to join the Church even when they had an inclination to do so.

In April 1966, President C. Douglas Barnes of the New Zealand North Mission visited Rarotonga and, under instructions from the First Presidency, directed the assimilation of the Rarotongan Mission into his area. Knowing that this was going to happen, the First Presidency had assigned Emile C. and Evelyn H. Dunn to serve as missionaries in the New Zealand North Mission. The First Presidency suggested to President Barnes that the Dunns should be assigned to Rarotonga, Elder Dunn to act as a district president and a counselor in the mission presidency.

Since that time the Cook Islands have been assigned to the Fiji Mission (in 1971) and the Tahiti Papeete Mission (in 1975). The Church in the Cook Islands has developed to the approximate level of many of the areas in French Polynesia. At the end of 1979 there were 718 members in ten branches of the Church in the Cook Islands.

CHAPEL CONSTRUCTION

President Gordon C. Young used funds that the Saints had collected over the years to build four or five chapels. He also started work on the new Auckland chapel, on the old Queen Street property. President Ottley supervised the completion of that chapel, which was dedicated in 1953 by Elder LeGrand Richards. It was the first modern, multipurpose chapel in New Zealand.

Even while the labor missionaries were building CCNZ and the temple, crews were deployed to other parts of the country to build chapels. Under the direction of President Ballif, Mr. Cowley, the Church attorney in New Zealand, succeeded in putting a law through the New Zealand Parliament that exempted the Church from certain taxes and other encumbrances. Prime Minister Nash and former Prime Minister Holyoak gave considerable support and assistance to the Church at that time. In fact, Church relations with the government were excellent then and have continued to be so.

Mr. Cowley also aided the Church in searching out titles for new property to be used for chapels and in discovering titles for lands that the Church owned but had lost track of. These land titles were lost through the dissolution of small branches, removal of elders from areas where they lived in small mission homes that were built on Church-owned property, and so forth. According to President Ballif, the Church owned dozens of properties that were unknown to Church leaders before his time. Many of these lands were sold or traded for new and more suitable building sites. Before President Ballif was released, he purchased forty-seven chapel sites. By the end of 1966, labor missionaries constructed forty-seven chapels, most of them on these same sites.[25] Since that time many more chapels have been constructed. These chapels are modern, functional buildings that contain not only worship areas but also cultural and recreational halls, classrooms, offices, and kitchen facilities. By 1977, there were 107 branches and wards in New Zealand, and most of these units were housed in their own facilities.

SEMINARIES AND INSTITUES IN NEW ZEALAND

In late June 1968, William E. Berrett, administrator of Seminaries and Institutes, visited New Zealand and discussed the possibility of starting the home-study seminary program there. Local priesthood leaders responded enthusiastically, and early in November, Rhett S. James, an institute teacher who had been in Tucson, Arizona, arrived in Auckland with his family to organize the program. Elder James had served his mission in New Zealand only eight years before. He established his office at CCNZ and went to work meeting with Church leaders throughout the Auckland Mission area and to a lesser degree in the south. As Elder James met with stake presidents and other leaders, he learned that few of the youth of the Church were being married in the temple; in fact, a large number of them were becoming inactive in the Church even after being graduated from CCNZ. In his capacity as division coordinator, Elder James saw how much good the institute program could do in holding the older youths in the Church; particularly could it help the students of marriageable age. He suggested that a full-time New Zealand staff should be trained, with local men directing the program. Administrator Berrett liked the plan.

Kaikohe was the first Church unit to hold seminary classes. By February 1970, over three hundred young people were enrolled. By March, Elder James had taught thirty-one teachers the basic elements of the seminary and institute programs. When the first year of classes ended, there were 558 students enrolled in the total program.

During 1971, four full-time and three part-time men were

employed in the program as teachers and administrators. Growth continued, and by the end of that year there were 1,187 students enrolled. In 1972, New Zealander Rex Kennerley, who had been engaged in the program from its inception, was appointed division coordinator in place of Elder James. Brother Kennerley was the first local member from outside the United States to be called to such a position.

The first four-year seminary graduation was held at Hamilton South Stake in 1973, and others soon followed. Also in that year there were over one hundred New Zealanders serving in the mission field, most of them the products of CCNZ, the seminary, and institutes. By the end of 1974, 2,300 young people were enrolled in seminary and institute courses. The benefits of the program were already apparent through increased activity among the young people and a rising percentage of temple marriages.[26]

THE CHURCH AND MAORI CULTURE—"MAORITANGA"

For several generations many New Zealanders thought of the LDS Church as a Maori church. Obviously, it was never that, but from the 1880s until the 1950s, the connection between the Mormons and the Maoris was firm. Since that time there has been an apparent shift of emphasis from the Maori to the pakeha, which Ian Barker, in his study of the Mormon-Maori connection, has interpreted as a near desertion by the Church of its Maori members. Mr. Barker would probably have seen the relationship of the Church and the Maoris more clearly if he had studied the Church's expansion in other nations. Rather than interpreting the institutional changes as shifts toward the pakeha, he would have seen them as part of a worldwide phenomenon. The Church has changed as an institution everywhere. The casual nature of Church organization that was so compatible with the Maori way of life was largely characteristic of the entire Church in prewar times. Mr. Barker is correct when he points out that Maori cultural patterns—Maoritanga—were more acceptable within the Church before the war. But now the Church demands that Maoris, like everyone else, conform to what might be called the Mormon cultural pattern. The Maoris, for example, were not alone in their rather offhand method of keeping records. The entire Church has placed more emphasis on this matter in recent years. Latter-day Saint funerals throughout the world, as another example, are now conducted in essentially the same fashion, and Maoris are expected, in spite of their liking for the old *tangi,* to conform to that fashion. Latter-day Saint chapels everywhere, for another example, look much alike; and again the Maoris feel some pressure, real or otherwise, to abandon their old-style meetinghouses. Further, the Maori language has largely been eliminated from interracial meetings. For this same reason even the missionaries have not been encouraged to learn the Maori language since World War II.

The old Hui Tau was a distinctly Maori tradition. Nevertheless, it was expensive and, considering the size of the Church, it no longer served the needs of the people. But other parts of Maori culture are encouraged by Church leaders in both Salt Lake City and new Zealand. Maori music, history, mythology, dance, and arts and crafts are taught at CCNZ. Many wards and branches sponsor Maori choirs and dance groups. The Maori language too is taught at CCNZ. It must be recognized, however, that the Church has not encouraged the continuation of many aspects of Maoritanga. In a way it could be said that only the "relics of the Maori past" remain. The Church has done much to integrate its Maori members into the mainstream of the Church.[27]

In 1964, Johannis Jacob Mol, of Australia National University at Canberra, studied the religious affiliations of the Maoris. He concluded that the Latter-day Saints have done a better job of integrating the various races of New Zealand, particularly Maoris and pakehas, than any other Church. Professor Mol concludes, "The Mormons are the most successful of all Churches in the implementation of a policy of integration. Although in some areas nearly all its members are Maori (in such a situation one cannot very well speak of a successful policy of integration), the fact that 50% of its members go to services every Sunday, which have many non-Maori overtones, and feel at home in this environment, is certainly an achievement of the first order. This applies to the absolute numbers of Maoris who are in meaningful interaction with pakehas in face-to-face religious groups."[28]

Perhaps the Church has succeeded because the pakehas have come into a predominantly Maori church, rather than the other way around.

Professor Mol did not include in his study the large number of Samoans and Tongans and smaller numbers of Tahitians, Cook Islanders, and others who have immigrated to New Zealand, especially to the Auckland area, and who have remained active in the Church. By 1984, there were over five thousand Samoan Latter-day Saints in New Zealand.

STALWART CHURCH LEADERS IN NEW ZEALAND

New Zealand has produced many faithful members of the Church, most of whose names have not found their way into this volume. Many, such as Ihipera Takare "Aunt Polly" Duncan, who hosted hundreds of missionaries and four Presidents of the Church and served for thirty-one years as president of the mission's Relief Societies, have been left out only because they did not play a significant role in the institutional development of the Church. Several persons, however, must be introduced.

Baden-Powell Pere, who served as president of the Auckland Mission from 1973 until 1976, was the first Maori or New Zealander to be called to such a position. Brother Pere, a well-known athlete, jet pilot, and educator, did much not only to help nonmembers find the Church but also to encourage inactive members to return to the fold.

Other New Zealanders who have served as mission presidents since the mid-1970s include Stanford W. Bird, who served in the Wellington Mission, and Kenneth M. Palmer, who presided over the Fiji Suva Mission. Probably the best-known Church leader in New Zealand is William Roberts, who was converted to the Church in 1952. His Church positions include branch president, stake president's counselor, stake president, regional representative, mission president in England, and president of the New Zealand Temple. After he retired from his lifetime employment with the government Lands and Survey Department, the First Presidency asked him to establish a Church distribution and printing center in Auckland. This center served the translation, publication, and distribution needs of the Saints not only in New Zealand but also in a large part of the Pacific. Elder Roberts was also responsible for Church real estate in the South Pacific. President Ballif said of him, "Roberts is wonderful. I don't think there's a better man in the Church anywhere."

Another New Zealander Saint who has brought considerable credit to the Church is Manuera Benjamin Riwai-Couch, a part-Maori who is a member of the New Zealand Parliament. Better known simply as Ben Couch, he moved quickly from a junior position in Parliament to the prime minister's cabinet. In 1978, he was assigned to take the portfolios for Maori Affairs and the postal system. In 1980, he dropped the postmaster assignment and added the ministry of police. As minister of police and minister of Maori Affairs he has had ample opportunity to deal with difficult and sensitive issues. He insists that he generally uses the principles of the gospel to guide his decisions.

Since 1975, Brother Couch has frequently hosted members of the First Presidency and other general authorities at government offices in Wellington. Largely because of him, Prime Minister Robert D. Muldoon has been very friendly to the Church and has welcomed Church leaders to his office. Ben Couch's personal code is, "If you believe something is true, you live it." He applies this idea in every part of his life.[29]

THE NEW ZEALAND AREA CONFERENCE

Unlike the area conferences in Australia, where the vastness of the continent required the general authorities to hold three separate conferences in 1976, the New Zealand meetings were held at one place, much like the old Hui Taus. This meeting in February 1976, however, exceeded the size of the largest Hui Tau by at least three times. Over sixteen thousand people jammed the Church College of New Zealand stadium for the entertainment and later for the regular sessions of the conference. Three thousand entertainers participated in the cultural show—more participants than had generally come to Hui Tau until the mid-1950s.

Before the meetings at Temple View, President Spencer W. Kimball was the host for a select group of dignitaries at a luncheon. Ben Couch, member of parliament from the Wairarapa, introduced President Kimball to Robert D. Muldoon, prime minister of New Zealand. The friendly relationship of the Church and the government was once again renewed.[30]

The Church leaders and Saints considered the conference a grand success. Twelve thousand people, nearly half of New Zealand's Latter-day Saints, had gathered together to be fed spiritually and socially. When the grandest of Hui Taus ended, the Saints were eager to improve themselves and to strengthen the Church.

THE YEARS SINCE 1976—APPRAISAL

There have been some events that are newsworthy in a historical sense during the years following the first area conference. For example, a second area conference was held in 1979, and a third conference—actually a multiregion meeting—was held in 1984. Also, each January since 1978, the Saints of New Zealand have put on a pageant, similar to pageants elsewhere in the world. In 1979 the New Zealand pageant was performed on the grounds of the temple in Temple View by over 700 actors, technicians, costumers, makeup artists, and so on. In addition to scenes depicting the restoration of the gospel, the pageant included segments about the Maori prophets who foretold the coming of the gospel to New Zealand. Crowds averaged around fifteen thousand per year. "I was very impressed with the missionary potential of the pageant and the role members and priesthood holders played in bringing non-members to see it," was Elder Loren C. Dunn's reaction following the 1979 performances. "The information center at the temple counted more than 2,000 persons visiting the center in one day and that is well above the average."[31]

The spiritual momentum of the first area conference did much to increase missionary success. During the three years that followed, convert baptisms averaged over two thousand a year, up considerably from previous years. Elder Dunn attributed the growth not only to the conference, but also to the greater preparation and spirituality of the missionaries who were in the field at that time. A major reason for improved missionary effectiveness was the establishment of missionary training centers for missionaries who had been called to teach in English-speaking areas. Language training centers had been in use for a decade before the missionary training centers were established in 1978. New Zealand, too, established a missionary training center for elders and sisters who had been called from Australia, New Zealand, and some other Island areas. Although the sessions lasted only one week, the local setting and special training helped the South Pacific missionaries to be more productive. By the late 1970s, local missionaries made up almost 30 percent of the missionary force in New Zealand and Australia.

Not everything that has happened to the Church in New Zealand has been positive. In the early 1980s, a member couple apostatized and began to vigorously fight the Church. They tied in with a group called Ex-Mormons for Jesus who used as much influence as possible to destroy the faith and beliefs of Church members in New Zealand. Some of the weak and a small number of the supposedly strong members of the Church were led away. Nevertheless, as with all periods of harassment and persecution, this one too passed without seriously damaging the Church. An interesting sidelight was the support a number of high-ranking government officials gave the Church during this era. Especially Prime Minister Robert D. Muldoon voiced his anger at the lies that were being circulated. He has expressed his admiration for the Church's concern for families and its position on moral issues.

In French Polynesia, Tonga, Samoa, and Australia, temples have

The Auckland Distribution Center housed the offices for most temporal affairs—translation services, supplies, real estate, and so on—during the 1970s. (Photo by R. Lanier Britsch.)

been constructed in the past several years, but the Church in New Zealand has had to measure its progress in more subtle ways. The New Zealand Temple is no longer the spiritual hub of the entire South Pacific. With the building of temples in so many areas, the Island Saints in all major areas have matured in a gospel sense. In New Zealand especially, it is now necessary to measure growth in terms of improved administrative efficiency and more complete development of all Church programs. The growth in numbers of converts has been impressive. In 1984, membership in New Zealand stood at just over 40,000. But the most important fact concerning the Church in New Zealand today is that it is a fully functioning part of the Church.

It is no longer necessary or desirable that outsiders direct the many departments of the Church there, such as Temporal Affairs, Real Estate, Distribution and Translation, the Church Educational System, Seminaries and Institutes, Social Services, and so forth. Local members are more capable of handling such affairs than imported help from America could possibly be. The local leaders know their people, their government, and their customs and social patterns, and they know the programs of the Church.

New Zealand (along with Australia) provides an excellent example of the complete program of the Church. In 1975, Elder Robert L. Simpson, then an assistant to the Quorum of the Twelve but changed to a member of the First Quorum of the Seventy when that quorum was created, was assigned to supervise the affairs of the Church in Australia, New Zealand, and the South Pacific islands. This move was part of a new initiative that divided the world into six administrative zones. This system has been fine tuned several times since then. Elder Simpson was asked to live in the area. Because New Zealand was conveniently located for transportation, he chose to reside in Auckland. His presence there was a great positive force in Church development. Not only was he available to guide local decisions and to explain general Church policies, but also he was a living manifestation that the leaders of the Church in Salt Lake City were conscious of the Saints in that area and cared enough about them to send one of the Lord's servants to direct his affairs among them. Only twenty-five years before, visits by general authorities were major historic events in New Zealand. Now, one of the Brethren was appointed to live there.

Elder Simpson was living in New Zealand in 1976, when the first area conference took place. He was able to coordinate the preparation necessary to make that event run smoothly.

While he was in that assignment, he spent roughly 70 percent of his time traveling. The distance encompassed in his territory was close to six thousand miles wide and several thousand miles from south to north. When President Kimball and the area conference visitors traveled the same paths that Elder Simpson traveled so often, they decided it was too much area to handle, and during the summer of 1976, his area was reduced to Australia and New Zealand.

To the extent that it was possible, Elder Simpson and Elders Loren C. Dunn and Jack H. Goaslind, Jr., who followed him were all advocates of training local leaders to be autonomous. Elder Simpson felt that there was a great benefit in having a general authority available for stake presidents to call to get immediate answers to their needs. As he traveled in his area Elder Simpson was "able to give directions that were more meaningful to this particular area of the world." He said, "To feel that we were way down in that part of the world operating the Church more or less as we felt it should be operated within the confines of the handbooks and the revealed word was just a very stimulating feeling for everyone."[32]

When he spoke of "everyone," he was referring to the local members who were serving as regional representatives, to the many

Church employees who were directing and working for the various departments of the Church in that country, and to the stake leaders who were eager to build the kingdom properly but who wanted to put a local stamp of approval upon it as far as it was possible within the guidelines found in the "handbooks and the revealed word."

The period of President Spencer W. Kimball's presidency has been exceptionally dynamic. Every major change that has been implemented in Salt Lake City has been duplicated—at least when appropriate and advisable—in New Zealand (and elsewhere in the Pacific). Changes in the frequency of stake conferences, the consolidated meeting schedule, the creation of the council form of church administration wherein stake presidents meet with other stake presidents and their regional representatives, and the separation of the responsibilities of the ecclesiatical and temporal affairs of the Church have all affected the Church in the Pacific. When the revelation that all worthy men of all races were eligible to receive the priesthood was announced on June 9, 1978, the Saints in New Zealand and other island areas also rejoiced in the expansion of blessings to all mankind.

Of course, modern electronic communication has greatly improved the ability of the central headquarters to communicate with the outlying parts of the Church. General conference meetings and other special meetings, such as those held for the women of the Church, are now available to New Zealand stake centers through satellite transmission. Also, it is possible for leaders in Salt Lake City to confer regularly by telephone with leaders in New Zealand. Elder Goaslind, who did not live in New Zealand while he administered that area, held at least weekly telephone conferences calls with his department heads in New Zealand. The difference felt by members in New Zealand, in 1984, when compared with the situation twenty-five or thirty years earlier, was almost breathtaking. Although New Zealand is a great distance away from the center of the Church in terms of miles, it has almost drawn abreast of the heart of the Church in terms of development and administration. The future appears positive.[33]

PART 5

SAMOA

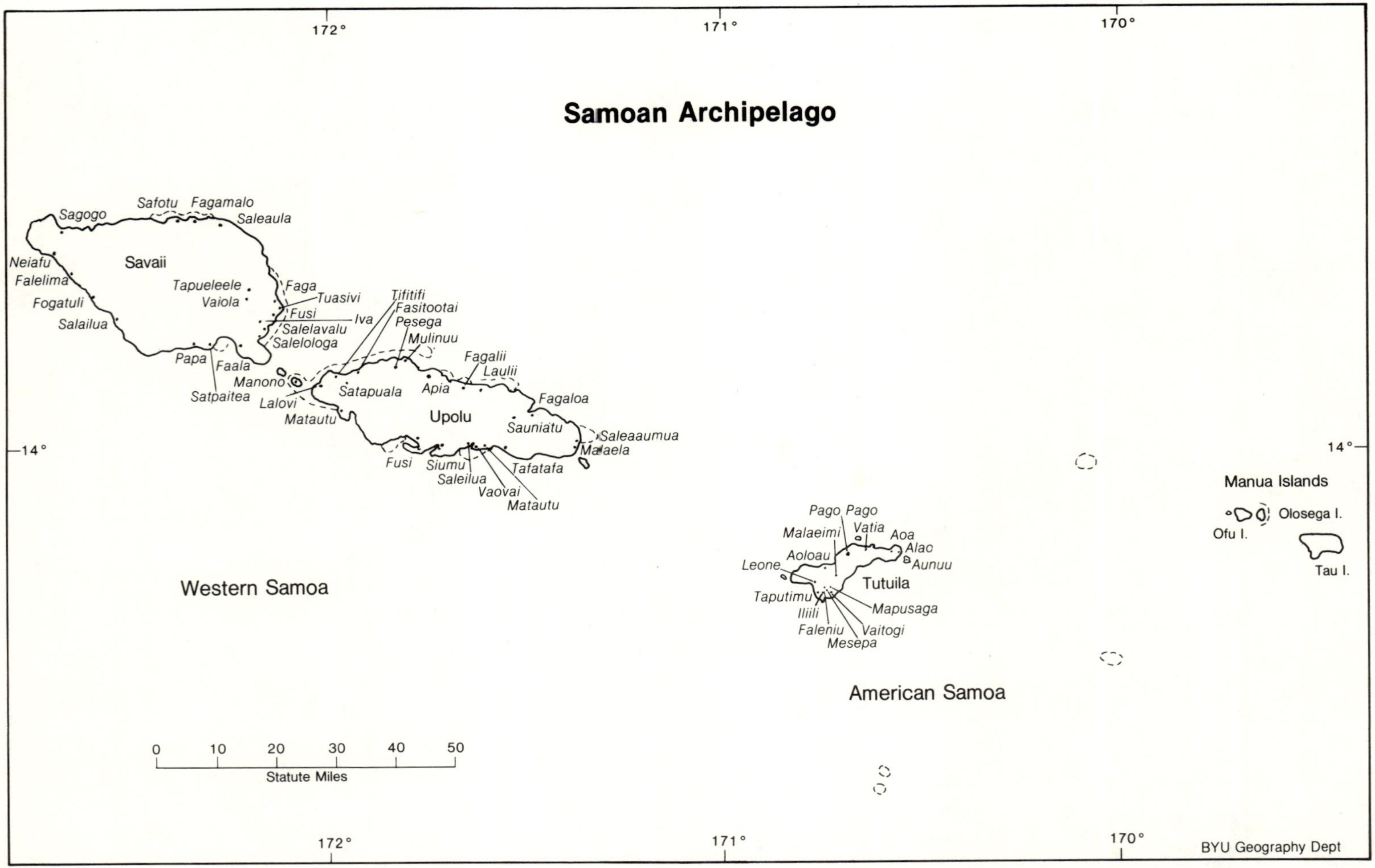
Samoan Archipelago
172°
171°
170°
14°
14°
Savaii
Sagogo
Safotu
Fagamalo
Saleaula
Neiafu
Falelima
Fogatuli
Salailua
Tapueleele
Vaiola
Faga
Tuasivi
Fusi
Iva
Salelavalu
Salelologa
Papa
Faala
Satpaitea
Manono
Lalovi
Matautu
Tifitifi
Fasitootai
Pesega
Mulinuu
Fagalii
Laulii
Satapuala
Apia
Upolu
Fagaloa
Sauniatu
Saleaaumua
Malaela
Fusi
Siumu
Saleilua
Vaovai
Tafatafa
Matautu
Western Samoa
0
10
20
30
40
50
Statute Miles
Pago Pago
Vatia
Aoa
Malaeimi
Alao
Aunuu
Aoloau
Leone
Tutuila
Taputimu
Iliili
Faleniu
Mesepa
Vaitogi
Mapusaga
American Samoa
Manua Islands
Olosega I.
Ofu I.
Tau I.
172°
171°
170°
BYU Geography Dept

CHAPTER 21

TWO BEGINNINGS IN SAMOA

Samoa, 1863–1889

The Latter-day Saint mission to the Sandwich Islands (Hawaii), which was founded in late 1850, ran into problems in 1857 and 1858. For a variety of reasons, principally the loss of faith by many of the Hawaiian converts and the fact that Brigham Young was deeply concerned about the impending Utah War, the Zion (Utah) elders were called home. After their departure in 1858, the local Saints were left to care for the Church. Three years later, in July 1861, the adventurer Walter Murray Gibson, who joined the Church in January 1860, arrived in Hawaii as a missionary. His appointed field of labor was Japan and Malaysia, but he had also been asked by President Young to visit the Hawaiian Saints. Gibson went far beyond the authority given him by the Church and ultimately defrauded the Hawaiian members and misused his ecclesiastical authority. He was excommunicated in April 1864.[1]

The influence of Walter Murray Gibson was felt far and wide. Not long after he had established himself as the supreme leader of the Saints in Hawaii, he decided to send missionaries to other islands of the Pacific. As early as September 1861 he reported to Brigham Young his designs to expand the bounds of the Church in the Pacific to the Society Islands and other points. His hope was to convert to Mormonism, and then train, a force of Polynesian elders to move into Malaysia and establish the Church and a political kingdom there.[2]

In a letter of August 30, 1862, Gibson told President Young that two elders, "intelligent native brethren," had been dispatched on a mission to the Society Islands and Tonga Islands. At that time he said that he intended to send other Hawaiian elders to the "Marquesas Islands, the Tonga Group, the Samoan Group, and [to] Malaysia and

Japan."[3] Accurate records of Gibson's activities in this sphere cease with the letter just quoted, but sometime during the fall of 1862, probably during October conference or in early December, two priesthood bearers were called to serve as missionaries to Samoa.

There is a sad irony surrounding the call of Kimo Pelio and Samuela Manoa as the first missionaries of the Church to the Samoan Islands. Both men were faithful servants of the Lord who had been ordained to the Melchizedek Priesthood even before Gibson came to Hawaii. But Gibson convinced many Hawaiian Saints that he was authorized to enlarge the priesthood activity in Hawaii; he ordained twelve apostles, some seventies, an archbishop, and bishops. He ordained Kimo Pelio one of the Hawaiian apostles, and Samuela Manoa a seventy. Brothers Pelio and Manoa were so faithful that they accepted Gibson's charge to open Samoa, but because Gibson fell from his position of glory, they were left to their own devices in Samoa.

Brothers Pelio and Manoa sailed from Honolulu on December 23, 1862, and arrived on the tiny Samoan island of Aunuu on January 24, 1863. After laboring on Aunuu for several months with only one baptism, they moved to nearby Tutuila and began teaching there. Before long they raised up a branch of forty-two baptized members, many of whom lived in Utumea. It is reported that Brother Pelio also extended his labors to Apia, on Upolu Island, and baptized several people there.[4]

When the mission was reopened in 1888, Elder Manoa reported that he and Elder Pelio had baptized around fifty people during all of their ministrations. It is doubtful that many more people than this were baptized, even though some sources have reported as many as two hundred baptisms.[5]

Problems arose for the Samoan Mission. The first was the fact that the mission was not sanctioned by the leaders of the Church in Salt Lake City. But local difficulties also arose.[6] When the mission was reopened, Elder Manoa reported that he had written to Hawaii a number of times asking for assistance. The question may be raised, why was the Church not paying attention to the little cluster of Saints in Samoa during these years? The best answer is probably that the Church was honestly ignorant of the few Saints who had been brought together in that distant place. Elder Manoa's letters may have ended up in places other than the Church headquarters in Laie. This author has been able to find only three references to Samoa in the Church Archives during these years, though there may be others. Harvey H. Cluff mentioned the Samoan group twice. The first reference is cited above; the second leaves us with a question. Elder Cluff wrote: "In the evening Elder

John A. West arrived [in Hawaii] . . . on his way to fulfill a mission on the Samoan Islands. He will stop here until his two companions arrive."[7] Apparently Elder West's two companions never did arrive, for he filled his mission in Hawaii.

The other reference is a letter from ten Samoan Saints who asked President Brigham Young to send "some of the servants of God." It arrived shortly after his death in 1877. Perhaps the pressure of serious difficulties relating to the transfer of the presidency caused this letter to be set aside unanswered and unfulfilled. Perhaps the First Presidency felt that careful thought needed to be given to the matter and simply waited to make a decision until more information was available.

JOSEPH HARRY DEAN REOPENS THE SAMOAN MISSION

The 1880s were difficult years for the Saints in Utah. The most serious problem was the polygamy issue. Many of the Church's strongest men were imprisoned during the later years of the decade. Joseph H. Dean, husband of two wives and father of five children by the first, Sally, spent part of 1886 and until May 13, 1887, in prison on a conviction of unlawful cohabitation. The day of his release he was once again hiding from the law because deputies were to arrest him on charges of illegal voting. A close friend, William O. Lee, allowed Brother Dean to stay in his home while plans were being made to take care of him. While he was there, a message came from Apostle Franklin D. Richards. He asked Elder Dean about the possibility of his filling a mission in Hawaii; it would be his second mission there. The First Presidency agreed that the mission call would relieve more problems for the thirty-one-year-old fugitive than it would cause.

On Monday, May 23, 1887, Joseph H. Dean and his second wife, Florence Ridges, were set apart to be missionaries. In his journal Elder Dean noted that they were "set apart to go to the Sandwich, Society, Navigator [Samoa], or any of the other groups of islands that the spirit might dictate through the authorities."[8] Within a few days Joseph and Florence had said their good-byes to Sally and the children, and they were on their way.

The records do not reveal what else, if anything, was said by the leaders of the Church to Elder Dean about Samoa. But it is evident from his journals that Elder Dean was interested in Samoa and the possibility of going there. By October 1887 he was aware of Samuela Manoa, and during conference he asked whether anyone knew his address. Brother Kaleohano told Elder Dean that he had received word from sailors of the Hawaiian man-of-war *Imiloa,* which had just returned from Samoa, that Samuela Manoa was still there, "that there were a good many Saints there, and that they felt that the Church had forgotten them entirely." This news increased Elder Dean's concern about Samoa.[9]

As soon as he knew that Brother Manoa was still alive and faithful to the Church, Elder Dean began gathering information about Samoa. From a man who had worked in Samoa, he learned about steamship connections, the almost total lack of mail service, the cost of sailing to Tutuila (which was close to Aunuu where Brother Manoa lived), the fact that there were 35,000 people living in the islands, and so on.

On October 26, 1887, Elder Dean wrote to Brother Manoa and asked whether he would be able to care for him and his wife. Florence was by this time five months pregnant, and Elder Dean must have been deeply concerned about housing arrangements, food, and other facilities. A few days later he wrote to Presidents Wilford Woodruff and George Q. Cannon and explained the possibilities for mission work in Samoa. In December a letter came back telling him to move ahead with the project. Elder Dean was busy with many matters relating to the Hawaiian Mission, but he continued to work toward going to Samoa.

On February 9, 1888, Florence delivered a ten-pound baby boy. On the following day Elder Dean received word from Brother Manoa. Elder Dean wrote in his journal, "Manoa will open his house for us and make us comfortable. He is very desirous to have us come and says he thinks the prospects are as good for converts as on Hawaii. That settles the matter and I will be able to take Florence along with me."[10]

Elder Dean's course was set. They were all going to Samoa.

In early May, Elder Dean decided to sail for Samoa on the seventh of June. During the remaining time he made reservations for their steamship passage (at a reduced rate because of their ecclesiastical status); arranged with a faithful Hawaiian brother, C.K. Kapule, to come to Samoa as a missionary as soon as he could arrange his affairs (Brother Kapule's wife had just died); and continued to search for information about Samoa. Finally the much-anticipated day for sailing arrived. Unfortunately the mail ship, the *Alemeda,* did not come until the tenth, three days late. Their departure was complicated even further because the captain was not sure he would stop the ship at Tutuila. However, a couple of miles west of Tutuila, the Deans were lowered over the side of the *Alemeda* into a small rowboat that had

A steamer, similar to those used by hundreds of LDS missionaries over the years, resting at anchor in Pago Pago Harbor, around 1900. (Courtesy LDS Church Archives.)

been sent by Brother Manoa and would take them to his home on Aunuu. Because of the roughness of the sea, the Deans were forced to spend three nights in Tutuila. But finally the long-boat was put ashore at Aunuu on June 21, 1888.

Samuela Manoa and his wife greeted Elder Dean, Florence, and the baby at the shore and took them to their frame house. Brother Manoa ushered Elder Dean into a separate room away from the crowd and, taking him by the hand, he said in Hawaiian, "I feel greatly blessed that God has brought us together and that I can meet his good servant here in Samoa." Twenty-five and a half years had passed since Brother Manoa had seen an authorized priesthood leader from Zion!

Hawaii was more advanced than Samoa, but the Deans were not troubled by the primitive physical circumstances. Samuela Manoa owned a western-style home and had a bed prepared for their use even though Samoans sleep on mats on the floor of their *fale* (large mushroom-shaped thatched houses). There also was a good kerosene lamp, earthenware dishes, and a concrete floor, but there was "no stove, no cows, no bread, nor anything to make it of. No running water, rainwater being all that they use. It seems that we will have to live on straight native fare." Probably the greatest disappointment was the mail. "The mail facilities seem to be at a fearful state. No inner island mail at all."[11] These inconveniences notwithstanding, Elder Dean and his wife were excited to be there and were eager to begin teaching the gospel.

The natives of Aunuu were equally eager to hear Elder Dean's message. On Sunday, June 24, Elder Dean gathered a large number of the villagers together and preached his first sermon. Brother Manoa translated from Hawaiian into Samoan after Elder Dean spoke each sentence. The whole process was very cumbersome, and the new missionary was eager to learn the language as fast as possible.

On the following day Elder Dean rebaptized Brother Manoa, confirmed him, and ordained him an elder. This was necessary because of Brother Manoa's questionable original authority from Gibson. The act of baptism must have been a spiritual experience for those who looked on, because a Samoan woman named Malaea applied for baptism almost immediately. Her faith seemed sincere, and so the good elder put his wet clothes back on and baptized her. She had not been baptized before, and therefore he counted her as his first Samoan convert.[12]

By July 3, Elder Dean had performed fourteen more baptisms. He soon expanded his work to include occasional visits to Tutuila, where he baptized the daughter of a Samoan judge on July 21.

On July 29 Brother Dean delivered his first sermon in the Samoan language. When the first group of American elders arrived in October, they reported that he was speaking quite fluently. Considering the kinds of problems that existed in Samoa, Elder Dean's success was encouraging.

THE RELIGIOUS AND POLITICAL SITUATION IN SAMOA BEFORE THE OPENING OF THE LDS MISSION

Before the arrival of Christian missionaries in Samoa, the people worshipped a pantheon of deities. The names of these gods were not the same as those in Hawaii, but there are evidences of a common origin. Unlike Hawaii, Samoa remained quiet and relatively undisturbed by the changes and attractions of the modern world until much later. Even as late as 1874 there were fewer than three hundred European and American residents in all of Samoa.

Christianity was introduced into Samoa after it was already established in Hawaii, Tahiti, and Tonga. In 1828 Christian converts from Tonga, which is five hundred miles south of the Samoan group, were the first emissaries of Christianity to enter Samoa. Two years later one of the greatest missionaries of the London Missionary Society (LMS), John Williams, visited Tonga and then, in company with a Samoan chief who had been converted to Christ while in Tonga, he moved on to Samoa. While there he converted a large number of people at Sapapali'i, Savai'i. Mr. Williams promised that he would soon return with teachers to train them in the doctrines of the new religion. When he returned two years later, he learned that the news of Christianity had spread over most of the main islands of the group. Once again he left for England to recruit more missionaries. He did not return until 1838 (and then for only a brief time), but by 1836 a new contingent of LMS missionaries arrived in Samoa. There they found thirteen thousand Methodists who had been converted by Tongan missionaries. This caused an open feud between the LMS group and the Methodists, which was resolved in favor of the LMS in 1839. After that time the LMS had almost complete control over the religious lives of the Samoan people. Some small minorities of Methodists, Seventh-Day Adventists, and a larger group of Catholics grew over the years. The Roman Catholic mission was founded in Samoa in 1845.[13]

Just as the Latter-day Saints owe a debt of gratitude to the Protestant missionaries in Hawaii and elsewhere in the Pacific, so do they in Samoa. By the 1840s most Samoans considered themselves Christian. Although some of the changes these early missionaries demanded of their converts had little to do with Christianity (they sometimes equated the cultural preferences of the Western world with Christianity and required their converts to conform to these preferences), nevertheless, most of the work of the early LMS missionaries must be listed on the positive side of the ledger. They founded schools and even started a seminary in 1844 to train Samoan ministers. By 1842 the Gospel of John was translated into Samoan, and in successive stages the remainder of the Bible was published in Samoan, this work being completed by 1860. This progress was made under difficult circumstances and at the cost of much sacrifice on the part of the missionaries.

When Elder Dean and his companions began teaching the gospel in Samoa, they found the political situation much more complex than the stable religious situation. An explanation of these religious and political matters is necessary in order to understand the situation in Samoa when the LDS mission was founded there.[14]

In June 1888, Samoa was on the verge of a civil or tribal war. During the next several years LDS missionaries were witnesses of several battles and sometimes were caught between the warring factions who were attempting to control the country. The Samoan political situation was complicated by the involvement not only of several tribal factions who were seeking the kingship, but also by the presence of three foreign powers, Germany, Great Britain, and the United States. The degree of their interest in Samoa varied, but all three nations were tenaciously defending their own involvements.

British interests there began with the work of the LMS. After the missionaries, came traders and others seeking land. German involvement began with merchants who arrived in 1845. Later trade developed into landholding and plantations. The actual land claims of the Germans were substantially larger than those of either the British or the Americans. American concern in Samoa was only slight until after the Civil War. In the 1870s, when steamships began to replace sailing vessels, U.S. merchants and traders brought the good natural harbor at Pago Pago, Tutuila, to the attention of the American government. By this time the United States did have a small interest in Samoan trade and landholdings, but a good harbor for repairs and a coaling station was an important concern for U.S. maritime and naval officials.

After a certain point in the relationships and contacts of the Samoans with Western nations, "a stable, strong, central government became the paramount need if order was to be maintained and progress made."[15] Unfortunately, this proved to be difficult to achieve. In Grattan's words, "native politics in Samoa . . . was peculiarly vigorous and productive of the disorders of war—a continuation of politics by other means, so to speak."[16]

In 1878 and 1879 all three Western powers entered into treaties with the reigning king of Samoa. But they went a step further to assure the security of their interests and in September 1879 formed a condominium government for Apia. For the next twenty years the only stable government of Samoa was controlled by the consuls of the three powers at Apia. "They were given power to make and enforce regulations, to tax buildings and lands for community expenses, and to appoint a magistrate. In times of civil war, Apia was to be neutral territory."[17] Unfortunately even this system did not bring peace to the little island nation.

In the mid-1880s Britain concluded that the only way to stabilize the situation would be through annexation by one of the powers, preferably Germany. The Germans concurred, but the U.S. government, for reasons that were partly altruistic and partly self-serving, desired

Samoa to remain independent and Pago Pago harbor to remain under U.S. control.

Because the Samoans could not agree who their king should be, an international conference was convened among the three powers in Washington, D.C., in June 1887. The United States stood in the way of cession of Samoa to Germany, and the meetings were adjourned temporarily. At this point Germany manipulated the Samoan political situation, deposed the most popular claimant to the kingship and deported him, and placed another legitimate though not so popular claimant, Tamasese, on the throne. The deposed king, Malietoa Laupepa, however, bequeathed his political power to a third legitimate claimant of kingship, Mata'afa. By combining his forces with those of Laupepa, Mata'afa had the support of a significant majority of the Samoans. The Americans in Samoa generally favored him, as did the LDS missionaries when they arrived.

At this point, war broke out between the German-supported forces of Tamasese and Mata'afa's faction. Within two weeks of the initial fighting of August 31, 1888, Mata'afa had clearly defeated his opponents. When word of these events reached the governments involved, each nation dispatched warships to the scene. Thus early in March 1889 Germany had three ships, the *Eber,* the *Olga,* and the *Adler* at Apia. The U.S. sent the *Trenton,* the *Nipsic,* and the *Vandalia,* and Britain sent the *Calliope.*

While these great ships lay in Apia harbor, a terrible hurricane struck on March 15 and unleashed its fury for twenty-nine hours. When it was over only the *Calliope,* which had steamed out to sea, was still afloat. Three LDS missionaries watched as the ships were destroyed and many lives were lost. The upshot of the disaster was the cessation of hostilities in Samoa and the return to the conference table.

The result of the second conference was the continuation of the tripartite government of Samoa, but with greater involvement by each nation. Samoan kingship was continued, a commission was established to examine land claims, a chief justice was appointed, and an outlander (a European outside the three powers) was appointed president of the municipality of Apia to preside over the three consuls.[18]

Ten years later only one part of the new government had worked to the satisfaction of all the parties involved. This was the land commission. The greatest weakness in the system as a whole was ambiguity in the phraseology dealing with the choice of future kings. Tamasese and Mata'afa were not satisfactory choices, and so the British suggested the reappointment of Malietoa Laupepa, who had been exiled several years before. This appeared to be the best course of action, but Mata'afa refused to go along with the new government and made war on Laupepa. Mata'afa was defeated in the summer of 1893 and was exiled.

An unstable peace was maintained until the death of Laupepa in 1898 when civil war once again loomed. None of the powers believed that the Samoan kingship should go on, nor did they have reason to believe that the tripartite arrangement should be continued. Discussions concerning how best to resolve the Samoan question continued from June 1899 until December, when a decision was made to divide the islands, with the U.S. taking Tutuila (with Pago Pago harbor) and some adjacent islands and Germany taking control of the remaining islands. Britain gained concessions elsewhere in the Pacific. This agreement was ratified in the United States Senate on February 16, 1900. Three days later Tutuila was placed under the control of the navy. In this way the U.S. gained American Samoa, and Germany took control of all the rest.

CONTINUING DEVELOPMENT DURING THE FIRST YEAR OF THE REOPENING

On October 30, 1888, four months after his arrival in Samoa, President Joseph H. Dean wrote to President Wilford Woodruff. His letter included a paragraph explaining why he had not expanded the work beyond Aunuu. First, he did not feel that he should leave the forty or so souls who had joined the Church there since he arrived. He wrote, "My policy has always been to labor as hard to keep a member as to get a new one, and not to spread my wings over more eggs than I can keep warm." Second, he mentioned that he had not quite mastered the Samoan language in the four months he had been there. Then, almost incidentally, he mentioned that he had been working with the members on a new meetinghouse.

President Dean's letter did not mention that he had organized a branch, baptized at least thirty-five people (who had an additional twelve children under eight), organized a Sunday School and a Relief Society, looked after the arrival and subsequent work of Elder Kapule when he came on August 13, and cared for and oriented Elder William O. Lee; his wife, Louisa; and their baby, Louie; Elder Adelbert Beesley; and Elder Edward James Wood after they arrived on October 10.

In addition, Elder Dean and his new flock were faced with a serious challenge. Whether true or not, a rumor was circulated to the effect that the reigning king, Tamasese, following the advice of his German adviser, Mr. Brandeis, had declared it illegal to join the Mamona (Mormon) Church. He allegedly threatened to arrest all who were baptized into the new church—President Dean along with the rest. Since this scare, which first came in late August, only one person, a young boy, had applied for baptism. The missionaries were not able to confirm the rumor and later gained assurance from the American consul that they and their congregations would be protected; nevertheless the civil war on Upolu Island was having a negative effect upon the work.[19]

The arrival of new missionaries made it possible to expand the work. Dean concluded that Aunuu was not suitable for a mission headquarters and was anxious to move to Tutuila as soon as housing could be arranged. But even Tutuila was not central enough, and before another year had passed, headquarters were moved to Fagalii, near Apia.

When a new group of elders arrived in early October, they set about immediately to complete the meetinghouse. It was eighteen by thirty-six feet and "very comfortable and commodious." The roof was of sugar-cane leaf thatch, the lumber and posts were of breadfruit and coconut, and the floor was covered with clean white coral pebbles. Elder Wood said it was of half American and half Samoan design.[20]

The elders also devoted as much time as possible to the study of the Samoan language. Their study was fairly unsystematic; most of the time they listened to the native speakers, jotted down the words they heard, looked them up in a dictionary, and then tried to use them.

The first conference of the Samoan Mission was held on October 28, 1888. Four days later President Dean took Elders Beesley and Wood with him to Tutuila. On November 2, they began a twenty-three day teaching marathon that required eighty-eight miles of walking and ultimately led them before 1,851 people in thirty-nine villages. When they were through, they had baptized three people, but the elders were sure that once the government problem was resolved, many people would come into the Church.[21]

Actually, the Tutuila tour was immensely valuable. By living with the Samoan people, the elders quickly became educated in the ways of this society. One of the first lessons they learned was the necessity of following local social customs when gospel standards would allow it. The use of kava is a good example. It is a mild narcotic drink derived from the roots of a pepper plant; kava played (and still plays) an important ceremonial role whenever guests came into a village. Elder Wood wrote that when they entered a village, "they first made 'ava' for us. It is always given to callers of importance as a welcome of the village to them.

"[When the drink is prepared] the *tulafale* (head talking man) then calls out the names of those to drink. Custom does not compel you to drink, but it is a grave breach of respect if you do not touch the cup and pass it back."[22]

When Elder Dean first arrived on Aunuu, he refused to drink kava because the missionaries in Hawaii had prohibited its use. But it was evident that kava drinking was an important social requirement in Samoa. To this day all leaders in the Church from missionaries to general authorities participate in the kava ceremony.

The elders also learned that it is best to begin a gospel discussion with the highest-ranking chief or chiefs (matai) of a village. The Samoan social system was and is partiarchal. The village elders make the rules of the community; young people listen and obey.

The missionaries learned to respect the intelligence of the Samoans, especially their knowledge of the Bible. The LMS had done a good work among the Samoan people, most of whom had learned to read by using the Bible as their text. The LMS had also taught the people to hold prayers and a form of family home evening.

Every evening the chiefs came to have prayer with Elders Dean, Beesley, and Wood. After prayer they had supper. Elder Wood wrote, "On looking around the little village it was a beautiful scene. We could see in every hut the family gathered around the fireplace, singing or reading or praying, seemingly unconscious of all surroundings. This grand custom is followed in almost every household on the islands."[23]

The elders realized that even though the people lived in huts and used ovens that were nothing but heated rocks in the ground, the people were very spiritual. Elder Wood noted that his and the other missionaries' own "testimonies were many times strengthened by having our food provided for us, having boats placed at our disposal, also in having the privilege of holding so many meetings and in nearly every instance of having good places to sleep."[24]

In early December 1888, the missionaries bought a small (twenty-two foot) sailboat that they christened the *Faaaliga*—"Revelation"—and used to go from place to place on Aunuu and Tutuila. The two-sailed boat was well made but was very small for sailing in open waters.

Soon after the end of the Tutuila tour, Elders Wood and Kapule

The waterfront at Apia, Samoa, during the 1890s. (Courtesy LDS Church Archives.)

were assigned there permanently. They worked from the village of Alao, which already had some LDS families. In early January, President Dean and his family also moved there. On January 25, 1889, they moved to Vatia, a "nice village" directly over the mountain north from Pago Pago.

Rents were high, and rumors of war reached the village only a few days after they moved there. The Samoans, including some of the members of the Church, asked the missionaries to live with them in their homes. The reason for this soon surfaced: missionaries and their properties were exempt from the ravages of tribal war. On February 7, Vatia was attacked by thirty followers of Mata'afa. As was customary in such circumstances, the warriors burned fales, destroyed property, and killed livestock. No people were killed on this occasion. By mistake some of the mission animals were killed and some personal property was destroyed, but the missionaries were not harmed.

After much hard work the elders built a twenty-by-forty-foot mission house. It was constructed of coconut wood and was made with only two axes and two natives adzes. In early March, even before the house was finished, the Lees moved from Aunuu to Vatia.

On March 12 and 13, 1889, Elders Dean, Beesley, and Wood embarked on a trip that was later described as the "most exciting and important boat voyage of our entire mission."[25] This voyage, to Apia,

Upolu, took them across forty miles of open water and approximately twenty-five miles along the coast of Upolu. This island is forty-four miles long and averages a width of thirteen miles. Almost half the Samoan people lived here. The little twenty-two-foot craft made it close to Upolu, only to be overturned near shore. Some islanders righted the craft, and, finally, after nearly two full days at sea, the elders reached Apia.

This trip to Apia was motivated by two desires. The first was to establish the Church on Upolu. A Samoan convert during the days of Manoa, named Ifopo, had encouraged the elders to come to his home on Upolu. Ifopo later proved to be a faithful convert to the Church by helping the elders in many ways to establish the Church in his area. The second purpose of the trip was to visit the American consul in Apia and establish relations with his office. This was prompted by the Samoan war and its possible implications for the Church.[26]

President Dean and his companions visited the American consul, Mr. Blacklock, to ask him if he had heard anything concerning the rumor that Latter-day Saints would be put in prison. He said he had heard nothing of the kind and assured them that he would guarantee their safety and the safety of their converts.[27]

It was while the elders were at Apia that the great hurricane struck. These elders found themselves in dangerous circumstances. A man named Moors housed them in the loft of an old barn and slaughterhouse near the harbor, where they remained until the storm ended. The barn was so full of holes that a candle could hardly be kept lit even before the storm; but perhaps the flimsy construction helped the building to remain standing through the entire storm. Elder Wood later wrote that he stood at the window most of the day and night watching the mighty ships and their crews meet destruction. There was nothing anyone could do. But when the storm ended, "the beach was swept clear of its row of buildings, only one small building still stood, buried in sand to the roof, which alone had saved it from total destruction." Inside were Elders Dean, Beesley, and Wood.[28]

After completing their business in Apia, they sailed toward the east end of Upolu. At Salea'aumua they located Ifopo, who welcomed them warmly, provided a feast, and ultimately applied for baptism. He had been baptized twenty-five years before, but it was considered best to do it again. With the performance of this ordinance the elders felt that the door to this large and beautiful island had been opened. They sailed that day for Tutuila.

The annual conference of the Samoan Mission was held in Aunuu on April 7. All of the missionaries were present (Sisters Dean and Lee excepted) and a fair number of Samoan Saints as well. The pattern for this conference followed the established procedure for such meetings elsewhere in the Church.

On June 16, 1889, four new missionaries arrived. They were Elders Hyrum E. Boothe, Brigham Smoot, Jesse J. Bennett, and Brigham Soloman. Unfortunately, they were not well prepared for life in Samoa. When they disembarked from the steamer, they did not want to get into the little mission boat because they didn't think it would hold them. When they arrived at Vatia, after the eight-mile trip along the coast, they found that the missionaries and the Samoan people were suffering from a famine that had come as a result of the hurricane. Then, two days later, Elder Smoot, who could not swim, stepped off the reef and drowned, but he was miraculously restored to life through the administration of his fellow missionaries.[29]

June 1889 marked the end of the first year of the Samoan Mission. By this time the missionaries had experienced almost every problem Samoa could offer. They had endured war, famine, a hurricane, and tropical storms. They had suffered sickness, apostasy, days in open boats, and storms at sea. Rumors had been circulated against them, and Protestant ministers had used both newspapers and their pulpits to republish the old lies about Joseph Smith and the Latter-day Saints. (Elder Lee mentioned that the Roman Catholics were to be commended because they did not persecute the Mormons.) The elders' housing was inferior to their homes in Zion, and living conditions resembled a perpetual camping trip. Nevertheless, the elders were in excellent spirits and eager to spread the gospel throughout the islands.

On June 18, 1889, Elders Lee and Bennett were assigned to Tutuila and Aunuu; Elders Beesley and Boothe were sent to Manua; and President Dean and Elders Wood, Smoot, and Soloman were given the task of opening proselyting work on Upolu.

The elders completed a coconut wood meetinghouse at Vatia before they separated to their new areas. The building was completed in late July, and in the first week of August the missionaries left for their new assignments. So ended the first year of the Samoan Mission.

CHAPTER 22

THE DEVELOPMENT OF SCHOOLS, PLANTATIONS, AND GATHERING PLACES

Samoa, 1889–1919

On August 8, 1889, Joseph H. Dean and his companions sailed to the east end of Upolu, where Ifopo lived. Ifopo was especially eager to have missionaries in his village and area, and so Elders Wood and Smoot left their trunks at his home. Two days later Ifo (as the elders called him) and the elders sailed to Apia.

Ifo wanted the brethren to set up their headquarters at his village. To do so would have provided free land, but it would have been a long distance from Apia. At this time Apia was being considered seriously as a regular stop for the San Francisco–to–Sydney mail steamer, and it was so designated within a few months. It was already the seat of the foreign powers in the country and was for all intents and purposes the capital of the nation.

In Apia the elders once again stayed in Mr. Moors's barn, where some interesting and inspirational experiences again occurred. At Apia the Spirit seemed to say, "Procure headquarters for the mission."[1] While the elders were considering the various possibilities, an unlooked-for proposition came to them. Elder Dean wrote:

> We made the question a matter of much prayer, and received an answer in the most unexpected manner possible. The very next day, after prayer meeting, while in Mr. Moors's store, he [Mr. Moors] casually remarked:
>
> "Mr. Dean, I've got the very piece of land you folks are looking for." This of course, was before we had mentioned our desires to anyone.
>
> "How do you know we are looking for a piece of land?" answered Brother Dean.
>
> "Well, of course I don't know," said Mr. Moors, "but judging

This home at Fagalii served as mission headquarters from 1889 until 1902. Note the mission sailboat, the Fa'aaliga, at the left. Shown left to right are Louisa, Laurie, and William O. Lee; Edward J. Wood; Langley A. Bailey; George McCune; Florence Dean (holding baby); Jasper Dean, Joseph H. Dean, Adelbert Beesley, Brigham Smoot. Photo taken in August 1890. (Courtesy LDS Church Archives.)

> from what others of your occupation have done, I should think a piece of land close to Apia is what you should have."
>
> He was assured that his idea had long been ours, but that buying in our position was almost out of the question.
>
> He told us that if it was our financial condition that made us hesitate, that could be overcome. "Give your note," said he. "I have been through Salt Lake, and had the pleasure of an interview with the Presidency of your church. Now, you go and look at the land, only a couple of miles up coast, and if it suits, you decide to take it and come and get what materials you want to put up a house, and I'll take your note for the amount."[2]

The next morning the missionaries rowed their boat to Fagalii, the site Mr. Moors had offered them. On August 14, 1889, President Dean signed an agreement with Mr. Moors to take over the property. Fagalii became the headquarters of the mission and remained the center of operations for a little over ten years.

After the land had been purchased, President Dean, his family, and Elder Soloman settled at Fagalii and began constructing a small house (which later grew in all directions as the needs of this headquarters building were expanded). Elders Wood and Smoot went to the east end of Upolu to Ifo's area and began proselyting in earnest.

THE FAGALII PERIOD, 1889 to 1900

During the fall of 1889, Elders Wood and Smoot baptized enough people to organize a small branch on the east end of Upolu. From there they expanded their efforts along the south side of the island, heading west. Protestant opposition was fairly strong, but the elders met with many groups of *matai* (chiefs) in their *fono* (councils) and usually found at least one willing listener in each area. In this way the Church began to take hold on Upolu.

The arrival of Elders George McCune, Langley Bailey, and George Abel on April 26, 1890, made it possible to further extend the work. In June 1890, Elder Dean, along with Elders Wood and McCune, went to Savai'i, the largest island of the Samoan group. Two converts who had been baptized on Upolu, Brother Afualo and Sister Afualo Emele, helped get the work established in their home village of Fogatuli. Before many days a small group of converts had been baptized. From there the elders moved to the north side of the island where they encountered serious opposition in the area of Salailua, but they remained to establish what Elder Wood called the most "wide-awake" branch in Samoa.[3]

By this time Elder and Sister Dean had spent a year in Hawaii and two years in Samoa. Their accomplishments had been significant, and they had had two children (the second had been born in June 1890). On July 14, Elders Henry L. Bassett and Caleb E. Summerhays arrived from Salt Lake City. They brought President Dean notice of his release. The Deans left for home on August 16, 1890. Elder William O. Lee was appointed president of the mission. When the Deans left Samoa, there were twelve male missionaries, one female (Sister Lee), and close to eighty baptized Samoan members of the Church. With their children the LDS congregation had grown to 124 souls.[4] Also by this time missionaries were laboring on all three of the major islands of the group and on some of the smaller islands as well.

From the time of President Dean's departure until 1897, the growth of the Church in Samoa was slow but steady. Then during 1897 more baptisms were performed (268) than during the previous three years. Between 1891 and 1899, membership in Samoa grew from 209 to 1,139.[5] Local wars hindered the teaching effort during 1893 and 1894 and again in 1899, but during the other years the growth pattern of the Church was apparently unaffected.

As is true in missions throughout the Church, the mission presidents in Samoa set the tone and pace of proselyting work. The presidents of the Samoan Mission were generally young men who were called to the office while they were serving in the mission. The three exceptions to this pattern from 1888 until 1899 were Joseph H. Dean, Edward J. Wood, and William G. Sears. The presidents who served after Dean were William O. Lee, 1890-92; George E. Browning, 1892-93; Ransom M. Stevens, 1893-94; Thomas H. Hilton, 1894-95; John W. Beck, 1895-96; Orlando Barrus, 1896; Edward J. Wood, 1896-99; William L. Worsencroft, 1899; and William G. Sears, 1899-1902.[6] Of these men, only Elders Wood and Sears had previously served missions in Samoa before they were called to serve as presidents. Mission presidents are generally called from among the returned missionaries from the respective mission fields. The linguistic ability and in-country experience gained while on a first mission is, of course, of considerable value for the mission president in carrying out his work. But in Samoa, as in almost every new foreign-language mission, there was not a reserve of returned missionaries who could be relied on to fill the position of president. For this reason the other presidents of the mission were not as mature nor were they as demanding of the missionaries as were presidents Wood and Sears.

THE PATTERN OF MISSIONARY WORK

The pattern of missionary work developed from a simple and not-too-carefully-worked-out system during the early part of the decade into a fairly well-structured operation by the end of the period. Until 1894 the method of teaching the gospel was for the pairs of elders to take walking tours around the islands. In the process they met with village chiefs, left pamphlets, bore their testimonies, occasionally baptized a person or two, and then moved on to another village. Over a period of time they were able to organize a number of branches, and when this happened, the elders began to spend much of their time with the members of these small groups. By 1895 most of the branches were still small, around fifteen to twenty-five members.

Until 1895 the proselyting areas of the elders were not carefully defined. The suggestion to divide the islands into specific areas came from Elder Andrew Jenson, assistant Church historian, who visited Samoa during the summer of 1895. Once the areas of responsibility were designated, the elders became more efficient.

Undoubtedly the most important changes made in the proselyting pattern were directed by President Wood. He insisted that the missionaries spend more hours in direct teaching. Prior to his time the elders made a monthly trip to Fagalii when the mail steamer came in. President Wood decided that this traveling wasted too much time and told the elders that the mail would be sent to them.

But the proselyting tool that brought the greatest changes and the most rapid growth in numbers of converts was the "magic lantern" shows. President Wood brought slide pictures of important people and places in Utah wherever he went. Hundreds of people from chiefs to toddlers came to his presentation. Through this means the elders were able to teach the gospel in villages that had been closed to them before.

The lantern show became so popular that chiefs requested President Wood to come to their villages. The result was a rapid increase in number of baptisms during 1897 and 1898. President Wood reported that the presidents of the Church, the apostles, the temple in Salt Lake City, the tabernacle, and other important Church people and sites were now common knowledge among the Samoan people. Prior to the lantern shows, many Samoans believed that the Mormons lived as semibarbarians outside the bounds of civilization.

When President Sears came to Samoa, he brought another innovation, a graphaphone or record player. This too attracted a good deal of attention.

During the first half of the decade, Church membership grew by ones and twos. But after 1896, it grew by fives, nines, and tens. The original pattern of conversion to Christianity, when the London Missionary Society came into Samoa, was by village mass movement. The chiefs usually made the decision to become Christians first, and the people followed close behind. This pattern did not apply to the Latter-day Saints until 1897, when the lantern shows attracted so much attention. But from this time on for the next couple of years, it was not unusual for villages to swing their allegiance to the LDS Church even though not all of the people were formally baptized.

The position of respect gained by the Church during these years was important. Samoan custom law, *fa'a-Samoa,* allowed chiefs' councils, *fono,* to determine which religions could be practiced within each village. In those villages where a decision was made not to allow the Latter-day Saints, the penalty for becoming a Mormon was the destruction of one's property, the burning of his *fale,* and expulsion from the village. The elders reported that they believed many people had turned their hearts to the Church but were afraid to join.[7]

A number of villages made the decision to invite the LDS missionaries. Among these were Fagaloa, Matautu, Laulii, Pesega, Vaitogo,

Tifitifi, and Leone. The last two not only asked the elders to come to their villages, but they also gave their meetinghouses to the Church.[8]

Schools were an important means of influencing the Samoan people. Even Joseph H. Dean and his missionaries discussed schooling as a possible way of strengthening the children of converts. By 1892, the elders were conducting one or two schools from two to four days a week. The sister missionaries were also much involved with the schools.

As the number of branches grew, so did the number of schools. By the end of the decade, the little chapel schools, where the elders taught fifteen to thirty-five students who sat on the meetinghouse floor, became inadequate. The elders began to build "central schools" where children from a broad area could come to study and live full-time. Before the turn of the century, such schools were constructed in Pago Pago on Tutuila, Tuasivi on Savaii, and Malaela on Upolu. In addition to helping young members live the gospel, the schools helped to develop future leaders of the Church. Local leadership was a matter of concern for the missionaries in Samoa during these years. As is the pattern elsewhere in the Church, the local Saints assumed important positions from an early date. By the time the Church had been in Samoa for four or five years, Samoan elders were filling missions, serving as branch presidents, and helping in other ways.

When branches were first organized, the Zion elders had taken charge of them, but as the number of branches grew it became difficult for the missionaries to care for all the groups. Accordingly, as Samoans were ordained elders, they were called to fill missions in their own country. Until the 1950s, these local elders were called to leave their own villages and serve, sometimes for long periods, as branch presidents in other places, a pattern of leadership peculiar to Samoa. The idea behind this tradition was that a prophet was without honor in his own village. It is evident from the records that this method had its beginning in the 1890s and was patterned on the procedure of the London Missionary Society. Usually these native missionaries had to move their own families to other villages and sometimes to other islands. As time passed, this became the established mode of operation in the Samoan Mission.

In addition to the Samoan elders, other Samoan priesthood bearers, and faithful sisters, there was another group of Saints in the islands. These people were a small but generous group of Caucasians and half-castes who were permanent residents of Samoa. Time and again the missionaries wrote gratefully of the large Kenison family, the

Mackies, the Rosenquists, and the Burgesses. Most of the men of these families made their livings by sailing and trading between the islands, and they frequently befriended and aided the missionaries. During the 1890s,Captain Kenison's name is mentioned more often than that of any other person except the mission presidents themselves in Andrew Jenson's "Manuscript History of the Church." Not only did Kenison and the other captains provide transportation, but they also gave food, shelter, and even money to support the efforts of the LDS missionaries in Samoa. Nearly all of the white community in the islands, members and nonmembers alike, provided encouragement to the missionaries.

The sacrifice of life was also made in order to establish the Church in Samoa. On September 18, 1895, Andrew Jenson made the following observation in a letter published in the *Deseret News* January 4, 1896: "Compared to time and number, the Samoan Mission history records more deaths among our missionaries than any other mission we have so far established as a Church—one Elder, two missionary sisters and three children, in seven years, out of eighty missionaries who, since 1888, have been sent from Zion to labor in Samoa and Tonga."[9]

The elder who died was Ransom Stevens, mission president. He died of typhoid. The two married sister missionaries died of complications related to childbirth.

The children died of various causes, all related to the Samoan environment. In addition to the six deaths noted by Elder Jenson, several other children and sisters passed away while in Samoa or shortly after their return home.[10]

THE OPENING OF TONGA AND THE REOPENING OF FRENCH POLYNESIA

When William O. Lee became president of the mission, he sent two elders, Brigham Smoot and Alva J. Butler, to Tonga, the Friendly Islands. These first elders left Samoa on July 12, 1891, and arrived at Nuku'alofa, Tonga, a day or two later. More missionaries were subsequently sent to work with them. (Unfortunately, even though a number of elders worked in various parts of Tonga for the next six years, because of the small number of baptisms the mission was closed early in 1897 by instruction from the First Presidency through President Edward J. Wood. (See the history of the Tongan Mission, chapter 25.)

On January 22, 1892, about six months after Tonga was opened, Elders Joseph W. Damron and William A. Seegmiller sailed from Apia for Papeete, Tahiti, where they had been assigned to reopen the Society Islands Mission. Their efforts there were more successful than those in Tonga. (See chapter 2.)

INTERNATIONAL INVOLVEMENT IN SAMOA

As mentioned previously, in December 1899 the British, Americans, and Germans decided to divide Samoa and allow the United States to control the area now known as American Samoa (of which Tutuila is the primary island), and to allow Germany to take possession of Upolu and Savai'i and the adjacent islands. The United States took control of Tutuila in early 1900, and Germany took over in Apia on March 1 of that year.

The war slowed the work of the mission considerably. Only about half as many baptisms were performed in 1899 as in 1898, and most of these were in the last half of the year. And in some of the areas of Upolu, particularly the western end, the people were so displaced and upset by the war that they were not eager to have the elders among them for a few months. Nevertheless, eastern Upolu, Tutuila, and Savai'i had not been seriously affected by the hostilities, and the people there warmly accepted the elders and their teachings.

From 1899 until the beginning of World War I in 1914, Western Samoa was a German territory, and Eastern Samoa (American Samoa) became and remains a U.S. territory. The presence of German and American officials had a profound effect not only on the history of Samoa but also on the history of the Church in that land.[11]

Dr. Wilhelm Solf, who had formerly served as municipal president in Apia, was appointed governor (1900-11) when Germany took over Upolu and Savai'i. Solf, a sincere Christian of high principles, was an excellent administrator. But unfortunately the qualities that made him a success in political office—that is, loyalty to his superiors, willingness to make regulations and carry them out, and even a certain amount of ego—caused him to be an obstacle to the LDS mission.[12]

In May 1901 a circular from Governor Solf caused a major crisis for the Latter-day Saints. He decreed that from July 1, 1901, on, no English-language schools would be allowed in German Samoa. This act was part of a plan for a government system of schools and led to a dark period in the history of the mission. English-language schools had been one of the most important proselyting and social-service methods of the Latter-day Saints.

The psychological impact of this decree on the mission was profound. Even though the education circular was not pointed at the Latter-day Saints alone, and though Governor Solf was not personally hostile toward the Mormons, the missionaries concluded that the Church was being persecuted. It is true that Solf was not overly warm toward the Church—he tried to reflect the attitude of his home government, which was one of cold nonrecognition—but when the various mission presidents met with him he was generally friendly, and he never took a position that was deliberately antagonistic toward the Church.

Still, the members of the mission force were sure that they were being singled out. At the time when the English-language issue occupied their attention, the missionaries held a deeply spiritual meeting in which they made many prophecies. One man, Elder Martin F. Sanders, did not respond at that time to the promptings of the Spirit. For the next six weeks he was harassed by his failure to speak. Then at a similar meeting on July 26, he "predicted that the Saints of Samoa were about to be gathered together."[13] The school problem, in combination with other concerns of the missionaries (primarily the fact that they could see so little moral progress among the Samoan members), kept this prophecy in the minds of the missionaries. Ultimately two gathering places were acquired, one on Upolu and one in Tutuila. It is unlikely that they would even have been considered if the school crisis had not occurred.

Because Governor Solf's edict regarding language was not rescinded, the mission was forced to adjust. The mission president closed the schools for at least two months to allow time for planning. Initially, two courses of action seemed available—one, to conduct some schools only in the Samoan language; and two, to organize other schools for foreigners and part-Samoans who did not fall under the governor's order. Both types of schools were opened with the governor's approval. "Foreign schools," as they were called, were operated at Fagalii, at Malaela on east Upolu, and at Tuasivi, Savai'i. In February 1902, a group of nonmembers asked President Joseph H. Merrill, who became president in December 1901, to start a foreign school at Pesega, near Apia. Again the governor approved on condition that English not be taught to the Samoans but only to the children of foreigners.[14]

The request for the Church to start a school at Pesega was fortuitous. In 1899 a fine Chinese brother named AhMu had offered to give the Church some property at Pesega. At that time the mission presi-

The home of AhMu, the Chinese member who donated the ground for the LDS complex at Pesega. (Courtesy LDS Church Archives.)

dent was giving serious consideration to the idea of moving the mission headquarters from Fagalii to Pesega. The First Presidency advised him to keep the headquarters at Fagalii. When the mission officers decided to build a combined church and school building at Pasega, they did not plan to move the mission president's home and headquarters as well. But as the months passed and the members made progress on the buildings, the new mission president became more and more convinced that Pesega would make a better location for the mission office than Fagalii. Although Fagalii had been the headquarters for a decade, there were few members living nearby, and the mission president did not believe that the environment was hospitable to spiritual growth. Not until June 26, 1902, did President Merrill discuss moving the headquarters, but on August 27, Pesega became the new home for the mission. It has remained the headquarters ever since. On October 5, the new meetinghouse was dedicated at annual conference.[15]

The Samoan schools and the foreign schools were started in the fall of 1901. In April 1902, President Merrill received word from Church headquarters in Salt Lake City that several missionaries who were of German birth or who spoke the language were being sent to

The old mission home at Pesega was constructed and dedicated in 1902. (Courtesy LDS Church Archives.)

Samoa in answer to his request. When these elders arrived, it was possible to begin offering classes in German to Samoans at two or three of the schools. Although six or eight German-speaking elders served over the next several years, their attempts to teach the language fell short of what was expected by Governor Solf. The Church leaders in Utah also had considerable difficulty finding qualified German speakers to send to Samoa. Because of these and other problems, in July 1905 the First Presidency approved the discontinuation of the effort to operate German schools and suggested that if Church members wanted their children to learn English, they could send them to American Samoa. Otherwise the mission was authorized to teach the people of German Samoa in their own language.

This decision brought to an end the Church's efforts to teach in the German language until 1913, when a second attempt was made to open German-language schools. This second effort, however, came to an abrupt halt when World War I broke out between Germany and Great Britain. The British took over Samoa on August 28, 1914, hardly a year after the mission opened the second group of German schools. Almost immediately after the British takeover, the mission began to open new English-language schools.

THE CREATION OF SAMOAN GATHERING PLACES

The missionaries first contemplated the idea of creating a gathering place for members of the Church in July 1901, but the mission leaders did not seriously consider it until early the next year. President Merrill caught the spirit of gathering soon after his arrival in the islands. He wrote concerning a conference held by the Savai'i Saints on April 12, 1902, "The spirit of gathering rested upon the people, and many of the natives expressed their earnest desire to be permitted to gather together at some place where they would be able to free themselves from the bondage of the ancient customs of their people."[16] By June the president said he had the matter of gathering "on his mind all the time."

The actual gathering process had its beginning in American Samoa even before these meetings. Close to the turn of the century, missionaries began teaching the gospel in Faleniu, Tutuila. This village was described by an elder as "a beautiful little village, located about three miles inland, near the west end of the island. A large rock wall surrounds the village, and the houses are so built that it is in lawn in the center, which makes an excellent play ground for the children."[17] Since the first conversions there, fifty members had been baptized, and the Protestant missionary had departed leaving the elders his dwelling house, meetinghouse, and his adherents. This kind of mass conversion was not unusual in the early years of the Church in Samoa. The important fact was that this branch became the nucleus for the gathering on Tutuila.

The countryside around Faleniu appealed to President Merrill as an especially fine place to establish a plantation. He wrote to the First Presidency and obtained permission to enter a lease for some acreage. In late February or early March 1902, he obtained twenty-two acres of "good land." Elder Merrill said, "The object of this leasing of land is to start a plantation for the church with the hope of gathering the Saints to one place."[18] It is doubtful that the purpose of gathering had been explained earlier to the Church leaders in Salt Lake City.

President Merrill was much concerned with the possibility of gathering after this date (March 1902), but his time was consumed by other matters such as the move to Pesega. In a talk in June he said he doubted that he would see the gathering during his time, but thought it would begin soon. He closed by making a prophetic statement. The gathering, he said, "will try the Saints and the elders." Ill with elephantiasis, President Merrill was released on January 2, 1903. Elder Martin F. Sanders was appointed to succeed him.

Elders' house or fale at Mapusaga, Tutuila, 1911. (Photo by John Q. Adams in the *Improvement Era.*)

Mapusaga branch chapel, 1911. (Photo by John Q. Adams in the *Improvement Era.*)

President Sanders was deeply committed to the gathering. Soon after he took office he began writing to the First Presidency about the matter. They considered it worthy of serious consideration and counseled President Sanders to study it carefully. They also advised that the proposed locations be large, healthful, productive, and attractive and that the move not offend either government involved.[19]

The First Presidency approved the acquisition of one hundred more acres near Faleniu in March 1903 but was still not prepared to recommend a full-scale gathering. A number of months passed before any additional land was leased, but the missionaries were moving ahead with plans. On May 30, President Sanders dedicated the original twenty-two acres near Faleniu as a gathering place. Here the Saints established a new Mormon village called Mapusaga.

In July 1903, the First Presidency suggested that two gathering places should be set up, one in American Samoa and one in German Samoa, and that these colonies should contain at least four hundred acres each.

From this time on until his release in November 1904, President Sanders spent a major part of his time looking for property. Agreeing that Mapusaga was the best place for gathering on Tutuila, he and his companions found an additional tract of land called "Malaeimi," which consisted of what they thought to be six or eight hundred acres of good plantation land. They leased it from a chief named Puailoa and entered it in the land court of Tutuila on October 31, 1903. Unfortunately another chief contested Puailoa's claim to the land, and this disagreement caused a long delay in concluding the lease. The problem was finally resolved in 1907. The lease of the 239 acres, when it was concluded, was for forty years at an annual rent of $180.

At the end of May 1904, President Sanders and the other elders found a suitable piece of land in German Samoa that was twenty-five miles east of Apia and several miles inland from the sea. They called it the land "behind Manunu."

President Sanders took an option on this land and informed the First Presidency concerning it and the financial terms that were available. The Church leaders considered the matter carefully and finally decided the best course would be to send President Samuel E. Woolley of the Hawaiian Mission to act as their agent in Samoa. He had been manager of Laie Plantation in Hawaii since 1895 and knew more about the problems of gathering Polynesian Saints on plantations than anyone else in the Church. They gave him authority not only to decide whether the proposed land was suitable for a gathering place, but also to decide whether the whole scheme was a wise move to make.[20]

President Woolley arrived at Apia on September 22, 1904, in company with Thomas S. Court, who had been called to replace Elder Sanders as president of the mission. On Monday the 26, Elders Sanders, Woolley, and Court traveled toward the mountain lands that were under consideration. All day on the twenty-seventh they tramped around the country. Rain fell constantly. President Woolley said it was "very wet and nasty" and that the underbrush was terribly damp and dense. A Samoan elder named Elisara carried the missionaries on his back across several streams early in the day, but by nightfall President Woolley and the others were so wet that they too walked through the rivers, sometimes up to their waists.

On October 1, Presidents Woolley, Sanders, and Court met at the mission office at Pesega and decided to buy the properties behind Manunu. President Woolley recommended not only that the Manunu lands be acquired but also that lands be obtained at Tuasivi, Savai'i. He suggested that the Church should have a home under each government—the American and the German. Lands, of course, had already been acquired on Tutuila.

That day, after the options had been signed and the land was in the hands of the Church, Elder Woolley wrote concerning his feelings about the new plantation: "I feel that everything has worked our way and everyone who knows the land says we have one of the choice lands of Samoa . . . . There is a good waterfall on the land and a large stream of water. It will take a number of years to develop the property into a paying proposition, yet it will enhance in value each year, so I feel that it is a paying proposition, and as agent for the First Presidency I recommend it."[21]

Four days later President Sanders leased approximately three hundred acres of land near Tuasivi, Savai'i. Unlike the other two gathering places, it was never developed.

The land deals ultimately turned out in an interesting way. The mission leaders originally estimated that the Manunu lands consisted of 488 acres. After the survey it was discovered that there were actually 725.5 acres. Prior to signing the contracts for the larger property, President Sanders had entered an agreement to purchase an adjoining 125 acres from another party. Since this property was not clear of title problems, the Church did not buy it. The total amount paid for the land that was to be named "Sauniatu" came to $7,170 (including $555 for surveying).[22]

LDS missionaries posing in front of a plaited frond chapel on Savaii, 1902. (Courtesy LDS Church Archives.)

The Samoan members and missionaries cleared the first land on November 8, 1904. In later years, residents of Sauniatu celebrated this day as Founders Day. Almost twenty years later Elisara, one of the first settlers, still vividly remembered the gallant efforts of the first inhabitants. He said that six inches of rain fell that day, almost half of Utah's average yearly precipitation. Everything was so wet that kindling a cooking fire was impossible, so the soaked but dedicated Saints swung their axes all day without eating. Within a few days they constructed several tiny huts for shelter. "Not higher than five feet, not much wider and but little longer, [they] were made of banana leaves for roofing, and cocoanut leaves partially closed them in." Rain leaked in, and mosquitoes had good fare, but the pioneers worked on.[23]

The settlers soon had two Samoan-style houses under construction—one for Elisara and the other for Tafaoga. The first missionary and priesthood meetings were held there on January 23-24, 1905. The day following, Elder Wilford W. Emery, conference president, offered a dedicatory prayer on the land and the growing community. Four veteran Samoan elders, Opapo, Elisara, Tafaoga, and Sio spoke during the meeting. From this time on the mission record makes more and more frequent references to the wisdom, strength, and power of the local Saints. Following the dedicatory meeting, the village leaders and the missionaries selected the name "Sauniatu"—"prepare for the things of the Lord"—for the colony.[24]

Over the next three years the missionaries expended great effort trying to get the Samoan Saints to gather in Sauniatu. During 1905 in particular, the missionaries and Samoan elders devoted a major part of every conference meeting to preaching the need to move to Sauniatu. The most faithful Saints responded well. By October 1905, the Samoan Saints had built seventeen houses (fales) at Sauniatu and by the end of the year 151 people called the new colony home. When the general conference of German Samoa was held in April 1906, the people had constructed eleven additional fale, along with a new meetinghouse.

The development of Sauniatu, however, was a difficult matter. The Saints had to clear the land, plant crops, build roads (the rough, winding road from Fusi at the seashore through the undergrowth to Sauniatu was not completed until 1908), plant coconuts and other trees, build walls, and found a school.

In addition to encouraging the success of Sauniatu, President Court also supported the expansion of Mapusaga on Tutuila. Progress there moved more rapidly after the lease of the Malaeimi lands in 1907.

But the growth of Sauniatu and Mapusaga brought serious problems to the mission. There was a falling away among those members who did not want to gather at the Mormon colonies. Savai'i was hardest hit by apostasy, but Upolu and Tutuila had their share of such problems. From mid-1905 on, for the next year or so, it was not unusual to see entries in the mission record to the effect that 12, 38, 110, or some other number of people had asked to have their names removed from the records of the Church. A number of members preferred to renounce all allegiance with the Church rather than leave their ancestral homes and lands. The leaders of the outer branches moved to Sauniatu, while some members remained to administer the programs of the Church. Often those members who stayed behind faltered and fell away.

In his report of December 31, 1908, Elder John Q. Adams, mission secretary, describes the problems even the more faithful Saints had in making the move to Sauniatu:

> Unlike the white foreigner, whose home is as a rule decided by his purse, the native domicile descends as a sacred legacy from father to son. Almost invariably, the piece of land occupied by a family at present is the identical spot on which for generations back, have dwelt their ancestors. It is apparent what aversion a demand

> compelling radically opposite change from this tradition of the forefathers would naturally occasion. Such a proposition faced the Saints when the call came to pull up stakes and journey to a new, wild, uncleared section. As a natural and expected consequence, obedience to the call was not universal by any means.[25]

The founding of Sauniatu took a great toll among the members, and a number of branches were closed. Membership on Savai'i sank so low that for a while there were only three small branches in operation. The school at Tuasivi, which had been successful for a long time, was closed in 1905; too many of the children had gone to LDS schools on Tutuila. Missionaries who visited members and others on Savai'i were seldom received warmly.

The revival of the branches outside Sauniatu, Pesega, Mapusaga, and Pago Pago did not begin until 1908. William A. Moody followed Thomas S. Court as mission president in April 1908. Soon after he arrived, he noticed that the branches outside of the gathering places badly needed attention. He reported his feelings to the First Presidency, and they encouraged him to rebuild the old branches. In fact, they wrote, "We too are of the opinion that too much stress was made to induce the breaking up of established homes in the old branches of

Twenty-five people crowded into this Samoan longboat in order to go to conference on Upolu Island in 1910. (Photo from the *Improvement Era*.)

the church for the purpose of making new ones at the gathering places named."[26] They asked President Moody to "heal the wounds" and "build new bridges" to the disaffected Saints. "To judge from your correspondence," they wrote President Moody, "we are inclined to the belief that the colonizing effort has been undertaken at too much of a sacrifice."[27] Not until 1911 or 1912 did the whole mission regain its former strength.

The rebuilding process succeeded largely because President Moody worked hard and demanded equal effort from his missionaries. The missionaries found it effective to resume the practice (started early in the mission's history but dropped for a time) of touring the mission with a group of Saints. Such trips, called "malaga" or "taamilosaga," usually included several Samoan men who could preach well, a school band or choir or both, and a number of well-wishers who went along for the fun. Such tours created much interest during President Moody's time and continued to be useful during the following years.

Latter-day Saint school bands were the best in the islands. The band from Mapusaga was used regularly for important government occasions on Tutuila, and the Sauniatu band regularly won top recognition in German and then British Samoa after 1914. During this period there were at one time six LDS bands in Samoa.

After President Moody's time, three important developments occured at Sauniatu. First, two families came to the islands to serve as agricultural missionaries. Elder Henry S. Gibbon and his wife were appointed to manage the operation at Mapusaga, and Elder David Wilcox, along with his wife, Elizabeth, and their three daughters, was appointed to manage Sauniatu. Second, during the time of President Christian Jensen, Jr. (1911), families at Sauniatu were allowed to work their own two-acre plots in addition to the Church-held lands. Third, a substantial concrete chapel was constructed and dedicated April 6, 1917. It is still in use.

THE REOPENING OF THE TONGAN MISSION AREA

From 1891 until 1897 the Samoan Mission operated a conference (district) in Tonga. But because the missionaries made almost no converts, they were removed for a decade. On March 19, 1907, however, President Thomas S. Court sailed to the Vava'u Group in

Sauniatu chapel, 1932. (Photo from the *Improvement Era.*)

northern Tonga to investigate the possibility of sending missionaries there again. He returned to Apia on April 11, with the report that the prospects in Tonga seemed excellent. Two days later he called Elder William O. Facer to serve in Tonga, and two weeks later President Court asked Elder Heber J. McKay from the Tutuila Conference to go there. On June 1, Elders Facer and McKay sailed for Tonga. By the end of July they had established a school that was "growing very well."[28]

Between 1907 and 1916, the Church grew considerably in Tonga, creating administrative difficulties. The Tongan area demanded a great deal of each mission president's time, and yet it did not receive as much attention as it should have. It became necessary, therefore, to divide the two areas. In February 1916, President Edward J. Wood of Alberta Stake; President Joseph H. Dean, the first missionary to Samoa; and Ernest C. Wright, newly appointed mission president in Samoa, arrived in Samoa from America. The First Presidency had given President Wood the assignment to choose a mission president for Tonga from among the elders presently serving in the mission. He selected Willard L. Smith and his wife, Jenny, to lead the new mission in Tonga. They had already served for a year on Tutuila. The Smiths were set apart on April 3 and sailed for Tonga soon afterward. The new mission was created in this way.

TRANSLATION AND PUBLISHING WORK

The Book of Mormon was the most important item published in the Samoan language during this period. In 1900 the First Presidency authorized President William Sears to translate it. Through the efforts of four missionaries, President Sears, Frank E. Morris, George C. Spilsbury, and Edwin Smart, the first draft of the translation was completed by March 28, 1901. They reworked it during the next five months, and by September it was ready to be transcribed in final form before being sent to Salt Lake City for printing. Elder Frank E. Morris was released from his mission early so that he could supervise the shipment and printing of the new translation. He left Samoa on April 2, 1902. By June 1903 the first small shipment of the Samoan Book of Mormon, O le Tusi a Mamona, arrived at Pago Pago, and the first large shipment followed in December, ready for general distribution.[29]

The historical records contain few references to other publishing projects until the last three or four years of this period. When President Wood visited Samoa, he was accompanied by Joseph H. Dean and Ernest C. Wright. Both men were excellent translators. Elder Dean's purpose for returning to Samoa was to translate a group of hymns into Samoan and to set them to music. He was assisted in this task by his son Harry, who was serving a mission in Samoa at that time, and by a native missionary named K. Saupaia. The older Dean sailed from the islands on November 3, 1916, having completed the work as far as possible. The hymn book was published as *O Pese a Siona* in 1918.

President Wright's publishing efforts were in a different direction. He was unusually eager to have converts brought into the Church, but he was disappointed by the situation he found in the mission. The elders were not working very hard. They preferred to have the Samoan elders do the tracting and the teaching of the gospel while they themselves acted as resident ministers and schoolteachers.

President Wright changed all this by writing and publishing a number of tracts and requiring his missionaries to distribute them. The first was titled "The Godhead." Brother Wright ordered 10,000 copies in January 1917. Over the next six or eight months ten others of his tracts were published in similar quantities. He set a goal of distributing 75,000 tracts during that year and then pushed his missionaries until they accomplished it.

CHURCH SCHOOLS

Through these early years, Church schools played a vital role in the history of the Church in Samoa. The work "school" referred to many different kinds of efforts, ranging from three or four small children learning the alphabet in their own vernacular beneath a palm tree, to German-language schools, or to fairly well-developed English-language schools that offered a reasonably wide curriculum. The number of schools in operation varied greatly over the years. Early in the century (1904) there were four "advanced" schools and ten smaller elementary schools. During the time of Superintendent Richard T. Haag, 1913-14, the number of schools grew to twenty-six, with 628 pupils. By 1919 the number of schools had dropped to eighteen, but the numbers enrolled seem to have been larger than in Haag's time.

The schools brought the Church much favorable recognition. It was not unusual for the ranking administrative officers of both Samoas to compliment the mission presidents for the work the schools were accomplishing among the people.

Most of the teachers were American missionaries. But a great number of local Saints were called as schoolteachers after they had been graduated from the Church schools at Sauniatu and Mapusaga. These graduates became the backbone of the Church in Samoa.[30]

THE PEOPLE

From the days of Joseph H. Dean until the end of 1919, the Samoan people contributed greatly to the Church's success. Their leaders called them early to positions of authority and depended on them to maintain the branches. The mission leaders regularly consulted the chiefs on all matters of importance, such as the creation of schools, the building of homes and meetinghouses, and even the distribution of missionaries. Many Samoan priesthood bearers and their wives served missions among their own people and bore witness to the truthfulness of the gospel. Their numbers, when wives are included, exceeded those of the foreign elders. In August 1917 there were twenty-nine foreign missionaries, but there were thirty-six local Samoan missionaries (eighteen married couples) serving the Church. By 1920 many of the members of the Church had been born and reared according to the *Mamona,* Mormon, way of life, and had been educated in Latter-day Saint schools. The Church in Samoa was ready to move into a new era of steady growth and greater influence.

CHAPTER 23

STEADY GROWTH THROUGH DIFFICULT TIMES

Samoa, 1920–1948

The second decade of the twentieth century ended with Samoan LDS membership at 3500. A year later, according to the best statistics available, the total population of both Samoas stood at 45,200, and the Church claimed between 5 and 6 percent of the population. During the next three decades the general population nearly doubled. And as it grew, so too did the Church membership. By 1950, 7,362, approximately 8 percent of all Samoans, were baptized Latter-day Saints. The growth of the Church, however, was not dramatic during this period. The high year for convert baptisms was 1946, when 305 people were brought into the Church. The average number of converts for the thirty years was 189 per year. Nevertheless, the steady rate of growth increased the ratio of Latter-day Saints to the total population.

MISSIONARY WORK

Government regulations in Western Samoa during most of this period limited the number of foreign missionaries to twelve. Three to six other American missionaries were assigned to American Samoa. The average number of foreign missionaries in the two Samoas from 1920 until 1946 was between sixteen and eighteen. During this time the number of branches grew from twenty-eight to fifty-eight. Obviously the foreign missionaries were not able to act as branch presidents for so many units of the Church. Thus, the responsibility for the branches fell upon the local Saints.

Local elders, priests, and even teachers or deacons were regularly called to act as presidents in the branches. During this entire time almost every village branch was presided over by a missionary couple

The new meetinghouse at Tuasivi, Savaii, as it appeared in 1904. (Photo from the *Instructor*.)

who were assigned to move there. It was not unusual for them to remain in these callings for six to twelve years without being transferred or released. Between thirty-five and fifty couples were generally involved in such assignments. They were responsible for conducting all branch affairs and also for most of the missionary work that was performed in their village areas.

The livelihood of the local missionaries was taken care of by a program developed by President Willard L. Smith in 1930. (Before then the local missionaries had been forced to rely on the generosity of the villagers among whom they worked.) President Smith asked the members in each village to set aside two parcels of land, one to be used for the erection of a dwelling house and also, if needed, as the site for a chapel; the other to grow food on. In this way the missionary and his family could be self-supporting. Most of the village chiefs soon responded to President Smith's request by signing contracts agreeing to the plan.[1]

The white or *palangi* missionaries were used as district presidents (there were three districts until 1944, when President John Q. Adams expanded the number to five), as plantation managers during part of this time, and as schoolteachers. They also did a good deal of traveling from branch to branch.

The presidents of the Samoan Mission, in addition to administrative work connected with regular Church and missionary functions, were also responsible for two and later three plantations, three residential schools and their attendant villages, and a large school system.

Two mission presidents had an especially lasting effect on the Church in Samoa: John Q. Adams, who served from late 1919 to 1923, and again from 1943 to 1948; and Willard L. Smith, who served from 1927 to 1934 (he was the first president of the Tongan Mission from 1916 to 1920). President Adams started and almost ended the period, and President Smith filled a major part of the middle years.

One of the continually popular proselyting techniques in Latter-day Saint missionary work in the Samoan Islands was the use of touring groups of students. This method was used regularly until after World War II. Little use was made of the scriptures as proselyting tools.

It is difficult to explain the reluctance of the mission presidents and paalangi elders to ordain Samoan men to the Melchizedek Priesthood. The implication was that the white missionaries did not trust the Samoans with much authority. This was a carryover from the paternalistic attitudes of the past and had a tinge of white supremacy. The accompanying table reveals that in 1920 there were fewer than two Samoan Melchizedek Priesthood holders per branch. As late as 1950 the number was still fewer than four Melchizedek Priesthood holders per branch, hardly a sufficient number to operate the full program of the Church.

Samoan Mission Statistics, 1920-1950[2]

Year	Total Membership	Samoan Melchizedek Priesthood	Percent of Membership	Number of Branches
1920	2,647	45	1.70	28
1925	3,695	42	1.14	30*
1931**	3,835	51	1.33	NR
1935	4,835	63	1.30	47***
1940	5,575	114	2.04	54
1945	6,436	191	2.97	64
1950	7,362	218	2.96	58

*1924 report of number of branches.

**1931 was used rather than 1930 because the membership census was corrected during that year.

***1936 report of number of branches.

In summary, the missionary methods in Samoa did not change much from 1920 to 1950. Growth was relatively slow, but it was faster at that than the rate of growth of the population in the two Samoas. Most converts were proselyted by local missionaries, who did the major share of the branch work. The foreign elders confined themselves primarily to teaching, plantation supervision, and administrative assignments.

ELDER DAVID O. MCKAY'S VISIT TO SAMOA

On November 8, 1920, President Adams received word that Elders David O. McKay and Hugh J. Cannon were making a worldwide tour of missions and would be coming to Samoa within a few months. The magnitude of this event is difficult for readers almost six decades later to grasp. But this was without question the supreme moment in Samoan LDS history to that time. Elder McKay was the first general authority to visit the South Pacific islands. After his visit, almost twenty more years passed before another general authority came to this area.

The missionaries and Saints made elaborate preparations for Elder McKay's arrival. On May 3, 1921, a telegram came from Elder McKay, then in New Zealand, informing the Saints that he would be at Apia harbor in one week. President Adams sent messengers to all branches on Upolu and Savaii. When the honored guests disembarked at 9:00 A.M. on May 11 and were rowed ashore in two Samoan longboats, they were greeted by one of the most excited groups of Saints ever assembled, as well as a great many people who were not in the Church but who knew who Elder McKay was. Members and nonmembers alike crowded around the guests, the Sauniatu band played, and a grand parade proceeded past the shops and business houses of Apia. Almost everything came to a standstill as the first apostle to visit Samoa greeted the people.

When the guests arrived at Pesega they were formally welcomed by an assembly of thirty high chiefs. After the speeches, the *taupou* (the highest chief's virgin daughter) passed the kava to Elders McKay and Cannon as a manifestation of respect. The Saints and guests held a great feast in the afternoon and presented special entertainments in the evening. For the next four days conference meetings were held during the days, and programs of various kinds at night.

The sojourners were in the islands for twenty-eight days. During that time they sailed to American Samoa, where they held a series of meetings and visited with the Saints of Pago Pago and Mapusaga. They also visited a number of schools and branches on Upolu.

But the most important event happened at the gathering place, Sauniatu. Elders McKay and Cannon and President Adams spent most of May 31 studying the school and plantation. During the afternoon Elder McKay and his companions administered to and blessed a number of children and others. Then, realizing they had to cover twenty-five miles of difficult terrain on horseback before nightfall if they were to be back at Pesega on schedule, the group of leaders stepped into the living room of the missionary home expecting to make a hasty retreat toward Apia and Pesega. But the Saints of the village desired to shake hands with the apostle of the Lord. The Relief Society sisters crowded the room and the porch. As Elder McKay left the mission home, the Sauniatu band began playing "Good-by, My Feleni," which is equivalent to Hawaii's "Aloha Oe." The grand old Samoan patriarchs Elisara and Saimasina wept as they clasped Elder McKay and Elder Cannon. In fact, everyone wept.

As the visitors walked to their horses, the people gathered again, and the scene was reenacted. President Adams recounted the concluding events in these words: "Once more we set out, on our horses this time, and looking back we saw that they were following us slowly, the band playing their touching air. Framed and over-arched in the vista of a tunnel-like tropical lane of greenery, and rhythmically advancing to the softened tone of the faraway instruments—was ever such a picture presented to mortal eyes? And we all knew that in both parties not a dry eye could be found."[3]

At this, feeling the devotion of the Sauniatu Saints, Elder McKay said, "Let us return and hold prayer with them under the trees." He dismounted and hung his umbrella on a kapok tree. Then, raising his arms in prayer, he gave the people a blessing. He blessed them for their faith and love. He prayed for their health, for their prosperity, and for the righteousness of their leaders. He prayed for peace and harmony in the village, that above all. "Our Father, may they have clear understanding of the truth and make rapid progress in gaining a knowledge of thee and thy divine work."[4] He sealed these blessings upon the people by the authority of the "holy apostleship." Quickly turning away, he and the others lost sight of the group who lingered for one last look at their apostle. Brokenly, Elder McKay spoke to President Adams, "And these are they whom the world calls bad."[5]

Before the day was over the Saints of Sauniatu erected a lava-rock marker on the spot where Elder McKay gave the blessing. A year later they constructed a monument nearer the village in commemoration of the apostolic visit. Each year for many years thereafter a special service was held at Sauniatu on May 31, "McKay Day."

THE CONVERSION OF TAPUELEELE VILLAGE

While Elder McKay was in Samoa, he assured the missionaries, foreign and Samoan, that if they would faithfully do their assigned work, the time would not be far distant when a whole village and perhaps even villages would join the Church as one body.[6] On a number of earlier occasions, village chiefs had joined the Church, and they were later followed by their families and others. But until this time an entire village had never become Latter-day Saints in a single day.

Tapueleele village is about four miles inland up the mountain on the east end of Savai'i. As long as anyone could remember, all residents of this place had belonged to the London Missionary Society church. The people of Tapueleele supported a minister and had built a small but attractive chapel. Until June 1922, no one considered changing religions. At that time, however, an influential Latter-day Saint named David Crighton, of Tifitifi, west Upolu, decided to build a new home for the missionaries in his village. He hired a group of carpenters from Tapueleele, Savai'i, to do most of the work. He constantly discussed the beliefs of the Mormons with these people. Before long some of the chiefs had been won over in friendship.

During August 1922, a number of the Tapueleele chiefs saw a performance by a touring group of Sauniatu school children. Soon after, the conference presidents of Savai'i and Upolu, Ralph A. Knowlton and Gilbert Tingey, visited the village of Tapueleele. They were well received, but there the matter rested for a time. Soon, however, word traveled as far as Pesega that Tapueleele had joined the Church. President Adams described the news in this way: "Without one word from us, all the chiefs of the village decided that they wanted the L.D.S. Church and one of its schools in their precinct, and in decorous fashion they met in solemn conclave and then and there decided to oust their minister, turn over the well built little frame church and native-built but large minister's house to the 'Mormons.' "[7]

President Adams regularly sent missionaries, local and foreign, to the village for the next few months. It soon became evident to the elder in charge that the chiefs' decision to join the Church was sincere and permanent. In consultation with the elders involved, President Adams decided that the next Savai'i Island conference should be held at Tapueleele on December 2 and 3, 1922. The conference was a wonderful success, for several reasons: there had been enough food, the people of Tapueleele were quickly integrated into the LDS fold, and an impressive baptismal service had been held at "the foot of a high, foamy waterfall in a great cleft in the lava of the adjacent forest." The moss-lined glen had afforded an exceptional setting in which the fifteen converts of that day were baptized. Others were baptized during the weeks that followed. Another reason for the success of the meetings was the unexpected donation by the village chiefs of one hundred acres of land upon which they desired a school to be built.[8]

The mission president soon started a school there, with Emma Burgess, a part-Caucasian Samoan girl, as the first teacher. Under her direction the children progressed well in the rudiments of education. But progress on the one-hundred-acre tract of land was much slower. The government required a careful legal procedure when property was exchanged, and the Church did not take control of the tract until late in the decade while Willard L. Smith was president of the mission.

The mass conversion of Tapueleele was the most dramatic story of its kind, but other villages came into the Church in almost the same manner. There was the mass conversion of Tafatafa, Upolu, in 1932. The chiefs of this village had become angry with their Wesleyan minister and asked him to leave. Later they invited the Latter-day Saint missionaries to visit their village and teach them the restored gospel. The elders held meetings there for three months but delayed baptizing anyone because they thought the villagers' anger with their pastor might be transitory and he would be asked back. This turned out not to be so, and the villagers joined the Church. Mission leaders assigned Taaga, a Samoan elder, to preside over the new branch. The chapel and dwelling house of the former pastor were turned over to the Church.[9]

THE EFFECTS OF THE HAWAII TEMPLE

The completion of the first temple in the Pacific at Laie, Hawaii, had a direct effect on the Church in Samoa. By the end of 1922 one Samoan family had moved to Laie to do temple work. A year later the number had increased sufficiently that Hawaiian Mission President Neff found it necessary to organize a Samoan Society to keep them active in the Church.[10] In Samoa the Relief Societies raised $439.20 to support temple work for the Samoans during 1923.

Samoan Mission records reveal that three native missionaries, their families, and nine schoolboys immigrated to Hawaii in 1923; and in 1924, four missionaries, three women, and ten boys and girls departed from Samoa for Hawaii. Interest in temple work continued through the '20s, but by the last three years of the decade, President Smith became concerned about the exodus.[11]

By late 1930 the judge of American Samoa shared that concern, though for different reasons. Large numbers of people from Western Samoa were passing through American Samoa en route to Hawaii and not coming back. (Because of the political status of Tutuila as an American property, it was easy for residents of that island to go to Hawaii. This continues to be true in the 1980s). Many of these people claimed they would return to Samoa but did not. To curtail this problem, the judge ruled that residents of Western Samoa could go to Hawaii only if they gave bond that they would return to Samoa by a prearranged date. President Smith saw this as a good move because it would keep some of the Saints in Samoa who were needed there to operate the Church.[12]

By 1933 President Smith was opposed to emigration under any circumstances. He believed that the most worthy Saints were too busy on missions to have time to plan temple trips and that they did not have the money to make the voyage. Some members who had gone to Hawaii had given the Church a bad name because they did not return when they said they would. President Smith concluded that it was better for the members to work on family records in Samoa and to have their endowment work done after they died. His attitude was probably not shared by some Samoan members, but nevertheless it was the operating principle of the highest leader of the Church in the Islands.

Genealogy work received a boost from May 1936 to May 1937, during the time of William A. Waddoups. His term as mission president was short because he was sent on to New Zealand to strengthen genealogy and temple work there.

PLANTATIONS AND CENTRAL SCHOOLS

When President Adams arrived in the islands as mission president, he came better prepared than any of his predecessors to handle the management of the plantations. He had studied coconut farming before going to Samoa as mission president and had also learned enough about cattle raising to make intelligent decisions in that area. He was aware from the start that coconuts did not thrive in Sauniatu and Mapusaga. On his first visit to Mapusaga, he found the plantation "in chaos." A $900 debt had been accumulated, and there was little harmony in the village. When he visited Sauniatu in April 1920, President Adams found the villagers discouraged. The chiefs asked whether the gathering place could be moved to the east end of Upolu. Twice that month, in fact, the chiefs requested that Sauniatu be moved. By the second date President Adams had thought the matter through, and he believed the village was worth maintaining where it was. He asked the people there to remember the sacrifices of the early Saints at Nauvoo, Illinois, and to try to emulate their example.

The issue of whether to move Sauniatu was not resolved until Elder McKay visited the village and blessed it and those gathered there. From that time on there was no serious discussion among the Samoan members concerning the question of moving. Members encouraged others to come, and the population doubled in 1922, though it dwindled later.

President Adams tried to help Sauniatu to be more prosperous by directing the draining of parts of the plantation (an undertaking that was only marginally successful) and advising the villagers about where to plant. These efforts notwithstanding, Sauniatu never produced well and was nearly always a financial burden on the Church. In the early 1930s, the First Presidency suggested that Sauniatu be sold, rented, or given away, but President Smith could neither sell nor rent it, nor could he figure out to whom to give it.

Mapusaga was not such a problem. President Adams spent several months there working with the Saints to restore confidence in the system and teaching the foreign elders how to administer the operation.

During the presidencies of John Q. Adams and Ernest L. Butler (1923-27), Saints were encouraged to gather at Sauniatu and Mapusaga, but the earlier emphasis on gathering was not continued. It was becoming evident that the major reason for the existence of both villages was to support the residential schools there. Gathering places were no longer needed because improved relations with the governments of both Samoas had largely eliminated the need for gathering. In fact, the mission presidents were on pleasant social terms with most of the government administrators of Western Samoa and many of the

U.S. Navy governors of American Samoa. During this era governments were more a help than a hindrance to the Church.

During the Adams-Butler period, central or "advanced schools" were operated at Sauniatu and Mapusaga. The Mapusaga school was called Vaiola-Penina (Vaiola, the boys' school, meaning "living waters," and Penina, the girls' school, meaning "pearls"). The students who attended either school were assigned to families who lived permanently in the villages. The students were controlled by the *matai,* male family heads. The normal pattern was for students to attend school during the early hours of the day, usually only until 1:00 P.M., and after that they were to work under the direction of the matai. Special fale were set aside for the boys and girls to sleep in. An adult resident supervised both groups and slept with them for their protection.

Some major changes in this pattern took place during the presidency of Willard L. Smith (1927-34). President Smith believed that Mapusaga and Sauniatu were useful only for their support of the schools.[13] He decided that some of the families who had long resided at Sauniatu should be called back to their native villages.[14]

President Smith's most important change was to remove the students from the control of the matai and house them in compounds where they were under the direct control of local missionaries who had been called to act as head residents and overseers. To do this it was necessary to construct a number of new dwelling houses, tin roofed fales.[15] This change allowed the children to spend a greater part of their time working on school matters. They were still required to spend time on the village plantations and to keep their villages neat and clean, but they were removed from the sometimes dictatorial control of the matai.[16]

During this era a new residential school was established near Tapueleele, Savai'i, on the large tract of land donated by the village chiefs. President Adams had suggested that the land be made into another gathering place for the Saints of Savai'i. But President Butler could not act upon the suggestion because of legal entanglements—the governor did not sign the papers declaring the Church to be in control of the property until 1928—and by the time President Smith took over, he did not want to create another gathering place.

President Smith chose the land the Church took over. Because he did not want the village heads of Tapueleele to have too much control, he selected a tract that was somewhat removed from the village. The piece of land the mission leaders selected was bordered by acreage that was available from the War Reparations Estate, administered by the New Zealand government of Samoa. They purchased fifty acres of land at 2.5 pounds per acre. This site became the village of *Vaiola,* the name chosen for the new school.

In late 1928 or early 1929, Elder Charles I. Sampson and a small group of school children cleared the area and planted about thirty-six acres of coconuts. Elder Sampson lived in a small hut at first. But the students, villagers, and he soon constructed Samoan fales for residential and school purposes, one of which he occupied. The children of Tapueleele, the only ones interested, came to live with him, and together they created the village and school. Elder Sampson and the local and foreign missionaries who followed him had to work very hard. President Smith described the early years in this way: "We had to build houses, make roads, teach school, all this with the planting and caring for the plantation in three or four short years. . . . The elders in the beginning especially certainly worked hard, those who follow will never know what it has taken to fell trees and make them into lumber."[17]

At first the elders and students attempted to raise coconuts, but the rhinoceros beetle caused much damage, and they decided to plant cocoa. This turned out to be a temperamental crop. But a successful combination of coconuts and cocoa was produced as the years passed.

Although Vaiola school had a slow start, continued support from mission leaders helped it to succeed. In April 1932 the leading Church chiefs from Savai'i built two dwelling houses for the school children.

With the creation of Vaiola school, the Church now had three central residential schools, one on each large island. Together they served the needs of the Church until after the Second World War.

FURTHER EDUCATIONAL DEVELOPMENTS

According to several mission presidents the schools, central and village, were the most important proselyting tools of the Church.[18] They were needed in order to compete with the LMS, the Wesleyans, and the Catholics, all of whom sponsored fine schools.[19] Neither Samoan government provided much public education. The U.S. naval government of American Samoa did more for education than did the government of Western Samoa, but both governments depended on the various churches to provide most of the education of the Samoan people.

Education in LDS schools was rudimentary. Foreign missionaries staffed some grades of the central schools, but young graduates of the Church schools did most of the teaching. Before World War II, almost none of the Samoan teachers had a high-school education.

President Butler and each president after him emphasized teacher training. Beginning in 1924 the mission leaders made efforts to bring order and uniformity to the curriculum. That year eight of the Samoan teachers participated in the Government School Institute, and the following year the mission held two one-week training sessions for the Latter-day Saint Samoan teachers. Latter-day Saint mission leaders were much involved in public education during the 1920s. President Butler was a member of the school board appointed by the government of Western Samoa, and Conference President A.W. Bonham was secretary of the committee on textbooks appointed by the governor of American Samoa. He and other Church leaders hoped to establish uniformity in textbooks for Latter-day Saints schools throughout the mission.[20]

Because the schools took so much of the missionaries' time, in 1928 the Church asked the government of American Samoa to take over financial support of the school at Mapusaga and to pay the native teachers there as they did the teachers in the government schools. Later that year, government and Church leaders approved a plan and signed a contract turning support and supervision of the school over to the government. The government agreed to pay $100 a month for the services of two elders and also to pay the Latter-day Saint Samoan teachers.[21]

Because of complaints from non-Mormons, the contract was soon reduced so that it supported only one elder at $50 per month, but the pay to the Samoan teachers was continued. This arrangement prevailed until the end of 1933, when the navy administrators decided Mapusaga's location did not serve well the needs of the public school system. The mission president continued to operate the school without government assistance.

In November 1929 the American government asked Elder Orval J. Doney to conduct the annual teachers institute that was to run from December 10, 1929, to February 10, 1930. Elder Doney also conducted similar teacher training sessions for the Church in Western Samoa.

In summary, the schools required a tremendous amount of supervision and creative energy from mission leaders and local teachers as well as a large amount of money for school buildings and dwellings.

But the schools served two very important purposes. The young Samoan Saints gained a basic knowledge of reading and writing, and many people were brought into the waters of baptism.

THE VISIT OF ELDERS GEORGE ALBERT SMITH AND RUFUS K. HARDY TO SAMOA

The year 1938 marked the fiftieth anniversary of Latter-day Saint missionary work in Samoa. Elaborate plans were made to celebrate the jubilee. Elder George Albert Smith of the Council of the Twelve and Elder Rufus K. Hardy of the First Council of Seventy arranged a tour of the South Pacific missions so that they could be in Samoa during the celebration.

The visit of Elders Smith and Hardy was only the second visit by general authorities to the Islands. Great feasts, special entertainments, beautiful decorations, and much speechmaking were planned for the honored guests, who arrived in Apia on June 8. The major attraction of the celebration was a four-day conference that culminated on Sunday, June 19. Not only did Elders Smith and Hardy speak but A.C. Turnbull, the non-Mormon administrator of Samoa, also attended the session and spoke briefly. His visit to the conference was the first of its kind by any New Zealand administrator of the islands.

The official celebration was important, but not as significant as were the visits made by Elders Smith and Hardy to government offices, to important Samoans, to special dinners, and to the homes of influential Samoans and Europeans in Apia. The official visit of Elders Smith and Hardy lasted from June 8 to July 1.[22]

DEPRESSION, WAR, AND THE AFTERMATH

The Great Depression of the 1930s did considerable economic damage to Samoa, but because most of the people were already living at barely a subsistence level they hardly noticed the change. But for those of the middle and upper classes, money was scarce. A surprising effect of the Depression was that nonmembers became more friendly to the Church. President Willard L. Smith thought this was because ministers of other churches found it more difficult to collect their support money and therefore applied greater pressure on their people for the customary church funds, causing many non-Mormons to be attracted to the lay priesthood system of the Latter-day Saints, where no support money was required.[23]

The Depression years led directly into the Second World War. Western Samoa, because it was under British Commonwealth protection and administration, was placed officially in a state of war in 1939. Even before the Pacific war began on December 7, 1941, the First Presidency considered it best to bring the missionaries back to the United States. On October 14, 1940, the newly arrived Samoan mission president, Wilford W. Emery, received a telegram from President Heber J. Grant requesting that the missionaries be sent home on American ships as soon as possible. By October 26, all but three of the Samoan missionaries were on their way home. The last three left November 29, 1940. Even Sister Emery left for a few months.[24]

With the exodus of the foreign missionaries, President Emery made a number of changes before the end of October 1940. Iulai AhMu was sustained to take President Emery's place in case he was called home. Aloese, a Samoan sister, was called as mission Relief Society president. In the districts, Samoan brethren were called to preside. Percy Rivers, who had changed his name from AhMu, was called as mission secretary.[25]

At about the same time, President Emery made arrangements for the care of part of his temporal responsibilities. Caucasian missionaries had managed the three plantations almost continuously, but now the plantations lacked adequate leadership. President Emery solved the problem by signing a contract with the attorney general of American Samoa to have the government oversee the whole operation. Of special concern was the herd of about 350 cattle. The attorney general agreed to provide care for the herd until the missionaries returned, pay all expenses, and bank for the Church any money that might be made from transactions.[26] President Emery also wanted to place the Mapusaga school under government control, but he did not succeed.

Like the rest of the world, the Saints in Samoa were disturbed to learn of the Japanese bombing of Pearl Harbor. The news brought fear and concern to Samoa. The governments, believing an attack against Samoa was possible, encouraged the people to prepare habitations in the bush if necessary. Supplies of almost all kinds quickly became hard to obtain, and the governments imposed rationing.

Although Tutuila was attacked only once (by a Japanese submarine), and Western Samoa escaped completely, both Samoas were brought into the war, primarily as areas of support for the troops in the war zone, farther west. Thousands of marines were stationed on Tutuila and Upolu. President Emery wrote on April 1, 1942, that "the government has taken every home and church that is available on

Tutuila for government purposes."[27] Two weeks later President Emery received orders to give up the missionary home and chapel in Pago Pago. Only a week after this, on April 22, he learned that he would have to give up the mission headquarters at Pesega. This ruling was not immediately put into effect, but some months later eight or nine marine officers moved into the mission home with John Q. Adams, President Emery's successor. By May the entire Pesega complex was occupied by hundreds of servicemen. It was necessary to close the Pesega school for a number of months because of the presence of the military.

Large trucks, small trucks, jeeps, and other vehicles were constantly passing Pesega, loaded with equipment and material that had been unloaded at Apia. It was now being taken to Satapuala, at the west end of Upolu, where an airport was being constructed. This, the first airport in Western Samoa, typified the great changes that came to Samoa during the war years. New technology was paraded daily before the eyes of the Samoans. Unfortunately, new forms of vice and corruption were also introduced. Many people began to smoke. Money was available in greater amounts than at any time in Samoa's history. Lonely servicemen sought female companionship, and as a result many Samoan women, some LDS, fell into moral transgression.

The most dramatic story involving the Church took place at Mapusaga. By October 1942 a mobile hospital had been established there to care for servicemen who had been injured in the Solomon Islands. So much activity surrounded the scene that President Emery said, "Mapusaga is just like a little city at the present time." At that date the Samoan Saints were still living there. The next August, however, President John Q. Adams received word that Mapusaga was being entirely taken over by U.S. forces and that the village, including the local Saints, was being moved away, up the mountainside. President Adams was unable to obtain permission to travel to the island of Tutuila at that time, but he hoped that the movement of the village would somehow prove a blessing. Brother Adams, who was by nature rather paternalistic, was angered by the refusal of the Marine Corps attorney general to act on his repeated applications for a permit to come to Tutuila. Not until May 1944, almost a year after Mapusaga was moved, did President Adams obtain permission to go to the island. When he arrived at the site of old Mapusaga, he found it abandoned not only by the Church members but also by the military. In March 1944 the marines had been moved to the war zone. When they left they dismantled or destroyed what they had built and what had been left of the village as well. All that remained were 107 concrete slabs of different sizes and shapes and the water system underground.

Why the village was moved is not clear. In the mission record, President Adams gave two conjectures. First, he believed that the Marine colonel in charge disliked Samoans and Mormons and used his influence to weaken the Mormon village. The second conjecture was more serious. President Adams wrote that if the Saints in Mapusaga had been true to the commandments, the village would never have been moved. "There were gambling, drunkenness, excessive dancing and frequent ribald so-called amusements (especially with the U.S. troops), adultery, disobedience, insincerity prevalent. That these conditions prevailed none can deny. That the place needed cleaning out isn't controversial."[28]

When President Adams first saw the new village, called Mapusaga Fou, or New Mapusaga, he found a collection of hastily thrown together homes of every sort of material. The people had had to rebuild their homes without help; all the military did was haul the material.

The site of Mapusaga Fou was a mile up the mountain from the old village. It was in a beautiful setting, but the Church did not own the land, and from the beginning it was questionable that the village could remain in that place. The chiefs who owned the land wanted the village moved as soon as possible.

The issue of leased land at Mapusaga had occupied the attention of many a mission president. During the 1930s two presidents had tried repeatedly to renew the leases on the two pieces of land that constituted the plantation and on which the village stood. Leases on both parcels—22 acres where old Mapusaga stood and 360 acres of plantation land—had been made early in the century. The lease on the smaller piece expired in 1943; the lease on the larger was due to expire in 1946. Without the renewal of these leases the Church would be out of business in that historic area.

On July 17, 1944, President Adams began negotiating for the twenty-two acres with the group of Faleniu chiefs of the LMS Church who owned the land. Breaking with past custom, the chiefs did not want to lease it again but desired instead to sell it. Two years before, they had offered the land to President Emery for five thousand dollars. Now President Adams reminded the chiefs of the use that had been made of the property as a school for their children over the past forty years. This apparently made an impression, and they asked him to name his price. He offered one thousand dollars, and to his surprise they agreed. Before the transaction was completed some days later, two chiefs who had not attended the meeting balked at the offer, but they were finally persuaded, and the sale took place.

The large piece of ground, called Malaeimi, was originally leased from Puailoa for fifteen dollars a month. Puailoa died before the lease expired, but his wife, Salataima, an active member of the Church, wanted to arranged a new lease. Her brother, Chief Lanufua of Nuuuli, dissuaded her from signing, and only after President Adams applied great pressure did she go against her brother's desire and sign a new lease arrangement. Under the new lease, which began in January 1946, she received thirty dollars a month and two beef cattle each year for the next forty years.

After the leases were signed, President Adams decided to change the name of the old Mapusaga site to Mesepa (after the biblical Mizpah), and to make it a village for the gathering of Saints who desired to prepare themselves to go to the temple. His plan was to invite to Mesepa only those members who could seek the spirit of temple work, prepare family records, save funds, and go directly to the temple at Laie. He put part of this plan into effect, but later mission presidents did not understand his purposes, and the village soon returned to its former status as a regular Church community.

While President Adams was busy recreating the mission, he also decided to rename the village and school at Vaiola. He named it "Nifae" after the Book of Mormon prophet Nephi. This name was used until the early 1950s, when the people and the mission presidents decided to restore its traditional name of Vaiola, "living waters."[29]

The war benefitted most Samoans economically. The U.S. Navy enlarged its use of Pago Pago Harbor as well as other parts of the islands. These developments provided much labor at good wages for the Samoans.

As a result of the war, some interesting facts became evident to Church leaders. One was that the Samoan priesthood bearers were not only capable of leading the Church but were able to enlarge it as well. The largest number of converts ever baptized before the late 1950s was the 305 people baptized in 1946 by a missionary force that was entirely local. The Samoans were also able to continue the schools during the war. The total number of schools dropped to thirteen in 1944, but the Samoan members continued to operate them.

Still, there were some problems during the war. The Church-owned buildings fell into disrepair because of the unavailability of repair materials. It was almost impossible to find workers to do repairs because most skilled people were hired in war-related jobs.

President Adams had to make some adjustments in Church organizations because of the war. He arranged three districts (earlier called conferences) into five, making it easier for the groups to gather at conferences. These districts were all presided over by Samoan priesthood holders.

He also made arrangements to have all auxiliary meetings take place on Sunday so that the people would not have to travel so much. This procedure was changed again in 1948, when Elder Matthew Cowley asked that Primary, MIA, and Relief Society be held on weekdays.

The conclusion of the Pacific War brought still other changes to the Church in Samoa. The foreign missionaries returned. The amount of American money available from defense-related jobs declined. The more nearly normal situation made it possible to repair buildings and expand Church schools and facilities. But the most important change was the trend toward more direct involvement in Samoa by the general authorities.

Not until the postwar years was the full program of the Church introduced in Samoa. The auxiliaries had been functioning for years, but in a locally designed manner. But after the war the First Presidency and general authorities took a much more direct interest in the Pacific missions. Elder Matthew Cowley, appointed to preside over the area, regularly visited the various missions, including Samoa, and helped enlarge the interest of the other Church leaders toward the Saints in Samoa. In November 1948 Church architect Edward O. Anderson visited Samoa to look at the chapels, most of which were still fales, take pictures, and study the entire building situation. Until the postwar years little effort had been expended to introduce the lesson manuals of the various auxiliaries. But in 1948 President Golden H. Hale took steps to have some manuals translated into the Samoan language.

The postwar Church in Samoa, in other words, was in a state of transition. The past was gone. The war had destroyed the old era. But the great growth of the next era was just beginning.

CHAPTER 24

BUILDING CHAPELS, MEMBERSHIP, AND STAKES

Samoa, 1948–1984

When John Quincy Adams penned his final entry in the mission record book in February 1948, he listed some of the accomplishments of the previous five years. He counted 1,205 people baptized, 820 babies blessed, seven new buildings under construction or completed, eleven new branches organized, and fourteen schools in operation (he emphasized that there were 240 students in Pesega). A 10,000-gallon water tank had been made at Nifae-Vaiola, and members were journeying, some with the intention of staying, to the temple in Hawaii. He said much more, but of a long-range significance was his observation that "Eastern and Western Samoa seethe with the freedom urge."[1]

Almost his last entry stated that "not an excommunication has been done." A number of Saints had been disfellowshipped, but the policy since the early years of the century had been to treat the Polynesians with special understanding in relation to moral issues. That is not to say that the mission presidents did not constantly teach a strict standard of sexual morality, for they did. But since the days of President Joseph F. Smith, the mission presidents had operated under instructions that directed them to take local cultural patterns into consideration. The idea was to treat the people with patience and long-suffering.[2]

The lack of ecclesiastical action to counter moral laxity was symptomatic of the general state of affairs during the war years. It was impossible for President Emery or President Adams to supervise closely the districts and the numerous branches. This was especially so in President Adams's time; he found it impossible to visit Tutuila for over nine months, and he also found that he could best operate under a schedule of extended visits to Vaiola, Pesega, and Sauniatu. He could not carefully direct affairs throughout the mission. The Saints did quite well, but some matters of procedure were neglected and some programs were curiously modified.

During the last few months of President Adams's administration, he was forced to hold several meetings with the branch presidents on Upolu and Savai'i and to reprimand them sharply for borrowing tithing money and not paying it back. Smoking became a serious problem for some of the members. President Adams believed that all the evils of the outside world had come into the country and the Church during the war.

The next three mission presidents were occupied constantly with the problem of bringing the Church members in Samoa into line with the accepted behavior of Latter-day Saints elsewhere in the world. To observers outside the faith, both in the islands and elsewhere, such an attitude appeared narrow and paternalistic, but to members of the Church the ideal of a single standard of behavior with regard to morality and consistency in Church government and internal administration applied to the Islands as well as the rest of the world. Local customs could be adopted and the programs of the Church adapted only when principle was not involved.

The loose control of the war years became evident to President Golden H. Hale soon after his arrival in Samoa. At a meeting of branch presidents in October 1948, someone asked, "Why can't we be paid for our missionary work?" Brother Hale assured them that there were no paid jobs in the Church and encouraged them to plant good gardens and be humble, and the Lord would take care of them.[3]

President Hale worked to eliminate unorthodoxy in the Church, but his successor found that both Roman Catholic and Protestant ways of doing things continued. For example, President Earl S. Paul found an oil painting of the Angel Moroni with wings spreading from corner to corner of the Sauniatu chapel, and it was removed by his orders. He also found white cloths with typical Protestant crosses hanging over more than one LDS chapel pulpit, and these too he had removed.[4]

President Hale put the American missionary force back to work doing almost exactly the same things they had done before the war. But the mission made much new progress on several fronts. The First Presidency authorized a new school for Pesega, and missionaries and teachers improved the school (an important story that will be told later) and helped the local leaders increase their effectiveness.

But these changes notwithstanding, when President Earl S. Paul arrived in Samoa in April 1951, he felt that few significant changes had occurred since his first mission, which had ended in 1916. The roads on Upolu were better, but the Church seemed essentially the same. The buildings in use by the Church were basically the same as before. But by the time President Paul left the mission two years later, revolutionary changes were under way.

The eleven years from 1951 to 1962 saw more development in the Church in Samoa than during the previous sixty-three years. Consider the statistics in the accompanying table.

The mission secretaries or clerks during this period seem to have had a difficult ime arriving at an accurate census of membership. Three facts shoı ld be noted. First, between 1952 and 1960, approximately forty-one hundred Samoan members of the Church immigrated to other countries, primarily to Hawaii, the U.S. mainland, and New Zealand. This was not a new trend, nor did it cease after 1960. The Church has not maintained records of the number of members who have left Samoa during the last eighteen years, but the total is large. Estimates vary widely about total Samoan (not LDS alone) emigration from American Samoa, but conservative estimates now place the number of American Samoans in Hawaii and the West Coast states at forty-five thousand—almost three times the number living in American Samoa. Large numbers of Samoans from Western Samoa have also migrated to New Zealand.[6] The point is that thousands of LDS Samoans have left the islands since 1950, and many excellent leaders have been among them.

Second, the number of men ordained to the Melchizedek Priesthood increased from 276 in 1951 to 764 in 1961. This figure is significant because it indicates that a growing number of men were worthy to hold administrative authority and that leadership was coming into Samoan hands.

Third, the growth of the Church during 1959, 1960, and 1961 was astonishing. In no other place in the Pacific did the Church double such a large base figure in so short a time. The growth that came during these three years was founded on significant advancements in Church organization and administration, education, and construction that began in the early 1950s. The result of these advancements was the creation of Apia Stake in 1962.

CHURCH ORGANIZATION, ADMINISTRATION, AND MISSIONARY WORK

One of the first concerns of President Paul was to bring the Church organization in Samoa into line with the order of the Church

Samoan Mission Statistics, 1951-1961[5]

Year	Total Members	Convert Baptisms	Melchizedek Priesthood	Branches/ Districts	Number of Missionaries	
					foreign	local
1951	7,808	276	257	62/6	48	
1952	6,472*	208	269	49/6	33	
1953	6,598	184	332	47/6	31	
1954	7,080**	152	391	54/14 †	68	
1955	6,853***	111	447	50/14	84	
1956	7,500	267	484	58/14	148	
1957	7,525+	437	485	58/13	123	76
1958	8,368	450	540	63/11	110††	15
1959	10,345	1,101	638	75/11	182	119
1960	12,260	2,361	700	76/12	122	68
1961	16,649	4,382	764	84/12	101	80

* 1,711 members emigrated to other countries this year.
** Gained 1,012 from the Cook Islands and Fiji, but lost 651 to emigration.
*** Lost 406 to emigration.
+ Lost 655 to emigration.
† (10 dist. in Samoa)
†† (Fiji & Cook Is. assigned elsewhere)

as specified by the general authorities. He was disturbed that the old system of sending Samoan priesthood holders from their own homes to other places as missionary branch presidents was still in vogue. This system caused at least two problems: First, these missionaries were displaced from their own *aiga,* or extended family group, and thus were dependent on the branch members for their support over a long period of time. Second, the branch presidents did not have counselors. They operated in much the same fashion as the Protestant ministers.

The reorganization of the branches began within two weeks of President Paul's arrival. On April 15, 1951, he organized the Pesega Branch, with Selu Fruean as president, Iulai AhMu as first counselor, Joseph Hunt as second counselor, and Samuela Atoa as clerk. It was the first complete branch presidency in the mission.[7]

The next step was much more difficult. President Paul called branch presidents to the mission office to discuss the problem. He explained in detail the proper order of the Church. Then he announced that all branch presidents were released to return to their home villages. New branch presidencies were to be called, each with a president and two counselors. Most of the branch presidents gratefully accepted the new procedure, but one man objected, saying "But President Paul, the scriptures say a prophet is without honor in his own home." In answer President Paul assured them that they were not called as prophets but as branch and district presidencies.

President Paul and his associates worked vigorously during the next year to reorganize all of the branches. To help the new officers learn their duties, the missionaries translated a handbook of instruction into Samoan. The Saints studied the new materials with enthusiasm, and before long the branches were operating quite smoothly.[8]

Church records had been a problem in Samoa since the beginning of the mission. Membership statistics were frequently more a guess than an accurate census. Other reports were traditionally made by the mission president and his co-workers. The Samoans themselves seem to have had little concern for such procedures. One of the problems that made it so difficult to keep accurate membership records was the Samoan tradition of having only one name and of changing it as new rank or circumstances warranted. Mission leaders made an effort to convince all families that uniform family names should be chosen and kept permanently. Most families chose the name of the family high chief as their new surname. President Stone, finding that genealogy work was difficult because names were changed so often, encouraged people to maintain single family names.

Once the branches were firmly in the hands of the Samoan members, the next step was to place the districts under their jurisdiction. The first all-Samoan district presidency since the war was installed on March 2, 1952. Selu Fruean was called as president of Pesega District, and Laita Leatutufu and Samuela Atoa were installed as counselors. Amuia Hunt was the first clerk. By the following October all of the districts were in local hands. President Paul also created one new district, making a total of six.[9] Foreign missionaries continued to act as district supervisors, with the responsibility of advising district and branch presidencies, but otherwise the positions of leadership were in local hands.

During his tenure, President Howard B. Stone began translation work, pushed training programs of various kinds such as organ and chorister courses, organized elders quorums for the first time, and started the Senior Aaronic Priesthood program to activate men over nineteen years of age. President Stone is remembered in Samoa for his contribution to the building program, but he was also very progressive in improving the organizations of the Church.

When President Stone was released, the Samoan Mission was responsible not only for the proselyting missionary work and the ecclesiastical organization of all units of the Church, but also for four large schools and the three plantations at Mapusaga, Sauniatu, and Vaiola. A large building program was also underway. To this should be added the missionary work in Fiji and the Cook Islands, which were under the Samoan Mission.

Brother and Sister Stone were released February 1, 1957. Their successors were President and Sister Charles I. Sampson from Provo, Utah. Brother Sampson recognized the rapid progress that had taken place during recent years, but he became aware of several serious needs that remained. First was the need for more printed materials in the Samoan language. Translation committees had long been functioning, but there were problems with the dissemination of the manuals, lessons, handbooks, and so forth after they were translated. The biggest problem was the outmoded duplicating machine that had produced all written materials for the Church in Samoa. President Sampson obtained a Xerox Offset Press from New Zealand at considerable cost. Before long, William Fruean, one of the local missionaries who had had previous experience with such equipment, had the press in operation, printing hundreds of thousands of pages of Church-related material. (Incidentally, Milford Cottrell, principal of Pesega school, helped get this purchase through for school use as well.) During this time mission leaders made a decision to follow a lesson schedule one year behind the English manuals so that the translators would have ample time to complete their work and get the printing done.[10]

President Sampson next turned his attention to proselyting.

During his first week he wrote, "The missionaries from Zion are spending far too little time in proselyting and teaching the Gospel, and are consuming almost the full day in the job of supervision and jobs, of course, here in the offices and the school."[11]

President Sampson also observed that the foreign missionaries were monopolizing class time in the branches. He decided that the district and branch presidencies would have to be put entirely on their own. "It was clear," he wrote, "that young Mormon missionaries from the States had very little if any experience in church administration and could best put their efforts into regular proselyting endeavor."[12] From that time on, contacts with local members were to be limited to obtaining referrals and helping fellowship new members.

To make this method of operation work, the missionaries printed another handbook of instructions and directed training sessions for the local leaders. The results were excellent. The Samoan leaders continued to develop, learn, and take more responsibility, and the foreign and local missionaries devoted more time to teaching investigators. Membership began to grow rapidly. In 1956 there were two hundred baptisms. In 1957 this number doubled. Over eight hundred converts joined in 1958, and eleven hundred in 1959. Many of these converts were students at one of the Church schools, but there were also adults who bolstered the local leadership as they became Latter-day Saints.

It has often been said among the Saints and missionaries of Samoa that President Stone built the chapels and President Sampson filled them with people. The schools continued to be an important influence, and the combination of new buildings and more active missionary work produced a rich harvest.

The conversion of the village of Lotofaga illustrates this well. In March 1957 a young woman came to the mission office with a request from her father, a high chief in Lotofaga, that the gospel be brought to his village. President Sampson asked why this request was being made. She told him there were some problems with the local denominations, and the village chiefs had been debating what to do. An elderly chief named Ama remembered his boyhood days when he had attended school at Sauniatu. He had been baptized a Latter-day Saint, but on his return to his native village his parents had insisted that he attend their Protestant church. His affection for the Church had persisted, however, and he had now persuaded the other chiefs to consider it as an alternative.

President Sampson told the woman that teachers would be sent to her village every Sunday for a few months to teach them the gospel, and then, if the people of Lotofaga desired baptism, it would be granted. Mulivae Purcell and Iete Teo of Pesega were assigned to teach them. Two American lady missionaries were assigned to work with the children. In the early part of May, over forty people were baptized, and a number of small children were blessed. More converts followed later.[13]

Mass conversions such as those at Lotofaga excited members of the Church and encouraged them to support and encourage missionary work in Samoa. But the increased numbers of missionaries and teachers entering the country during 1957 and 1958 disturbed the leaders of other churches. An event that triggered problems for the Church was the arrival on February 28, 1958, of a charter plane carrying forty Latter-day Saint teachers and labor missionaries, their families, and several new proselyting missionaries. The high commissioner for Western Samoa, Mr. Guy Richardson Powles, received complaints that the Mormons, whose proselyting missionary force had recently grown to over 120, were attempting to convert all of Samoa through sheer weight of numbers. Commissioner Powles obtained the opinions of LMS, Methodist, and Roman Catholic officials about the large influx of Latter-day Saints and found that the other churches were upset because the status quo had been disturbed. After careful discussion of the attitudes and facts as presented by both sides, the executive council of the Samoan government decided on May 9, 1958, to limit proselyting missionaries for all churches to one to every two hundred members in each mission. The most recent government census listed about 5,400 Samoans as LDS. (Mission statistics listed 6,357 in March 1958.) Thus the Church was limited to twenty-seven foreign proselyting missionaries. Fortunately, labor missionaries and teachers were not included in this quota.[14]

Although the matter of missionary quotas received much attention in the Samoan legislature and in the local press, open debate did not bring a change in the new government policy. To some members of the Church it appeared that the recent momentum of the mission would be curtailed. But President Sampson was not discouraged. On the day of the decision he told the mission office staff that he did not believe the new policy would affect the missionary effort. "In a mission presidency meeting shortly after our meeting with the government," he wrote, "we were considering our problem, when it came to our minds like a revelation that many Samoans over the years had gone to New Zealand and to the States. Maybe there were enough Samoan citizens in foreign countries, worthy and able, to replace our

Samoan LDS missionaries tracting in the area near Sauniatu, 1974. (Photo by R. Lanier Britsch.)

American missionaries."[15] They made their wants known to the First Presidency, and it was not long before Samoan names began to appear on the roster of missionaries who were coming to Samoa. Ima Teo, Luele Teo, Whitney Teo, and Alema Fitisemanu were among the first to come. President Sampson also continued the practice of calling many local men and women to serve missions in Samoa. As a result the conversion statistics continued to climb. Local Samoan elders and sisters became the backbone of the rising generation of Latter-day Saints in their own country.

When President Sampson removed proselyting missionaries from district and branch assignments, he did not leave the local leaders without support. There was a reserve of experience and strength to call on because in earlier decades the Samoan priesthood brethren had handled almost all branch assignments and many district callings. But to help inexperienced leaders, President Sampson organized a series of leadership training sessions. A manual of Church government, called *Fa'asino Ala,* was prepared, printed, and distributed. Because the Doctrine and Covenants was not yet available in Samoan, the Church government manual was especially needed.

President Sampson fostered proselyting work until the end of his mission in 1961. He was replaced by J. Phillip Hanks, twenty-eight years old, a teacher at the Church College of Western Samoa. President Hanks believed many young people had been brought into the Church during the past several years who did not understand the gospel. He chose to emphasize the teaching of families. The rate of baptisms dropped, but the stability of the new members improved. President Hanks, like President Sampson, stressed leadership training. By the early 1960s this became a monumental task, for there were ten districts and between eighty and ninety branches. Preparing language materials and conducting leadership sessions with the presidents and counselors of all these groups required great effort and enormous blocks of time.[16]

THE ADVANCEMENT OF CHURCH EDUCATION IN SAMOA

"We have a large school here at Pesega this year," wrote President Golden H. Hale in his 1949 report to the Presiding Bishopric; "the enrollment is over the 500 mark and we are having such a time to house them. It is certainly urgent that we get started in our new school as soon as possible . . . . At present we are holding one class here on the veranda of the mission home and [one] in the garages, and wherever we can put them."[17] School enrollment at Pesega had grown rapidly. In 1947, only 250 children had attended the school; but now, with twice that many, President Hale felt almost overrun by students and wanted them housed in modern facilities away from the mission home. Through the efforts of Elder Matthew Cowley, the First Presidency approved a new school facility in March 1949.

In August 1950, George R. Biesinger, whom Elder Cowley had selected to direct construction projects in New Zealand and the Islands, arrived in Apia to announce plans for construction. The groundbreaking took place that month. The proposed structure was to have twenty-five classrooms, an auditorium, outdoor recreation facilities, and a capacity of six hundred students. Through special effort by the builders, the auditorium was far enough along that it was used for a mission conference in October 1951. Two people, Elder H. B. Paulsen, Church building supervisor, who replaced Biesinger in early 1951, and Brother Maliatoa Fitisemanu, a strong supporter of the school, provided direction for the project. The entire project was under the general supervision of the mission presidents—Elders Hale, Paul, and finally Howard B. Stone. It was President Stone who guided the Samoan building program through its most productive years.

When President Stone took over the mission in January 1953, he assessed the progress on the school building (as well as a number of small chapels that were also under construction) and concluded that labor costs were greater than the output warranted. In February, he decided to discharge the hired laborers and to implement a volunteer labor program that was identical to the system used in Tonga.

By December 1953, the Pesega School, which was primarily an elementary school with a few junior-high-school students, was completed and ready for dedication. Elder LeGrand Richards of the Council of the Twelve Apostles dedicated the Pesega School on December 5. (He also visited Tonga and dedicated the Liahona College at this same time, and he dedicated three Samoan chapels while on this visit.) The labor missionaries also built thirteen small chapels to take the place of some of the fale chapels.

During the 1920s, '30s, and '40s, the Church supported more than a dozen elementary schools that met in fale. These were consolidated into the elementary–secondary school in Pesega and the elementary–junior high schools at Sauniatu and Vaiola. These three schools were the only Church schools until 1960, when the new Mapusaga High School opened in Tutuila.

Originally the fale schools were a proselyting tool. But though the missionary teachers were sincere and desired to help their pupils, educational standards were often poor. In 1954, Wendell Wiser, a missionary in New Zealand who had a doctorate in chemistry, was transferred to Samoa to be principal of Pesega School. He instituted reforms that led to great improvements in the standards of the school. Brother Wiser established entrance and grade-placement examinations. He also standardized textbooks and instructional materials.[18]

In 1955 the First Presidency asked Milford C. Cottrell and his family to go to Pesega. Brother Cottrell was the first professional educator to be asked by the Church to go to Samoa, and his family was the first nonmissionary family to be sent there for the educational system. During his term as principal, from 1955 until 1958, he organized the first Form V and VI classes, equivalent to grades eleven and twelve in the American system. However, the greatest changes were brought about by the Pacific Board of Education, which took over the schools in 1957. In 1958 the First Presidency approved a policy to replace all missionary teachers with trained professionals. Some missionary teachers had been competent, but the majority had not been college graduates. The creation of the Pacific Board relieved the mission presi-

Samoan boys working in the bush, 1974. (Photo by R. Lanier Britsch.)

dent of the heavy responsibility of supervising the schools. It also upgraded the schools themselves by staffing them with qualified teachers, making them a more effective proselyting tool.

In 1957 the Pacific Board approved further enlargement of the campus. The new wing was not finished until February 1961, but the completed library, science laboratory, homemaking room, bookkeeping room, band and chorus room, and administrative offices contributed much to the quality of the educational program. In 1960 the Pacific Board changed the name of the school to the Church College of Western Samoa. The elementary grades became known as Pesega Elementary School.[19]

President David O. McKay, who emphasized education, directed much money toward building Church schools. In few places in the world was Church education money more seriously needed than in Western Samoa.

During the late '50s the government was severely restricted financially and had to curtail public education and medical programs. About 40 percent of the total teaching staff at government schools was dismissed. Hence all mission schools were overcrowded, not only those of the Church. During that time 40 percent of the students at Pesega were non-LDS. Higher and higher percentages of Latter-day Saints filled the schools as years passed, but for a time the school met not only a Church need but also a national one.[20]

By May 1962, the approximate time when Apia Stake was created, the enrollment of the schools in Pesega, Sauniatu, and Vaiola (the latter two were still small and poorly developed) was over twelve hundred, with faculties of over sixty teachers and administrators.

The general Church education policy in Samoa since 1962 has been one of restrained growth, with emphasis on quality. There has been a sustained movement toward localization of the entire system. By 1973, the system had a local superintendent, Samuelu Atoa, and most faculty members and administrators were local people. In the late 1970s when Jeffrey R. Holland became commissioner of education, he combined the responsibilities of religious education (seminaries and institutes) and Church schools under one administrative head. In Samoa, this brought a change from superintendent to CES associate area director. In this office, the local leadership policy has not been absolutely inflexible. Successively, Larry Oler, Sam Atoa, Keith Buhler, and Lanu T. Palepoi have led the Church schools in Samoa. In 1978 there were six elementary schools and one Church high school in Western Samoa, with a combined enrollment of 1,613, of whom 571 were students at Church College of Western Samoa.[21] Of course growth in Church schools has continued since then. The Vaiola School on Savai'i has been upgraded to a high school from a middle school. In 1984 there were 1,584 children attending Church elementary schools and 881 attending the two high schools.

One further part of the story of Church education in Samoa deserves attention here. During the early part of the century the Samoan Saints created gathering places not only on Upolu but also at Mapusaga on Tutuila. In 1947 the mission reestablished a school on the Malaeimi plantation property, which had been leased by the Church since early in the century. Although President Paul supervised construction of a small frame schoolhouse there, it proved inadequate for the needs of the growing Church population in the area. Before the Pauls left the islands in January 1953, President Paul learned that this property could be bought fee simple, and he tried to buy the Malaeimi lands so that the Church could build a secondary school. (Most land in American Samoa was subject to communal ownership and could not be sold to a private owner.) But before he was able to obtain the necessary permission from Church headquarters and the government in American Samoa, he returned home.

When President Paul reported to President McKay, he told him how important he thought the three-hundred-acre plantation could be to the development of the Church. President McKay contemplated the matter for several months and then asked President Paul to return to Samoa and act as agent for the Church in purchasing the land. During the summer of 1953, he succeeded in acquiring it for $30,000. The former owner was Sister Salataima Puailoa, a strong member of the Church.[22]

Four years of planning and delays passed before construction on the new Mapusaga High School got under way. Then another three years of work by labor missionaries were required before the one-million-dollar campus was completed and ready for occupancy. The initial student body consisted of 188 ninth and tenth graders, all of whom had been chosen by means of government tests. Fewer than one-third of the young people who started their education at Mapusaga that September 19 were members of the Church.

The campus was elaborate by island standards. The original school had a main building erected around a central courtyard. Included in the complex was a chapel with an attached gymnasium-cultural hall, an auditorium, eleven classrooms, offices, and a library. Later, other structures were added, including homes for the faculty, dormitories, and a vocational education building. The original buildings were dedicated on January 2, 1962, by Wendell B. Mendenhall, chairman of the Pacific Board of Education.

Latter-day Saints might ask why their tithing dollars were used to support and educate so many non-Mormons. Over the years the number of Latter-day Saint students increased as the student body grew (1965, 47 percent LDS; 1967, 60 percent LDS; 1969, 73 percent LDS). The non-Mormon students did cause problems in religion classes until the percentage of Mormon students passed the two-thirds mark, but after that the school became not only a fine academic institution but also a good proselyting tool. (Academic standards actually went up because the administration announced that low-achieving students would not be accepted for the 1967-68 school year. It happened that the number of Latter-day Saint students rose to a new high at the same time.) Mapusaga High School was approved by the government because the Church promised to educate as many of the Samoan young people as possible. Indeed, the major justification for the

A view of Mapusaga High School, 1974. (Photo by R. Lanier Britsch.)

school was the fact that the government high school, Samoana, could accept only 40 percent of the eligible students. Mapusaga High School performed an important social, economic, and educational service.

In 1965 the government built a large new high school in Pago Pago, the population center of the island. This development was part of what James Bishop, a U.S. State Department officer, called the "greatly increased spending by an embarrassed U.S. government."[23] Since this new facility provided enough space for all students of high-school age, it appeared to the Church Board of Education that Mapusaga High School was no longer needed. After careful study in Tutuila, however, it was discovered that almost half of the students at Mapusaga were from Western Samoa and, as aliens, could not enroll in the public schools of American Samoa. Thus for a time the school was necessary. But in 1970 the governor of American Samoa signed an executive regulation that allowed alien children to attend government schools without paying a prohibitive tuition. From that time until late 1973, the Church Educational System was looking to divest itself of the school. In 1974 the Church Educational System sold the buildings but leased the land to the government to be used as a community college.[24]

Church education in Samoa has changed when necessary. Worldwide demands on the Church Educational System now limit new schools to areas where elementary and secondary education is not available from government sources. Present policy emphasizes the expansion of seminary and institute classes.

During 1978 a new early-morning seminary program was introduced in Samoa. Now students are also enrolled in home-study seminary classes. The entire student body of the Church College of Western Samoa receive daily religious education.[25]

Church schools have played a large role in the history of the Church in Samoa. President J. Phillip Hanks, echoing the sentiments of many mission presidents, assessed the role of the schools in these words: "I found that most of the leadership in the branches and districts came out of the schools. It was obvious who had been in the Church schools and who had not. I would say that these Church schools were *the* most important thing in providing Church leadership."[26]

THE LABOR MISSIONARY PROGRAM IN SAMOA

President Howard B. Stone directed the labor missionary program in Samoa from 1953 until his release in 1957. The system was used after that time, and the momentum of his administration carried it until the program was discontinued.

The big years of the program were from 1953 until 1959. During that time the building missionaries completed the school at Pesega, over thirty chapels, a mission home, several missionary homes, the new wing of the Pesega School, twenty-five homes for faculty members, dormitories, and other buildings on the campus. This work was done by 120 labor missionaries from Samoa and an additional twenty-five from the States. It should be added that the Samoan Mission also had responsibility for new buildings in the Cook Islands and Fiji.[27]

President J. Phillip Hanks, who served as a missionary, as a school teacher at Pesega, and finally as mission president between 1953 and 1965, believed that the building program was important to the growth and development of the Church. He wrote:

> This program was a blessing to the people in many ways: First, it provided buildings which they could be proud of. Second, it provided a great deal of on-the-job training for many, many young men who put it into use for a life's occupation. Third, the personality of the Church and Church members changed during those years. For many decades the Church was looked down upon by the local populace as a poor church. This resulted in slow progress,

Faaala chapel is typical of the LDS meetinghouses throughout Samoa. (Courtesy LDS Church Archives.)

David O. McKay village, part of Sauniatu, was constructed to honor the prophet's two visits to Samoa in 1921 and 1955. (Photo by R. Lanier Britsch.)

> persecution, and shame on the part of some of the weaker members . . . . But with the newer buildings being built, the Church began to take upon itself more prestige. . . . The effect upon the local members was one of pride and confidence. No longer did the members have to walk ashamed of their poverty. Now they could walk with head erect, look people in the eye, and actually have the envy of other denominations. This brought faster growth. Thousands were baptized during this period of time.[28]

By the mid-1960s, over fifty new concrete-brick chapels had been constructed in Samoa, mostly by labor missionaries. Since that time many other chapels have been built. In 1984, there are 103 units of the Church in Samoa. Because transportation facilities are generally poor, it is necessary to construct chapels close enough to the people so that most ward or branch members can walk to meetings. To illustrate, there are seventy-one chapels in Samoa compared to only forty-one in Hawaii for a similar Church membership. In April 1982, the Church instituted a new building program based on the percentage of full-tithe payers. This program, the so-called tithing faithfulness program, provides for the complete cost of new buildings as well as maintenance in stakes that qualify. Because of poor record keeping in most wards, only a few units have qualified for new buildings under the new program. Also, because cash is in short supply in Western Samoa, a tithing-in-kind program was experimented with in 1982 and following. It seems to be bearing good results. Most Samoan chapels are still small, single-unit structures.

THE VISIT OF PRESIDENT DAVID O. MCKAY TO SAMOA IN 1955

President David O. McKay (accompanied by Sister McKay, Franklin B. Murdock, and Patrick and Lela Dalton [she had come along from Tonga as stenographer]) arrived in Pago Pago on the M.V. *Tofua* on January 14, 1955. The McKays were given an elaborate and warm welcome at Tutuila. During their brief stay, they visited Mapusaga and spoke to the assembled Saints.

That afternoon they boarded the *Tofua* again and sailed for Apia. They arrived after dark, but the lateness of the hour did not diminish the royal greeting the prophet received. Dignitaries from the government, the two Samoan kings, and thousands of Saints welcomed the first president of the Church ever to tour the islands.

President McKay's visit to Upolu Island included feasts, conference sessions, tours of chapels, and a King Kava ceremony. At

Chapel at Siumu, Upolu, under construction. Ward members contributed large amounts of time and labor to pay for their share of the building. 1974. (Photo by R. Lanier Britsch.)

one of the conferences he told the assembled LDS *matai* or chiefs from Upolu and Savai'i: "Be sure to honor your native titles but do not put them before the Holy Priesthood of God." (President Stone noted in the mission records that in the past some matai had refused to give their high titles away in order to accept callings in the Church.) President McKay was impressed with the faith of Maliatoa Fitisemanu, who had been influential in building the Pesega School and had helped translate the Doctrine and Covenants into Samoan. Earlier in his life he had been offered a high position in society if he would renounce his religion. His reply to those who made the offer was, "I would rather be a deacon in the Mormon Church than the king of Samoa."[29]

President McKay's visit to Sauniatu was a spiritual highlight. He loved Sauniatu, and the Saints there loved him in a special way. Concerning Sauniatu he said, "This indeed is the most beautiful place I have ever seen. It is indeed the vision which I saw on my first trip to Samoa thirty-four years ago. Such beauty, such grandeur and such splendor I have never heretofore known." While he spoke to the members at Sauniatu, he told them they soon would be able to "enter a house of the Lord in some location not far away, and this would be one of the greatest blessings they could obtain." Following the meeting a sister with a very sick baby asked President Stone to have President McKay merely touch her child and it would live. President

McKay touched the baby on the head and said, "The Lord bless this baby and its parents." The baby lived, and the father soon asked for a call as a missionary.[30]

Following his stay in Samoa, President McKay traveled on to Fiji and then to New Zealand. There he selected the site for the New Zealand Temple.

In April 1958, when the new temple was dedicated, fifty Samoan Church members went to New Zealand to participate in the services. There they enjoyed a separate dedication session for Samoans held in their own language. When the temple opened for ordinance work, the Samoans were among the first to receive the blessings offered by the temple. Over the years before 1958, many more Samoans had traveled to Hawaii for temple purposes than had members from Tonga and the other island groups. The New Zealand Temple, however, made it possible for larger numbers of worthy Samoan members to obtain their own endowments and to do work for their dead.

THE CREATION OF APIA STAKE

The number of Saints in the Apia area had grown to nearly twenty-five hundred and made up nine branches. Seven of these units were fairly large. On March 18, 1962, the area was organized into a stake. (It is of interest that Western Samoa became an independent nation only three months before, on January 1, 1962.) Elder Mark E. Petersen of the Council of the Twelve and Elder John Longden, an assistant to the Council of the Twelve and area supervisor for the South Pacific, presided and called the new stake officers. They selected Percy J. Rivers, a counselor in the mission presidency who later served as stake patriarch, regional representative, and a member of the first Samoa Temple presidency, to be the first Samoan stake president. They called Ralph Sharp as first counselor and Samuela Atoa as second counselor. Seven branches were made wards and two remained branches.

Seven years passed before the Pago Pago Stake was organized on June 15, 1969, with Patrick Peters as president. Between then and 1974, five other stakes were organized. Samoa is the first country in the world to be covered by stakes.[31]

THE PERIOD SINCE 1975

During the past three decades the Samoan Saints have been visited by leaders of the Church on many occasions. But until the First Presidency instituted area conferences, the local people did not have an equivalent to general conference in Salt Lake City. In February 1976, eleven general authorities, including President Spencer W. Kimball and President N. Eldon Tanner, visited both American and Western Samoa. They held meetings with about one thousand Saints in Pago Pago on the sixteenth and then flew to Apia. The local people did everything they could to make the area conference an extraordinary occasion. Feasts, kava ceremonies, gift giving, dances, and entertainment occupied an entire day. On the eighteenth the general authorities met with 130 missionaries, of which 104, or 80 percent, were local people.

Over fifteen thousand people, mostly members, assembled to hear the Church leaders speak. President Kimball stressed the importance of doing genealogy and missionary work "as necessary preliminaries to having a temple built locally." He repeated the doctrine, taught most forcefully by President Joseph F. Smith, that the Polynesian people "are descendants of the Nephite Hagoth," and he charged every missionary to play an important part in the gathering of Israel. President Kimball emphasized the importance of living all the laws of God. "There should be an upsurge in spirituality in every phase of the Church in Samoa after this conference; otherwise we will feel that perhaps our coming here has been useless."[32] Over the next four years 4,525 new members joined the Church in Samoa, an increase of more than 17 percent. By 1980 there were 26,104 Latter-day Saints there, living in ten stakes.

President Kimball complimented the Saints for their high percentage (70 percent) of temple marriages. He was also pleased with the large percentage of members at the conferences (about 73 percent). This was the largest percentage of membership to attend an area conference anywhere in the Pacific.[33]

Soon after the Samoan area conference, on October 15, 1977, President Kimball and the general authorities announced that a small temple would be constructed in American Samoa. It was to serve the needs of Saints in the Samoa, French Polynesia, Tonga, and Fiji areas. This was the first of the now-numerous "small" temples. The Brethren wanted to build another temple in Polynesia, and because of air routes through Pago Pago, it seemed at the time to be the logical place to construct another temple. But the further evolution of the concept of small temples to serve the needs of smaller bodies of Saints, coupled with land-title problems that delayed the construction of the temple in American Samoa, brought changes in April 1980.

At that time, President Kimball announced that not one but three new temples would be constructed in Polynesian lands—Samoa, Tonga, and French Polynesia. Because the great majority of the members in Samoa lived in Western Samoa, the temple would be built there. This was a blessing, because as a rule the members in American Samoa have much larger incomes and can afford to fly to Western Samoa much more easily than can Western Samoans afford to go to American Samoa. The site for the Samoa Temple did not surprise anyone. It was to be placed in the midst of the Pesega complex that already included the Church College of Western Samoa, the Pesega Elementary School, the Samoa Apia Mission headquarters, and a stake center. When the temple was constructed, it was realized that the front door stands almost in the same place where AhMu's home (AhMu was the early Saint who contributed this land to the Church) had stood.

President Kimball visited Samoa again on February 19, 1981, to break ground for the temple. He was joined by head of state Susuga Malietoa Tunumafili II in turning the first shovelfuls of soil for the project. Actual construction did not begin until about November, but considerable groundwork was done in preparation.

The actual construction process was generally quite straightforward. Costs were higher in Samoa than in Tonga because import duties were greater, but aside from that, the Samoan Temple moved along at close to the same tempo as its Tongan duplicate. As was true for the Tongan Temple, members came from all parts of the country to spend one, two, or more days contributing their labor and service to the project. Missionaries, too, contributed their diversion days. As seems to be the rule with Pacific temples, there was a tremendous flurry of activity toward the end in order to complete it by the appointed deadline. The most difficult part of the project was building a forty-foot scaffold around the spire and then manually hoisting the statue of the Angel Moroni into place.

The Samoa Temple was formally opened to the public, before its dedication, on July 18, 1983. Again His Highness S. Malietoa Tunumafili II was there. This time he was accompanied by the prime minister, Eti Tofilau, and by Galea'i Poumei, president of the senate of American Samoa. They helped Elder John H. Groberg, area executive administrator, cut a ribbon that had been drawn across the temple gate. The following day the temple was opened to the public. During the two weeks it was open, many thousands of nonmembers toured the holy house, and many were touched by the sacred purposes of the structure.

The Apia Samoa Temple was dedicated by President Gordon B. Hinckley on August 5, 1983. (Courtesy Norman Faldmo, Jr.)

Because of his failing health, President Spencer W. Kimball was unable to travel to Samoa to dedicate the new temple. He sent President Gordon B. Hinckley, second counselor in the First Presidency, to preside at the event. President Hinckley, who at that time was carrying a heavy leadership load, inspired the gathered Church members with his love, concern, and deeply emotional counsel and prayers. "There has never been another day quite like this in the history of Samoa. There will never be another day like it again," said he. "I am confident the veil is thin, and that on the other side there are many missionaries who served here in years past, and many people of simple faith who accepted the message and endured much for it." He was accompanied by Elders Howard W. Hunter, Marvin J. Ashton, and L. Tom Perry of the Council of the Twelve; Elders W. Grant Bangerter and John H. Groberg of the First Quorum of the Seventy (who supervised most of the preparations for this event); and Bishop H. Burke Peterson of the Presiding Bishopric.

In the dedicatory prayer, which was offered in seven sessions between August 5 and August 7, 1983, and was heard by close to sixty-five hundred faithful Saints, President Hinckley said, "We are grateful for these beautiful islands of Samoa, and for thy faithful saints who

The Apia, Samoa Temple is situated among other Church structures at Pesega, Apia, including a stake center (near left), mission home and office (near right), and school buildings (behind). (Courtesy Norman Faldmo, Jr.)

dwell here. Jacob, son of Lehi, declared anciently: 'Great are the promises of the Lord unto them who are upon the isles of the sea' (2 Nephi 10:21). We have witnessed the fulfilling of thy covenant, for thou hast not forgotten them." Indeed, the Church has provided far more temples per capita for the Polynesians than for any other people.

The first temple presidency consists of Charles I. Sampson, whose years of service in Samoa are noted earlier in this book; Percy Rivers, the first Samoan stake president, regional representative, and stalwart; and Van Livingston, a former missionary to Samoa. These men have encouraged the Saints to follow President Hinckley's counsel not to leave the temple idle. Since shortly after it was opened, the temple has been used beyond its estimated capacity.

Ever since 1977, when the first announcement of a forthcoming temple was made, there has been an undeniable surge of growth and activity in Samoa. The number of local missionaries has grown steadily, particularly during the presidency of R. Carl Harris from 1981 to 1984. In December 1983, there were 213 missionaries serving in Samoa, most of whom were Samoans, but with some Tongans. The three Samoans who served as mission presidents before President Harris—Patrick L. Peters, Faaesea P. Mailo, and Lueli Uiva Te'o—each did much to increase the momentum of the work. As in Tonga, the missionaries generally live in the homes of the Saints (this is changing now with the placement of twelve-by-twelve-foot sleeping huts in many places throughout the mission). Between 1976 and 1981 the missionaries averaged 1,950 convert baptisms a year, with a high of 2,598 baptisms in 1980. The past three years have been close to that six-year average, with 1983 rising to 2,344 convert baptisms. At the end of 1983 there were officially 40,705 members of the Church in Samoa (although this figure is probably about five thousand high because of record-keeping problems). These members were living in 103 wards and branches that make up eleven stakes. Between 18 and 20 percent of the island Samoan population belongs to the Church.[34]

PART 6

TONGA

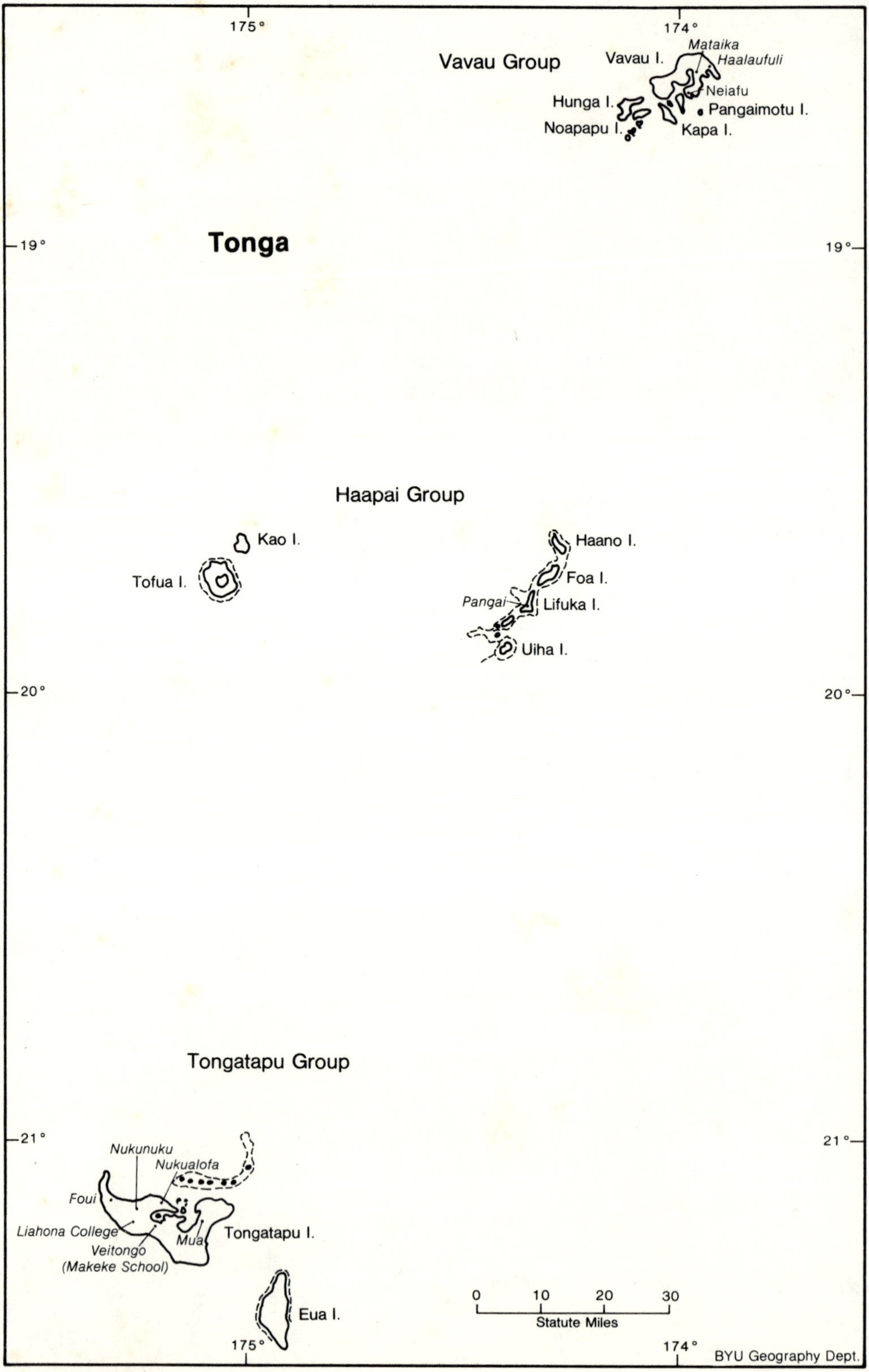

Tonga
Vavau Group
Vavau I.
Mataika
Haalaufuli
Neiafu
Hunga I.
Pangaimotu I.
Noapapu I.
Kapa I.
Haapai Group
Kao I.
Tofua I.
Haano I.
Foa I.
Pangai
Lifuka I.
Uiha I.
Tongatapu Group
Nukunuku
Nukualofa
Foui
Liahona College
Veitongo
(Makeke School)
Mua
Tongatapu I.
Eua I.
0
10
20
30
Statute Miles
175°
174°
19°
20°
21°
BYU Geography Dept.

CHAPTER 25

YEARS OF EXTREME STRUGGLE

Tonga, 1891–1924

The first Latter-day Saint attempt to establish the restored gospel in Tonga began on July 15, 1891, when Elders Brigham Smoot and Alva J. Butler arrived in Nuku'alofa, Tongatapu. They had been sent to Tonga by President William O. Lee of the Samoan Mission.

Their arrival seemed well-timed. The Tongan legislative assembly was holding its annual meeting, and nobles and officials were gathered from all three island groups, Vava'u in the north, Ha'apai in the center, and Tongatapu in the south. During the next several weeks many Tongan nobles met with the elders and discussed the Church. The legislative gathering proved to be a rapid way of teaching the gospel to many important people.

But in the long run the arrival of the elders in Tonga was poorly timed. In fact, it could be concluded that the efforts of the elders were foredoomed to failure because of the Tongan religious and political situation. Some background is necessary to understand the circumstances Elders Smoot and Butler and later missionaries encountered.

The first successful Christian mission to Tonga came under Wesleyan Methodist leadership. After two abortive attempts, the first by the London Missionary Society in 1797 and the second by Walter Lawry in 1822, John Thomas and John Hutchison finally succeeded, in 1826, in establishing a functioning mission. By 1829 seven converts had been baptized, and on August 3, 1831,[1] the chief of Ha'apai, Taufa'ahau, was baptized. Taufa'ahau, who took the Christian name Jiaoji, or George, became a close ally of the missionaries and even an impressive evangelist in his own right.[2]

George became king of the whole of Tonga in 1852. He took the title George Tubou I. He was instrumental in the Christianizing of Tonga, a movement that was complete by the 1840s.

Even before King George was baptized, an important decision had been made about missionary jurisdiction in Tonga and other nearby areas. In 1830, John Williams of the London Missionary Society and his associate, John Barff, called at Tongatapu and met with Nathaniel Turner and William Cross of the Wesleyan Missionary Society. They decided that Samoa would henceforth be considered an LMS area and that Tonga and Fiji would be the responsibility of the Wesleyans. The London offices of both bodies ratified this agreement.[3] After 1830, LMS missionaries honored the comity agreement and left Tonga to the Wesleyans. When Roman Catholics arrived, they were considered intruders. The same was true of the Seventh-Day Adventists and the Latter-day Saints, neither of which groups respected the old agreement.

The Christianization of Tonga was a disruptive force from the beginning. Virtually all aspects of life, including the old socio-political structure, kin groups, and so forth, were affected. The abandonment of polygamy disrupted many once-stable families. Misuse of chiefly powers caused hardships for Tongans who were not part of the aristocracy.

King George instituted a fairly extensive legal code in 1862. It contained a clause that emancipated the people, who had been virtually the slaves of the chiefs. Missionary influence was evident throughout the code: A recently arrived Wesleyan missionary named Shirley W. Baker had been a significant advisor to the king while the document was being drafted. But the code proved to be heavily weighted in favor of the king and his newly appointed nobles.

In 1875, however, King George gave his people a constitution that granted complete religious freedom and religious toleration. It, like the law code of 1862, was strongly influenced by the missionaries.

During his later years King George came increasingly under the influence of Baker. The office of prime minister and several others fell into Baker's hands. For various reasons, both political and religious, Baker convinced King George that the relationship between the Tongan Wesleyan Church and the headquarters in Sydney was an undesirable arrangement. In 1885, Baker engineered a split with the Sydney office and created a new church, the Wesleyan Free Church of Tonga.[4]

The king wanted all Tongans to leave the Wesleyan congregation and join the new group. But convictions were strong, and a small but vocal minority refused to make the move. Even persecution failed to bring some loyal Wesleyans into line. Baker used government positions and higher wages as enticements and won some people over, but others in high positions remained faithful to the old church even though they were stripped of their titles. Persecutions continued and, from 1887 until 1890, Tonga was in religious upheaval.[5]

The persecutions did not last long. The British high commissioner in Suva, Fiji, ordered Baker off the islands on July 5, 1890. Six days later the new prime minister pardoned all people who had been loyal to the Wesleyan Church.[6]

Elders Smoot and Butler arrived in Tonga only one year after Shirley Baker was deported. Memories of the persecutions and troubles of the past few years were still vivid, and all Tongans knew the king wanted unity and harmony within the new Tongan Free Church. One can hardly imagine a more difficult time for Latter-day Saint missionaries to attempt to establish the Church in Tonga.

It is surprising that when Elders Smoot and Butler obtained an audience with the king, he listened attentively to the Articles of Faith and then wished the elders success and said his people were "perfectly free to join whichever church suited them best."[7] Perhaps he did not anticipate that many Tongans would feel free to join the new faith.

Church records reveal that the reactions of the people in Tonga toward the Church were mixed. Many high-ranking dignitaries expressed sincere interest in the teachings of the Church, but the European ministers of religion circulated hostile stories about polygamy and wild reports concerning Joseph Smith and Brigham Young.

Elders Smoot and Butler held their first religious service at Pea on August 1, 1891. After the meeting, the elders learned that every person in attendance had broken the law that stated that no public services could be held by any denomination in any village unless at least six adult members of that denomination resided in the village.[8]

Until that law was repealed the following November, the continuance of the mission was in question. But it was not the only problem the elders encountered while getting the Church established. When they decided to build their own headquarters, where they could live, hold a school, and conduct church meetings, they applied for permission to lease some ground. But opposing ministers delayed approval of the lease until late October.

In November, the elders chose a plot of land at Mu'a. Early in December the elders went to work on their new headquarters. By January 14, 1892, they completed a large room that was to double as a meeting hall and schoolroom. Ten days later they held the first Latter-day Saint meeting at Mu'a. By May 15, the entire structure was completed and dedicated. During May, three new missionaries arrived, Elders Kinghorn, Hunter, and Merrill.

Although the elders had been holding meetings in the Tongan language since January, the arrival of the new missionaries made the need to master the language all the more evident. Language study was hampered by the lack of dictionaries, word lists, grammars, and the like. The only text was the Tongan-language version of the Bible. Considering the circumstances, it is remarkable that Brigham Smoot completed a tract in Tongan by September 16, 1892. This pamphlet, "The Kingdom of Heaven," served the needs of the Tongan conference until missionary work was discontinued in 1897.

During the 1891-97 period, the missionaries preached the gospel in every village on Tongatapu, opened the work in Ha'apai (May 1893) and Vava'u (September 1895), and taught the gospel on virtually every island in each of those groups. They opened schools in each group, the first at Mu'a on July 15, 1892. They made converts; the first was Alipate, who was baptized at Mu'a on September 11, 1892. The elders gave the priesthood to the Tongans. Additional elders and sisters arrived, but only sixteen Tongans joined the Church during this period, and two of them later apostatized. In early 1897, the First Presidency recommended that the Tongan Conference be closed. The missionaries left Tonga and arrived in Apia, Samoa, on April 18, 1897.[9]

Why did the first Latter-day Saint missionary effort in Tonga fail? The main problem was the opposition and power of the Tongan Free Church. Most Tongans believed that they would be disloyal to the king if they joined another alien denomination. They also feared that their local nobles, who controlled the land, might treat them unfairly.

THE REOPENING OF LATTER-DAY SAINT MISSIONARY WORK

Ten years passed before the Church formally opened missionary work again in Tonga. On March 19, 1907, President Thomas A. Court of the Samoan Mission sailed to the Vava'u group. His purpose was to "investigate the prospects for opening up the work of the Lord in that country, and to purchase some horses also if he found any suitable ones."[10] When President Court returned to Samoa, he reported that the prospects were "very bright" and that he intended to send elders there soon. On April 13, President Court assigned William O. Facer, who was working on Upolu, to go to Tonga with a companion who would be chosen from among the Tutuila elders. President Court told the assembled Upolu missionaries that friends he had made in Vava'u had asked the Church to send elders to open a school and preach the gospel. According to Ermel J. Morton's account of the Tongan Mission, the man who asked President Court to send missionaries to Vava'u was Iki Tupou Fulivai, harbormaster.[11]

On April 27, President Court asked Elder Heber J. McKay to accompany Elder Facer to Tonga and to act as conference president. Elders McKay and Facer arrived in Neiafu, Vava'u on June 13, 1907.[12]

By July 31 the elders had opened a school and begun to attract students to it. In October two people asked for baptism, but the elders did not believe they were ready. In November Vava'u was hit with a whooping-cough epidemic that took the lives of many children. One of Iki's children suffered terribly with it.[13] The elders administered to him, and soon the child was healed. Word of this power and gift soon spread throughout the group, and before long the elders were blessing children almost daily.[14]

By January 1908, Elder McKay reported that fifteen people regularly attended Sunday meetings, twenty-eight children attended day school, and thirteen young men usually met three evenings a week for night school.[15]

Although some baptisms may have been performed before May 1908, the first documented baptisms took place at that time.[16] In June, the elders reported that the people of Vava'u often attended preaching meetings in such large numbers that homes and meeting halls were inadequate to hold them all. Requests were coming in to the elders to visit villages away from Neiafu, and Elder McKay sent Elder Woolley to Mataika to work. The people there had offered to give an elder a place to stay, food to eat, and even money if he would preach to them. Along with regular preaching meetings, Elder Woolley soon organized a Sunday School and a day school.

In March 1909 Elders McKay and Facer went several times to the village of Ha'alaufuli and then, because the people showed so much interest in the gospel, Elder McKay assigned Elder Facer there permanently. Facer opened a school and immediately had fifty students in regular attendance. A week after he opened the school, ten people asked for baptism. Between early April and July 26, twenty-two more people joined the Church. Elder Facer organized an active branch at Ha'alaufuli.

On July 24 and 25, the elders brought the three branches, Neiafu, Mataika, and Ha'alaufuli, together for the first conference of the Vava'u Conference of the Samoan Mission. The Tongan Saints celebrated Pioneer Day on July 24, and on the following day, Sunday, they held three sessions of conference. The elders had their hands full, but with the help of three additional elders who arrived at about that time—Elders Ormond, Olson, and Wright—the work moved ahead even faster in the months that followed.[17]

In November and December of 1908, President William A. Moody, who replaced President Court, visited the Tongan area to supervise the elders. Other Samoan Mission presidents regularly visited Tonga until 1916, when it became a separate mission.

Latter-day Saint missionary work was started in Tongatapu on March 17, 1911, when Elders W.F. Winn and George W. Seely arrived at Nuku'alofa. There they met Fale Kava, a Tongan boy whom they had known in Vava'u. The next evening the elders held their first meeting in Nuku'alofa at Fale Kava's home. Forty people attended.[18]

Ten days after they arrived, the elders opened a school at Nuku'alofa. Attendance was not good, and this school was discontinued in June. But before this school closed, another was started at Fo'ui. Later, the elders started schools at Nukunuku and Ma'ofaga. The elders chose Ma'ofaga to be their headquarters. Here they leased land and constructed a chapel and a school. The building was completed in December 1912. On October 23, 1912, still another school was started at Mu'a. Other schools followed.

During June and July 1911, President Don C. McBride of the Samoan Mission visited Tongatapu Island. On July 9, he conducted the first priesthood meeting on the island and officially created the new Tongatapu Conference of the mission. The first baptism on that island came on July 13, 1911.

The following summer, 1912, the next Samoan Mission president, Christian Jensen, visited Tonga. At least three branches were organized—Fo'ui, Nukunuku, and Ma'ofanga—and two Samoan girls, Malia and Lillie Josephs, who were serving as missionaries, were called as presidents of the Relief Society and Primary Association, respectively. They were assigned to establish and organize these auxiliaries.[19]

Although the membership of all three branches was small at this time, schools were operated at all three places and at others that were opened later. In late December 1912, the Tongan missionaries dedicated a new schoolhouse.

THE CREATION OF THE TONGAN MISSION

Although the number of converts in Tonga was not large and the number of missionaries in the country was relatively small, by early

1916 it was evident to the mission president in Samoa and the First Presidency in Salt Lake City that the work in Tonga could progress more quickly if it were made a separate mission.

In January 1916, the First Presidency asked Edward J. Wood, past president of the Samoan Mission, to go as their representative and organize the Tongan Mission. Brother Wood was then president of Alberta Stake in Canada. He arrived in Samoa on February 23, 1916. He selected Willard L. and Jenny Smith to go to Tonga as mission president and mission mother. They arrived at Nuku'alofa on May 11, 1916,[20] and took charge of approximately 450 Tongan Saints, eleven branches, two conferences, and ten other missionaries.

Evidently, almost immediately after arriving, President Smith requested more missionaries. In a letter from the First Presidency to Willard L. Smith, dated June 8, the brethren informed him that they would "endeavour to send five elders as soon as possible." But they went on to explain that in ratio to the small population (22,000), Tonga would then have more missionaries per capita than any nation except Samoa. Of course, the insular geography of Tonga had to be considered, and the brethren sent the additional elders as soon as possible.[21] By the end of 1917 there were twenty Latter-day Saint missionaries in Tonga, but during that fall the First Presidency informed President Smith that the Church was having difficulty obtaining visas for Great Britain and its protectorates, of which Tonga was one. Initially the cause was World War I, but when the war ended in Novem-

School at Houma, Tongatapu, 1917. (Photo from the *Improvement Era*.)

ber 1918, the British continued to exclude Mormon missionaries. The issue was not resolved until May 1920, when the British Home and Foreign Offices became convinced that they had overstepped their bounds and were creating an international issue.[22] In the meantime the few missionaries who entered Tonga found it necessary to come through American Samoa and Vava'u, where there was no immigration authority. Once the missionaries were in the country, the Tongan authorities did not remove them.[23]

The accompanying table illustrates the numbers of Latter-day Saint missionaries in Tonga from 1916 until 1925, along with other information.

Tongan Mission Statistics, 1916-1925[24]

Year	Total Members	Convert Baptisms	Melchizedek Priesthood	Total Branches	Total Districts	Total Missionaries
1916	450 est.	65	2	11	2	12
1917	517	60	2	14	2	20
1918	633	118	2	13	3	12
1919	739	91	3	14	3	8
1920	820	71	2	15	3	8
1921	947	106	6			14
1922	1,008	69	9	17	3	17+17 local
1923	1,002	28	11	17	3	13+19 local
1924	1,051	35	17	15	3	6+13 local
1925	1,080	40	19	—	—	—

After the visa problem was solved in England, the number of missionaries rose in 1921 and 1922 but dropped again in 1923 because serious problems arose between the Church and the Tongan government.

Several other items must be mentioned. In 1917 President Smith sent elders to reopen Ha'apai. He also assigned elders to work on a Tongan translation of the Book of Mormon. Evidently a satisfactory translation was not produced, for no manuscripts were put into print. President Smith also encouraged genealogy work, and he helped the Saints construct three or four chapels.[25]

As can be seen in the table, almost no Tongan men were ordained to the Melchizedek Priesthood during Elder Smith's presidency. The

First Presidency counseled him to ordain only those men who had proven themselves worthy after years of faithful service in the Church.[26] Still, under his leadership, the Tongan Mission almost doubled in membership, and four new branches were created.

After five years of service, the Smiths were replaced by M. Vernon and LaVera Wilcox Coombs of Cardston, Canada. They, with their children, had no difficulty obtaining visas because they were residents of a British Commonwealth country. (Tonga had become a British protectorate in 1900.) They arrived in Tonga on August 9, 1920. Without question, President Coombs's mission was the pivotal era in early Church history in Tonga.

THE VISIT OF ELDER DAVID O. MCKAY

When Elder David O. McKay arrived at Nuku'alofa on May 8, 1921, his ship, the *Tofua,* was quarantined. This was strange because there were no epidemics in either New Zealand or Fiji at that time. The best decision seemed to be to sail on to Samoa, so Elder McKay invited President Coombs to go with him. Following their visit to Upolu and Tutuila, they sailed back to Tonga on the *Tofua* and were placed under quarantine again by the local health officials. Elder McKay had to wait from June 11 to 22 on the small island of Makaha'a, off the coast of Tongatapu.

During the wait, President Coombs explained the local political, social, and religious situation to Elder McKay in some detail. Shortly before this time, Brother Coombs had applied for a land lease for a new boarding school. But this and other lease applications had been denied. It appeared to him that the government had turned hostile to the Church. He even believed the quarantine was part of a Tongan Free Church plan to keep an illustrious Mormon leader out of the country.

After being released from quarantine, Elder McKay met with the Saints in several conference sessions. President Coombs arranged for him to meet with Prince Uiliami Tungi, minister of lands and consort to the queen. To Elder McKay's enquiry about his attitude toward the Church, Tungi said, "I have nothing against your efforts here, but the Wesleyan and the Tongan Free Church feel that you are taking away too many of their members."[27] As will be seen later, Prince Tungi had stronger feelings against the Church than those he expressed to Elder McKay.

Elder McKay visited not only Tongatapu but also Ha'apai and

Vava'u. The story of his harrowing sea voyage to Ha'apai has been told in his secretary's book *Cherished Experiences from the Writings of David O. McKay.*[28] Elder McKay sailed from Vava'u to New Zealand on July 4, 1921.

THE MORMON EXCLUSION LAW OF 1922

After Elder McKay departed, the Church's relationship with the government steadily deteriorated. During September, government officials, using the pretext of an influenza epidemic, denied the Church the right to hold a conference. Yet the Wesleyans and Free Church held similar but much larger meetings at the very time the Church conference had been scheduled.[29] On January 24, 1922, a lease application[30] for property on which to construct a mission house at Lifuka, Ha'apai, was rejected. (This was the second application to be refused.) When President Coombs wrote to Prince Tungi, minister of lands, for an explanation of the lease refusal, he was informed that the government, that is, the cabinet, had under consideration a proposal to prevent Mormons from entering Tonga. Until the matter was resolved, the government did not consider it desirable to grant any more leases to the Church.[31] In March, President Coombs asked the minister of lands to reconsider the leases, but his request was denied.

From Elder Coombs's perspective, the anti-Mormon issue began in September 1921 in Ha'apai. However, the records of the British high commissioner in Suva, Fiji, reveal an altogether different series of events. The question of excluding Mormons from Tonga was first raised in official circles during the fall of 1919.

The feelings of the Tongan government toward the Church surfaced as a result of an application of entry made by Laverne Clarke, the young wife of Francis L. Clarke, a missionary.[32] Her application was handled by British officials in the United States, England, Fiji, and, finally, in Tonga. The Tongan government response to the application was negative. Premier Tu'ivakano told the British consul and agent, Islay McOwan, that the cabinet had discussed the matter and that "it [was] not considered advisable to allow any more members of the Mormon Church to come to Tonga." The premier made Tongan intentions very clear by explaining that when the seven missionaries in Tonga left, no replacements would be allowed. Two denominations were all that were needed. In closing, Tu'ivakano suggested that Tonga needed a passport law to control entry into the country of "undesirables."[33]

Mr. McOwan told Tu'ivakano that without just cause and sufficient reasons he could not suggest such a course to his superior, the high commissioner.

On December 18, 1919, Tu'ivakano again wrote to McOwan on this subject. He admitted that the cabinet was "not able to bring any specific charge against the Mormons" but mentioned rumors from England that Mormon missionaries were exporting "numbers of young girls to . . . America," and that other civilized nations, that is, England and New Zealand, were not favorably inclined toward the Mormons.[34]

It was late in February 1920 when the Tongan government finally gave permission for Sister Clarke to enter Tonga. Her husband's current residence there was the expressed reason for allowing one last Mormon.[35]

Information about Tonga's anti-Mormon plans accompanied Sister Clarke's visa approval when it was sent to London. Even though the British government had decided to allow Latter-day Saint missionaries into the United Kingdom, Lord Milner, colonial secretary, acted as the Tongan government had requested. Hence, the New York passport control office was instructed not to grant visas to Mormon missionaries intending to go to Tonga.[36]

Word of these actions did not reach Tonga until late February 1921. By then Tu'ivakano and the cabinet had decided to handle the problem themselves. Tu'ivakano asked for British permission to pass a law banning Latter-day Saint missionaries as undesirable immigrants. "They can hardly be looked on as Christians, and therefore religious liberty would not apply to them," he explained. The British government seemed to agree. "After consultation with His Majesty's Ambassador at Washington," replied Winston Churchill, the then colonial secretary, "the Secretary of State for Foreign Affairs considers that no objections are likely to be raised by the United States Government to the exclusion of these missionaries from Tonga, on the understanding that the contemplated legislation is to be confined to the exclusion of those who may wish to enter in future and not to the expulsion of those who already reside in the island."[37]

Thus encouraged, Tongan leaders acted quickly. On June 29, 1922, the assembly enacted legislation prohibiting Mormons from entering Tonga and imposing a 100 pound fine, deportation, or both on violators. Latter-day Saints already in Tonga, however, would be allowed to remain there.[38] The new law went into effect on July 18. Lawrence Leavitt and his wife, another missionary couple, arrived just before the deadline. They were the last Latter-day Saint missionaries to enter the country for more than two years.

The exclusion law naturally caused serious problems. Since Church leaders call laymen as full-time preachers for a relatively short time and then keep a cycle of replacements coming, the breaking of the cycle threatened to eliminate the mission in a brief time. During the two years following the enactment of the law, President Coombs saw his mission staff dwindle to a total of five foreign (American and Canadian) missionaries. Two died of typhoid fever at Ha'apai, several missionaries left the islands because of elephantiasis, one departed because of a hernia, and another left because he was "a complete physical wreck." Still others left because of financial or domestic complications at home.[39] If Tongans had not been called as missionaries, conversions to the Church would have ceased.

The steady decline of the missionary force was a strain on President Coombs and the Tongan members. As the elders went home, the schools, which had been conducted at virtually every location where elders lived, were consolidated, until by early 1924 only one school remained open in each island group. There were other problems: On Tongatapu, President Coombs had responsibility for nine branches. Travel between them was usually done by horseback, or, for Mrs. Coombs, in a horse-drawn carriage. But travel in the Tongan islands had never been easy. Small sailboats were the common means of transportation, but as word spread concerning the legal status of the Latter-day Saints, missionaries found it virtually impossible to hire boats and boatmen. President Coombs vividly described the growing abuse of the Latter-day Saints: "We have been stoned out of houses, in Ha'apai the natives will absolutely not allow us to ride in their boats. In Vava'u the natives politely requested to us to leave their houses, and the natives everywhere have informed us that they are strictly forbidden to converse with a Mormon missionary."[40]

When the exclusion law was first passed, the causes were a mystery to Church members and missionaries alike. By careful probing, President Coombs pieced together most of the legislative assembly debates and eventually succeeded in acquiring a transcript of the proceedings. He learned that the Mormons were "guilty" of teaching and practicing polygamy, teaching the people to be disobedient and disrespectful to government authorities, claiming to belong to the church of Jesus Christ, claiming to be saints, and being rude. As the months passed, the list of accusations grew.[41]

The transcript of the debate, which President Coombs did not acquire until December 1923, revealed that the polygamy question was the main issue, but there were others: "Disturbances are caused by this Church" and "many of their religious doctrines clash with the doctrines of other churches which have been brought to Tonga."[42] President Coombs never satisfied himself as to why the polygamy issue was raised in Tonga. The doctrine, which had been abandoned by the Church in 1890, had never been taught in the islands.

President Coombs concluded that there were only three possible ways in which the Church could obtain repeal of the law. One, which proved fruitless, was to apply pressure on the British high commissioner to have him invalidate the law.[43] The high commissioner, it turned out, did not have authority to veto Tongan legislation. A second approach was through the U.S. State Department. Efforts were made in behalf of the Church by Senator Reed Smoot of Utah, but because communications were slow among authorities in Tonga, Samoa, and Washington, President Coombs was not aware of these efforts. His third and most successful tactic was to persuade the Tongan legislative assembly by petition and personal appeal that the law was unconstitutional and should be repealed.

President Coombs became convinced that petitions were the best approach to the problem. He spent hundreds of hours writing petitions and finding people to sign them. He believed that on the basis of Tongan constitutional articles IV and V, the Mormon exclusion law was unconstitutional.[44] President Coombs spoke with Chief Justice Strong about the Mormon position on the matter but found that Strong held a different interpretation of the laws.

The question of repealing the Mormon exclusion law was brought before the Tongan legislative assembly on July 3, 1924. The final debate was surprisingly short. The three most vocal opponents of the repeal petition were Prince Tungi, Tu'ivakano, and Chief Ata. President Coombs expected Chief Justice Strong to oppose the repeal also, but to his surpise Strong switched sides and supported the Latter-day Saints. "My views of the Mormons during the last two years have undergone a complete change," he explained. He also said that "he had learned that the evidence on which he had condemned the Mormons was false and erroneous." In view of the squabble between the Free Church and the Wesleyans, it was difficult for him to see what harm the Mormons could do. In his opinion Mormons conducted themselves as peacefully as most other Tongans.

Strong's change of attitude gave President Coombs the first hint that the Church might win. Before the morning session ended, five more speeches were given in favor of the repeal petition. Shortly after lunch, it was proposed that the issue be referred to the privy council. If this had happened, it was virtually certain that the Church would lose: There were only two known friends of the Church on the seven-member privy council. But this proposition was defeated. The question was then put to a vote of the assembly. When the tally was counted, the vote stood at eleven in favor of repealing sections 7 through 9 of the 1922 Passport Act, and eight against. President Coombs had won.[45]

The irony of this outcome was that though Brother Coombs had carefully enlisted the support of many friends, had gathered as many Church members together for a show of force as was possible, had skillfully written a set of arguments using the Tongan constitution as the basis,[46] and had personally talked to many government officials to try to change their minds, the law was repealed not because he had fought his case well, but because of problems between the Wesleyans and the members of the Free Church. "The trouble between the Tongan Free Church and the Wesleyan Church," noted President Coombs, "has caused intense feeling among all people. All the nobles except one . . . are with the Queen and the Wesleyan Church. The representatives . . . are generally against the Queen and the Wesleyan Church and hence will readily support any cause objectionable to the queen and nobles. The representatives, to a man, voted to grant our petition; two nobles, the Governor of Ha'apai and two members of the Privy Council also voted for us."[47]

President Coombs sent a telegram to Salt Lake City informing President Grant of the good news. On October 25, 1924, Brother Coombs received a letter from the First Presidency congratulating him on the "splendid accomplishment" but informing him of a tentative decision to withdraw missionaries from Tonga. Church leaders in Utah felt that the expenditure of time and money in Tonga was out of proportion to the results obtained. No new missionaries would be sent until a final decision was made.

The next day President Coombs posted a letter to the First Presidency that contained his most profound expressions of affection for the Tongan people and the mission. "But oh, Brethren," he wrote, "if it is not too late, let me plead for my people. This is the hardest proposition that I have ever faced in my life, and Brethren, I would rather lay down my life for them than to run off and leave them leaderless. They are my people, I have made my greatest sacrifices for them and have used my God-given talents in their behalf; I have bought them with seven years of my youth. I have rejoiced when they have rejoiced and have gone down in sorrow with them. I do not want to persuade you against your better judgement, but if we could have only four missionaries we could, at least, hold our own."[48]

President Coombs also told the Church leaders of recent increases in church attendance and better adherence to the commandments, and he reminded the First Presidency of a newly completed chapel. Perhaps his strongest argument was that the Latter-day Saints were getting a reputation as quitters, having left Tonga once before in 1897.

His arguments had the desired effect. On November 28, 1924, the First Presidency wrote, "We are in receipt of your letter of October 26 containing a very earnest appeal for the continuation of the Tongan mission and have decided that it shall continue." Missionaries would be sent "at once."

President Coombs did not receive this letter until February 14, 1925. By that time virtually all of the major problems of the mission had been resolved.

CHAPTER 26

THE LOCAL SAINTS CREATE A FIRM FOUNDATION

Tonga, 1924–1951

Only a month after the Tongan legislative assembly repealed the Mormon exclusion law, President M. Vernon Coombs found a suitable piece of land on which to build a new, expanded central school. Between June 1922 and July 1924, the number of small elementary schools dropped from over ten down to three—one in each island group. Now that the way was clear to increase the number of missionaries, President Coombs desired to enlarge the school system as soon as possible. He envisioned a large (100- to 150-student) boarding school that would serve the older Latter-day Saint students from throughout the kingdom. The Makeke school, as it was called, became the foundation for an enlarged school system in later years.

There was little that was dramatic in the founding of the Makeke (literally "arise and awake") school. It was founded only because President Coombs believed in the idea, found land to lease, and encouraged Church leaders in Salt Lake City and priesthood holders in Tonga to support it. Brother Coombs leased the land on August 25, 1924, and then obtained permission from the Presiding Bishopric to expend the $250 it cost for the seventy-five-acre piece. The land was situated nine and one-half miles from Nuku'alofa, near Veitongo. It was bordered on one side by the government road, and on the opposite end by the sea. Fortunately, President Coombs did not have to obtain government sanction of the lease because the previous leaseholder, Mr. Miles, had already received permission for a foreigner to have it.

When President Coombs obtained Makeke, the First Presidency was considering closing the mission. When he learned this, he closed all Church schools. Between December 1924 and January 1926, there were no Church schools on Tongatapu. In February 1925, he received word that the mission would continue, and in July the First Presidency

Tonga missionaries gather on the steps of the new Makeke School, 1928. (Courtesy Jay A. Cahoon.)

sent him a telegram with a one-word message—"Build."[1]

Even though President Coombs did not receive permission to build the school until July 1925, he had not let the land lie unused. Within a few weeks of taking possession of Makeke, he assigned work crews to clear the land of weeds and brush and to plant crops—sweet potato, papaya, coconut, yam, and vegetables. The priesthood brethren spent many weeks constructing a hog-proof fence. They also moved some old buildings from behind the mission home in Nuku'alofa and built a cistern.

On October 7, several months after Coombs obtained permission to build, he, Elder Orrin Fisher—the only other foreign missionary on the island besides Sister Coombs—and the local missionaries and priesthood holders ceremoniously mixed a batch of concrete and poured part of the foundation for the schoolhouse. From that day until the building was completed in January or February 1926, the mission president, Elder Fisher, and Elders DaCosta Clark and Maurice Jensen (when they arrived in November) devoted almost all of their time to building. President Coombs did not feel that their time was wasted because they were working side by side with Tongans and were learning the language quite rapidly. Week by week, President Coombs assigned each branch on the island to take its turn providing six men to work on the project.

By January 1926, the school was well enough along for small classes to begin. The Saints from Tongatapu had constructed two large Tongan houses for dormitories. President Coombs asked Samuela V. Fakatou, who had recently graduated from the Maori Agricultural College in New Zealand, to be teacher, along with Elder Jensen, who was placed in charge of the school and plantation. Felisione Manisela was called to be chaperon and superviser of outside work. President Coombs dedicated the new school on February 20, 1926.[2] The student body was small at first but grew to over fifty in three or four years.

GENERAL CONDITIONS IN THE TONGAN MISSION

When M. Vernon and LaVera Coombs returned home in June 1926, they were replaced by Elder Jay A. Cahoon and his wife, Ada. Although the Cahoons were both only twenty-one years old and remained in the mission for only sixteen months, they did an excellent job.

Tonga was a young mission. There were only a little over one thousand members of the Church in Tonga in early 1926. The mission had seldom had more than a dozen missionaries assigned to it at one time. The value of mission property was still under thirty thousand dollars, there being only six permanent chapels. Although there were

Chapel and mission home at Nuku'alofa, Tonga, 1928. (Photo from the *Improvement Era*.)

President and Sister Jay A. Cahoon (center first row) and missionaries in Tonga, 1927. (Photo from the *Improvement Era.*)

481 members in Tongatapu, 202 in Ha'apai, and 397 in Vava'u, there were hardly enough Saints on any one island to justify a single ward. The average branch had only sixty members. From outward appearances it was not a stable mission. Yet by the 1970s, 19 percent of the population of Tonga was LDS—a greater percentage than the Church could claim in any other nation in the world.

During 1922, 1923, and 1924, President Coombs called seventeen, nineteen, and thirteen local missionaries respectively. His purpose was to compensate for Zion elders who were not allowed in the country. He continued to call Tongans, usually married couples, after the exclusion law was repealed. He also called six to nine "home missionaries" every six months in Tongatapu and Vava'u, and fewer home missionaries in Ha'apai. This system continued on through the 1930s and until 1946. Then, because only the mission president, his wife, and three other missionaries were allowed in the country, the mission president started calling between twenty and forty local missionaries. After that, even much larger groups of local missionaries were called. The local missionaries communicated well with their own people, learned to teach and defend the gospel, and, perhaps most important, strengthened their own testimonies of and commitment to the Church. And Tongan returned missionaries strengthened the local branches and districts.

Because there were so few Zion elders, local elders were called to serve not only as branch presidents but also as district presidents. Herman Wolfgramm was called to preside over the Vava'u district in 1925. By the mid-1930s, the three districts were led by young local men, all of whom were graduates of the Maori Agricultural College in New Zealand. Although the foreign missionaries were usually involved in the schools, during the 1930s and 1940s Makeke and the smaller schools generally had mostly Tongan teachers.

When World War II started, local Saints were already in charge of most activities and held most leadership positions. There was to be no transition from missionary church to local church.

During the 1920s and the 1930s, however, the missionaries, foreign and local, did not proselyte with the same enthusiasm that they were to show in the postwar years. The foreign elders were almost always involved in schoolteaching or administrative work, and the local missionaries usually spent their time friendshipping members as well as nonmembers.[3] The accompanying table illustrates the steady, almost patterned growth of the Church in Tonga during the quarter century under consideration:

Tongan Mission Statistics, 1926-1951[4]

Year	Total Members	Convert Baptisms	Melchizedek Priesthood	Total Branches	Total Districts	Zion + Local Missionaries:
1926	1,096	47	20	18	3	6 + 6
1931	1,267	50	34	18	3	8 + 6
1936	1,553	30	67	20	3	9 + 15
1941	2,072	69	83	24	3	2 + 13*
1946	2,422	51	136	31	3	5 + 18
1951	3,124	53	163	36	4	5 + 25**

*Ave. 1936-40, 13 + 12
**Ave. 1946-50, 5 + 30

THE DEPRESSION YEARS

Because Tonga has a subsistence economy—most of the people live on what they produce—the world-wide Depression did not have a serious effect on the people there. Most members of the Church earned cash by growing and processing copra, but the copra price dropped to its lowest level in history during 1934. Tithing records reveal that the people had very little money, but in 1934, President Wiberg encouraged them to pay their tithes "in kind," and this procedure improved the tithing record.

More serious than the effects of the international economy were the problems caused by nature. Every year or two, one part of the kingdom or another was hit by either a hurricane or a drought. Zion missionaries frequently wrote of the terrible damage caused by bad storms (hurricanes usually destroyed the coconut crop for two to three years) or of the need for rain. President Coombs often complained that the roads were so muddy he needed tire chains to travel to Makeke, or that the dust on the roads was ankle deep. In 1925 President Coombs and Elder and Sister Cahoon were caught in a hurricane at sea, with waves over thirty feet high, on an overloaded forty-five-foot sailing ship. Their planned two- or three-day trip from Tongatapu to Vava'u took them ten days. Such problems at sea were not unusual.

During 1932 two elders died in the Tongan Mission. Elder Mervin Proctor died on Tongatapu of Vincent Angina infection, and Elder Victor Lee died of typhoid fever (a needless death because inoculations had been available in Tonga since 1924) at Ha'alaufuli, Vava'u. They were the fourth and fifth missionaries to die in Tonga.[5]

In August 1932, Floy B. Cutler, wife of President Newel J. Cutler, contracted yellow jaundice and had to go to Hawaii for medical care. President Cutler, who went with her, left an elder in charge of the mission. During the next year, four of the five Zion elders, including the missionary in charge, entered into what President Reuben M. Wiberg, the next mission president, called "secret combinations and whoredoms." These four elders were dishonorably released from their missions and later excommunicated or disfellowshipped from the Church, but their licentious behavior had become known not only to most older members of the Church, but also to many non-Mormons as well. The damage to the reputation of the Church was the most serious result of the elders' misbehavior. When President Reuben M. Wiberg released the only remaining foreign elder in January 1935, he was the sole Zion missionary in Tonga for the next five months. With the exception of the mission president, the Church was operated entirely by Tongans.[6]

President Wiberg assigned the district presidents to carry out a combined fellowshipping and census program. The district presidents asked priesthood brethren to visit lost, inactive, hostile, and disaffected members, and many of those responded by renewing their

Thousands of baptisms have been performed along the shores of the islands of the Pacific. Here an elder performs the sacred ordinance for Jone Hettig in Tonga in 1928. (Courtesy Jay A. Cahoon.)

activity. The visiting brethren also found that some people had died and that others had apostatized. President Wiberg excommunicated fifty-seven people in 1934, most of them for apostasy, and another fourteen were excommunicated in 1935, when the program was completed.[7]

At this time Church leaders in Salt Lake City sent President Wiberg a series of films on the relationship of the Book of Mormon to the ruins of ancient America. The films, which were seen by hundreds of people, raised interest in the Latter-day Saint position as to the origins of the Polynesian peoples. The illustrated lectures helped to counteract the effects of the apostate missionaries.[8]

In early 1935, President Wiberg changed the emphasis in the Mutual Improvement Association. Until this time, it offered the youth little more than another theological lesson meeting. To demonstrate what "Mutual" was all about, leaders of the Vava'u district sponsored contests in public speaking; debating; storytelling; choral, quartet, and solo singing; and instrumental work in conjunction with district conference. During the following May, all three districts competed in several of the talent areas at an all-mission conference.

All-mission conferences were an innovation during the mid-1930s. In the May 1935 conference, each auxiliary conducted training sessions or separate conferences, choirs from each district sang, and over 860 Saints and friends attended the fourteen sessions. During the conference, a mission board of education was elected, with Samuela V. Fakatou as chairman. Brother Fakatou was still teaching at Makeke. At the same time, President Wiberg called and sustained him as mission translator. Three new missionaries arrived from Zion while the meetings were in progress. From May 1935 onward more and more Zion elders arrived, and through the combined efforts of these missionaries and the now well-experienced Tongan Saints, the Church grew more rapidly during the next five years.[9]

EMILE C. AND EVELYN H. DUNN BEGIN THEIR TEN-YEAR PRESIDENCY

Tonga suffered destructive hurricanes in February and December 1935. The coconut crop was almost entirely destroyed by the two blows, and several Church buildings were damaged, particularly those in Vava'u. When Emile C. and Evelyn H. Dunn arrived at Nuku'alofa on March 12, 1936, they found the islands cleaned up, but evidence of the last hurricane remained.

President Wiberg sailed from Tonga on the same ship that the Dunns had arrived on. It was only afterward that President Dunn learned that President Wiberg had decided not to open the Makeke school at its normal time. The Saints evidently would not all pay the school budget of one pound (four dollars) per family, and President Wiberg had thought it best to close the school for a while. Because he knew the importance of the school, President Dunn called the board of education together a week after he arrived, and together they formulated plans to reopen the school. They decided to ask each able family in the mission to contribute five shillings to build new seats and blackboards. They also decided to require students to deposit enough money before school started to buy their school books. The board established the age limit for students at twelve to twenty-one years inclusive, and finally they set May 19 as the opening day of school. Evidently the Church members conformed to the rules, for the school was soon refurbished and painted, and classes were carried on as usual until December, when it closed for the normal vacation period.[10]

On February 22, 1937, another destructive hurricane hit Tongatapu. Most of the coconut and yam crops were ruined, some homes were wrecked, and six large Tongan dormitory houses at the Makeke school were blown down. It took the students, teachers,

Saints, and missionaries a month to clean up and rebuild. Because the students and their supervisors had planted the school plantation well, they did not suffer for want of food.

The school year was unusually successful. Seventeen or eighteen years before, the Church had purchased ten brass musical instruments and Elder Stirling Ivie May had organized a band. Now President Dunn suggested that the Vava'u Saints donate the band instruments to the Makeke school. They did so, and before the year was over, Jone Tuita and Elder Verl W. Teeples organized a band. The school continued to grow during the next several years. By the end of the 1940 school year, there were 112 students enrolled, and the school had gained official recognition from the government as a college. This gave the older boys, who were liable to pay a poll tax to the government, the privilege of paying only half the tax while attending school. Six of the students sat for the government examination that year, and four of them succeeded in passing the tests.

During 1936 and the following several years, the Church established Boy Scout troops and Beehive classes for the girls of the same age. Before long these groups were asked to participate in government ceremonies and festive occasions.

The MIA organizations of the mission created much interest in the Church during these years, as did the other auxiliaries—the Relief Society, the Primaries, and the Sunday Schools. In 1936, Sister Evelyn H. Dunn helped the MIA people produce a pageant titled "The Conversion of King Lamoni." They did not follow writer Carl Wood's script precisely; conditions and facilities in Tonga would not allow such accuracy. But the pageant was a grand success. The costumes were made of Tongan tapa cloth, and other local materials were used to provide the sets. Before the production ceased, it had been produced in all three island groups, and hundreds of nonmembers as well as members of the Church had seen it. Before long, MIAs throughout the mission put on plays and smaller pageants that had been created entirely by local members.[11]

The people of Tonga experienced a severe drought during the first six months of 1938. Many people went hungry, including members of the Church. But most Latter-day Saints had plenty of taro planted, which helped tide them over until they could raise some sweet potatoes. President Dunn may have been exaggerating a little when he wrote that "The only people who were selling produce to the markets and steamers were the Mormons," but, in any event, most Church members had enough food to survive the drought without suffering.

Several years before, President Wiberg had asked the Saints to plant a "good garden of taro and to always have some." Even the Makeke school carried on without problems because the leaders there had planted enough food for an emergency.[12]

THE APOSTOLIC VISIT OF GEORGE ALBERT SMITH

Seventeen years had passed since Elder David O. McKay's first general authority visit to the missions of the Pacific. Now word came of the imminent arrival of Elders George Albert Smith and Rufus K. Hardy. The Saints in Tonga had only ten or twelve days to get ready, but during that time they cleaned the Tongatapu chapels and cleared part of the Makeke plantation forest to make room to hold a pageant and feast.

When the *Matua* docked at Nuku'alofa at 7:00 A.M. on May 10, only Elder Smith was on board. Elder Hardy was seriously ill and had been forced to remain in the hospital in New Zealand. Elder Smith's Tonga visit must have sapped much of his energy, for he had to do double duty in Elder Hardy's absence. He hardly had time to freshen up before the first session of the Tongatapu District conference began at 10:00 A.M. the same day. From then until he left the islands on June 8, almost the only rest he enjoyed during daylight hours came while he was aboard ship traveling between the three island groups.

Elder Smith covered a multitude of subjects in his twenty-seven major addresses and several minor talks—for example, the importance of the Tongans' heritage as descendants of Lehi and Israel and the importance of supporting Tongan Queen Salote Tupou. Throughout his stay he repeated to the missionaries in each area the importance of teaching the truth accurately and avoiding contention.

After visiting Vava'u and Ha'apai, Elder Smith returned to Tongatapu for a few days. During that time he visited with local business and political leaders, the most important of whom was Queen Salote. Elder Smith spent an hour with her and explained the connection between the American Indians and the Polynesian people. He promised to send her a copy of the Book of Mormon.[13] He later sent one, and he also sent her and her consort, Uiliami Tungi, a beautiful Navajo blanket.

On the morning of June 8, the *Matua* again docked at Nuku'alofa. President Rufus K. Hardy of the First Council of the Seventy was on board. President Dunn and others took him to Makeke and one or two scenic sights, then to a short meeting at the Nuku'alofa chapel. After a

The royal palace in Nuku'alofa, Tonga. (Courtesy Ralph A. Britsch.)

hurried lunch the two general authorities sailed from Tonga aboard the *Matua*.

"Whether it is the visit of the brethren," wrote President Dunn at the end of 1938, "or the increased effort of the missionaries, or both, with an increased blessing from the Lord, we have made a very noticeable growth in numbers in the mission this year."[14] One hundred and seventeen new members were baptized in 1938, almost double the previous year. Not until 1954 did the Tongan Mission have over one hundred convert baptisms again. Undoubtedly, Elder Smith's encouragement and teaching did have an inspiring effect on the missionaries. The timing of his visit was especially good because there were more full-time missionaries in 1937, 1938, and 1939, than at any other time since 1923. As was true in Australia and New Zealand, momentum was growing in the Tongan Mission. Unfortunately, World War II was just ahead, and with the start of the war the missionary momentum was seriously curtailed.

THE TRANSLATION OF THE BOOK OF MORMON AND OTHER MATERIALS

Every missionary had plenty to do teaching prospective members, directing affairs in branches and districts, helping with auxiliaries, working or teaching at Church schools, and so forth. But in addition to these obligations, the missionaries—under the direction of the mission president—were also responsible for translation work.

Until President Wiberg called Samuela Fakatou to be mission translator in 1935, most translating of missionary tracts and Sunday School, MIA, Primary, and Relief Society lessons was done by missionaries. Frequently the wife of the mission president was the main translator. The Tongan Mission was dependent on its own resources for both production and distribution of printed materials.

After 1935, Sam Fakatou and other local leaders who were fluent in English were called to do much of the translation work. Their products were generally of a high quality because of their better knowledge of the Tongan language.

There were several reasons why the Book of Mormon was not translated into Tongan before this time. One was lack of the appropriate personnel. Another reason was the problems faced by the mission in 1922 through 1924 and again in 1934 and 1935 when missionary numbers dropped so low. Elder Stirling I. May translated half of the Book of Mormon around 1920, but his unfinished manuscript was unfortunately packed away in some dark corner of the mission office, and no later mission president knew of it.

While Elder George Albert Smith was in Tonga, President Dunn asked him for permission to prepare a translation of the Book of Mormon in Tongan. Elder Smith supported the project, and before long President Dunn assigned Elder Ermel J. Morton to handle it. Elder Morton had entered the mission in 1936, and by mid-1938 he was fluent in the language. By April 1939, Elder Morton completed his first draft of the translation. After that, he, the Dunns, and several other missionaries revised the manuscript and typed it in what they thought was its final form. In August the project was completed, and Elder Morton took it to the First Presidency in Salt Lake City.[15]

Elder Morton and his co-workers assumed that the new book would be in print before many months. Unknown to them, however, the Crown Prince, later to reign as King Taufa'ahau Tupou IV, returned to Tonga from Australia at about this time and brought with him some new ideas about how the Tongan language should be written. For example, although the pronunciation of the language was not revised, the spelling of the word "Toga" was changed to the present "Tonga." As Morton began the work of revision, he soon realized that he needed a better understanding of the idiom and grammar of the language. After a year of study he resumed his work and completed the revision of the original manuscript on March 15, 1945. The

Tongan version of the Book of Mormon was finally published by the Deseret News Press in Salt Lake City in April 1946.[16] The book was available in Tonga later that year.

THE WITHDRAWAL OF THE FOREIGN MISSIONARIES AND WORLD WAR II

When World War II started in Europe during 1939, life went on as usual in Tonga. President Dunn sent missionaries to open the work in Niua Tobutabu, far to the north of the Vava'u group, in 1939, and to Eua, southeast of Tongatapu, in 1940.

The Saints continued building chapels and other facilities. They made regular use of a new recreation hall that the Church constructed in Ha'alaufuli. The only significant evidence of the Church's concern about the war came in President Dunn's repeated admonitions to the people to plant gardens and to try to maintain a supply of extra food. In 1939 the Tongan government denied landing permits to two Zion elders. Later landing permits were granted, but a quota of ten pairs of missionaries plus the mission president was established. However, before the next year ended, all of the Zion elders except the mission president and his family had been removed because of the war.

President Grant's telegram instructing President Dunn to send the missionaries home arrived in Tonga on October 15, 1940. It came as a surprise to President Dunn. Because communications between Tonga and the outside world were poor, international developments had not taken on as much meaning as they had in Australia and New Zealand. He began making arrangements for the ten foreign elders to leave the country. The Saints all over the mission were deeply saddened by the news. Nevertheless, as they had done many times before when elders had been transferred or released, they prepared feasts and celebrated, though sorrowfully, the departure of the Zion elders.

Through the assistance of Arthur G. Armstrong, the British agent and consul, President Dunn sent a number of wireless messages to President Wilford Emery in Samoa. President Emery arranged for the Tonga missionaries to sail from Apia to Pago Pago, there to meet the *Mariposa,* which would transport them to Hawaii.

Mr. Armstrong, who had helped President Dunn work out several problems, was concerned about the departure of the missionaries and told Brother Dunn he hoped the mission would not be completely closed down. Armstrong expressed his appreciation for what Americans in Tonga were doing to help the Tongan people.[17]

President Dunn had an appointment with Queen Salote (relating to another matter) on October 24, the day the missionaries sailed from Tonga on the *Matua*. During this interview the queen asked President Dunn why the missionaries were being removed. This gave him an opportunity to explain why the Church believes in the need for living prophets. The missionaries were being withdrawn, he explained, because the prophet had been inspired to call them back.

Others besides the queen wondered about the withdrawal of the elders. Even before the end of the day when the message to withdraw arrived, rumors were spreading to the effect that the Mormon Church was being discontinued and would die. However, nowhere in the southwest Pacific did the removal of the Zion elders have less effect upon the Church and its continued progress than in Tonga. The *Matua* departed from Nuku'alofa bearing the ten elders on October 24, 1940. President and Sister Dunn and their three children remained in Tonga.

President Dunn called Tevita Mapa as president of Tongatapu District, Tevita Finau as president of Ha'apai District, and Vuna F.F. Wolfgramm as president of the Vava'u District. They each chose local counselors to assist them. Three foreign missionaries had been working at Makeke College, so President Dunn called on his wife, Evelyn; Samuela V. Fakatou; Tevita Pita; and Jiaosi Bolauni (Brown) to take over teaching responsibilities there. Sister Dunn had the students in the sixth form (seniors) live at the mission home in Nuku'alofa, where she primed them for the government school-leaving examination. Brother Fakatou directed the work at Makeke College.[18]

During the years of Emile Dunn's presidency, he had placed some foreign missionaries in leadership capacities, such as Mission Young Men's MIA president and Mission Genealogy Society secretary. Beyond these, he called local members to fill all positions except those his wife held, namely, president of the Relief Society, Primary, and Young Women's MIA. Because most of the Tongans who were in district and mission leadership positions were not familiar with recordkeeping procedures, President Dunn called a secretary in each district to compile and prepare all historical and financial reports. This procedure worked well during the entire war.

Between October 24, 1940, and December 7, 1941, the Tongan Saints carried on much as usual. "Union" meetings were held monthly in each district (the union meeting was a combined leadership meeting that involved people from all auxiliaries and the genealogy committees), and the district Melchizedek priesthood quorums continued to meet regularly. The impact of World War II still had not been felt in Tonga.

But on December 7 and 8, 1941, the Japanese attacked Pearl Harbor in Hawaii, Clark Air Base in the Philippines, and other points in Southeast Asia. Within hours of these events, the Tongan government interned all Japanese and Germans who were living in the islands. The distant war was now a Pacific war.

Within a week of the Pearl Harbor attack, the Tongan government, acting on advice from the British, ordered all white women and children (even the wives of Tongans) evacuated to New Zealand. President Dunn asked that an exception be made in the case of his wife and children. The consul told him emphatically that not a single woman or child would be left behind when the *Matua* sailed in two or three days. On December 20, Sister Dunn and her children, Hyde, Karen, and Ofa, sailed from Tonga. They arrived in New Zealand on December 30. Sister Dunn and the children lived with the Matthew Cowley family for the next fourteen months until they returned to Tonga. President Dunn called local presidents for each of the auxiliaries Sister Dunn had led. The Church in Tonga was again almost entirely on its own.

The government immediately imposed wartime precautions, such as blackouts. These blackouts caused the Church some problems. Regular night meetings were canceled, and missionary cottage meetings were difficult to conduct without light. To counter the negative effects of the blackouts, the Saints built a large Tongan-style house—large enough to hold five hundred people—in the nutmeg grove at Makeke. Evidently their lights could not be seen there from the air, for evening meetings were held on occasion. The local missionaries tried to do their work and to hold cottage meetings in the afternoon and early evening. Most members of the Church in Nuku'alofa moved into the country, causing the branch in the town to be temporarily discontinued.

On April 20, 1942, a convoy of thirteen American war ships anchored off Nuku'alofa. For the next several years, the island of Tongatapu was not the same. Soldiers, sailors, and marines were ever-present. Local people were employed or commandeered to help the military effort. American money flowed freely, and the Tongan people were wealthier than at any previous time in their history. Tithing was frequently paid in American money during this period. U.S. army officers obtained permission from President Dunn to move into the mission home and elders' quarters.

During 1942 and 1943, Tongan members of the Church had their first introduction to foreign Latter-day Saints who were not missionaries. A number of Mormon servicemen were stationed on Tongatapu. These men attended Church meetings when they could and helped the members whenever possible.

After October 1942, the American military began pulling its men out of Tonga, a slow process that actually took a great many months. Even after July 1943, when most American soldiers had been moved closer to the war zone, ships regularly stopped at Nuku'alofa to get supplies and to provide rest for those on board.

Through all of the changes caused by the war, the Saints continued to hold their meetings and to expand the missionary work. Between 1942 and 1945, President Dunn kept an average of fifteen Tongan elders (along with their wives and families) in the mission field. Ten of these men were generally assigned as branch presidents in the area where they served. In September 1943, four missionaries were assigned to serve on Niuafo'ou Island (Tin Can Mail Island). The Church now had missionaries on "all of the groups of islands in Tonga."[19]

In 1944 two new branches were organized, and the next year two dependent branches were added, one of which was at Tongamama'o,

A contemporary fale on Tongatapu, Tonga. (Courtesy Ralph A. Britsch.)

Niuafo'ou. The new members there soon learned how the Church tries to take care of its own. The island was badly shaken by a volcanic eruption in November 1943, and a serious drought followed. To help the people survive, the Church sent food from Tongatapu, Ha'apai, and Vava'u. After a hurricane hit the island of Niautoputapu, the Saints assisted the people there in the same way.[20]

For the most part, the war had moved past Tonga by late 1943 or early 1944. From then until it ended in August 1945, the Saints did their best to hold to the faith and make the Church grow. Even when the war ended, however, many months passed before life returned to normal. Many products were difficult to obtain because transportation in the Pacific had been almost halted during the war, and peacetime shipping firms could not quickly restore normal operations.

President Dunn and his family remained in Tonga until June 1946, when they were replaced by Evon W. Huntsman and his wife, Martha. The Huntsmans were accompanied by Liddell and Hortense Roberts and their three children. The Dunns had served for over ten years. During their term the Church had grown by 35 percent, a large increase considering the years that were included.

THE POSTWAR YEARS AND THE BUILDING OF LIAHONA COLLEGE

World War II brought many changes to the Pacific islands, including technological and political ones. Although communications between Tonga and other areas after the war were slow and often poor, they were better than before. Transportation facilities were improved somewhat during the war. The military constructed an airport that remained in use after the servicemen were gone, and the docks were improved. New political attitudes were stirring some of the Pacific peoples to action. Although Tonga was an independent kingdom, some Tongans resented what they called the "overwhelming European influence." Anti-European and anti-colonial feelings were certainly not limited to the Pacific at this time. Throughout the Third World, colonial people struggled for freedom from the powers that controlled them.

In July 1946, only a month after President Huntsman assumed office, he applied to the government for five landing permits for incoming elders. These permits were granted on July 6, and relations between the Church and the government seemed to be harmonious. Three days later, two new missionaries arrived at Nuku'alofa—Elders Bevin Blake and John B. Laycock, whose landing permits had been granted earlier. The next day, however, President Huntsman learned that the cabinet was in the process of reevaluating missionary landing permits. The old problem of getting missionaries into Tonga was surfacing again. But the next day they learned the worst: No more landing permits would be granted; the five permits were canceled; and from that day on, only one foreign missionary would be allowed for every two thousand members of the Church. Although these rules were to apply uniformly to all religious denominations, the Latter-day Saints were the only group who were seriously engaged in missionary work at that time.[21]

Because there were only 2,422 Latter-day Saints in Tonga in 1946, the quota system would have allowed only one foreign missionary and his family, if he were married. President Huntsman believed the quota system was an outgrowth of interfaith rivalry. He may have been partially correct, but from discussions he had with Premier Ata and others, it became clear to him that they honestly could not see the need for foreigners in the country. Tonga was already Christianized, they reasoned, and there was no necessity for "European" missionaries.

President Huntsman and the Saints did everything they could to change the cabinet's decision, including petitioning the legislative assembly, talking to the British consul, and pleading with Queen Salote, but all to no avail. In September 1946, an elder arrived on the *Matua,* but he was not allowed to land. In early November, Elder Rudolph H. Wolfgramm, a Tongan who had become a naturalized American citizen, arrived in Tonga with his wife, Edna. Because they were originally from Tonga, they were allowed to land for three months. President Huntsman hoped he could get the quota system changed during that time, but the government would not modify its stand. On January 26, 1947, Elder and Sister Wolfgramm were ordered to leave the country. Two days later the First Presidency wired President Huntsman and asked him to apply for two more landing permits. Although he thought it was futile, he did so, and on February 4 he was told by the government that the two permits would be granted, but only as replacements for foreign missionaries who were already in the country. This was important because from that time on the government allowed four elders and their families. This included the mission president.

Recognizing that Elder Wolfgramm and his wife could be of greater service to the Church than he, Elder Laycock suggested that he be sent to another mission so that the Wolfgramms could stay. The government and the First Presidency approved this move, and Elder Laycock sailed from Tonga for Hawaii on February 22.[22]

When Elder Matthew Cowley made his first visit to Tonga in June 1947, he saw the situation from a different perspective. During several sessions of a conference that were held while he was there, Elder Cowley admonished the Saints to avoid religious prejudice, to support the government, and to try to see everything from the viewpoint of the government. "If you people will support one another in your positions and your work in the Church," Elder Cowley told the assembled members, "you won't need many missionaries out here from Zion, for you have the same priesthood as the elders do that come from Zion, and God will have his spirit with you if you are following the principles of the priesthood."[23]

Elder Cowley said that he had observed a growing anti-white attitude all over the islands and that he doubted the Church could get more missionaries into Tonga for some time. Elder Cowley's attitude helped the Saints to accept the quota system and to move ahead with other matters of importance.

Before Emile C. Dunn left the islands, he spent twelve days with Evon Huntsman discussing the needs of the mission. One matter was the critical need to improve the Makeke school or college. The students, now around 150 in number, were living in dilapidated dormitories with dirt floors. They were crowded together, and the plantation was not adequate to provide for their needs. President Dunn explained this to President David O. McKay the following October, but long before that, President Huntsman had begun looking for more property so that the school could expand. After looking at many leaseholds, he had found an excellent plantation of 276 acres near Halaloto, seven and one-half miles from Nuku'alofa. The lease owner, Frank Cowley, was asking 10,000 pounds ($35,000) for the plantation, which included 150 acres in coconuts, seventy cattle, and a few other items. On February 19, 1947, President Huntsman recommended to the First Presidency that the property be acquired, and on April 14 approval came from Salt Lake City. Brother Huntsman soon secured the land. When Elder Matthew Cowley came to Tonga in June, he inspected the Frank Cowley property, approved it, and sent word to the First Presidency to send the necessary money to a New Zealand bank.

President Huntsman almost immediately began calling the plantation "Liahona," after the brass direction ball mentioned in the Book of Mormon. For the first year that the Church had this property, mission records refer to it both as the Makeke College and as the Liahona Plantation. The reason for this was that President Huntsman first thought of the new land as a large garden plot for the school; then he decided that it would be better to move the old buildings to the new property. The records do not make clear who it was that decided a new, modern school should be built at Liahona. The idea may have come directly from President McKay or Elder Cowley. In any event, during late September 1947, President Huntsman received instructions from the First Presidency to request landing permits for Emile C. and Evelyn H. Dunn and their two girls, Karen and Ofa. A year after their release from the mission presidency, the Dunns were being called back to Tonga to build a new school at Liahona.[24]

When the Dunns arrived at Nuku'alofa, they knew they were to build several modern, concrete-block dormitories and classroom buildings, but they did not have a final plan for the campus. President Huntsman wanted to move the buildings in time for the Makeke College 1948 school year. But the moving of the buildings took a while, and school started a little late. One hundred and sixty students were enrolled that year.

Months went by and the new buildings were not under way. A great deal of work had to be done clearing land, erecting temporary

Liahona High School. (Photo by R. Lanier Britsch.)

buildings, working on a water system, and so forth, before the new buildings could be constructed. Because the college was to be built of concrete block, a building material that had not been used before in Tonga, Elder Dunn had to import a block-making machine from the United States. This machine and several other pieces of construction equipment arrived in Tonga during July 1948, along with 32,000 bags of cement, 100,000 board feet of lumber, and a lighting plant. Brother Dunn spent most of his time during the remaining months of 1948 making concrete block.

Brother Dunn did much more than work on the new college. President Huntsman's health was not good during the early months of 1948, and it did not improve as the year went on. On July 14 he was released and Elder Dunn was appointed in his place. During President Huntsman's two years in Tonga, he had accomplished a number of important things, among them purchasing the Liahona lease; moving Makeke College; and dividing Tongatapu district, with its twenty-one branches, into the Hahake (east) and Hihifo (west) districts in December 1947.

During 1948 Church architect Edward O. Anderson visited the proposed Liahona campus and drew plans for buildings and the general physical plant layout. While Elder Anderson was in Tonga, he officiated at the groundbreaking on November 5. Before the end of that year President Dunn had taught one of the local Saints how to make block, a rather technical operation, and soon other priesthood brethren were engaged in that part of the work. Before the school was completed, the mission presidents called almost all of the local missionaries to work full-time as builders at Liahona. During 1949, 1950, and 1951, proselyting almost stopped. The school was the greatest attraction to non-Mormons; they were amazed at the size, quality, and nature of the project.

Saints from Vava'u and Ha'apai came by boat and stayed a month or two at a time, and the members from Tongatapu came regularly, staying for a week or so. They all brought their own food. This was the beginning of the program that was later called the Building Missionary Program. Although the Tongan Saints were not called as building missionaries at this time, they functioned in that way.

The Tongan men could handle many of the construction jobs. They had been doing carpentry for many years, but the blocklaying was new to Tonga, and help was needed. Elder Reuben M. Flynn was sent from Utah to handle that job. He taught Tonga workers to lay the blocks well enough that by August 29, 1949, when Elder Cowley arrived, he was able to preside at the cornerstone ceremony.

In 1949, two Zion missionaries and their families were allowed in the country as replacements for elders who had been released. They were Thomas P. Wilding, a former Tongan missionary who had building experience, and Franklin A. Spencer, a skilled mechanic. In 1950, Elder Cowley sent several other builders from New Zealand, among them George R. Biesinger and Lionel Going. Brother Biesinger was in Tonga for a short time, but Brother Going took over as project supervisor in April 1950 and remained until the school was completed in 1953.

In July 1950, President Dunn was released. His replacement was Evon W. Huntsman, who wanted to return to complete his earlier mission call. When the Dunns left Tonga, they had completed almost thirteen years as mission leaders. In addition, President Dunn had served four years in Tonga during his first mission.

By the end of 1951 all of the buildings were completed, and most of the local priesthood members and some of the local missionaries had been released to return home. Elder Going kept a few key men on the project to help make desks, tables, and beds, but most of the work was done. On February 11, 1952, Liahona College would open its doors. Over two hundred students, about 35 percent of them nonmembers, were expected.[25]

CHAPTER 27

SETTING THE PACE FOR WORLDWIDE CHURCH GROWTH

Tonga, 1952–1984

"I have called and set apart twenty new local missionaries," wrote President Evon W. Huntsman at the end of 1951, "and sent them to all five of the main islands of the mission, instructing them that they are to spend all the time possible in carrying the Gospel message to everyone who will accept it."[1]

The missionaries' time would no longer be required at Liahona. President Huntsman closed his report to the Presiding Bishopric by saying, "With the new college, new missionary force, and a new mission president to inject new life into the mission, 1952 should be a banner year." 1952 was a banner year, one of many over the following years.

Between 1952 and 1968 the Church in Tonga grew from 3,280 members, four districts, and thirty-five branches, to almost 12,000 members (real growth of 264 percent), a stake, eight wards, ten districts, and fifty branches. The slow, trying years, the years of struggle, persecutions, disappointments, and difficulties, finally came to an end. Even the annoyances caused by government restrictions and the petty harassments of other churches seemed to work more to the Church's good than to its detriment. During this era the Tongan Saints matured and advanced in matters relating to leadership, Church organization, and spiritual enlargement; the constructing of chapels and other buildings for Church purposes; the improvement of the system for teaching the gospel to nonmembers; and the growth and improvement of the Church school system in Tonga. The rapid growth of the 1950s and 1960s was to a great degree an outgrowth of the work that had been done by earlier missionaries and members, but leaders in Tonga and Utah made many changes in the way Church matters were handled, and these changes also brought significant results. The accompanying table illustrates the growth of the Church in the Tonga Mission during this era.

Tongan Mission Statistics, 1952-1967[2]

Year	Total Members	Convert Baptisms	Melchizedek Priesthood	Total Branches	Total Districts	Missionaries Foreign	Missionaries Local
1952	3,280	71	189	35	4	4	19
1955	3,979	82	190	45	5***	12	18*
1958	4,906	166	282	50	7†	15	33**
1961	6,358	519	446	56	8	14	57
1964	8,697	830	724	59	12	16	146
1967	11,366	823	940	57	11	20	54

*4 foreign proselyting missionaries, 8 missionary teachers at Liahona, 18 local full-time missionaries.

**5 foreign proselyting missionaries, 10 missionary teachers at Liahona, 33 local full-time missionaries.

***Niue added

†Fiji added

This table includes the years prior to the creation of the first stake in Tonga in 1968.

D'Monte W. and Joan Coombs and their children arrived in Nuku'alofa in February 1952. President Coombs was to lead the mission for nearly four years. The son of M. Vernon Coombs, who presided over the Tongan Mission from 1920 to 1926, he had spent his early years among the Tongan people. He still remembered the language and many cultural traits of the people.

Perhaps his lifelong familiarity with the Tongan people, along with his determination to see the Church grow, gave him the courage he needed to handle many uncomfortable problems that had been allowed to go unattended. Specifically, President Coombs held Church courts and tried many members who were accused of adultery and fornication. Prior to this time almost no Tongans had been disfellowshipped or excommunicated for immorality. Brother Coombs, however, believed that the "membership was riddled" with the problem of sexual immorality and apostasy, and he determined to clean it up. He held many courts, excommunicated a few, disfellowshipped a number, and called many men and women to repentance. After President Coombs excommunicated the highest tithe-payer in the mission for adultery, many persons who were guilty of the same offense voluntarily confessed their sins, corrected their behavior, and were forgiven by the Church. President Coombs established a new standard of behavior for the Tongan Saints.[3]

But not all of Elder Coombs's contributions and responsibilities related to uncomfortable problems; he also helped to establish correct organizational procedures. A high percentage of the local missionaries acted as branch presidents in the villages where they were assigned, and the local branch members were responsible for the support of the Tongan elders and their families. Seeing that this situation had to be changed, President Coombs began, in March 1952, to have the district presidents install local brethren as branch presidents. By the end of the year, twenty-two branches had been reorganized with local leaders. President Coombs continued this procedure until almost all branches had their own people in charge.

By this method, President Coombs freed many missionaries for full-time proselyting. He had noted, however, that married elders were not as free to move about because of family obligations. With these facts in mind, President Coombs and his counselors decided, on December 31, 1952, to begin calling young Tongan elders, unmarried men, to fill local missions.[4] Six married couples would still be needed to lead new or weaker branches, but during 1953 the presidency called eight young men to serve missions.

In September the mission sponsored a missionary training school. In a series of eight cottage meetings, experienced elders demonstrated the use of visual aids, specific scriptures, and carefully worded questions. Most of the Tongan elders were less than comfortable with this new method of teaching. Furthermore, Tongan custom frowned on young people asking older people direct questions. Several years were required before the lessons and teaching method were adapted to the Tongan situation.[5] Nevertheless, during D'Monte Coombs's presidency, the missionary system was reorganized to fit the best teaching methods that had been developed in the Church to that time.

Mission presidents and general authorities who visited Tonga during the 1950s and 1960s agreed that the most effective missionary tool was Liahona College. Many non-Mormon youths attended the residential high school, and a high percentage of these students eventually joined the Church. But students were not the only people who

Air view of Liahona High School. (Courtesy LDS Church Archives.)

were affected; visitors, from the queen on down, toured the campus.

The initial campus was completed and ready for dedication many months before Elder LeGrand Richards of the Council of the Twelve visited Tonga in November and December 1953. There was time to make elaborate preparations for the important event. Among the numerous guests of honor that December first was Queen Salote Tupou. This gracious lady, who had reigned since 1918, spoke to the assembled throng of Saints who came from all over her kingdom. She told the people that she considered the dedication services to be a truly happy occasion "because it is predicated on achievement." Queen Salote, too, taught the people. "The building of this institution," she proffered, "the purpose of this school, is to build up Christian civilization; that civilization in which we are united; the kind of civilization from which we obtain peace; the civilization whereby we are truly free. That is Christian civilization, the civilization whereby we have faith in God and the knowledge of the will of Jesus Christ."[6]

Elder Richards told the Saints to send their children to the college. He added that he hoped the Church could build new facilities as quickly as the student body required them. Hardly a year passed before the Church authorized a number of new buildings to be constructed at Liahona.

PRESIDENT MCKAY'S SECOND VISIT TO TONGA

There was a great contrast between David O. McKay's visit to Tonga as an apostle in 1921 and his visit as president of the Church in 1955. His first visit was marred by what appeared to be a trumped-up quarantine of his ship designed to discourage his entry into the country. In 1955, however, the British consul as well as many top government officials freely offered their assistance to help make President McKay's visit pleasant. Queen Salote was not on Tongatapu when President McKay, his wife, Emma Ray, and Franklin D. Murdock arrived on January 11, but the first family was well represented by Prince Tungi (now King Taufa'ahau Tupou IV) and other distinguished people. President McKay met with Prince Tungi and established a warm relationship. In truth, Tungi had already helped the Church on a number of occasions, particularly by giving approval for teaching missionaries to enter the country and work at Liahona.

Tongan Church members gave President and Sister McKay a welcome that was ordinarily reserved for royalty and nobles. He thanked them by paraphrasing Robert Burns's poem on returning home:

> When death's dark stream I ferry o'er,
> A time that surely *shall* come,
> In Heaven itself I'll ask no more,
> Than just a Tongan welcome.

President McKay's two-day stay in Tongatapu and half-day visit in Vava'u were profoundly meaningful and important to the Tongan Saints. This was the first visit to their land by a president of the Church. Emotions were high as the prophet of God spoke to the assembled throngs at Liahona and Ha'alaufuli, dined with them at sumptuous feasts, and enjoyed the music, dances, and speeches that were provided for him, his wife, and Elder Murdock.

President McKay was on a special mission at this time. He had been commissioned by the Council of the Twelve and the First Presidency to select a temple site somewhere in the South Pacific. He obviously had this responsibility in mind when he said to the Vava'u Saints, "Do you know what I saw today, in vision? A temple on one of these islands, where the members of the Church may go and receive the blessings of the temple of God. You are entitled to it."

Lela Dalton, clerk of the meeting, wrote that on hearing this "the entire congregation burst into tears."

While President McKay was on the Liahona campus, President

Coombs explained the need for more dormitories. President McKay instructed him to apply to the Church Building Committee for them. In Vava'u President McKay learned that several chapels were soon to be constructed, and when he found that the buildings would not have recreation halls, he told President Coombs and the assembled Saints that the new chapels should be built with facilities for athletics, drama, and other activities. One- or two-room chapels would no longer suffice.

From Vava'u, President and Sister McKay and Elder Murdock sailed to Niue, where high seas prevented their landing, and on to Samoa. The official tour of Tonga ended on January 13, 1955.

THE ISLAND OF NIUE

Before moving on, we will digress here to introduce Niue, an island that has been attached to several different missions, but which at this writing was again under the leadership of the Tonga Nuku'alofa Mission.

The tiny island of Niue, like the Cook Islands, is linked to New Zealand both politically and financially. The Niueans are British subjects and New Zealand citizens, and they are free to enter New Zealand without restriction. The little island lies roughly 300 miles east of the Tongan Group, 580 miles west of Rarotonga, and 350 miles southeast of Samoa. The population is small, 3,578 in 1978. The people are Polynesians who speak their own distinct language.

During 1951, Elder Fritz Bunge-Kruger visited Niue Island and later suggested to President Gordon C. Young in New Zealand that the Niuean people might be ready for the gospel. President Young asked Elder Bunge-Kruger to take his family, now consisting of a wife and six children, to Niue and preach the restored truth. He did this in September, but before going, he bought a sixteen-millimeter movie projector, a screen, and other necessary equipment and made arrangements with MGM and Warner Brothers in Wellington, New Zealand, to supply him with films on Niue.

For three months after he arrived there, Elder Bunge-Kruger showed films in all the villages of the island. Then he decided it was time to start doing some missionary work. As he had done before on Rarotonga, he published a little newsletter containing information about the Church. His efforts were met with immediate interest among some old friends of his from American Samoa, where he was born, but he also had negative reactions from the local London Missionary

Society minister, who tried to get him removed from the island. Elder Bunge-Kruger soon started a Sunday School. It proved popular, and before many weeks were over, one hundred children were attending each Sunday.

After the Bunge-Krugers had been on Niue for about six months, President Sidney J. Ottley, the new president of the New Zealand Mission, sent two full-time missionaries there. Shortly after they arrived, forty people were baptized into the Church. The Bunge-Krugers remained on the island for fifteen months, but long before they departed the full-time elders had taken over most of the work.[7]

Niue, like the Cook Islands, has been a Church orphan in a sense. Since the beginning of work there, it has been part of the New Zealand, then the Tongan, then the Fiji, and again the Tongan Missions. Like the Cook Islands, Niue has so few people that the Church has not grown rapidly, and the same kinds of anti-Mormon pressures exist there as in Rarotonga. Today Niue has four independent and five dependent branches with several hundred members.

THE LABOR MISSIONARY PROGRAM IN TONGA

In his position as leader of the Church, President McKay had a grasp of programs that were underway all over the world. When he told President Coombs to apply for new buildings at Liahona and for new chapels throughout the mission, he did so knowing that the volunteer labor program that had been used to build Liahona College had been adopted in New Zealand to build a similar school there and that the Twelve intended to change the status of the volunteers to that of missionaries. This was done in February 1955. Wendell B. Mendenhall, who had helped with the Church College of New Zealand project, was called by the First Presidency to head the Church Building Committee and direct the labor missionary program.

Before President McKay had left for the Pacific, the Church Committee on Expenditures had approved twenty-one new concrete block chapels for Tonga, at a cost of $265,859. President Coombs did not receive authorization to move ahead, however, until after President McKay's visit. It was then necessary, considering the President McKay's advice to build recreation halls, to apply for money to make these additions. In April, President Coombs received an additional appropriation of $125,958 to build recreation halls.

In the meantime, he and his counselors had established a policy that, before starting new chapels, the branches would need to provide

$1,750 and do the work without pay. Another year passed before the work was ready to start. President Coombs was released in December 1955, and Fred W. Stone was called to take over. By the end of January 1956, President Stone had called and set apart fifty labor missionaries. The Tongan labor missionaries, who had been joined by experienced American builders, began work on new buildings at Liahona in January, and on March 1, President Stone directed the groundbreaking for a new chapel at Matahau. By the end of 1956, Tongan labor missionaries had nearly completed a new vocational and technical education shop and additional dormitories were well underway at Liahona. In March 1959, ten chapels had been completed and dedicated, and others were under construction. By June 1959 the labor missionaries had completed a new mission home.

The twenty-one chapels were completed by 1960, and in March thirty-one Tongan labor missionaries traveled to Hawaii, where they had been called to construct several new buildings at the Church College of Hawaii. During the big years of the labor missionary program, between 1955 and 1962, the Tongan Saints constructed many new and comparatively elaborate chapels. Because of the building momentum of the late 1950s, the Tongan Latter-day Saints saw their chapel style change from one-room frame or Tongan-style buildings to modern structures. The labor missionary program contributed greatly to the extensive building program in Tonga.[8]

DEVELOPMENTS IN CHURCH EDUCATION

When President McKay toured the Pacific missions in 1955, he became acutely aware of the growing and almost unmanageable size of the mission presidents' responsibilities. The steady growth of Church-supported schools in Tonga, Samoa, and New Zealand accounted for much of the administrative burden on these leaders. In 1956, President McKay made all school principals responsible directly to him, but this was only a partial solution to the problem. He eventually proposed to his counselors and the Council of the Twelve that a special board of education be created to administer all Pacific schools of the Church. He reasoned that a central board could bring uniformity and economy to the schools. In 1961, after the new program had been in effect for four years, the Pacific Board of Education wrote, "This concept was clearly logical. The Church schools of the Pacific fitted with perfect naturalness into an integrated system of education, made homogeneous by Church membership, geography, similar administration problems and a student body predominantly Polynesian. Such a system under centralized control relieved the First Presidency of supervisory detail while remaining directly responsible to their authority."[9]

The Pacific Board of Education was formed June 21, 1957, with Wendell B. Mendenhall as chairman (he was chosen because of his familiarity with the extensive building projects in Samoa, Tonga, New Zealand, and elsewhere in the Pacific), Owen J. Cook as executive secretary, and Edward L. Clissold, D'Monte W. Coombs, and Ermel J. Morton as board members. Wayne F. McIntire replaced Elder Morton in 1960. The Pacific Board, which operated from 1957 until 1965 when the Unified Church School System (formerly called LDS Church School System) assumed its functions, was both a policy-making and administrative body.

The Pacific Board of Education had to face many problems that had developed in the island schools. For one, Liahona College was a more complex institution than Makeke College had been. The physical plant was larger, more modern, and more complicated and expensive to maintain. The curriculum at the new school was broader and more sophisticated. The faculty was larger and had innovative ideas concerning curriculum. These and hundreds of other developments required attention from the new board.

Two important questions facing the board were the place of primary education and the role of missionary teachers in the system. Primary schools were originally the heart and soul of the missionary system in Tonga. Between the 1930s and 1956, however, secondary education had replaced the primary schools. Believing that many younger children needed schooling and that primary schools could help the missionary cause, President Fred W. Stone asked Elder James P. Christensen (who later became a mission president) to open primary schools in Vava'u. He did this in early 1956, and Elder John H. Groberg (who later became a mission president and a member of the First Quorum of the Seventy) opened a school in Pangai, Ha'apai. By 1957 the three schools had 230 students, and the next year 250 children. In 1958, however, the Pacific Board and the First Presidency decided that the Church would prefer the governments of various lands to assume the responsibility for the primary education of their own children. The efforts of the Church would be concentrated at Liahona College. Since then the Church has not operated primary schools in Tonga.[10]

When Liahona College opened in 1952, it did so with several

Tongan teachers and five foreign teaching missionaries, men and women who had been called on missions to teach at Liahona College. They were not allowed by the government to proselyte. By 1958, sixteen missionary teachers were engaged at Liahona. Although these teachers were generally competent, the quality of teaching was somewhat irregular. With the intention of making all Pacific Church schools better and more nearly uniform, the Pacific Board decided in 1958 to replace all missionary teachers with hired, trained professionals. In addition to the other benefits, this system would relieve the mission presidents of the responsibility of directing the teachers as well as the proselyting missionaries.

In February 1958, twenty-six teachers who had been recruited in America arrived in Tonga, and the last missionary teacher left Tonga in June 1959. Because of the American educational backgrounds of the Pacific Board, the principals, and the faculties, the English language was emphasized. It was believed this was necessary if students were to obtain good employment or go on to higher education. Carrying this American emphasis further, in April 1961 the board changed the name of Liahona from a college to a high school and changed from the British-New Zealand system of "forms" to "grades."

But when Rondo S. Harmon became principal of Liahona in 1963, he soon recognized that the school was producing graduates who were generally unsuited for life in Tonga. Too much emphasis was being given to university preparation, and particularly to preparation to enter the Church College of Hawaii and other American schools. Harmon did not believe that CCH degrees were of much value in Tonga, because few jobs were available for people with American degrees.

Principal Harmon chose to emphasize vocational and agricultural training that was designed to Tongan needs. He stressed the preparing of students to pass the "school leaving" examination—called the school "C" or certificate, which was patterned after the New Zealand system. When Brother Harmon returned to the United States in 1967, his replacement, Orson H. White, also emphasized the policy of preparing the Tongan students for life in Tonga.

Curriculum was important, and the growth of the student body and the need to enlarge the physical plant received considerable attention from the Pacific Board and local administrators. The original student body at Liahona was a little over 200, but by October 1958, 485 students were enrolled. During that year labor missionaries completed the second classroom building, a dining hall, and some other facilities. But continued success among the proselyting missionaries caused the student body to grow, and the fine reputation of the school also attracted many non-Mormons.

By 1964, more qualified students wanted to attend Liahona than could be accepted. In that year, an administrator accepted more seventh-grade students than the school could house. When the students began to arrive, Principal Harmon and his associates decided to send all seventh-grade students from Tongatapu back home. Since there were many chapels that could serve as schools, Liahona would send teachers to those chapels, and the students could then live at home. This plan received the support of the LDS Church Schools administrator, Harvey L. Taylor, in 1965. During the next two years, the eighth and ninth grades were added to the new chapel-school system. These schools are frequently called "side schools," but within the Tongan system they are called the "middle schools." By 1968 there were eleven middle schools. A relatively large number of Tongan graduates from CCH taught in these schools.[11]

The creation of the middle schools allowed the entire system to grow from 775 students in 1963 to 1,650 students by the end of 1968. Because of this rapid growth, Administrator Taylor appointed Principal Harmon to be superintendent of the new Liahona School System in 1966. (The name of the system was soon changed to Church Schools Tonga.) Brother Harmon established an administrative office with staff members to handle the many needs of the seventy-five teachers and numerous students and staff members in the system. Tupou Pulu, the first Tongan to graduate from CCH, was made supervisor of middle schools. Tongans handled most of the staff positions.

At about the same time, Archie Cottle, who had spent several terms in Tonga as a Church builder, and his associates completed several additions to the campus at Liahona. The new buildings included a large auditorium-gymnasium, improved music facilities, an enlarged library, and a large athletic field. Other additions to the campus were made later in the decade and are still being made.

The main reason for the existence of the early primary schools, Makeke College, Liahona College, and the middle schools, was to change students' lives and to help them develop testimonies of the gospel. When President McKay visited Tonga in 1955, he told the missionaries and teachers that he believed in education because he could see endless good from good teachers.[12] President McKay considered the schools an adjunct to the mission.

From the 1930s on, the mission had operated a branch of the

Church at Makeke College, and when Liahona opened its doors, branches were organized there. By 1964 there were four branches, and President Dalton organized the school into a separate district. This arrangement was not maintained for long because the American teachers at the school were needed in district leadership positions beyond the confines of Liahona. For this reason the Liahona District of the Church was combined with Hihifo District in July 1966.

It has been unusual for non-Mormons to graduate from Liahona, because most nonmembers join the Church while they attend the school. Formal religion classes are an important part of the curriculum.

About 1964, President Dalton, Principal Harmon, and the senior class advisor decided to call every graduate who was willing and worthy (which was most of them) to fill a short-term mission. "We called the senior class for about a three- or four-week period," said President Dalton, "assigned them to be companions of the regular missionaries, and sent them out to function as regular missionaries. Those youngsters loved that experience so much that they all wanted to be full-time missionaries."[13] President Dalton later called many of these young people, male and female, to serve full-time missions. At the end of 1965, there were 214 Tongan missionaries serving in Tonga. During that year, 1019 converts were baptized members of the Church. Many of them had been converted by graduates of Liahona High School. As Elder Matthew Cowley said in 1947, "Your school is your greatest missionary."[14]

POINTING TOWARD STAKEHOOD

Efforts of many kinds ultimately culminated in the creation of the first Tonga stake in September 1968. It could not have happened in 1958, when the first stake was organized in New Zealand, because there were not enough Latter-day Saints in Tonga to sustain and support a stake. And numbers of members were not all that was lacking; the Tongan Saints needed more knowledge of Church organization, and, at that time, the general authorities wanted a higher percentage of the members to be endowed in the temple before stakes could be organized. But in the next ten years the Tongan Saints grew in numbers, in administrative ability, and in number of endowed temple attenders.

Unlike the Polynesian Saints in New Zealand, Samoa, and Hawaii, where relatively large numbers of members traveled to the temple in Hawaii, most Tongan Saints were unable to go to the temple until after the New Zealand Temple was dedicated in 1958. After that time, however, Tongan Saints journeyed to New Zealand yearly in groups of fifty to one hundred and fifty people. Year by year the Tongan Church was strengthened by the members who had covenanted with the Lord to live a higher spiritual and moral law.

In 1966 President John H. Groberg traveled to the New Zealand Temple with a large group of members. The Tongan Saints remained in the temple as long as it was open. They did work for their own kindred dead and then devoted their time to doing names that were supplied from Salt Lake City. But, since President Groberg felt strongly that Tongan Saints should do temple work only for their own dead, during 1967 he pushed genealogical research among the people who planned to go to the temple that year. When the 1967 excursion departed, the participants were prepared to do thousands of Tongan names in the temple. Because President Groberg had emphasized genealogical research, the Tongan Saints came that much closer to being prepared for the independence of a stake.

Until 1959, the Tongan Saints did not have access to the entire Doctrine and Covenants in their own language. In that year the Church published Ermel J. Morton's translation of it and of the Pearl of Great Price. Elder Morton, who served as principal of Liahona College from 1951 until 1957, completed the translation of these sacred books in 1956, but three years were required for checking and proofreading. Elder Morton also translated a number of other items, including tracts, George Q. Cannon's *History of the Church for Young People,* "Joseph Smith's Own Story," and a Tongan grammar. After leaving Tonga in 1957, he, along with Elder Groberg, was assigned to translate the temple ceremony into Tongan. Elders Morton and Groberg carried out this assignment in the Idaho Falls Temple.

Every mission president devoted considerable energy to the matter of providing translated lessons for the organizations of the Church. In 1967 William Roberts from New Zealand visited Tonga as coordinator of the Translation and Distribution Center that was being established in Auckland. Elder Roberts interviewed a number of Tongans as prospective full-time translators for the Church. No longer would the mission president be required to supervise the production of Church materials, nor would the mission auxiliary leaders have to do the translating. Elder Roberts appointed John Latu as translation coordinator for Tonga. Elder Roberts also hired translators both in Tonga and in New Zealand. In the long run, however, the translators in Tonga did the best work because they were constantly in contact with the language. By the late 1970s the translation and printing functions were done in Tonga,[15] and in the early 1980s this work was transferred to Salt Lake City.

Presidents Stone, M. Vernon Coombs (who returned in 1959), Dalton, and Groberg directed many organizational changes both within the missionary system and in the districts. The mission presidents started using methods similar to those employed in the other missions of the Church. At Liahona, not only President Dalton but also President Groberg emphasized missionary work. President Groberg organized the Liahona Missionary Committee, which helped direct many intensive training sessions for missionaries who had been called. They also supervised missionary preparation classes at Liahona.

When John H. Groberg became mission president in July 1966, only six foreign missionaries were allowed in Tonga. By the time he left in 1969, he had succeeded in raising the quota to twelve. His success was grounded on a special relationship he had developed with Prince Tungi and his family during his first mission. President Groberg had become acquainted with the royal family in Ha'apai while they vacationed there. He was so close to them that he even told the children bedtime stories. Once, while sailing between islands, Elder Groberg and Prince Tungi found themselves the only passengers who could stand the high seas without getting sick. For several hours they played the piano for each other and conversed freely. As mission president, Elder Groberg continued the warm relationship with Prince Tungi and his wife. When Tungi became king on July 4, 1967, President and Sister Groberg were among the small number of guests who were invited to attend the formal coronation ceremonies. The Grobergs retain a sincere love for the royal family.

Queen Salote too was generally considerate of the Church, especially during her later years. But because of her strong relationship with the Wesleyan Free Church of Tonga, many Tongans believed that it was anti-Tongan to leave the Wesleyan Church and join the Mormons. After her death, however, the LDS Church grew rapidly.[16]

While the missionaries were enlarging the membership, district leaders were busy making changes and improvements in their organizations. President Dalton formed district councils that functioned in much the same manner as stake high councils. In 1964 the mission held the first youth conference. In the same year, President Dalton directed a mission-wide leadership training course. Step by step the Tongan Saints learned the skills and abilities that were necessary to operate independently.

After President McKay's visit to Tonga in 1955, the Tongan Saints received periodic visits by general authorities and General Board members. Elder Marion G. Romney came in 1958. Then, during the 1960s, Elders Longden, Petersen, Stapley, Monson, and Young came to visit. Elder Thomas S. Monson, who was area supervisor for the South Pacific area, visited Tonga in November 1965. In his major address to the Tongan Saints, he encouraged them to prepare themselves and the Church for stakehood. The next three years saw the Saints move steadily toward that objective.

THE CREATION OF NUKU'ALOFA STAKE AND THE JUBILEE CELEBRATION

By 1968 the Church in Tonga had the size, experience, and priesthood strength needed to maintain a stake. During April, Elder Monson visited the mission and concluded that Tonga was ready; he recommended to the Council of the Twelve that the first stake should be created. President Groberg received notice on June 16 that Elder

Nuku'alofa, capital city of Tonga. (Photo by R. Lanier Britsch.)

Monson's recommendation had been approved. On August 11, he announced that Elder Howard W. Hunter and Elder Monson would be coming to Tonga on September 4 to organize the stake.

When they arrived, they were met by a large group of Saints and the Liahona band. Elders Hunter and Monson almost immediately set to work interviewing priesthood leaders to determine who the stake president should be. After a day and a half of interviews and discussions, they had decided who should lead and where the stake boundaries should be set. The new stake president was Orson H. White, superintendent of Church Schools Tonga. He had had considerable administrative experience in the Church, having been in several bishoprics. He chose as his counselors Tonga Toutai Paletu'a and 'Uliti Uata. Jay A. Cahoon, a former mission president who was working at Liahona as a builder, was called as patriarch. The Nuku'alofa Stake was formed from Loto and Hihifo Districts. Nine branches became eight wards. Hihifo District continued to exist.[17]

September, October, and November 1968 were three of the busiest months in the history of the Church in Tonga. Beginning with the creation of the stake, President Groberg, President White, the missionaries, and the Saints were involved in what seemed to be a never-ending round of meetings, feasts, and planning sessions. President Groberg, after learning that the missionaries had baptized 108 people during September, challenged the elders and sisters to prepare themselves mentally and spiritually to baptize 500 people in November. "It was emphasized," the mission secretary wrote, "that we should not strive for figures but strive for the spirit of the Lord, and if it is His will, then surely this goal could be achieved." Other events of this brief period included a visit to the mission and stake by Bishop Victor L. Brown of the Presiding Bishopric; J. Thomas Fyans, then of Translation and Distribution Services; and several other representatives from departments of the Church. There were also several district meetings; a mission presidents' seminar in Noumea, New Caledonia; and a visit to the stake and mission by Elder Henry D. Taylor, assistant to the Council of the Twelve, during which he conducted the first quarterly stake conference and held conferences at Eua and Ha'apai. All of this, however, took second place to another event, the fiftieth anniversary Golden Jubilee Celebration.

The timing of this event seemed to be inaccurate no matter how one figured it, and many people told President Groberg that a better, more accurate time should be chosen. Celebrations could have been held in 1941 (fifty years after 1891, when the first elders arrived in

Tonga), 1957 (fifty years after missionaries reopened Tonga in 1907), or in 1966 (fifty years after the mission was officially formed), but they were not. The idea for a Golden Jubilee came to President Groberg several years before he was called as mission president. As a young bishop in Idaho, he sat in his office one day trying to solve some problems relating to a chapel he was building. In a moment of inspiration, the Spirit whispered to him, "You'll go to Tonga, and there you'll preside over the mission and you'll conduct a fiftieth anniversary jubilee—and don't forget that."[18] He did not forget.

When preparations were underway for the Jubilee, President Groberg learned that fiftieth anniversaries had special significance for the Tongan people. In earlier times, anyone who lived fifty years was considered old. When the Jubilee was proclaimed as a Golden Anniversary, not only the common people but also the nobles and royalty enthusiastically supported and encouraged the celebration. Surprisingly, President Groberg also learned that November 1968 was an appropriate time for the festivities. He wrote, "It was not until about September or October 1968 that we received a letter from the widow of the first Tongan Mission President—Willard L. Smith—with this note: 'I thought you would be interested in the following which I have copied from my husband's diary. "November 1918 - We held the first mission wide conference of the Tongan Mission this month -etc." ' "[19] And so in 1968, even without President Groberg's knowing it, he and his associates had chosen to hold the Jubilee fifty years after the first mission conference!

On October 30, President Groberg learned that President N. Eldon Tanner of the First Presidency had agreed to attend the Jubilee. Saints and friends of the Church began to gather from the outer islands several weeks before the celebration began on November 25. Members of the four Tongatapu districts built large Tongan houses for the visitors at Liahona, but so many people came that additional shelters had to be constructed. The king and premier notified Groberg that they were ready and willing to participate, and a history of the mission by Ermel J. Morton would be ready in time for distribution at the meetings.

The actual celebration lasted from November 25 to December 1, 1968. President and Sister Tanner; Lavern Parmley, president of the Primary Associations of the Church; and Kathryn S. Gilbert of the Relief Society General Board arrived in Tonga on November 27. The Liahona band played, choirs sang, leaders gave excellent talks, and the members danced and ate.

The most important day of the celebration was "Remembrance Day," November 29. During services that began at 9:00 A.M., the king's choir (made up almost entirely of Wesleyan ministers) sang, Viliami S. Kioa gave a brief history of the mission, President Groberg and President Tanner spoke, and the king, Taufa'ahau Topou IV, made the concluding remarks. (His wife, Queen Halaevalu Mata'aho, spoke to the assembled Relief Society sisters at an earlier session.) In the afternoon, 6,507 people attended the feast and 11,067 people attended the dance festival on the palace grounds in the evening. The Golden Jubilee was a huge success, but President Groberg was especially pleased because he believed it had been a spiritual event and not just a celebration.

Soon after the festivities ended, President Groberg learned that the missionaries had baptized 507 people in November. During the year, 1,767 converts were baptized, more than at any time before. The year 1968 must be judged a great year in Tongan LDS history.[20]

FROM 1969 TO THE PRESENT

The years since 1968 have been impressive in many ways. The Church has continued to grow in numbers, but more importantly, the Tongan Saints now operate virtually every part of the Church. The Church is a Tongan Church.

Since the first stake was organized in 1968, nine other stakes have been created in Tonga. The first two additional ones were organized on Tongatapu on July 26, 1970. The third was created there one year later, and the fourth was organized in Vava'u in December 1975 and on and on. Tongans preside in all ten stakes.

During the last twelve or fifteen years every home in Tonga has probably been visited by the missionaries between 150 and 200 times, on the average.[21] Nevertheless, growth continues at a rapid pace. By December 31, 1983, there were officially 31,723 Latter-day Saints in Tonga (although Elder Groberg estimates that this number is approximately 5,000 members high because of record-keeping inaccuracies). According to recent estimates, between 25 and 30 percent of Tonga's one hundred thousand people are Latter-day Saints. This is the highest percentage of members in any nation in the world.

Tonga now produces more missionaries than can be effectively used within the country. No area in the world produces more missionaries in proportion to Church population than Tonga. In 1977 and 1978, Church leaders in Tonga and Salt Lake City began calling

Young Tongan missionary sisters dressed in a combination of modern dresses and traditional apron or *tavalu*. (Courtesy Ralph A. Britsch.)

Since about 1908 the Church has made use of small, easily transportable missionary quarters. Similar houses are in use in Samoa. (Photo by James J. Pinegar.)

Tongan elders to serve missions in other countries. (Many Tongans had served missions elsewhere before that time, but they were usually called from other states or countries.) In 1978, six Tongans were sent to Bolivia; twelve went to the Philippines; four were called to the Suva, Fiji Mission; and a number accepted missions in the Honolulu Hawaii Mission, in which they were assigned to preach the gospel in Micronesia. Some of these elders are supported by members of their families who live in the United States; a few are partially supported by their stakes in Tonga; but most receive assistance from the general missionary fund of the Church.[22] Year by year larger and larger numbers of Liahona High School graduates have gone on missions. In 1983, 100 percent of the graduating class accepted calls to serve missions either in Tonga or in other parts of the world. Because their numbers are so large and because of the financial burden, the length of missions for Tongans in Tonga (and Samoans in Samoa) was changed in 1982 to twelve months.

Tongan missionaries generally live in the homes of members; the wards feed them, give them referrals, see that they keep the mission rules, and so on. (A similar system operates in Samoa. A major difference is that in Samoa older couple missionaries have been called to supervise the younger missionaries.)

The large number of former missionaries in Tonga is giving great strength to the Church there. When Elder Groberg organized the tenth stake in 1983, every significant position was filled by a returned missionary. One cannot imagine a stronger situation for growth and development.

In 1974, Tonga Toutai Paletu'a, who had served as a counselor in the mission presidency, as a patriarch, and as a stake president, was called as president of the Tonga Nuku'alofa Mission. He was released in 1977 and was soon called as regional representative of the Council of the Twelve. He was replaced by Sione T. Latu, another experienced Tongan leader. Still another Tongan, Pita F. Hopoate, followed President Latu. The succession of Tongan presidents was broken when Melvin Butler was called to lead that mission. At this writing, President Butler is the only non-Tongan in a major position (stake president, regional representative) in the Church there. The growth of the Church in Tonga has never moved faster than in the past ten years. From 1977 to 1980, under President Latu, convert baptisms reached an all-time high, averaging 2,780 baptisms per year. There were 2,261 convert baptisms in 1983.

Church schools in Tonga have also seen growth and change. From

Saineha High School at Neiafu, Vava'u, Tonga was dedicated by Elder John H. Groberg in 1978. (Courtesy Norman Faldmo, Jr.)

the mid-1960s until 1978 the school system was called Church Schools Tonga; it is now called Church Educational System Tonga. The new designation includes not only the ten middle schools and two high schools but also a rapidly growing seminary program. Saineha High School, Liahona's sister institution in Neiafu, Vava'u, was dedicated by Elder John H. Groberg in May 1978. This new school, with its seventeen classrooms and other facilities, is large by the standards of the area. Two hundred and sixty students came under the tutelage of the seventeen faculty members in its first year. Saineha, like all other Church schools in Tonga, is administered by a Tongan principal.

Almost two thousand young people are now enrolled in Church schools in Tonga. The superintendent of the system from 1975 to 1981 was James William Harris. Brother Harris, a Tongan, was educated in New Zealand, at the Church College of Hawaii (where he was student-body president and valedictorian of his class in 1963), and at Brigham Young University, where he earned a master's degree in educational administration. In 1981, Vuki Tangitau, who holds advanced degrees from the Provo campus of BYU, was appointed associate area director.

Until 1978, school administrators in Salt Lake City and Tonga believed they were providing well for the religious education of the Tongan Saints. It was determined, however, that many Latter-day

In the 1980s the Church has made use of prefabricated frame chapels that have been imported from New Zealand. (Photo by James J. Pinegar.)

Saints, both young and old, were not directly involved in the Church schools and therefore were not receiving religious training on a weekday basis. In February 1978, early-morning seminary classes were introduced in chapels throughout the islands, and before the end of the year, 830 students were enrolled. Pene Muti was director of religious education within the Church Education System Tonga at that time.[23]

PHYSICAL FACILITIES

Replacing old coconut-frond fale chapels and building attractive modern structures to house the constantly growing wards and branches of Tonga has been a major continuing undertaking. As was noted earlier, the Church building missionaries constructed the first concrete brick meetinghouses in the islands. Although new chapels have been built almost continuously, small branches and wards have either had trouble qualifying financially for chapels or their numbers have been so small that it did not seem wise to building administrators to spend money on small buildings. But a breakthrough in small meetinghouse construction occurred in 1980, when small prefabricated wood buildings of approximately twenty by forty feet in dimension were created (for groups of around twenty members) and shipped in from New Zealand. The number of Latter-day Saint meetinghouses grew from fifty-six in 1979 to sixty-eight in 1980 to eighty-seven in 1981. Many of the new buildings were larger meetinghouses of masonry construction, but the new small chapels contributed significantly to the large growth.

In 1983, eighteen new meetinghouses were either under construction or completed. At that time there were seventy-six permanent meetinghouses for the 103 wards and branches. As is true in Samoa, walking is the main mode of transportation, so the Church has attempted to place chapels no more than three miles apart.

When the tithing faithfulness program for financial support from Church headquarters was introduced in April 1982, all Tongan stakes qualified for new buildings. Also in 1982, the stakes in Tonga implemented the full Church operations and maintenance program as practiced in the United States. Local unpaid physical facilities representatives (PFR) who are called by stake presidents have taken responsibility for chapel maintenance, a task that was formerly in the hands of paid employees of the Presiding Bishopric's Office. The director of temporal affairs's office in Honolulu supervises construction and maintenance in Tonga, Samoa, Guam-Micronesia, and Hawaii. Most construction projects are now being done by the awarding of contracts to private contractors, in contrast to earlier years in which labor was voluntary.

On March 3, 1982, the Tongan Islands were hit by one of the most destructive hurricanes in the kingdom's history, "Hurricane Isaac." Glen Lung, assistant to the director of temporal affairs for the Hawaii and South Seas area, wrote:

> Hurricane Isaac, which wreaked such terrible destruction, such that over 90 percent of the homes in Ha'apai Islands were destroyed, was also a blessing. As is so often the case in disaster it brought out some of the best in human behavior and demonstrated the great strength of the LDS Church. Immediately, it was noticeable that except for minor roof damage, not one LDS chapel was destroyed. They were quickly repaired and used as temporary shelters for nonmembers as well as members. The Church quickly allocated over a million dollars of relief funds plus large commodity shipments which were distributed through normal church procedure. Members were expected to work in return for the church assistance rendered. With help from the Presiding Bishopric's Office, many small simple new homes were built for the Saints. The whole population was so impressed by the Church members and the welfare program that missionary work surged forth.[24]

A modern chapel near the campus of Liahona High School. (Photo by R. Lanier Britsch.)

Missionaries stand in front of a small temporary chapel in the island of Tongatapu, 1983. (Photo by James J. Pinegar.)

TONGAN AREA CONFERENCE

Although the weather was extremely wet on February 24 and 25, 1976, when President Spencer W. Kimball conducted the first area conference of the Church in Tonga, 71 percent of the Tongan Church members attended the two days of sacred services. This was only the second visit by a president of the Church to Tonga, although President Kimball had visited Tonga in 1972 while he was a member of the Council of the Twelve. Even though the huge feast was somewhat waterlogged, more than ten thousand members and friends attended it. The Liahona band, two hundred *lakalaka* dancers, and more than one thousand others performed in the cultural activity during the first afternoon.

The principal reason for the conference was for the president of the Church and other general authorities to teach the gospel to the members in Tonga who were unable to attend conferences in Salt Lake City. The other general authorities there were President N. Eldon Tanner and Elders Bruce R. McConkie, Marion D. Hanks, William H. Bennett, Robert L. Simpson, Robert D. Hales, Loren C. Dunn, and Bishop Victor L. Brown. President Kimball urged the Tongan Saints to stay in Tonga, "to make Zion bloom where you are." He asked the Tongan members to cooperate in the principle of establishing Zion in Tonga and to teach the gospel through the Church schools.[25]

The Tongan Saints were working toward President Kimball's goal of a local Zion even before he issued the challenge. Perhaps more than in any other country in the Pacific, the Saints in Tonga were working toward self-government and also to extend their missionary influence to other areas. In April 1974, President Kimball revealed his vision for the expansion of the gospel to all the world.[26] In that great talk, he suggested that nation by nation the various peoples should produce enough missionaries to handle the needs of their own countries and then send them to other lands where more missionaries are needed. Tonga may have provided the model for such action.[27]

THE NUKU'ALOFA TONGA TEMPLE

If there is a single outward manifestation that marks the maturity of the Church in a geographical area, it is the building of a temple. As much as in any area of the Pacific, the building of the Nuku'alofa Tonga Temple signifies that the Church has fully come of age in the Friendly Islands. Church activity in Tonga is unusually high, as is evident from the high rate of tithe paying, the high average attendance

President Spencer W. Kimball turned the first ceremonial shovelfuls of dirt to commence construction of the Tongan Temple, February 18, 1981. (Courtesy Ralph A. Britsch.)

at sacrament meetings, and the high level of missionary work done by the Tongan members. Almost all offices in the Church are held by Tongans. Any hints of paternalism are long since gone. The Church in Tonga is a mature and powerful organization.

For many years before the announcement of a temple came, the Saints in Tonga had hoped the First Presidency and Council of the Twelve would decide to build a temple there. The cost of flying to New Zealand was high, and even the wealthiest members had trouble going to the temple frequently. When Tonga Toutai Paletu'a, first president of the new temple but then a regional representative, heard the announcement that a temple was going to be built in his country, he cried for joy. "We all cried," he said. "We felt such joy. I was so thrilled I had to call my wife and tell her. I couldn't hold back the tears. I felt like my dream had come true."[28] President Paletu'a was attending general conference in Salt Lake City in April 1980 when he heard the good news. At that time he had no idea that a year later he would be called to preside as president of the temple.

On February 18, 1981, President Spencer W. Kimball visited Tonga to break ground and dedicate the site for the temple. His visit was short; he was on a quick trip of thirteen days that included groundbreakings in Tahiti and Samoa as well as Tonga. The land

The Tonga Temple was dedicated by President Gordon B. Hinckley on August 9, 1983. (Courtesy Norman Faldmo, Jr.)

chosen for the temple is immediately to the side of Liahona High School. As is true in Laie and Pesega, the Church leaders chose to place the temple next to an important Church school. The close relationship of spiritual and secular learning was once again symbolically represented to the Church and the world.

Over seven thousand people gathered to watch as President Kimball turned the first shovelfuls of black soil. The event was further dignified by the presence of King Taufa'ahau Tupou IV, who participated in the ceremony. The King had approved the site and authorized the ninety-nine year lease on the land. Elder Adney Y. Komatsu, executive administrator of the area, also attended the groundbreaking.

Generally, the Brethren have called an experienced member from the United States as the first president of a foreign temple. But while President Kimball was in Tonga for the groundbreaking, he felt inspired to call Brother Paletu'a to that position. President Kimball asked Paletu'a to see him when he came to general conference in April 1981. The call was extended at that time.

Plans for the temple were completed by November 1981, and construction began. The Tonga Temple is nearly an identical twin to the new temple in Samoa. Both temples are 12,500 square feet in size. With the exception of the short delays caused by Hurricane Isaac, the project moved forward without significant problems. In fact, it was completed and ready for visitors nine or ten days before it was scheduled to open to the public. Seeing this as a wonderful opportunity to have thousands more nonmembers go through the building before it was closed to outsiders, Elder Groberg, who was again assigned as executive administrator of the area, decided to move up the day for having the official opening ceremony.

Because Elder Groberg had promised the king that he would personally show him through the building and explain its purposes, on July 9, 1983, the King of Tonga once again visited the Liahona complex. As the king and queen arrived, they rode past one-half mile of roads lined with Latter-day Saint school children dressed in green and white school uniforms. The children waved and chanted the traditional greeting of respect for their royalty—"Tue, Tue, Tue." The occasion was marked by elaborate festivities—bands, choirs, dances, and the presentation to the king of a statue of himself, and so on. But the significant fact was that the temple was now open to visitors. Before its doors were closed to those without recommends, over 50 percent of the Tongan people toured the sacred edifice.

Because of health problems, President Kimball was unable to attend the dedication services. President Gordon B. Hinckley presided over and conducted the first session in the temple on August 9. In a

Elder John H. Groberg poses at the open house of the Tonga Temple with temple president Tonga Toutai Paletu'a (at Groberg's left) and his counselors. (Courtesy John H. Groberg.)

Young Tongan guides pause in prayer at the beginning of several days of open houses before the dedication of the Tongan Temple. Note the extremely long tapa cloth upon which they are seated. (Courtesy John H. Groberg.)

King Taufa'ahau Tupou IV, King of Tonga, and Elder John H. Groberg have been friends for many years. Here they are seen conversing in the office of the royal palace. (Courtesy John H. Groberg.)

powerful address he acknowledged a group of prisoners who, with their guards, had visited the temple open house. According to the *Church News* account, he said as he thought of them he also thought there must be many good Tongan spirits on the other side of the veil who, as it were, are prisoners who cannot go forward. "I think I can hear in my mind their wardens cry out to the Tongan Saints, 'won't you do something to help them?' " He asked those assembled to remember their forebears. "All you are and all you have came through them. The house is here, the keys are here. Unlock that door that these good Tongans may go forward into immortality and eternal life." In the dedicatory prayer, President Hinckley said, among many other profound sentiments, "We thank thee for the coming forth of the Book of Mormon with its record of the forebears of the people of Tonga." Once again the leaders of the Church affirmed the long-held belief that the Polynesian people are descendants of Lehi.

Because of pressing responsibilities elsewhere in the world, President Hinckley left Tonga the next day, but six more dedication sessions were held in the Liahona High School gymnasium. Fifteen thousand people, over half the Tongan Church members, were able to attend and to hear Elders Howard W. Hunter, Marvin J. Ashton, and L. Tom Perry of the Council of the Twelve repeat the dedicatory prayer and speak.

Like the Saints in Samoa, who have worked hard to keep their temple busy, the Tongan Saints have used the new temple far beyond its projected capacity. In December 1983, Tongan members of the Church did over five thousand endowments for their kindred dead, twice the capacity of the temple. As Elder Glen Lung, regional representative in Hawaii, said concerning the Polynesian Saints, "Nothing daunts their pursuit of righteousness."[29]

PART 7

FIJI AND OTHER ISLANDS

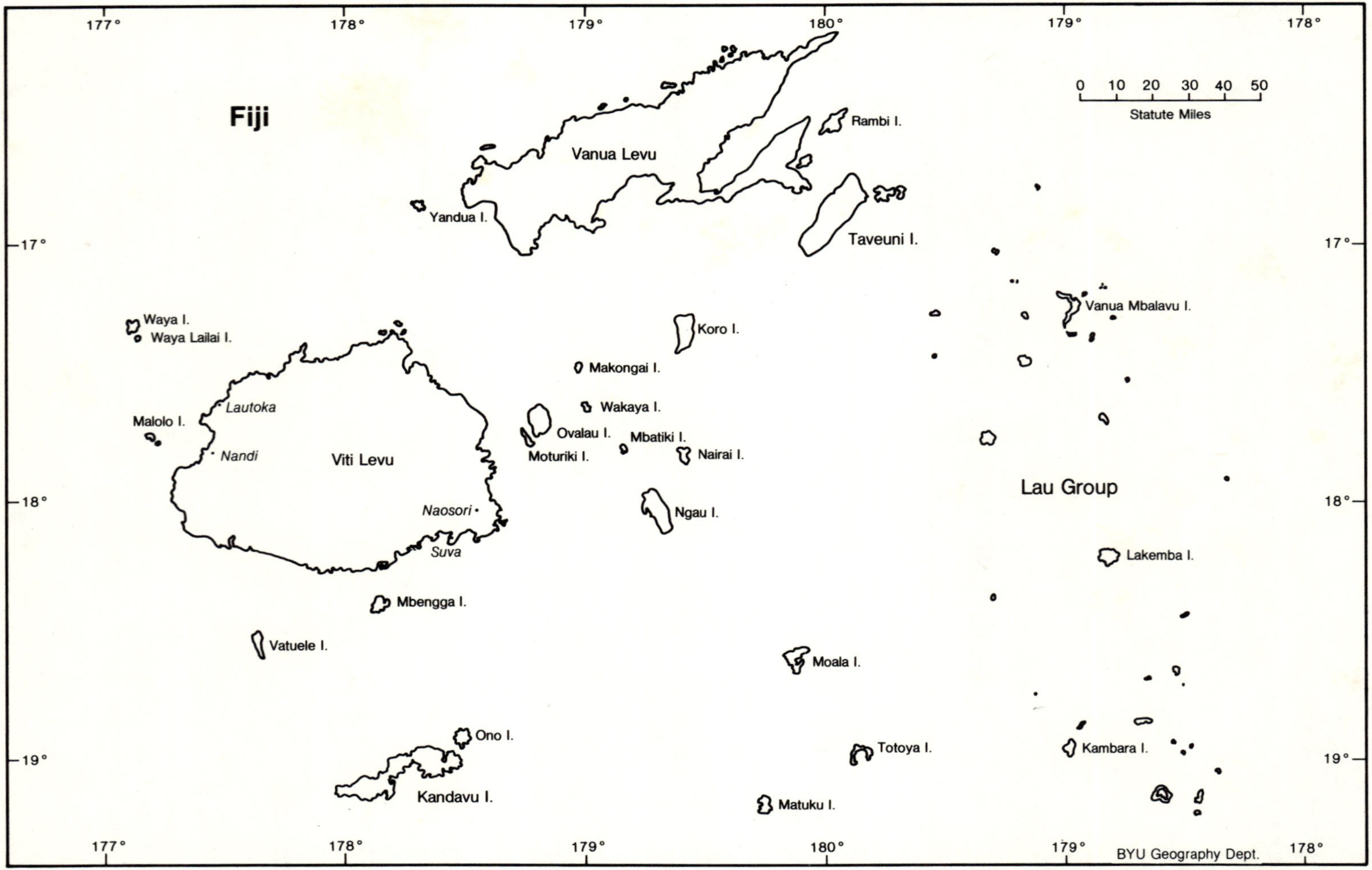
Fiji
177°
178°
179°
180°
179°
178°
17°
18°
19°
0 10 20 30 40 50
Statute Miles
Vanua Levu
Rambi I.
Yandua I.
Taveuni I.
Vanua Mbalavu I.
Waya I.
Waya Lailai I.
Koro I.
Makongai I.
Lautoka
Wakaya I.
Malolo I.
Ovalau I.
Mbatiki I.
Nandi
Viti Levu
Moturiki I.
Nairai I.
Lau Group
Naosori
Ngau I.
Suva
Lakemba I.
Mbengga I.
Vatuele I.
Moala I.
Ono I.
Totoya I.
Kambara I.
Kandavu I.
Matuku I.
BYU Geography Dept.

CHAPTER 28

THE NEWER, THE SMALLER, AND THE NON-POLYNESIAN AREAS

"As we have slowed down to look around," wrote President Ebbie L. Davis in 1973 as he reflected on his missionary responsibility, "it has become increasingly clear that there is so much to do here that we are going to get very little done. There are so many programs—construction, real estate, translation, leadership training, increasing [numbers of] missionaries, Church schools, localization of leadership, new areas to open, etc.—that we will only be able to push all of them forward a little way, rather than pushing a few [programs] a long way. . . . With our six separate national governments to deal with, five kinds of money, ten major languages, and the great distances between our areas in the mission, at times it seems like an impossible task. Half of the mission president's time is usually spent away from the office and home. We have all three major South Pacific ethnic groups in our mission. There are Polynesians in Rarotonga and Niue; Melanesians in Fiji, the New Hebrides, and the Solomons; and Micronesians in the Gilberts and Nauru. Variations and adaptations are required in the missionary program and the leadership training program for all of these distinct peoples. It seems quite clear that this is a Mission of Missions. Some day divisions will have to be made along ethnic and cultural lines, if not national lines. Until their time comes it will be the responsibility of the mission president to try his best to make sure all areas get equal and appropriate time and care for their particular needs."[1]

President Davis was describing the Fiji Suva Mission in 1973, but his words, with only a few name changes, might well have described the Micronesia-Guam Mission area in 1980. In fact, in an interview with President Ferron C. Losee in 1984, he reported almost the same situation. He said that his mission field fulfilled the prophecies relating to "those on the isles of the sea." He pointed out that the Micronesia-

Guam Mission covers a vast amount of territory—it is six thousand miles across—and has numerous cultural groups. At least nine major languages are spoken in different island groups (plus English, Japanese, and some Filipino dialects). There are six governing bodies in the Micronesia-Guam Mission. All of the problems of newness that President Davis mentioned concerning Fiji certainly apply there.

THE FIJI MISSION AREA: HUB OF THE SOUTHWEST PACIFIC

For the first 110 years that the Church was in the Pacific, missionary work was limited to the peoples of Polynesia and Australia. It was not until 1954 that missionary work began in the Melanesian Islands, specifically in Fiji. Anthropologists generally classify the peoples of Fiji, New Caledonia, Vanuatu (formerly the New Hebrides), the Solomons, and New Guinea as part of the Pacific Negroid family. Great diversity exists, however. As a rule, the peoples of this area have black rather than brown skin, curly or kinky hair rather than the generally straighter hair of Polynesia, and smaller but taller body build. There is little question that Latter-day Saint missionaries were kept away from the Melanesian areas during earlier times because of the restriction against blacks holding the priesthood. Until the mid- to late-1950s, however, no one with high ecclesiastical authority in the Church had seriously looked into the question of the eligibility of the Melanesians to hold the priesthood. Even after missionaries were assigned to Fiji in 1954, there was some question about this matter, but President McKay was satisfied by anthropologists at the National Museum in Suva that the Melanesian peoples were in no way related to African negroes. In 1958 he authorized Church leaders to ordain Fijians, who have a considerable admixture of Polynesian blood, to the priesthood. Although some Fijian families had joined the Church before that time, this move by President McKay did much to give the work momentum among the local people.

The history of Fiji is filled with all the drama and interest of the old South Pacific. The local people were regarded by foreign visitors, settlers, and missionaries, as treacherous and dangerous cannibals. From 1860 to the end of the century, however, a complete social revolution took place. Credit for this change goes to dedicated civic and government leaders, both Fijian and British, and to Christian missionaries. Lasting missionary efforts had been started by Methodist preachers in 1835. By 1840 a printing press had been imported from

Britain, and portions of the New Testament were soon published in Fijian.[2]

The accomplishments of the missionaries were many. As Latourette says, "Their preaching, their training of teachers, their translation and printing of the Bible, their creation of a system of elementary schools, their systematic preparation of inquirers for church membership, and their own devotion had marked results."[3] Among these results were the cessation of tribal warfare and the end of cannibalism. Before the turn of the century, the vast majority of Fijians had espoused Christianity as taught by one or another of the various denominations.

There are some interesting similarities between the history and geography of Hawaii and of Fiji. Hawaii lies 22 degrees north and Fiji 17 degrees south of the equator, and their climates are similar. Although Hawaii has only seven islands of importance and Fiji has thirteen (along with another ninety-two that are inhabited and two hundred that are not), the islands of Viti Levu (on which Suva, Nandi, and Laotoka are situated) and Hawaii, "The Big Island," are almost identical in size. Even the total populations of the two areas are similar, Hawaii with 965,000 and Fiji with 612,046 in 1980. Hawaii and Fiji have both relied on sugar and tourism as important sources of income.

This development of the sugar industry in both states has determined, to an unusual degree, their racial and, therefore, cultural configurations. Before the 1860s and the American Civil War, the southern states of the United States produced a large percentage of the world's supply of cotton. But during the Civil War, while the U.S. supply almost ceased, planters in Hawaii and Fiji invested heavily in cotton. Before their efforts had produced a profit, however, the American south was back in business, and Hawaii and Fiji had to look for a better agricultural industry. Sugar was the answer in both places.

Just as in Hawaii, where the plantation magnates brought laborers in from China, Japan, the Philippines, and elsewhere, the sugar producers in Fiji imported first other Melanesians and then thousands of Indians. The Fijian government made arrangements with the British government of India in 1878 to bring in Indian laborers for a period of five years. If the laborers stayed for that time, they were free to go home at their own expense. If they remained for an additional five years, however, their return passage would be paid. Or they could remain in Fiji if they wished. Although there were abuses in the so-called "indenture system," thousands of Indians preferred life in Fiji to that at home in India. By 1916, when recruitment stopped, there were almost forty thousand Indians in Fiji. The Indian part of the population has grown rapidly, far outdistancing the Fijian. By 1978 there were 272,447 Fijians and 306,957 people of Indian extraction.

Most of the Indian immigrants were Hindus and members of castes, highly restricted groups, which, because of religious and economic sanctions, remained separate from one another. But by crossing the sea, the laborers lost caste as far as the people in India were concerned. Furthermore, the conditions on ships and in company housing in Fiji made keeping of caste rules, especially separate eating, impossible. As a result the caste system disappeared among Indians in Fiji.

Belief in Hinduism and Islam, however, has not diminished. Among the Indian population, about 70 percent are Hindu, 25 percent are Muslim, and the remainder are Sikhs and Christians.[4]

Because the Indian people in Fiji have remained much to themselves and have maintained their native languages (Hindi, Urdu, Tamil, and Telugu) and religious beliefs, and because the original immigrants were generally illiterate, for many decades the Indians lagged behind the Fijians in literacy and education. More recently, however, there has been a surge among them to acquire all the education possible. Indians now hold a significant number of government positions as well as places in business, education, and industry. Most Fiji Indians now speak a composite language called Hindustani, which is closely related to Hindi.

Between 1874 and 1970, Fiji was a British colony. Suva was the site of the administrative offices not only for Fiji, but also for all other British areas of the Western Pacific. But in 1970 Fiji gained independent dominion status. The constitution guarantees rights similar to those found in the U.S. Constitution. English is the language of government.

LATTER-DAY SAINT MISSIONARY WORK IN FIJI

Latter-day Saint missionary work in Fiji began officially in May 1954, when the First Presidency assigned this area to the Samoan Mission. The following August, President Howard B. Stone sent Elders Boyd L. Harris and Sheldon L. Abbott to begin working in Suva. They organized the Suva Branch on September 5, 1954. Only two missionaries were allowed into the country by immigration officials, and these elders probably would not have been allowed had there not been a small group of Tongan members of the Church living there.[5] For several decades, Cecil B. Smith, a part-Tongan, and Mele (Mary) Vea Ashley and their families had carried on Church meetings on a small scale. When the first missionaries arrived in Suva, they spent their time working with all people who were interested in their message, but they concentrated their efforts on the Tongan and Samoan minority. This population base was too small for much success.

The work in Fiji did not receive the necessary encouragement for it to grow until January 1955, when President David O. McKay stopped over in Suva. He, like many missionaries and mission leaders before him, traveled through Fiji without considering it seriously as a mission field. Because he was delayed for a day in Suva, he happened to meet Elders Harris and Abbott on the street. Evidently he was not aware that there were missionaries or members of the Church there. On Sunday, January 9, President and Sister McKay and Elder Franklin D. Murdock attended a sacrament meeting at the home of Brother Cecil Smith. In attendance were twenty-eight members of the Church. President McKay told the little group that he considered the occasion significant. He said that when he and Hugh J. Cannon visited Suva in 1921, they did not feel that the time was right to introduce the gospel. Now, however, he felt inspired to tell the Saints that it was time to begin building up the kingdom of God in Fiji. He emphasized example, personal missionary work, and good deeds. Find a piece of land upon which to build a chapel, he suggested.[6]

In late March, the Church purchased a large piece of land at Des Veuex and Berry roads, on a hill overlooking the city and harbor. President McKay, Brother Murdock, and Wendell B. Mendenhall had seen the land. When the Church Building Committee prepared plans for the chapel, they did so with the small size of the branch in mind. President McKay, however, decided that the Suva chapel should be a manifestation of the Church's interest in the area and asked that a large building be constructed. The completed chapel is almost as big as a standard stake center. It has all of the normal Latter-day Saint chapel features, such as a cultural hall with a stage, a kitchen, classrooms, and so on. The Suva chapel is designed to allow free movement of air, and it also has some other adaptations to the tropical climate. For many years the little branch rattled around in the structure, and even they wondered whether President McKay had made a mistake.

While the building was under construction, the First Presidency decided to transfer Fiji to the Tongan Mission because the Tongan mission president regularly passed through Fiji to travel from one area of his mission to another. Also, new Zion elders who were heading for

View of Fiji's first LDS chapel. It was built far beyond the size of the small branch that inhabited it because President McKay had faith that the Church in Fiji would grow. (Photo by R. Lanier Britsch.)

Tonga always came through Fiji. The transfer took place on January 15, 1958.[7] Ninety-three people, a record attendance, were at the meeting.

This record was soon replaced, however, when President McKay visited Suva in May on his return from the New Zealand Temple dedication. On May 4, he dedicated the chapel. Over three hundred people attended the feast, cultural entertainment, and actual dedication services. In his talk, President McKay told the assembly that the time would soon come when not only the chapel but also the recreation hall would be filled to overflowing with members of the Church.

When President McKay arrived in Suva on May 2, he voiced his strong concern that the government was still allowing only two proselyting missionaries into the country. The day following the dedication, President McKay, along with Mission President Fred W. Stone, Wendell B. Mendenhall, and the Church attorney, Morris Scott, visited Sir Ronald Garvey, governor of Fiji. Garvey had attended the meeting and told the visitors that "he was very much impressed with the dedication services of the Suva chapel and [that] he now has a better appreciation of what the Church is doing." After receiving assurances that Mormon missionaries would never be a "charge or a burden" on the colony, and hearing that it is the Church's method to call on all people, Christian or other, Governor Garvey promised President McKay that he would discuss the matter with the council and give a hasty answer. Two weeks later the Church received word that the missionary quota had been increased by six. This remains the quota to the present.[8]

When additional elders arrived, it was possible to broaden the field of activity. Within a year, elders were working in Laotoka, Fiji's second largest city, at Naosori near Suva, and in the Lau group of islands, in the direction of Tonga. In February 1959, President M. Vernon Coombs ordained Gideon Dolo, a Fijian, an elder, and sent him to the Lau group as a missionary along with the foreign elders. He was the first Fijian to hold the Melchizedek Priesthood.[9]

The story of the conversion of the Sokia family, who have become stalwarts in the Church, illustrates well the workings of the Lord among the Fijian people. In about 1948, a relative of the Sokia family who worked for the Carnegie Library in Suva picked up a discarded book that was titled *What of the Mormons?* He later gave it to Kini Sokia, who, with her husband and young family, read the story of the Latter-day Saints and the restored Church. The Sokia family then knew nothing about George Albert Smith, the man who had sent the book to the library. They cherished the book much as they loved the Bible. Kini, however, was a staunch Roman Catholic, and her husband was an inactive Methodist.

A year or two after Latter-day Saint missionaries were assigned to Suva, the elders called at the Sokia home. When they introduced a tract called "Joseph Smith Tells His Own Story," the Sokias made the connection between their book on the Mormons and the message the missionaries were presenting. The Sokia family studied the gospel carefully, and by 1958 every member joined the Church. Even before their conversion Sister Sokia took her children to Primary. They were the first three to graduate from that organization in Fiji.

Over the years since that time, this family—the second Fijian family to join the Church—has been part of the foundation of the Church in Fiji. The oldest son, Josefa, for instance, has grown up in the Church and has held important responsibilities in it. Like any other active Latter-day Saint boy, he held the offices of the Aaronic Priesthood and then served in the MIA and Sunday School. Later he became branch clerk, branch president, district clerk, and district president; in 1974, when he was twenty-eight years old, he was called as a member of the mission presidency. He directed the seminary program for a time.[10]

Progress during the 1960s was steady but not dramatic. By 1966, 150 people regularly attended district conferences in Suva. But three years later the number had grown to almost 500 and the district was divided.[11]

In July 1971, the First Presidency approved the creation of the Fiji Mission, and Elder Howard W. Hunter presided at its organization. At that time there were only seven branches of the Church in Fiji, but Niue and the Cook Islands needed a "home," and they were added to the mission. Total mission membership at the end of 1971 was 3,097.

Sherman Lindholm, who, with his wife, was serving a mission in Suva, was asked to lead the mission during its first year. In 1972, Ebbie L. Davis, who was a teacher at Liahona High School in Tonga, was called to fill the first three-year term as mission president.

By 1972, President McKay's prophecy concerning the large Suva chapel was fulfilled: At every district conference that year the building was filled with Latter-day Saints—Fijians, Indians, Rotumans, Tongans, Samoans, New Zealanders, Australians, Europeans, and Americans.

The growth and development of the Fiji Mission since 1972 has been rapid and varied. President Davis and President Kenneth M. Palmer, who followed him, directed the expansion of the Church into several new areas. They also presided over a redivision of the mission, in 1975, along new lines. They strengthened the educational efforts of the Church, a matter we will discuss shortly, and emphasized translation work in the seven languages that were spoken in the mission. Temple work, too, was stressed.

As was true in other parts of the South Pacific during February 1976, the Saints of the Fiji Suva Mission were encouraged and strengthened by the first area conference in their country. President Spencer W. Kimball, President N. Eldon Tanner, and Elders Haight, Simpson, and Hales spent only six hours with the Fiji-Mission Saints, but during that time the visitors observed a cultural program that included songs and dances from Rotuma, New Caledonia, the Gilbert Islands (now called the Republic of Kiribati), and Fiji. The Saints presented President Kimball with a *tabua,* a sperm-whale tooth, a gift of great prestige.

The general authorities presented the Saints with their special witness of the gospel and taught them concerning their responsibility to be involved in missionary work and in works of brotherly kindness, and to lengthen their stride in building the kingdom of God. Elder Simpson stressed the importance of the Fiji Suva Mission as a leader in taking the gospel to all Pacific peoples. President Kimball emphasized, among other things, the importance of living the Ten Commandments

A Fijian chief performs a ceremonial greeting before President and Sister Spencer W. Kimball and President and Sister N. Eldon Tanner during the first area conference in Fiji, 1976. (Courtesy LDS Church Archives.)

as well as the commandments Jesus taught in the Sermon on the Mount. He said, "There is no greater example of the type of life we Latter-day Saints should follow than the life of the Savior." The 980 people in attendance left the meetings with a new resolve to live more Christ-like lives.[12]

In 1979, about thirty missionaries were assigned to Fiji proper. Of that number, six were from North America, four were allowed from Tonga, and the rest were local missionaries. An additional ten missionaries were laboring in New Caledonia, which had been part of the mission since 1975; eight elders from the British Commonwealth were then working in the New Hebrides (now called Vanuatu), and an other eight missionaries were teaching the gospel in the Gilbert Islands.

Beginning early in the mission's history, considerable effort was dedicated to translation projects. Because of the diversity of languages spoken in various parts of the Fiji Suva Mission, it was difficult to make much headway on many fronts, but some undertakings were more important than others. In 1980 the Church published the Book of Mormon in Fijian. Translation work was done in Fiji and in Salt Lake City.

The development of Church schools in Fiji and the establishment of the Church in New Caledonia, the New Hebrides, and the Gilbert Islands deserve our attention. Both public and private education are provided in Fiji, but most schools are operated either by local committees or by church groups. The leaders of the Church in Suva recognized in the mid-1960s that the Suva chapel afforded an excellent facility for a Church school. Most of the young people of the Church found it necessary before that time to attend schools that were operated by other religious denominations. In an effort to create a Latter-day Saint setting for elementary education, the Church School System approved the creation of the LDS Elementary School in Suva. Brother Charles Mohi was imported from New Zealand to serve as the first principal, and local teachers, mostly LDS, were hired to teach the classes. The school was opened in February 1969.[13] Although there were some periods of adjustment to the local education system during the first three or four years, by the end of 1973 the school had well over a hundred students, and the educational standard satisfied the Church and the government.

Later, the school was divided into schools "A" and "B," with the older grades meeting in a newer chapel in north Suva and the lower grades remaining at the original chapel.[14]

As early as 1970, mission leaders in Tonga and Fiji were talking about opening a high school in Suva or Naosori. Young Latter-day Saints needed the school, and President James P. Christensen and the Fiji missionaries believed that a high school could help attract many young people into the Church. The school could also provide a much-needed service to the people of Fiji. But the idea did not gain support

An aerial view of the LDS Fiji Technical College, Suva, Fiji. (Courtesy Norman Faldmo, Jr.)

among the First Presidency until early 1974. Shortly after he became president of the Church, Spencer W. Kimball sent Commissioner of Education Neal A. Maxwell to Fiji to do a feasibility study. He, along with Alton Wade, who administered Church schools in the Pacific at that time, made a positive recommendation to President Kimball, and the new school, the LDS Fiji Technical College, opened in a beautiful new campus in 1975. The college's curriculum is oriented toward trades and vocations, but it also includes an academic emphasis. Most of the faculty are local people. Howard Wolfgramme was the first principal. Perhaps the most exciting fact is that about half of the student body is composed of Indians (this is also true for the elementary school). These students, many of whom are members of the Church, may well be the future missionaries of the Church to India.[15]

The seminary program of the Church was established in the Fiji Suva Mission in 1973. Since that time the enrollment has grown steadily. In 1978, 128 students were enrolled in home-study classes in seminary, 137 were taking institute courses by individual study, and another 147 students, those who were enrolled at the technical college, were taking daily religion courses.[16] By 1984, 372 students were enrolled at the college.

Church growth in Fiji has been steady and impressive. A number of Latter-day Saints hold positions of prominence in government, education, and business. For example, Ro Tevita Logovatu, a social welfare officer in the Fijian government and paramount chief of the Rewa District surrounding Suva, is an active member of the Church and a graduate of Brigham Young University–Hawaii Campus. Nemani Delaibatiki, also a member, is editor of one of Fiji's two major daily newspapers.

On June 12, 1984, Elder Howard W. Hunter of the Quorum of the Twelve Apostles organized the Suva Fiji Stake. He called Inosi Naga, a convert in 1974, as stake president. President Naga is CES administrator and director of religious education in Fiji. Brother Naga is a man of spirituality and knowledge of the gospel, and he is a fine administrator.[17]

CHURCH ACTIVITY IN NEW CALEDONIA

Church activity in New Caledonia began during the 1950s, and in 1984 the area had over six hundred members. At the time of its beginning, a few Tahitian Latter-day Saints migrated to the French Overseas Territory to work in a nickel smelter. In July 1961, the First Presidency authorized President Kendall Young of the French Polynesia Mission to go to Noumea, the capital of New Caledonia, and organize the sixty Tahitian members into a branch. In October President Young visited Noumea and called Teahu Manoi, an elder in the priesthood, to be the first president of the Noumea Branch.

President Young investigated the possibility of opening missionary work in the territory. He learned that the populace, which consisted at that time of 80,061 people, was divided among Europeans of French extraction (28,454), Melanesians (32,334), and "others" (12,016). By the early 1970s the population had risen to well over one hundred thousand people.

President Young concluded that it was time to preach the gospel in New Caledonia and took the necessary steps to gain government recognition of the Church there. But it proved difficult for him to obtain visas for missionaries. In 1967, President Karl M. Richards of the French Polynesia Mission met with the high commissioner and governor of New Caledonia, Monsieur Jean Risterucci, and convinced him of the need for Mormon missionaries in Noumea. High Commissioner Risterucci approved visas for six missionaries in February 1967, with the understanding that the number would soon be raised to ten. President Richards then asked the First Presidency to authorize missionary work in New Caledonia. In August 1967, Elder Paul H. Dunn of the First Council of the Seventy traveled to Noumea and recommended that it was time to move into New Caledonia. On October 6, 1967, the First Presidency approved this action.

On May 2, 1968, Elder Thomas S. Monson of the Quorum of the Twelve visited Noumea and, under instructions from President David O. McKay, dedicated the land of New Caledonia for the preaching of the gospel. Two months later, on July 15, 1968, the first Latter-day Saint missionaries arrived in Noumea. They were Harold and Jeannine Richards and their daughter Jacquelina. Harold was the son of President Karl M. Richards. Harold had learned French on his first mission in France. Jeannine was a native of France. Their knowledge of the French language and people was essential for success in this area where French was the official language of government and the language of a significant part of the people.

Although the high commissioner had granted the Church permission to have six missionaries, the established churches, particularly the Roman Catholics, opposed this move and successfully delayed the entrance of additional elders until January 1969. At that time Elders James A. Tatton and Lyle W. Parker received visas and entered the country.[18]

When President Richards first met with High Commissioner Risterucci, the commissioner suggested that the Church should buy land and build a large and impressive chapel. With this in mind, Harold Richards bought a choice piece of land. But unfortunately, someone in the Church Building Department decided that the branch in Noumea was too small to justify more than a "first phase" building, a small building that consisted of little more than a chapel area. Because of this tactical error the Church had a difficult time gaining support from French administrators in Noumea.[19]

Although mission leaders in Tahiti were concerned about the Saints and missionaries in New Caledonia, the distance between the two countries was too great for the mission president to visit there very often. The Church did grow during the first five years of the 1970s, but not to the extent that might have been possible with closer supervision. In September 1973 and again in October 1974 Elder Groberg, who was the regional representative, and the mission presidents discussed which mission could better serve the needs of New Caledonia—Tahiti or Fiji. In June 1975 the First Presidency transferred New Caledonia to the Fiji Suva Mission.[20]

The New Caledonian members were soon incorporated into the mainstream of the mission. District and branch leaders attended regional meetings in Suva (a thing that would have been impossible in Papeete), and when the first area conference was held in February 1976, fifty members from New Caledonia traveled to Suva to participate. In May 1976, President Kenneth M. Palmer divided the Noumea Branch into two units. At that time the Noumea Saints also approved a decision to enlarge the chapel. The division of the Noumea Branch gave the district presidency a reason for being. Before long, district officers were directing regular leadership meetings, and a district council, similar to a stake high council, was organized. Mission records reveal that by 1976 the full program of the Church, including seminary, was operating in New Caledonia.

In July 1978, there were 382 members of the Church in this area and a third branch, the Tontouta Branch, had been organized. Through careful and regular negotiations with government officials, President Palmer arranged to have one expatriate (non-French) missionary in New Caledonia for every two French missionaries. This arrangement has made it possible for the Church to increase the number of missionaries and to expand missionary work beyond the Noumea area.

The next big step will be to extend the work among the Melanesian people of New Caledonia. In 1978 the First Presidency called Georges L. Bourget of eastern Canada to replace President Palmer as mission president. President Bourget combined the advantages of Commonwealth citizenship with a native fluency in both English and French. Since that time the church has continued to grow. In 1984 there were over eight hundred members in New Caledonia.

VANUATU (THE NEW HEBRIDES) AND THE SOLOMON ISLANDS

Through the efforts of Presidents Davis and Palmer, the Church established missionary work in the New Hebrides. Although the New Hebrides are made up of eighty islands and a population of close to 90,000 people (approximately the same as Tonga), the Church has moved into this area only since 1974. The organization of the Fiji Mission created the impetus to open missionary work in this area.

The New Hebrides are racially part of Melanesia. The islands were governed until 1980 by a condominium administered jointly by the United Kingdom and France. English, French, and a variety of local dialects are spoken, as well as Bislama, a kind of pidgin English that is rapidly becoming the universal language of Melanesia. The condominium was headed locally by French and British resident commissioners, who were assisted by a joint advisory council but who also lead dual governments.

The first known Latter-day Saints to live in the New Hebrides (since World War II, when thousands of American servicemen were stationed there) were several Tongan families who migrated to Port Vila (or simply Vila) in the late 1950s. These members were not organized into a branch, however, until July 15, 1973, when President Ebbie L. Davis created the Port Vila Branch with Lanipoto Fehoko as president. At that time the First Presidency had not approved the area for proselyting. But because the area was part of the Fiji Mission, President Davis traveled from island to island and determined that although not all of the major islands of the New Hebrides were prepared for the gospel, some parts were.

President Davis visited a Mr. Townsend, the British resident commissioner, and discussed the possibility of bringing missionaries into the country. Mr. Townsend encouraged President Davis to pursue the matter as soon as Church leaders approved the move. Eight months later, in June 1974, the First Presidency gave its blessing to opening the New Hebrides, the Solomons, and the Gilbert and Ellice groups.

When President Davis visited Mr. Townsend on June 11, 1974, he found that the resident commissioner was still favorable to the Latter-day Saints' desires, but he informed President Davis that he could approve visas only for British Commonwealth citizens. The French resident commissioner could approve visas for French citizens. All other people would have to be approved by both commissioners, and this would probably prove difficult. The first LDS missionaries to enter the New Hebrides were Tongans who were Commonwealth citizens. They arrived in Port Vila on January 12, 1975. A week later, on January 26, 1975, President and Sister Davis flew to Port Vila, where they, along with Branch President and Sister Fehoko and Elders Mokofisi and Malohifo'ou, met together to dedicate the New Hebrides Islands to the preaching of the gospel. Together they climbed a small hill in Port Vila, and President Davis offered the dedicatory prayer to turn the key for the establishment of the Church there.

Four months later, two Canadian elders, Elders Olsen and Lowry, were transferred from the Canada Montreal Mission. At that point the immigration officer in the New Hebrides decided that four Latter-day Saint missionaries were enough. His action was symptomatic of greater problems yet to come. The Church did grow slightly—by 1978 there were 83 members and in 1984 there remained 120—but the new government of Vanuatu was hostile to the missionaries and soon missionary work was curtailed. Before the work stopped, missionaries were working in Vila in Efate and at Santo, Espirito Santo Island.[21]

Although Presidents Davis and Palmer both tried to obtain permission from the government of the Solomon Islands to establish the Church in that area, neither was successful. In 1974, the Solomons were in the final stages of obtaining complete independence from the British when President Davis applied for visas for missionaries. He was told that the visas could not be granted because three other churches had recently moved into the islands, and that rather than bringing peace, they had caused intervillage wars. Government leaders desired peace and unity at the time of independence; therefore they had decided not to allow any new churches. At this writing there are no LDS missionaries in the Solomon Islands.[22]

KIRIBATI

To most older people the name "Gilbert Islands" means little more than a few vaguely remembered dots in the South Pacific where thousands of servicemen lost their lives during World War II. Tarawa, with its population of fifteen or twenty thousand people, is only a series of coral islets that make a forty-mile chain beside a triangular shaped lagoon. The highest point on the atoll is fifteen feet above sea level. Until 1975, however, Tarawa served as the administrative center for the Gilbert and Ellice Islands, a British Crown Colony. It is now the capital of the Republic of Kiribati. Hardly fifty thousand people reside in the entire republic.

The minute size of these Micronesian islands and their unimportant status on the world globe notwithstanding, since 1972 Kiribati has played an interesting and faith-promoting role in the development of the Church in the Pacific. In 1972 there were no Latter-day Saints in the Gilbert Islands; in 1984 there were over five hundred baptized members (plus children), two branches, and a Church secondary school. In 1976 Church service education missionaries were sent to Tarawa, and in 1978 the first educational missionaries arrived there.

Living conditions may be as primitive in Kiribata as in any other area in the Pacific. In a letter of December 1978, Elder Richard M. Pratt, who, with his wife Adeline, was teaching school in Kiribati, described the status of the Church, the islands, the school, and the people on Tarawa:

> This is our tenth day in the islands, and words fail to tell the true story. [Elder Pratt was undoubtedly suffering from culture shock.] It is as primitive as a thousand years ago in the ways they live, yet there are elements of civilization such as the narrow oiled road that stretches the length of the island on the lagoon side. . . . The other signs of modern culture are the bank, the post office, and 2 or 3 tiny all-purpose stores 30 minutes and 30 cents from our village of Eita.
>
> The island is thickly covered with coconut trees. They are the staff of life. Without the coconut tree, life would cease to exist here, literally. They eat it, wear it, drink it, build their huts from it, and burn the rest to cook their rice and fish. Our [five] acre campus, leased for 99 years by the Church, spreads from the ocean on the south to the road on the north next to the lagoon. . . .
>
> Our buildings consist of 12-15 native-constructed buildings, completely made of coconut, except the two teachers' homes have the luxury of concrete floors. . . . There are no glass windows, no doors that can be locked. The upper half of the walls are open to allow free passage of air. The often-blowing trade winds make the heat bearable. . . .
>
> The center of the campus is dominated by the main building, some 30 by 40 feet in size, and called by the natives "maneaba." [*Maneaba* means central gathering place.] Its steep roof, supported on 12 coconut posts, is gracefully designed and resembles a bird in flight. This covered area is the chapel, assembly hall, and center of all

> campus and branch activities. The graveled floor is covered with thin coconut-leaf mats. These are picked up and stored after each Sunday service. About 120 natives sit on the thin mats, no chairs, sing without accompaniment, and rejoice in the gospel from 9 until 1:30. The meetings follow each other, for these people are too poor to afford more than one bus fare a Sunday. Some come Saturday night and sleep on the gravel. It is just as good as they have at home.[23]

Although Elder and Sister Pratt found the standard of living far lower than in the developed part of the world, they also found a people who desired more education for their young people. It was their desire for schooling that created the opportunity for the Church to enter Kiribati.

In 1972 officials in Church Schools Tonga began receiving letters from Waitea Abiuta, the headmaster of a small secondary school known as A.K.A.S., an abbreviation for Auriaria Kokoi Ataria School. Waitea, who represented a number of parents and board members of the A.K.A.S., asked Church education leaders to allow their children to attend Liahona High School. These letters were considered seriously by Tongan, Fiji Mission, and Church Education System leaders, and in September 1972, President Ebbie L. Davis visited Tarawa.

President Davis, of course, saw this situation as an opportunity to start missionary work in the Gilbert Islands. He investigated carefully but found that the department of immigration had a policy that "when a church has 50 adult members it will be officially recognized and will be allowed to bring foreign proselyting missionaries into the Gilbert Islands."[24] In effect this policy made it impossible to establish a new church, or so it seemed. In his survey of Gilbert affairs, President Davis learned that only 6 or 7 percent of all children ages twelve through seventeen were offered any educational opportunities. The A.K.A.S. school had successfully avoided the government's policy by sending students to various church schools outside the Gilbert Islands. Now the board was attempting to send students to Liahona High School. President Davis decided to recommend that twelve Gilbertese students be enrolled on a trial basis. This recommendation was accepted by Church school officials, and in late 1972, George Puckett, superintendent of Church Schools Tonga and an associate, went to Tarawa and selected twelve students. The following year, twelve more A.K.A.S. students were accepted.

During 1972 and 1973, President Davis sensed a certain amount of hostility from the government toward the Church and A.K.A.S. In July 1974, however, the attitude of the government officials seemed to change for the better, probably because local Gilbertese administrators were replacing British officials. Mr. Tanentoa, the Gilbertese minister of education, told President Davis that he favored the expansion of secondary education and welcomed LDS efforts in this field.[25]

By the end of 1976, sixty Gilbertese students had been enrolled at Liahona High School. All of these students were non-Mormons when they arrived in Tonga; however, all but three or four joined the Church. Once again Liahona High School played a significant role in missionary work.

From his first visit to the Gilberts in September 1972 until he was released as mission president, President Davis made frequent visits with government officials in an effort to obtain visas for missionaries. In late 1974 he and Elder John H. Groberg, regional representative for the area, talked with President Tonga Toutai Paletu'a of the Tonga Nuku'alofa Mission about using Gilbertese converts from Liahona High School as missionaries in their native islands. President Toutai supported the plan, and by October 1975, six Gilbertese students had been ordained elders and were prepared to serve missions. President Palmer, the new mission president in Fiji, flew to Tarawa with the missionaries on October 19, 1975. The following day the little group met in a cemetery on Betio, Tarawa, and President Palmer dedicated Kiribati to the preaching of the gospel.

As is frequently true when the Church moves into new areas, opposition arose from both Roman Catholic and Protestant church leaders. When school opened at A.K.A.S. in early 1976, only seventeen students enrolled. Students who were converted after the six missionaries returned to the country were almost the only students in the school. The other students left because of the indirect association between the Church and the school. Waitea, the headmaster, two board members, two teachers, and thirteen students had joined the Church since October. On Sunday, January 24, 1976, Waitea was ordained an elder and set apart as president of the Tarawa Branch. The A.K.A.S. school buildings were used for church meetings. The sudden drop in enrollment caused a crisis for the school, for it had debts that were being paid through student tuition. In order to save the school and also to maintain the Church's base of operation, the Church Educational System provided a modest amount of financial help to keep the school solvent. CES also decided to send a professional teacher, Grant Howlett, and his wife, Pat, to Tarawa from Liahona High School. The Howletts were called on a Church service basis. They and their five children arrived in the Gilberts in August 1976.

Brother Howlett became headmaster of the school and established excellent relations with the ministry of education. Through his guidance, the A.K.A.S. school remained open, and the enrollment increased from seventeen to seventy-three students by early 1977. Even though the Roman Catholic bishop demanded that members of his church withdraw from the school, Brother Howlett offered the students so much that the enrollment did not decline.

Only a short time after Elder Howlett arrived, he began hearing reports that Waitea, the headmaster, was not living a moral life. After a careful investigation Elder Howlett confronted Waitea with the accusations. Waitea confessed his failings and was later excommunicated. This left the school entirely in the hands of Elder Howlett and the Church. The local government withdrew the school from official registration and made it necessary for the Church Educational System to either take over the school or allow it to be closed down. The Church decided to take over the school, lease the property on which it stands, and change the name to the Moroni Community School.

On January 1, 1978, George and Ana Moleni from Liahona High School, and their five children arrived on Tarawa. The Molenis both held college degrees and were experienced teachers. They were called to assist Grant Howlett both in the school and in the branch. Nine months later, the Pratts arrived to begin their two years as education missionaries. Through their united service, the student body of Moroni Community School grew to 120. In 1984 the student body was 240 and being held at that number.

After the first six Gilbertese elders opened missionary work, several similar groups followed. But anti-Mormon influence upon the department of immigration caused that agency to change its longstanding policy of allowing churches with fifty adult members to bring foreign missionaries into the country. Almost as soon as the Church was officially registered as a legal body during 1977, the department of immigration declared that the Church would have to use only Gilbertese missionaries. In an effort to train and strengthen these young men, President Palmer developed a policy of sending all foreign elders from the Fiji area to Tarawa for the last three or four weeks of their missions. Gilbert Island immigration laws allowed short stays of this kind. In this way the local elders were helped considerably, and the Church continued to grow rapidly. There were 105 baptisms in 1977 and 95 in 1978.[26] In October 1980, construction began on a new chapel that was completed in 1982. Even though some fixtures had not arrived from Australia to be installed, the new branch president, Buren Ratieta (the

The principal's home at Moroni Community High School, Tarawa, Kiribati. This structure has been remodeled to provide greater comfort to its occupants. (Courtesy Norman Faldmo, Jr.)

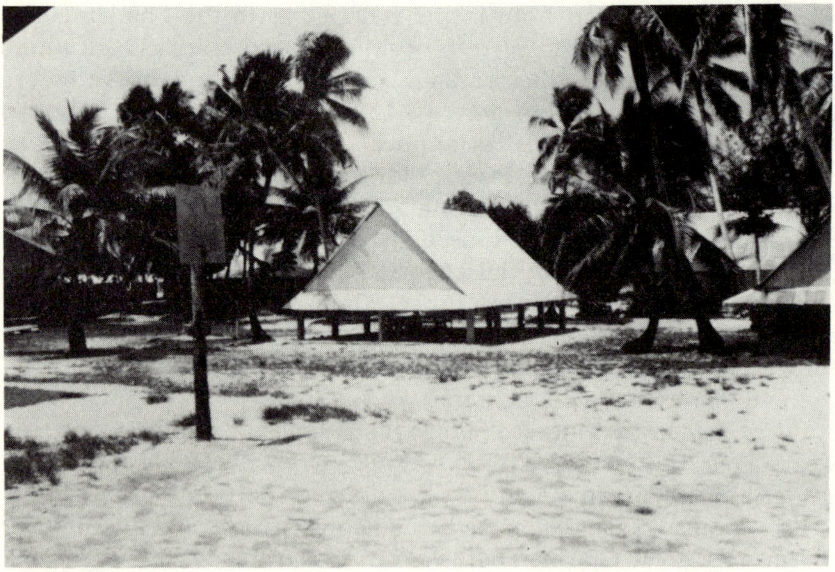

Originally covered with palm frond, the *maneaba*—central gathering place—now has a corregated metal roof. The entire Moroni Community High School has been remodeled and improved since the Church Educational System took it over. (Courtesy Norman Faldmo, Jr.)

first native of Kiribati to so serve since Waitea was released in 1976) held the first services in it in February 1982. Almost 250 people attended. The president of the Republic of Kiribati attended when that building was dedicated. During the festivities that followed, he told the audience that he and other leading government officials had objected to the Church being established in Kiribati because it is so influential. He said they feared that the Church would divide the people. But his attitude changed after he saw the great contribution the Church made to the social, educational, and cultural development of their country. They are now happy to welcome and cooperate with the Latter-day Saints.

A manifestation of his trust in the Church is his appointment of Baitika Toun, a branch president and member of the parliament, as minister of education in the president's cabinet. It is significant that the Church, once rejected on the basis of legal technicalities and prejudice, now stands in a position of trust.

THE MICRONESIA-GUAM MISSION

Some Latter-day Saints have lived in Guam, and many others have been aware of Guam and the islands of Micronesia since World War II. At that time the Marshall, Caroline, and Mariana Islands, with their tiny islands of Majuro, Kwajalein, Ponape, Truk, Yap, and larger Saipan and Tinian—were forever ingrained on the minds of Americans and the world as Allied troops fought through these islands. Since World War II, servicemen's groups and branches of the Church have continued on Guam.

Guam is a territory of the United States. America's westernmost outpost, it played a large role in U.S. defense during the Korean and Vietnam conflicts, and it remains strategically important to the United States. Estimates in 1980 place the population of Guam around 120,000. Military personnel are much in evidence, but the local people, the Chamorros, number well over sixty thousand. English is the official language of the island, but the Chamorro language is still widely spoken. Guam was controlled by the Spanish for over two hundred years. During that period the local people were converted to Roman Catholicism, which remains important. The United States took over the island in 1900.

LDS presence on the island of Guam has been evident since 1944, when the first servicemen's group was organized. On August 25, 1955, President Joseph Fielding Smith visited Guam and dedicated it to the preaching of the gospel. In January 1957, the first full-time mission-

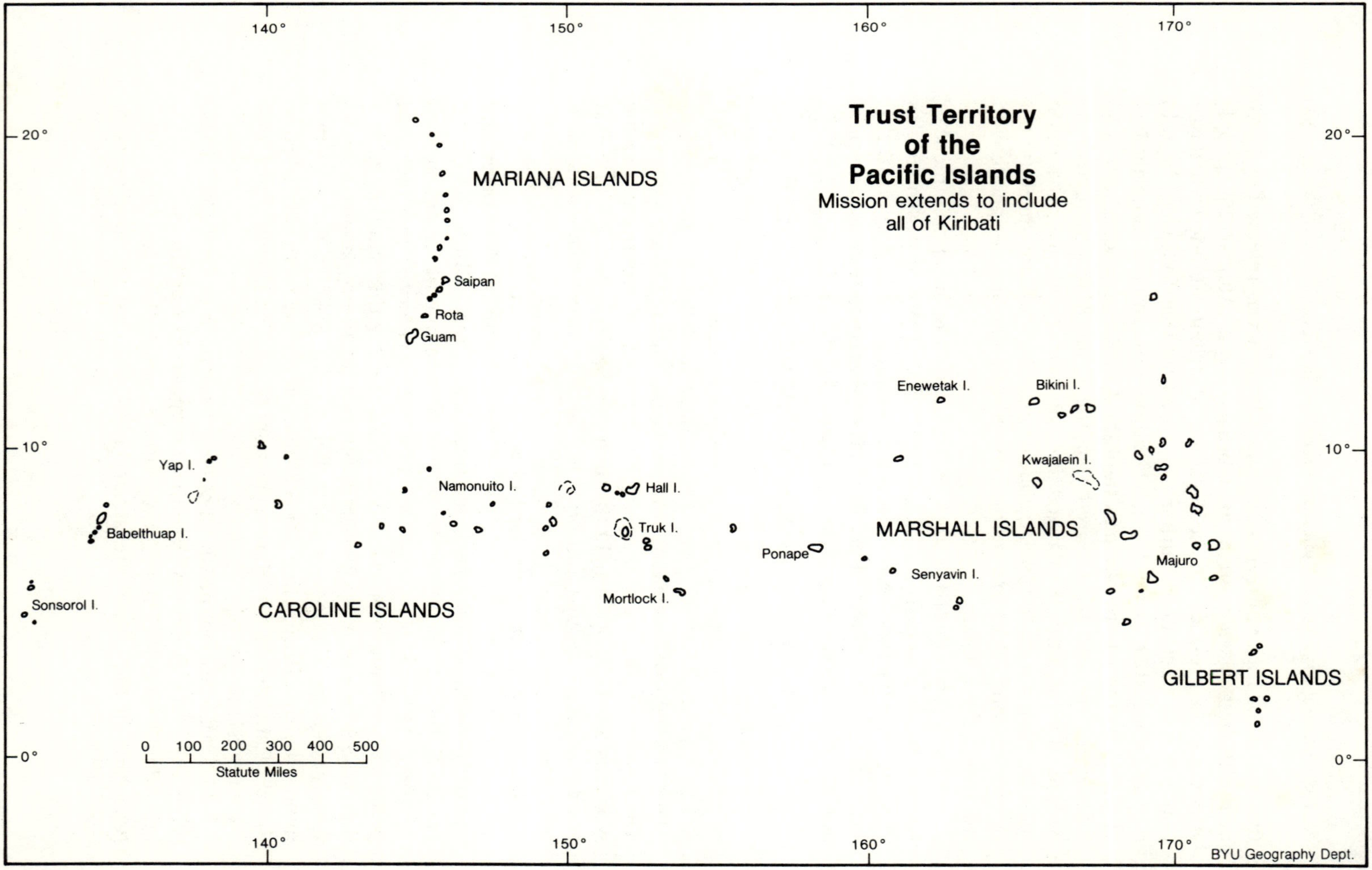

Trust Territory
of the
Pacific Islands
Mission extends to include
all of Kiribati
140°
150°
160°
170°
20°
10°
0°
MARIANA ISLANDS
Saipan
Rota
Guam
Enewetak I.
Bikini I.
Kwajalein I.
Yap I.
Namonuito I.
Hall I.
Babelthuap I.
Truk I.
MARSHALL ISLANDS
Ponape
Majuro
Senyavin I.
Mortlock I.
Sonsorol I.
CAROLINE ISLANDS
GILBERT ISLANDS
0 100 200 300 400 500
Statute Miles
BYU Geography Dept.

LDS Chapel in Guam. (Courtesy David Walden.)

aries arrived. Elder Mark E. Petersen of the Council of the Twelve dedicated the first chapel in 1959. Until the 1970s, however, the missionaries confined their efforts almost entirely to Americans who were interested in the Church.

Before being made the headquarters of the Micronesia-Guam Mission in 1980, Guam was part of the Japanese, the Northern Far East, the Southern Far East, and the Hawaii Honolulu Missions, and the Kaneohe Hawaii Stake, even though Guam is separated from Hawaii by thirty-three hundred miles of ocean. In the spring of 1980, Guam and Micronesia became a separate mission, with Ferron C. Losee as president. Guam, like many parts of the Fiji Suva Mission, has been, if not an orphan, at least a stepchild. After the early 1970s, however, Guam received considerable care and interest from the Hawaii Honolulu Mission and the Kaneohe Hawaii Stake. The Hawaii Honolulu Mission sent missionaries to Guam in 1970, and after that time the Church there grew from a branch to two wards, which were made part of the Kaneohe Stake. During the mid-1970s, missionaries broadened their proselyting base to include the Chamorro people.

In January 1975, President Robert E. Crandall of the Hawaii Honolulu Mission sent Elders Callis Carleton and Jeffery Frame to Saipan, headquarters of the U.S. Trust Territory, in the Mariana Islands. This was the first real move into Micronesia proper. Elders Carleton and Frame, like elders who have opened new areas elsewhere in the Pacific, encountered opposition from the Roman Catholic clergy and also had difficulty arranging for an appropriate place for meetings. These problems notwithstanding, they proselyted the people of Saipan (who number about thirteen thousand) and soon baptized their first convert, a Mr. Taylor. Through the help of Alfred "Mustang" Gonzales, a member who was working on a new airport, the elders found a quonset hut for Sunday meetings and began holding services. Before long, replacements came for the original elders, and two additional missionaries brought the force to four.

Brad Nago, one of the most important early converts, had come with his family to Saipan to work on the airport. There he met Brother Gonzales, and the two men became good friends. The story is told that Brad Nago saw Brother Gonzales at a cafe one day, and they talked about Brother Gonzales's planned return to Hawaii. Brother Gonzales told Brad Nago that he needed a replacement as branch president for the little dependent Mormon branch that had been formed. Brother Gonzales jokingly informed cigar-smoking Brad Nago that he was the man for the postion. Subsequently, Nago and his family studied the gospel and were baptized in January 1976. He replaced Brother Gonzales as president of the Saipan Branch. By July 1978 there were sixty-nine members in this new unit.

Through the enthusiastic encouragement of Elder John H. Groberg, area supervisor for Hawaii and the South Pacific, President William W. Cannon of the Hawaii Honolulu Mission led the expansion of the mission into all seven districts of the U.S. Trust Territory. Over forty missionaries, many of whom are from Tonga and Samoa, were soon proselyting on or near Saipan (one branch with 122 members), Palau (one branch with 75 members), Yap (one branch with 100 members), and Majuro (three branches with 325 members). (Figures in parentheses are for 1983.) In March 1979 there were 500 members of the Church in these islands,[27] but by 1983 the number had grown to over 3,000 in nineteen branches. Kiribati was assigned to this mission in late 1980.

Because the Trust Territory was under United States protection and control, the Church had no difficulty bringing missionaries into the area. The timing for entry was right, however, because of political changes that are taking place there.

Micronesia—not including Kiribati—was administered by the United States as the U.S. Trust Territory of the Pacific Islands from 1947 to 1982. In mid- to late-1982, the United States and the governments of the Republic of Palau (sometimes spelled Bilau), the Federated States of Micronesia (which includes the states of Yap, Truk, Ponape, and Kosrae), and the Republic of the Marshall Islands signed a Compact of Free Association, which was designed to terminate the trusteeship. The Commonwealth of the Northern Mariana Islands is a legal part of the Trust Territory until the Trusteeship Agreement is terminated; it will then become a United States territory. There has been considerable confusion in Micronesia during the late 1970s and the early 1980s as the new governments have come into being and taken control. Land purchases for chapels in particular were difficult because local laws were not clearly established and government officers were not prepared to make many important decisions. Most recently, however, relations with the new governments have been amicable.

The entire population of Guam, Kiribati, and the present and former Trust Territory is only three hundred thousand people spread over thousands of islands in millions of square miles of ocean. There are nine distinct cultural groups and at least nine different languages. Considering these facts, the Church cannot expect to bring large numbers of people into the kingdom. Nevertheless, through the programs of the Church, including seminary and possibly schools, the Church can expect to greatly enrich the lives of many people in this far-flung part of the world.[28]

PAPUA NEW GUINEA

The newest major area of the Pacific to be opened to Latter-day Saint missionary work is Papua New Guinea. Aside from Australia, it is the most densely populated area in the Pacific. New Guinea is the second largest island in the world. Its dense jungles, mangrove swamps, savanas, and high mountains topped with snow evidence a land of diversity and challenges for the Church.

Papua New Guinea's rivers, forests, and mountains have created an isolating effect that has helped preserve a multitude of nations and tribes within a nation. It has been suggested that the seven or eight hundred languages account for a sixth of the world's tongues. Most used are English, Tok Pisin (pidgin), and Hiri Motu. Tok Pisin has rapidly become the lingua franca of the country. The vast majority of people in Papua New Guinea are Melanesians, but within that classification are found a rich variety of cultures and customs.

The nation of Papua New Guinea became independent on September 16, 1975, following almost one hundred years of colonial status under Germany, Britain, and Australia. It is part of the British Commonwealth of Nations. Papua New Guinea includes not only the east end of New Guinea (the west half is called Irian Jaya, part of Indonesia), but also six hundred other islands.

Latter-day Saint missionaries had visited New Guinea for twenty-five years or more before seriously attempting to gain a permanent foothold. Shortly after becoming president of the Australia Brisbane Mission in July 1980, Dennis D. Flake sent Elder and Sister L. Douglas Johnson to Port Moresby, Papua New Guinea, to open missionary work there. Port Moresby (population 122,000) is the capital city. The Johnsons and other couples who have followed them have devoted their time to gaining legal recognition for the Church, to making friends, and to meeting with those who have invited the missionaries to share the gospel with them. The Church gained legal status in May 1981 and has the right to lease land for chapels and other church buildings. No land is held free and clear. To date, Latter-day Saint missionaries have not ventured far beyond the capital, but several branches of expatriates have been formed in several mining districts on islands. In addition to the three or four branches in Port Moresby, there are small branches at Lae, Arawa, and Rabaul.

In April 1983, Elder L. Tom Perry of the Quorum of the Twelve and Bishop H. Burke Peterson of the Presiding Bishopric visited Port Moresby, and Elder Perry offered a prayer dedicating that land. At the same time, these Church leaders and the mission president held planning meetings to plot the future development of the Church in Papua New Guinea. It was decided to move slowly and baptize only as many members as could be trained in doctrine, government, and Church administration. The idea was to prepare the members to govern themselves and then move more quickly to spread the gospel beyond Port Moresby and its immediate hinterland.

Although the missionary couples who have labored there have maintained a low profile and have not proselyted openly, many people have asked to be taught, and the Church had grown to over 750 by late 1983. A chapel was constructed in 1983 and 1984. Two local young men had been called from Port Moresby to serve missions in Australia. They were Elders George Mauhi and Robert Goisisi.

Although the plan of the Church leaders was to contain growth to limited numbers within the Port Moresby area, there were signs that because of the transient nature of the people the gospel was finding its way into villages and homes outside the capital.[29]

Key to Abbreviated Titles

Church Publications

CN *Church News*

DN *Deseret News* or *Deseret Evening News*

IE *Improvement Era*

HC *History of The Church of Jesus Christ of Latter-day Saints* (commonly called *Documentary History of the Church)*

MS *Millennial Star*

WE *Woman's Exponent*

Manuscript Collections and Reports in Church Archives

FMHR Fiji Historical Record

FPMR French Polynesia Mission Record

JHC Journal History of the Church

MFSR Mission Financial and Statistical Reports

MHAM Manuscript History of the Australasian/Australian Mission

MHBY Manuscript History of Brigham Young

MHFP Manuscript History of the French Polynesia Mission

MHHM Manuscript History of the Hawaiian Mission

MHNZ Manuscript History of the New Zealand Mission

MHSM Manuscript History of the Samoan Mission

MHTM Manuscript History of the Tongan Mission

SMHR Samoan Mission, Historical Record

Libraries and Archives

AH Archives of Hawaii, Foreign Office, Box 15, Honolulu, Hawaii

BYU-SC Special Collections, Harold B. Lee Library, Brigham Young University, Provo, Utah

CA Church Archives, Historical Department of The Church of Jesus Christ of Latter-day Saints, Salt Lake City, Utah

WPA Western Pacific Archives, Suva, Fiji

NOTES

CHAPTER 1

1. See Joseph Smith, *History of the Church of Jesus Christ of Latter-day Saints,* ed. B. H. Roberts, 7 vols. (Salt Lake City: The Church of Jesus Christ of Latter-day Saints, 1902-1932), 5:349, 386; hereinafter cited as *HC;* Louisa Barnes Pratt, "Journal of Louisa Barnes Pratt," Kate B. Carter, comp., *Heart Throbs of the West* (Salt Lake City: Daughters of Utah Pioneers, 1967), 8:228.
2. *HC,* 5:404-6.
3. Jane Tudor, ed., *Pacific Islands Yearbook,* 11th ed. (Sydney: Pacific Publications, 1972), p. 185.
4. Doyle L. Green, "Mission to Polynesia: The Story of Addison Pratt and the Society Islands Mission," *Improvement Era* 52 (July 1949): 436; hereinafter cited as *IE.*
5. Ibid., p. 437; see also Andrew Jenson, Manuscript History of the French Polynesia Mission (MHFP), July 21, 1844, Church Archives, Historical Department of the Church of Jesus Christ of Latter-day Saints, Salt Lake City, Utah; hereinafter cited as CA.
6. Green, "Mission to Polynesia," p. 437.
7. Most of these men, all of whom were shipbuilders, left the islands for California in the days of the Gold Rush of 1849. Some later returned to their adopted island home.
8. See Aarne A. Koshinen, *Missionary Influence as a Political Factor in the Pacific Islands* (Helsinki, 1953, reprinted ed., University Microfilms International, 1978), pp. 110-12ff.
9. Ibid., pp. 164-66; C. Hartley Grattan, *The Southwest Pacific to 1900* (Ann Arbor: University of Michigan Press, 1963), pp. 216-20; for a summary of the L.M.S.–Roman Catholic conflict see also Kenneth Scott Latourette, *A History of the Expansion of Christianity,* 7 vols. (New York: Harper and Row, Publishers, 1943), 5:06.
10. MHFP, August 15, 1844.
11. Ibid., September 16, 1844.
12. Ibid., October 17, 1844 to January 25, 1845.
13. When Pratt was reunited with his wife in Salt Lake City in 1848, he was fully apprised of the "letter" situation. A number of Church leaders had sent letters to the Pacific elders regularly, as did Sister Pratt. It must be counted as bad luck that these messages did not arrive.

    But more important, it must be remembered that the Prophet Joseph Smith was killed in June 1844 and that the Saints were persecuted, mobbed, and finally driven out of Nauvoo and eventually west to Utah. During this time Sister Pratt and her daughters suffered privations and would have given much for a mouthful of island fruit, fish, or coconut, or for a few degrees of warmth while they shivered in a sod hut at Winter Quarters. All this was brought to Addison's awareness only after he joined the Saints in Utah.
14. MHFP.
15. Ibid., February 20, 1845.
16. S. George Ellsworth, "Zion in Paradise: Early Mormons in the South Seas" (Logan, Utah: The Faculty Association, Utah State University, 1959), p. 13.

17. MHFP, May 1, 1845; also Green, "Mission to Polynesia," *IE* 52 (October 1949): 635.
18. Ibid.
19. MHFP, December 4, 1845.
20. MHFP, September 24, 1846.
21. Ibid., November 14, 1846.
22. Ibid., January 1, 1847.
23. Ibid., March 28, 1847; Green, "Mission to Polynesia," *IE* 53 (March 1950): 178-80; Louisa Barnes Pratt, *Journal,* pp. 245-46. She says the date of arrival was August 1848 rather than September.
24. Ellsworth, pp. 23, 25; also L. B. Pratt, *Journal.*
25. James S. Brown, *Giant of the Lord: The Life of a Pioneer* (Salt Lake City: Bookcraft, 1960, orig. pub. 1902), pp. 183-88.
26. Ellsworth, "Zion in Paradise," p. 28; Mrs. Pratt colorfully describes her island experiences in her journal, mentioned above.
27. *Millennial Star* (Liverpool) 14: 109; hereinafter cited as *MS.*
28. Koskinen, *Missionary Influence,* p. 181.
29. John Davies, *The History of the Tahitian Mission, 1799-1830,* ed. C. W. Newbury, (Cambridge: Published for the Hakluyt Society, at the University Press, 1961), pp. 338-39.
30. Koskinen, *Missionary Influence,* pp. 108, 112.
31. *MS,* 15:406-07.
32. Brown, *Giant of the Lord,* pp. 237-51.
33. Elder Brown did not obtain an exact understanding of what happened, nor did later writers such as Eugene M. Cannon and F. Edward Butterworth have all the correct details; see Brown, pp. 279-80, and *MS,* 15:407; MHFP, December 31, 1853 (but written in the 1890s); F. Edward Butterworth, *The Adventures of John Hawkins: Restoration Pioneer* (Independence, Missouri: Herald Publishing House, 1963), pp. 203ff.

CHAPTER 2

1. Young to Gibson, March 5, 1851, Brigham Young Letterbooks, CA.
2. Brown, *Giant of the Lord,* pp. 279-80; MHFP, December 31, 1953 (but written in the 1890s), CA; Butterworth, *Adventures of John Hawkins,* pp. 203ff. Andrew Jenson served as assistant LDS Church historian for almost five decades. He visited Tahiti in 1895 and gathered historical data. He also interviewed many missionaries and read many missionary journals in an effort to document the development of the LDS Church in French Polynesia. See also MHFP, 1867; Ellsworth, "Zion in Paradise," p. 31.
3. Butterworth *Adventures of John Hawkins,* and *Roots of the Reorganization: French Polynesia* (Independence, Missouri: Herald Publishing House, 1977), pp. 92-94. Butterworth hardly footnotes, but he supplies information that is unavailable elsewhere.
4. MHFP, by date.
5. William A. Seegmiller, Journals 1891-1895, dates as given, CA.
6. Ibid.; Joseph W. Damron, Jr., Missionary Labors of Joseph W. Damron, Jr., in his own handwriting, CA.
7. In 1838 the Colombian government gave France the right to construct a canal through the Isthmus of Panama. From then until the French attempt to build a canal failed in 1889, there was considerable discussion of the economic advantages that could be had in the Pacific. See Grattan, *The Southwest Pacific to 1900,* p. 217.
8. Seegmiller, January 28, 1892; Damron, same date; see also C. Hartley Grattan, *The Southwest Pacific Since 1900* (Ann Arbor: University of Michigan Press, 1963), pp. 411-12.
9. Damron, Missionary Labors.
10. Ibid., First Presidency to Damron and Seegmiller, March 29, 1892, First Presidency Letterpress Books, CR-1-20, vol. 24, CA.
11. First Presidency to James S. Brown, April 14, 1892, CA.

12. MHFP, June 3, 1892.
13. Damron, Missionary Labors.
14. Brown, *Giant of the Lord,* pp. 511-16.
15. Damron, Missionary Labors.
16. Letter from Damron, January 15, 1893 *(Deseret News* hereinafter cited as *DN* (Salt Lake City) 46:557.
17. Ibid.; Brown, *Giant of the Lord,* pp. 518-19; MHFP, January 1-7, 1893.
18. Brown, *Giant of the Lord,* pp. 526-28.
19. MHFP, July-August, 1893.
20. See MHFP, March 30, 1895, to November 9, 1895. Details of the day-to-day encounters with Martin and others are given.
21. F. J. West, *Political Advancement in the South Pacific* (Melbourne: Oxford University Press, 1961), p. 86; see also Stephen H. Roberts, *The History of French Colonial Policy, 1870-1925* (Handmen, Connecticut: Archon Books, 1963 [first published in 1929 by P. S. King and Company, Great Britain]), pp. 511-16.
22. MHFP, December 31, 1895.
23. Paper titled "Daniel T. Miller," 2 pp., Ms d 5207, CA.
24. MHFP, May 31, 1895; April 6, July 31, and August 31, 1896, CA.
25. MHFP, June 11, 1897.
26. MHFP, by dates mentioned; also William Henry Chamberlain, Diaries 1897-1900, Ms d 1691, CA.
27. *DN,* 56:411.
28. MHFP, Miller to First Presidency, December 14, 1897; May 14, 1898.
29. MHFP, September 10, 1898; July, September 1899.
30. MHFP, November 28, 1897; December 14, 1897; May 14, 1898.
31. French Polynesia Mission, Historical Record 1900-1930, CR 3039 Series 11 (7432), September 7, 1901, CA; hereinafter cited as FPMR.
32. Ibid.
33. Ibid., November 20, 1903.
34. Latourette, *Expansion of Christianity,* 5:207-8.
35. MHFP, September 27, 1899; FPMR. July 29, 1904, CA.

CHAPTER 3

1. See Bengt Danielsson, *Raroia* (Chicago: Rand McNally & Company, 1953), passim.
2. MHFP, Joseph F. Smith to Daniel T. Miller, June 11, 1897, CA.
3. First Presidency to Thomas S. Court, July 7, 1905, Samoan Mission Historical Report (6132), CA.
4. See Danielsson, *Raroia,* p. 131ff.
5. FPMR, January 27, 1903, CA; see also H. J. Sheffield, Missionary Experience of Heber James Sheffield in Tidal Wave and Cyclone in the Society Islands, 1903, CA.
6. Danielsson, *Raroia,* p. 136.
7. MHFP, July 11, 1897; March 12, 1898; April 10, 1900; and May 1, 1900, CA.
8. FPMR, October 5, 1906.
9. Ibid.
10. *DN,* May 23, 1914.
11. MHFP, June 18, 1914.
12. Mission Financial and Statistical Reports, Tahitian Mission, by year, CA; hereinafter cited as MFSR. In the 1910 and 1912 reports the mission president stated that the figures were guesses at best. This may account for the relatively large total membership jump between those years.
13. *DN,* May 23, 1914.
14. FPMR, by dates.

15. See *DN,* February 5, 1916, and May 19, 1917.
16. FPMR, June 13 and December 21, 1916; September 10 and November 21, 1917; and December 17, 1918, CA.
17. Vahineiti Piimoua Fuller Oral History, interview by R. Lanier Britsch, 1974, typescript, James Moyle Oral History Program, CA.
18. FPMR, by date.

CHAPTER 4

1. Kennard to wife and family, June 11, 1920, copy in possession of author.
2. Ibid.
3. Grattan, *Since 1900,* p. 514.
4. MFSR, Tahitian Mission, by year, CA.
5. FPMR.
6. MHFP, August 31, 1929; November 30, 1930; FPHR, April 28, 1931; July 20, 1935; April 4-6, 1943; April 1945; December 1946; February 17, 1949, CA.
7. MHFP, May 31, 1929.
8. FPMR, December 20, 1923; MHFP, May 31, 1925.
9. MFSR, Tahitian Mission, 1940; FPHR, April 30, 1940.
10. FPMR, December 24, 1936; October 14, 1938.
11. MHFP, May 31, 1927.
12. FPMR, May 18, 1935.
13. MFSR, Tahitian Mission, 1925 and 1926.
14. FPMR, April 11, 1921; August 9, 1921.
15. Ibid., June 22, 1939.
16. Rufus K. Hardy, "Conclusion of Tahitian Mission Trip," *DN* August 19, 1939.
17. Ibid.
18. Ibid.; see also Doyle L. Green, "Tahiti . . . ," *IE* 42 (October 1939): 592-93, 632-33.
19. FPHR, November 15, 1931.
20. Ibid.
21. Ibid.
22. Ibid., by date.
23. Ibid., July 5, 1940; MHFP, August 31, 1940.
24. MHFP, September 4, 1940.
25. Ibid.
26. Ibid., June 6, 1941.
27. Ibid., April 27, September 29, 1942.
28. Ibid., December 20, 1946.
29. Ibid., August 27, 1946.
30. Ibid., by date.

CHAPTER 5

1. Judy Tudor, *Pacific Islands Year Book,* 11th Ed., p. 161.
2. MFSR, French Polynesia Mission, by year, CA.
3. MHFP, March, June, September, and December 1950; MFSR, French Plynesia Mission, 1950,CA.
4. MHFP, French Polynesia Mission, June 30, 1950.
5. Ibid., passim.
6. Raituia T. Tapu Oral History, interview by R. Lanier Britsch, 1974, typescript, pp. 8-9, James Moyle Oral History Program, CA; FPHR, July 23, 1959, p. 472, in Mission Office, Papeete, Tahiti.

7. MFSR, French Polynesia Mission, 1953.
8. MHFP, March 31, 1955.
9. Ibid.
10. Ibid., June 30 and September 30, 1955.
11. Ibid., September 9, 1956; *Church News,* August 24, 1957; hereinafter cited as *CN.*
12. MHFP, March 4, 1956.
13. Ibid., March 31, 1957.
14. Brief History of Paea Branch, typescript in possession of author; MHFP, by date; David W. Cummings, *Mighty Missionary of the Pacific* (Salt Lake City: Bookcraft, 1961), pp. 241-47.
15. Karl M. Richards, "A History of the French Polynesian Mission," typescript in possession of the author.
16. MHFP, December 16, 1963–January 5, 1964.
17. Claire T. Manea, interview by R. Lanier Britsch, Papeete, Tahiti, January 4, 1974; Gordon B. Hinckley, Journal, by date, in possession of President Hinckley, Salt Lake City, Utah.
18. Harvey L. Taylor, "The Story of the LDS Church Schools," 2 vols., typed manuscript, prepared for the Church Commissioner of Education, 1971, pp. 188-211, CA; Church Educational System, *Overview 1978,* p. 38.
19. Bruce M. Lake, interview, November 2, 1982, Salt Lake City, Utah.
20. "Conference in Tahiti," *Ensign* 6 (May 1976): 144.
21. Del Van Orden, "New Day Dawns for Temples in Pacific," *CN,* February 28, 1981; "Building of Temples Shifts to High Gear," *CN,* March 13, 1982; "Tahiti Temple Leader Called," *CN,* September 4, 1982; "Tahiti Temple Elicits Raves and Whispers," *CN,* October 23, 1983; John L. Hart, "Polynesia's Fifth Temple Dedicated," *CN,* November 6, 1983.

CHAPTER 6

1. Samuel Eliot Morison, *The Oxford History of the American People* (New York: Oxford University Press, 1965), p. 548.
2. Eugene E. Campbell, "The Mormon Gold-Mining Mission of 1849," *Brigham Young University Studies,* 1 & 2 (Autumn-Winter, 1959-1960): 19-31; see also Henry W. Bigler, Journal, September 25, 1850, CA; and William Farrer, Biographical Sketch, Hawaiian Mission Report and Diary, 1821-1906, September 25, 1850, p. 35, typescript, in Special Collections, Harold B. Lee Library, Brigham Young University, Provo, Utah; herinafter cited as BYU-SC.
3. Farrer, Mission Report and Diary, December 13, 1850. For information concerning Hawaiian history see Ralph S. Kuykendall, *Hawaiian Kingdom,* 3 vols. (Honolulu: University of Hawaii Press, 1947); Gavan Daws, *Shoal of Time: A History of the Hawaiian Islands* (Hawaii: The University of Hawaii Press, 1968); and Gerrit P. Judd, *Hawaii: An Informal History* (New York: Collier-Macmillan, 1961).
4. George Q. Cannon, *My First Mission,* 2nd ed. (Salt Lake City: Juvenile Instructor Office, 1882), p. 19.
5. Farrer, Mission Report and Diary, January 13, 1851.
6. Ibid., January 18, 1851.
7. Cannon, *My First Mission,* p. 22.
8. Farrer, Mission Report and Diary, January 26, 1851.
9. Cannon, *My First Mission,* p. 27; Farrer, Mission Report and Diary, January 27 & 30, 1851.
10. Ibid., February 2, 1851.
11. Ibid.; also Cannon, *My First Mission,* p. 29.
12. Andrew Jenson, Manuscript History of the Hawaiian Mission, February 27, 28, 1851, CA; hereinafter cited as MHHM.
13. Ibid., February 20, 1851.
14. Cannon, *My First Mission,* p. 38.
15. Ibid.
16. MHHM, August 6, 1851; also Cannon, *My First Mission,* p. 46.
17. MHHM, August 17 & 18, 1851.

18. Farrer, Mission Report and Diary, dates as mentioned; and MHHM, dates as mentioned.
19. The wives of all three elders were apparently not considered missionaries. They merely accompanied their husbands on their missions. Consider the following quotation from a letter from Parley P. Pratt to Brigham Young: "We have sent to those islands three additional missionaries who sailed on the sixth day of August for the Port of Honolulu." Parley P. Pratt, *Autobiography of Parley P. Pratt* (Salt Lake City: Deseret Book Company, 1938), pp. 375, 384, 386.
20. Farrer, Mission Report and Dairy, dates mentioned; Cannon, *My First Mission,* p. 47; MHHM, dates mentioned; *MS,* 14:492-93.
21. MHHM, August 22, 1951.
22. Ibid., September 22, 1851.
23. R. Armstrong to R. C. Wyllie, Honolulu, October 8, 1851, Archives of Hawaii, Foreign Office, Box 15, hereinafter cited as AH; also in Letters to Brigham Young, Ms d 1234, CA. See also Margaret Comfort Bock, "The Church of Jesus Christ of Latter-day Saints in the Hawaiian Islands" (M.A. thesis, University of Hawaii, 1941), pp. 12-15.
24. Cannon, *My First Mission,* p. 50; Farrer, Mission Report and Diary, December 5, 1851.
25. Cannon, *My First Mission,* p. 69. There is an internal inconsistency in Cannon's version of the beginning of this work. He states that he started translating in the last days of January 1851. But this seems highly unlikely since he had been in the islands only six weeks at the time. On the previous page he states that the work of translation was begun after the branches at Wailuku and Waiehu had been organized. This did not happen until the fall of 1851. Elder Cannon apparently remembered the process taking two and a half years, for he wrote: "The translation was finished on July the 22nd, 1853—about two years and a half from the time I commenced it" (p. 70). However, it is more likely that the work took one and a half years to complete. This is confirmed by Andrew Jenson, who states that translation work began January 27, 1852. See Andrew Jenson, comp., *Church Chronology,* 2nd ed., rev. and enl. (Salt Lake City: Deseret News Press, 1899), p. 45.
26. Farrer, Mission Report and Diary, June 14, 1852 through August 6, 1852.
27. Cannon, *My First Mission,* pp. 70-71.
28. John Stillman Woodbury, Journal, July 25, 1853, BYU-SC.
29. Farrer, Mission Report and Diary, November 6, 1853; Bigler, Journal, January 5, 1854.
30. A couple of references do indicate that the books were slow in coming. The first is a letter from John T. Caine to Brigham Young, written April 13, 1856. Here Caine acknowledges to President Young the receipt by the missionaries in Hawaii of 1,500 copies of a letter from Elder Cannon in the Hawaiian language. It gave "a brief history of the rise of the Church, the coming forth of the Book of Mormon &c." It was, according to Caine, "the first publication setting forth our principles ever issued in the Hawaiian language." Caine mentioned that Elder Cannon wrote saying that the Book of Mormon had been printed but was not bound at the time. (John T. Caine to Brigham Young, April 13, 1856, Ms d 1234, CA.)
31. Bigler, Journal, November 24, 1857; Bigler to Brigham Young, December 3, 1857, and May 21, 1858, Ms d 1234, CA. Statistics of the last conference held while the foreign elders were still there listed "1800 copies Book of Mormon in Hawaiian, unbound." MHHM, April 25, 1858.
32. Woodbury, Journal, April 9, 1853.
33. Ephraim Green, Diary, April 18, 1853, typescript, BYU-SC.
34. Farrer, Mission Report and Diary, April-May 1852.
35. Ralph S. Kuykendall, *The Hawaiian Kingdom, 1778-1845,* 3 vols. (Honolulu: The University Press of Hawaii, 1938), vol. 1: *Foundation and Transformation,* pp. 351-360; see also "Notes on Conference between Mr. Armstrong and certain Mormon ministers," August 20, 1853, Foreign Office and Executive file, AH; see also Bock, "Church in the Hawaiian Islands," p. 21.
36. Woodbury, Journal, May 7 & 8, 1854.
37. The polygamy issue is amply documented by Bock, "Church in the Hawaiian Islands," pp. 25-27, who used numerous sources from the Archives of Hawaii; for further data see Woodbury, Journal, typescript pp. 314-17, 320, 339-41, 345, 389. Even before this law became

public, Francis A. Hammond wrote that he had met with Levi Haalelea, a member of the privy council, who told Hammond "how he fought against a bill that has just been passed by the legislature and house of Nobles to have the power of marrying retained only in the hands of the Minister of Interior and make a source of revenue by affixing a license to it &c. He said the bill was got up on account of our ordaining so many natives to the priesthood, and his fighting stoutly against it caused Armstrong, the framer of the bill, to call him a Mormon. They have also passed a law to have all ministers of the gospel taxed. This too was got up for our benefit as we had ordained many natives to the priesthood and under the old law they could all get clear from their taxes." Francis A. Hammond, Journals, 1852-1884, July 24, 1854, Ms f 338, CA.

38. Woodbury and Hammond both commented on this problem.
39. Ibid., November 1853.
40. Benjamin F. Johnson, *My Life's Review* (Independence, Missouri: Zion's Printing and Publishing Co., 1947), pp. 157-58.

CHAPTER 7

1. Leonard J. Arrington, *Great Basin Kingdom: An Economic History of the Latter-day Saints, 1830-1900* (Cambridge: Harvard University Press, 1958), pp. 23-28.
2. Woodbury, Journal, p. 125; Johnson, *My Life's Review,* pp. 164, 168-69.
3. Johnson, pp. 167-69.
4. Ibid.
5. F. A. Hammond to William Farrer, February 24, 1854, in Farrer, Journal and Letters, 2:81; see also Hammond, Journal, February 23, 1854.
6. Brigham Young to Philip B. Lewis and missionaries to the Sandwich Islands, April 1, 1854, Brigham Young Letterbooks, Ms f 219, CA.
7. Johnson, *My Life's Review,* p. 182.
8. Cannon, *My First Mission,* pp. 20-21.
9. Ephraim Green, Diary, various dates 1854-1855. Unless otherwise noted, the following paragraphs on Lanai have been taken from his diary.
10. Ibid., Smith, p. 183.
11. Hammond, Journal, July 25, 1855.
12. Silas Smith to Brigham Young, July 3, 1856, CA.
13. The information in the several preceding paragraphs was taken from letters from Silas Smith to Brigham Young dated as follows: July 3, July 31, October 11, December 6, 1856; and May 17, 1857, Ms d 1234, CA.
14. Bigler, Journal, September 13, 1857.
15. Ibid., October 4, 1857; and *Manuscript History of Brigham Young,* October 4, 1857, CA; hereinafter cited as MHBY.
16. Ibid., November 20, 1857.
17. Ibid., December 22, 1857.
18. Bigler and Woodbury to Brigham Young, December 3, 1857, Ms d 1234, CA.
19. *Directory: Church of Jesus Christ of Latter-day Saints Hawaiian Mission* (Honolulu n.p., 1934), p. 10.
20. MHHM, April 25, 1858, and October 6, 7, 8, 1858.
21. The most frequently cited books, articles and theses concerning Gibson include Gwynn Barrett, "Walter Murray Gibson: The Shepherd Saint of Lanai Revisited," *Utah Historical Quarterly* 40 (Spring 1972): 142-62; R. Lanier Britsch, "Another Visit with Walter Murray Gibson," *Utah Historical Quarterly* 46 (Winter 1978): 65-78; Gavan Daws, "The Shepherd Saint," *Shoal of Time: A History of the Hawaiian Islands* (Honolulu: University of Hawaii Press, 1968), pp. 220-25; Frank W. McGhie, "The Life and Intrigues of Walter Murray Gibson" (M.A. thesis, Brigham Young University, 1958); James A. Michener and A. Grove Day, "Gibson, the King's Evil Angel," *Rascals in Paradise* (London: Secker and Warburg, 1957),

pp. 120-54; Joseph B. Musser, "Walter Murray Gibson—Oceanic Adventurer," *U.S. Naval Institute Proceedings* 52 (September, 1926): 1709-32; Brigham H. Roberts, *Comprehensive History of the Church,* 6 vols. (Salt Lake City: Deseret Book Company, 1930), 5:97-100; Esther L. Sousa, "Walter Murray Gibson's Rise to Power in Hawaii" (M.A. thesis, University of Hawaii, 1942); Samuel W. Taylor, "Walter Murray Gibson: Great Mormon Rascal," *The American West* 1 (Spring 1964): 18-27, 77; Lorrin A. Thurston, *Memoirs of the Hawaiian Revolution* (Honolulu, 1936).

22. *DN,* November 18, 1860.
23. *Pacific Commercial Advertiser* (Honolulu), October 17, 1861.
24. Gibson, Diary, November 5, 1861, CA; Gibson's diary is also reproduced as an appendix in Frank W. McGhie, "Life and Intrigues."
25. Ibid., January 31, 1862.
26. Ezra T. Benson to Cannon, April 12, 1864, MHBY, CA.
27. Joseph F. Smith to Cannon, May 4, 1864, MHBY, CA.
28. Captain Gibson remained in Hawaii until shortly before his death in 1888. Although he did not die a wealthy man, he did enjoy a considerable amount of financial as well as political and social success during the post-Lanai years of his life. He was a firm supporter of causes that were popular with the Hawaiian royalty. For several years, from 1882 until 1887, he was prime minister of the Hawaiian kingdom. He seems to have held no grudge against the leaders of the Church for excommunicating him, as many men in his circumstances might have done. On the contrary, he spoke warmly in later years of his respect for the Latter-day Saint cause. He died in a Catholic hospital in San Francisco.

CHAPTER 8

1. Joseph F. Smith to Brigham Young, July 5, 1864, MHBY, CA.
2. Brigham Young to Joseph F. Smith, July 28, 1864, Letters of Brigham Young, CA.
3. See Gustive O. Larson, "The Mormon Reformation," *Utah Historical Quarterly* 26 (January 1958): 45-63.
4. Brigham Young to King Kamehameha V, March 24, 1865, Letters of Brigham Young, CA.
5. Daws, *Shoal of Time,* pp. 174-78.
6. Hammond, Journal, 1864-1865, January 26, 1865, CA.
7. Brigham Young to Daniel H. Wells and Brigham Young, Jr., February 28, 1865, Letters of Brigham Young, CA.
8. Brigham Young to William King, March 29, 1865; Brigham Young to Hammond and Nebeker, December 29, 1864, Brigham Young Letterbooks, CA; Hammond, Journal, March 9, 1865.
9. Hammond, Journal, May 1, 1865.
10. Ibid.
11. Kamehameha V to Brigham Young, May 10, 1865, copy in possession of author.
12. MHBY, 1866, p. 313, "Sandwich Islands Conference Report," April 6, 7, and 8, 1866, CA.
13. Nebeker to Brigham Young, October 17, 1865, and November 19, 1866, CA.
14. Brigham Young to Nebeker, July 16, 1867, CA.
15. Brigham Young to Nebeker, February 6, 1868, Letters to Brigham Young; Nebeker to Brigham Young, February 24, 1868 and March 15, 1868, CA.
16. Previous authors have generally devoted much time to the operation of the plantation over the years. Although Laie plantation was the physical location of the headquarters of the Church in Hawaii, the history of the operations of the plantation are outside the central concern of this book. For more detailed treatment of the plantation see Bock, "Church in the Hawaiian Islands," chapter 3; Joseph B. Musser, "Laie—Home Place of the Church in Hawaii," typescript, CA; and Antoine R. Ivins, "Laie Plantation," typescript, CA.
17. Harvey Harris Cluff, Autobiography, p. 160, handwritten copy, CA.

18. Native Saints in the Sandwich Islands to Brigham Young and Counselors, June 25, 1874, Letters to Brigham Young, CA.
19. Edward Partridge, Jr., Journal, Number 4, June 15, 1882, CA.
20. Harvey H. Cluff, Autobiography, p. 123; Smith to Brigham Young, November 9, 1874; Pack to Brigham Young, April 19, 1877, CA.
21. Bock, "Church in the Hawaiian Islands," p. 75; MHHM, April 1872; A. L. Smith to Brigham Young, November 9, 1874; Ward E. Pack to Brigham Young, April 19, 1877, CA; MHHM, 1894, CA.
22. MHHM, February 23, 1889.
23. Alma L. Smith to Brigham Young, October 14, 1875, CA.
24. Harvey H. Cluff, Autobiography, p. 158.
25. MHHM, March to May 1892.
26. Harvey H. Cluff, Autobiography, p. 129; *Woman's Exponent* (Salt Lake City), 3:12:1, letter of October 5, 1874; hereinafter cited as *WE*.
27. *WE,* 9:10 (August 1, 1880): 74.
28. MHHM, May 6, 1877.
29. *WE,* 12:11:86; 23:3-4 (August 1 and 15, 1894): 173; 24:2 (June 15, 1895).
30. Jerry K. Loveland, "Dedication of the Old Laie Chapel," typescript in possession of Eugene Campbell, Brigham Young University, Provo, Utah. The manuscript quotes at length from the original minutes of the dedication by William G. Farrell, conference clerk.
31. *WE,* 3:12:1.
32. MHHM.
33. MHHM, October 5, 1887.
34. It is probable that Saints at Laie were discouraged about the Laie plantation during the time when President Smith was among them. Some writers and speakers have implied that the continued existence of the Laie settlement was in serious question. (See David W. Cummings, *Centennial History of Laie,* 1965.) There is no evidence in the records of the mission or of the missionaries at that time that this might have been so.

    On the other hand, there is little reason to doubt that President Smith made this statement. According to Castle H. Murphy, who was in Hawaii when President Smith visited there on several occasions after the turn of the century and with whom this writer has conversed, such statements as these are in harmony with the kinds of things he said in Murphy's presence.

    The principal problem with the document quoted above is that it was written after the fact by a woman who was young at the time it was spoken. She stated that though she was young when President Smith made the prophecy, her memory of the event was reinforced by the retelling of it by her grandparents. Although her testimony tends to lend authenticity to the fact that he did make the prophecy, it also leads one to question the exactness of the statements she remembered after so many years.
35. MHHM, February 1885 to June 25, 1887; Smith, *Life of Joseph F. Smith,* pp. 262-86; Joseph Fielding Smith, Jr., and John J. Stewart, *The Life of Joseph Fielding Smith* (Salt Lake City: Deseret Book Company, 1972), pp. 39-44.
36. *WE,* 26:18-19 (February 15, and March 1, 1898).

CHAPTER 9

1. All of the foregoing information concerning the mission years of Matthew Noall, unless otherwise indicated, has been taken from MHHM; see dates. See also Matthew and Elizabeth DeEtte Laker Noall, Journals, Reports, and Letters to the First Presidency, etc., Western Americana Collection, University of Utah Library, Salt Lake City; and Matthew Noall, *To My Children* (Salt Lake City: Utah Printing Company, n.d.).
2. Hawaiian Saints began emigrating to Utah in the 1870s, and by 1889 approximately seventy-

five islanders resided in the northwest section of Salt Lake City. Unfortunately, they were generally in poor economic condition. Desiring to improve the situation of the Hawaiian Saints, President Joseph F. Smith spearheaded the purchase of a large ranch in Skull Valley, west of Tooele, Utah, which served as a gathering place, a Zion, if you will, for the Hawaiians. Settled in August 1889, the islanders named their new community Iosepa, "Joseph" in Hawaiian, after Joseph F. Smith. Iosepa was reasonably successful, growing to 228 residents at its greatest size. Although many reasons have been given for its closing in 1917, the best is that most of the inhabitants moved back to Hawaii when the temple was constructed. See Dennis H. Atkin, "A History of Iosepa, The Utah Polynesian Colony" (M.A. thesis, Brigham Young University, 1958). Some useful information concerning the Hawaiian government's attitude toward the colony is found in Bock, "Church in the Hawaiian Islands," pp. 77ff.

3. The main source for information on the years 1895 to 1915 is Samuel E. Woolley, Journals, CA.
4. Ivins, "Laie Plantation," p. 6.
5. Bock, "Church in the Hawaiian Islands," p. 90.
6. Musser, "Laie—Home Place of the Church in Hawaii," n.d. (probably written between 1935 and 1940), pp. 12-13. See also MHHM, August 22, 1918.
7. Ivins, "Laie Plantation."
8. George Q. Cannon, Journal of Travels to the Hawaiian Mission Jubilee, December 17, 1900, typescript of dictation taken by Clawson Y. Cannon, p. 9, copy in possession of R. Lanier Britsch. Other important sources of information about the Jubilee are Woolley, Journals, by date; and MHHM, by date, CA.
9. Woolley, Journal, December 23, 1900.
10. Ibid., p. 14; see also Woolley, December 27, 1900.
11. Italics added. Hawaiian Mission, General Minutes, April 6, 1911, p. 8, CA.
12. "Civic Pride is Part of Mormon Policy as Evidenced by Settlement at Laie: Homes, Roads and School Are Credit to the Territory," *Pacific Commercial Advertiser,"* Sunday, March 21, 1920.
13. MFSR, Hawaiian Mission, CA.
14. General Minutes, Hawaiian Mission Conference, April 3, 1915, CA, CR, 3695, 11, Box 1, fd. 5.
15. Smith, *Life of Joseph F. Smith,* p. 421.
16. *Conference Reports* (Salt Lake City), October 1915, pp. 8-9.
17. MHHM, December 11, 1919.
18. MHHM, by date. See also *IE,* 19:79-80; 19:953-58; 23:149-53; 23:281-88; and 29:258-62.

CHAPTER 10

1. Nearly all of the information in this section is derived from the mission president's annual report, which was part of the Mission Financial and Statistical Report, CA.
2. J. Reuben Clark, Jr., "The Outpost in Mid-Pacific," *IE* 38 (September 1935): 532-33.
3. MFSR, Hawaiian Mission, 1921.
4. J. Pia Cockett, "Visit of President David O. McKay in 1921," typescript in CA, CR 3695, 1, Box 1. See also Reuben D. Law, *The Founding and Early Development of the Church College of Hawaii* (St. George, Utah: Dixie College Press, 1972), pp. 19-21. Law quotes a transcript of D. Arthur Haycock, president of the Hawaii Mission, in which President McKay retold this story again in 1955. President McKay also related this story in New Zealand shortly after it happened.
5. Richard C. Harvey, "The Development of the Church of Jesus Christ of Latter-day Saints in Hawaii" (M.A. thesis, Brigham Young University, 1974), pp. 76-77.
6. MHHM.
7. MFSR, Hawaiian Mission, 1922, 1923.

8. Bernard Francis Pierce, "Acculturation of Samoans in the Mormon Village of Laie, Hawaii" (M.A. thesis, University of Hawaii, 1956), pp. 16-22.
9. First Presidency to Castle H. Murphy, November 20, 1934, First Presidency Letter Books, CA.
10. Clark, "Outpost in Mid-Pacific," p. 535.
11. Ibid.
12. Edward L. Clissold Oral History, interview by R. Lanier Britsch, 1976, typescript, pp. 6-7, James Moyle Oral History Program, CA.
13. Elwood L. Christensen Oral History, interview by R. Lanier Britsch, 1974, typescript pp. 17-20, James Moyle Oral History Program, CA.
14. Clark, "Outpost in Mid-Pacific," p. 533.
15. J. Christopher Conkling, "Member Without a Church: Japanese Mormons in Japan From 1924 to 1948," *Brigham Young University Studies* 15 (Winter 1975): 210. Conkling's data is from Mission Financial and Statistical Reports, Central Pacific Mission, 1937 through 1948, CA.
16. Ibid., p. 211.
17. Eldred L. Waldron to R. Lanier Britsch, June 15, 1976, in possession of the author.
18. *Ka Elele O Hawaii,* December 1942, p. 38, CA.

CHAPTER 11

1. Clissold, Oral History, pp. 16-17.
2. "Stakes of Zion," *Deseret News 1976 Church Almanac* (Salt Lake City: Deseret News, 1976), pp. C12-C30. See also later editions.
3. Daws, *Shoal of Time,* p. 191.
4. Roscoe E. Cox, "Religious Education in Hawaii," *IE* 44 (December 1941): 728.
5. William E. Berrett, Interview, June 23, 1976; Frank W. McGhie, "Religious Education in the Hawaiian Islands," typescript in possession of writer.
6. Ibid., Berrett.
7. Leon R. Hartshorn, "Mormon Education in the Bold Years" (Ed.D. dissertation, Stanford University, 1965), p. 120.
8. David O. McKay, Diary, February 7, 1921, quoted in Reuben D. Law, *The Founding and Early Development of the Church College of Hawaii* (St. George, Utah: Dixie College Press, 1972), pp. 27-28; see also David W. Cummings, *Mighty Missionary in the Pacific* (Salt Lake City: Bookcraft, Inc., 1961), pp. 257-58; and Harvey L. Taylor, "The Story of L.D.S. Church Schools," bound typescript, 2:78ff, in CA. These three books are the principal sources relating to the history of CCH. Taylor's study is brief but useful. Law's work is primarily a stringing together of documents generated by himself and others during the years of his presidency. Cummings's book is written in a flamboyant, exaggerated manner. An in-depth, scholarly study remains to be done on the founding and history of the institution.
9. Edward L. Clissold, "Address," Dedication of the Church College of Hawaii, December 17, 1958, typescript in CA; see also Law, *The Founding and Early Development,* pp. 37-39.
10. Ibid., Clissold.
11. Law, *The Founding and Early Development,* pp. 66-69.
12. Ibid.
13. Clissold, "Address."
14. Taylor, "L.D.S. Church Schools," p. 88.
15. Law, *The Founding and Early Development,* passim, pp. 239-58.
16. "Church College of Hawaii Becomes BYU Campus," *Ensign* 4 (June 1974): 65.
17. Clissold, interview, June 11, 1976; and *Building Missionaries in Hawaii* (n.p., n.d.), p. 132.
18. Alf Pratte, "The Time to 'Do It' Is Now . . . ," and "Hawaii Temple Rededicated," *Ensign* 8 (August 1978): 74-78.

CHAPTER 12

1. Latourette, *The Expansion of Christianity,* 5:132.
2. Andrew Jenson, *Encyclopedic History of the Church* . . . (Salt Lake City: Deseret News Publishing Co., 1941), pp. 35-36.
3. John Murdock, Journal, CA.
4. Wandell to B. Young et al., February 11, 1852, CA; *DN,* November 27, 1852.
5. Andrew Jenson, Manuscript History of the Australia Mission, April 1855, CA; hereinafter cited as MHAM.
6. Peter Crawley, "The First Australian Mormon Imprints," *Gradalls Review* 2 (Fall 1973) 1:43.
7. MHAM, by date.
8. MHAM, by date; *Zion's Watchman,* mission periodical, p. 261, CA.
9. MHAM, July-August 1852.
10. MHAM, "Minutes of Conference," July 6, 1852.
11. MHAM, by date.
12. MHAM, November 1853; *MS,* 16:141.
13. *DN,* November 17, 1852.
14. MHAM, passim.
15. *MS,* 10:81-88 (March 15, 1848). President Young's letter was dated December 24, 1847.
16. *DN,* 5:100.
17. MHAM, p. 156; Amasa Potter, "The Lord's Blessings," *Faith Promoting Series, Twelfth Book* (Salt Lake City: Juvenile Instructor Office, 1884), p. 90.
18. MHAM, September 7, 1855.
19. Ibid.
20. See Susa Young Gates, "A Remarkable Life" (the life of Mary Chittenden) in *Heroines of "Mormondom," the Second Book of the Noble Women's Lives Series* (Salt Lake City: Juvenile Instructor Office, 1884), pp. 37-85.
21. *DN,* December 8, 1854.
22. Ibid., June 6, 1855.
23. *MS,* 21:442.

CHAPTER 13

1. MFSR, Australia, by year, CA.
2. Journal History of the Church, October 30, 1902, CA; hereinafter cited as JHC.
3. Marion G. Romney Oral History, interviews by James B. Allen, 1972 and 1973, typescript, p. 6, James Moyle Oral History Program, CA.
4. Clarence H. Tingey Oral History, interviews by R. Lanier Britsch, 1973, typescript, pp. 21-22, James Moyle History Progam, CA.
5. Ibid., pp. 16-20.
6. JHC, October 30, 1902; February 12, 1903.
7. Ibid., March 23, 1913.
8. Tingey, p. 12; MFSR, Australia, 1918.
9. JHC, September 24, 1918.
10. Malcomb R. Thorp, "The British Government and the Mormon Question, 1910-22," *Journal of Church and State;* 21 (Spring 1979): 305-23; JHC, March 4, 1919; June 27, 1919; August 4, 1919; May 3, 1920.
11. *IE,* 21 (1918): 453.
12. MFSR, Australia Mission, 1922.
13. JHC, November 23, 1923.
14. MFSR, Australia, 1921.
15. Leonidas D. Mecham, *Australian Missionaries,* p. 11; see also *Austral Star,* 2 (October 1930): 4-5.

CHAPTER 14

1. MFSR, Australia, by year.
2. MHAM, 1924-1927.
3. MFSR, Australia, 1927.
4. Ibid., by year. The actual number of foreign missionaries in Australia as of December 31 each year was: 1929—31; 1931—28; 1932—23; 1933—18; 1934—15; 1935—29, 1936—47.
5. MFSR, Australia, 1929.
6. A complete set of the *Austral Star* is held by the Church Library, CA.
7. MHAM, June 1930.
8. *Austral Star,* August 20, 1930.
9. MHAM, June 30, 1931.
10. MFSR, Australia, 1933 and 1935; *Austral Star,* June 20, 1933.
11. *Austral Star,* March 20, 1931; Tingey, Oral History, pp. 28-29.
12. MHAM, December 31, 1931.
13. Ibid., 1935, 1936, and 1937.
14. Calculated from yearly Financial and Statistical Reports, 1925, 1930, 1935, 1940, 1945, and 1950.
15. Ibid.
16. Ibid.
17. MHAM, June 1939.
18. Manning Clark, *Short History of Australia* (New York: The New American Library, 1969), p. 237.
19. Andrew Jenson, Manuscript History of the Tongan Mission, October 15, 1940, CA.
20. MFSR, Australia, 1940.
21. Mecham, *Australian Missionaries,* pp. 39-40; Elvon W. Orme, interview, August 31, 1978.
22. Ibid.
23. MHAM, September 31, 1946.

CHAPTER 15

1. James B. Allen and Glen M. Leonard, *The Story of the Latter-day Saints* (Salt Lake City: Deseret Book Company, 1976), pp. 569-70.
2. MHAM, December 31, 1951; Young Adults of Australia, "The Gospel in Australia: Our Heritage," *The Latter-day Saints* (n.p., 1975), p. 9.
3. Allen and Leonard, *The Latter-day Saints,* p. 567.
4. Garry P. Mitchell, "The Church in Australia," *Ensign* 6 (February 1976): 18.
5. H. Earl McBride, "President McKay in Brisbane," *Austral Star,* March 1955.
6. Ibid.
7. Mecham, p. 44. Sister Liljenquist made this report.
8. MHAM, March 31, 1957.
9. Mecham, p. 62; *The Gospel in Australia,* p. 6.
10. Cummings, *Mighty Missionary of the Pacific,* pp. 215-40, passim.
11. *Deseret News 1983 Church Almanac,* pp. 146, 147, 150, 160, 161.
12. Mitchell, "The Church in Australia," p. 13.
13. Bird to Mecham, October 24, 1975, in Mecham, *Australian Missionaries,* pp. 134-35; see also J. Martel Bird Oral History, interview by Charles Ursenbach, 1976, typescript, pp. 125-30, James Moyle Oral History Program, CA.
14. Bird, Oral History, pp. 113-14.
15. Mitchell, "The Church in Australia," p. 13.
16. Bird, pp. 112-13.
17. *Ensign* 6 (May 1976): 138-43.
18. *CN,* June 24, 1984.

19. Rex D. Pinegar, interview, June 29, 1984; Area Book for Australia/New Guinea, December 7, 1983, Management Information Center, The Church of Jesus Christ of Latter-day Saints; Loren C. Dunn, interview, January 10, 1984.
20. *CN,* October 18, 1980.
21. "Ground Broken for the First Temple in Australia," *Ensign* 12 (October 1982): 77.
22. *CN,* August 21, 1982.

CHAPTER 16

1. In this chapter I have relied heavily on the following works: Brian W. Hunt, "History of the Church of Jesus Christ of Latter-day Saints in New Zealand" (M.A. thesis, Brigham Young University, 1971); and Ian R. Barker, "The Connexion: The Mormon Church and the Maori People" (M.A. thesis, Victoria University of Wellington, 1967).
2. See chapter 12.
3. Andrew Jenson, Manuscript History of the New Zealand Mission, April 1, 1855, CA; hereinafter cited as MHNZ.
4. *DN,* June 6, 1855; January 26, 1888.
5. *MS,* 29:379.
6. Ibid., 29:430.
7. Ibid., 32:346.
8. Ibid., 32:347.
9. Ibid., 32:425.
10. MHNZ, May 25, 1870.
11. Ibid., July 12, 1870.
12. MHNZ, October 4, 1871; *MS,* 34:24.
13. MHNZ, November 25, 1875.
14. Grattan, *The Southwest Pacific to 1900,* pp. 388-89.
15. Ibid., p. 158.
16. Latourette, *The Expansion of Christianity,* 5:182.
17. See Ian R. Barker's sections on this topic, pp. 37-42.
18. Johannis Jacob Mol, "The Religious Affiliations of the New Zealand Maoris," *Oceania* 35 (1964-65): 136.
19. Barker, "The Connexion," p. 37.
20. *DN,* December 8, 1853, p. 96.
21. MHNZ, November 26, 1876, ff.
22. *Juvenile Instructor,* January 1887, p. 6.
23. *DN,* 29:679; MHNZ, October 7, 1880.
24. William M. Bromley, "Introduction of the Gospel to the Maoris," *Juvenile Instructor* 22 (1887): 6-7, 26-27, 57.
25. MHNZ, December 25, 1882; *DN,* 1883:192.
26. MHNZ, February 18, 25, 1883.
27. Alma Greenwood, "My New Zealand Mission," *Juvenile Instructor* 20 (1885):191. This series of articles is the best source concerning the introduction of the gospel to the Maoris of the Wairarapa and Hawkes Bay.
28. Ibid., p. 207.
29. Ibid.
30. Ibid., p. 222.
31. Ibid., p. 251.
32. MHNZ, August 13, 1884 ff.
33. Ibid., January 19, 1885.

CHAPTER 17

1. Eric G. Schwimmer, *The World of the Maori* (Wellington, New Zealand: A. H. & A. W. Reed, 1966), p. 61.
2. Hirini Whaanga, "A Maori Prophet," *Juvenile Instructor* 37 (1902): 152.
3. Ibid., pp. 152-53.
4. Hunt, "Latter-day Saints in New Zealand," p. 28.
5. Stuart Meha, "The New Zealand Mission," typescript, pp. 3-4, Mendenhall Library, Church College of New Zealand.
6. William Bromley, Journal, June 16, 1881, CA.
7. *DN,* November 23, 1881, p. 683.
8. Nolan P. Olsen, "New Zealand—Our Maori Home," *IE,* 35 (May 1932): 446.
9. Matthew Cowley, "Maori Chief Predicts Coming of L.D.S. Missionaries," *IE,* 53 (September 1950): 697. See also *Matthew Cowley Speaks* (Deseret Book Company, 1954), pp. 200-205.
10. Cowley, "Maori Chief Predicts . . . ," p. 698.
11. For a complete explanation of how the covenant was preserved by the members of the Ngatikahungunu tribe and how a photograph of the same came into the possession of Matthew Cowley, see ibid., pp. 755-56.
12. *Proceedings of the Diocesan Synod of the District of Wellington,* First Session of the Ninth Synod, October 1881, p. 16, from Barker, p. 40.
13. Greenwood, "My New Zealand Mission," p. 222.
14. Barker, "The Connexion," p. 43.
15. Ibid., p. 36.
16. For more information about the Io concept see Schwimmer, *The World of the Maori,* pp. 114-16.
17. First Presidency to Members of the Church in the New Zealand Mission, in General Conference Assembled, Copy books, CR 1-20, Reel #42, CA.
18. *DN,* 1886:460.
19. MHNZ, March 10-11, 1887.
20. Ezra Foss Richards, Journal, March 13, 1887, BYU-SC.
21. For the best coverage of the Book of Mormon translation and publication project, see Hunt's thesis, chapter 5.
22. Hirini Whaanga, "A Maori Prophet," p. 153.
23. Christie R. Bunnell, comp., Autobiography of Lars Christian Rasmussen, in possession of the author, pp. 3-5.
24. MHNZ, April 8, 1897, CA.
25. Australian East Mission, Historical Record 1891-1897, CR mh 10872, (2881), CA.

CHAPTER 18

1. 1901 and 1905 statistics are from MHNZ, December 31, by year; the remaining figures are from Mission Financial and Statistical Reports, by year, CA.
2. MFSR, New Zealand, 1912. In 1917 the numbers were not too different. Of sixty-three missionaries, nineteen were working with pakehas, twenty-nine with Maoris, and the remainder were engaged in nonproselyting activities. MHNZ, August 12, 1917.
3. MHNZ, April 6-9, 1900; April 29 ff, 1901.
4. Ibid., November 6, 1901. See also New Zealand Mission, Historical Record, pp. 282-84, CA.
5. MHNZ, December 19 and 30, 1902.
6. Ibid., December 5, 1903 to February 9, 1904, passim.
7. Ibid., by date.

8. Ibid., February 12, 1898; August 3, 1902; March 15, 1903; August 29, 1903.
9. Ibid., April 6, 1902; also February 16 and March 9, 1902.
10. Ibid., by date.
11. Ibid., by date.
12. For the most complete discussion of these subjects see Hunt, "LDS in New Zealand," chapters 6 and 7.
13. Sondra Sanders, Journal, Book One, p. 146, CA; see also Hunt, p. 62 ff.
14. Hunt, p. 65.
15. The word college has a different meaning in New Zealand than it does in the United States. Whereas in the U.S. it refers to post-secondary education, in New Zealand it denotes post-primary or post-secondary education. In the U.S. the MAC would have been called a high school.
16. MHNZ, April 2, 1904.
17. MHNZ, November 1906, but the letter was dated September 24, 1906.
18. *MS,* 75:369.
19. Hunt, "LDS in New Zealand," pp. 73-74.
20. *New Zealand Official Yearbook, 1937,* p. 852.
21. *IE,* 16:172.
22. MHNZ, August 11, 1917.
23. Ibid., August 1917 to February 28, 1918, passim.
24. Henry A. Smith, *Matthew Cowley—Man of Faith* (Salt Lake City, Utah: Bookcraft Publishers, 1954), p. 53.

CHAPTER 19

1. C. H. Grattan writes: "During the 1920s prices for New Zealand exports were unstable with a downward trend. They moved erratically from 1921 through 1924, ending at a lower level than in 1920, moved upward to above the 1920 level in 1925, fell off sharply in 1926 and 1927, 'recovered' a bit in 1928, began a downward trend in 1929 which carried them to their lowest levels in 1931, 1932, and 1933, while in 1934 a recovery began." *The Southwest Pacific Since 1900,* p. 271.
2. MFSR, New Zealand, by year.
3. MHNZ, April 22, 1921. I have relied heavily on the "Manuscript History" and also on the Mission Financial and Statistical Reports, New Zealand, for this section and the several topics that have preceded it.
4. Gordon Claridge Young Oral History, interviews by Lauritz G. Petersen, 1972, typescript, pp. 9-10, James Moyle Oral History Program, CA.
5. MHNZ, by date.
6. R. M. Burdon, *The New Dominion: A Social and Political History of New Zealand, 1918-39* (Wellington: A. H. & A. W. Reed, 1965), p. 289.
7. MFSR, New Zealand, 1929.
8. Ariel S. Ballif Oral History, interviews by R. Lanier Britsch, 1973, typescript, p. 7 and p. 73, Oral History Program, CA. See also MHNZ; April 5-10, 1928.
9. MHNZ, September 1928.
10. Ibid., September 22 and October 14, 1928.
11. Hunt, "LDS in New Zealand," pp. 85-86.
12. First Presidency to the New Zealand Mission President, October 2, 1930, CA.
13. Journal History, February 5, 1931, CA.
14. Smith, *Matthew Cowley,* p. 213.
15. MFSR, New Zealand, 1936.
16. Ibid., 1933.
17. MFSR, New Zealand, 1936.
18. Ibid., 1937.

19. MHNZ, August 8, 1937.
20. Smith, *Matthew Cowley,* p. 114.
21. MHNZ, May 31, 1938.
22. Ibid., June 16, 18, 1940.
23. MFSR, New Zealand, 1940.
24. Smith, *Matthew Cowley,* p. 132.
25. MFSR, New Zealand, 1946.

CHAPTER 20

1. MFSR, New Zealand, 1948.
2. Young Oral History, pp. 20-21.
3. Ibid., p. 17.
4. Ibid.
5. Smith, *Matthew Cowley,* pp. 155-57.
6. Young Oral History, p. 12.
7. Ibid., p. 23.
8. MFSR, New Zealand, 1949, 1950.
9. The fullest account is David W. Cummings, *Mighty Missionary of the Pacific,* chapters 2-12; see also Jeannette McKay Morrell, *Highlights in the Life of President David O. McKay* (Salt Lake City: Deseret Book Company, 1966), chapter 20.
10. Ballif Oral History, p. 56; Taylor, "LDS Church Schools," p. 165.
11. Cummings, *Mighty Missionary,* p. 52.
12. Morrell, *Highights of David O. McKay,* p. 197.
13. Cummings, *Mighty Missionary,* p. 102.
14. Bruce M. Lake, interviews, September 28 and November 2, 1982, Salt Lake City, Utah.
15. Alexander P. Anderson to R. Lanier Britsch, July 22, 1976, in possession of R. Lanier Britsch.
16. See chapter 3.
17. Fritz Bunge-Kruger Oral History, interviewed by R. Lanier Britsch, 1974, typescript pp. 1-4, The James Moyle Oral History Program, CA.
18. Darold M. Marlow, "Rarotonga," *IE,* 69 (June 1966): 410-11.
19. MFSR, New Zealand, 1949.
20. Young Oral History, pp. 39-41.
21. Andrew Jenson, Manuscript History of the Samoan Mission (MHSM), June 30, 1954, CA.
22. Ibid., September 30 and December 31, 1955; see also David W. Cummings, *Mighty Missionary,* pp. 195-97.
23. MHSM, December 31, 1960; Marlow, "Rarotonga," p. 446.
24. Ibid., Marlow, pp. 446-47; C. Douglas Barnes, taped recollections and documents, in possession of R. Lanier Britsch.
25. Ballif Oral History, pp. 49-50; Barker, "The Connexion," p. 147.
26. New Zealand Division, Seminary and Institute Department, "Seminaries and Institutes in New Zealand," *New Zealand Church History, Unit 9* (1974).
27. See Barker, "The Connexion," passim.
28. J. J. Mol, "The Religious Affiliations of the New Zealand Maoris," *Oceania* 35 (1964-65): 136-43.
29. Mervyn Dykes, "Ben Couch, Cabinet Minister in New Zealand Parliament," *Ensign* 13 (April 1983): 25-28.
30. Iain B. McKay, "Conference in New Zealand," *Ensign* 6 (April 1976): 75-77.
31. *CN,* February 3, 1979.
32. Robert L. Simpson Oral History, interviews by Gordon Irving, 1978, typescript, p. 33, James Moyle Oral History Program, CA.
33. In addition to the sources cited in this chapter, several others were used in its preparation. See Jack H. Goaslind, Jr., Oral History, interviews by Gordon Irving, 1981-82; William R.

Perrott Oral History, interview R. Lanier Britsch, 1974; Leo W. Russon Oral History, interview by R. Lanier Britsch, 1974; and Douglas H. Strother Oral History, interview by R. Lanier Britsch, 1974, James Moyle Oral History Program, CA. Also Loren C. Dunn, interview by R. Lanier Britsch, January 10, 1984, Salt Lake City, Utah. C. Douglas Barnes provided taped information.

CHAPTER 21

1. See chapter 7.
2. Walter Murray Gibson to Brigham Young, September 2, 1861, Letters to Brigham Young, CA.
3. Gibson to Brigham Young, CA.
4. Jenson, *Encyclopedic History of the Church,* p. 765.
5. Ibid., and also referring to a statement made by Harvey Harris Cluff, Autobiography, October 6, 7, and 8, 1871, p. 128, CA.
6. It is difficult to be sure of the facts in this situation. The only source was Brother Manoa himself, and his story is not easily corroborated.
7. Cluff, Autobiography, August 12, 1872, p. 134, CA.
8. Joseph H. Dean, Journals, May 23, 1887, CA.
9. Ibid., October 9, 1887.
10. Ibid., February 10, 1888.
11. Ibid., June 21, 1888.
12. Andrew Jenson, Manuscript History of the Samoan Mission, June 24, 1888, CA; hereinafter cited as MHSM.
13. Latourette, *The Expansion of Christianity,* 5:214-18; and Alan R. Tippett, *People Movements in Southern Polynesia,* chapter 4.
14. Grattan, *The Southwest Pacific to 1900,* p. 483.
15. Ibid.
16. Ibid., p. 488.
17. Ibid., p. 504.
18. The best LDS source relating the political situation from 1888 to 1899 is by William O. Lee, "Political Samoa," *IE,* 2 (June 1899): 434-41.
19. Journal History of the Church, October 30, 1888, CA.
20. Edward J. Wood, "My Samoan Experience," *The Juvenile Instructor* 23 (1893): 348. This is a portion of an eleven-part series that gives a great deal of information on a variety of subjects.
21. MHSM, November 1 through 23, 1888, CA.
22. Wood, "My Samoan Experience," p. 408.
23. Ibid., p. 409.
24. Ibid., p. 491.
25. Ibid., p. 539.
26. MHSM, March 12-19, 1889, CA.
27. Ibid.
28. *Cardston News* (Alberta, Canada), October 27, 1936; Wood, "My Samoan Experience," p. 632.
29. MHSM, June 16-18, 1889; and Wood, "My Samoan Experience," pp. 634-35.

CHAPTER 22

1. Wood, "My Samoan Experience," p. 701.
2. Ibid.
3. Ibid., pp. 774-75.

4. MHSM, August 6, 1890.
5. Ibid., passim.
6. Jenson, *Encyclopedic History,* p. 776.
7. MHSM, November 15, 1895.
8. Ibid., August 8, 1897 and May 4, 1898.
9. Ibid., September 18, 1895.
10. A number of friends and relatives of those who died or who lost family members became upset about the deaths in Samoa and questioned the general safety of all the missionaries. The mission president simply replied that people also die in Utah, and that the work had to be done in Samoa. Two thoughtful articles have been printed concerning these deaths: Loren C. Dunn, "Faithful Laborers," *Ensign.* 5 (May 1975): 25-26; and William A. Moody, "At Rest On the Hill Overlooking the Sea," *IE,* 14 (1911): 113-17.
11. MHSM, December 31, 1898, and March, April, and May 1899.
12. E. von Vietsch, *Wilhem Solf: Botschafter Zwischen den Zeiten* (1961).
13. Samoan Mission Historical Record, July 26, 1901, CA; hereinafter cited as SMHR.
14. Ibid., February 2, 1902.
15. Ibid., per dates above.
16. *DN,* May 10, 1920.
17. *DN,* August 24, 1901.
18. SMHR, March 14, 1902.
19. First Presidency to Sanders, March 31, 1903, copied in SMHR.
20. First Presidency to Woolley, August 4 and 5, 1904, First Presidency Letter Press Copybooks, CA.
21. Samuel E. Woolley, Journals, October 1, 1904; see also SMHR by dates, CA. Copies of most of the legal papers related to this transaction are entered in SMHR.
22. SMHR, February 17, 1906.
23. Ibid., November 16, 1921.
24. Ibid.
25. Ibid.
26. First Presidency to Moody, July 28, 1908, Letterpress copybooks, CA.
27. Ibid.
28. SMHR, by date.
29. *DN,* June 6, 1903 and December 12, 1903; see also SMHR, May 1904.
30. SMHR, by dates; also *DN,* May 12, 1904; April 18, 1914; and November 4, 1919.

CHAPTER 23

1. MHSM, August 31, 1930.
2. MFSR, Samoa, by year.
3. *DN,* June 1921.
4. President David O. McKay, "Sauniatu," *IE,* 69 (May 1966): 366.
5. John Q. Adams, "Samoa's Love and Affection: In Appreciation of the Memorable Apostolic Visit of May, 1921," *IE* 26:645.
6. Ibid.
7. *DN,* January 1923; also SMHR, copy of *DN* article.
8. Ibid.; also MFSR, Samoa, 1922.
9. MHSM, March 31, 1932.
10. MFSR, Hawaii and Samoa, 1922, 1923.
11. Ibid., Samoa, 1928.
12. MHSM, December 31, 1930.
13. MFSR, Samoa, December 31, 1930.
14. MHSM, November 30, 1920; and June 13, 1933. A thirty-page letter from Willard L. Smith explaining the workings of the mission to his successor is included in the MHSM at this point.

15. MHSM, August 27, 1931.
16. Ibid., "Smith to successor."
17. Ibid.
18. Ibid., March 31, 1933.
19. Ibid., June 30, 1931.
20. MFSR, Samoa, 1924 and 1925.
21. Ibid., 1928; and MHSM, February 20 and August 1928.
22. MHSM, June 8–July 1, 1938.
23. Ibid., December 31, 1931.
24. SMHR, 1938-1951, by date.
25. Ibid.
26. Ibid., November 25, 1940.
27. Ibid.
28. Ibid., July 16, 1944.
29. Ibid., July, August, October 1944.

CHAPTER 24

1. SMHR, February 1948.
2. Ibid., July 7, 1905.
3. SMHR, October 1-3, 1948.
4. Earl S. Paul, interview June 8, 1976, Salt Lake City, Utah.
5. MSFR, Samoa, by year.
6. James Bishop, "American Samoa: Which Road Ahead?" *Pacific Studies* 1 (September 1977): 48-49.
7. Earl S. Paul, "Item of Interest of 1951 Mission," p. 1; copy in possession of the author.
8. Earl S. Paul, "Mission No. 3," p. 6; in possession of the author.
9. MHSM, by date.
10. Charles I. Sampson, "Mission Summary," pp. 2-3, in possession of the author.
11. Charles I. Sampson, Samoan Mission President's Daily Diary, January 19 to February 9, 1957, CA.
12. Sampson, "Mission Summary," p. 3.
13. Ibid., p. 4.
14. MHSM, June 13, 1958.
15. Sampson, "Missionary Summary," pp. 5-6.
16. J. Phillip Hanks, "Missionary Summary," p. 4, in possession of R. Lanier Britsch.
17. MFSR, Samoa, 1949.
18. Taylor, "LDS Church Schools," p. 66.
19. Ibid., p. 68.
20. MHSM, June 30, 1958.
21. Ibid., p. 69; Church Educational System, *Overview 1978*, p. 13.
22. Earl S. Paul, Papers, "Fourth Mission," copy in possession of R. Lanier Britsch; MHSM, addendum to December 1953 report.
23. Bishop, "American Samoa: Which Road Ahead?," p. 47.
24. Taylor, "LDS Church Schools," pp. 44-46, 49, 55, 59; interviews at Mapusaga, January 1974.
25. Church Educational System, *Overview 1978,* p. 38; Alton L. Wade, interview, January 31, 1979, Salt Lake City, Utah.
26. Hanks, "Mission Summary," p. 1.
27. Cummings, *Mighty Missionary,* p. 214.
28. Hanks, "Mission Summary," p. 1.
29. MHSM, March 31, 1955; see also David O. McKay, "Sauniatu," p 366.
30. Ibid.
31. MHSM, by date.

32. George Hunt, "Conference in Samoa," *Ensign* 6 (April 1976): 74.
33. *Deseret News 1979 Church Almanac,* p. 120.
34. R. Carl Harris et al., *Samoa Apia Mission History, 1888-1983* (Apia, Samoa: Samoa Apia Mission, 1983), passim; John H. Groberg, interview by R. Lanier Britsch, January 12, 1984, Salt Lake City, Utah; Dell Van Orden, "New Day Dawns for Temples in Pacific," *CN,* February 28, 1981, pp. 3-4; "Island's Leaders Impressed by Samoa Temple," *CN,* July 31, 1983, p. 3; Gerry Avant, "Members Rejoice at Samoa Rites," *CN,* August 14, 1983, pp. 3-5; Glen Y. M. Lung, "Statistical Growth of the LDS Church in Samoa and Tonga (for 1981)," *Proceedings of the Third Annual Conference of the Mormon Pacific Historical Society* (Laie, Hawaii: Brigham Young University—Hawaii Campus, 1982), pp. 20-21; Glen Y. M. Lung, "Statistical Growth of the LDS Church in Samoa and Tonga (for 1982)," *Proceedings of the Fourth Annual Conference of the Mormon Pacific Historical Society* (Laie, Hawaii: Brigham Young University—Hawaii Campus, 1983), pp. 23-24; Glen Y. M. Lung, "Statistical Growth of the LDS Church in Samoa and Tonga (for 1983)," taped, Laie, Hawaii, March 3, 1984.

CHAPTER 25

1. H. G. Cummings, ed., *Sources of Tongan History: A Collection of Documents, Extracts, and Contemporary Opinions in Tongan Political History, 1616-1900* (Nuku'alofa, Tonga, 1972), 58. Reproduced is the baptismal register from the archives of the Free Wesleyan Church of Tonga, Nuku'alofa.
2. Ibid., especially pp. 52-93; also, see Sione Latukefu, "King George Tubou I of Tonga," in *Pacific Island Portraits,* J. W. Davidson and Deryck Scarr, eds. (Wellington and Auckland: A. H. & A. W. Reed, 1970), pp. 55-75; Martin Jerrett-Kerr, *Patterns of Christian Acceptance: Individual Response to the Missionary Impact, 1550-1950* (London: Oxford University Press, 1972), 171-88; and Noel Rutherford, *Shirley Baker and the King of Tonga* (Melbourne, 1971). Rutherford's volume centers on the life of Baker but adds many insights concerning George Tubou I that cannot be gained elsewhere. The best summary of the Christianizing process is found in Alan R. Tippett, *People Movements in Southern Polynesia,* chapters 3 and 4.
3. Tippett, *People Movements,* 78-79, 111-26. Tippett has carefully reconstructed the elements in the comity agreement in the Tonga-Samoa area. See also Richard Lovett, *The History of the London Missionary Society, 1795-1895,* 2 vols. (London, 1899), 1:284-85.
4. J. E. Carruthers, *Memories of an Australian Ministry* (London: Epworth Press, 1922), pp. 146-49.
5. Rutherford, *Shirley Baker,* p. 131.
6. Cummings, *Sources of Tongan History,* pp. 385-86.
7. Andrew Jenson, "Manuscript History of the Tongan Mission," July 16, 1891, CA; hereinafter cited as MHTM.
8. Ibid., August 1, 1891.
9. Ibid., by date; and MHSM, April 18, 1897.
10. SMHR, March 19, 1907, CA.
11. Ermel J. Morton, *Brief History of the Tongan Mission of the Church of Jesus Christ of Latter-day Saints* (Suva, Fiji: Fiji Times Print, 1968), p. 10.
12. MFSR, Tonga, 1907.
13. SMHR, November 19, 1907.
14. Ibid.
15. Ibid., by date.
16. Ibid.
17. Ibid., July 25-26, 1909.
18. Tongatapu District, Tongan Mission, Record of Work, 1911-1923, CR9197 (old number 3210), CA; hereinafter cited as Tongatapu District Record.
19. Ibid.

20. SMHR, by date; and Morton, *Brief History,* p. 12.
21. Morton, *Brief History,* p. 12.
22. Malcolm R. Thorp, "The British Government and the Mormon Question, 1910-22," *Journal of Church and State* 21 (Spring 1979): 305-23.
23. Reynolds to Smith, March 5 ,1920, Tongan Mission Papers, CR9197-2, Box 2, CA.
24. MFSR, Tonga, by year.
25. Morton, *Brief History,* pp. 13-14; see also Tongan Mission Papers, CR9197, Box 2, fd. 2, CA.
26. Ibid.
27. Mark Vernon Coombs, Journal and Memoirs, 1920 to August 1926, typed copy, p. 60, CA.
28. Clare Middlemiss, comp., *Cherished Experiences from the Writings of David O. McKay* (Salt Lake City: Deseret Book Company, 1955), pp. 103-14.
29. Coombs, Journal, pp. 78-83.
30. The landholding system of Tonga is rather unusual. All land is the property of the crown, but it is divided into large estates that are assigned to hereditary nobles. There is no privately held land in the kingdom. Land can be leased by Tongans and foreigners, but it is subject to the approval of the cabinet. The cabinet did not have to approve leases that were transferred from one holder to another. It was this type of arrangement that appealed to President Coombs when he was seeking land for a school.
31. Coombs to Heber J. Grant, January 24, 1922, CA. Here Coombs quotes a letter from U. M. Umafuke, acting minister of lands. See also Coombs, Journal, p. 117.
32. Lord Milner, secretary of state for the Colonies, to Cecil Rodwell Hunter, high commissioner for the Western Pacific, October 6, 1919, archive file 2532/1919; Roger Greene to Islay McOwen, January 5, 1920, archive file 2532/1919. Both letters are held by Western Pacific Archives, Suva, Fiji, hereinafter cited as WPA.
33. Tu'ivakano to McOwan, November 13, 1919, file 2532/1919, WPA.
34. McOwan to Tu'ivakano, November 18, 1919, file 2532/1919; Tu'ivakano to McOwan, December 18, 1919, file 2532/1919, WPA.
35. Tu'ivakano to Vice Consul Masterton, February 25, 1920, file 2532/1919; Rodwell to Milner, March 24, 1920, file 2532/1919, WPA.
36. Milner to Rodwell, August 12, 1920, file 2532/1919; Foreign Office to Passport Control Officer, New York, August 18, 1920, file 2532/1920, WPA.
37. Winston Churchill to High Commissioner, December 19, 1921, file 1009/1921, WPA. It is not clear from the records I have reviewed whether the British ambassador in Washington, D.C., actually contacted the U.S. State Department on this matter, or, if he did, at what level discussion took place. Considering the response of Secretary Charles Evans Hughes when he learned about the law's passage, it appears doubtful whether he was contacted about the then proposed legislation.
38. *Tongan Government Gazette,* number 21, Tuesday, July 18, 1922, p. 113; see also MFSR, Tonga, 1922.
39. Coombs, Journal, passim.
40. Coombs to Grant, June 30, 1923; and August 4, 1923, Tonga Papers, CA.
41. Coombs, Journal, p. 118. Much social disruption was caused when the practice of polygamy was stopped in the 1830s and 1840s; thus, it is not surprising that this would be at the head of the list of complaints against the Latter-day Saints.
42. "Translation of Transcript of the Minutes of the Legislative Assembly of Tonga, June 30, 1922," Tonga Papers, CA. This problem was considered a serious one by Prince Tungi long before the legislative debate took place. In an interview with Elder David O. McKay of the LDS Church's Council of Twelve Apostles, which was held during Elder McKay's visit to Tonga in 1921, Elder McKay asked Tungi this question: "Upon what grounds do you object to our missionaries?" Prince Tungi replied: "The other churches were here first and their ministers think that you are taking too many of their people away from them." Coombs, Journal, p. 120.
43. Coombs was misinformed concerning the power of the high commissioner (as was the U.S. vice consul in Apia). The high commissioner's authority did not extend to beyond consul-

tation and advice. He could not invalidate the passport law even if he deemed it desirable to do so.

44. Cummings, *Sources,* p. 193.
45. Coombs, Journal, pp. 194, 196-97.
46. Coombs argued his case under three general headings. He pointed out that on constitutional grounds the exclusion law was not legal because (1) the section did not effect all classes equally; (2) it was retrospective in its ultimate effect; and (3) it was provocative and incitive of discrimination against the Latter-day Saints.
47. MFSR, Tonga, 1924.
48. Coombs to First Presidency, October 26, 1924, Tongan Papers, CA.

CHAPTER 26

1. Coombs, Journal p. 201ff.
2. Ibid., passim.
3. Jay A. Cahoon Oral History, interview by R. Lanier Britsch, 1973, typescript, p. 11, The James Moyle Oral History Program, CA; MFSR, Tonga, 1929.
4. MFSR, Tonga, by year.
5. Ibid., 1932; and Morton, *Brief History,* p. 30.
6. Ibid., 1934.
7. Ibid.; MHTM, August 31, 1934.
8. MHTM, August 31, 1934.
9. Ibid., May 31, 1935
10. MFSR, Tonga, 1936.
11. Emile C. and Evelyn H. Dunn Oral History, interview by R. Lanier Britsch, 1978, typescript, pp. 16-17, James Moyle Oral History Program, CA.
12. MFSR, Tonga, 1938.
13. MHTM, May 31 and August 31, 1938.
14. MFSR, Tonga, 1938.
15. Morton, *Brief History,* pp. 36-37; Dunn Oral History, p. 22.
16. Ibid., p. 39.
17. MHTM, November 30, 1940.
18. Ibid., and MFSR, Tonga, 1940.
19. MFSR, Tonga, 1943; see also MHTM, February 28, 1943, and November 30, 1943.
20. MFSR, Tonga, 1944.
21. MHTM, by date.
22. Ibid.
23. Ibid., June 24, 1947.
24. MHTM, passim; and Dunn Oral History, pp. 36ff.
25. Together Emile and Evelyn Dunn have since served missions in Rarotonga and at the London Temple. Information for this section has been drawn from the following sources: MHTM, passim; MFSR, Tonga, 1947-51; Morton, *Brief History,* pp. 44-49; Taylor, "LDS Church Schools," pp. 125-29; and Dunn Oral History.

CHAPTER 27

1. MFSR, Tonga, 1951.
2. Ibid., by year.
3. Ibid., 1952, 1953, 1954, 1955.
4. MHTM, December 31, 1953.
5. MFSR, Tonga, 1953, 1954.

6. MHTM, December 31, 1953.
7. Bunge-Kruger Oral History, pp. 4-8, see notes to chapter 5.
8. Ibid., passim.
9. Pacific Board of Education Report to the First Presidency, December 1, 1961, p. 15, in possession of author.
10. Taylor, "LDS Church Schools," p. 136.
11. Patrick D. Dalton, Jr., Oral History, interview by R. Lanier Britsch, 1974, p. 16, Oral History Program of the Church, CA.
12. MHTM, March 31, 1955.
13. Dalton Oral History, p. 15.
14. MHTM, June 26, 1947. Most of the information for this section is derived from Taylor, "LDS Church Schools," pp. 134-59. Taylor's principal sources appear to be MHTM and private records to which he had access.
15. John H. Groberg Oral History, interview by R. Lanier Britsch, 1975, passim, James Moyle Oral History Program, CA.
16. Ibid., pp. 6-7.
17. MHTM, by date.
18. Groberg Oral History, p. 4.
19. John H. Groberg, papers in his possession.
20. Ibid., passim; MHTM, by date, and Morton *Brief History,* passim.
21. Charles Woodworth, interview, January 16, 1974, Nuku' alofa, Tonga.
22. John H. Groberg, interview, January 16, 1979, Orem, Utah.
23. Alton L. Wade, interview, January 31, 1979, Salt Lake City, utah.
24. Lung, "Statistical Growth . . . in Samoa and Tonga (for 1981)," pp. 20-21; Lung, "Statistical Growth . . ." pp. 23-24.
25. Marie Paongo, "Conference in Tonga," *Ensign* 6 (May 1976): 138-39.
26. See Spencer W. Kimball, "When the World Will be Converted," *Ensign* 4 (October 1974): 12.
27. Groberg Oral History, p. 14.
28. Gerry Avant, "Tongans Sing, Dance, Weep at Dedication," *CN,* August 14, 1983, p. 7.
29. Lung, "Statistical Growth . . . in Samoa and Tonga (for 1983)," taped, John H. Groberg, interview by R. Lanier Britsch, January 12, 1984, Salt Lake City, Utah; Dell Van Orden, "New Day Dawns for Temples in Pacific," *CN,* February 28, 1981, pp. 3-4; "Tongan Royalty Tour Temple," *CN,* July 24, 1983, p. 4; "Tonga Sons, Daughters Serve with Devotion" (Dedicatory Prayer), *CN,* August 14, 1983, p. 4.

CHAPTER 28

1. Fiji Mission, Historical Record, June 28, 1973, CA, hereinafter cited as FMHR.
2. Latourette, *The Expansion of Christianity,* 5:220-21.
3. Ibid., p. 223.
4. Tudor, *Pacific Islands Year Book,* 11th ed., pp. 267, 291.
5. MHSM, September 30, 1954.
6. Middlemiss, *Cherished Experiences,* pp. 111-12; Mary and Margaret Ashley, taped recollections, January 26, 1974 Auckland, New Zealand, in possession of R. Lanier Britsch.
7. MHSM, March 31, 1958.
8. MHTM, June 30, 1958.
9. Ibid., March 31, 1959.
10. Kinisimere W. R. Sokia Oral History, interview by R. Lanier Britsch, 1974, typescript, pp. 1-3, James Moyle Oral History Program, CA; Josefa N. T. Sokia Oral History, interview by R. Lanier Britsch, 1974, typescript p. 12, James Moyle Oral History Program, CA.
11. Groberg Oral History, 1975, p. 33.
12. FMHR, February 23, 1976; Maraia Sokia, "Conference in Fiji," *Ensign* 6 (April 1976): 77.

13. Taylor, "LDS Church Schools," p. 148.
14. Alton L. Wade, interview by R. Lanier Britsch, January 31, 1979, Salt Lake City, Utah.
15. Ibid.; Ebbie Davis, interview by R. Lanier Britsch, August 1975, Provo, Utah.
16. Church Educational System, *Overview 1978,* p. 38.
17. Mike Foley, "Schools, Saints Aid LDS Image in Fiji," *CN,* January 8, 1983, p. 7; "First Stake Created In Island Nation of Fiji," *CN,* July 10, 1983, p. 4; and "Converts: Island's Pearls: Fijian Who Once Hid From Elders Is Now Stake Leader," *CN,* October 16, 1983, p. 6.
18. Karl M. Richards, "Noumea-New Caledonia," a brief unpublished sketch, copy in possession of R. Lanier Britsch.
19. Karl M. Richards Oral History, interview by R. Lanier Britsch, typescript, pp. 49-56, James Moyle Oral History Program, CA.
20. FMHR, September 23, 1973; October 31, 1974; and June 7, 1975.
21. Ibid., by date.
22. Ibid., see especially June 9, 1974; February 4 and 6, 1975.
23. Richard M. Pratt to Ward H. Magleby, December 31, 1978, copy in possession of R. Lanier Britsch.
24. Alton L. Wade, "Gilbert Island Update," May 17, 1977, Church Educational System papers.
25. FMHR, July 16, 1974.
26. This section has been written from the private records of Alton L. Wade, CES administrator of the South Pacific; from Fiji Suva Mission, Historical Reports, by date; and from Richard M. Pratt's letter, noted above.
27. Alf Pratte, "Message is taken to the Pacific Isles: Gospel is Taught to the Micronesians," *CN,* March 24, 1979, p. 3.
28. Sources for this section include John H. Groberg Oral History, interview by Gordon Irving, 1978, typescript pp. (1) 26, 47, and (2) 26-27, 51, James Moyle Oral History Program, CA; John H. Groberg interview by R. Lanier Britsch, January 16, 1979, Salt Lake City, Utah; Alf Pratte, "The Gospel Moves to Micronesia," *Ensign* 8 (February 1978): 76-77; Robert E. Crandall to R. Lanier Britsch, June 25, 1976, in possession of R. Lanier Britsch; Judy Tudor, *Pacific Islands Year Book,* pp. 235-63, passim; Ferron C. and Fay Losee, interview, February 23, 1984, Provo, Utah; Micronesia-Guam Mission, Missionary Conference, October 15-18, 1982, Barrigada, Guam (this record includes brief reports and historical summaries from all parts of the mission).
29. "Branch Thrives as Church Taken to New Guinea," *CN,* June 27, 1981, p. 5; "Crossing Cultures to Modern Nation, First Missionaries from New Guinea," *CN,* October 2, 1983, p. 13; Dennis D. Flake, telephone interview by R. Lanier Britsch, February 22, 1984.

SOURCES CONSULTED

GENERAL REFERENCES AND BIBLIOGRAPHICAL GUIDES

Allen, James B., and Leonard, Glen M. *The Story of the Latter-day Saints.* Salt Lake City: Deseret Book Company, 1976.

Arrington, Leonard J. *Great Basin Kingdom: An Economic History of the Latter-day Saints, 1830-1900.* Cambridge: Harvard University Press, 1958.

———, and Bitton, Davis. *The Mormon Experience: A History of the Latter-day Saints.* New York: Alfred A. Knopf, 1979.

Clement, Russell T. *Mormons in the Pacific: A Bibliography.* Laie, Hawaii: The Institute for Polynesian Studies, 1981.

Forman, Charles W. *The Island Churches of the South Pacific: Emergence in the Twentieth Century.* Maryknoll, New York: Orbis Books, 1982.

Garrett, John, *To Live among the Stars: Christian origins in Oceania.* Geneva, Switzerland, and Suva, Fiji: World Council of Churches in association with the Institute of Pacfic Studies, University of the South Pacific, 1982.

Roberts, Brigham H. *Comprehensive History of the Church, Century One.* 6 vols. Salt Lake City: Deseret Book Company, 1930.

Smith, Joseph. *History of the Church of Jesus Christ of Latter-day Saints.* Edited by B. H. Roberts, 7 vols. Salt Lake City: The Church of Jesus Christ of Latter-day Saints, 1902-1932.

UNPUBLISHED SOURCES

CHURCH RECORDS AND MANUSCRIPTS

Unless otherwise noted, all items cited in this section are found in the Historical Department Archives of The Church of Jesus Christ of Latter-day Saints, Salt Lake City, Utah.

Australia East Mission. Historical Record, 1891-1897.

Bigler, Henry W. Journal.

Brigham Young Letterbooks.

Bromley, William. Journal.

Bunnell, Christie R., comp. Autobiography of Lars Christian Rasmussen. Copy in possession of R. Lanier Britsch.

Cannon, George Q. Journal of Travels to the Hawaiian Mission Jubilee. Typescript of dictation taken by Clawson Y. Cannon. Copy in possession of R. Lanier Britsch.

Chamberlain, William Henry. Diaries 1897-1900.

Cluff, Harvey Harris. Autobiography. Handwritten copy.

Coombs, Mark Vernon. Journal and Memoirs, 1920 to August 1926. Typed copy.

Damron, Joseph W., Jr. Missionary Labors of Joseph W. Damron, Jr. In his own handwriting.

Dean, Joseph H. Journals.

Farrer, William. Biographical Sketch. Hawaiian Mission Report and Diary, 1821-1906. Typescript, in Special Collections, Harold B. Lee Library, Brigham Young University, Provo, Utah. Hereinafter cited as BYU-SC.

Fiji Mission. Historical Record.

First Presidency Letterpress Books. Vol. 24.

French Polynesian Mission. Historical Record, 1900-1930.

French Polynesian Mission. Quarterly Historical Reports.

Gibson, Walter Murray. Gibson's diary is reproduced as an appendix in Frank W. McGhie, "Life and Intrigues . . ."

Green, Ephraim. Diary. Typescript in BYU-SC.

Hammond, Francis A. Journals, 1852-1884.

Hawaiian Mission. General Minutes.

Hinckley, Gordon B. Journal. In possession of President Hinckley. Salt Lake City, Utah.

Manuscript Histories. Andrew Jenson, assistant church historian, directed the compilation of a number of manuscript histories. For the earlier years these histories consisted of journal entries taken from diaries, journals, and other writings of missionaries to various fields. They also frequently included documents and newspaper clippings of significance. During the later years these histories included but were not entirely limited to quarterly historical reports that were submitted by the missions. The Manuscript Histories used in this study include "Australia Mission," "French Polynesia Mission," "Hawaiian Mission," "New Zealand Mission," "Samoan Mission," and "Tongan Mission."

Matthew and Elizabeth DeEtte Laker Noall. Journals, Reports, and Letters to the First Presidency, etc. Western Americana Collection. Mariott Library, University of Utah Library, Salt Lake City.

Manuscript History of Brigham Young.

Mission Financial and Statistical Reports, by mission.

Murdock, John. Journal.

New Zealand Mission, Historical Record.

Partridge, Edward, Jr. Journal.

Richards, Ezra Foss. Journal. BYU-SC.

Samoan Mission, Historical Record.

Samoan Mission, Historical Report.

Sampson, Charles I. Samoan Mission President's Daily Diary.

Sanders, Sondra. Journal. Book One.

Seegmiller, William A. Journals 1891-1895.

Tongan Mission Papers.

Tongan Mission, Tongatapu District, Record of Work, 1911-1923.

Woodbury, John Stillman. Journal. BYU-SC.

Woolley, Samuel E. Journals.

Record collections in two other archives were useful in completing this study: Western Pacific Archives, Suva, Fiji; and State of Hawaii, Archives, Honolulu, Hawaii.

THESES AND DISSERTATIONS

Atkin, Dennis H. "A History of Iosepa, The Utah Polynesian Colony." M. A. thesis, Brigham Young University, 1958.

Barker, Ian R. "The Connexion: The Mormon Church and the Maori People." M. A. thesis, Victoria University of Wellington, 1967.

Beck, Raymond Clyde. "Palawai Basin: Hawaii's Mormon Zion." M. A. thesis, University of Hawaii, 1972.

Bock, Margaret Comfort. "The Church of Jesus Christ of Latter-day Saints in the Hawaiian Islands." M. A. thesis, University of Hawaii, 1941.

Boone, David F. "The Worldwide Evacuation of Latter-day Saint Missionaries at the Beginning of World War II." M. A. thesis, Brigham Young University, 1981.

Hartshorn, Leon R. "Mormon Education in the Bold Years." Ed.D. dissertation, Standford University, 1965.

Harvey, Richard C. "The Development of the Church of Jesus Christ of Latter-day Saints in Hawaii." M. A. thesis, Brigham Young University, 1974.

Hunt, Brian W. "History of the Chruch of Jesus Christ of Latter-day Saints in New Zealand." M. A. thesis, Brigham Young University, 1971.

McGhie, Frank W. "The Life and Intrigues of Walter Murray Gibson." M. A. thesis, Brigham Young University, 1958.

Pierce, Bernard Francis. "Acculturation of Samoans in the Mormon Village of Laie, Hawaii." M. A. thesis, University of Hawaii, 1956.

Sousa, Esther L. "Walter Murray Gibson's Rise to Power in Hawaii." M. A. thesis, University of Hawaii, 1942.

Stanton, Max E. "Samoan Saints: The Samoans in the Mormon Village of Laie, Hawaii." Ph.D. dissertation, University of Oregon, 1973.

ADDRESSES, ARTICLES, AND STUDIES

Area Book for Australia/New Guinea. December 7, 1983. Management Information Center, The Church of Jesus Christ of Latter-day Saints, Salt Lake City, Utah.

Brief History of Paea Branch. Typescript in possession of R. Lanier Britsch.

Clissold, Edward L. "Address." Dedication of the Church College of Hawaii. December 17, 1958. Typescript in CA.

Cockett, J. Pia. "Visit of President David O. McKay in 1921." Typescript in CA.

Hanks, J. Phillip. "Mission Summary." In possession of R. Lanier Britsch.

Ivins, Antoine R. "Laie Plantation." Typescript, CA.

Loveland, Jerry K. "Dedication of the Old Laie Chapel." Typescript in possession of Eugene Cambell, Brigham Young University, Provo, Utah. The manuscript quotes at length from the original minutes of the dedication by William G. Farrell, conference clerk.

McGhie, Frank W. "Religious Education in the Hawaiian Islands." Typescript, CA.

Meha, Stuart. "The New Zealand Mission." Typescript, Mendenhall Library, Church College of New Zealand, Temple View, N. Z.

Micronesia-Guam Missionary Conference. October 15-18, 1982. Barrigada, Guam. Contains short historical summaries of mission areas.

Musser, Joseph B. "Laie—Home Place of the Church in Hawaii." Typescript, CA.

Pacific Board of Education Report to the First Presidency. December 1, 1961. Copy in possession of R. Lanier Britsch.

Paul, Earl S. "Items of Interest 1951 Mission." Copy in possession of R. Lanier Britsch.

———. "Mission No. 3." In possession of R. Lanier Britsch.

———. Papers, "Fourth Mission." Copy in possession of R. Lanier Britsch.

Richards, Karl M. "A History of the French Polynesian Mission." Typescript in possession of R. Lanier Britsch.

———. "Noumea-New Caledonia." A brief unpublished sketch. Copy in possession of R. Lanier Britsch.

Sampson, Charles I. "Mission Summary." In possession of R. Lanier Britsch.

Sheffield, H. J. Missionary Experience of Heber James Sheffield in Tidal Wave and Cyclone in the Society Islands. 1903. CA.

Taylor, Harvey L. "The Story of the LDS Church Schools." 2 vols. Typed manuscript prepared for the Church Commissioner of Education, 1971.

Wade, Alton L. "Gilbert Island Update." May 17, 1977. Church Educational System papers.

ORAL HISTORIES

Ballif, Ariel S. Oral History. Interviews by R. Lanier Britsch. 1973. Typescript. Oral History Program, CA.

Bird, J. Martel. Oral History. Interviews by Charles Ursenbach. 1976. Typescript. The James Moyle Oral History Program, CA.

Bunge-Kruger, Fritz. Oral History. Interview by R. Lanier Britsch. 1974. Typescript. The James Moyle Oral History Program, CA.
Cahoon, Jay A. Oral History. Interviews by R. Lanier Britsch. 1973. Typescript. The James Moyle Oral History Program, CA.
Clissold, Edward L. Oral History. Interview by R. Lanier Britsch. 1976. Typescript. James Moyle Oral History Program, CA.
Christensen, Elwood L. Oral History. Interview by R. Lanier Britsch. 1974. Typescript. James Moyle Oral History Program, CA.
Dalton, Patrick D., Jr. Oral History. Interview by R. Lanier Britsch. 1974. Tyepscript. James Moyle Oral History Program, CA.
Dunn, Emile C., and Dunn, Evelyn H. Oral History. Interview by R. Lanier Britsch. 1978. Typescript. The James Moyle Oral History Program, CA.
Fuller, Vahineite Piimoua. Oral History. Interview by R. Lanier Britsch. 1974. Typescript. The James Moyle Oral History Program, CA.
Goaslind, Jack H., Jr. Oral History. Interviews by Gordon Irving. 1981-82. Typescript. The James Moyle Oral History Program, CA.
Groberg, John H. Oral History. Interview by R. Lanier Britsch. 1975. The James Moyle Oral History Program, CA.
———. Oral History. Interview by Gordon Irving. 1978. Typescript. The James Moyle Oral History Program, CA.
Perrott, William R. Oral History. Interview by R. Lanier Britsch. 1974. The James Moyle Oral History Program, CA.
Richards, Karl M. Oral History. Interviews by R. Lanier Britsch. 1973. Typescript. James Moyle Oral History Program, CA.
Romney, Marion G. Oral History. Interviews by James B. Allen. 1972 and 1973. Typescript. James Moyle Oral History Program, CA.
Russon, Leo W. Oral History. Interview by R. Lanier Britsch. 1974. The James Moyle Oral History Program, CA.
Simpson, Robert L. Oral History. Interviews by Gordon Irving. 1978. Typescript. The James Moyle Oral History Program, CA.
Sokia, Kinisimere W. R. Oral History. Interview by R. Lanier Britsch. 1974. Typescript. The James Moyle Oral History Program, CA.
Sokia, Josefa N. T. Oral History. Interview by R. Lanier Britsch. 1974. Typescript. The James Moyle Oral History Program, CA.
Strother, Douglas H. Oral History. Interivew by R. Lanier Britsch. 1974. The James Moyle Oral History Program, CA.
Tapu, Raituia T. Oral History. Interview by R. Lanier Britsch. 1974. Typescript. The James Moyle Oral History Program, CA.
Tingey, Clarence H. Oral History. Interview by R. Lanier Britsch. 1973. Typescript. Oral History Program, CA.
Young, Gordon Claridge. Oral History. Interviews by Lauritz G. Petersen. 1972. Typescript. Oral History Program, CA.

INTERVIEWS, LETTERS, AND TAPED RECOLLECTIONS

Anderson, Alexander P., to R. Lanier Britsch. July 22, 1976. In possession of the R. Lanier Britsch.
Ashley, Mary and Margaret. Taped recollections. January 26, 1974. Auckland, New Zealand. In possession of R. Lanier Britsch.
Barnes, C. Douglas. Taped recollections and documents. In possession of R. Lanier Britsch.
Berrett, William E. Interview. June 23, 1976. Provo, Utah.
Clissold, Edward L. Interview. June 11, 1976. Salt Lake City, Utah.
Crandall, Robert E., to R. Lanier Britsch. June 25, 1976. In possession of R. Lanier Britsch.
Dunn, Loren C. Interview. January 10, 1984. Salt Lake City, Utah.
Davis, Ebbie. Interviews. August 1975 and January 1979. Provo, Utah.

Flake, Dennis D. Telephone interview. February 22, 1984.
Groberg, John H. Interview. January 16, 1979. Salt Lake City, Utah.
———. Interview. January 12, 1984. Salt Lake City, Utah.
Lake, Bruce M. Interviews. September 28 and November 2, 1982. Salt Lake City, Utah.
Losee, Ferron C. and Fay. Interview. February 23, 1984. Provo, Utah.
Lung, Glen Y. M. "Statistical Growth of the LDS Church in Samoa and Tonga (for 1983)." Taped. Laie, Hawaii, March 3, 1984.
Manea, Claire T. Interview. January 4, 1974. Papeete, Tahiti.
Orme, Elvon W. Interview. August 31, 1978. Salt Lake City, Utah.
Paul, Earl S. Interview. June 8, 1976. Salt Lake City.
Pinegar, Rex D. Interview. June 29, 1984. Salt Lake City, Utah.
Pratt, Richard M., to Ward H. Magleby. December 31, 1978. Copy in possession of R. Lanier Britsch.
Wade, Alton L. Interview. January 31, 1979. Salt Lake City, Utah.
Waldron, Eldred L., to R. Lanier Britsch. June 15, 1976. In possession of R. Lanier Britsch.
Woodworth, Charles. Interview. January 16, 1974. Nuku'alofa, Tonga.

PUBLISHED SOURCES

BOOKS

Allen, Helena G. *The Betrayal of Liliuokalani, Last Queen of Hawaii, 1838-1917.* Glendale, California: The Arthur H. Clark Company, 1982.
Brewer, W. Karl. *Armed with the Spirit: Missionary Experience in Samoa.* Provo, Utah: Young House of Brigham Young University Press, 1975.
Brown, James S. *Giant of the Lord: The Life of a Pioneer.* Salt Lake City: Bookcraft, Inc., 1960. Orig. pub. 1902.
Building Missionaries in Hawaii. n.p., n.d.
Burden, R. M. *The New Dominion: A Social and Political History of New Zealand, 1918-39.* Wellington: A. H. & A. W. Reed, 1965.
Butterworth, F. Edward. *Roots of the Reorganization: French Polynesia.* Independence, Missouri: Herald Publishing House, 1977.
———. *The Adventures of John Hawkins: Restoration Pioneer.* Independence, Missouri: Herald Publishing House, 1963.
Cannon, George Q. *My First Mission.* 2nd ed. Salt Lake City: Juvenile Instructor Office, 1882.
Carruthers, J. E. *Memories of an Australian Ministry.* London: Epworth Press, 1922.
Clark, Manning. *Short History of Australia.* New York: The New American Library, 1969.
Cowley, Matthew. *Matthew Cowley Speaks.* Salt Lake City: Deseret Book Company, 1954.
Cummings, David W. *Centennial History of Laie,* 1965.
———. *Mighty Missionary of the Pacific.* Salt Lake City: Bookcraft Inc., 1961.
Cummings, H. G., ed. *Sources of Tongan History: A Collection of Documents, Extracts, and Contemporary Opinions in Tongan Political History, 1616-1900.* Nuku'alofa, Tonga, 1972.
Danielsson, Bengt. *Raroia.* Chicago: Rand McNally & Company, 1953.
Davies, John. *The History of the Tahitian Mission, 1799-1830.* Edited by C. W. Newbury. Cambridge: Published for the Hakluyt Society, at the University Press, 1961.
Daws, Gavan. *Shoal of Time: A History of the Hawaiian Islands.* Honolulu: University of Hawaii Press, 1968.
Gates, Susa Young. "A Remarkable Life." The life of Mary Chittenden in *Heroines of "Mormondom," the Second Book of the Noble Women's Lives Series.* Salt Lake City: Juvenile Instructor Office, 1884.
Grattan, C. Hartley. *The Southwest Pacific to 1900.* And *The South West Pacific Since 1900.* Ann Arbor: University of Michigan Press, 1963.
Harris, R. Carl., et al. *Samoa Apia Mission History, 1888-1983.* Apia, Samoa: Samoa Apia Mission, 1983.

Jenson, Andrew, comp. *Church Chronology.* 2nd ed., rev. and enl. Salt Lake City: Deseret News Press, 1899.

———. *Encyclopaedic History of the Church* . . . . Salt Lake City: Deseret News Publishing Co., 1941.

Jerrett-Kerr, Martin. *Patterns of Christian Acceptance: Individual Response to the Missionary Impact, 1550-1950.* London: Oxford University Press, 1972.

Johnson, Benjamin F. *My Life's Review.* Independence, Missouri: Zion's Printing and Publishing Co., 1947.

Judd, Gerrit P. *Hawaii: An Informal History.* New York: Collier-Macmillan, 1961.

Koshinen, Aarne A. *Missionary Influence as a Political Factor in the Pacific Islands.* Helsinki, 1953. Reprinted, University Microfilms International, 1978.

Kuykendall, Ralph S. *Hawaiian Kingdom.* 3 vols. Honolulu: University of Hawaii Press, 1947.

Latourette, Kenneth Scott. *A History of the Expansion of Christianity.* 7 vols. New York: Harper and Row, Publishers, 1943.

Latukefu, Sione. "King George Tubou I of Tonga." In *Pacific Island Portraits.* Edited by J. W. Davidson and Deryck Scarr. Willington and Auckland: A. H. & A. W. Reed, 1970.

Law, Reuben D. *The Founding and Early Development of the Church College of Hawaii.* St. George, Utah: Dixie College Press, 1972.

Lovett, Richard. *The History of the London Missionary Society, 1795-1895.* 2 vols. London, 1899.

Michener, James A., and Day, A. Grove. "Gibson, the King's Evil Angel." In *Rascals in Paradise.* London: Secker and Warburg, 1957.

Middlemiss, Clare, comp. *Cherished Experiences from the Writings of David O. McKay.* Salt Lake City: Deseret Book Company, 1955.

Morrell, Jeannette McKay. *Highlights in the Life of President David O. McKay.* Salt Lake City: Deseret Book Company, 1966.

Morison, Samuel Eliot. *The Oxford History of the American People.* New York: Oxford University Press, 1965.

Morton, Ermel J. *Brief History of the Tongan Mission of The Church of Jesus Christ of Latter-day Saints.* Suva, Fiji: Fiji Times Print, 1968.

Noall, Matthew. *To My Children.* Salt Lake City: Utah Printing Company, n.d.

O'Brien, Robert. *Hands across the Water, The Story of the Polynesian Cultural Center.* Laie, Hawaii: Polynesian Cultural Center, 1983.

Potter, Amasa. "The Lord's Blessings." In *Faith Promoting Series, Twelfth Book.* Salt Lake City: Juvenile Instructor Office, 1884.

Pratt, Louisa Barnes. "Journal of Louisa Barnes Pratt." Compiled by Kate B. Carter. *Heart Throbs of the West,* vol. 8. Salt Lake City: Daughters of Utah Pioneers, 1967.

Pratt, Parley P. *Autobiography of Parley P. Pratt.* Salt Lake City: Deseret Book Company, 1938.

Roberts, Stephen H. *The History of French Colonial Policy, 1870-1925.* Hamden, Connecticut: Archon Books, 1963. First published in 1929 by P. S. King and Company, Great Britain.

Rutherford, Noel. *Shirley Baker and the King of Tonga.* Melbourne: Oxford University Press, 1971.

Smith, Henry A. *Matthew Cowley—Man of Faith.* Salt Lake City: Bookcraft Publishers, 1954.

Smith, Joseph Fielding. *The Life of Joseph F. Smith.* Salt Lake City: Deseret Book Company, 1938.

Smith, Joseph Fielding, III, and Stewart, John. *The Life of Joseph Fielding Smith.* Salt Lake City: Deseret Book Company, 1972.

Snow, Eliza R. *Biography and Family Record of Lorenzo Snow.* Salt Lake City: Deseret News Company, 1884.

Schwimmer, Eric G. *The World of the Maori.* Wellington, New Zealand: A. H. & A. W. Reed, 1966.

Thurston, Lorrin A. *Memoirs of the Hawaiian Revolution.* Honolulu, 1936.

Tippett, Alan R. *People Movements in Southern Polynesia: Studies in the Dynamics of Church-planting and Growth in Tahiti, New Zealand, Tonga, and Samoa.* Chicago: Moody Press, 1971.

Tudor, Jane, ed. *Pacific Islands Yearbook.* 11th ed. Sydney: Pacific Publications, 1972.
Vietsch, E. von. *Wilhelm Solf: Botschafter Zwischen den Zeiten.* 1961.
West, F. J. *Political Advancement in the South Pacific.* Melbourne: Oxford University Press, 1961.

ARTICLES, BOOKLETS AND PAMPHLETS

Baldridge, Kenneth W. "Search for a Site: Selection of the CCH Campus." *Proceedings of the Fourth Annual Conference of the Mormon Pacific Historical Society.* Laie, Hawaii: Brigham Young University-Hawaii Campus (BYU-HC), 1983.
Barrett, Gwynn. "Walter Murray Gibson: The Shepherd Saint of Lanai Revisited." *Utah Historical Quarterly* 40 (Spring 1972): 142-162.
Bishop, James. "American Samoa: Which Road Ahead?" *Pacific Studies* 1 (September 1977): 47-53.
Britsch, R. Lanier. "Another Visit With Walter Murray Gibson." *Utah Historical Quarterly* 46 (Winter 1978): 65-78.
Cambell, Eugene E. "The Mormon Gold-Mining Mission of 1849." *Brigham Young University Studies (BYU Studies)* 1 & 2 (Autumn-Winter, 1959-1960): 19-31.
Chase, Lance D. "Character as Destiny: The Hawaiian Mission Crisis of 1874." *Proceedings of the First Annual Conference of the Mormon Pacific Historical Society.* Laie, Hawaii: BYU-HC, 1980.
———. "Life in Early Laie, 1850-80." *Proceedings of the Second Annual Conference of the Mormon Pacific Historical Society.* Laie, Hawaii: BYU-HC, 1981.
"Church College of Hawaii Becomes BYU Campus." *Ensign* 4 (June 1974): 65.
Church Educational System Overview 1978. Salt Lake City: Church Educational System, 1978.
Clark, J. Reuben, Jr. "The Outpost in Mid-Pacific." *The Improvement Era* 38 (September 1935): 532-533. Hereinafter cited as *IE.*
Clement, Russell T., and Tsai, Sheng-Luen. "East Wind to Hawaii: Contributions of Chinese and Japanese Mormons in Hawaii." *Proceedings of the Second Annual Conference of the Mormon Pacific Historical Society.* Laie, Hawaii: BYU-HC, 1981.
Conkling, J. Christopher. "Members without a Church: Japanese Mormons in Japan from 1924 to 1948." *BYU Studies* 15 (Winter 1975): 191-214.
"Conference in Tahiti." *Ensign* 6 (May 1976): 144.
Cox, Roscoe E. "Religious Education in Hawaii." *IE* 44 (December 1941): 728.
Cowley, Matthew. "Maori Chief Predicts Coming of L.D.S. Missionaries." *IE* 53 (September 1950): 697.
Crawley, Peter. "The First Australian Mormon Imprints" *Gradalis Review* 2 (Fall 1973) 1:43.
Deseret News 1976 Church Almanac. Salt Lake City: Deseret News, 1976.
Directory: Church of Jesus Christ of Latter-day Saints Hawaiian Mission. Honolulu: n.p., 1934.
Dunn, Loren C. "Faithful Laborers." *Ensign* 5 (May 1975): 25-26.
Dykes, Mervyn. "Ben Couch, Cabinet Minister in New Zealand Parliament." *Ensign* 13 (April 1983): 25-28.
Ellsworth, S. George. "Zion in Paradise: Early Mormons in the South Seas." The Faculty Association: Utah State University, 1959.
Forman, Charles W. "Tonga's Tortured Venture in Church Unity." *The Journal of Pacific History* 13 (Parts 1 and 2, 1978): 3-21.
Green, Doyle L. "Mission to Polynesia: The Story of Addison Pratt and the Society Islands Mission." *IE* 52-53 (1949-1950).
Greenwood, Alma. "My New Zealand Mission." *Juvenile Instructor* 20 (1885): 114ff. This is a multi-part series.
"Ground Broken for the First Temple in Australia." *Ensign* 12 (October 1982): 77.
Hunt, George. "Conference in Samoa." *Ensign* 6 (April 1976): 74.
Kimball, Spencer W. "When the World Will Be Converted." *Ensign* 4 (October 1974): 3-14.
Larson, Gustive O. "The Mormon Reformation." *Utah Historical Quarterly* 26 (January 1958): 45-63.
Lee, William O. "Political Samoa." *IE* 2 (June 1899): 434-41.

Lung, Glen Y. M. "Statistical Growth of the LDS Church in Samoa and Tonga (for 1981)." *Proceedings of the Third Annual Conference of the Mormon Pacific Historical Society.* Laie, Hawaii: BYU-HC, 1982.

———. "Statistical Growth of the LDS Church in Samoa and Tonga (for 1982)." *Proceedings of the Fourth Annual Conference of the Mormon Pacific Historical Society.* Laie, Hawaii: BYU-HC, 1983.

Marlow, Darold M. "Rarotonga." *IE* 69 (June 1966): 410-11.

McKay, David O. "Sauniatu." *IE* 69 (May 1966): 364-66.

McKay, Iain B. "Conference in New Zealand." *Ensign* 6 (April 1976): 75-77.

Mitchell, Garry P. "The Church in Australia." *Ensign* 6 (February 1976): 13-19.

Moody, William A. "At Rest on the Hill Overlooking the sea." *IE* 14 (1911): 113-17.

Mol, J. J. "The Religious Affiliations of the New Zealand Maoris." *Oceania* 35 (1964-65): 136-43.

Musser, Joseph B. "Walter Murray Gibson—Oceanic Adventurer." *U.S. Naval Institute Proceedings* 52 (September 1926): 1709-1732.

New Zealand Division, Seminary and Institute Department. *New Zealand Church History.* Unit 9, 1974.

Olsen, Nolan P. "New Zealand—Our Maori Home." *IE* 35 (May 1932): 446.

Paongo, Marie. "Conference in Tonga." *Ensign* 6 (May 1976): 138-39.

Perrin, Yves R. *A History of The Church of Jesus Christ of Latter-day Saints in French Polynesia, 1844-1982.* Originally published in French in Papeete, Tahiti, 1982. Translated into English by permission by the Missionary Training Center, Provo, Utah, 1984.

Pratt, Alf. "The Time to 'Do It' Is Now . . . " and "Hawaii Temple Rededicated." *Ensign* 8 (August 1978): 74-78.

———. "The Gospel Moves to Micronesia." *Ensign* 8 (February 1978): 76-77.

Sokia, Maraia. "Conference in Fiji." *Ensign* 6 (April 1976): 77.

Spurrier, Joseph H. "Jonathon Napela: Quiet Hero of Hawaii." *Ensign 8* (August 1978): 49-51.

Stanton, Max E. "Samoan Saints: Settlers and Sojourners." *Proceedings of the Second Annual Conference of the Mormon Pacific Historical Society.* Laie, Hawaii: BYU-HC, 1981.

Taylor, Samuel W. "Walter Murray Gibson: Great Mormon Rascal." *The American West* 1 (Spring 1964): 18-27, 77.

Thorp, Malcomb R. "The British Government and the Mormon Question, 1910-22." *Journal of Church and State* 21 (Spring 1979): 305-23.

Whaanga, Hirini. "A Maori Prophet." *Juvenile Instructor* 37 (1902): 152.

Wood, Edward J. "My Samoan Experience." *The Juvenile Instructor* 23 (1893): 348. This is a portion of an eleven-part series that gives a great deal of information on a variety of subjects.

Young Adults of Australia. "The Gospel in Australia: Our Heritage." 1975.

PERIODICALS

Austral Star. Mission periodical. Sydney, Australia.

Cardston News. Alberta, Canada.

Church News. Salt Lake City, Utah.

Conference Reports. Salt Lake City, Utah.

The Contributor. Salt Lake City, Utah.

Deseret Evening News. Salt Lake City, Utah.

Ensign. Salt Lake City, Utah.

Improvement Era. Salt Lake City, Utah.

Juvenile Instructor. Salt Lake City, Utah.

Ka Elele O Hawaii. Hawaiian mission periodical. Honolulu, Hawaii.

The Liahona. Salt Lake City, Utah.

Millennial Star. Liverpool, England.

New Era. Salt Lake City, Utah.

Pacific Commerical Advertiser. Honolulu, Hawaii.

Tongan Government Gazette. Nuku'alofa, Tonga.

Woman's Exponent. Salt Lake City, Utah.

Zion's Watchman. Mission periodical. Sydney, Australia.

INDEX